'O'Keefe skilfully highlights Australia's distinctive strategic culture as a critical driver of its foreign policy. This well-structured, pragmatic analysis offers significant insight for students keen on understanding the practicalities of foreign policy making – an invaluable addition to any bookshelf.'

– *Mark Dinnen*, *Bond University, Australia*

'Building on the concept of strategic culture, this book provides a much-needed, theoretically informed and empirically rich analysis of contemporary Australian foreign policy.'

– *Matt McDonald*, *University of Queensland, Australia*

'*Australian Foreign Policy* provides an accessible and essential primer for students of Australia's foreign relations, challenging us to think more critically about the significant events, relationships and ideas that shape Australia's future.'

– *Danielle Chubb*, *Deakin University, Australia*

T0379986

Australian Foreign Policy

Relationships, Issues, and Strategic Culture

Michael O'Keefe

BLOOMSBURY ACADEMIC

LONDON • NEW YORK • OXFORD • NEW DELHI • SYDNEY

BLOOMSBURY ACADEMIC
Bloomsbury Publishing Plc
50 Bedford Square, London, WC1B 3DP, UK
1385 Broadway, New York, NY 10018, USA
29 Earlsfort Terrace, Dublin 2, Ireland

BLOOMSBURY, BLOOMSBURY ACADEMIC and the Diana logo are trademarks of
Bloomsbury Publishing Plc

First published in Great Britain 2023

Copyright © Michael O'Keefe, 2023

Michael O'Keefe has asserted his right under the Copyright, Designs and Patents Act, 1988,
to be identified as Author of this work.

For legal purposes the Acknowledgements on p. xiii constitute an extension of this
copyright page.

Cover design: Eleanor Rose
Cover image © Salt pool, Western Australia © Getty Images

All rights reserved. No part of this publication may be reproduced or transmitted in
any form or by any means, electronic or mechanical, including photocopying,
recording, or any information storage or retrieval system, without prior
permission in writing from the publishers.

Bloomsbury Publishing Plc does not have any control over, or responsibility for,
any third-party websites referred to or in this book. All internet addresses given in
this book were correct at the time of going to press. The author and publisher regret
any inconvenience caused if addresses have changed or sites have ceased to exist,
but can accept no responsibility for any such changes.

A catalogue record for this book is available from the British Library.

Library of Congress Cataloging-in-Publication Data

Names: O'Keefe, Michael, author.
Title: Australian foreign policy : relationships, issues, and strategic culture / Michael O'Keefe,
La Trobe University, Australia.
Description: [New York] : [Bloomsbury], [2023] | Includes bibliographical references and index. |
Summary: "How does Australia's unique geographical, cultural and historical position influence its
approach to foreign policy? What key challenges does Australia face on the world stage, and how
can it overcome them? Reflecting the messy reality of foreign policy decision-making, this book
helps you to understand the changes and continuities in Australia's approach. For example, does
the US withdrawal from Vietnam in 1973 and collapse of South Vietnam continue to cast a
shadow over Australian foreign policy, or is it relevant only in understanding the dynamics of the
cold war? Using an Australian Strategic Culture framework, O'Keefe sheds light on the
characteristics that make Australia behave in a way different to any other country. Equipping you
with analytic skills to understand the main debates, this book is essential reading if you are a
student of Australian foreign policy, as well as of broader Australian domestic and international
politics"-- Provided by publisher.
Identifiers: LCCN 2023013455 (print) | LCCN 2023013456 (ebook) | ISBN 9781350369368
(paperback) | ISBN 9781350369375 (hardback) | ISBN 9781350369382 (pdf) | ISBN
9781350369399 (epub)
Subjects: LCSH: Australia–Foreign relations–1945- | Australia–Foreign economic
relations. | National security–Australia. | Geopolitics–Australia.
Classification: LCC JZ1990 .O54 2023 (print) | LCC JZ1990 (ebook) | DDC 327.94--dc23/
eng/20230601 LC record available at https://lccn.loc.gov/2023013455
LC ebook record available at https://lccn.loc.gov/2023013456

ISBN: HB: 978-1-3503-6937-5
       PB: 978-1-3503-6936-8
       ePDF: 978-1-3503-6938-2
       eBook: 978-1-3503-6939-9

Typeset by RefineCatch Limited, Bungay, Suffolk

To find out more about our authors and books visit www.bloomsbury.com
and sign up for our newsletters.

This book is dedicated to the pragmatism of the Apcar line, and to Nicky, Jacquie and Alex who have inspired me to try to make sense of the present for their future.

CONTENTS

Figures and Tables ix
Maps x
Boxes and Case Studies xi
Acknowledgements xiii
Abbreviations xiv

Introduction 1

1 The Australian foreign policy context: Strategic culture as theory 5

2 Australia's strategic culture 17

3 Background to the United States: The making of the 'unbreakable' alliance 39

4 United States: Alignment in the twenty-first century 53

5 Background to China: Trading partner and potential threat 84

6 China: Strategic competitor 89

7 Background to Japan: Threat and trading partner 123

8 Japan: 'Special' strategic partner? 130

9 Background to Indonesia: The fractured history of diplomacy and the dynamic of diplomatic slight and escalation 155

10 Indonesia: Proximity and the unrealizable potential of dissimilar neighbours 170

11 Background to the South Pacific: The diversity of the South Pacific as seen from Canberra 198

12 South Pacific: Australia's 'hegemonic' credentials under challenge 211

13 The politicization of official development assistance as a foreign policy tool 240

14 Realism and the limits of climate securitization in Australian foreign policy 259

15 Asylum seekers as a threat to Australian sovereignty: Buttressing realism and the intergenerational appeal of strategic culture 279

Overview and conclusion: Australia's foreign policy DNA 306

Notes 319
Bibliography 355
Index 389

FIGURES AND TABLES

Figures

6.1	Australia's two-way trade pre-COVID19 by region	98
6.2	Gross domestic product (GDP) forecasts to 2030	101
8.1	Japan and Australia – by numbers	142
10.1	Australian ODA to Indonesia	184
14.1	Australian pre-COVID19 energy imports and exports, 2019	262
15.1	Nationality of asylum seekers in 2015	283
15.2	'Offshore processing' in PNG and Nauru	284
15.3	Medical transfers from 'regional processing centres'	302

Tables

2.1	Distinguishing middle and medium powers	35
6.1	Australia's top 10 pre-COVID19 export markets	99
6.2	Australia's pre-COVID19 trade and investment relationship with China	100
8.1	Australia–Japan policy agreements by administration	131
8.2	Japan's pre-COVID19 global merchandise trade relationships	142
8.3	Major Australian pre-COVID19 exports and imports	143
8.4	Australia's pre-COVID19 investment relationship with Japan	143
10.1	Australia's pre-COVID-19 pandemic trade and investment relationship with Indonesia	191
10.2	Indonesia's pre-COVID19 pandemic merchandise trade relationships	192
10.3	Australia's pre-COVID19 pandemic investment relationship with Indonesia	192
13.1	ODA delivered through UN agencies, 2022–23	253
14.1	Australian pre-COVID19 electricity generation, 2018	272

MAPS

2.1	The Japanese threat, 1942	22
3.1	Japanese advances in the south-west Pacific from December 1941 to April 1942	44
7.1	Australia under attack: Australia bombed, strafed and shelled	128
11.1	Pacific demography	203

BOXES AND CASE STUDIES

Boxes

1.1	Mutually Assured Destruction (MAD)	14
2.1	Core beliefs characterizing Australia's Strategic Culture	17
2.2	Credible contingencies	27
2.3	The core elements of Strategic Culture and indefensibility	28
2.4	The Domino Theory of Communist expansionism	30
4.1	AUKUS (2020)	58
4.2	Five Eyes at a glance	61
6.1	Australia versus China at the World Trade Organization (WTO)	102
6.2	FIRB's national interest test	105
7.1	The White Australia Policy	124
8.1	Japan's slow return to 'normal nationhood'	133
8.2	Australian submarines and shared interests	148
8.3	The prohibition on belligerency	149
9.1	The Howard letter (1998)	162
9.2	International Force East Timor (INTERFET), September 1999	163
9.3	The US doctrine of pre-emption	166
10.1	The Bali Nine drug smugglers	180
10.2	The Asian Values debate	193
11.1	Colonialism, Neo-Colonialism and Phosphate Mining on Nauru	200
12.1	RAMSI at a glance, 2003–17	225
13.1	Aid and official development assistance	241
13.2	The SDGs and ODA	252
15.1	The politicization of terms to describe asylum seekers	286
15.2	The language of detention	288
15.3	Key events in the 'Children Overboard' affair	297
15.4	Key events in the SIEV X tragedy	298

Case studies

6.1	China's claims in the South China Sea	110
6.2	China's influence activities in Australia	120
8.1	Whaling – domestic politics, environmental credentials and a clash of cultures	137
10.1	Drug trafficking and death sentences – public opinion, sovereignty and cultural sensitivity	180
12.1	Metropolitan versus geographic identity: West Papua and Pacific identity	214
12.2	The acrimonious 2019 PIF as a turning point in Australia's relations with PICs	216
12.3	The Pacific Maritime Security Programme and Pacific Support Force	224
12.4	Australian sanctions against Fiji	233
12.5	Nauru's role in Australia's 'Pacific Solution'	236
13.1	Politicizing ODA to win a United Nations Security Council (UNSC) seat	245
13.2	Humanitarian assistance	246
13.3	Countering Chinese influence in the Pacific	253
13.4	COVID-19 diplomacy and China	255
15.1	Australia's see-sawing foreign policy on asylum	294
15.2	Children as pawns in policy	297
15.3	Sovereignty, Threat Perceptions and Unauthorized Air Arrivals in a 'War on Terror'	299
15.4	Humanizing asylum seekers through the rise and fall of the Medivac Bill 2019?	301

ACKNOWLEDGEMENTS

My greatest inspiration for this book has been the countless students who I have taught Australian foreign policy. Every year I learn something from them and they show me how I can teach better. Despite all the trouble in the world, they also renew faith in the capacity of critical thinking to shape the future of Australian policy-making.

Thanks to my colleagues at La Trobe University and elsewhere for their interest and engagement in the subject of Australian foreign policy and Strategic Culture.

This book was supported by a La Trobe University grant through the Social Sciences Research Platform.

My thanks to Bethany Evans and Kerry Woodward for research assistance and Bronwyn Hislop for copyediting along the way. Both Milly Weaver and Tallulah Griffith at Bloomsbury have also been fantastic at bringing this project to fruition.

Of course, all errors and omissions are my own.

ABBREVIATIONS

ABC	Australian Broadcasting Corporation
AANZFTA	ASEAN–Australia–New Zealand Free Trade Area
ABS	Australian Bureau of Statistics
ACSC	Australian Cyber Security Centre
ADF	Australian Defence Force
ADMM-Plus	ASEAN Defence Ministers' Meeting Plus
AFP	Australian foreign policy
AIFFP	Australian Infrastructure Financing Facility for the Pacific
AIMF	Australia–Indonesia Ministerial Forum
AIRPD	Australia–Indonesia Partnership for Reconstruction and Development
AMS	Agreement on Maintaining Security
ANA	Afghan National Army
ANZUS	Australia–New Zealand–United States treaty
APEC	Asia–Pacific Economic Cooperation
APTC	Asia–Pacific Training Coalition
ARF	ASEAN Regional Forum
ASD	Australian Signals Directorate
ASEAN	Association of Southeast Asian Nations
ASIO	Australian Security Intelligence Organization
AusAID	Australian Agency for International Development
AUKUS	Australia–United Kingdom–United States trilateral agreement
AUSFTA	Australia–United States Free Trade Agreement
Austrade	Australian Trade and Investment Commission
BRI	Belt and Road Initiative

ABBREVIATIONS

CCP	Chinese Communist Party
CER	Closer Economic Relations Agreement
CFTA	China–Australia Free Trade Agreement
COIN	Counterinsurgency Operations
COP	Conference of the Parties
CPRS	Carbon Pollution Reduction Scheme
CSP	Comprehensive Strategic Partnership
CTBT	Comprehensive Nuclear Test Ban Treaty
DCP	Defence Cooperation Programme
DFAT	Department of Foreign Affairs and Trade
DOD	Department of Defence
EAS	East Asia Summit
ECP	Enhanced Cooperation Programme
EEC	European Economic Community
EEZ	Exclusive Economic Zone
ERF	Emissions Reduction Fund
EXIM	Export Import Bank (China)
FBI	Federal Bureau of Investigation
FDI	Foreign Direct Investment
FFA	Forum Fisheries Agency
FIRB	Foreign Investment Review Board (Australia)
FOIP	Free and Open Indo-Pacific
FONOP	Freedom of Navigation Operation
FSM	Federated States of Micronesia
FTA	Free Trade Agreement
FTAAP	Free Trade Area of Asia-Pacific
GCF	Green Climate Fund
GDP	Gross Domestic Product
GFC	Global Financial Crisis

GNI	Gross National Income
HADR	Humanitarian Assistance and Disaster Response
IA-CEPA	Indonesia–Australia Comprehensive Economic Partnership Agreement
IAD	Indonesia Australia Dialogue
ICJ	International Court of Justice
IGO	intergovernmental organization
INTERFET	International Force East Timor
IPCC	Intergovernmental Panel on Climate Change
ISAF	International Security Assistance Force
IWC	International Whaling Commission
JAEPA	Japan–Australia Economic Partnership Agreement
JCLEC	Jakarta Centre for Law Enforcement Cooperation
JSF	Joint Strike Fighter
KOPASSUS	Special Forces Command (Indonesian: Komando Pasukan Khusus)
LNG	Liquified Natural Gas
MAD	Mutually Assured Destruction
MDG	Millennium Development Goals
MNE	Multinational Enterprise
MOFA	Ministry of Foreign Affairs (Japan)
MOU	Memorandum of Understanding
MSG	Melanesian Spearhead Group
NAFTA	North American Free Trade Agreement
NAM	Non-Aligned Movement
NARA	Basic Treaty of Friendship and Cooperation
NATO	North Atlantic Treaty Organization
NCP	New Colombo Plan
NGO	Non-Government Organizations

ABBREVIATIONS

NPDI	Non-Proliferation and Disarmament Initiative
NPM	New Public Management
NPT	Treaty on the Non-Proliferation of Nuclear Weapons
OAE	Office of Aid Effectiveness
ODA	Official Development Assistance
OECD	Organization for Economic Cooperation and Development
ONA	Office of National Assessments
PACER	Pacific Agreement on Closer Economic Relations (2001)
PACER+	Pacific Agreement on Closer Economic Relations (2017)
PALMS	Pacific Australia Labour Mobility Scheme
PCA	Permanent Court of Arbitration
PIC	Pacific Island Countries
PICTA	Pacific Island Countries Trade Agreement
PIDF	Pacific Islands Development Forum
PIF	Pacific Islands Forum
PIFS	Pacific Islands Forum Secretariat
PMSP	Pacific Maritime Security Programme
PPP	Purchasing Power Parity
PRC	People's Republic of China
PRRP	Pacific Regional Programme
PSF	Pacific Support Force
PSIDS	Pacific Small Island Developing States
Quad	Quadrilateral Dialogue between Australia, the US, Japan and India
R2P	Responsibility to Protect
RAA	Reciprocal Access Agreement (between Australia and Japan)
RAAF	Royal Australian Air Force
RAMSI	Regional Assistance Mission to the Solomon Islands
RAN	Royal Australian Navy

RCEP	Regional Comprehensive Economic Partnership
RIMPAC	Rim of the Pacific
SAS	Special Air Service Regiment
SC	Security Council
SDCF	US–Japan–Australia Security and Defence Cooperation Forum
SDF	Self Defence Force (Japan)
SDG	Sustainable Development Goals
SIEV	Suspected Illegal Entry Vehicle
SOE	State-Owned Enterprises
SOLAS	International Convention for the Safety of Life at Sea
SPARTECA	South Pacific Regional Trade and Economic Cooperation Agreement
SPC	South Pacific Commission
SPC	Secretariat of the Pacific Community
SPREP	Secretariat of the Pacific Regional Environment Programme
SWP	Seasonal Worker Programme
TAC	Treaty of Amity and Cooperation
TNI	Tentara Nasional Indonesia (Indonesian National Military)
TPP	Trans-Pacific Partnership Agreement
TPV	Temporary Protection Visa
TSD	Trilateral Security Dialogue
UAE	United Arab Emirates
UAV	Unmanned Aerial Vehicle
UN	United Nations
UNFCCC	United Nations Framework Convention on Climate Change
UNDP	United Nations Development Programme
UNCLOS	United Nations Convention on the Law of the Sea
UNHCR	United Nations High Commissioner for Refugees
UNICEF	United Nations Children's Fund
UNPKO	United Nations Peacekeeping Operations

UNSC	United Nations Security Council
USP	University of the South Pacific
USSC	United States Studies Centre
WMD	Weapons of Mass Destruction
WTO	World Trade Organization

Introduction

The traditional approach to explaining Australian foreign policy (AFP) has been to rely largely on descriptive methods to produce historical narratives, arenas for popular debate or theoretical accounts. The orthodox focus has been on a chronological explanation of the evolution of diplomatic relationships or agendas. One problem with this approach is that while we know what happened and when, we don't necessarily learn *why* it happened, or *how* it is significant today. Therefore, these linear explanations of Australian foreign policy are incomplete and unsatisfying, and this text will provide a hybrid approach of history and theory to make sense of AFP.

By way of example, the US withdrawal from Vietnam and subsequent collapse of South Vietnam cast a shadow over AFP. Was this because it was symptomatic of President Richard Nixon's 1968 Guam Doctrine that heralded an end to US troops intervening in South East Asia, which potentially left Australia vulnerable to Communist threats? If so, then this episode should be consigned to Cold War history, but does the long shadow of Vietnam have relevance today? Was the Australian march to Singapore with the British in the Second World War and alongside the US to Saigon in the Vietnam War connected to a unique Australian Strategic Culture that transcends geopolitical eras? Was the fall of Saigon in 1975 akin to the fall of Singapore in 1942 insofar as these distant events directly challenged enduring pillars of AFP? If so, does the march to and withdrawal from Gallipoli in 1915 or Bagdad in 2003 fit this pattern of Strategic Cultural behaviour and does this influence present foreign policy? Answering these types of questions will provide a much richer understanding of AFP and assist in contextualizing future challenges, such as how to manage the rise of China.

These examples highlight that the nature of the evolution of AFP at liminal moments, where foreign policy appears to have changed course, have not been sufficiently explained in the descriptive literature on AFP. Descriptive approaches exaggerate the significance of present events where change is often more apparent than real. Put simply, this means that we experience the 'arrogance of the present' where current events take on greater importance in analyses because they are not contextualized historically. So, in order to make sense of the impact of strategic change we need analytic tools that allow us to zoom out and review foreign policy in context. To date, when this departure from descriptive methods has been used it has focused on International Relations theory and to a lesser extent area studies perspectives.

When International Relations theories are introduced as analytical frames or lenses we can understand how Australia fits into the international system of states alongside other states. What we don't learn is why Australia chooses particular foreign policy settings to deal with challenges and opportunities that present themselves. The continuity and change in AFP are not revealed if we do not interrogate the granular detail of AFP. For instance, the rise of China is often treated in an almost ahistorical manner, with explicit or implied references to the inevitability of an existential threat developing. If a broader Strategic Cultural approach is used, then the rise of China might fit a broader historical pattern of path dependency in policy-making whereby the Soviet Union, Indonesia, Japan, Germany and Russia have all filled a similar role as a source of existential threat in AFP. This insight, in relation to the central place of threats in AFP, can provide a useful explanation for particular decisions. That said, it is only a partial explanation and a pluralistic approach, which includes other perspectives, is required to make sense of AFP.

This book will elevate the place of Australia's unique Strategic Culture as both an *explanation* and *determinant* of foreign policy. It will highlight the enduring influence of Australia's highly militarized Strategic Culture on foreign policy and provide the basis for contextualizing key diplomatic relationships and responses to issues such as climate change. It will highlight the dominance of inertia and path dependency in foreign policy and explain the rare examples of dramatic change. In so doing, it will move beyond Realist and Liberal Internationalist *caricatures* as explanations of state behaviour by introducing an additional explanation for the foreign policy behaviour of the Australian State. As such, Strategic Culture will be introduced to produce a pluralistic approach that focuses on explanations for particular state behaviour that can extend, coexist with or supplant orthodox theoretical perspectives.

Contemporary issues and challenges (such as climate change, asylum seekers and overseas development assistance) will be examined and viewed through this lens to clarify the significant continuity in foreign policy that is unwelcome to orthodox descriptive/linear or theoretical explanations of AFP. Notable myths in the making that will be challenged are that US decline will prompt greater Australian independence, or even that a closer security relationship with China is possible.

A note on method and structure

A modified debates method will be used in this book. Traditionally, debates pit two 'sides' against one another, in this case in an attempt to best explain AFP. This oppositional debates mode of argument can easily lead to 'sides' speaking past one another in 'non-debates', or to the type of polarity that creates caricatures of reality that end up undermining the cases they are attempting to establish. The debate becomes about sides or theories rather than explaining reality and misses the point of using theory as an explanatory reflection of reality. Theory must be a tool that assists us in understanding reality and examples should not become

INTRODUCTION

'square pegs rammed through round holes' in order to make a flimsy case for the dominance of one theoretical explanation for policy.

This book will overcome these problems and avoid getting bogged down in polemical arguments by referring closely to government declaratory policy (public statements) and operational policy (how governments utilize resources). It will also include public commentary, public opinion and academic analysis that attempts to explain and contextualize foreign policy decisions on a given relationship or issue.

In practice, this will mean that a baseline of what the Australian foreign policy position is on a particular issue will be produced from information drawn from official government documents (declaratory policy) and current trends/events. This largely descriptive picture of 'facts' will be compared and contrasted with the historical trends for each diplomatic relationship or issue, the government's operational policy, public commentary from think tanks, newspapers, etc., public opinion and academic explanations. In the case of theory, a pluralistic approach will be taken whereby Strategic Culture will be introduced as an explanation that in particular cases can complement, extend or replace other perspectives to explain and contextualize foreign policy.

As such, what the government says it is doing and what it actually does will be connected with current affairs to provide a statement of the 'facts' on a given issue. The 'facts' are often contested and this is where we leave descriptive texts behind because it is how we contextualize the facts that is important. The 'facts' will be compared and contrasted with what other key actors think the government is doing and what should be done. All of this is viewed through various analytical lenses to see how we can make sense of continuity and change in AFP and how we can prepare for the future. Taken together this method provides a clear picture of the present state of play in foreign policy and the tools for readers to position themselves in debates.

The text is structured in three sections. The first provides a historical and theoretical background to the subject. The second concentrates on Australia's key bilateral relationships with the US, China, Japan, Indonesia and the South Pacific. From Canberra's perspective, dividing AFP into siloed bilateral relationships is an artificial split because these relationships are interconnected, but it reflects diplomatic practice and serves the purpose of allowing the key themes that play out in AFP to be revealed more fully. The themes provide background assumptions about how policy-makers use foreign policy to achieve Australia's national interests with respect to particular states. The third section focusses on pressing issues in international affairs, namely overseas development assistance, climate change and refugee flows.

Each chapter is framed by the pressing foreign policy priorities and challenges in the bilateral relationship in question and the inevitable questions they raise. Competing priorities and interests in relation to the capacity to achieve Australia's interests are revealed in relation to the key themes that explain AFP. The chapters on bilateral relations are split into a self-contained historical background to set the scene and then a detailed analysis of recent and current policy. The influence of Strategic Culture will be appraised in the context of the particular priorities and challenges in each bilateral relationship with reference to other enduring themes in AFP. As such, this method will accomplish something that most analyses do not – a historically grounded, context-specific explanation of AFP behaviour towards key bilateral partners and issues.

1

The Australian foreign policy context: Strategic culture as theory

Introduction

This chapter seeks to contextualize Australian foreign policy (AFP) within the study of foreign policy in general. The point is to identify the building blocks of analysis needed to understand what is distinctive about Australian foreign policy. This approach differs from much of the literature in that it assumes from the outset that AFP is distinctive while acknowledging that it is formed and implemented within an international system of states.

Core thematic issues dealt with in this chapter include: What is the 'art of the possible' for policy-makers? This begs several subsidiary questions such as: What are the core attributes of landscape within which analysis of AFP occurs? What are the boundaries of the arena in which policy-makers form and execute AFP? How do systemic factors shape AFP? How can Realism and Liberal Internationalism assist in explaining foreign policy? How can reflection on a state's unique strategic culture extend Realist and Liberal Internationalist perspectives? These questions lead directly into the discussion of Australia's Strategic Culture in the next chapter.

How can we explain Australian foreign policy?

The number of academic books and articles and newspaper columns that have attempted to answer this question is staggering and too large to count. In addition, highly polarized foreign policy debates are divisive and produce contradictory explanations and prescriptions. This makes it very difficult to produce a considered answer. This background 'noise' must be filtered out to make sense of Australian foreign policy.

At the outset, it is essential to acknowledge that all opinions are written *from particular perspectives that influence the scope of their answers*. What is considered relevant or not, how issues are prioritized, what foreign policy approaches are promoted, and where the boundaries between foreign policy and other policies lie, all are shaped by the 'lenses' through which analysts look at foreign policy.

These perspectives and vantage points shape perceptions of what is believed should be the scope of foreign policy and, most importantly, what is possible in foreign policy.

What is deemed possible can be described as the 'art of the possible'; the range of options that can be considered when undertaking diplomacy to achieve the national interest. Before examining the 'art of the possible' in AFP, we must briefly identify the key aspects of the international system that shape debate over how to explain foreign policy. We first need to understand the boundaries developed by the dominant analyses of foreign policy.

The building blocks of foreign policy analysis: Bounded rationality, formal equality and sovereignty

In the discipline of International Relations, most analyses of foreign policy use *systemic* or universalist approaches to understanding day-to-day international affairs. These perspectives assume universal truths about states and their behaviour. They assume both that all states are motivated by achieving the national interest and that the nature of the international system is the prime determinant of the behaviour of the actors (or states) within it.[1]

The international system and bounded rationality

International Relations perspectives 'zoom out' to view the globe as an international system or society of states that shapes the behaviour of the states within to provide boundaries to their rationality.[2] The system shapes how all states view the 'art of the possible' in relation to foreign policy. The system provides the diplomatic playing field, albeit one that is not a level playing field. For example, norms prohibiting wars of conquest and territorial expansion have shaped post twentieth-century international affairs, but war and conflict persist.

Equally, powerful states have not always obeyed these norms or rules that are designed to guide state behaviour and encourage peaceful interaction. This rule-breaking in the name of the national interest highlights assumptions about the anarchic nature of the system that are only moderated by international cooperation and norms *if* states agree to adhere to them. The background context of anarchy leads states to various strategies to protect their security, with armament and alliance coexisting alongside efforts to create international order through norms and international law.[3] As such, evaluating how Australia views armament, alliance and international order is a key aim of this book.

In this conception of the international 'system', states are most often viewed as *rational* actors interacting with other rational actors to try to maximize the benefits accruing to them.[4] While this approach, borrowed from economics, is problematic for a range of reasons, it came to dominate thinking (a discussion of the irrationality of Cold War thinking and Strategic Culture follows).[5] The focus on national self-interest identifies power, and differentials in power, as key drivers

THE AUSTRALIAN FOREIGN POLICY CONTEXT

of international affairs.[6] It does not put a great deal of weight on values or ethics in shaping international interaction, which is in contrast to Strategic Culture. This orthodox view espoused by historical theorists such as Machiavelli and Hobbes, and modern proponents such as US Secretary of State Henry Kissinger, represents the essentially Realist foundations of foreign policy.[7] From this perspective, the dominant assumption underpinning much of the literature on foreign policy is that morality is not as important as the national interest, unless it assists in achieving the national interest. As Hans Morgenthau noted: 'universal moral principles cannot be applied to the actions of states . . . [other than] the moral principle of state survival'.[8]

In this context, bounded rationality meant that states were shaped by the rules or norms of behaviour prescribed by the international system. This perspective was borrowed from the field of economics and transposed onto states.[9] The primary unit of analysis was *states*, which are also described as nations, nation-states or countries. Each of these descriptions has a slightly different technical definition developed for other purposes, so 'states' will be used throughout. States are considered groups of people with a government that represents them when dealing with other states in the international system. States (generally) accept the legitimacy of the rules or norms of the international system and generally abide by them. The rules and the acceptance of them make it a *system*. The fact that the rules are not always obeyed makes the 'system' as imperfect as its members.

The formal equality of unequals in the international system

Most International Relations perspectives also assume the formal equality of states.[10] This means that they treat all states as formally alike, possessing both shared interests and approaches to achieving them, often within a shared understanding of the boundaries of acceptable behaviour. Shared interests include furthering their national interests and protecting the system and their place in it. Shared approaches to international affairs include developing and respecting the rules of the system, diplomacy in the achievement of interests and settlement of disputes, and the use of force against other states as a last resort. A key reason to introduce Strategic Culture into considerations of foreign policy is that formal equality does *not* acknowledge that states are actually far from equal. States may share assumptions about the nature of the system but their foreign policies are shaped by their relative capabilities.

Sovereignty

The 'glue' that holds the system together is the sovereign principle. Sovereignty is interpreted in different ways depending on the analytical vantage being used but generally refers to supreme authority and control over a polity and acknowledgement by other states of this control.[11] Westphalian sovereignty defines the political *independence* and territorial *integrity* of states within the present international order that was born out of the Peace of Westphalia in 1648.[12]

Political independence refers to the capacity of a government to make decisions that support its interests without undue influence from other states. There is much debate over the nature of undue influence in international affairs with an extreme view being that economic and political globalization has challenged the independence of states to the point where the concept of sovereignty is untenable. Similarly, territorial integrity, whereby a government exercises control over a defined geographic area through 'a monopoly of violence', has also been challenged by global trends, such as transnational crime or terrorism, though not to the same degree as political independence.

State sovereignty is based on the *formal* equality of states as actors within a system governed by rules and the reality of dramatic inequality (in power, natural resources and human capital, for instance) is not the focus. The universality of international law provides a clear example of the preference for formal equality because all states should conform to the law, but more powerful states often bend rules that do not suit their national interests. Australia's treatment of asylum seekers and its response to climate change in the face of international criticism fits this pattern of behaviour. Therefore, while the theory focuses on a sense of international order between equals, in reality this is far from the day-to-day lived experiences of states and peoples. This highlights the weakness of universalist theories in accurately describing the realities of states and peoples.

Formal inequality in the United Nations

The operation of the United Nations (UN) provides a sound illustration of how 'sovereign *in*equality' plays out in the reality of international affairs. The UN Charter (1948) contains considered and comprehensive rules guiding state behaviour to encourage conditions that support the development of social and economic prosperity whilst also prohibiting rule-breaking such as expressions of naked aggression (for example, war and invasion).

Differentials in power are clear from the voting structure of the UN. In the UN General Assembly, all states have one vote and practise diplomacy to convince others to democratically support resolutions that develop shared interests. In contrast, in the Security Council, a group of powerful states effectively control 'high' policy, such as legitimizing international intervention and sanctions, and have veto powers over all resolutions, thereby nullifying the democracy of the General Assembly.[13] The operation of the Security Council shows that some states are more *equal* than others.

Powerful states have more capacity to shape international order to support their interests. The assumption behind this inequality might be that supporting their interests may support the interests of others, but clearly this is not always the case. This assumption has been tested on numerous occasions by deadlock in the Security Council over how to respond to key issues and conflicts, such as that in Ukraine. In a broader sense, the veto has limited the application of the Responsibility to Protect (R2P) innocent civilians through peace-making interventions.[14] The principle of R2P threatens to dilute sovereignty by justifying armed international intervention to protect civilians from gross human rights violations and some

THE AUSTRALIAN FOREIGN POLICY CONTEXT

states, such as China and Russia, openly recognize that this could undermine their interests.[15]

Realism, liberal internationalism and the 'art of the possible' in foreign policy

The vantage point from which international affairs is observed shapes the 'art of the possible' in foreign policy. The 'art of the possible' provides a useful way of capturing the options inherent in a particular theoretical perspective of foreign policy and allows its capacity to explain foreign policy to be evaluated. The term has been used to describe an approach called *Realpolitik*, whereby policy-makers are involved in a constant evaluation of national interests, and that these evaluations are assumed to be rational.[16] *Realpolitik* excludes ideological or ethical thinking to self-consciously focus on national interests. This narrow perspective is most associated with Realist thinking and it has a long history of shaping how foreign policy-making is viewed.[17] Realism is narrow insofar as it does not emphasize the influence of values or national histories on decision-making, and the 'art of the possible' is used in this book to show that other factors, namely Liberal Internationalism and Strategic Culture, provide insights into how *particular* states *actually* behave.

A counter-response to the naked self-interest of Realism is the Liberal Internationalism of the twentieth century that injected liberal values into considerations of foreign policy-making. Liberal Internationalism enriches the understanding of international affairs by filling gaps evident between the reality of day-to-day diplomacy and narrow Realist perspectives. Liberal Internationalism softens the emphasis on naked self-interest and focuses on the importance of utilizing the system within which states operate, and the rules and values that bind states in cooperation and also predispose them to avoid conflict.

Liberal Internationalism explains the influence of ideologies and ethical values, such as democracy, representation and universal human rights, in the international arena. In the eyes of US Realists, the Liberal project in foreign affairs has been tarnished by failures of US administrations to include a credible democratizing project in foreign policy when other pressing national interests are at stake, as evidenced in the withdrawal of US forces from Afghanistan.[18] This tension between Liberal values and practice in foreign policy has also been identified in Canberra's willingness to selectively apply norms in a process described as Australian 'exemptionalism'.[19] However, despite these obvious flaws in the application of Liberal values, it is clear that they still provide a potent motivating force for international cooperation on issues such as human rights or climate change.

When viewed from the vantage of a *particular* state, both Realism and Liberal Internationalism are systemic theories that seek to primarily explain international affairs from the standpoint of 'like' political units operating in a 'like' diplomatic environment. That is, the landscape is the international system and it is populated by functionally equivalent states maximizing their interests in competition with one another. This level of abstraction allows sovereignty and formal equality to act as the foundations of the system or society of states. They are systemic perspectives as state behaviour is generalized to the point where their place as generic actors in the system is emphasized more than any individual peculiarities they possess. The systemic perspective is akin to biological classification where all are members of a species are biologically equal; all human beings are biologically equal.

In debates about International Relations, systemic perspectives also often become caricatures of themselves as they can be essentialized into opposing poles. Realism can signify national power and self-interest while Liberal Internationalism can represent norms and values. This bipolarity obscures the rich development of nuance within each theoretical position that attempts to engage in a theoretical dialogue with opposing critiques and/or with the realities of practical diplomacy and foreign policy that did not neatly or consistently conform with either perspective. Neorealism and the English School would best capture this nuance that qualifies naked self-interest with the existence of an international (if not global) policy-making context.[20]

Another intimately connected issue is that the bipolar debate between the two dominant theories (Realism and Liberal Internationalism) has led to a form of competition between them that shaped how new/alternative perspectives, such as critical theories and Constructivism, were framed.[21] New approaches are often compared to existing theories in a binary way (black or white) that limits their impact as explanations of foreign policy behaviour. This competition does no justice to the alternative viewpoints that advocate for multiple perspectives that are viewed as existing simultaneously (nation, state, gender, class, faith, etc.).

As critical theories advocate an emancipatory project for human beings rather than attempting to explain past state behaviour, they do not form the focus of analysis.[22] For example, Realist, Liberal Internationalist and Strategic Cultural perspectives can be clearly identified in AFP, but identifying critical theory as a driver of policy, in relation to issues such as gender or climate change, is more problematic. Furthermore, mentions of these issues are often illusory insofar that they might appear prominently in declaratory policy statements, but don't necessarily trump more orthodox drivers of AFP. In Chapter 13, we will see that gender figured prominently in Australia's approach to overseas development assistance (ODA), but that national interest considerations, such as the geopolitical context with China in the South Pacific, are identified as the priority.

While debate and theoretical clarification have tightened how these systemic approaches relate to the reality of day-to-day foreign affairs, one unifying characteristic is that they did not emphasize variations in national foreign policy approaches as key variables worthy of study. National attributes were assumed to be subject to the greater influence of the institutional constraints imposed by power differentials and the structure of the international system. The 'art of the possible' was largely defined by relative power and the nature of the playing field. The importance of national variations becomes readily apparent when we reflect on the purpose of foreign policy as many answers did not focus on the international system, but rather groups of people that inhabit it.

Extending the 'art of the possible' in the explanation of AFP

A key contribution of this book is to enrich foreign policy analysis by including the influence of national Strategic Culture into considerations of international affairs. The 'art of the possible' in the foreign policy of a particular polity is shaped by its unique Strategic Culture as well as considerations of national interest and ideology/values. In this sense, a polity is a political entity consisting of a group of people with a shared national identity and understanding of government, who also face the world with attitudes about how foreign policy should be conducted. Not all polities are alike and while their foreign policies exist within the bounded rationality of the international system, they differ markedly.

The diversity in approaches to foreign policy highlight the human element in decision-making and the historical Strategic Cultures within which they operate. The diversity is revealed if we pose the fundamental question of *what is the purpose of a state's foreign policy?* Or, more specifically, why was any given decision made by a given government at a liminal historical moment in international affairs (such as the outbreak of war or the emergency response to a pandemic). Why did Prime Minister Scott Morrison's coalition government sign the AUKUS defence agreement in 2021 that would deliver nuclear submarines and revolutionarily pivot AFP into a new era? How did Canberra weigh up the costs of negotiating it secretly with the Trump and Biden administrations with full knowledge that it would be a turning point in relations with Australia's number one trading partner, China? Systemic theories provide an explanation of the playing field within which the negotiations occurred, but history and culture, Strategic Culture, explain why the decision was made and how if seamlessly fits with AFP.

What is the purpose of foreign policy?

Answering the seemingly simple question about the purpose of foreign policy is much more difficult than it might seem as it raises many more questions. The two most important subsidiary questions are what is the aim of foreign policy and how can it be achieved?

While these questions are not always explicitly mentioned in foreign policy analysis, they always frame what is being discussed.[23] Taken together, variations in the definition of both the aim of foreign policy and how to achieve it capture the diversity in approaches to foreign policy. This diversity and the tensions that they cause is a direct challenge to the systemic approaches to explaining international affairs.

The abstract national interest versus particular national interests

In traditional International Relations theories, there is a general consensus on the aim of foreign policy – furthering the national interest. While this concept *appears* to provide the 'glue' that holds together foreign policy analysis, its capacity to clarify the purpose of foreign policy is illusory. The abstract thought that all states have interests that drive them is certainly true, but this realization raises even more questions. Namely, what precisely is the national interest? Who defines it? How can it change? What happens when the national interests of two states conflict? Apparent conceptual consensus about the abstract theoretical value of the national interest provides less grounding than it might appear because the national interest itself is contested and the national interests of states are often in competition as interests are defined by individual states to maximize gains to that state rather than to the international system.

When we move beyond abstractions, then particular national interests can be defined. Individualized national interests are important determinants of foreign policy because they reflect the identity of particular nations/states rather than the international community or some sense of global identity. International affairs is a competitive arena and national interests often pit states against one another as they are trying to achieve the same things for their citizens and that can come at the cost of citizens of other states. For example, Australia's response to climate change and asylum seekers, discussed in Chapters 14 and 15, clearly reveals Canberra's definition of the national interest in relation to Australian citizens and their welfare and prosperity versus that of the citizens of other states.

Systemic theorists may be content to focus on *the* national interest as an abstract driver of foreign policy, but the diversity of policy prescriptions developed in Africa, the Indo-Pacific, Europe and South America highlights that there are as many national interests as there are states. National interests may coincide because possessing shared interests is commonplace due to shared experience, but equally national interests may conflict. As such, thinking about the national interest in relation to a *particular* polity such as Australia at a *particular* point in time is essential to understanding foreign policy. In this way, we're really thinking about national interests versus *the* national interest as a driver of foreign policy, and understanding national interests requires tools that emphasize particular attributes of states.

By way of example, if we abstractly treat the national interest as a series of ongoing rational evaluations of interests, then it should change over time based on changing circumstances and conditions. Furthermore, on the occasion of liminal moments in history, such as the end of the Cold War, we should see dramatic change in the face of strategic transformations. This means that in the natural state of international affairs, we should observe significant alterations in foreign policy priorities and strategies. However, this does not gel with the high level of continuity in foreign affairs, especially in AFP.

In the reality of day-to-day diplomacy, incremental change is the more natural condition than revolution. There is significant continuity in national foreign policies, which challenges the influence of rational evaluations of naked self-interest in altering the national interest. This brings alive the continuity in Lord Palmerston's famous dictum: 'We have no eternal allies, and we have no perpetual enemies. Our interests are eternal and perpetual, and those interests it is our duty to follow.'[24] Most presume this means that interests change, but in AFP the interpretation that infers continuity is most apt when viewing Australia's alliance

THE AUSTRALIAN FOREIGN POLICY CONTEXT

with the US. Reliance on 'great and powerful friends' is a key attribute of Australian Strategic Culture and the 'unbreakable alliance' is a major focus of Chapter 4.

Drilling down to the national interests of particular states

Various perspectives on foreign policy are founded on differing assumptions about what forms the national interest, and how these interests should be prioritized.[25] These differences are compounded by different expectations about the role of government and the tools that can be used to achieve interests. Furthermore, these underlying assumptions, expectations and tools differ widely both within and between states.

If we acknowledge the central place of national interest in foreign policy-making, and that *the* national interest of a particular state influences its definition of the 'art of the possible' in that polity, then we must broaden analysis beyond systemic explanations for foreign policy behaviour. The diversity we see in the national interest must lead us to question the deterministic dominance of systemic perspectives. In this context, determinism suggests that systemic patterns of cooperation and conflict between states drive foreign policy outcomes. However, if all states are *not* alike and if they define the national interest differently, then should we not need to refer to their peculiarities in order to explain foreign policy?

A key reason for broadening our analytical frame is that no single systemic theory can explain *all* state behaviour. For instance, classical Realism is incapable of explaining the apparent 'irrationality' that states often exhibit when they are *not* maximizing their self-interests. For example, the Morrison government's escalating trade conflict with China was certainly inflamed by signing the AUKUS agreement and boycotting the 2021 Beijing Winter Olympics. In these cases, self-interest is not so 'naked' and rather is clothed in an array of beliefs and values that are influenced by a state's Strategic Culture: values, history and geography. Furthermore, decision-makers act on imperfect information[26] and often this can occur in haste due to the nature of crisis decision-making.

The Cold War roots of modern Strategic Culture

From the 1970s, a theoretical perspective was developed to explain the apparent Cold War 'irrationality' on the part of the US and Soviet Union that could have led to nuclear annihilation.[27] At the height of the Cold War, the doctrine of mutually assured destruction (MAD) was developed whereby the US and USSR possessed enough nuclear weapons to survive a first strike by the opposition and therefore field a credible response to a full-scale nuclear attack (Box 1.1).[28] To develop a strategy that would lead to annihilation seemed irrational. How could MAD be in the national interest? Why could statesmen and women not rationally evaluate their interests to avoid MAD? Why were the norms and structures of international collaboration unable to prevent the development of this strategy of annihilation?

BOX 1.1: MUTUALLY ASSURED DESTRUCTION (MAD)

- Developed during the Cold War as the superpowers developed nuclear war-fighting strategies.
- The logic of nuclear deterrence was that the possession of nuclear forces would prevent war (due to the destructive capacity of nuclear weapons).
- Once nuclear parity between the superpowers was gained, the debate shifted to the credibility of deterrence.
- Having credible second-strike capacity would deter an opponent from attacking first in an attempt to win.
- A credible second strike required redundancy – survivability in the case of an enemy first strike to allow retaliation.
- In order to guarantee a credible second strike, many more nuclear weapons were needed (to allow for those destroyed by an enemy's first strike).
- Multiple delivery systems (air, sea and land) were also needed to guarantee survivability for a second strike.
- The resulting overwhelming destructive power of nuclear arsenals ensured that in a nuclear war, both sides would be annihilated and the world would be destroyed.

In this MAD scenario, the allies of the superpowers would also be targeted so as to ensure the complete destruction of the enemy (and this is an issue that influenced US–Australia relations and will be discussed in Chapter 13).

Put simply, the question raised by MAD was how can we explain individual state behaviour that did not correspond with systemic theoretical explanations? How could it be in the interests of a state to see the annihilation of its people in order to ensure the annihilation of the enemy? How could brinkmanship of the sort seen in Cold War flashpoints, such as the Cuban Missile Crisis (1962) or proxy wars, such as the US–Vietnam War (1965–75) and Soviet-Afghan War (1979–89), occur? How could it be in the interests of a state to see the destruction of the international system?

As noted earlier, the orthodox explanation of International Relations was that the nature of the international 'system' of states provided the playing field and, to borrow from psychology and economics, bounded the rationality of states so that they all behaved in similar ways.[29] This involved furthering their own interests and shaping and protecting the system within which they could flourish. The Cold War highlighted that these systemic explanations were not rich enough to explain apparent irrationality in cases such as MAD. In this case, ideology was at stake for both the US and Soviet Union and it was potent enough to bring the world to the point of annihilation. Furthermore, these ideological preferences reflected a level of continuity and inertia that meant that they were more than simply policy preferences to achieve the national interest – they were ingrained in national cultures.

Strategic Cultures within *the international system*

The idea that a particular state's unique Strategic Culture had an equally significant influence over behaviour as systemic factors has become more influential over time. Snyder's identification of the persistence of cultural beliefs amongst policy-makers during the Cold War was identified by an increasing number of analysts.[30] Strategic Culture reflected on and blended the history, geography and culture of a particular state. It was endearing for many analysts as they reflected on how particularistic variables influenced how states behaved in particular situations in international affairs. Examples abounded, such as the 1962 Cuban Missile Crisis, where the US defined non-negotiable aspects of its sphere of interest in the face of a test posed by Soviet attempts to station nuclear missiles in Cuba.[31] The superpowers appeared to be on the brink of nuclear war and the lack of compromise on the part of the US was perceived to verge on irrational. Winning a nuclear war involved everyone losing.

By extension, it was a valuable insight to reflect on how these Strategic Cultures shape and influence international affairs *from the bottom up*. This was in sharp contrast to the *top-down* approaches of systemic theories that did not delve into the particular attributes of the states that collectively form the international system.

Strategic Culture defined

Kerry Longhurst captured Strategic Culture well when she described it as:

> A distinctive body of beliefs, attitudes and practices regarding the use of force, which are held by a collective and arise gradually over time, through a unique protracted historical process. A strategic culture is persistent over time, tending to outlast the era of its original inception, although it is not a permanent or static feature. It is shaped and influenced by formative periods and can alter, either fundamentally or piecemeal, at critical junctures in that collective's experiences.[32]

Strategic Culture conceived this way could be seen as akin to Constructivism.[33] However, it accepts the ideational approach associated with Constructivism and extends it to the actions of a specific state at a given time.[34] Its analytical gift is to elevate the importance of the actions of a *particular* polity in responding to foreign policy challenges and opportunities.[35] Its proponents did not set itself up as a binary explanation of foreign policy behaviour to attempt to challenge or supplant systemic theories.[36] As such, Strategic Culture is not focused on 'winning' an abstract theoretical debate, but rather on accurately depicting the messy reality of foreign affairs *in a particular state*.

Conclusion

Strategic Culture is therefore a bridge between systemic theoretical perspectives and descriptive accounts of foreign policy practice.[37] The point is not to undermine the role of systemic theories in explaining the context within which states act, but rather to acknowledge that a hybrid, pluralistic approach that draws on several theoretical perspectives is the appropriate way of explaining the behaviour of *particular* states. This means that Strategic Culture acknowledges the systemic factors that shape foreign policy-making and incorporates Realist and Liberal Internationalist tendencies when they are evidenced in a particular example of foreign policy decision-making. The following chapter will detail Australia's unique Strategic Culture.

2

Australia's Strategic Culture

Introduction

An essential aspect of Strategic Culture is the distinctiveness it identifies in the geography, history and culture of particular polities. That is, while two or more states may share similar attributes, no two Strategic Cultures are identical. The abiding belief from the first settlement that Australia is a geographically large island with a small, largely Western population, perched on the boundary of a potentially threatening region,[1] is unique. The implications of this feeling of vulnerability amongst the first British colonists still resonates today.

To understand Australia's distinctive Strategic Culture, we have to identify and situate Australian foreign policy (AFP) within Australia's immutable geography and history to identify core beliefs and the practices developed from them (Box 2.1).

BOX 2.1: CORE BELIEFS CHARACTERIZING AUSTRALIA'S STRATEGIC CULTURE

- Geographic isolation from Anglo-American culture and alienation from Asia.
- Exaggerated threat perceptions sourced from Anglo-American culture and centred on Asia.
- A sense of indefensibility arising from geography and demography.
- A fear of abandonment by Anglo-American allies in the face of indefensibility from a threatening region.

Core practices derived from these beliefs include:

- Securitization of foreign policy.
- A habit of dependence on 'great and powerful' Anglo-American friends.
- Hedging alliances through defence self-reliance and Liberal Internationalism.
- Strategic denial of the proximate region from unwelcome Asian powers.[2]
- Inertia in the face of geostrategic change.

No book has been produced on Australian Strategic Culture, but it has been the topic of numerous journal articles. Key proponents include Cheeseman, Lantis, Charlton, Bloomfield, Nossal and Poore.[3] Graeme Cheeseman's 'Australia: The White Experience of Fear and Dependence' is the archetypal discussion of this issue.[4]

At the outset, we also have to understand that in order to be persistent and self-perpetuating, Strategic Cultural beliefs are interconnected and mutually reinforcing, as are the practices developed to respond to them. As such, they also overlap with Realist and Liberal Internationalist accounts of foreign policy; no one approach tells the story of AFP but rather a pluralistic account is needed. The preceding beliefs and practices will be the subject of the following analysis.

Geographic isolation from Anglo-American culture and alienation from Asia

> For most of the two hundred years since European settlement [in 1788], Australia has fought against the reality of our own geography. We thought of ourselves, and were thought of by just about everyone else, as an Anglophonic and Anglo phallic outpost – tied by history, language, culture, economics and emotion to Europe and North America.[5]

This quote from a former Australian foreign minister captures succinctly the dominant attitude of 'Australia' towards its geography. Whilst located in what could variously be called Asia, the Asia-Pacific, Indo-Pacific or Oceania, Australia has never quite felt at home. This may seem odd, but it is the foundation stone of Australian Strategic Culture. The former foreign minister may suggest that attitudes have changed but this is far from the case. Australians have not embraced an Asian, Indo or Oceanic identity and neither have Asians or Pacific Islanders accepted Australia as part of their regions.

Furthermore, this alienation from Asia predates the granting of independence from the United Kingdom in 1901. The lineage of alienation coined by Geoffrey Blainey as the 'Tyranny of Distance'[6] is much older, stretching from colonization in 1788. Australian colonists arrived in an unfamiliar and 'alien' environment that almost defeated early attempts at settlement. As with many settler societies, such as the US, the indigenous population and 'unforgiving' environment were seen as threats that needed to be 'tamed' so that Western ways of governance and farming could be introduced. Over the first 100 years of settlement, exploration revealed a diverse continent that stretched the imagination of the European colonizers, but the harsh environment remained threatening. Once the indigenous population had been subjugated and the environment had been 'tamed', then the colonists shifted to view the Asian neighbourhood as a source of threat.[7]

The situation becomes more complex and fraught when we reflect on cultural differences. Anglo-Saxon attitudes were an essential part of colonization, but it was not as much about colonizing the indigenous population as it was about subjugating them and establishing and maintaining an imperial outpost. Once the indigenous population had been 'pacified', the threat to European ways no longer came from within. Initially, threat perceptions did not arise from Asian states, but rather from other European empires in Asia. With the decolonization of most of Asia in the 1950s and 1960s, Australia's threat perceptions did not decline but rather they shifted to regional threats.

Immigration policy in the new nation mirrored colonial attitudes, with the White Australia Policy dominating attempts to control the complexion of Australia's population.[8] Language and cultural tests were used to exclude and long after the White Australia Policy was dismantled in the 1960s, echoes of this approach could be seen in citizenship tests such as that introduced by the Howard government in 2007.[9] The post-Second World War immigration boom captured by Prime Minister Arthur Calwell's call to 'populate or perish' had a clear emphasis on increasing the British population of Australia that stretched to Anglo-Saxon Europeans, and was further stretched by the inclusion of Southern Europeans. The attitudes that made these approaches popular and the populist politics associated with them highlight the deep-rooted domestic basis for Australia's Strategic Cultural fear of Asia.

The rise of Imperial Japan and the very real threat it posed in the Second World War confirmed the bias in Australian mindsets (this episode is discussed in detail in Chapter 8). Japanese culture was 'alien' to the European values that Australia held dear and was perceived to pose a real threat. Despite tensions rising in the 1930s, analysts did not predict that Japan would attempt to dramatically expand its empire to include most of Asia and the Pacific. With the fall of Singapore in 1942,[10] European imperial forces in Asia had been quickly defeated and Canberra's worst fears came to pass. Ultimately, the Japanese attack on US forces at Pearl Harbour on 7 December 1941 awoke the 'sleeping giant', which sealed Tokyo's defeat in 1945. Canberra also gained a new ally (see Chapters 3 and 4).

With the post-Second World War wave of decolonization, Australia became aware of the strength of other Asian cultures, such as Indonesia, and this further entrenched threat perceptions and the sense of alienation from its geography. One by one the European empires in Asia retreated or fell (in Indonesia, Hong Kong, Malaya, the Philippines) and Australia was left as the only Western outpost in an increasingly nationalistic Asia. Asian values essentialized through concepts such as communalism and authoritarianism that reinforced Australia's cultural difference.[11] The combination of Asian values with Communism during the Cold War further alienated Canberra.

Australia has been described as 'the odd man out' in Asia, and despite numerous attempts to break down barriers they remain and may actually have been reinforced over time.[12] From the standpoint of culture, it is arguable whether Australia *is* in fact in Asia. Australia's geography is inescapable, with close maritime borders with Indonesia and Papua New Guinea, but the dramatic mismatch in identity is not as easily bridged.

Debating Asia

There has been much debate about Australia's place in Asia and it came to a head with the Asian values debate in the 1990s (see also Chapter 10).[13] The values that bind Australia to the UK or US (such as individual rights, universal human rights, democracy) are not necessarily valued or institutionalized to the same degree in all Asian states. A key assumption drawn from this sense of cultural difference was that Australian values and security were potentially under threat. Ultimately, this proved not to be the case, but it prompted commentators to ask 'is Australia an Asian Country?'[14]

Australia viewed Asia as a block of countries, even if states in Asia did not necessarily view themselves this way. Intermittently in the post-Second World War era, Canberra made attempts at political and economic integration,[15] but these only really succeeded in the economic sphere where self-interest prevailed. In international trade, growth was the key aim of all states and competition between Asian states to build export-oriented industries was the norm, so there was little sense of 'Asianess' driving regional diplomacy. Furthermore, historical animosities (which formed part of their own strategic cultures) between states such as China and Japan or Korea and Japan, often threatened to lead to conflict and disorder rather than supporting the creation of a cohesive Asian identity. So, it was debatable whether there really was an 'Asia' for Australian policy-makers to contrast themselves with, nonetheless a strong point of contrast was identified.

Debates about whether Australia was an Asian nation tested the underlying basis of Strategic Culture (shared history and values), and despite significant efforts by the Labor governments of the 1980s and 1990s to break barriers to closer engagement with Asia, the distinctiveness prevailed. Anglo-Saxon attitudes derived from the colonial era, and more recently Anglo-American inclinations from the post-Second World War era, remain an essential part of Australia's identity. Furthermore, despite immigration and shifting demographics, which have enriched Australian multiculturalism and increased the 'Asian' population in Australia, Australia is not an 'Asian' nation.[16] Australia's identity as an outsider has been reinforced by historical events and has supported the maintenance of exaggerated threat perceptions.

(Exaggerated) Threat perceptions from Asia (and the Indo-Pacific)

Australia's threat perceptions are derived from geographic proximity to, and cultural alienation from, Asia. Whether threat perceptions are exaggerated is a matter of debate. As noted in the preceding section, British colonists felt a threat from European colonizers in Asia almost from the very beginning of colonization. In fact, soon after the colony was established in January 1788, two French frigates arrived at Botany Bay. The British were surprised as they were in the process of relocating to a more suitable site at Sydney Harbour and made their territorial claim clear.

Over the next 150 years, threat perceptions in the Australian Colonies mirrored those in mother England. This was evidenced in relation to the provision of volunteers from all six Australian Colonies to fight against Dutch settlers in the Boer War from 1899 to 1902[17] and from the newly independent nation to fight the Germans in the European Theatre during the First World War from 1914 to 1918. In fact, only a few hours after the First World War was declared, Australian

AUSTRALIA'S STRATEGIC CULTURE

forces fired on and interned a German ship trying to escape Port Phillip Bay. Australia's second, more significant action occurred with the invasion of the German colony of New Guinea on 11 September 1914.

In the nineteenth century, the outposts of unfriendly European empires, such as Germany, had little capacity to threaten the Australian Colonies or the fledgling nation founded in 1901. However, threat perceptions are not necessarily aligned with reality and the government and population felt profoundly threatened. The disconnect between capacity, intentions and realistic strategic calculations is why threat perceptions ingrained in Strategic Culture can be described as exaggerated. Furthermore, they are ingrained and fit the theory of Strategic Culture insofar as they are replicated by historical processes that extend beyond the initial source of threat.

As the Australian nation grew in power and confidence, the next threat perceived was from an Asian empire, namely Japan, and this piqued Australia's sense of cultural alienation. Japan attacked and destroyed most of the US Pacific fleet at Pearl Harbour on 7 December 1941 and land forces quickly captured Singapore, the bastion of UK power in Asia, on 15 February 1942. The Americans arrived after losing the Philippines and General Douglas MacArthur's command reported that Australia was vulnerable: 'The forces available in Australia were inadequate to meet the Japanese threat' and 'limitations of manpower and productive capacity ... made support from overseas essential.'[18] The map reproduced here clearly shows the geography of threat in 1942, and also clearly connects to the isolation and perceptions of indefensibility that are other elements of Australia's unique Strategic Culture.

The events of 1942 piqued Australia's threat perceptions, and for possibly the only time in history, they heralded an existential threat to Australia that was not exaggerated – that is, the Japanese initially planned to invade Papua New Guinea (PNG) to contain the threat posed by Australia. See Map 2.1. Plans to invade Australia were under-developed and quickly superseded by Japanese losses in PNG and the Solomons. This was a liminal moment for Australian policy-makers that connected alienation from Asia, threat perceptions and a sense of indefensibility (to be discussed in the next section) to form a potent attribute of Strategic Culture.

Ultimately, the Japanese were defeated in the Second World War, and in the process Australia gained a new 'great and powerful friend', namely the US (the Australia–US relationship will be discussed in detail in Chapters 3 and 4). However, the removal of Japan as an existential threat did not reduce Australian threat perceptions. In fact, being threatened became a general state of being in search of a specific threat. As such, the perceived threat of Japan in the Second World War was quickly replaced by the threat of Communism and this persisted throughout the Cold War. In this way, heightened or exaggerated threat perceptions became a permanent fixture of Strategic Culture.

The Communist threat was first identified in Europe, but the distance from Australia did not make it any less a driver of policy. As will be noted below, Australian policy-makers habitually identify with threats to the strategic interests of 'great and powerful friends' and respond with strategies that involve a pluralist Liberal Internationalist, Realist and Strategic Cultural response. As the Cold War

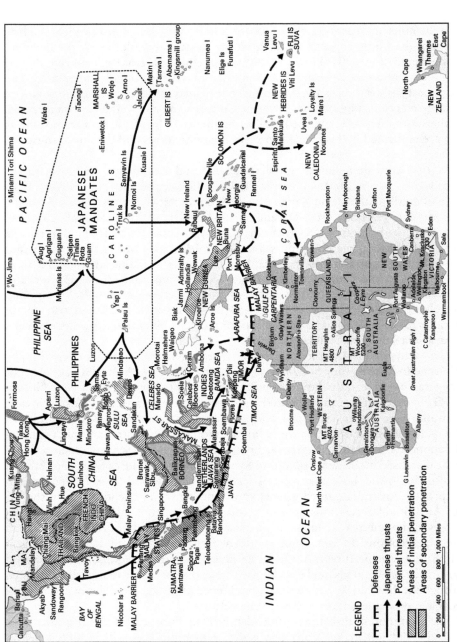

MAP 2.1 *The Japanese threat, 1942.*[19]

began in the late 1940s, Australian policy-makers were key drivers in establishing the UN to institutionally protect international peace and security, but at the same time, hedged by maintaining a physical 'forward defence' strategy that saw Australian troops deployed alongside the US in Korea and Commonwealth forces in Malaya from the early 1950s.

These conflicts brought 'international' Communism to Asia. Despite the large distances from conflict zones to Australia and the lack of local military capacity, Australia still perceived a heightened threat. These conflicts were considered part of the Domino Theory whereby decolonizing states were seen as being susceptible to Communist insurrection and could fall like a row of dominos that knock each other over.[20] The Communist threat appeared imminent and drove AFP. As with alignment with the strategic interests of allies, the adoption of the Domino Theory highlighted the direct influence of UK/US strategy on AFP. This influence continues to this day and is evident in the response to the rise of China, including the most recent hardening of strategic calculations that occurred after President Trump was elected in 2017.

As the Cold War unfolded, various Communist threats were identified in Asia and dealt with in a familiar pattern that resonated with responses to the Boer War and the First and Second World Wars. Australia followed the UK and then US in supporting 'friendly' anti-Communist authoritarian regimes, such as that of President Suharto in Indonesia, to maintain political stability. Where a breach in order occurred, Australia most often provided troops, such as in the case of Korea, Malaya or Vietnam, thereby becoming involved in wars in mainland Southeast Asia during every decade from the 1940s to the 1970s.

As the Cold War came to an end in the late 1980s, foreign policy and defence strategy were reviewed, but the liminal moment prompted by the collapse of the Soviet Bloc in 1989 did not see a dramatic change in threat perceptions. As with the end of the Second World War, Australian policy-makers looked for Liberal Internationalist alternatives in relation to strengthened global governance through a revitalized UN and the creation of regional institutional architecture, such as the Asia-Pacific Economic Cooperation (APEC) forum or the Association of Southeast Asian Nations Regional Forum (ARF). However, as with the end of the Second World War, Australia was also committed to using military force as a key foreign policy tool, in this case to support the US in the first Gulf War in 1990 and greater UN interventionism throughout the 1990s. The inertia in Australia's foreign policy highlights the enduring and self-perpetuating nature of Strategic Culture.[21]

The hope of a new world order dawning at the end of the Cold War slowly waned as UN interventions got bogged down in increasingly complex peace-making operations, such as those in Yugoslavia (1991), Somalia (1992) and Rwanda (1994). The final flicker of hope was extinguished by the 9/11 attacks on New York and Washington, DC in 2001. The US-led international response in the 'War on Terror' has endured in the foreground and then background of international affairs to this day. In the 'War on Terror', Canberra was firm in supporting US strategic interests and deployed forces in a habitual manner that was in tension with both Realist and Liberal Internationalist explanations for foreign policy.[22] The details of how these events brought Australia and the US closer together are dealt with in detail in Chapter 3, but suffice to say the swift declaratory support by Prime Minister John Howard, who was in Washington, DC at the time, and the subsequent provision of military forces to US-led operations in Iraq, Afghanistan and elsewhere, provides a clear example of the pluralistic application of elements of Strategic Culture, Realism and Liberal Internationalism. This combination of approaches to international affairs is most noteworthy in the threat perceptions and support for the US.

The 'War on Terror'

Prime Minister Howard quickly framed the terrorist attacks as 'a massive assault on the values not only of the United States of America but also of this country'.[23] Therefore, the threat was identified as targeting Australia and the Liberal values that Australia and the US shared. The attacks were also seen as triggering provisions of the Australia, New Zealand, United States (ANZUS) alliance that required joint action to counter shared threats.[24] Canberra's response was as much aimed at the US/international audience as it was domestic public opinion where Strategic Cultural threat perceptions were inflamed. As such, Canberra's actions reinforced the value of Australian diplomatic support for US strategic interests, including creating what had been aptly termed 'Coalitions of the Willing' in relation to support for the Gulf War in 1990 and subsequent US-led interventions.

International terrorism was framed as an existential threat to the Liberal 'rules-based order' of which Australia was a firm supporter and also a direct threat to Australia. It was not clear how credible this threat was in 2001 or at key times when decisions were made to escalate support for the 'War on Terror', but it remained a clear message in declaratory policy. This framing was aligned closely with (exaggerated) threat perceptions that characterized Australia's Strategic Culture and spoke to the domestic audience. The messaging was generally welcomed by the electorate and justified a significant militarization of Australian public policy and this was not the first time, since the Hawke government had a similar response to the end of the Cold War.[25] Militarization was measured by a dramatic rise in the tempo of military operations overseas and in defence spending, but also through a raft of legislation in relation to intelligence gathering and surveillance. In addition, militarization was apparent in connections drawn to other divisive domestic issues, such as the 'unauthorized arrival' of asylum seekers (which is discussed in Chapter 15).

The rising threat from China

The rise of China is significant insofar as it was perceived by Canberra as a strategic threat which prompted a return to more orthodox geopolitical competition. It was not so much that China was rising, as this had been occurring since the 1990s, but rather that it went from an economic saviour to be perceived as a potential military threat. It was difficult to pinpoint a moment when this occurred, but China's rejection of the International Tribunal's finding on the Spratly Islands in 2016 and its subsequent militarization of the South China Sea in the face of denials provides a useful timeframe.[26]

Canberra's firming opinion of China could be connected to US foreign policy, but this is another case where Australia led. Critics often point to Australia being a dependent follower of the US, but this is another example where Canberra identified its interests and acted on them. Furthermore, it was not just in Australia's interests to stand up to Chinese coercion, but also to tie the US more closely to the region, and to build closer links with like-minded states. This is precisely what Canberra did with AUKUS (Australia, UK, US), the Quad (Australia, India, Japan, US), bilateral relations with the US and Japan and ratcheted up competition with China in the South Pacific. Australian policy documents, such as the 2016 Defence White Paper and 2017 Foreign Policy White Paper, actually pre-empted the Trump administration's increasing confrontation with China.[27] This highlighted Canberra's fragile sense of security and the strong relationship between Australia's exaggerated threat perceptions and the fear of abandonment, whereby the perceptions of drift in US engagement in the Indo-Pacific prompted a response in Canberra.

Permanent threats in the absence of permanent enemies

If threat perceptions simply involved a rational calculus posited by Realism, they could be ameliorated through the development of military power and by norms protecting sovereignty through Liberal Internationalist organs of global governance. If these orthodox strategies worked in Australia's case, then it would be unlikely that exaggerated threat perceptions would be a core facet of Australia's Strategic Culture. There are many other states that also have heightened threat perceptions, but many are likely to face a clear and present danger that justifies these threat perceptions. Not many states fit this mould, perhaps the US and USSR during the Cold War, and Israel also stands out. Presently, Ukraine is being threatened by Russia and several North-East Asian states feel this threat from China. By contrast, Australia has only faced this type of existential threat for a brief period during the Second World War and therefore Canberra's threat perceptions appear exaggerated.

Australian Strategic Culture identifies potential threats from the 'north' in every decade since independence in 1901 (and also during pre-independence colonial times). As the Cold War faded in the late 1980s, identifying threats from other states, especially neighbouring states in Asia, became more diplomatically unpalatable, and the tone of declaratory policy softened. However, propping up the ANZUS alliance though expeditionary operations alongside the US and defence spending remained priorities.[28] This permanent tempo led to Smith and Kettle's critique that Canberra had 'threats without enemies'.[29] This focus on military threats did not change during the 'War on Terror' when the threat from fundamentalist Islamic terror was identified because being threatened was habitual in AFP. As the 'War on Terror' faded in the 2010s, Canberra identified China as a major strategic threat from 2018.

Threatening capabilities versus intentions

The shift from identifying specific threats to being concerned about the general capabilities of Indo-Pacific states occurred in the late 1980s. As noted, the liminal strategic moment provided by the end of the Cold War in 1989 afforded policy-makers the opportunity to reappraise strategy. The Dibb Review, produced in 1986, highlighted that there were no credible high-level threats to Australia, but that lower-level threats could develop 'from or through' Indonesia.[30] This analysis was highly contested as it posed a major challenge to the high-level threat perceptions that have shaped Strategic Culture. The idea of lowering the level of credible threats to less than a high-level existential threat challenged the very basis of the militarized strategic calculations that had come to dominate AFP. In this case, the Indonesian archipelago had variously been described as a 'protective barrier' against threats or as a source of threat itself, and this tension was difficult to reconcile with increasingly sensitive relations with Jakarta.[31] However, despite sensitivities in relations, the alienation from Asia and feelings of indefensibility continued to fuel exaggerated threat perceptions.

No state with the capability or intention to militarily threaten Australia exists anywhere in Asia or the Indo-Pacific, and Indonesia certainly does not meet these criteria. However, the influence of Strategic Culture was enduring and threat perceptions were not based simply on rational calculations. In the end, policy-makers planned to be able to defeat any regional state and therefore the lack of any *actual* threatening intentions was sidestepped in favour of a focus on the possession of military capabilities. Australia would prepare to counter any regional state that could potentially threaten it if hostile intentions developed in the future.[32] This hedging against future potential threats skewed planning in favour of high-level scenarios because Australia's military establishment focused on 'threats without enemies'.[33]

The 1986 Dibb Review: rational policy-making meets Strategic Culture

The 1986 Dibb Review had responded to the lack of enemies by producing a scale of threats to Australia based on their credibility or likelihood of occurring (Box 2.2).[34] This rational approach to planning was in tension with the biases evident in Strategic Culture and also traditional approaches to defending Australia held by the defence establishment. In a play on Blainey's focus on distance, this tension in defence planning has been described as a 'Tyranny of Dissonance'.[35] That is, the defence establishment was not inclined to accept strategic guidance that ran counter to long-held orthodoxies about the worst-case scenarios that Australia might face. Dibb eschewed the types of high-level threats that had driven defence planning since federation in 1901. These types of existential threats involved the nightmare scenario of a direct invasion of Australia and justified high levels of defence spending on equipment designed for countering equally armed opponents. By contrast, a rational/technocratic approach did not reflect upon the ingrained beliefs inherent to Strategic Culture and produced an unpalatable alternative that was strongly resisted.

AUSTRALIA'S STRATEGIC CULTURE

BOX 2.2: CREDIBLE CONTINGENCIES

- Low-level or escalated low-level threats as the most credible.
- High-level threats required long lead times to develop (10–15 years, if at all).
- Credible low-level threats involved scenarios such as small-scale harassment of offshore oil rigs.
- While low-level contingencies were the most credible, this did not mean that they were likely to occur.
- Challenged high-level capabilities-based threat planning.

The 1987 Defence White Paper that followed and purportedly implemented the Dibb Review did not integrate the graduated credible threat spectrum. The equipment and doctrine proposed ignored the focus on low-level threats through a clever fix.[36] The argument used was that equipment designed to counter high-level threats could be used to counter low-level threats, but the opposite would not be true. Therefore, foreign policy remained aligned to a militarized version of Strategic Culture and low-level contingencies were quietly forgotten.

Despite the lack of credibility, or to put it another way, the incredible possibility that Australia would face an existential threat from another state (directly targeted against it), exaggerated threat perceptions remain a persistent and distinctive element of Strategic Culture. Furthermore, they continue to be exaggerated beyond credible contingencies that are likely to present themselves, such as regular natural disasters and political crises in the South Pacific. Exaggerated threats are so enduring that they have outlived specific sources of threat that no longer figure in strategic calculations, such as European empires, Imperial Japan, Communism in Asia or the 'War on Terror'. This process is aptly characterized by defence doctrine that has focused on 'threats without enemies'.[37] That is, preparing to counter threats that refer to the capabilities of regional powers without reference to their intention to threaten Australia. Clearly, this approach to not identifying threats was a declaratory policy tactic aimed at reducing diplomatic sensitivities by not identifying a particular threat, but the fact that it has driven defence strategy during key liminal moments in AFP, such as the end of the Cold War, highlights its salience in Strategic Culture.

Furthermore, while there was debate over Canberra's apparent 'China Choice' in the 2000s, it is clear to all that China is being viewed as a threat to the rules-based international order or the US if not directly to Australia (this debate is discussed in Chapter 6). This debate connects directly to present AFP and assumptions about the coming war with China and decisions to purchase high-level equipment such as nuclear-powered submarines. The Albanese government has clearly stated that it would support the US alliance, but also greater defence spending to support defence self-reliance, which was the focus of the 1986 Dibb Review. This is recognition of the changing strategic environment and could also be seen as a hedging strategy against US decline. The 2020 Strategic Update noted the prospect of high-intensity military conflict in the Indo-Pacific is less remote than at the time of the 2016 Defence White

Paper, including high-intensity military conflict between the United States and China.[38] This means that the government is not identifying China as a direct military threat to Australia but rather a threat to the US and Indo-Pacific 'rules-based order'. Furthermore, strategic warning time was reduced to below 10 years, meaning that Australia has to acquire and field military capabilities sooner rather than later.

A sense of indefensibility arising from geography and demography

Intimately connected to Australia's exaggerated threat perceptions is a heightened sense of indefensibility. As noted earlier, from colonization Australia's settler society *perceived* an existential threat from European empires in Asia and the Pacific, such as France, Germany and Russia. Threat perceptions were coupled with the distance from the 'mother country' (the United Kingdom), the geographic size of continental Australia, and small population, to produce feelings of isolation in a potentially unfriendly neighbourhood (Box 2.3). However, as noted above, for most of Australia's history it was *potential* threats that drove strategic calculations rather than credible existential threats.

Australia is a great distance from the UK. At the time of colonization this was a greater strategic distance, as travel by ship took three months, so the Colony could not expect help if a threat presented itself. When the first air link was created in 1918, it took 28 days and while this has been reduced to less than a day, travel by ship today still takes 40 days. Basing a British naval squadron in Singapore in the 1920s did provide some assurance to Canberra, but the fragility of the assumptions behind this assurance was revealed by the fall of Singapore to the Japanese in 1942. Any illusions of local support from other British colonies, whether Hong Kong or Singapore, was quickly dashed. However, despite the fragility of these assumptions, the habit of encouraging a 'great and powerful friend' to garrison forces in the region has continued. The ramping up of US Marine rotations forces in Darwin and the announcement in 2022 that US B52 strategic bombers would be based there are the latest examples of this habit.

Australia is the world's only island continent, which is not a strategic issue in itself, but coupled with threat perceptions it raises concerns about defensibility.

BOX 2.3: THE CORE ELEMENTS OF STRATEGIC CULTURE AND INDEFENSIBILITY

- Alienation and threat from region
- Distance from allies
- Large size of the Australian continent
- Small population
- Rich natural resources

Australia is the world's seventh largest state, with a landmass of nearly 7.8 million square kilometres. Its coastline is approximately 34,000 kilometres long (not including offshore islands), which gives it the sixth longest coastline on earth. These geographic realities needn't be problematic, but if they are perceived to be vulnerabilities, then this feeds into perceptions of indefensibility. No regional states have the capability or intention to invade Australia, so these geographic realities are actually strengths, but only if the defence establishment chooses to view them as such.

The population of Australia is approximately 26 million, placing it 55th in the world and represents about a third of one per cent of the global population. Comparatively, Australia's population is much smaller than most Indo-Pacific states that form the target of the threat perceptions that characterize Strategic Culture. Australia's population density is 3.3 per square kilometre, with only three states having a lower density. The average density for Asia is approximately 150 per square kilometre, ranking it as the most densely populated region on earth. Australia's population is highly urbanized, with over 90 per cent living in large cities, mostly on the eastern seaboard. Despite the size of the continent, over 50 per cent of the population lives within seven kilometres of the coast.

Australia has the world's largest exclusive economic zone (EEZ), which provides a huge bounty of offshore and undersea resources. Sovereignty dictates that the EEZ needs to be policed and for Canberra the focus of these efforts are illegal fishing and transnational crime (especially human trafficking). Furthermore, as an island with an export-oriented economy, Australia's strategic geography demands that defence is extended to its proximate approaches and trade routes linking it to major markets in the Indo-Pacific, Europe and North America. This explains Australia's emphasis on maritime forces (air and sea) versus the land forces required for continental defence. This focus was reiterated in the 2023 Defence Strategic Review, which queried whether Army projects in the pipeline should be cut in order to fund maritime capabilities, such as submarines.

The relatively small size of the population and large coastline has been connected to feelings of indefensibility since before Australian independence. In 1901, when Australia's Strategic Culture was in its infancy, these strategic factors mutually reinforced a sense of indefensibility because the Australian Colonies had no military forces and little capacity to fund or organize themselves in the face of perceived threats from other European empires in Asia. Furthermore, as the nation grew attempts to 'populate or perish' through selective immigration policies failed to deliver sufficient population growth that could counter deep-seated insecurities.

This indefensibility was reinforced throughout history by liminal events that happened elsewhere, but piqued the threat perceptions in Australia. Events around the time of Australia's independence such as the Boer War in South Africa (1899–1901), the Russo-Japanese War (1904–5) and the First World War (1914–18) had a significant impact on threat perceptions, the sense of indefensibility and the key prescription to insecurity – reliance on a 'great and powerful friend' (which is discussed below). A good example of this habitual response was the adherence to the US belief in the Domino Theory[39] during the Cold War whereby Australia was feared to be 'The Last Domino' (Box 2.4).[40]

BOX 2.4: THE DOMINO THEORY OF COMMUNIST EXPANSIONISM

- Developed by US strategists to explain the spread of Communism during the Cold War.
- Popularized by US President Dwight Eisenhower in 1954 (at the time France was defeated by the Vietnamese).
- Washington (and Canberra) feared that the 'loss' of China to Communists in 1949 would spread throughout Asia.
- The Asian possessions of European empires were decolonizing and could be prone to Communist ideology.
- Asian states were seen as dominos lined up and ready to fall with each 'loss' influencing the others to fall under Communist influence.
- In the 1960s, the Domino Theory was influential in the Australian response to the Malayan Confrontation, the Suharto coup in Indonesia, and commitment alongside the US to the Vietnam War.
- The rapprochement with China in 1972 led to a reappraisal of the conceptualization of whether international Communism was a unified force.

International events to the present day, such as China's rapid military modernization and militarization of the South China Sea in the 2000s, have acted to perpetuate this belief in indefensibility.

Debating indefensibility

The accuracy of the belief in indefensibility is questionable for the same reasons as Australian threat perceptions can be said to be exaggerated (discussed earlier). In the absence of a credible threat, there is nothing to defend against, but if threat perceptions persist, then a credible response is needed. Early colonists were confident that the Royal Navy would defend their interests from European empires in Asia[41] and this confidence persisted after federation in 1901. However, this debate point over whether Australia was in fact militarily threatened becomes tautological because the facts are not as important as government and public perceptions at liminal moments in history. This highlights the importance of *perceptions* and *misperceptions*.[42]

As the *perception* of threat or indefensibility is real, then threat itself does not have to be 'real'. Perceptions drive policy regardless of their credibility and this is clearly what has occurred in Australia since before federation in 1901. For example, after the Second World War, it was discovered that Japan never seriously contemplated invading Australia. Speculative debate within the Japanese military about whether to invade Australia was quickly resolved in the negative, but the perception that a Japanese invasion was imminent drove policy. The fear of the 'alien' other to the north became reflexive in Strategic Culture. Therefore, the accuracy of the belief in indefensibility is not the point, but rather the fact that *belief* in indefensibility is a key enduring element of Australia's Strategic Culture. This belief reinforces other aspects of Strategic Culture to produce a potent driver of a highly militarized foreign policy that is self-perpetuating and enduring.

The fear of abandonment by Anglo-American allies in the face of indefensibility from a threatening region

In Australia's Strategic Culture, the core characteristics – geographic alienation, heightened threat perceptions and feelings of indefensibility – are intimately connected to what academic Allan Gyngell called the a fear of abandonment.[43] Within the logic of Strategic Culture, this fear is the seemingly natural outcome of these factors, which has led to a seemingly natural range of responses that culminate in the militarization of foreign policy. However, they are not natural, but rather the unique construct of geographic, historical and cultural experiences.

Fear of abandonment has influenced AFP at most liminal moments in Australian history. When Prime Minister Curtin looked to the US for support in 1942,[44] it was largely due to the fall of Singapore and the sense that the guarantee of Royal Navy support that had hitherto allayed fears had been broken. Similarly, the ANZUS alliance was in part a response to fears of possible US disengagement after the defeat of Japan at the end of the Second World War. Through this lens, the 2021 Australia, United Kingdom, United States (AUKUS) agreement, and initiatives to encourage US deployments on Australian soil, could be seen as attempts to reaffirm US and UK support in countering China.

The fear of abandonment made Australian policy-makers highly attuned to the strategic calculations of its 'great and powerful friends'. For example, at the beginning of the Second World War, Australia deployed the majority of its front-line forces in support of the British in the Middle East and North Africa, and then fought to hastily redeploy them closer to home after the outbreak of war in Asia. This response is evidenced in the fact that Canberra responded to calls for greater 'burden-sharing' by US policy-makers in the 1960s, 1980s and 2000s. Canberra was keen to be seen to be paying its alliance premiums whether this involved deploying forces alongside the US overseas or increasing defence spending, something that is discussed in detail in Chapters 3 and 4.

The prescription for abandonment has involved attempts at greater self-reliance through increased defence expenditure, paying strategic insurance premiums to the 'great and powerful friend' (e.g. deployments overseas), and building or strengthening international institutions of governance (UN, APEC, ASEAN-RF, Quad). This prescription involves a blend of Realist, Liberal Internationalist and Strategic Cultural approaches to AFP and highlights the need for a pluralistic approach for understanding AFP.

Institutionalizing Strategic Culture in Australia's psyche

Each individual attribute of Australia's Strategic Culture is not necessarily unique to Australia, but the uniqueness of Australian Strategic Culture comes from how they are arrayed together. This level of interconnectedness is only possible because of the protracted historical process that began with colonization in 1788 and saw Strategic Culture replicate itself continually over successive generations of citizens and policy-makers alike. A key measure of this continuity in Strategic Culture is the steadfast support for the US alliance in AFP and public opinion, and the very slow shift in opinion on other foreign policy issues.[45]

Responses to countless historical events over more than 200 years have acted to reinforce the centrality of these attributes to how Australians view themselves and the strategic environment they inhabit. Furthermore, in entrenching Strategic Culture these responses have tested the tools available to policy-makers and the room to manoeuvre in international affairs: the 'art of the possible'. In particular, the seemingly predictable response to liminal strategic moments by successive generations of policy-makers has institutionalized Strategic Culture in Australia's psyche.

During any liminal moment, such as the end of the Cold War, there *could* have been a breach in the trajectory, but in fact these events have consistently reinforced and strengthened Strategic Culture. This is not to say that alternative options have not been canvassed, but rather to identify the adaptability of Strategic Culture to how strategic change is viewed in Australia.

Militarization of security and foreign policy

It is clear from the centrality of heightened threat perceptions and habitual responses to them that AFP is militarized[46] and this reflects Australia's Strategic Culture. However, within the defence establishment there are different emphases over how to respond to the high-level threat perceptions that have been identified as integral to Australia's Strategic Culture. In defence planning there is an ongoing tension between the defence of Australia (continental defence) and countering threats further afield (forward defence). These perspectives can be used to justify different equipment to cater to different contingencies, such as fighter aircraft, tanks or submarines.

Two constants stand out in defence decision-making since the Second World War: the capacity to operate alongside the US and the ability to counter equally armed opponents. These constants highlight the influence of the forward defence school of thought where Canberra will provide expeditionary forces to operate alongside the US in distant theatres, but interestingly, Australia has not operated alongside the US against equally armed opponents (since Japan in the Second World War). This tension highlights the inertia in high-level threat perceptions from Strategic Culture that have had an enduring influence on defence planning. Similarly, while the geographic focus of these threats and deployments has wavered from Asia to the Middle East, the constant has been threats *from* Asia (and now the Indo-Pacific). This fear of the North is a constant. Even before independence, the Australian Colonies feared other empires operating in the region (such as Germany or Russia).[47] These threats drove early attempts to defend Australia, such as developing fortifications to defend the approaches to Sydney or Melbourne and led to the creation of fledgling Australian naval forces before the First World War.

In Australia's formative years, foreign policy was handled by the Home Office in London, something that persisted long after federation in 1901. As such, there was no independent foreign policy and the development of uniquely Australian interests was not as much stunted as beyond the 'art of the possible' for later colonial or early-Australian policy-makers.[48] An independent foreign policy was only formed in response to the liminal moment posed by the threat from Japan in 1941 where interests between Canberra and London diverged. With the fall of Singapore and statements from the Admiralty about defending England before defending the Colonies (that is Australia), the latent fears of abandonment prompted attempts at greater self-reliance and ultimately an alliance with a new 'great and powerful friend', namely the US (which is dealt with in detail in Chapter 3). This necessitated a dramatic shift from the 'British embrace', which highlighted where Realist national interests in finding a new ally trumped sentiment towards the 'mother country'.[49] As noted, threats from Asian states began with Japan and shifted to Communism in Asia (China, Vietnam, etc.). Indonesia was also a source of threat for much of the twentieth century, including a period when the potential for Indonesia to be a Communist threat exercised the minds of Australian policy-makers (relations with Indonesia are covered in depth in Chapter 10). It is interesting to note how threat perceptions seamlessly shifted between states, but never wavered from being focused on Asia (other than in the case of the 'War on Terror', which was still focused on Asia). From this perspective, the threat from China that firmed in the 2020s fits a familiar pattern and one that rekindles threat perceptions from the Cold War, albeit with less focus on the ideology of Communist China and more focus on the military power and economic coercion of mercantilist China (discussed in Chapter 6).

These high-level threat perceptions drove a desire to keep the US engaged with Australia's strategic interests in the Indo-Pacific region. This was more pronounced at liminal strategic moments when there were fears that the US might look inward or prioritize other issues, especially in relation to the Cold War emphasis on Europe. For instance, at the height of the Cold War, Australian policy-makers were keen to engage the US in fighting Communism in Vietnam and at end of the Cold War, in the early 1990s, Australian policy-makers supported America's engagement with the 'new world order'. Similarly, the present focus is on the 'rules-based order' in the Indo-Pacific, which represents strategic concepts developed to guide US grand strategy.

Australian political culture and strategic culture

Within Australia's distinctive Strategic Culture there are two additional themes that need to be introduced to produce a nuanced account of AFP. The first is the influence of the Liberal/Labor ideological divide in domestic politics. In addition, we need to be aware of the limits of these perspectives and therefore a reflection on both the limits of theory on the agency of policy-makers and the influence of party politics on AFP is warranted to complete the picture.

Party ideology and AFP: a Labor tradition of Liberal Internationalism and 'middlepowermanship'?

The Labor tradition in AFP is more closely associated with Liberal Internationalism than Liberal or Coalition governments (involving the Liberal Party and National Party).[50] Labor's embrace of what Canadian diplomat John Holmes described as 'middlepowermanship'[51] has often involved what's been described as 'good international citizenship' whereby progressive norms are brought to centre-stage in foreign policy. This view was elevated in AFP by Foreign Minister Gareth Evans in the 1990s.

Due to the complexity in international affairs, these aims are probably best understood as values that a government commits to rather than laws that must be followed. This approach is epitomized by a faith in progressive aspects of international order and justice that is much broader than the Liberal's support for norms and rules that promote free trade and security. Prime Minister Malcolm Fraser captured the Liberals' realism in contrast to his predecessor Gough Whitlam's idealism: we 'must be prepared to face the world as it is, and not as we would like it'.[52] The shift from idealism to realism (denoting being realistic rather than the theory of Realism) is a recurring theme in relation to changes of government,[53] and the fact that the shift occurs seamlessly highlights the pluralism within AFP.

Furthermore, while Liberals have more actively supported the alliance with the US, Labor is associated with an activist foreign policy that can be viewed as a counter to the militarized elements of Strategic Culture. This fits the ideological mould whereby the Liberals are generally conservative whilst Labor countenances alternatives to the orthodox militarized paradigm. However, we must not take these generalizations too far as Labor governments have also supported the alliance with the US and many of the apparent ideological differences have been more of declaratory policy emphasis rather than differences in operational policy, such as decisions at liminal moments about whether to deploy expeditionary forces alongside US military forces. As such, the US alliance is the most bipartisan aspect of AFP.

The ideational aspects of 'middlepowermanship' are in contrast with the Liberal acknowledgement that Australia is a *medium* power.[54] *Middle* power has connotations of creative policy advocacy based on intellectual imagination and vision.[55] This vision of foreign policy has a selfless aspect that focuses on Liberal Internationalist values such as humanitarianism and privileges multilateral approaches to achieve national interests. As such, the Labor tradition challenges the 'art of the possible' shaped by the Liberal focus on material power, where Australia could be said to be a medium power, with a preference for bilateralism and Realist perceptions of national interests. However, the Labor tradition does not challenge the foundational role of the US alliance in AFP, which makes it what academic Allan Patience has described as a 'dependent middle power'[56] at best (Table 2.1).

In other areas, there is more distance between the parties on AFP. Labor prime ministers and foreign ministers have been active advocates of Australia's position as a middle power whereby creative niche diplomacy and coalition-building with like-minded states was perceived as the best way of achieving the national interest. Despite debate over the definition of middle powers both academically and

TABLE 2.1 *Distinguishing middle and medium powers*

Middle power	Medium power
A measure of relative power presuming power equates to influence	A measure of relative power presuming power equates to influence
Focus on military, economic *and* ideational power	Focus on military and economic power
Acknowledges 'soft power' as a diplomatic tool supporting the national interest	Acknowledges 'soft power' as a diplomatic tool supporting the national interest
Elevates progressive Liberal Internationalist values in foreign policy	Elevates sovereignty but acknowledges Liberal Internationalist values with respect to national 'exemptionalism' to achieve the national interest
Advocates for progressive norms through active 'middlepowermanship'	Does not attempt to lead international agendas
More associated with Labor governments	More associated with Liberal/Coalition governments

practically,[57] these ideational aspects of leadership through the exercise of 'soft' power can be identified as shared attributes of middle powers.[58]

The ideational aspect is important because middle powers claim to be and are accepted as middle powers. As such, 'middlepowermanship', the generally Liberal Internationalist acts undertaken by middle powers, are more closely associated with Labor governments. For example, the Rudd and Gillard government's foreign policy in the early 2000s was described as 'middle power dreaming'.[59] Notable differences between the parties that fit this typology are the Asian engagement agenda promoted by the Hawke/Keating governments in the 1980s and 1990s, the climate change agenda promoted by the Rudd government in the early 2000s, and the Albanese government's willingness to conform to climate change targets in 2022.[60] Both of these issues are treated more positively in Labor party rhetoric even if the realities of foreign affairs and exigencies of electioneering limit the possibility of revolutionary shifts. The limits in achieving middle power norms has led to some disappointment amongst Labor supporters in failing to attain Liberal values,[61] but the limits of Liberal Internationalism are also analytically useful as they point to the influence of other variables, such as Strategic Culture and the need for a pluralistic approach to explaining AFP over time.

Foreign Minister Gareth Evans epitomized the activist foreign minister who strongly advocated 'middlepowermanship'. Evans focused on active engagement with the Asia-Pacific region of which he argued Australia was inextricably a part, support for democratic forms of international governance, and the elevation of traditional, not military security issues and conflict resolution mechanisms.[62] Evans' tenure straddled the end of the Cold War and his government's response to the liminal moment posed by this dramatic strategic change was to engage with the reinvigoration of the international order. Prime examples of Labor 'middlepowermanship' at this time in the early 1990s include the APEC, Cairns Group, Cambodian Peace Plan and Antarctic environmental protection.

Strategic change was met with hope for new internationalism that left the division of the Cold War behind and opportunities were sought to reorient AFP to focus on 'comprehensive engagement' with Asia.[63] A concerted effort at creating an Asian identity was attempted in the 1990s and institutionalized through APEC and the ARF. In writing about AFP, Evans noted that Australia needed to move beyond narrow nationalism to focus on internationalism and becoming an 'Asia-Pacific nation'. According to this expression of Labor's Liberal Internationalism, being an effective middle power was the best way of achieving Australia's national interests with Asia.[64]

By contrast, the Liberal Party's conception of a *medium* power involves a more instrumental perception of national interests and measure of economic and military power. As such, the Liberal Party's tradition could be more closely connected with Realist calculations of how relative national power can be applied to maximize gains for the national interest.[65] Furthermore, these calculations did not focus on the ideational power inherent in the Liberal Internationalist vision of convincing others of the ethical value of foreign policy initiatives. As such, the Liberal Party seems less interested in applying Liberal Internationalist values in the international arena, versus Liberal ideas within the domestic jurisdiction in relation to the rights of citizens (Chapter 15 identifies this tension in discussing the treatment of asylum seekers as non-citizens).

The limits of theory in explaining political agency: Realism and 'realism'

While there do seem to be tendencies between the Liberal Party and Labor Party to view the international arena differently, a word of caution is warranted. A strong caveat is needed with respect to discussion of how theory influences AFP. Most theory is an explanation of past foreign policy outcomes undertaken by observers who were not part of the policy-making process that led to decisions being made. This distance from foreign policy-making itself allows a level of abstraction and generalization that identifies broad patterns and trends. These generalizations allow an understanding of a 'system' to be developed, but for foreign policy practitioners, such as politicians and senior bureaucrats, theory is only convincing and useful if its application or 'footprint' makes sense of day-to-day international affairs.

Attempts to adequately capture the day-to-day reality of foreign policy-making leads to theoretical debate within and between academic camps, such as between Realists and neo-Realists and Liberal Internationalists, to improve explanations that are seen to diverge from the reality of foreign policy *in action*. As such, Liberal Internationalism can be seen as a response to Realism's overwhelming focus on power and competition between states, seeking to insert Liberal values, non-state actors and patterns of cooperation into considerations of foreign policy. Critical theorists go a step further by attempting to look beyond national interests to include cross-cutting themes such as feminism, but these approaches are often distant from the realities of day-to-day policy-making.

Most foreign policy analysts see these theoretical turns as providing valuable pluralistic insights that explain the messy reality of foreign policy-making. However, this embrace of pluralism may not be as welcome amongst abstract theorists seeking to stake out the ground for a particular theoretical explanation for AFP. This level of theoretical debate is beyond the scope of this book, which is not as concerned about these debates as with the usefulness of theories in explaining the reality of foreign policy-making, *in Australia*. Therefore, the focus on Strategic Culture can be viewed as an attempt to refine and extend existing theoretical perspectives by elevating the influence of local factors such as geography, history and culture on day-to-day policy.

This does not mean that Strategic Culture stands in opposition to Realism and Liberal Internationalism, but rather that it can be used in a pluralistic manner alongside insights from these theories to better make sense of AFP. For example, practical initiatives such as the Quadrilateral Dialogue (Quad), reinvigorated in 2020 and supported by the Morrison and Albanese governments, could be interpreted as an elevation of Liberal values supporting the 'rules-based order' in the Indo-Pacific.[66] Equally, the Quad could be seen as an attempt to contain China, which would conform with Realist thinking about alliances, and as the target is China, then the Quad could also be interpreted as responding to the threat from the North that drives Australian Strategic Culture.

Theoretical determinism: policy-makers are not theorists!

Once theory is used practically, it is tempting to treat theoretical explanations of past behaviour as predictors of future behaviour. We must be cautious about this sort of *determinism* because of the diversity of approaches to foreign policy-making that are exhibited locally. Theory can assist in understanding the past and point to future developments, but it does not determine the agency of policy-makers *who are not theorists*.

A connection is often made between theory and policy-makers, as in the earlier discussion of the Labor tradition in foreign policy. However, most policy-makers are unlikely to be aware of the twists and turns in theoretical debates or that they are likely to be labelled as exhibiting behaviour that appears to conform with a particular theory. For instance, Prime Minister John Howard reacted to the end of the Cold War by strengthening the US alliance and supporting the US war in Iraq. This could be viewed through a Realist lens but it does not mean that when he made this decision he referred to a copy of Hans Morgenthau's *Politics Among Nations*.[67] Howard may have been a Realist, but that does not mean that he identified as such.

Even when policy-makers mention theory, they may not be using the term precisely. For example, Howard described his approach as 'positive realism', but it was clear that he was referring to being realistic and pragmatic and this was contrasted to his Labor opponents who he was accusing of being idealistic and unrealistic.[68] Liberals may search for greater realism than the apparent idealism of Labor, but they are not necessarily Realists![69] The idealism of Labor can partially be explained by a history of more Liberal Internationalist declaratory rhetoric that was not necessarily backed up by consistent changes in operational policy. That is, declaratory policy was what Labor said about foreign policy, and how themes were described in policy statements rather than substantive shifts in policy.

Theoretical perspectives may interact with policy, but in the eyes of the policy-makers themselves, theory did not necessarily consciously influence or inform it. So analysts must be cautious when we apply theoretical traits to policy-makers or their policies because they are abstractions applied after the fact to describe outcomes and therefore should not be treated as being historically deterministic.

The search for alternatives versus an emphasis on additional options

Regardless of comments in the previous section, there are also grounds to be cautious about how much Labor's apparent preference for Liberal Internationalist alternatives represents a challenge to the status quo that is reflected in Strategic Culture. It may simply be that Labor's willingness to countenance alternatives is more apparent than real as it has not led to a wholesale change in AFP. This means that in practice canvassing options occurs within the context of the 'art of the possible' shaped by numerous factors, including Australia's relative power and the limitations posed by structure of the international system. Canvassing options occurs within the context of underlying trends in Strategic Culture.

This means that a search for options does not lead to a zero-sum decision; it was not black or white/alliance or not. However, due to the highly politicized nature of domestic electoral politics, it is likely that exploring options could be characterized as a divisive zero-sum equation. This way, any dramatic shift in AFP would be seen by the electorate as a breach with elements of Strategic Culture that neither public opinion nor either of the political parties actually believes is negotiable, such as the US alliance. Therefore, inertia remains one of the most powerful forces in AFP. The best predictor of what Canberra will do tomorrow is what it did yesterday.

Conclusion

Australian Strategic Culture can be compared and contrasted with the two dominant theoretical approaches used to explain foreign policy: Realism and Liberal Internationalism. As noted, when these perspectives are explicitly related to AFP, this is generally done in an abstract fashion. As such, a pluralistic approach taken in this book offers Strategic Culture as an explanatory framework for AFP while also including insights from the more dominant systemic International Relations theories. Australia's Strategic Culture will be shown to contain elements of these theories in a manner that reflects its explanatory purpose rather than theoretical purity.

The distinctive takeaway from this chapter that is unorthodox in the study of AFP is that systemic theory can be demystified and de-ideologized. The addition of Strategic Culture to analyses allows theory to be reformulated in a pluralistic toolkit that can be used to explain the key tenets of Australian foreign policy.

3

Background to the United States:
The making of the 'unbreakable' alliance

Introduction

The diplomatic relationship with the US is the most important in Australian foreign policy (AFP) and in many ways frames this book. This chapter will provide a historical background on how this came to pass by connecting diplomatic relations to the evolution of Strategic Culture. We will see that the ANZUS (Australia, New Zealand, United States) alliance has endured many strategic changes that could have made it redundant to one or all parties. However, the 'ties that bind' Australia and the US are so strong that they transcend naked Realist calculations or the lofty hopes that Liberal Internationalist norms would bring lasting peace.

The relationship with the US has led to much debate in Australia and these debates over issues such as hosting US bases/joint facilities, dependence on US equipment and doctrine, and impacts on Australia's reputation provide a telling insight into the influence of Strategic Culture on AFP. This chapter provides background to the next, which concentrates on the present state of diplomatic relations. How the Australia–US relationship is institutionalized forms the focus of this chapter and informs the structure of all chapters so that comparisons and contrasts can be drawn.

Thematic questions addressed in this chapter include: How has the US alliance become 'unbreakable'? Does alliance renewal through liminal moments in history question the Realist emphasis on there being 'no permanent alliances, only permanent interests'? How has the alliance survived in the face of domestic opposition to following the US into wars throughout the twentieth century? How strong is anti-Americanism in Australia? How have tensions between US universal ideology and Washington's pursuit of its national interests been resolved?

The making and strengthening of the 'unbreakable alliance': the alignment of interests at liminal moments in history

Due to its central place in AFP, the Australia–US relationship is of particular interest during times of dramatic strategic change. Strategic change, such as the end of the Second World War, the US withdrawal from the Vietnam War in 1973, the end of the Cold War in 1989, the post-2001 War on Terror, and the challenge China poses to international order brings foreign policy assumptions into the spotlight. Policy and public debates occur with heightened vigour that can prompt new possibilities to be canvassed. The rise of China as a strategic competitor to the US and potential threat to Australia is a 'liminal' moment whereby the status quo is threatened, but opportunities also develop.[1]

Liminal moments are when a transition between two eras may be occurring (such as the end of an empire, rise of another, start of a war or when peace is declared). As such, liminal strategic events test the continuity evident in Australia's Strategic Culture. There are few revolutions in AFP and at first glance this continuity may be surprising, and it is why Strategic Culture is such an important perspective to bring into any analysis of AFP. The question is: in what sense will continuity with the past be maintained and how it will influence Canberra's response to China?

The Australia–US relationship was borne from the darkest days of the Second World War and this baptism of fire has cast a long shadow over diplomatic relations ever since. However, the alliance has never faced a challenge of the sort posed by the rise of China. In the 2010s, speculation was rife that Australia would have to make a choice with bitter consequences, regardless of the path taken. This chapter argues that posing Canberra's dilemma as a China choice was divorced from the reality of Australia's strategic planning. If there was a choice to be made, then Australia had already firmly chosen the US due to the long-held calculations of the national interests that reflect an overlap between Realism and Strategic Culture and Liberal Internationalism. This is despite the fact that on occasion the US itself challenges the Liberal Internationalist order and values that are often singled out as binding relations. AFP is also sometimes in tension with these values, such as in the case of the treatment of asylum seekers, leading to 'exemptionalism'.[2] This reinforces the importance of using a pluralistic approach to explaining foreign policy. The question of what the future may hold in respect to Australia's bilateral relationship with China is also examined in Chapter 6.

The most important contextual point to keep in the forefront while we survey the history and character of the Australia–US relationship is the asymmetry between the two countries. By all measures other than geography, Australia is a medium or middle power. In contrast, the US remains an unsurpassed global superpower. This unrivalled strength since the end of the Cold War is under challenge from China, but the US has faced challengers before, such as from Europe and Japan and has undergone renewal.

The US is the international hegemon that established and supported the Liberal International system, although this also appears to be under challenge, giving rise to the liminal moment that is exercising the minds of strategists in Canberra. US military and economic strength and its universalist culture has buttressed the international system. Its economic primacy is under more challenge than other elements of hegemony. Furthermore, its capacity for renewal has been demonstrated numerous times over the last century, so we must be circumspect in elevating the significance of any of these trends, lest we fall into the trap of the analytical 'arrogance of the present'. It would be ahistorical to exaggerate the significance of

BACKGROUND TO THE UNITED STATES 41

current events or to devalue the role of historical trends such as the US capacity for renewal or the plateauing of rising powers.

The US retains the position of the world's largest economy (gross domestic product [GDP] per capita), gained in the 1890s, although China is predicted to overtake it in the next decade. China has already overtaken the US when GDP is measured using purchasing power parity (PPP), but US per capita wealth and the stock of wealth in the US greatly surpasses China and will do so for the foreseeable future. By contrast, Australia's PPP is ranked nineteenth in the world. The US population of 338 million is the world's third largest and forms a large consumer market that is on par with China's, even though China has a population four times the size of the US. In contrast, Australia's population of 26 million ranks fifty-third in the world.

The US also has unrivalled ideational and cultural power insofar as it stands as the beacon for democracy, capitalism and the Liberal world order that dominates international institutions and norms. This position is maintained no matter how imperfect US leadership is. US movies, media, music and fashion also have unparalleled reach and these elements of soft power buttress and partially offset the imperfect application of hard power to suit America's national interests. It is noteworthy that Europe, Japan and China do not have the potential to produce an ideational challenge to US cultural soft power.

US defence spending is relatively stable at US$767 billion per annum, which represents 38 per cent of the global total. Its nearest competitor, China, spends US$270 billion, or 13 per cent of the total. By contrast, Australia spends US$28 billion or 1.4 per cent of global spending, placing it in twelfth position internationally.[3] The US military incudes 1.348 million active personnel and 858,000 reserves, making it the third largest military on earth. The strength of the Australian Defence Force (ADF) stands at 59,000 with 21,000 reserves, making it the sixty-sixth largest military on earth. Comparisons between the size of militaries and their quality are notoriously difficult to make due to a range of factors, such as doctrine, equipment, training and operational experience. However, it is acknowledged that Australia and the US have fielded well-equipped, highly trained forces in recent conflicts that use ever-evolving doctrine honed through extensive operational experience. This cannot be said for many other militaries, including China's, and is treated as a key practical benefit of the alliance.

Background/history

The US became Australia's security guarantor and major trading partner after the Second World War. With the benefit of hindsight, this shift appears natural as the UK declined, the British Empire lost global reach, and Europe became the focus of British foreign policy and trade.[4] However, this seemingly seamless transition between 'great and powerful friends' was far from natural and obscures the significant diplomatic efforts on both sides of the Pacific that led to both the creation of the ANZUS alliance and its institutionalization into an enduring aspect of AFP. At this liminal period from 1942 to 1951, policy-makers in Canberra displayed key characteristics of Strategic Culture: heightened threat perceptions and indefensibility in the face of the fear of the North. Alliance with a 'great and powerful friend' and development of the US brokered 'rules-based order' provided the prescription for Australia's insecurities.

It is with this 'natural' transition that we see the role of Australia's Strategic Culture in shaping AFP on display. First and foremost, the shift to the US was driven by strategic considerations rather than trade or culture. Over time, diplomacy, trade and culture have buttressed the security relationship and have helped make it holistic and enduring, but these elements were secondary to the strategic calculus when Canberra saw no other option but to choose to transition from the UK to the US as security guarantor. This was a dramatic shift in sentiment given that diplomatic relations with the US were only established in 1940, with embassies not opening until 1946. The prime aim was to secure Australia from the existential threat from Japan at the nadir of the Second World War. In 1942, the British were firmly focused on defending the UK from Nazi Germany. Singapore, the bastion of UK power in Asia, fell on 15 February 1942 and the security guarantee that had hitherto cemented the historical bonds of colonialism was shattered. The greatest fear of Australian policy-makers that frames Strategic Culture was playing out: Imperial Japan posed an existential threat from the 'north' which Australia could not hope to counter alone.

Fortuitously for Canberra, the Japanese attack on the US naval base at Pearl Harbour on 7 December 1941 brought the US into the war against Japan, and Australian and US interests aligned. By the end of that month, Australian Prime Minister John Curtin famously stated that: 'Without any inhibitions of any kind, I make it quite clear that Australia looks to America, free of any pangs as to our traditional links or kinship with the United Kingdom.'[5]

At the time, Australia was vulnerable and the threat was not exaggerated. US war planning documents noted that: 'The forces available in Australia were inadequate to meet the Japanese threat' and 'limitations of manpower and productive capacity . . . made support from overseas essential.'[6] Thus, the threat from Japan was existential. After the war, historians discovered that Japan was not planning to invade Australia, but at the time all indications were that invasion was imminent and this aligned with the fears inherent to Strategic Culture. Therefore, this 'liminal moment' did not involve exaggerated fears, but the repercussions for AFP are felt until this day, as threats since 1942 have often been exaggerated.

Searching for allies would be a natural Realist response to an existential threat. Australia would always be a junior partner in an unequal relationship of mutual benefit, but the fact that Australia had also been so closely dependent on the UK and had not practised a credible level of defence self-reliance is an integral element of Australia's unique Strategic Culture. If threats are exaggerated, and Australia is ill-prepared, then Australia is seen to be indefensible without the help of a much stronger security guarantor. A central function of AFP has been to pay alliance premiums to ensure that the 'great and powerful friend' is willing and able to defend Australia from threats from the North.

BACKGROUND TO THE UNITED STATES

Close military cooperation in the Second World War evolved very quickly, with Australian forces stemming the Japanese advance on land on the Kokoda track in Papua New Guinea (PNG), while the US bogged down Japanese forces at Guadalcanal in the Solomon Islands. Australian warships fought alongside the US in the seminal naval Battle of the Coral Sea, destroying a Japanese invasion force headed for Port Moresby in PNG and contributing to the US victory at Midway. See Map 3.1. Taken together, these actions stemmed the tide of the war and prevented PNG from becoming a major staging ground for Japanese operations against Australia and Fiji.[7] As such, early relations were certainly 'forged in fire' and definitely spoke to the core attributes of Australian Strategic Culture.

The alignment of security interests forged in the defeat of Japan in the Second World War continued into the Cold War, and beyond into post-Cold War interventions.[8] The defeat of Japan was a liminal moment where Realism would tell us that an alignment can dissolve because its reason for being no longer existed, but the alignment of interests continued. The US quickly became embroiled in the Cold War with the Soviet Union, which spread to Asia through the perception that there was an international Communist conspiracy. With the 'loss' of China to Communists in 1949 and defeat of French forces at Dien Bien Phu in Vietnam in 1954, the consensus amongst US policy-makers was that Communism could spread quickly and threaten Western interests globally. This belief was expressed in the 'Domino Theory' of Communist expansionism, whereby post-colonial states in Asia were 'dominos' that could easily fall to Communism and affect their neighbours. Australian policy-makers accepted this perspective of the threat and this thinking strongly influenced Australia's participation alongside the US in the Vietnam War.[9] However, Canberra's interest in ensuring that the US remained engaged in the region was also a motivating factor.[10]

Prime Minister Harold Holt's famous June 1966 proclamation that Australia would go 'All the way with LBJ' captured Canberra's staunch support for the US. It was uttered when speaking at the White House while visiting President Lyndon B. Johnson (LBJ) and was meant to show solidarity. However, the reception in Australia to Holt's acclamation of alliance loyalty was mixed. This highlighted domestic division over the alliance and the Vietnam War, which became the most divisive issue of a generation. Holt's decision to greatly expand involvement in Vietnam had initial domestic support, but this waned.

This pattern of high-level support for US strategic interests, often against public opinion, was repeated with respect to other distant US wars, such as the Iraq War from 2003. Canberra's steadfast support was a response to the UK's ongoing withdrawal of troops in Asia, known as a withdrawal 'East of Suez' from 1968. Canberra's support was also influenced by Prime Minister Holt's close relationship with LBJ, and this was also the case with Prime Minister Howard and President George Bush, Jr. in Iraq in 2003. This demonstrates three recurring themes in the relationship with the US: the coincidence of interests, paying so-called alliance premiums in order to tie the US to Australia's interests, and the influence of close relations between leaders on policy.

The 'Domino Theory' represented the development of shared threat perceptions whereby Australia's commitment was a response to the strategic interests of its

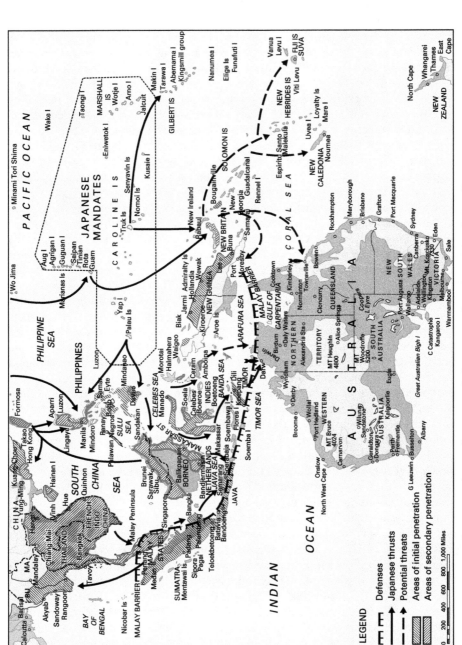

MAP 3.1 *Japanese advances in the south-west Pacific from December 1941 to April 1942.*[11]

'great and powerful friend' and to its own Strategic Culture. The Second World War threat from Imperial Japan had hardly faded before it was replaced with another existential threat. This threat from Communism was to bind Australia and US strategic interests throughout the Cold War from 1951 to 1989, when the Soviet Union collapsed. This meant that US foreign policy directly impacted Australia's security and US actions often compelled action from Canberra.

A prime example of this strategic dynamic was President Richard Nixon's 1968 Guam Doctrine, which signalled the US desire for greater burden-sharing from its allies in Asia. Australia responded by firming its commitment to fight alongside the US in Vietnam, with increased defence spending and greater self-reliance, but as with earlier support for the British Empire, this did not equate to strategic independence. It was framed as a greater capacity to provide (local) support for the US, and Australia's defence policy in the 1980s coined the term 'self-reliance *within alliance*', which led to domestic criticism over which element was dominant in the relationship.[12]

The alignment of security interests continued after the Cold War and beyond.[13] Canberra was a strong supporter of President George Bush, Sr.'s 'New World Order' in the 1990s, following the US into the Gulf War in 1990 and Bush, Jr.'s War on Terror in Afghanistan from 2001 and Iraq from 2003. In the 2010s, Australia facilitated the southern element of President Obama's 'Pivot to Asia' through the rotational basing of US Marines in Darwin. While President Trump's foreign policy unpredictability led some commentators to question the value of the alliance, Canberra walked in lockstep on strategic issues (in contrast to not supporting Trump's trade war).

While Trump's 'Free and Open Indo-Pacific' strategy lacked clarity until it was abruptly de-classified in the last days of the administration,[14] Canberra appears to have accepted the underlying assumptions of the US strategy by supporting freedom of navigation in the South China Sea and ramping up engagement with the South Pacific to counter China. The US 2017 National Security Strategy heralded a significant declaratory shift in Washington against China: '. . . the assumption that engagement with rivals and their inclusion in international institutions and global governance would turn them into benign actors and trustworthy partners . . . turned out to be false'. China was identified in relation to 'influence operations, and implied military threats [and] infrastructure investments' in ways that have been repeated in Australian foreign policy statements, especially regarding the South Pacific.[15]

China became increasingly assertive towards Australia, which became the target of discriminatory trade bans on beef, barley, wine, lamb and coal. President Joe Biden's administration stood with Canberra and connected any thaw in relations with China to removing its discriminatory trade actions against Australia, stating 'we are not going to leave Australia alone on the field'.[16] The US provided Australia with the opportunity to acquire nuclear submarines in 2020 and Canberra also supported the permanent deployment of US strategic nuclear forces to Darwin through the 2022 agreement to base B52 bombers. The implications of this shift to directly defending Australia's interests for AFP are profound and will be dealt with in greater depth in Chapter 6 where the focus is the relationship with China.

The birth of the Australia–US relationship provided the foundations for an enduring alliance. It also offers insights into what conditions might be necessary to prompt another transition in the future, as was the case in the shift from the UK to US as alliance guarantor from the signing of the ANZUS alliance in 1950.

Manus Island case study of shared regional security interests

The Manus Island naval base development in PNG provides a recent example of an alignment of interests, where Australia could be seen as paying the alliance premiums while also tying the US to Australia's area of primary strategic interest. In November 2018, Australia announced that it would redevelop the PNG naval base on Manus Island. Soon thereafter Mike Pence, the US Secretary of Defence, announced that the US would partner with PNG and Australia. The diplomatic implications were clear with respect to the coincidence of Australia–US interests in the South Pacific.

The original Australian decision was widely interpreted as an attempt to limit Chinese influence in PNG. It followed an announcement in August 2018 of Australian support for the development of the Black Rock peacekeeping facility in Fiji. The ostensible reason for US participation was 'to protect the sovereignty and maritime routes of Pacific Island nations'[17] but the clear target was to check Chinese influence. As such, Australia delivered the US an option to signal regional cooperation in protecting the 'rules-based order' that China's actions in the Spratly Islands were seen as disrupting.

Australia responded to Trump's call for allies to do more, representing the latest response to similar calls since US President Richard Nixon's 1968 Guam Doctrine of burden-sharing during the Vietnam War. The announcement provides a significant connection to the birth of the security relationship after the Second World War as it occurred 70 years after the US and Australia first agreed to jointly use the Manus Island base. At that time, fighting the Japanese in the Second World War was the object of threat perceptions. These have shifted to China, which highlights the intersection of Realist and Strategic Cultural strains in AFP; alliances are a central Realist approach to managing insecurity but the ANZUS alliance is seemingly permanent due to the permanent threats that drive Strategic Culture.

This Manus Island announcement also highlights the value of access and diplomacy with US policy-makers. In this case, Pence's announcement was a part of a side meeting at the APEC summit in PNG. One message downplayed by the Manus initiative was Prime Minister Morrison's opening statement on maintaining free trade, squarely aimed at highlighting the collateral damage to allies from the Trump Administration's trade war with China, showing the uneasy relationship between security and trade. The Biden administration's first comments on China's trade sanctions against Australia highlight that the US approach to strategic competition has hardened and therefore more cooperation along the lines of Manus Island is likely to occur.

Characterizing the 'unbreakable democratic alliance': Shared interests, affinity and adaptability

In US declaratory policy, Australia is described as 'a vital ally, partner, and friend of the United States' which shares a 'democratic alliance'.[18] In his first call to Prime Minister Morrison, President Biden described the ANZUS alliance as 'an anchor of stability in the Indo-Pacific and the world'.[19] From Australia's perspective, Australia identifies US regional engagement as 'essential' to 'the stability and prosperity of the Indo-Pacific' through its web of alliances with Australia, Japan and South Korea, and as such Canberra 'will continue to ensure the strength and vitality of our alliance'.[20]

The Australia–US relationship was 'forged in fire' during the Second World War, but a Realist appraisal might suggest this single-faceted character could have made it at risk of unravelling as interests changed. The theory of alliances points to vulnerability during times of strategic change,[21] which means that ANZUS could be challenged by the rise of China, but there is no sign that this is the case.

As a response to heightened threat perceptions identified in Strategic Culture, successive generations of Australian policy-makers have sought an *enduring* 'great and powerful friend' and much effort has been put into broadening the relationship. To be enduring, the relationship was identified by Canberra and Washington as being 'unbreakable' in the grand narrative of the relationship; in reality, this is based on its adaptive capacity. The democratic alliance involves culture and economics; common Anglo-Saxon historical roots in the British Empire; shared language; respect for fundamental human rights, such as freedom of expression and association; democracy; free-market/capitalist ideology; and commitment to rules-based international order.

Declaratory policy on ANZUS focuses on several key themes, such as cultural similarities and values and a continuous history of strong bilateral relations. The 'unbreakable alliance',[22] as various prime minsters have described it, is meant to set Australia apart from other US allies. It provides a self-perpetuating reason for Australian policy-makers to maintain and strengthen bilateral links in the face of whatever liminal moment occurs, whether that be the Second World War, the beginning of the Cold War, its end, the War on Terror, or the rise of China. The shifting of geo-economic power to Asia has led some commentators to question whether the 'unbreakable alliance' requires regular renewal.[23] Observers must be mindful that the US has other 'special' relationships with states in the region, such as Japan and Korea, and old allies such as the UK, so this places the onus on Australian policy-makers to ensure that Australia's interests remain uppermost in the minds of US policy-makers.

Military cooperation against shared threats

The most relevant theme for Strategic Culture is the birth of the Australia–US relationship through war, its maintenance through numerous military deployments, and ongoing close military cooperation. When he addressed the Australian Parliament in 1996, President Bill Clinton noted that 'Our bonds have truly been forged in the fires of war – war after war after war. Together we carried liberty's torch in the darkest nights of the 20th century.'[24] An example of this characterization was the Australian government's 'Centenary of Mateship' campaign in 2018, which remains front and centre in declaratory policy: 'a friendship first formed in the trenches of World War I during the Battle of Hamel on 4 July 1918'.[25] The public relations by-line for the mateship campaign was 'Forged under Fire' in reference to the history of fighting together that began in the First World War: 'Since that day' Australian and US forces 'have served alongside one another in every major conflict'.[26] This sentiment is echoed almost word for word in foreign policy statements such as the 2017 National Security Strategy of the United States of America.[27]

The development of this sense of shared military history was evidenced as early as the Second World War in guidebooks for US servicemen, which noted: 'Maybe there are fewer people in Australia than in New York City, but their soldiers, in this war and the last, have built up a great fighting record.'[28] The fact that it was commonplace to mention the history of shared warfighting highlights the centrality of shared security interests in how the relationship is perceived on both sides of the Pacific. When connected to the common belief that US intervention saved Australia from Japanese invasion, this provides a potent foundation for enduring relations. Australia's war minister in the Second World War, Francis Forde, captured the essence of what was to become the glue that holds the relationship together: 'We feel that our fate and that of America are *indissolubly* linked. We know that our destinies go hand in hand and that we rise and fall together. And we are proud and confident in that association.'[29]

Seventy-five years later, the question of just how indissoluble these links are remains a regular topic of debate, but the lesson of the Cold War and War on Terror is that analysts should not be surprised by the capacity of the 'democratic alliance' to be remade. For example, in the first contact with Marise Payne, the Australian foreign minister in 2021, the incoming US Secretary of State Antony Blinken noted how committed he was 'to strengthening the unbreakable bond between the two countries'.[30] This characterization of an unbreakable bond is first attributed to Prime Minister Robert Menzies in 1955.[31] It runs contrary to the Realist focus on states having changing interests versus permanent alliances, but does align with the heightened threat perceptions and indefensibility that characterize Strategic Culture.

Values and the 'rules-based order'

The Australia–US relationship is often described as a 'democratic alliance'[32] and this highlights the importance of ideological values and a like-minded approach to diplomacy. Australia's foreign policy elevates the role of values in shaping national identity with the focus on the rule of law and representative government. As such, foreign policy becomes an extension of domestic policy, which provides a Liberal Internationalist flavour that is tempered by a Realist focus on achieving national interests. Prime Minister Morrison championed the US 'moral purpose' and has explicitly connected Australian culture to the US by emphasizing a 'belief

BACKGROUND TO THE UNITED STATES

in the values and institutions that the United States has championed and we [Australia] share'.[33] Furthermore, in the face of growing tension with China, Foreign Minister Marise Payne noted that the government would not 'trade away' basic principles and democratic values'.[34] This emphasis fits neatly with Strategic Culture, where Australia's Anglo-Saxon roots are contrasted with the 'alien' cultures of Asia.

A secondary theme that has supported perceptions of shared interests focuses on the maintenance of what Australia's defence and foreign policy White Papers term the 'rules-based order'. This is a recent description of an enduring theme in relations and it is noteworthy that this is 'the' order not 'an' order that could be easily replaced by an alternative order, such as one developed by China. Australia has been a beneficiary of the international architecture sponsored by the US after the Second World War. This includes the Bretton Woods international trade regime that led to the development of the International Monetary Fund, the UN, the World Bank and so on.

With the threat of Communist insurgencies and the collapse of command economics of the Cold War long past, the focus has been on reducing barriers to free trade and maintaining a stable strategic environment conducive to free trade. To this end, Australia has a range of free trade agreements (FTAs), including its largest with the US. In 2019, Trump's escalating trade war with China involving tariffs on aluminium could have had an unintended impact on Australian businesses and this challenged the free trade status quo. However, Canberra successfully lobbied the Trump administration for an exemption. The exemption may be symbolic of close relations, but regardless, this was an example of US behaviour running counter to World Trade Organization (WTO) rules and thereby undermining the Liberal order. As such, the Trump administration shook faith in US leadership credentials.

The longstanding faith in the inviolability of the US and Australian commitment to free trade and sovereignty has been challenged by the Chinese actions in militarizing islets in the South China Sea and Russia's actions in Ukraine and Crimea. The US has been at the forefront of responding to these issues, which Canberra has supported but has implications for Australia. The US is clear that China has taken advantage of weaknesses in the capacity of international institutions applying the norms and rules and many like-minded states might agree, but the prospect of the Trump administration prosecuting a trade war against China left many allies behind.[35] For instance, Australia's declaratory condemnation of China has soured bilateral relations at times, but China remains Australia's number one trading partner. If Australia agreed to US pressure to conduct a freedom of navigation (FONOP) in the South China Sea, this could be seen as a provocation that might have unintended consequences.

The present geopolitical manoeuvring raises the question posed by each generation of Australian analysts, namely, are there times when support for US strategic interests is not in Australia's national interests? This is a potentially uncomfortable situation for Canberra because it is not always possible to find a coincidence of interests, yet the need to buttress the 'unbreakable' alliance reduces diplomatic room to manoeuvre.

The Australia–US identity: inconvenient facts, asymmetry and exceptionalism

A highly complementary and essentialised view of the similarities that connect Australia and the US acts to obscure any differences, especially when Australian interests are potentially undermined by the relationship. For instance, the common history is not so common as the US emerged out of a violent revolution in the American Colonies against the British (which coincidentally led to the colonization of Australia by the British in search of a new place to send convicts). Independence was willingly and peaceably granted to Australia by the UK 125 years later. There are also significant differences in democratic culture between the two states in relation to the institutions of governance and electoral politics. Australia has a strong party system, contrasting with the US presidential approach to government, which is based upon much weaker party affiliation and much greater loyalty from politicians to their local constituencies. Furthermore, clear differences exist in relation to divisive social and political issues such as gun control, abortion, climate change and religion.[36]

The commitment to capitalism is also quite different with a collective understanding of workers' rights being entwined in Australian history. The US approach is much more unfettered and can be captured by the universalist 'American Dream', whereby people are seen to succeed or fail based on their merits. By contrast, Australia's approach can be characterized more by egalitarianism, whereby the response to inequality includes a strong social welfare safety net and universal access to affordable health care to protect the needy. Furthermore, unlike the US, unionism and expectations of government intervention in the economy has been an essential part of Australia's political culture,[37] although this has waned over time. These key differences were displayed clearly in the different approaches of the two governments to the COVID-19 pandemic where Canberra provided significant government support while Washington largely left Americans to their own devices.

All the preceding differences could be differences amongst equals, but in key areas that count, Australia is far from the United States' equal. The asymmetry in economic and military power has been already mentioned but also exists in relation to the United States' universalist ideology. The US looks inwards and in diplomatic affairs sees itself as at the centre of international affairs and from this vantage Australia is but one ally searching for attention. This asymmetry is a core reason why Canberra's fears of abandonment drive AFP.

From the perspective of diplomacy and international affairs, the asymmetry is profound. Australia is a medium economic and military power interacting with the world's predominant power and often stands with the US against other great powers, such as the Soviet Union (during the Cold War) and presently against China. Through its Strategic Culture, Australia sits uncomfortably perched on the periphery of Asia, from which it is culturally alienated, while the US has placed itself at the centre of international diplomacy since the Second World War, largely by sponsoring the creation of and/or hosting of the post-war architecture of international governance, such as the UN. US exceptionalism also leads it to more readily set aside international norms when they challenge its national interests,

BACKGROUND TO THE UNITED STATES

whereas Australia is more circumspect due to its position as a medium power, and its Strategic Cultural concerns about being indefensible in a threatening region.

The asymmetry means that both states have national interests that potentially conflict with one another and with the 'rules-based order', but the US has greater capacity and willingness to use foreign policy to suit its preferences. Each state trumpets support of the 'rules-based order' whilst undermining norms that don't suit its preferences. However, the US is far better placed to ignore and shape rules. For Australia's part, the Liberal Internationalist emphasis on norms and rights has been strained by US *Realpolitik*, which highlights the centrality of Realism to foreign policy. An example of this is the respect for human rights, which are generally viewed as universal and inalienable. In the case of China, Indonesia and Myanmar, where core geostrategic interests are at stake, successive Australian governments have softened the approach to encouraging others to comply with the norms to the point where Canberra has been criticized for 'enabling authoritarianism'.[38] It remains to be seen if the Biden administration is able to reverse the view that the US is itself a threat to the Western Liberal International order,[39] but declaratory statements suggest that 'America is back'.[40] The Biden administration's leadership with respect to the Russian invasion of Ukraine is a case in point.

Debate over the closeness of the Australia–US relationship – anti-Americanism

The affinity with the US expressed in Australian declaratory statements and operational support for US strategic interests has existed alongside a virulent strain of anti-Americanism in Australia. This mirrors the colonial experience, where blind love of empire was not universal and where there were regular critiques of Mother England, especially when it was seen as not acting in Australia's interests. For example, in the First World War there were debates over conscription and many argued that only volunteers should be sent overseas to defend the British Empire. The domestic division was so strong that Prime Minister Billy Hughes' government lost two referendums and troops were not conscripted for overseas service. However, despite this setback there was no shortage of volunteers and Australian deaths were higher as a proportion of their military forces than was the case for Britain, Germany, France, Canada or the US.

This undercurrent of anti-Americanism in Australia relates to nearly every aspect of the relationship, with support for US bases and wars being notable examples. The strength of anti-Americanism has often connected to public perceptions of US presidents, and the wars they undertook (and that Canberra supported them in). In this manner, Australian public expressions of anti-Americanism have been loudest when Presidents Richard Nixon, Ronald Reagan, George W. Bush and Donald Trump were in the Oval Office. Unpopular wars where Australian policy-makers sent troops include the Vietnam War in the 1960s and 1970s and the 2003 Iraq War, which arguably coincided with the height of anti-American sentiment in Australia.

The strength of anti-Americanism has waxed and waned over the last century,[41] but has never led to a breach in the relationship and may be fading. Anti-US sentiment almost became mainstreamed in the 1980s, as epitomized in popular culture by Midnight Oil's hit song 'US Forces'. However, even at its height during the Vietnam War or second Gulf War, anti-Americanism has not necessarily impacted on the underlying security, economic and cultural relationship. For example, soon after the second Gulf War in the early 2000s, public opinion turned against supporting the war, but Prime Minister Howard lent unstinting diplomatic and military support to President Bush, Jr. It is not clear what impact this anti-US/war/Bush sentiment had on the several elections Howard won during this period and it doesn't appear that the Howard government was concerned enough about the potential for an adverse electoral impact to alter its strong alignment with US interests. At this time, Australia was criticized for being a 'Deputy Sheriff' to the US and it was suggested that this had negative reputational impacts in Asia.[42] However, it is unclear if this criticism had as much currency in Asia as it did amongst critics of the alliance in Australia.

Conclusion

From a theoretical standpoint, the longevity and strength of the US alliance could be seen as perplexing. The alliance was created after the Second World War to assuage Canberra's fears about the threat of a resurgent Japan. For 70 years it has adapted to respond to new threats that were shared in Canberra and Washington. This is not a coincidence as it involved alliance management by generations of policy-makers. For Canberra, this was particularly significant with respect to US calls for greater burden-sharing in the 1960s and 2010s. As such, the alliance reflects the close alignment of threat perceptions that has been developed independently. Furthermore, it is the glue that holds relations together and the foundation for a comprehensive range of diplomatic and trade relations that grew throughout the twentieth century. The current threat is China and the following chapter will provide an overview of present relations between Australia and the US in the face of this latest geopolitical challenge.

4

United States:
Alignment in the twenty-first century

Introduction

The diplomatic relationship with the US is so central to Australia's national interests that it has become a part of its foreign policy DNA. The relationship has grown out of the combat during the Second World War where a shared enemy was defeated. The US rose to become a superpower and bankroller of the Liberal International order that has so benefited Australia and many other states. However, relations were far from transactional and grew from a coincidence of interests to shared interests in protecting the Liberal order, especially in the Indo-Pacific.

That Canberra and Washington have forged a close partnership is no accident and for Australia it reflects the need to assuage high-level threat perceptions from the North, and feelings of isolation and indefensibility. Canberra also fears abandonment from its 'great and powerful friend' and has acted to maintain regional engagement. So much so that participation in US-led expeditionary operations in Asia and elsewhere has become a definitional part of Australia's Strategic Culture.

The key question is: Would the US defend Australia in its time of need? The strength of the US commitment has never been tested, and the only time the ANZUS alliance has been activated, it was by Australia to support the US after the 9/11 attacks in 2001. Doubt has led to regular criticisms of too great dependence on US alliance versus building greater self-reliance and deepening diplomatic relations with other states. Nonetheless, Australia's threat perceptions have provided an enduring rationale for keeping the alliance strong. The latest era of heightened geopolitical competition will test the alliance again, but if history is a guide, Canberra will not retreat from its reliance on 'great and powerful friends.'

Bilateral diplomatic relations can be analysed in several ways, and the institutionalization of key aspects of foreign relations (security, trade, diplomacy) is a clear marker of the health of a bilateral relationship. Institutionalization involves formalizing a relationship through various bilateral mechanisms. In practice, it involves a range of formal arrangements, such as treaties, and informal practices and conventions, such as regular ministerial meetings. Institutionalization

Security: An 'unbreakable' security alliance and enduring shared interests

The Australia–US relationship was 'forged with fire' in the face of the Japanese threat, but it was for policy-makers in Canberra to capitalize on the experience of the Second World War. When faced with the liminal strategic moment posed by the end of the war, Australia did not question whether to maintain alignment with the US. It was clear that the war had exhausted the UK, while the US had grown to become a superpower. Developments in Europe quickly captured Washington's attention as the Iron Curtain fell across Europe and the Cold War with the Soviet Union began. In Asia, meanwhile, China was 'lost' to a Communist revolution in 1949 and the US quickly became bogged down in the Korean War, which broke out in 1950.

The US wanted the Treaty of San Francisco (also known as the Treaty of Peace with Japan) signed to facilitate its post-war reconstruction efforts and to balance China and the Soviet Union in Asia. Australia's signature was needed, but there was concern in Canberra about the UK's capacity to defend Australia in a future conflict and lingering fears of the potential of the re-militarization of Japan.[1] As a compromise, the US negotiated the tripartite Australia, New Zealand, United States (ANZUS) Treaty to provide assurances of future support to Australia (and New Zealand) alongside the Treaty of San Francisco, and both were signed in 1951.

The ANZUS Treaty

Through the ANZUS Treaty the security relationship was formally institutionalized.[2] In declaratory policy since then, it has been commonplace to treat ANZUS as the cornerstone of Australian foreign policy (AFP). The text of ANZUS is relatively short and focused on sending a declaratory signal to both Australia and its potential adversaries. Article 3 obliges the parties to consult in times when territorial integrity or political independence is under threat. Article 4 declares the intent of the alliance:

> Each Party recognizes that an armed attack in the Pacific Area on any of the Parties would be dangerous to its own peace and safety and declares that it would act to meet the common danger in accordance with its constitutional processes.[3]

The 'Pacific Area' is not clearly defined, but Article 5 focuses on 'an armed attack on the metropolitan territory of any of the Parties, or on the island territories under its jurisdiction in the Pacific or on its armed forces, public vessels or aircraft in the Pacific'.[4] While it has not been tested, the implication is that it covers Australian territories such as the Cocos Islands and US compact territories such as the Marshall Islands. Of greater significance is that ANZUS technically covers US forces stationed in South Korea and Japan, which implies that Australia could be drawn into a conflict in Northeast Asia. That was not the key concern of Australian policy-makers when ANZUS was signed in 1951 but, given the rising geopolitical tension between the US and Japan in relation to China, it is a much more likely proposition now. Similarly, the likely response of US forces in Japan to any Chinese threat to Taiwan has been exercising the minds of policy-makers in Canberra.

Sheltering under the US nuclear umbrella

A key aspect of ANZUS is that it places Australia under the US 'nuclear umbrella'. This refers to the strategic concept of extended nuclear deterrence developed during the Cold War to explain how states allied with a nuclear power could gain the deterrent value of nuclear weapons without physically possessing them. In signing ANZUS, Australia joined North Atlantic Treaty Organization (NATO) states, along with Japan and South Korea, in being able to shelter under this US umbrella. This protects strategic stability by limiting the potential for miscalculation by nuclear armed adversaries because they have a clear statement of the intent of a nuclear power.

Another benefit of extended nuclear deterrence is that it limits the horizontal proliferation of nuclear weapons to other powers. For those sheltering under the umbrella, it provides security without having to devote resources to a costly nuclear weapons programme, and Canberra has clearly stated that it has no interest in developing nuclear weapons. Extended nuclear deterrence was dependent on the credibility of the umbrella both in the eyes of the recipient and potential adversaries. The weakness of this position is that it places states in a dependent position reliant on credibility of the nuclear guarantee. This explains why some great powers, such as the UK or France, have ensured that they possess their own nuclear deterrent.

Up until the 1970s, Australia half-heartedly considered developing nuclear weapons, but eventually signed and ratified the Nuclear Non-Proliferation Treaty (NPT) in 1973. In the face of the rise of China in the later 2010s and mixed signals from the Trump administration in relation to the commitment to alliances, especially NATO, debate has resurfaced.[5] The Australian government has not signalled any interest in changing the policy on its nuclear path and in 2019 the US reinforced the credibility of the guarantee of extended nuclear deterrence by explicitly mentioning that it applies to Australia for the first time in Congress. This was in relation to the threat from North Korea, but the obvious implication was that the US was shoring up its alliances.[6] The question of nuclear weapons was also raised in relation to the 2021 AUKUS agreement in relation to the Australian acquisition of nuclear submarines.

Activating the alliance

The ANZUS alliance has never been legally invoked in the treaty area, the Pacific. However, Prime Minister John Howard invoked it in response to the 9/11 terrorist attacks on the US in 2001. Howard was in Washington, DC at the time and his immediate and unequivocal support for the US had a strong impact on US leaders. While this attack was a direct threat to the US, Howard stated to the world that it was seen as a threat to Australia because it was a threat to the 'Western' world more broadly. As such, the invocation of ANZUS was not how the authors of the treaty would have imagined it would have been activated. In the 1950s, the assumption was that ANZUS would be activated when the US responded to a direct threat to Australia and not vice versa. This highlights the fact that over its 70 years, ANZUS has adapted to changing strategic circumstances and remained central to achieving Australian and US interests. However, it was not so with New Zealand (NZ).

In 1985, a diplomatic rift occurred when anti-nuclear sentiment in NZ led to objections to visits of US nuclear armed and/or powered vessels. The US would not compromise as the visits were seen as an essential part of extended nuclear deterrence. That is, a potential adversary needed to know that nuclear armed vessels may be present in an ally's territory in order to provide a credible deterrent. Furthermore, the timing of the rift at the height of the 'second' Cold War saw the US take the significant step of suspending its alliance obligations to NZ.[7] While this effectively ended the tripartite agreement, ANZUS was not abrogated and continued as a bilateral treaty between Australia and the US. Separate agreements were then signed to communicate the continuation of obligations between Australia and NZ. After the Cold War, there was a rapprochement between the US and NZ, but ANZUS was not reactivated as a tripartite treaty.

The 'demonstration effect' for Australia (and other US allies elsewhere) was that junior alliance partners need to fulfil their obligations. In this context, the alliance is seen as an insurance policy that requires the payment of regular in-kind premiums, such as credible levels of defence spending, allowing US access to Australian defence facilities, or deploying military forces alongside the US in conflicts of strategic significance to the US. Australia shares the costs of mutual security by paying alliance premiums and in return receives a guarantee of support if it is directly threatened. Australia's actions can be characterized as 'burden-sharing', which fits with the aims of US President Nixon's 1968 Guam Doctrine and also with similar calls by Trump in 2018. Paying alliance premiums assuages fears of abandonment that characterize Strategic Culture.

Debate over the alliance security guarantee

There has been regular debate over the value of close alignment with the US, most recently in relation to how to manage the rise of China.[8] A potent subset of this debate focuses on the credibility of the ANZUS security guarantee in the face of a threat from China. A key query about the credibility of ANZUS is the lack of institutionalization compared to other US alliances.[9] The key question that frames debate is, would the US defend Australia in its time of need? Questioning the US willingness to make a military commitment when Australia's very survival is at stake has the potential to shake the foundations of assumptions that have driven AFP since federation. The most important assumption is that Australia's indefensibility can be overcome by reliance on a 'great and powerful friend'. Any question of alliance credibility strikes directly at the fears inherent in Strategic Culture and the cynicism in Realism over the willingness of states to follow through on alliance commitments, especially when they might have to sacrifice their interests for others.

ANZUS commits the parties to consultation, which presumably would lead to joint action if the situation warranted it. However, this presumption of action can be criticized as it is seen as being less than a guarantee of support. The wording of ANZUS is weaker than the NATO treaty, signed in 1949, which explicitly commits to the 'use of armed force' but this does not necessarily question US resolve. Rather, this softer wording reflects domestic debate in the US over becoming involved in alliance entanglements.[10] This isolationist tendency has been a constant influence in US politics since the First World War but doesn't necessarily influence foreign policy. Defenders of the alliance argue that the 'spirit' of ANZUS is more important than the letter of the text. No alliance guarantee is watertight due to the vagaries of domestic legislative and political considerations, but the deterrent value of the alliance is maintained regardless of the tone of the text; a potential adversary cannot guarantee that the US will *not* support Australia if threatened.

Whether ANZUS provides a security guarantee for Australia has never been tested because Australia has not faced an existential threat since the Second World War. However, from the Australian perspective, when the US has asked for a reaffirmation of support, as with the anti-nuclear rift with NZ during the Cold War, or deployments to Iraq in the 'War on Terror', Australian policy-makers have been willing to pay the alliance insurance premiums.

Contemporary concerns over the credibility of the alliance guarantee peaked under the Trump administration,[11] due largely to perceptions of a lack of coherence in US foreign policy[12] rather than a Realist approach to disavowing alliances. One reason foreign policy observers were pleased with the election of President Joe Biden was that his administration would firm support for the alliance.[13] In the pressing case of China's threat to Australian trade interests, the US has followed through by providing firm support through strong declaratory statements and operational decisions such as the AUKUS nuclear submarine treaty or deployments of forces to Australia.

Benefits beyond the 'ANZUS umbrella': The practical aspects of day-to-day cooperation

In practice, ANZUS functions as an institutional 'umbrella' under which a wide range of defence cooperation occurs. These activities have changed over time to include issues such as cybersecurity, demonstrating the adaptability of the alliance. This day-to-day cooperation has been described by the government as the practical benefits of the alliance. This involves comprehensive cooperation through a large number of subsidiary agreements signed to facilitate access to defence equipment, intelligence-sharing and joint facilities, training exchanges and exercising. The

ANZUS umbrella also provides justification for Australian participation in wars and coalition operations alongside the US. These practical aspects of alliance will be dealt with in turn.

Privileged access to advanced defence equipment

The close relationship with the US has afforded Australia privileged access to defence technology and logistic support under the Australia–United States Defence Trade Cooperation Treaty. Access to sensitive technology has allowed the Australian Defence Force (ADF) to maintain a capability gap over potential adversaries. That is, if Australia cannot effectively defend itself independently, it needs to use force multipliers to try to counter threats and technological superiority over adversaries is one such potent multiplier. The use of military technology is central to overcoming the perceptions of indefensibility that characterize Australian Strategic Culture, and indefensibility aside, it aligns with the reliance on technology that is a key part of US Strategic Culture.[14]

The US is renowned for producing innovative military technology that often leads the world. Having access is important because this equipment is not always available widely and limitations are placed on the export of sensitive technologies to all but the most trusted allies. That said, competitors such as China have invested heavily in technology and technological superiority gaps are narrowing.[15] Australia has habitually relied on US defence equipment and there is little likelihood that it will diversify supply from potential competitors, as evidenced in Canberra's 2018 ban on Huawei technology. The cancellation of the French submarine contract in 2021 and signing of the AUKUS agreement to acquire US and/or British nuclear submarines is a case in point.

BOX 4.1: AUKUS (2021)

- A trilateral agreement between Australia, the United Kingdom and United States.
- Focused on nuclear powers sharing nuclear submarine technology with Australia.
- Delivers Australia a strong force multiplier to respond to the threat from China.
- Potential to be in tension with the Non-Proliferation Treaty.
- Potential to increase proliferation of weapons in Asia.

AUKUS and access to strategic strike options

Most commentary on AUKUS focuses on the submarine deal but Australia's decision to arm the submarines with cruise missiles also represents a major strategic shift. This will make Australia the only Indo-Pacific state other than the US and China with this capability and restores a long-range strategic strike option removed by the retirement of the F-111 aircraft in 2010. This means that Australia will once again be able to independently strike at targets long distances from its shores. As such, Australia's defence strategy has come full circle as a strategic strike deep into Asia was the justification for the original purchase of F-111s at the height of the Cold War in 1963. Australia has not had this capacity for over a decade, so it represents a shift in defence policy and would not have escaped the attention of neighbouring states and/or those further afield in the Indo-Pacific region. The fact that the decision was greeted by regional criticism highlights the raised threat perceptions (from China). The lack of domestic criticism over the submarine and cruise missile purchase shows how deeply embedded both high-level threat perceptions, and the use of force to resolve them, have become in AFP.

Access to US equipment facilitates interoperability with US forces and signals the closeness of the relationship to other security partners and potential adversaries alike. Interoperability allows Australia to both pay alliance premiums by contributing forces that can operate alongside the US in expeditionary operations, and also allows Australia to work closely with US allies in the region and beyond (such as Japan). In fact, it could be argued that participation in expeditionary operations is a definitional part of Australia's Strategic Culture.[16] Purchasing US defence equipment also supports the maintenance of the US as the world's largest arms exporter: seven of the top 10 arms manufacturers are American[17] and Australia therefore also gains extra cachet by supporting US domestic political priorities.

Debate over the suitability of US equipment

There has been regular criticism about whether acquiring US defence equipment is in Australia's interests. Debate focuses on whether purchasing US equipment locks Australia into US doctrine and whether the equipment is as good as claimed (to maintain technological superiority). What the debate misses is that Australia sources equipment from a wide range of suppliers. Such criticism would have more credibility if the ADF had not diversified the source of suppliers so that the US is the major supplier amongst many. For example, key equipment such as helicopters, ships and submarines has been bought from European manufacturers. Debate persists and this persistence may reflect other domestic issues, such as latent anti-Americanism wherein it is argued that dependence on US equipment could potentially allow the US to exercise undue influence over AFP. However, there is no evidence to support this ever having been the case. In fact, successive Australian governments have developed a range of initiatives to ensure the sustainability of US sourced equipment. For example, local content rules are included in all major defence purchases, which encourages the development of a domestic capacity to provide maintenance of equipment throughout its lifespan.

Focusing on dependence on US equipment as a driver of doctrine has some superficial appeal as using the same equipment does provide the option of deploying forces side-by-side through interoperability. However, suggesting that the equipment leads to dependence obscures the strong focus in Strategic Culture on deploying the ADF alongside US forces to pay alliance premiums. Therefore, the doctrine that the US uses, such as for counterinsurgency in the long wars in Afghanistan and Iraq, is directly relevant to the types of operations the ADF is tasked by Australian policy-makers to undertake. The criticism that purchasing US equipment influences Australian doctrine would have more credence if the ADF were equipped to fight contingencies that do not fit with Australian strategic guidance, but this is not the case.

From the standpoint of quality, no major equipment purchase since the Cold War has escaped criticism of quality, cost and suitability for Australian conditions, regardless of its source. It is almost a rule that elements in the defence community will be critical of any equipment purchase. The current Collins Class submarines and their proposed replacements are a case in point.[18] Similarly, the last A$9 billion acquisition of destroyers from Spain was dogged with cost overruns and safety concerns.[19] This pervasive nature of criticism on quality, cost and suitability may reflect division between the services (Army, Navy and Air Force) vying for their share of the defence dollar. Criticism also highlights the divisive lobbying process that occurs around defence purchases and the fact that when a decision is made, there are always winners and losers. Winners and losers are not simply US and European defence contractors who have much to gain by successful defence sales. State governments within Australia also have a strong vested interest in where equipment is produced due to the significant economic flow-on effects from the defence industry.

From a strategic standpoint, there is reason to question and debate the credibility of the type of 'existential' high-level threats against which Australia perceives itself indefensible. These threats to Australia's very survival justify the advanced defence equipment (such as submarines) that dominate defence procurement. However, these (exaggerated) threat perceptions remain a central tenant of Strategic Culture and are not driven by the possession of US equipment designed primarily for high-level warfare.

Intelligence-sharing and joint facilities

Due to obvious sensitivities, the Australian government has a policy of not disclosing information about intelligence activities. However, successive defence white papers and reviews have identified intelligence-sharing as a key benefit of alliance. The US has a global intelligence-gathering network that Australia gains access to through the Five Eyes Agreement (whose members are Australia, Canada, New Zealand, the United Kingdom and US). Five Eyes is a comprehensive agreement originating in the Second World War that integrates and shares signals, defence, geospatial and human intelligence gathered from across the network. Australia could not hope to gain access to the depth of intelligence on its own, but equally, due to the aforementioned sensitivities, it is not possible to acquire definitive evidence about just how critical access has been to protecting and achieving Australia's foreign policy interests.

In recent years, the Five Eyes agreement has risen in prominence, largely due to its position as a bulwark against potential threats from China. In Australia, Five Eyes has been mentioned in relation to intelligence about cyberattacks from China, both within Australia and impacting Australian interests elsewhere.

UNITED STATES: ALIGNMENT IN THE TWENTY-FIRST CENTURY

BOX 4.2: FIVE EYES AT A GLANCE

- An intelligence agreement developed by allies at the end of the Second World War.
- Inherently secretive, but mentioned positively by Canberra.
- Membership comprises Australia, Canada, New Zealand, the United Kingdom and US.
- Speculation about Japanese participation, highlighting how far Japan has become integrated in the 'Western' response to the rise of China.
- Comprehensive and adaptive with respect to all forms of intelligence from signals to human intelligence.
- Focus on counterterrorism shifting to cyberattacks and warfare.

Anonymous government sources have described China's attacks as 'a constant, significant effort to seal our intellectual property',[20] and Five Eyes is essential to the early detection of these attacks. The role of Five Eyes has not escaped Chinese propagandists, who categorize it as an 'axis of white supremacy', highlighting the effectiveness of both the network and the low state of bilateral relations at present.[21] In the 2020s, the possibility of including Japan in the Five Eyes agreement has been canvassed, which also received the ire of China. This speculation highlights Tokyo's increasing integration into the allied response to China, which is discussed in Chapter 8.

Australia shares its own intelligence within the network, but its biggest contribution comes from the joint intelligence facilities within Australia. Facilities at Northwest Cape, Pine Gap and Nurrungar (Woomera) were set up in the 1960s and 1970s to monitor the Soviet Union. One noteworthy use was to detect Soviet intercontinental ballistic missile launches at the beginning of a nuclear war to provide Washington with vital reaction time to respond under the doctrine of mutually assured destruction (MAD). This role in US nuclear warfighting was controversial in Australia, especially at the peak of anti-Americanism in Australia in the 1970s and 1980s (see Chapter 3). However, despite these sovereignty concerns, Australian governments maintained this vital contribution to US extended nuclear deterrence.

Over time, technological and strategic changes have undermined or lessened the need for such facilities, but in parallel to the alliance itself, the facilities were seemingly remade to cater to new security challenges. For instance, their prime role in detecting missile launches and targeting strikes was utilized throughout the Cold War (e.g. in Vietnam), but also in the first Gulf War in 1990 when Iraq launched Scud missiles at Coalition forces and Israel.

Debate over 'bases'

Despite the integral role of bases in the alliance during the Cold War, there was domestic controversy over the presence of 'US bases' in Australia.[22] Criticism focused on claims that they undermined Australia's sovereignty, that they could be used by the US for nuclear warfare/targeting (without Australia's consent), and that they made Australia a Soviet nuclear target, possibly including a target of pre-emptive strikes at the outbreak of a nuclear war. Demonstrations occurred at several facilities, especially in the 1980s and early 1990s, and highlighted the anti-nuclear anti-Americanism that existed amongst elements of left-leaning groups in Australia.[23] Efforts were made by successive governments to ensure that they were seen as jointly operated and staffed, with joint benefits accruing from them. This included highlighting the government's 'full knowledge and concurrence' in their operation[24] and renaming the bases as 'joint facilities' in all official communications, but the term 'US bases' has persisted.

Despite domestic criticism, the basing agreements were renewed by successive governments and the operations of the bases themselves were expanded. This was particularly the case for Pine Gap, which has doubled in size since the Cold War, in part because Nurrungar was closed in 1999 and its operations transferred to Pine Gap. A new facility was also opened at Kojarena in the 1990s and expanded in 2010. Declassified Cabinet papers reveal that the government acknowledged that 'there are potential sensitivities or criticisms associated with continued cooperation with the US in this area. Given our long track record of successful cooperation, and the wide public support for the alliance, they are assessed as limited and manageable.'[25]

The fact that these bases remain a central element of bilateral relations gives some insight into the dynamic of the 'unbreakable alliance'. Their reinvigoration highlights that they continue to have value for the US and Five Eyes, and therefore continue to provide Australia the opportunity to both pay alliance insurance premiums and accrue benefits from the relationship in relation to intelligence-sharing. While the government is restrained regarding discussing the joint facilities for security purposes, Minister of Defence Christopher Pyne noted in 2019: 'Australia is not only a beneficiary of the US policy of extended nuclear deterrence, it is an active supporter of it, through our joint efforts with the US at Pine Gap and at other facilities.'[26] The lowering of nuclear threat at the end of the Cold War removed the heat from the debate over hosting US bases/joint facilities and they continue to operate with little public attention.

Maintaining and strengthening the alliance through joint facilities highlights the high-level threat perceptions that have persisted in Strategic Culture despite dramatic strategic change associated with liminal moments such as the end of the Cold War. This is particularly the case with the expansion of joint facilities in the post-Cold War era, such as the post-9/11 elevation of the 'War on Terror' and also the more recent focus on geopolitical competition with China. As such, from Canberra's vantage the permanence of the alliance appears driven in part by permanently elevated threat perceptions. This is at odds with a focus on economic or other interests that might have seen the alliance downgraded had a purely Realist frame dominated the strategic calculus in Canberra.

Training and exchanges

Another mutual benefit of the alliance involves the wide array of training, exercising and secondments between US and Australian forces. These have occurred under the auspices of exchange agreements, the latest of which is the 2014 Australia–US Force Posture Agreement. These activities provide the ADF and US forces with opportunities to hone a wide array of warfighting skills and humanitarian assistance operations. In a broader sense, this form of military diplomacy builds and maintains the connections needed to practise interoperability while deployed on joint operations overseas.

Training, exercising and secondments involve a diverse range of activities that impact on all branches of the ADF at all levels. Activities include secondments, training and exercises with US forces in the continental US and wherever US forces are deployed internationally. There are also regular warship and aircraft visits; these are especially relevant in relation to US forces visiting Australia rather than Australian forces visiting the US. Under the Enhanced Air Cooperation programme, activities involving US B52 strategic bombers, fighters and transport aircraft have been institutionalized and include live fire training in the Northern Territory. In a major strategic shift in 2022, this arrangement was enhanced to include rotational basing of these nuclear strike aircraft.

Australian naval vessels also visit the US when participating in exercises, such as the biennial Rim of the Pacific (RIMPAC) exercise held off Hawaii and California. RIMPAC is the world's largest military exercise and in 2018 involved more than 50 vessels, over 200 aircraft and 25,000 personnel from 25 countries. Due to the COVID-19 pandemic, the 2020 exercise was pared down to involve 22 ships and 5,300 personnel from 10 states: Australia, Brunei, Canada, France, Japan, New Zealand, Republic of Korea, Republic of the Philippines, Singapore and the US.

A strategically significant training activity is the rotational deployment of US Marines to the ADF base in Darwin.[27] This initiative was announced as part of President Barack Obama's 'Pivot' to Asia, which was the United States' first operational policy activity directly attributed to countering the rise of China. The significance of the Pivot was underlined by Obama's speech to the Australian Federal Parliament in November 2011:

As President, I have, therefore, made a deliberate and strategic decision – as a Pacific nation, the United States will play a larger and long-term role in shaping this region and its future, by upholding core principles and in close partnership with our allies and friends.[28]

The agreement was a diplomatic victory for Obama, because it brought alive the US Pivot strategy,[29] and was also a victory for Canberra as it allowed Australia to pay alliance premiums. Australia would be seen to be a loyal ally providing support to the US while also keeping the US engaged in its area of primary strategic concern, which cements its Strategic Cultural interests in relation to indefensibility and alliance abandonment. The rotational aspect of the deployment spoke to the domestic political sensitivities for both partners; for the US, overseas basing is fraught due to the costs and impact on bases in the US, while for Australia, the sovereignty issues mentioned earlier in relation to joint intelligence facilities come to the fore. Therefore, this initiative does not involve basing US troops in Australia but rather rotating large groups of them through Darwin on a permanent basis, which might have the same net effect but does not trigger political sensitivities.

In 2019, over 2,500 US Marines were deployed through Darwin, which was a significant increase over the 200 first deployed in 2012. As both states move beyond COVID-19, this commitment continues to be strengthened. In terms of equipment, this deployment was the most capable to date and represented the full complement under the Obama agreement. These training activities bring significant training benefits to both parties, and to international collaboration as regional forces from Indonesia, Japan, Malaysia, the Philippines, Singapore and Thailand have been invited to participate. More significant are the command arrangements, whereby the US is reportedly willing to allow the Marines to come under Australian command if a regional contingency develops.

These recent activities highlight the present goal of both Canberra and Washington to strengthen the alliance rather than simply maintaining it. A Realist might conclude that this highlights the shared interests between the parties and that the focus is on the rise of China. As such, these activities achieve Australia's interests in both supporting US global interests while also connecting the US to its area of primary strategic concern, where the threats to the north that punctuate Strategic Culture are located. This fits a familiar pattern in relation to responses to the Korean War or Vietnam War, but also more routine activities such as practising freedom of navigation in the South China Sea or Taiwan Strait.

Coalition operations

Deploying forces alongside the US on military operations outside the Indo-Pacific is one of the most significant means Canberra has of paying alliance premiums. The significance of deployments may appear to focus on the practical aspects of contributing forces to coalition operations, but in fact in many cases the value of the contribution is as much political as operational. Forming post-Cold War 'Coalitions of the Willing' added an air of legitimacy to operations that were often initiated by the US to achieve its strategic interests. Significantly, these military deployments abroad also aligned with Australia's Cold War strategy of 'Forward Defence', where forces were sent to meet threats before they arrived on Australia's shores, in places such as Korea (1950–53), Vietnam (1962–75) and Malaya (1963–66).

While strategically significant, Australian contributions have not always have been pivotal to achieving operational objectives, but the government was acutely aware of the political importance of the contributions. This is not to question the professionalism or effectiveness of the ADF, but rather to note that Australia often provided small niche forces that operated within much larger coalitions. This meant that Australian forces did not necessarily have a material impact on the outcome of a campaign, operation or war involving greater contributions from the US or its other allies. It also meant that they could be insulated from the likelihood of heavy casualties, which would have had a negative domestic impact that could have outweighed the diplomatic benefits.

In the post-9/11 era, Australia contributed forces to two US campaigns: Afghanistan, from 2001 to 2021 and Iraq, in 2003 and from 2005 to 2009.

Afghanistan (2001–21)

Australia's twenty-year operation in Afghanistan began as a reflexive response to the Al-Qaeda attacks on the US and evolved into a counterinsurgency against the Taliban involving both active combat and nation-building. In the shadow of the 9/11 Al-Qaeda attacks on the US, Canberra quickly agreed to contribute forces to fight the Taliban in Afghanistan.[30] Prime Minister John Howard was on a state visit to Washington, DC when the attacks occurred and immediately pledged unequivocal allegiance. On his return to Australia six days later, he described the attack as 'a massive assault on the values not only of the United States of America but also of this country'.[31] Howard invoked the security provisions of the ANZUS Treaty for the first time and committed to support the US in the 'War on Terror':

> If that treaty means anything, if our debt as a nation to the people of the United States in the darkest days of World War II means anything, if the comradeship, the friendship and the common bonds of democracy and a belief in liberty, fraternity and justice mean anything, it means that the ANZUS Treaty applies and that the ANZUS Treaty is properly invoked.[32]

At this time, the precise nature of the US response to the terrorist attacks was unclear, but by November Australian forces would be deployed on Operation Enduring Freedom alongside the US in Afghanistan, searching for Osama Bin Laden and the Al-Qaeda forces that executed the September 11 terrorist attacks on New York and Washington DC. For the next 20 years, Australian forces would be involved in Afghanistan in various guises and capacities. In September, the ADF was first deployed unilaterally alongside the US and then by December under the UN mandated NATO-led International Security Assistance Force (ISAF). In addition, ADF logistic support forces operated out of the Persian Gulf, as did air-to-air refuelling aircraft. Further afield, fighter aircraft provided air defence out of the US base on Diego Garcia in the Indian Ocean. Nonetheless, it was the forces involved in active combat that were the most valuable to the US and the public focus of the operation.

Australian special forces deployed on Operation Anaconda in search of Bin Laden in September 2001 impressed their US coalition partners and cemented a place as valued allies. Over the next 20 years, Australia's commitment would vary enormously, from full Special Operations Task Groups, air force elements and naval support in the Persian Gulf, to having small groups of specialist advisors on the ground. The first period of high operational tempo occurred immediately after the 9/11 terrorist attacks through to 2002, when Special Air Service (SAS) Task Groups rotated through Afghanistan.

The second phase from late 2005 was a response to the deteriorating security situation whereby the Taliban had regrouped to mount a fully-fledged insurgency. This phase saw Australian forces increasingly involved in robust counterinsurgency

(COIN) operations and the force elements reflected this situation. This phase involved a Special Operations Task Group of SAS, Commandos and support elements along with infantry fighting vehicles and transport helicopters. The third phase from late 2006 involved replacing the Task Group with a Reconstruction Task Force that was part of the Dutch-led Provincial Reconstruction Team to Tarin Kot in Uruzgan Province. While these engineers already had protective cavalry and infantry forces assigned to them, they were enhanced with a Special Operations Task Group early in 2007. These engineers were involved in the construction of over 200 schools, medical clinics and roads.

The arrival of the Task Group brought the number of Australian personnel in Afghanistan to just under 1,000 and as other support elements joined the Reconstruction Task Force, this increased gradually to a peak of 1,550 by the middle of 2009. By early 2010, the Dutch withdrew and Australian forces took joint command of the Uruzgan Provincial Reconstruction Task Force with the US. This was the largest commitment of Australian military forces abroad since the Vietnam War. There were also approximately 800 personnel deployed in the Persian Gulf region supporting the troops in Afghanistan. The Australian commitment was the tenth largest in the ISAF.

By the end of 2012, Australia's commitment began to wind down, with troops handing over their forward operating bases to the Afghan National Army (ANA) who they had been mentoring for several years. Australian forces now operated out of the main base in Tarin Kot and security for the province became the responsibility of Afghan forces. In 2013, the drawdown at Tarin Kot continued with the base shutting in December. On making the announcement, Prime Minister Tony Abbott noted: 'Australia's longest war is ending. Not with victory, not with defeat, but with, we hope, an Afghanistan that is better for our presence here.'[33] However, 'victory' was elusive and the legacy of Australian involvement was not clear cut, for Australia or Afghanistan. A few hundred military trainers stayed on with the ANA for several years and the government provided a generous aid package.

Public opinion and the war in Afghanistan

Initially, public opinion supported the war as it was easily framed as being a key part of the 'War on Terror'. The Afghanistan deployment was also contrasted to the Iraq War, where troops were deployed in 2003. Afghanistan was seen as a 'good' or just war due to the direct response to the 9/11 attacks allowing self-defence to be invoked,[34] and because it operated under the auspices of the UN in a large coalition of forces. This legitimacy was not evident in the Iraq War as it did not have UN sanction, was led by the US and a smaller 'Coalition of the Willing', and focused on regime change. Nonetheless, support for the Afghanistan deployment waned over time and by 2008, a majority of respondents in Australian public opinion polls were against the war.[35] Despite the waning support, six successive prime ministers from the Coalition and Labor supported the intervention.

Australian combat deaths were relatively small but rose steadily during this period, but they accelerated after 2009 when support for the war had already lapsed, so it is unlikely that this factor strongly influenced public opinion. The issue of casualties was made more complex by the rise in 'green on blue' killings, where Afghans with whom the Australians were embedded killed several Australian troops in incidents from 2011. One such incident in May 2012 saw two soldiers killed in a 'green on blue' killing and another three killed in a separate incident on the same day. This led to isolated calls for the troops to be brought home early, which were resisted by Prime Minister Gillard.[36]

Throughout the long war, the government kept the media focus on the bravery and effectiveness of Australian special forces. This was a clear lesson from the Vietnam War where reports from journalists embedded with combat units provided raw accounts of the true nature of the war which negatively influenced public opinion. Through tight control of access afforded journalists in Afghanistan, the ADF was able to carefully manage the news about the war in Australia. However, as the operation was winding up in the late 2010s, revelations of abuses by Australian forces were aired, the implications of which for public support of future operations are yet to be seen.

When Prime Minister Scott Morrison announced the withdrawal from Afghanistan in September 2021, it had been Australia's longest war. In the final analysis, over 26,000 ADF personnel had served in Afghanistan, many on multiple rotations. Forty-one were killed in combat and accidents, 260 were wounded and the war cost approximately A$11 billion. In addition, veterans have been over-represented as regards mental health problems, suicide and homelessness.[37] Australia's experience pales in comparison with the 2,300 US personnel killed and the estimated 241,000 people killed in Afghanistan and Pakistan,[38] but the point for policy-makers is whether paying the alliance premiums was worth this cost. Prime Minister Morrison declared they were when he read the names of the fallen on the announcement of the final withdrawal: 'These brave Australians are amongst our greatest ever, who have served in the name of freedom.'[39]

Morrison was following President Biden's lead and this was reminiscent of Prime Minister William 'Billy' McMahon following President Richard Nixon's announcement of the withdrawal from Vietnam in 1971. As with Vietnam 50 years earlier, this decision led to reflection over Australia's role and the elusiveness of victory. Afghanistan was framed as being an 'unwinnable war'[40] and the fact that the contribution continued so long, and at such cost, highlights that the non-operational aspects of Australia's contribution were uppermost in policy-makers' minds. It would be an exaggeration to focus on the Liberal Internationalist values framing the UN/NATO operation as they do not explain the willingness to follow the US into fighting an unwinnable war. Moreover, the pattern from Vietnam and elsewhere highlights that paying alliance premiums has been a potent consideration in Canberra and this aligns neatly with both the Realist focus on smaller states maximizing power through alliances and the Strategic Cultural emphasis on indefensibility and the need to engage allies to counter threats from the North.

Iraq (2003 and 2005–8)

In marked contrast to Afghanistan in 2001, there was much debate over the justification for war against Iraq in 2003. Furthermore, there was debate over the US operational plan for conducting the war, and once the war was underway criticism focused on the execution of the operation. Concerns concentrated on the credibility of claims that Iraq possessed weapons of mass destruction (WMD), the Bush doctrine's aim of toppling President Saddam Hussein to achieve regime change, and the potential national, regional and international consequences of the war.[41]

The legitimacy afforded to the Afghanistan intervention was missing in the case of the Iraq War, as it did not have UN sanction, was led by the US and a smaller 'Coalition of the Willing', and focused on regime change. The framing of the war in relation to removing the threat of WMD was an attempt to gain international support, but it failed to get majority support in the United Nations Security Council (UNSC). If successful, this support would have provided a moral victory for the US, as regardless of the vote, France threatened a veto of any resolution that would lead to war. With this impasse the die was cast: the US withdrew the resolution and gave Iraqi President Saddam Hussein a 48-hour ultimatum to leave Iraq or face invasion, which occurred on 19 March 2003.

The justification for war and its execution was of central importance to Canberra because of latent anti-war sentiment in Australia. Criticism was likely for any war that did not gain UN sanction and therefore Prime Minister Howard advised President Bush to exhaust all avenues for a UNSC resolution, even when they appeared to be doomed. However, once the US decided to unilaterally invade, Howard nonetheless offered troops to the 'Coalition of the Willing'. He noted: 'George, if it comes to this, I pledge to you that Australian troops will fight if necessary.'[42] This highlights the relative importance of Liberal Internationalist values in Australian foreign policy: gaining international legitimacy would have been ideal but ultimately it was not necessary. A lack of legitimacy was not seen as an impediment to supporting US strategic interests and paying alliance premiums. Howard used the United States' 48-hour ultimatum to gain domestic legitimacy by securing cabinet approval for the operation, but Australian support was never in doubt. Apparently and controversially Australian special forces used this same timeframe to secrete themselves deep into Iraq in order to be in place to protect key infrastructure and to locate and destroy the feared Scud missile launchers as soon as zero hour for war was reached.[43]

Australian combat and support forces deployed to the invasion of Iraq included 500 special forces in active combat, air force elements including fighter aircraft, maritime patrol aircraft, air-to-air refuelling aircraft and transport aircraft, and naval vessels in the Persian Gulf. This made Australia the fourth largest contingent in the 'Coalition of the Willing', which spoke to Howard's commitment to supporting US strategic interests. However, this deployment of approximately 2,000 personnel can be contrasted with the US commitment of 178,000 personnel to the invasion, and the British commitment of 45,000 personnel. As such, Australia's commitment followed the familiar pattern of providing legitimacy for US intervention while not necessarily materially impacting on the conduct of the war. That said, by all accounts Australian special forces operating deep within Iraq did have a significant impact in the first crucial days of the war.

The combat phase of the war lasted from March to May 2003 as Iraqi forces were quickly defeated on the battlefield. During this time Australian special forces were actively involved in interdicting Scud missile launchers that had strategic significance as it was feared they would be fired against Israel, which could expand the conflict. Meanwhile, Australian air force and naval elements supported coalition operations. These forces were withdrawn soon after the active combat phase of the operation ended in May, leaving the US and other coalition members to manage the occupation and insurgency that developed. The withdrawal was carefully stage-managed so as to not appear to be abandoning the US and it conveniently coincided with the ADF deployment to the Solomon Islands in 2003. That is, Howard had an agreement with Bush to support the invasion as part of the 'Coalition of the Willing' but not to be involved in the occupation of Iraq, so Canberra could then withdraw its forces because Australia's regional security concerns close to home were seen to be requiring attention (the RAMSI operation in the Solomons in 2003 is dealt with in Chapter 12).

Despite the clear exit strategy as the US occupation of Iraq unravelled into an entrenched insurgency, Canberra finally agreed to repeated US requests to redeploy troops. Australian forces returned to Al Muthanna province in Southern Iraq in 2005, but their role was limited to supporting Coalition and Iraqi forces rather than actively engaging in combat. As such, it was a measured commitment that reflected Australia's diplomatic aims in paying alliance premiums rather than providing significant forces to achieve core US operational priorities. The Australian battlegroup supported a lightly armed deployment of Japanese engineers and when they withdrew, shifted to providing overwatch for Italian forces. An Australian Army Training Team also deployed to work with Iraqi forces and the combined size of Australia's contribution rose to 1,400 personnel. These forces were withdrawn in 2009 to deliver an election promise of Kevin Rudd's newly elected Labor government. Overall, the deployment cost approximately A$5 billion over 20 years, which is not an inconsiderable sum, but minor compared to the annual defence budget topping A$40 billion in 2021 alone, when the operation ended.

No Australian personnel were killed in active combat in Iraq, but four did die of wounds or in accidents in the theatre. There were so few combat deaths from the war in Iraq that it is unlikely that they negatively impacted on public support for the war in Australia. However, in contrast, over 4,500 US soldiers and 3,500 contractors, over 300 allied personnel, 12,000 Iraqi security services and, while the figures are difficult to verify, approximately 200,000 Iraqi civilians were killed,[44] bringing Australian casualties into stark relief. These figures again highlight the relatively small scale of Australia's commitment and their role in achieving diplomatic gains for Canberra rather than military gains for the US on the battlefield.

The level of domestic criticism of the war was on par with Vietnam, including from within political elites such as an influential open letter by former senior military and diplomatic figures. Criticisms focused on the legality of the war (the lack of UN mandate; the weakness of the evidence for weapons of mass destruction), the Bush doctrine's shift from WMD to regime change, and the lack of planning for reconstruction. While the government defines the national interest, the crux of the criticism was that associating with an unjust war lowered Australia's reputation, undermined international law and made Australia a greater terrorist target.[45] While public opinion more generally was also against the war, a notable difference between earlier generations was that protest was nowhere near as divisive as during the Vietnam War.[46] In addition, the war did not have a negative electoral impact for Prime Minister Howard, who won several elections to the backdrop of a majority opinion against the war.

Debate: is military support for the US always in Australia's interests?

There has been persistent debate over whether these deployments alongside the US have been in Australia's interests. Debate focuses on the impact on Australia's international reputation, whether Australia's alliance premiums will be repaid by the US when needed, and whether the ADF force structure is skewed by these operations. The most fundamental point to be made about Australia's interests is that they are defined by policy-makers in Canberra, and as successive governments have chosen to deploy forces to join US operations and to provide ongoing support, this means that they are ipso facto in Australia's national interests. This does not mean that public opinion has not shifted against particular operations, but rather that on balance, Canberra decides that despite some public disquiet the benefits of paying alliance premiums outweigh the costs.

It is a perennial claim by a few commentators that Australia's international reputation has been damaged by the close alliance with the US. The argument runs that Australia's deployments alongside the US make it a 'deputy-sheriff' and that this is viewed negatively by some regional states. The problem is how to quantify this argument, which also applies to its antithesis, that Australia's reputation is enhanced by the close alliance. There has been almost no diplomatic fallout in relation to these deployments and the only declaratory policy of regional states that includes such criticisms is from Malaysia's former prime minister, Mahathir Mohamad, who was critical of Australian foreign policy in a number of ways.[47] Connecting Prime Minister Mahathir's comments to any diplomatic or material impact, such as reducing trade or defence cooperation, was not possible. However, it is likely that this perception that Australia was too closely aligned to the US may have influenced the Association of Southeast Asian Nations (ASEAN) in not inviting Australia to join its ranks.

A second major objection to contributing to alliance operations was that there is no guarantee that Australia's alliance premiums will be repaid by the US when Canberra needs it most. This is a counterfactual question because a situation when Australia has needed US military aid to defend itself has never arisen. This makes it difficult to prove definitively that declaratory support will be realized operationally. However, as tensions rose with China in 2020–21, the US went further than previously by openly clarifying the status of its military alliances in protecting its allies from Chinese aggression. The incoming Biden administration noted that 'we are not going to leave Australia alone on the field'.[48] The apparent lack of US support for the Australian-led East Timor operation has been critiised. However, this peacekeeping operation was hardly an existential threat to Australia and the US was involved to the greatest extent possible politically. Ground troops were not provided, other than specialist communicators, but significant logistic support was provided and seven naval vessels including the cruiser USS *Mobile Bay* (which was placed in charge of air defence for the operation) and three amphibious assault ships were deployed. Significantly, the amphibious assault ship USS *Belleau Wood* was deployed to Dili Harbour with its contingent of Marines from the 31st Marine Expeditionary Unit during the key month of October 1998. As such, the US forces provided a potent deterrent to any escalation of conflict by Indonesian forces and were not absent from the operation, but rather let Australia lead.[49]

The third criticism is that the ADF force posture is skewed by the close relationship with the US. This is a two-pronged criticism relating to the source of equipment and its use. There has been a persistent claim that Australia's order of battle is dominated by US suppliers, but this is simply not the case. Key equipment, such as the Joint Strike Fighters, have been sourced from the US, but this is hardly surprising given the competitive advantage that the US has in fifth-generation fighter capabilities. Similarly, US transport aircraft and large helicopters are state of the art. Otherwise, the only other key capability is the army's Abrams tanks. In contrast, combat naval vessels have been sourced primarily from European manufacturers with the integration of some US sensors and weapons systems, but this is likely to change with the 2021 Australia, United Kingdom and United States (AUKUS) nuclear submarine agreement. Attack and transport helicopters are of European origin, as are infantry fighting vehicles, which are produced in partnership. Thus, key capabilities are procured from the US but in dollar terms or strategic terms, there is no over-reliance on a single source of supply.

The second aspect of the criticism over the way equipment is used is made partially redundant by the fact that ADF equipment is sourced from a range of suppliers. However, it is true that the forces have participated for many years in expeditionary operations that have involved integration in larger US-led coalitions whereby the independent operations were unnecessary (e.g. relying on US helicopter medical evacuation, or fuel or ammunition in Afghanistan). For instance, the government review of operations in Afghanistan identified 'our reliance on the United States for some of the critical military enablers in the field'.[50] These criticisms were aired even before the dramatic increase in the tempo of operations in Afghanistan and Iraq. There was much soul-searching due to deficiencies discovered whilst leading the International Force East Timor (INTERFET) Operation in East Timor in 1998, which led to investments in various logistic support capabilities. However, subsequent operations over the next 20 years in Afghanistan and Iraq did nothing to alleviate the practice of integrating Australian forces into US-led coalitions. This means that there is some validity to the criticism that these deployments fostered a lack of capacity to undertake independent operations.

The deployment of forces alongside the US has long been lauded from both capitals as a key contributing factor to the close alliance and close mateship between Australia and the US. When this has occurred close to home, as in Korea and Vietnam, this aligned with Australia's own defence strategy of 'Forward Defence' and when it was to support the US further afield, it has paid alliance premiums. The strategy has come with some costs, such as combat deaths and injuries, a lack of operational independence and possibly reputational damage, but these costs have been measured and borne by successive Australian governments. Canberra has been willing to pay alliance premiums and this aligns with both a Realist and Strategic Cultural approach to foreign policy. The need to guarantee security through the deterrent value of the alliance and the practical benefits of cooperation have assuaged fears of indefensibility against threats from the North and have been more palatable than the need to dramatically increase defence spending if Australia were to assuage its fears through greater self-reliance.

Security: mini-conclusion

While the birth of the Australia–US relationship seems natural, with hindsight it also seems inevitable that the relationship between the two would strengthen over time. If there is any sense of inevitability, it is due to the coincidence of shared interests and interaction of Realist and Strategic Cultural influences in AFP. It is commonplace in international relations to accept Lord Palmerston's dictum about states having 'no eternal allies . . . and no perpetual enemies',[51] but rather eternal and perpetual interests. Therefore, we might have expected the alliance to have been challenged by changing interests over the last 70 years in Australia and the US to the point where it could have unravelled. However, the level of continuity in relations appears to challenge the orthodoxy. The ANZUS alliance has outlived its initial purpose (as a guarantee to Australia against the threat of a resurgent Japan) and has morphed more than once to meet the challenges of the day. For example, ANZUS became an effective tool to coordinate activities during the Cold War, where international Communism was the threat, especially in relation to Australia's perception of 'Domino Theory' threats on its 'doorstep'. A similar dynamic occurred in relation to the 9/11 attacks on the US and the intervention in Afghanistan. This aspect of AFP is intriguing and is the cause of significant concern and confusion. This continuity highlights the coincidence of shared interests and the strength of Australian Strategic Culture in influencing AFP. This means that we would expect Canberra to respond positively to future requests for US support, such as freedom of navigation operations (FONOPs) in the South China Sea, but to do so in a measured manner.

Public opinion

A test of the health of diplomatic relations is the underlying approval of the general public and this has remained almost constant throughout the life of the alliance.[52] In fact, the level of continuity in relation to support for the alliance stands in contrast to public attitudes on most other foreign policy issues.[53] Relations with the US and issues related to the relationship have been regularly polled,[54] with the Lowy Polls providing 15 years of consistent data. Polling provides an insight into the complexity of relations and the latest poll shows how important the alliance remains to Australians despite who occupies the White House. Less common are polls in the US of attitudes to Australia, but the notable examples highlight a high level of affinity (97 per cent seeing Australia as a friend or ally) that mirrors Australian attitudes to the US.[55]

In 2022, 65 per cent of Australians trusted the US to behave responsibly in international affairs, but this had shrunk from 83 per cent in 2011. Other allies and security partners such as the UK and Japan topped the list of trustworthiness at 87 per cent and only 12 per cent trusted China.[56] In 2022, respondents were aware of the military threat that China posed to Australia (75 per cent) and saw the ANZUS Alliance as being the best insurance policy (87 per cent). Polling shows clearly how the election of Biden in 2022 reduced the pressure that the Trump administration placed on diplomatic relations. In 2022, 77 per cent of respondents believed that the US alliance made it likely that Australia would be brought into a war with China but 76 per cent also believed that the US would defend Australia against China and 64 per cent believed that the alliance made Australia safer. This highlights the complex relationship between insecurity and security in Australian Strategic Culture.

Negative polling on the Trump administration

In 2020, the Lowy Poll found that Australians were displeased with the Trump presidency. In particular, Trump's challenge to the international order undermined faith in the US and this is not surprising considering the strong emphasis on 'rules-based order' in the Liberal Internationalist strain in AFP. In 2020 under the Trump administration, only 51 per cent trusted the US and this was the lowest level of trust since the Lowy Poll began in 2006.[57] Furthermore, only 30 per cent trusted Trump, with the only world leaders below him being those in China and North Korea.[58] This is a very significant reflection of the US role as the moral bankroller of the Liberal International order and also the shared values that respondents agree underpin the alliance. Furthermore, in 2018, 42 per cent of respondents saw the Trump presidency as a 'critical' threat to Australia's security, and 36 per cent saw US foreign policy as a critical threat, both of which are sad indictments of the perceived disruption to the status quo that the Trump presidency has caused.[59] By 2022, the focus was back on shared threats with 65 per cent identifying China as the critical threat today and a 75 per cent chance that war will occur within the next 20 years.[60]

Perceptions of threat and the alliance guarantee

In 15 years of Lowy Institute polling, the proportion of Australians supporting the alliance has never dropped below 90 per cent. Despite the view of Trump, Australians maintained their strong support in the alliance, with 78 per cent saying that the alliance was 'very' or 'fairly' important for Australia. While support has fluctuated marginally, this reflects the average response over the last 15 years. In addition, the disinclination to support US military operations overseas that became apparent after Trump's election eased to the point where by 2020, a majority supported committing troops alongside the US (68 per cent, conditional on deployments having UN support – the figure remained below 50 per cent for unilateral action). By 2022, a small majority agreed that they were in favour of supporting the US in a war over Taiwan, and 64 per cent stated that ANZUS could draw Australia into a war in Asia which was not in its interests.[61] Despite this point, support for the alliance remains strong.

As noted earlier, deploying troops in support of US interests is a key means of paying alliance premiums, so it is important to note that with the election of the Biden administration the initial shock response to the Trump administration has eased. This is noteworthy as it highlights the importance of the deployment being seen as just, and that this sense of justice comes not simply from the particular deployment, but also from the perceived alignment of the president with the core values that bind the alliance. Other practical aspects of the alliance, such as hosting US forces, also have strong majority support (61 per cent in 2013).[62]

The previous low point in support for the alliance occurred in 2006 under the second presidency of George W. Bush, coinciding with the wars in Iraq and Afghanistan. As noted elsewhere, this adds another element to the affinity between the prime minister and the president that can also influence a willingness to deploy forces, regardless of the perceived impact on public opinion (as was the case with John Howard and George H. Bush during the Gulf War). The present relationship is stronger than ever and due in part to efforts of the respective governments to manage public opinion. For instance, the United States Studies Centre (USSC) at the University of Sydney was funded with a mission of improving public perceptions of the relationship. The model has been more akin to a US think tank than other Australian university research centres and this has included lobbying and outreach, much of which has been very successful.[63] Lobbying is central to the USSC's mission, so when the Australian government implemented the Foreign Influence Register (ostensibly aimed at monitoring Chinese influence), the USSC was one of the first organizations to register.

The election of President Joe Biden saw a predictable improvement of public opinion towards the US due to the perception that a Democrat would be more respectful of international norms and less likely to practise the type of US exceptionalism identified with Trump. Furthermore, this improvement in opinion about the US is likely to be more significant given the increasing concern over the potential threat from China and the resultant need for US support. In this manner, public opinion identifies Liberal Internationalist, Realist and Strategic Cultural influences within AFP. Interestingly, Australian public opinion led the US on identifying China as a potential threat and on the issue of whether Australia and China were engaging in a new Cold War, which means that encouraging the new president to bind the US to Australian regional security interests has taken on greater importance.[64]

Diplomatic support in international fora

Multilateral diplomacy is centred on the UN system and its agencies, but there is a constellation of smaller regional and issue-based intergovernmental organizations (IGOs) that target particular policy areas. As noted in Chapter X, there has been a long tendency towards Liberal Internationalism in AFP, largely led by Labor governments, that supports active membership of the international community, including numerous international and regional IGOs. As such, the relative level of engagement with membership of IGOs can provide insights into trends in AFP. UN voting patterns are publicized and the UN General Assembly operates as an open democracy, with the Security Council exercising veto powers. This provides some evidence of diplomatic collaboration and/or alignment at the highest level.

Australia's tenure as a semi-permanent member of the UN Security Council

In contrast, most IGOs do not publicize voting patterns and/or govern by consensus, so it is more difficult to track the strength of bilateral diplomatic alignment within them.

Australia's tenure as a semi-permanent member of the UN Security Council

In 2008, Prime Minister Kevin Rudd announced that Australia would campaign for a non-permanent seat on the Security Council, which Julia Gillard continued when she assumed the prime ministership. This was a highly politicized campaign, both within the UN and Australia. International criticism highlighted Australia's perceived closeness to the US, which was a divisive issue, but ultimately did not derail the bid. Domestic criticisms from the conservative Liberal-National Coalition highlighted the costs of the campaign, treating it as a waste of money that could be better spent elsewhere. This division is a clear example of the different emphasis placed on Liberal Internationalism versus more Realist approaches by the two political parties.

Ultimately, the Australian campaign succeeded, and it became a non-permanent member of the Security Council in 2013. However, by this stage, the Rudd/Gillard governments had lost an election to the Liberal-National Coalition. There was some concern that Australia would simply mirror the US, but despite the change in government, Australia displayed its internationalist credentials in working with Luxembourg, the other non-permanent Security Council member, to negotiate key resolutions supporting humanitarian activities during the war in Syria.[65] The subsequent Security Council Resolution 2139 is a good example of niche diplomacy that defines the vision of 'middlepowermanship' espoused by Prime Minister Rudd and other Labor policy-makers. However, this did not undermine relations with the US as it also represents a coincidence of interests with the US.[66]

While on the Security Council, Australia did not do anything against core US interests and the belief that Canberra would follow Washington had some credence. This speculation was well founded with respect to Australia's UN General Assembly voting history. In the General Assembly, Australia is one of the most closely aligned states with the US with a 60 per cent coincidence in voting patterns. The majority of the time, Australia votes the same way as the US and also does not often disagree with issues that the US supports. Voting on 'important' issues is even closer, with an 85 per cent coincidence.[67] The only states that vote more closely with the US than Australia are Canada, Israel, the Marshall Islands and Micronesia. This is a telling list as one is a neighbour, one is arguably the strongest beneficiary of US security guarantees, and two have Compact of Associations with the US. Australia does not meet any of these criteria yet votes in a similar fashion, making it one of the strongest supporters of US public diplomacy.

The US is sensitive to the role of the UN in global governance, and support for contentious issues, such as Israel, are closely scrutinized in Washington, DC. Australia's voting record in the UN provides clear evidence of the coincidence of interests with the US while also providing the opportunity for Canberra to publicly demonstrate support for US diplomacy and therefore pay alliance premiums. Furthermore, Australia's voting record also closely mirrors that of the United Kingdom, which highlights the very complex historical relationship and claims of shared identity and outlook that characterize Strategic Culture.

High-level diplomatic visits

A key element of public diplomacy is the outward 'optics' of the relationship. Strong relations are evidenced in many of the interactions discussed in this chapter, but high-level visits are significant as they provide highly symbolic messaging to domestic and international audiences alike. Being invited by the president of the United States to a meeting in the Oval Office and, for a select few, a ceremonial press conference on the South Lawn of the White House, are potent symbols of close relations.

Most Australian prime ministers have had the honour of an Oval Office meeting, the latest being Prime Minister Morrison with President Trump in September 2019 (subsequent meetings were disrupted by the COVID-19 pandemic). These visits often involve large delegations of political and business leaders (such as State premiers, cabinet ministers and company CEOs) and provide an opportunity for comprehensive engagement with the US polity and business community. An even greater symbol of friendship is to be invited to speak to a joint session of the US Congress or Australian Parliament, an honour afforded to three prime ministers – Bob Hawke (1988), John Howard (2002) and Julia Gillard (2011) – and three presidents – Bill Clinton (1996), George Bush, Sr. (2003) and Barack Obama (2011) – in the recent past.

Public diplomatic events are stage-managed to display cordial relations, push agendas and influence key audiences in both Australia and the US. For example, when elections near, a domestic audience can interpret a meeting at the White House as a testament of the prime minister's credentials as a statesperson on the international stage. From the standpoint of the messaging required to demonstrate a strong alliance, high-level visits can ensure that allies, friends and potential adversaries alike can appreciate the health and strategic value of the Australia–US relationship.

Due to the prohibitive distances involved for national visits, senior officials often use attendance at major international fora to maintain links and ensure that US policy-makers are reminded of Australia's interests. Conspicuous events include those at the UN in New York, APEC, the G20, Quad, etc. Lobbying a particular diplomatic agenda requires access and these side meetings between prime ministers/presidents and ministers/secretaries are often publicized as examples of having access to the highest echelons of the US government.

Below this high-level public diplomacy is a much wider range of links involving routine visits by lower-level politicians and officials designed to further specific aspects of the relationship. These involve everything from official visits by foreign ministers or ministers for trade, tourism and investment, to study tours by federal cabinet ministers or members of Parliament, to research a specific aspect of their portfolio, to intensive diplomacy in the lead up to an international summit/agreement. Taken together, this web of international diplomacy reinforces the strength of the Australia–US relationship by providing the tangible benefits of being around negotiating tables when issues directly impacting Australia's interests are at stake. This access is unparalleled in Australia's other bilateral relationships and reflects Realist, Liberal Internationalist and Strategic Cultural agendas alike.

Prime ministerial/presidential relations

Given the focus on shared interests and experiences and mateship, it is worth noting the influence that cordial relations between leaders can have on the relationship. Often, but not always, there has been an ideological connection between Liberal/Coalition prime ministers and Republicans, and between Labor leaders and Democrats. Examples include John Howard and George H. Bush in relation to the 2003 war with Iraq, the 'New World Order' and Australian US Free Trade Agreement (AUSFTA). In contrast, George W. Bush and incoming Labor Prime Minister Kevin Rudd did not build close relations, which was clear from the G20 response to the global financial crisis (GFC). Kevin Rudd and particularly Julia Gillard developed close relations with Democrat President Barack Obama. More recently, Labor Prime Minister Anthony Albanese appears to have developed cordial relations with President Joe Biden. This closeness reportedly influenced Canberra to answer the US call to base troops in Darwin as part of Obama's Pivot to Asia 2012. Obama reportedly had good relations with one Liberal prime minister, Malcolm Turnbull, but not another, Tony Abbott.

While he was elected as a Republican, there was no sign that Coalition leaders built an affinity with President Trump. A telling moment in interpersonal relations occurred in the infamous 2017 Trump-Turnbull phone call, the full transcript of which was published by the *Washington Post*. The transcript highlights a very tense and awkward exchange whereby Trump was clearly unhappy about having to follow through on the arrangement made with Obama to transfer some refugees from the Australian detention centre on Manus Island in Papua New Guinea to the US (see Chapter 4). Trump derided the arrangement as the 'worst deal ever' and described the phone call as the 'worst call'.

The fact that the transcript was leaked highlights how fraught the Trump White House was and painted Turnbull in a good light. There was no sign of an Australian leader kowtowing to the US president. Relations between Prime Minister Morrison and President Trump were outwardly strong, not least because of the efforts of the Australian ambassador to the US, Joe Hockey, to cement closer ties. In his speech on the South Lawn of the White House in September 2019, Prime Minister Morrison elevated the importance of shared values at an opportune time as it resonated with US domestic debate over increasingly open challenge from China.[68] However, the volatility of Trump's foreign policy was on display when revelations that comments by the Australian ambassador to the UK, Alexander Downer, had prompted a FBI investigation into the Trump administration's Russian connections, leading to veiled threats about limiting Australian access to US intelligence.

Prime ministerial/presidential relations and domestic politicking in Australia

Domestic debates in Australia over the alliance have also influenced US perceptions of Australia's commitment.[69] While bipartisanship in foreign policy is the norm in Australia, there have been some notable domestic disagreements and differences of approach, which represent a breakdown in the foreign policy consensus. These disagreements are often rooted in a different emphasis on Realism or Liberal Internationalism and may represent differences of opinion over Australia's interests in a particular scenario, such as whether to deploy forces to the war in Iraq in 2003. There has also been a history of Australian Labor leaders arguing for greater independence from the US and this connects to the more Liberal Internationalist strain in AFP. However, this sentiment has been more openly expressed as an election platform while in opposition rather than as policies while in government.

Labor opposition leader Mark Latham probably provided the clearest example of this critique of the alliance in 2004:

> The conservatives have always positioned the American Alliance as some sort of insurance policy, the premium for which is paid through Australian military commitments . . . Every dollar Australia spends on adventurism overseas, such as the conflict in Iraq, is a dollar that cannot be committed to the Australian homefront.[70]

Latham was not elected, so it is impossible to test whether this sentiment would have lasted the transition to government. For those elected, this sentiment has not had a significant impact on relations even when opposition leaders, such as Bob Hawke in the 1980s, became prime minister. In these circumstances, incoming Labor governments may have proposed additional foreign policy initiatives alongside the close alliance, such as an emphasis on greater defence self-reliance, but not at the detriment of the alliance. For example, Prime Minister Bob Hawke conducted a review of ANZUS which reaffirmed its central place in AFP.[71] Similarly, while in opposition, Kevin Rudd reflected on the balance needed between Australian and US interests,[72] but did not criticize the alliance once he was elected prime minister. In 2022, the incoming Albanese government called for a similar review. The 2022 Defence Strategic Review also affirmed the centrality of ANZUS to AFP.[73] The election of the Biden administration was greeted with relief by most political commentators and public opinion,[74] as there is the promise of more consistent leadership from Washington and greater engagement with Australia's area of primary strategic concern, the Indo-Pacific. This aligns with the Realist and Strategic Cultural focus on strengthening the alliance as well as the Liberal Internationalist interest in elevating respect for the Indo-Pacific 'rules-based order'.

Debate over the value of access in Washington

It is very difficult to quantify the benefit of close access to senior US policy-makers, and not clear whether access is always direct enough to influence outcomes to suit Australia's preferences. The presumption is that being around the table, or at least being consulted, when decisions are made will influence outcomes to suit Australia's preferences. As influence is largely intangible, it has been the source of debate by critics of the close relationship with the US. Evidence for both sides is drawn from examples where the US acts in a manner that is viewed as being for or against Australia's interests. However, due to the sensitivities involved, it is seldom clear what level of lobbying occurred and whether it was successful.

It is assumed that cordial relations are the minimum required for a healthy alliance, but the continuation and strengthening of the Australia–US relationship through so many prime ministers and presidents highlights a self-perpetuating element. This continuity and inertia underscores the importance of the existence of shared interests and threat perceptions and also adds credence to the influence of Strategic Culture on AFP. When close relations are built between Australian and US leaders, as was the case between John Howard and George H. Bush, or Julia Gillard and Barack Obama, then access can have a demonstrable impact on relations. In these cases, relationships facilitated the AUSFTA and US Marine deployments to Darwin. However, the implication of the influence of interpersonal relations is that the strong relationship is only one factor that can lead to access and that it does not *guarantee* access. Despite any misgivings, it is clear that successive governments have worked on the assumption that maintaining close high-level diplomatic relations is a core Australian interest.

Trade

The securitized nature of the relationship developed from its birth, but it has always been paralleled by trade and investment. Prior to signing a free trade agreement, trade grew slowly and steadily throughout the twentieth century. Trade with the US benefitted from the post-war boom in the 1950s and then proportionately alongside the resources boom in trade with Asia from the 1980s. Australia's trade with the US (and Asia) was boosted by the decline in trade with the UK due to its accession to the European Economic Community (EEC) in the 1970s. The global financial crisis of the late 2000s led to a decline in trade that was generalized as the global economy contracted rather than being specific to the relationship with the US. This recovered, only to be set back again by the COVID-19 pandemic.

The institutionalization of economic relations through the AUSFTA

While the security relationship was institutionalised through the ANZUS Treaty in 1951, a free trade agreement was not finalized until 2005. A trade treaty was proposed in 1945, but did not get traction on both sides of the Pacific. Much of the credit for finalizing the free trade agreement was due to the relationship between Prime Minister John Howard and President George W. Bush, who initiated negotiations in the early 2000s. The AUSFTA is a comprehensive preferential trade agreement governing trade and investment between the parties.

80 AUSTRALIAN FOREIGN POLICY

It is managed by a Joint Committee Meeting that meets regularly to oversee the operation of the agreement. The AUSFTA was modelled on the North American Free Trade Agreement (NAFTA) and provides the institutional foundation for the bilateral economic relationship.

Debate over trade institutionalization

There was much debate over AUSFTA on both sides of the Pacific and its creation is testament to the political will devoted to achieving a mutually agreeable outcome. Predictably, domestic debate focused on costs and benefits. The broadest argument against the AUSFTA was that while it might increase trade between the signatories, it would cause trade diversion for both countries (by limiting trade with others) that would reduce trade overall. Particular issues included the protection of intellectual property rights, exemptions (particularly for Australian sugar), and access to cheap pharmaceuticals under Australia's Pharmaceutical Benefits Scheme.

Despite these concerns, the Howard government went ahead with the agreement, asserting that the overall economic benefits justified it and noting that it was an extension of the ANZUS relationship. This connection made a bridge between trade and security, suggesting that there was surplus value from ANZUS that influenced thinking on other aspects of the relationship with the US.

Domestic debate was reminiscent of the attitudes towards the costs and benefits of ANZUS (e.g. 'US bases' in Australia and involvement in 'US wars') but was far more focused, as trade is tangible and security far more intangible (until it is directly threatened). The fact that a free trade agreement had not been signed earlier highlights that trade and security have been kept separate for some time. Furthermore, trade did not feature heavily in Australian Strategic Culture. For example, at the time of the sale of the Port of Darwin to a Chinese company in 2015, strategic concerns were raised but side-lined over trade benefits. Former US deputy secretary of state, Richard Armitage said that the US was 'stunned' by the sale, and relations with the US were reportedly damaged by being 'blindsided'.[75] The implication of alarmist commentary was that China could spy on US forces based in Darwin as part of the Pivot or, in times of war, sabotage operations.

In a short time, attitudes in Canberra hardened. The Australian Foreign Investment Review Board (FIRB) learned the lesson and created the Critical Infrastructure Centre. Following the US lead, a range of Chinese interests were banned on strategic grounds. Huawei is a prominent example, but CKI's A$13 billion pipeline bid demonstrates how widespread national security concerns became. The operation of the FIRB with respect to China is covered in Chapter 6.

Over a decade after the AUSFTA was signed, it is clear that the agreement has worked in the United States' favour, with the trade surplus growing from US$14 to US$25 billion. In the aftermath of pulling out of the Transpacific Partnership Agreement (TPP) in 2017, the Trump administration reportedly investigated whether to end or renegotiate AUSFTA. Given that the agreement had so clearly benefited the US, the response from the Australian foreign minister, Julie Bishop, was surprise. At this time, the Trump administration's agenda included reviewing

UNITED STATES: ALIGNMENT IN THE TWENTY-FIRST CENTURY

trade agreements and alliances. As such, the Trump administration's change of heart on renegotiating the AUSFTA may be linked to the Turnbull/Obama refugee transfer arrangement, which Trump also threatened to back out of because it was the 'worst deal ever'[76] for the US. It may have been that Trump was convinced that the 'dumb deal' on refugees was more than adequately compensated for by the trade surplus gained through AUSFTA.

Present economic relations

In 2017, the US became Australia's third largest two-way trading partner in goods and services, behind China and Japan. This reflected a rise in trade with Japan. In 2021, two-way trade with the US was valued at A$68 billion or under 10 per cent of Australia's total trade. The US is the number five destination for Australian exports and the second largest source of imports. In services, the US remains Australia's second largest two-way trading partner. Over the last decade prior to the COVID-19 pandemic, trade with the US remained relatively stable, while trade with China doubled in percentage terms.[77]

The complexion of trade with the US has changed over time but has focused on a range of merchandise consumer products such as niche industrial goods and services.[78] In addition, the balance of trade has favoured the US with a net surplus. This makes the nature of trade with the US quite different to the complementarities with Asia (primarily resources and manufactured goods).[79] Investment has always been a key component of the economic relationship and, significantly, it has been complementary *two-way investment*, which has almost tripled since the free trade agreement was signed (see below).

As noted, Australia carries a trade imbalance with the US of approximately A$20 billion. Beyond the trade imbalance, the relative significance of trade between Australia and the US is also asymmetrical. Australia's exports to the US represent less than 1 per cent of total US imports (or thirty-fourth largest) and US exports to Australia represent approximately 2 per cent of total exports (or sixteenth largest).[80] In contrast, exports to the US make the US the fifth largest market for Australia while imports make the US Australia's second largest source of imports.[81] This trade asymmetry mirrors the security relationship, which Canberra has facilitated through the AUSFTA.

Foreign investment has been a significant aspect of the economic relationship and it contrasts Australia's trade relations with other partners. Despite the dramatic growth in trade with Asia (primarily China) that has accompanied the resources boom, investment has not followed suit. In 2022, at over A$1 trillion the US remains the largest investor in Australia (followed by the Japan and UK) and this relative position has not changed for decades. Furthermore, Australian investment in the US is also over A$1 trillion, making it the largest single destination by far.

Foreign investment provides a significant boost of much needed capital to support economic growth in Australia. In addition, the contrast with major Asian trading partners highlights a positive correlation between risk and profitability as US businesses are comfortable investing in Australia and vice versa. This can be contrasted with China, where two-way trade is much larger, but there is little two-way investment.[82]

Foreign investment leads to economic activity such as employment creation, which provides measurable benefits. Australia maintains a positive FDI (foreign direct investment) imbalance, insofar as US multinationals employed four times as many people in Australia as Australian multinationals did in the US. Furthermore, this employment generated three times the sales for the Australian economy (US$156 billion versus US$54 billion in the US).[83] These tangible benefits for Australia of US FDI contrast with the trade deficit with the US and provide context to the overall economic relationship.

Cultural and 'people-to-people' links

Residency by people born overseas provides an insight into the depth of 'people-to-people' links between Australia and the US. The COVID-19 pandemic has dramatically impacted travel but prior to the outbreak there were approximately 150,000 Americans residing in Australia. This makes Americans the fifteenth largest group, while China has grown over the last 20 years to be the second largest. By contrast, there are over 90,000 Australians residing in the US, which represents a much larger proportion of Australia's population in the US than vice versa.[84] This is another example of asymmetry where Australians are drawn to the US and this mirrors the practice with Britain during imperial times.

Tourism is another gauge of 'people-to-people' links because it identifies an interest in cultural exchange. Prior to COVID-19, when restrictions completely disrupted tourism, nearly 800,000 US tourists visited Australia each year. This places the US third behind New Zealand and China. The rise of Chinese tourists is a recent phenomenon while US tourists have visited in large numbers for some time. US tourism has an economic impact to the tune of A$7 billion a year, which is not insignificant. In terms of tourist income, this represents the third largest market behind China and Europe. By contrast, well over a million Australians visit the US each year, making the US the second most popular destination behind Indonesia (Bali).[85] Again, the pattern of asymmetry is noteworthy. These markets have not recovered from the COVID-19 pandemic but the trajectory remains relevant to future growth.

Education was also an avenue for expanding cultural links. Prior to the impact of COVID-19 pandemic restrictions, Australia was the eighth largest market for US education, with 11,900 students enrolled. By contrast, 4,900 Australian students were enrolled in US institutions, which does not even place Australia in the top 25 markets for the US. As with tourism, there was an economic element to education due to the significant size of the sector. Before the pandemic, Australian education institutions earned approximately A$400 million from US students, which made the US the sixteenth largest market. This represented 1.3 per cent of the market and is dwarfed by a number of states including China, which spends over A$10 billion (or 30 per cent of the market).[86] Therefore, educational connections were also asymmetrical, but less significant than other 'people-to-people' links. It remains to be seen whether international education and tourism rebounds after the pandemic, but as China has limited its citizens' mobility for political reasons, then the relative size of the US market is likely to increase.

Taken together, immigration/emigration, tourism, travel and education act to buttress the already significant 'people-to-people' links developed since the Second World War.

Conclusion

The key question posed by the Australia–US relationship is: how has this military alliance seemingly broken the first rule of alliances, that of permanency versus changing national interests? It is clear that a potent mix of history, ideology and myth-making has ensured that the alliance has been reinvented through each generation and strategic challenge since the Second World War. The latest challenge to be weathered was the credibility gap created by the Trump presidency, whereby unpredictable behaviour caused some to question the US commitment to the 'unbreakable alliance'. Future relations will be shaped by the rise of China, and Canberra has stood firm in the face of China's economic coercion and had the confidence to do so as it had the public support of the Biden administration.

The relationship with the US highlights that a pluralistic perspective is necessary to understand the complexity of AFP. The security links with the US developed out of perceptions that the US was Australia's saviour against the Japanese in the Second World War, but becoming a 'great and powerful friend' is not simply about military power and the values that the US stands for have their lineage in the same Anglo-Saxon European history as Australia. The rules in the US brokered 'rules-based order' have been backed by the US and like-minded states, with Australia being a willing participant from the very development of core institutions after the Second World War. It is these essentially Liberal values that Australia has always felt are under threat from the 'alien' region that it finds itself adjacent to through an accident of colonial history. Australia's geography, history and culture combine in a potent policy mix that has led to deep-seated and exaggerated threat perceptions and a sense of indefensibility, and the US alliance has been the antidote to these concerns. As such, the US alliance is part of Australia's foreign policy DNA and this will likely be tested more significantly by the rise of China than at any other time in Australian history.

5

Background to China:
Trading partner and potential threat

Introduction

Australia and China marked 50 years of diplomatic relations in December 2022, but celebrations were muted. The impromptu visit by the Australian foreign minister, Penny Wong, to Beijing signalled a thaw in relations, but the basis for warm relations is weak. This chapter provides a background to present relations, which are dealt with in detail in Chapter 6. This chapter is much shorter than most background chapters due to the lack of significant connections between Australia and China prior to the end of the Cold War. During that period, the focus of diplomacy was on China's central role as a source of threat to Australia as clearly represented in Strategic Culture. Unlike other relationships born of conflict, such as that with Japan, there has been no tectonic shift in relations with Beijing and this forms the basis for diplomatic tension that presently characterizes relations.

Colonial relations

China came to prominence in the Australian imagination before Australian nationhood in 1901. The influx of thousands of Asian miners to the Victorian and New South Wales (NSW) Gold Rushes of the 1850s and 1860s was not received positively by existing settlers in the Colonies. Most Chinese miners flocked to the central Victorian goldfields centred around Ballarat. The authorities tried to limit Chinese arrivals by imposing an arrival tax in Victoria, which diverted many would-be miners through South Australia and on a long and dangerous trek into Victoria. In NSW, the Colonial government responded to public opinion with the Chinese Immigration Restriction and Regulation Act (1861), a precursor to the White Australia Policy.

The interactions between Chinese and other miners stoked latent racism and there were numerous incidents, such as the 1861 Lambing Flat riots in NSW. Most Chinese returned home when the major gold finds were exhausted by the 1860s, but enough remained to provide a significant diaspora population in Victoria and NSW. However, they were never welcomed into the fabric of Australian society and remained marginalized despite their long association with Australia.[1]

BACKGROUND TO CHINA

The swift arrival of large numbers of Chinese (and Japanese) to the predominantly white colonies was part of the creation of Asia as the 'other' of Strategic Culture as stereotypes were developed or reinforced during this time. At federation in 1901, the events at Lambing Flat and elsewhere on the goldfields were amongst the foundational myths used to support the White Australia Policy.[2] It is also worth noting that the stereotypes of 'Asiatics' focused squarely on Chinese, and did not in practice differentiate between Chinese and Japanese immigrants (see Chapter 7). These generalizations mirrored those of the 1850s US Gold Rush.

China as the communist threat to the north

Australia's awareness of the People's Republic of China (PRC) was piqued during the Cold War. The Communist victory in the Chinese civil war in 1949 shocked the US and its allies and was described as the 'loss of China'. The view of the victory of Chinese Communists through the lens of US foreign policy interests highlighted the growing bipolarity of the Cold War. Canberra's approach aligned with the US response of continuing to recognize the Chinese Nationalists who had fled to Taiwan as the legitimate government of China. This diplomatic position persisted until 1972, despite the diplomatic reality that Communist China on the mainland had become the heir to nationhood.

The 'loss' of China also occurred soon after the Soviet Berlin Blockade (1948–49) and coincided with the Soviet and Chinese support for North Korea in the Korean War (1950–53). These events encouraged perceptions of international Communist conspiracy that influenced the creation of the Domino Theory (discussed in Chapter 3). The Australian commitment to the KOREAN War was much more significant than the few aircraft deployed to the Berlin Blockade. Both operations could be seen as supporting the post-Second World War US-sponsored Liberal world order. The Korean War was particularly significant for the Liberal Internationalist strain in Australian foreign policy (AFP) as it was the first UN intervention and the first of many UN operations that Australia would materially support. Australia sent over 17,000 troops to support UN forces defending South Korea from the Communist North.[3] The enemy faced on the battlefield was China and North Korea, placing China alongside Japan as an Asian state against whom Australia had fought a war.

Australian army, air force and naval elements were involved in active combat against Chinese forces, some of it bitter and costly to both sides.[4] Australian forces were attached to the Commonwealth Brigade in the last significant action alongside the British before shifting to coalition operations with the US in later conflicts. Australian casualties included 340 dead and 1,216 wounded.[5] These are significant figures for Australia's memory of the war, but are not as significant in context. For example, the US had 36,652 soldiers killed and 92,134 wounded in action.[6] These figures eclipse Australia's losses and highlight the differential context for Australia and its 'great and powerful friend'.

At this time McCarthyism swept America and the sentiment that there could be 'Reds under the beds' was mirrored in Australia. 'Reds under the beds' referred to the threat of internal Communist takeover that was a domestic version of the Domino Theory. The 'loss of China' in 1949 brought these fears into relief, as did the 1950s Korean War, Malayan Confrontation in the early 1960s and Vietnam War from the mid-1960s to mid-1970s. In all cases, China was framed as the enemy, which fit the 'alien' other from Asia that characterized Strategic Culture.

In the early 1950s, fear of Communism verging on paranoia swept Australia, influenced by McCarthyism and by domestic events such as the 1954 Petrov Affair where two Soviet spies defected in Canberra reinforcing fears of Soviet espionage, which was eerily reminiscent of the defection of a Chinese spy in 2019.[7] Robert Menzies' 1949 election campaign included a pledge to ban the Communist Party of Australia and upon election the new Menzies government enacted legislation to follow through. This was based on fears of international Communism and the influence of the Australian Communist Party on unions, including support for the 1949 coal strike. Australia's defence strategy focused on the forward defence against Communism in Asia, which also aligned with paying alliance premiums to the US. China became international Communism's face in Asia and the Korean War further reinforced Canberra's high-level threat perceptions from the 'alien' 'north'.

China's support for the north vietnamese in the 1970s

The next major regional conflict, the Vietnam War, was a proxy war between the US (and Australia) and Communist China and the Soviet Union. From humble beginnings involving 30 advisors in 1962, Australia deployed over 60,000 troops by 1972. Of these, 521 were killed and over 3,000 were wounded. A far larger number suffered trauma that came to be known as 'post-traumatic stress disorder'.

While Australia's commitment was far smaller than that of the US, it had far-reaching domestic political impacts that reverberate to this day. For Canberra, Vietnam became the local source of international Communist threat and an opportunity to engage the US with its regional strategic interests. It also provided the opportunity to support the US by paying alliance dues (see Chapter 3). In this geopolitical context, Vietnamese forces were identified as the enemy on the ground, but there was widespread recognition of China's military support for North Vietnam, and as such China remained the embodiment of the Asian enemy that characterized Strategic Culture. This persisted even after Beijing weakened support for the North Vietnamese and also outlived the diplomatic recognition of China in the middle of the Vietnam War.

The recognition of China in 1972

It was not until the Whitlam government was elected in 1972 that political recognition shifted from Taiwan to the PRC and this heralded the beginning of modern diplomatic relations with China. The Whitlam government also announced the withdrawal of the last Australian forces from Vietnam in 1972 and recognized North Vietnam. It was noteworthy that it took the first post-Second World War change in government from Coalition to Labor to achieve these outcomes, potentially pointing to a harder anti-Communist foreign policy by Conservative governments. However, despite differences in declaratory policy tone, Labor governments also generally closely followed decisions by the US and Whitlam's recognition fit this pattern with respect to the earlier change in policy by Richard Nixon's administration.

Normalization of bilateral relations with China hinged on Australia accepting what came to be known as the 'One China Policy'. The official communique noted:

> The Australian Government recognizes the Government of the People's Republic of China as the sole legal Government of China, acknowledges the position of the Chinese Government that Taiwan is a province of the People's Republic of China.[8]

Normalization of relations focused on trade, which grew slowly as China's economy grew. Furthermore, growth was driven by Chinese demand for natural resources as it became more outward looking and connected to the Western world. Trade grew slowly at first and then dramatically from the early 2000s, mirroring China's growth trajectory. Diplomatic relations lagged and were punctuated by events that reinforced the bias in Strategic Culture against the 'North'.

The Tiananmen Square massacre (1989)

From April to June 1989, a student protest occurred in Beijing which culminated in widespread suppression by Chinese security forces. Estimates vary widely and cannot be verified but range from a few hundred to a few thousand dead and up to 10,000 arrests. These events, variously called the Tiananmen crackdown, Tiananmen incident or the Tiananmen massacre, highlighted how far the Chinese Communist Party (CCP) would go to protect its grip on power. This could not have been in greater contrast to the fall of the Berlin War in November of the same year, which symbolized the end of the Cold War with the Soviet Union. The CCP actively strengthened authoritarian control from Xinjiang to Hong Kong to avoid another Tiananmen Square incident. Furthermore, the legacy of this event domestically and bilaterally can be seen in the Chinese government's crackdown in Hong Kong from 2020 and threats against Taiwan in 2022.

The Hawke government reacted strongly to the Tiananmen massacre by issuing critical statements and cutting diplomatic ties. Prime Minister Bob Hawke himself made an emotional speech in Parliament condemning the acts in the strongest language. This was a case of prime ministerial leadership in foreign policy as cabinet papers reveal that Hawke made the decision without consultation with Cabinet and against subsequent advice from several government departments. Ultimately, there was not much Australia could do in a practical sense to censure China, but over 20,000 Chinese students in Australia were granted protection visas that were later converted to permanent residencies. This was extended to their families and another 10,000 Chinese nationals gained residency,[9] providing the basis for a large increase in the Chinese diaspora over time.

Conclusion

Beijing has long used cultural diplomacy to build diplomatic relations and gain influence. Historically, the Chinese government has preferred to focus on the fact that Australia and China were on the same side in the First and Second World Wars rather than on the conflicts of Korea and Vietnam. However, the inconvenient truth is that prior to the Communist takeover of China in 1949, Canberra had little contact with Beijing and relations since have been overshadowed by the heightened threat perceptions in Strategic Culture.

President Xi Jinping noted in his 2014 speech to the Australian Parliament that: 'Chinese and Australians fought together in two world wars and jointly upheld world peace and human justice.'[10] However, the Korean and Vietnam Wars reinforced the predilection to perceive Asian threats inherent to Strategic Culture and have become part of Australia's policy DNA. It is this attitude that has been the direct or indirect target of much Chinese cultural diplomacy since the end of the Cold War and the shallowness of these attempts at garnering broad influence was revealed as relations broke down in the 2020s. The impact of the tensions is discussed throughout the next chapter to highlight that Canberra made its 'China Choice' some time ago, and Beijing is choosing to punish Australia through trade sanctions and diplomatic isolation.

6

China:
Strategic competitor

Introduction

December 2022 marked 50 years of diplomatic relations between Australia and China, and the anniversary prompted hopes of a thaw in relations. In 2022 as with 1972, a new Labor government is in power in Canberra and the prospects for another rapprochement are promising. Over the last decade Australia and China have grown in parallel and apart and the challenge for Canberra and Beijing will be to try to continue separating trade and security in order to build shared prosperity. However, a new Cold War has dawned and the ability to move beyond transactional economic links is severely constrained.

The rise of the People's Republic of China (PRC) has been a defining feature of international politics for some time, redrawing the regional strategic calculus. Despite this dramatic geoeconomic and geostrategic change, the implications for international affairs remain unclear and will play out for some time. Australia finds itself in the curious position of its major trading partner also being its major source of threat – largely unstated, but increasingly less so. Australian Strategic Culture has led to a curious mix of both increased defence self-reliance and greater support for the strategic interests of 'great and powerful friends' in the past. China[1] has become a truly shared threat amongst traditional 'Western' allies as the rise of the Quadrilateral Dialogue (Quad) and the birth of AUKUS (Australia, United Kingdom and United States) agreement attests. Due to the heightened threat perceptions inherent in Australia's Strategic Culture, this means that the rise of China and strategic issues have increasingly become the focus of Australian foreign policy (AFP).

In contrast to strategic issues, trade provides mutually beneficial links between Australia and China. Furthermore, the benefits for Australia have significantly impacted its trade trajectory. China has played a long game in cultivating closer trade relations with suppliers of strategic resources needed to fuel its growth and the Australian economy has eagerly met Chinese demand. A long-held assumption was that Australia's dependence on the Chinese market meant it had more to lose than China if trade was disrupted and that this would allow Beijing to exert influence over Canberra. However, from the early 2020s, China began to leverage this dependence through a range of trade 'sanctions' that sought to punish Canberra for strategic decisions; Canberra did not compromise, leading to a deterioration of relations.

The central question became whether this trade and security deficit was sustainable and how far Australia would go as the trade relationship was impacted by strategic issues. Could Australia continue to carefully navigate this path or would China force its hand, leading to a 'China Choice'?[2] While the debate is polarized, it does not involve simple bipolarity, but rather a range of contending visions of Australia's present relationship with China and the US and future options for maintaining national security during a period of rapid change and geostrategic competition. Authors such as Allan Gyngell and Richard McGregor acknowledge Australia's vulnerability due to its economic dependence on China, but prescribe a range of options and solutions that would better position Australia to weather economic coercion from Beijing.[3] In contrast, authors such as Hugh White have taken a Realist stance that argues that the rise of China and decline of the US demand a compromise in relation to 'Western' values, such as defence of the Liberal 'rules-based order' that has been elevated within Australia's national interests. As such, White acknowledges the dramatic differentials in power between Australia and China, and the prospect of US decline, and prescribes shifting beyond reliance on the US alliance.[4]

A refreshing aspect of the debate has been attempts to understand China's domestic politics and national interests, such as Linda Jakobson and Bates Gill's *China Matters*, but this nuanced approach has not had the impact that it might if the debate was not so politicized.[5] Speculation over the future of relations has escaped the narrow strategic debates amongst policy-makers and as with discussion of the US alliance debate has been popularized in the media by numerous authors. A key proponent has been Clive Hamilton, who argues that Chinese influence in Australia is significant, insidious and must be countered. As such, Hamilton and commentators such as Peter Hartcher argue that China's coercive influence can be resisted and that Australian values can be defended.[6]

The question of how to manage the so-called 'China Choice' between trade and prosperity and security looms large in Australian foreign policy. This chapter concentrates on the state of play in the relationship today and how relations have developed to date. This chapter stands alongside the chapters on Strategic Culture itself and those on relationships with the US and Japan, all of which point to the significance of how Australia's approach to China will define its future security and prosperity.

A distinctive and controversial aspect of the approach in this chapter is China's asymmetrical trade relationship and the limits of Australia's influence. As such, it will ask whether it is as much China's Choice as well as Australia's *China* Choice that will frame future relations. This strikes at the heart of how to do business with an authoritarian state, such as China, with a semi-command economy where trade is a potential economic weapon, and where the highly globalized interdependence of trade relationships do not relax the strategic threats. Theories about complex interdependence may have to be written if worst-case scenarios play out the way some commentators imagine they might. That is, that China

CHINA: STRATEGIC COMPETITOR 91

used trade sanctions to unilaterally punish Australia, while also damaging its economy, points to a level of irrationality that is not assumed in the literature on how interdependent economies interact. Similarly, Australia's posturing despite this vulnerability points to the fear of the 'north' inherent in Strategic Culture, but the potent mix of geoeconomics and geopolitics is unlike any liminal moment in history that Canberra has faced to date.

Bridging the cultural divide: Not quite 'friends'

China has used cultural diplomacy to influence trading partners in the developing world, but has also used it to counter US influence in states like Australia. These 'influence operations' have not necessarily worked the same way in Australia as elite dominated authoritarian states. In fact, the insidious nature of 'influence operations' has come to frame present government and public attitudes to China in Australia. As cultural diplomacy increased in importance, the history of Chinese immigrants on the goldfields and their influence on settler society was popularized through institutions such as the Gum San Chinese Heritage Centre in Ararat in regional Victoria. Some of the emphasis on cultural diplomacy in Australia was supported by Chinese government-funded Confucius Institutes as a form of soft power to influence attitudes and this influence was to become more prominent and problematic domestically in Australia over time.

China's position as an enemy in the Korean and Vietnam 'hot' wars and throughout the Cold War forms a formidable barrier to developing warm bilateral relations. When coupled with the history of racism against Chinese in Australia that dates to the Gold Rush in the 1850s, manufacturing cultural affinity is incredibly challenging (see previous chapter). The challenge is recognized by both governments and has been a major declaratory policy priority in both states' foreign policies. An orthodox strategy encouraging 'people-to-people' links through tourism, immigration and educational exchanges has been developed, but public opinion has been slow to shift. Relations remain largely driven from the top down as governmental versus societal priorities. As noted in Chapters 7 and 8, this is also the case with Japan, but not with the US (discussed in Chapter 4).

Tourism and immigration

Travel restrictions implemented in response to the COVID-19 pandemic caused an unprecedented collapse in international travel. The assumption is that travel will recover as states recover from the pandemic, so statistics from prior to the pandemic are used as an indicator of the trajectory of relations. In 2018, China was the largest tourism market for Australia in both number of arrivals and total spending. Over 1.4 million Chinese visited Australia and of these 1.3 million were tourists who spent A$11.6 billion. By contrast, 538,000 Australians travelled to China, making it the sixth most popular destination.[7] In raw numbers, China represents the largest single source of tourists by far, but in percentage of population terms (0.01 per cent) this is far less than other key markets, which shows that there is the opportunity for growth. However, any conclusions about the impact of tourism on 'people-to-people' links is tempered by the complexion of travellers. For example. the majority of Chinese travellers had travelled to Australia before, pointing to connections with the diaspora population in Australia. This means that a few Chinese are undertaking many trips to Australia rather than an increasing number of new travellers with no links to Australia. Furthermore, many of these Australian travellers were members of the diaspora population rather than tourists from non-Chinese backgrounds. Therefore, a word of caution is needed when drawing connections between the numbers of travellers and developing warmer 'people-to-people' links.

The Chinese diaspora population in Australia is not inconsiderable, with approximately 1.4 million people of Chinese descent living in Australia (5.5 per cent of the population). Over 50 per cent of Chinese in Australia (677,000) were born in China, representing 2.6 per cent of Australia's population. Chinese-born Australians are the third largest migrant group, behind those from the UK and India.[8] According to the 2016 census, approximately 50 per cent of people of Chinese descent speak Mandarin at home. In the 2021 census, Mandarin was the most spoken language at home after English. While Mandarin is the most popular language taught in schools, not many students in Australia are studying it at the highest level and of these less than 10 per cent are not from a Chinese-speaking background.[9] In 2019, Labor parliamentarian Chris Bowen lamented that only 130 Australians of non-Chinese background had the highest level of language proficiency, which highlights the deficit in this regard. Attempts to increase Asia literacy over the decades since Prime Minister Paul Keating trumpeted the charge in the 1990s have not resonated with the broader public.

Tourism and immigration statistics identify a high volume of 'people-to-people' interaction, but the maintenance of language barriers highlights that this does not necessarily equate to greater cultural understanding or affinity. The COVID-19 pandemic froze non-essential travel and it remains to be seen whether numbers increase in the future, but it is clear that Beijing was already using tourism as a lever to pressure Canberra by advising against travel to Australia. This was reinforced by stories about the racist treatment of ethnic Chinese during the pandemic.[10] This suggests that tourism is unlikely to recover until relations improve. More significantly for the terms of trade, Beijing also advised against study in Australia.

Educating Chinese students in Australia

As globalization has increased exponentially over the last decade, there has been huge growth in the international education market and this was led by Chinese students.[11] Student mobility between Australia and China has been quite one-sided, with far more Chinese students visiting Australia. Prior to COVID-19 travel restrictions, approximately 200,000 Chinese students studied in Australia every year. This represents approximately 30 per cent of the A$35 billion (2018) Australian market and dwarfed the 13,000 Japanese and 11,500 US students enrolled in Australian higher education institutions.[12] In comparison, Australian students made up 1.1 per cent of inbound students in China, or approximately 4,400 students.[13] These figures are not surprising considering the lack of interest in studying Mandarin in high school.

The 2015 China-Australia free trade agreement (CFTA) reduced barriers to Chinese students studying in Australia and numbers increased, but barriers to exporting educational products to China did not benefit.[14] Canberra's New Colombo Plan, where Australian students were provided with scholarships by the Australian government to increase Asia literacy, has been supported by the highest echelons of the Chinese government, which was necessary if success was to be achieved in an authoritarian state.[15] However, the numbers involved are small.

The complementary motives of China and Australia in encouraging educational exchange mirrored broader trade relations. China was interested in technology and knowledge transfer, and in influencing domestic politics in Australia (through Confucius Institutes, for example), while Australia was interested in increasing income from international education by growing its share of the market.[16] Australian governments have used educational soft power as a diplomatic tool, as evidenced by the support for Australian Studies Centres in China.[17] China does not seem concerned with their operations in China while Canberra has increasingly queried the operations of Confucius Institutes in Australia.

With China forming the major source of Australia's higher education market, there was always potential for political tension to spill over into this major market. The focus on student mobility has significant economic benefits for Australia and has also been an enduring theme in bilateral statements supporting the development of closer 'people-to-people' links. As such, international education fits with Liberal Internationalist values, but the risk to the lucrative education and tourism markets of spill over from tensions in the broader diplomatic relations would be identified by Realists as a vulnerability.[18] The market has been jeopardized by the fracture in relations and it is likely that student numbers will not recover post-COVID-19 after travel restrictions were lifted due to directives from Beijing to deter prospective international students.[19]

The government has stood firm in defending Australian sovereignty against Chinese influence operations but this has come at a cost. Canberra's willingness to weather the storm of China's trade sanctions highlights that the 'China Choice' is firmly grounded in the national interest and Australian Strategic Culture. A Realist calculus in relation to economic interests may be far more compromising than the path that Canberra has chosen and despite all the talk of the 'rules-based order', this stance is not Liberal Internationalist, but rather a pluralistic Realist Strategic Cultural reflection on how to counter threats to sovereignty from the 'alien' 'north'.

Public opinion

The Chinese press operates as an extension of the Communist Party and provides an insight into official views of Australia. Expert commentators and retired military officers quoted in the press can be viewed as mouthpieces for the government and as such their statements can be illuminating. As trade tensions grew in the early 2020s, so did the level of criticism from the Chinese press and low-level officials. These were obviously designed to influence Canberra but had the unintended impact of negatively impacting public opinion. Comments about China's capacity to buy commodities from states other than Australia fit this mould.[20]

Lowy Institute polling in 2022 showed a broad decline in sentiment towards China. In 2018, China was the sixth most trusted state to act responsibly in international affairs (52 per cent), with the US a few percentage points ahead (55 per cent), which highlighted the depth to which support for the US dropped under President Trump (see Chapter 4). By 2022, trust in China had dived to 12 per cent, a dramatic 40 per cent decline since 2018. In 2018, President Xi Jinping was the fifth most trusted leader (43 per cent) and was well ahead of Trump (30 per cent). However, by 2022, the Chinese president was trusted by just 11 per cent of respondents and President Joe Biden was trusted by 58 per cent. Similarly, in 2018, 63 per cent of respondents were worried about Chinese influence in Australian politics while 58 per cent were concerned about US influence. By 2022, 86 per cent were concerned about Chinese influence and 54 per cent were concerned about US influence.[21]

China-focused polling was negative, but so too were the implications of China's behaviour on respondents' threat perceptions. For example, after Russia in the Ukraine, the second, third, fifth and sixth highest critical threats (65, 64, 55 and 49 per cent respectively) were perceived from Chinese foreign policy, conflict over Taiwan, the rise of authoritarian governments and foreign interference.[22] All of these threats are identified with China in the Australian press.[23] On trade and investment, in 2018, 72 per cent believed that there was too much Chinese investment in Australia and this figure has risen markedly in recent years (up from 50 per cent in 2009).[24] By 2021, 67 per cent thought that Chinese investment in Australia contributed to a negative view of China. Furthermore, there was very high disapproval of the Chinese government gaining a controlling interest in Australian companies (92 per cent).[25]

Polling on China as a threat reflects tensions in threat perceptions. Polling in 2022 suggests that there is no need to make a 'China Choice' as most respondents to the Lowy Institute Poll no longer think that good relations with both the US and China are possible.[26] Furthermore, in a reversal of earlier attitudes, 63 per cent saw China as a military threat versus 33 per cent seeing China as primarily an economic partner.[27] However, at the same time, in 2022, 75 per cent believed that China will become a military threat to Australia in the next 20 years and this has also been rising (up from 41 per cent in 2009).[28] Respondents also believed that it is highly likely (77 per cent) that the US and China will go to war and that Australia will be drawn into the conflict due to the ANZUS alliance.[29] China's posturing over Taiwan registers negatively by the Australian public, but in 2018 less than 41 per cent of respondents thought that Australia should support the US in a conflict with China, a figure that is slowly rising, despite trying to remain neutral being the preference in 2021 (57 per cent).[30]

A word of caution is needed when interpreting these results as polls do not drive policy. However, it is clear that the Australian public has firm beliefs about the geopolitical struggle and does not shy away from the possibility of fighting a war alongside the US against China. That said, there was non-specified faith in being able to manage the status quo, despite the increased focus on issues such as Chinese foreign investment, interference operations and trade sanctions. Furthermore, in a vote of confidence in the government's handling of the relationship, the public squarely blames China for deteriorating relations.[31]

Diplomatic collaboration in international and regional fora

Beijing has become increasingly interested in being seen to be a '*responsible* great power' and to engage at a level commensurate with its economic and military might.[32] Due to China's status as a permanent member of the United Nations (UN) Security Council, much of this activity relates to the UN or regional organizations that Australia is not a member of, such as the China-backed Shanghai Cooperation Organization. As such, there is not a high volume of cooperative interaction towards multilateral goals that can be analysed to test the strength of shared international interests. The limited scope of institutionalized multilateral and bilateral collaboration is noteworthy and is in stark contrast to relations with allies, such as the US, or close friends, such as Japan.

Beijing's ambitious Belt and Road Initiative (BRI) has framed international affairs in many states in Asia and Africa, but the Australian government and businesses have been almost silent on the implications for Australia. The BRI was President Xi Jinping's signature international relations project designed to link markets in Asia and Europe and involves significant investment and economic development opportunities. Given that it is China's largest diplomatic initiative with momentous economic implications, this lack of engagement is telling.

While the federal government has not engaged with the BRI, the Labor government of the State of Victoria signed up to the BRI in 2019. It did so without consultation with the federal government, which revealed the potential tensions between local and federal interests in AFP. These tensions came to a head when Canberra repealed Victoria's signing onto the BRI on national security grounds in 2021, leading to another low point in relations with China.[33] This was an entirely predictable outcome and Canberra's willingness to strain relations points to a firming of Australia's position towards Beijing's diplomatic pressure and trade restrictions. Attempting to sign up state governments was akin to a 'divide and conquer' policy that would not be countenanced in Canberra.

In his seminal speech to a joint sitting of Australia's Parliament in 2014, President Xi Jinping noted that 'We maintain good cooperation in multilateral mechanisms, including the United Nations, APEC and the G20.'[34] This declaratory policy description stands in contrast to the US or Japan, where a stronger word would be used to describe cooperation. It is also clear that the range of shared interests that have built close multilateral relations with other states, such as security, climate change and maintaining Liberal Internationalist regional architecture, are under-developed in relation to China. Even the issue of overseas development assistance (ODA) that often united donors has caused tension in relation to fears about China's debt diplomacy in the South Pacific.[35]

Prime ministerial relations and high-level diplomacy

Australia and China have over thirty government consultation and dialogue mechanisms at all levels of government. Public diplomacy between Australia and China has grown in the last decade, but this has been from a small base. The turning point was the signing of the April 2013 Comprehensive Strategic Partnership and President Xi Jinping's subsequent visit to Australia in 2014.

The Comprehensive Strategic Partnership was a watershed in relations because diplomatic contacts were institutionalized through annual Leaders' meetings. At the ministerial level, regular economic and strategic dialogues were also announced. For example, in November 2018, the fifth Australia–China Strategic Economic Dialogue occurred. These activities outwardly appeared to provide the architecture for developing closer relations. For the first few years, meetings occurred regularly and a free trade agreement (FTA) was signed in 2015. However, tensions regularly surfaced in relations and diplomatic relations warmed and cooled in a regular pattern. For example, retractions and corrections on Australia's part and China delaying meetings signalled China's displeasure with Australian policy stances.[36] Beijing officially suspended the Strategic Economic Dialogue meetings in May 2021, which signified a new low point in relations and Canberra's failure to compromise in relation to China's grievances.

A 'top-down' approach

At the highest levels in both governments, there was recognition of a cultural disconnect. The emphasis on 'people-to-people' links has been driven by high-level diplomacy rather than at all levels of society. When addressing the Australian Parliament, President Xi Jinping noted that:

> We should intensify people-to-people exchanges and be friends . . . Likewise, if the China-Australia relationship is to flourish, it must be supported by stronger people-to-people ties. We should create more opportunities to boost exchanges and cooperation in education, culture, science, technology and tourism as well as between local governments and to build more bridges of understanding and friendship between our two peoples.[37]

Prime Minister Tony Abbott and President Xi Jinping were central to the completion of the long FTA negotiations. Considering the highly hierarchical structures of an authoritarian state such as China, it was natural that diplomatic priorities were driven from the top (as were most portfolios). This was even more the case with the centralization of power when Jinping became 'President for Life' in February 2018. Recognizing the realities of authoritarian governments was essential to Australia's approach to China as it was the Chinese Communist Party's *diplomatic* choice to trade with Australia and undertake educational exchanges and other activities, rather than being driven by market-driven forces. This became abundantly clear when Canberra fell out of favour with China in the late 2010s and despite Prime Minister Turnbull's attempted 'reset' in relations in 2018, relations unravelled.[38] The early 2020s witnessed increasingly undiplomatic language and trade tensions escalated leading to China imposing over A$20 billion in trade sanctions.

Prior to the COVID-19 pandemic and rising tensions, there were also an increasing number of reciprocal visits by ministers and senior bureaucrats. This demonstrates that the 'top-down' approach to building 'people-to-people' links was working, at least at the top level. Recent meetings have covered the gamut of government activities, including the portfolios of foreign affairs, trade, tourism and development, and industry. However, the overwhelming focus has been on trade and investment. Comparatively speaking, these interactions were nothing like the volume of interaction with states such as Japan or the US.

A thaw in relations under Labor?

Ministerial contact between China and Australia had been frozen by Beijing after a series of decisions by the Scott Morrison government, including introducing foreign interference legislation aimed at Chinese influence operations, blocking Chinese telco Huawei from operating in sensitive Australian infrastructure projects, and prompting an investigation into the origin of the COVID-19 pandemic, which alluded to Chinese government involvement. In addition to high-level diplomatic isolation, China introduced A$20 billion in sanctions against Australian products and Canberra responded by making a complaint against China to the World Trade Organisation (WTO).

The election of the Anthony Albanese government in 2022 appeared to prompt a thaw in relations. During the election campaign Albanese, then the opposition leader, walked a fine line to connect Labor foreign policy with the legacy of engagement going back to Whitlam, who coincidentally visited China while in opposition and then led the rapprochement with China prompted by shifting recognition from Taiwan to China. The thaw was evidenced in the slow re-engagement on the side of several major multilateral meetings. For example, the Australian foreign and defence ministers met the Chinese defence minister at the Shangrila Dialogue in Singapore in June 2022. Significantly, Prime Minister Albanese met President Xi Jinping on the sidelines of the G20 in November and Foreign Minister Penny Wong went on to meet Foreign Minister Wang Yi in Beijing just before Christmas 2022.

Diplomatic collaboration with China can be contrasted with the bilateral and multilateral trade and security collaboration that characterizes Australia's relations with Japan and the US. The missing piece of the puzzle with China is security diplomacy. Bilateral cooperation focused on trade fits neatly within an instrumentalist neo-Realist frame of thinking about maximizing interests. It also points to the lack of shared Liberal Internationalist values that has seen multilateral cooperation develop in a range of sectors in Australia's foreign relations with other states. Furthermore, if the abiding constraint on security diplomacy is based on threat perceptions founded on cultural and political differences, then Australia's Strategic Culture constrains the relationship.

Characterizing the relationship: An overwhelming focus on trade and investment

Trade background

Australia's prosperity over the last 30 years has been entwined with Asian dynamism. In the 1980s and 1990s, it was the industrialization of the so-called Asian 'Tigers' that fuelled demand for Australian natural resources. By the mid-1990s, Japan had outgrown the other tigers to become Australia's core trading partner. Then China's growth outstripped all Asian states and by 2007 became Australia's largest export market. The complementary nature of Australia's resource and agriculturally focused economy with Asian manufacturing powerhouses was a recipe for unprecedented growth. However, despite the increasing volume of trade, a free trade agreement with China took some time to negotiate, and came well after free trade agreements with other Asian states, which was telling.

The data in Figure 6.1 and Table 6.1 highlight the shift in Australia's trade to Asia and the role of China as the epicentre of Australian trade.

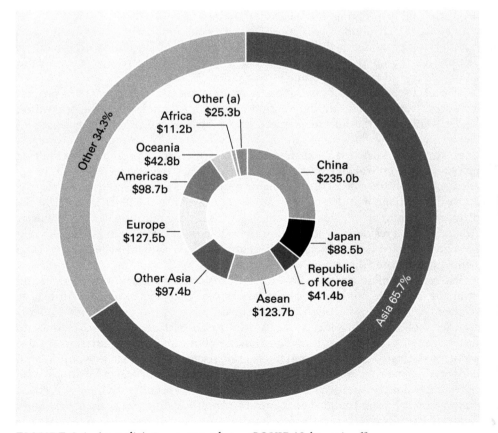

FIGURE 6.1 *Australia's two-way trade pre-COVID19 by region.*[39]

TABLE 6.1 *Australia's top 10 pre-COVID19 export markets (A$ billion)*[40]

Rank	Markets	Goods	Services	Total	% Share
1	China	134.7	18.5	153.2	32.6
2	Japan	59.1	2.6	61.7	13.1
3	Republic of Korea	25.6	2.2	27.8	5.9
4	United States	14.7	10.0	24.7	5.3
5	India	16.2	6.6	22.8	4.9
6	New Zealand	10.0	6.0	16.0	3.4
7	Singapore	10.6	5.4	16.0	3.4
8	Taiwan	12.4	1.5	13.9	2.9
9	United Kingdom	7.9	5.6	13.5	2.9
10	Malaysia	8.9	2.6	11.5	2.5
Total		300.1	61.1	361.1	76.8

Trade foreground

The CFTA was signed in 2015. Negotiations began in 2005 and the conclusion of the agreement after a decade of negotiations highlighted the major domestic challenges in convincing Australian business and the general public that a free trade agreement with China was in Australia's interests. In the face of numerous delays, Prime Minister Abbott was a central driving force to concluding the agreement and it was signed after President Xi Jinping's speech to a joint sitting of the Australian Parliament in 2014, coming into force the following year. The CFTA reduced tariffs on the majority of two-way trade and reinforced the already very strong trade relationship.

Department of Foreign Affairs and Trade (DFAT) statistics (Table 6.2) identify the complete dominance of China in almost all aspects of Australia's trade. China is Australia's largest two-way trading partner, largest export destination and largest source of imports. The only area that lagged was investment, where traditional markets (the UK and US) dominated. China became Australia's number one trading partner in the mid-2000s and consistent trade surpluses with China have been the most significant reason for Australia's prosperity for almost two decades. Figure 6.2, from the 2017 Foreign Policy White Paper, shows that the Treasury sees this trajectory being maintained for the foreseeable future.

As Australian prosperity is so closely linked to China, the question for Canberra is whether bilateral trade will continue to flourish. Will China's economic slowdown in the 2020s follow the trend of its Asian 'Tiger' neighbours or can Beijing defy the pattern through initiatives such as the BRI or a more sustainable economy that is more reliant on domestic consumption? In either scenario,

TABLE 6.2 *Australia's pre-COVID19 trade and investment relationship with China*[41]

Australian merchandise trade with China, 2019–20 (A$m)		Total share	Rank	Growth (yoy)
Exports to China	151,504	39.6%	1st	12.3%
Imports from China	81,052	26.1%	1st	3.6%
Total merchandise trade (exports + imports)	232,556	33.5%	1st	9.1%
Major Australian exports, 2019–20 (A$m)		**Major Australian imports, 2019–20 (A$m)**		
Iron ores & concentrates	84,683	Telecom equipment & parts		9,380
Natural gas	15,722	Computers		7,276
Coal	13,707	Furniture, mattresses & cushions		3,371
Beef, f.c.f.	2,839	Refined petroleum		3,034
Australia's trade in services with China, 2019–20 (A$m)		**Total share**	**Rank**	**Growth (yoy)**
Exports of services to China	16,246	17.6%	1st	–12.8%
Imports of services from China	2,429	2.8%	11th	–26.4%
Major Australian services exports, 2019–20 (A$m)		**Major Australian services imports, 2019–20 (A$m)**		
Education-releated travel	10,494	Personal travel excluding education		895
Personal travel excluding education	2,828	Transpoet		539
Australia's Investment relationship with China, 2019 (A$m)			**Total**	**FDI**
Australia's Investment in China			85,268	*15,511*
China's Investment in Australia			78,152	*45,992*

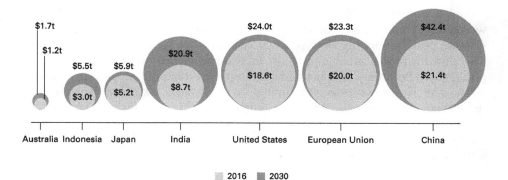

FIGURE 6.2 *Gross domestic product (GDP) forecasts to 2030.*[42]

Australia could continue to benefit from China's growth trajectory, but due to China's authoritarian system of government, this is reliant on Beijing's approval, and the trade conflict of the early 2020s demonstrated how exposed the Australian economy was to diplomatic pressure. Coming on the heels of the supply chain disruption wrought by the COVID-19 pandemic this prompted calls to diversify Australia's trading partners.

Weaponizing trade as a diplomatic lever

China's economic coercion grew incrementally as a sign of displeasure at Australian foreign policy. Initiatives included introducing political interference legislation, tightening foreign ownership laws, banning China's telecommunication companies from the 5G network, supporting the Permanent Court of Arbitration's findings against China's interpretation of sovereignty in the South China Sea, sponsoring an investigation into the origins of the COVID-19 pandemic, highlighting human rights violations of the Uighur people in Xinjiang, and diplomatically rebuking Beijing over the crackdown against dissent in Hong Kong. China's strategy appears to be one of punishment whereby the authoritarian government could use its control of the economy to disadvantage Australian businesses. China's approach could also be viewed as a wedging strategy by trying to put pressure on the Australia–US alliance.[43]

The high volume of trade with China has fuelled Australian prosperity for decades, but this dependence on China also involves strategic vulnerability. The Chinese government exercises a great deal of control over all aspects of politics, society and economics in China and this extends to access to imports and exports. A free-market system would see market forces regulate supply based on demand, but the Chinese government influences both. This means that it can directly influence how much of a particular commodity is imported from a particular market into China. As Xu Liping, an expert at the Chinese Academy of Social Sciences, noted: 'Australia needs to understand that many of Australia's exports to China are commodities, and there are many alternatives.'[44] The Chinese market therefore sources items such as barley and wine from elsewhere, with a devastating impact on Australian businesses.

Veiled threats mentioned by Chinese diplomats became a reality as Beijing weaponized trade in its diplomatic conflict with Australia. For example, in 2019, Chinese ports reportedly slowed down customs clearances for Australian coal. The slowdown was attributed to an increase in environmental inspections at ports, which began in 2015, but had only impacted Australian coal once before in 2016. The slowdown was not limited to Australian coal, but Russian and Indonesian coal imports were not impacted. Chinese officials denied that Australian coal was being targeted, but speculation linked the slowdown to tensions in relations,[45] which prompted discussion of whether Prime Minister Turnbull's 2018 'reset' in relations[46] had been a success.

Sanctions by stealth

Though imposed incrementally, a large number of tariffs and other trade restrictions added up to appear like sanctions against Australia. Commodities impacted included barley, beef, coal, copper, lamb, lobster and wine, and the restrictions grew to involve approximately A\$20 billion in trade. The impact on sectors differed but some were hit hard, such as the 96 per cent decline in wine exports after China imposed tariffs of over 200 per cent. Prior to the tariffs in 2019, Australia was the market leader ahead of France, with a third of sales,[47] and it is unclear whether this market will recover. The impact on the Australian wine industry cannot be underestimated and other sectors were similarly affected. Significantly, iron ore was not targeted, presumably due to the lack of alternate sources of supply.

Canberra responded to China's economic coercion by following one of the few avenues of recourse available: through diplomatic signalling, bandwagoning and by lodging complaints against the Chinese in the World Trade Organization (WTO). This highlights the free trade aspects of the 'rules-based order' whereby the Australian government does not use trade measures to signal diplomatic displeasure, other than economic sanctions imposed for legitimate reasons, generally under a legitimate mandate (such as under a UN mandate). The response to economic coercion highlights both Canberra's respect for free trade and the self-imposed limitations this brings, as well as the contrasting approaches to the 'art of the possible' in diplomacy that authoritarian states such as China employ.

BOX 6.1: AUSTRALIA VERSUS CHINA AT THE WORLD TRADE ORGANIZATION (WTO)

- China introduces A\$20 billion in sanctions against Australian exports.
- Initial negotiations fail as Beijing makes it clear that Australia is being punished for diplomatic activities and compromises would be needed.
- Australia takes complaints against China to WTO.
- Focus on wine and barley, although other products were impacted.
- Chinese sanctions treated by Canberra as 'anti-dumping and countervailing measures'.

The WTO case had also been working its way through the system and Canberra was confident of success in highlighting the illegality of China's sanctions. This Liberal Internationalist approach appeared to succeed but the lack of redress was of little benefit to Australian businesses after the damage was done to the Australian economy. The WTO episode highlights the strengths and weaknesses of the mechanisms that prop up the 'rules-based order', especially when an authoritarian state chooses to 'weaponize' trade.

Major allies and friends such as the US, UK and Japan supported Australia from the standpoint of defending the 'rules-based order'. A firm statement of US support came soon after the election of the Biden administration when spokesperson Kurt Campbell noted that: 'we are not going to leave Australia alone in the field'.[48] Australia's principled stance also gained support from the G7, European Union and the North Atlantic Treaty Organization (NATO), which reinforced the importance of upholding the international trade regime. This came against the backdrop of sanctions from China against European states due to their publicly aired concerns over human rights abuses in Xinjiang.

International support may have emboldened Canberra, despite the economic costs. For example, Prime Minister Morrison told the G7 meeting in June 2021 that:

> ... there is not a country that would sit around that table that would seek a concession on any of those 14 points as something they would also tolerate. So I think you just set out clearly that there are differences in world view here and they may never be able to be resolved.[49]

Due to the dependence on China, diversifying export markets is one of the options that the government has encouraged and exporters have pursued as it became increasingly clear that China was responding negatively to Australia's 'China Choice'. However, the limits of the government's power to protect businesses was on display with respect to Chinese sanctions in 2020. Similarly, the limited capacity to support diversification of markets was also clear.

Australian trade as collateral damage from the US trade war with China?

The Trump administration's trade war between the US and China had the potential to spill over into Australia's bilateral trade relations with both states. The relationship with the US is covered in Chapters 3 and 4, but there was speculation that any compromise on China's part would have mixed results for Australia. For example, in 2019, China's National People's Congress passed a foreign investment law that sought to compromise on key US claims that Chinese restrictions were producing an uneven playing field. Compromise highlighted a willingness to negotiate that had been absent from other 'rules-based order' issues that Australia was concerned with, including freedom of navigation on the high seas.

The problem with a compromise by China was that it subverted market forces and the economic logic behind global supply chains.[50] That is, China's diplomatic interests to either support or undermine Australian exports prevailed over rational market forces. A negative impact of China using trade as a diplomatic lever was predicted to be the flow-on effect on coal exports. The Australian government has been sensitive to China's demand for coal and the slowdown in processing customs clearances at Chinese ports was met with speculation that imports were a symbol of how badly the broader diplomatic relationship was faring. There were clear signs that China planned to increase imports of Virginian coal as part of a trade compromise with the US.[51] This form of preferencing would be politically expedient because it would have benefited President Trump's supporter base, but it would also challenge free trade and Australia's interests.

Australia's export-oriented trade strategy relied on free trade and this key plank in AFP references Liberal Internationalist values with respect to the 'rules-based order'. The Trump administration and China's behaviour was narrowly Realist as it was anti-competitive in support of national interests versus upholding free trade in the 'rules-based order'. As such, from the perspective of Australia's trade interests, China preferencing coal from the US would rival the US sanctions on Chinese steel that were aimed at China and that Australia narrowly avoided. It appeared that Australia could become collateral damage in the trade war between the US and China, and concerted efforts were needed by Canberra to ensure that Australia's interests were maintained. Ultimately, it was the election of the Biden administration that positively changed dynamics with regard to how the US viewed defending Australia's interests.

Chinese foreign direct investment in Australia

As of 2021, China was the eighth largest foreign investor in Australia, with 2.2 per cent of total foreign investment.[52] This is a decline from the peak of 2015 where China and the US were the top investors in Australia, but even at China's peak, the US was the largest. China's investment in Australia's Foreign Investment Review Board (FIRB) approved projects was below Australia's investment in China and well below investment from traditional markets (the UK and US). However, despite this relative position, the perception in Australia was that Chinese investment in Australia was much higher, which highlighted concerns over Chinese influence. Furthermore, with respect to Strategic Culture, perceptions count.

Is Chinese investment a threat to Australia?

Multinational companies based in one state routinely invest in business activities in other states and this is a key aspect of a Liberal free trade system. However, the level and type of investment in Australia has become a contentious issue in the last 15 years. In 2009, the government introduced a national interest test for investment by foreign governments in Australia. From this date, foreign applications were reviewed by the FIRB and individually approved by the treasurer. Several applications under the new test saw major projects modified, such as Chinalco's attempt to raise its stake in Rio Tinto. More telling was the refusal on 'national security grounds' of China Minmetal's attempted takeover of an Australian company operating adjacent to the Woomera missile range in South Australia.[53]

BOX 6.2: FIRB'S NATIONAL INTEREST TEST

- A regulatory mechanism to manage national interest/national security risks of a foreign investment.
- 'The national interest, and what would be contrary to it, is not defined in the Act.'
- Factors influencing decisions include 'National security, Competition, Other Australian Government policies . . . Impact on the economy and the community, Character of the Investor.'
- Attempt to provide transparency, but a high level of discretion remains.

The FIRB's national interest test was strengthened in 2015 and tightened in 2020. The point being to provide Canberra more oversight over foreign applications to purchase land or businesses deemed sensitive to Australia's national security.[54] A key reason for this legislation was the leasing of the Port of Darwin to Landbridge, a Chinese company, in 2015. In hindsight, this has been viewed as being strategically problematic, not least by Australia's close ally, the US. This was in part due to the increased basing of US marines in Darwin as part of President Barak Obama's strategic Pivot to the Indo-Pacific. The strategic issues were revisited when the Albanese government undertook a review of the lease in 2022.

While Chinese state-owned enterprises (SOEs) were not directly targeted, there has been some concern from Beijing about the application of foreign ownership rules. This came to a head in 2018 when China's Huawei telecommunications company was banned from investing in Australia's national broadband network, despite not being a SOE, and the justification was also on national security grounds.[55] The Department of Defence also banned the use of the Chinese WeChat messaging app on its phones.[56] Canberra mirrored US actions which could reasonably have been predicted to have damaging impacts, but went ahead nonetheless.[57] China commentators noted that investment was a test of the strength of the bilateral relationship and that 'capital xenophobia' sends mixed messages about whether Australia was serious about facilitating increased trade.[58] In an ominous veiled threat, it was observed that 'misunderstandings about specific investment cases can easily grow into larger diplomatic problems'.[59]

Public opinion and Chinese land ownership

Government policy has been firmly supported by public opinion. There are ongoing concerns about Chinese ownership of Australian resources, which arose during the minerals boom years in the mid-2000s. For example, in 2021, 79 per cent of respondents to the Lowy Poll believed that Chinese investment in Australia had had a negative impact on relations.[60] From 2005 to 2012, Australia was the number one destination for Chinese foreign investment, but this dipped at the end of the boom. The Australian government largely applied a Liberal Internationalist approach to market-based mechanisms and allowed this influx of investment[61] until national interest-based concerns over ownership of strategic assets prompted greater regulation. At its peak in 2017, China invested A$7.3 billion in the mining sector, which represented more than half of all foreign investment.[62] However, investment declined thereafter, predating the impact of the COVID-19 pandemic.[63]

Beyond the mining sector there were also significant concerns over Chinese ownership of residential property and agricultural land. Both of these concerns were not new and were highly politicized.[64] There was continuity with previous 'Asian' investors, such as criticism of Japanese investment in the 1990s.[65] In contrast, there were no concerns about the high level of UK or US investment in these sectors, and by 2022, China had dropped to the eighth largest investor in Australia.[66] The fact that Chinese investment was lower than that of other trade partners yet still prompted government and public concern highlights links with Strategic Culture because fear of the 'alien' north did not apply to investment from culturally similar allies. The shift in the focus of criticism from Japan to China was a recent phenomenon that mirrored increased overall Chinese investment and resonated in public opinion. The concerns in relation to residential and agricultural land were similar, but differed in important ways.

In the case of residential land, the national interest was personalized at the local level. There was public concern over regulation of foreign ownership and concern about the impact of investment on housing affordability for Australians. For example, a majority of respondents in one study believed that foreign/Chinese investors should not be able to invest in key residential markets (namely Sydney).[67] This concern had some basis as Chinese residential and commercial property investment reached A$24 billion in 2014–15, a 900 per cent increase in eight years.[68] From 2016, there was a decline in Chinese demand for property, but the Chinese continued to be the number three foreign investor in this sector and negative public perceptions remained.[69]

Chinese investment in agricultural land was also significant in domestic politics, but there was a mismatch between perceptions and reality. Public opinion towards investment, especially by Chinese SOEs, was consistently negative. In 2015, concerns over foreign ownership led to a reduction in the threshold for FIRB approval for agricultural land sales from A$252 to A$15 million. In addition, a register of foreign-owned land was created to allow a strategic overview to be produced. In 2020, foreign investors owned 13.8 per cent of agricultural land, a slight rise over the preceding five years. That is, Australian entities owned 86 per cent of Australian agricultural land. The foreign ownership figure was far below any critical level whereby foreign ownership might challenge Australia's sovereign interests. In a reversal of positions over the preceding five years, China was the largest landowner (2.4 per cent) after the UK (2.1 per cent), but again these percentages were quite small overall. In contrast, in 2020, China had declined from being the largest investor in agriculture in 2017 (A$2.2 billion) to the sixth largest investor (A$301 million).[70] The stock of land held by China remained relatively stable despite the impacts of the COVID-19 pandemic. However, the trajectory of growth declined, pointing to the influence of China's trade sanctions and preferences against Australia.

CHINA: STRATEGIC COMPETITOR

Public opinion on Chinese investment in Australia was critical of Canberra for allowing too much, especially in relation to agricultural land. While polls do not necessarily drive policy, they reflect commonly held beliefs in the electorate and these cannot be explained by a combination of a Realist focus on maximizing economic interests or a Liberal Internationalist focus on free trade that is often assumed to drive trade. Rather, attitudes akin to the Strategic Cultural fear of Asian economic 'invasion' persisted and were firming. This was despite the comparatively small level of Chinese investment and was in stark contrast to how investment from the UK or US was treated.

Characterizing the relationship: 'Tit for tat' diplomacy

Trade has been the overwhelming focus of foreign relations with China and until the 2020s, diplomatic tensions between Australia and China were generally moderate. Tensions have occurred at times and relations between Canberra and Beijing are currently at a low point. Relations have been unravelling from some time and Turnbull's so-called China 'reset' in 2018 highlights the last significant attempt at a rapprochement by Canberra. The then prime minister's explanation for the policy succinctly captured the mixed interests and motives faced by Australian policy-makers:

> We act to advance Australia's prosperity, ensure the independence of our decision-making and secure the safety and freedom of our people. And in doing so, we support an international order based on the rule of law, where might is not right and the sovereignty of all nations is respected by others.[71]

This quote highlights the intersection of a Realist focus on national interests and an acknowledgement of relative power and anarchy in the international arena; a Liberal Internationalist emphasis on values and the 'rules-based order'; and the respect for sovereignty shared by all schools of thought on foreign policy. Strategic Culture seems absent, but it is ever present in relation to exaggerated threat perceptions from an 'alien' other in Asia and a feeling of indefensibility.

Despite declaratory policy acknowledgements of the need for diplomatic compromise, the preceding quote by Prime Minister Turnbull demonstrated that values-diplomacy has also been an enduring element in AFP. The tensions that have been evident stem from the Liberal Internationalist emphasis on human rights and the maintenance of a 'rules-based order'. If there were no values in foreign policy, as Realists would contend, then these issues would not have been pursued by Australian policy-makers, especially when they had the potential to damage Australia's prosperity and potentially its long-term security. Since federation in 1901, these values have been heralded by prime ministers and foreign ministers from both sides of politics, highlighting the consensus over when and against whom to direct value-laden critiques.

The low points in foreign relations over the last 30 years have coincided with Australia's public criticism of Chinese actions or support for causes that are central to China's definition of national interests. Examples include Prime Minister Bob Hawke's support for Chinese students in the aftermath of the Tiananmen massacre in 1989; Prime Minister John Howard's meeting with the Dalai Lama in 2007;[72] Australia's willingness to allow exiled Uighur leader Rebiya Kadeer to visit and Prime Minister Kevin Rudd's subsequent meeting with her in 2015;[73] the Rio Tinto spying scandal and arrest of Stern Hu in 2015;[74] Prime Minister Julia Gillard's willingness to accept Obama's request to station US Marines in Darwin in 2015;[75] Australia's ongoing freedom of navigation operations in the South China Sea;[76] Australia's support for the US in relation to banning Huawei's operations in 2018;[77] and Australia's support for an investigation into the origin of the COVID-19 pandemic in 2020.

Each action struck at China's perception of the nature of the friendly relationship and involved diplomatic censure and actions to signal displeasure to Australia. Beijing's actions ranged from diplomatic rebukes, to trade restrictions, to arrests of Australian or dual-Australian citizens. This pattern was evident in China's treatment of many Western states, including the US, Canada and New Zealand. Furthermore, it has become more pronounced as China's confidence has grown. So, too, has the domestic counter-reaction to China, which highlights the limitations of Realist predictions about the need to focus on economic interests or strategic asymmetry over other more Liberal Internationalist values in relation to the 'rules-based order' and human rights.

China's responses often included impacting trade through limiting imports or using SOEs to limit contracts and this reinforced domestic assumptions about their role as agents of Chinese foreign policy. That is, from the perspective of a Liberal free trade regime, despite being founded or based in a particular state, transnational companies were viewed as self-interested actors attempting to maximize profits for their shareholders. Identifying SOEs as agents of the state stoked domestic concerns evidenced in Strategic Culture, but also connected with concerns about rising Chinese influence in the South Pacific and the potential for 'debt-trap' diplomacy to undermine Australia's interests in the proximate region.[78] Once commentators discerned the pattern of economic influence operations, they identified numerous examples, even if they were coincidental. In diplomacy, the public identification of 'tit for tat' relations in the press was tantamount to retaliation itself and it has been used by both states over the years.

The infamous dossier of 14 disputes

A prime example of the 'tit for tat' dynamic was the Chinese embassy's dossier of 14 disputes released in 2020. In a manoeuvre that could only be predicted to inflame the already tense diplomatic situation, the 14 points were released directly to the Australian media. In a classic case of megaphone diplomacy, they were reported widely domestically and by Australia's allies and friends, as well as by China itself. The 14 disputes squarely blamed the Morrison government for undermining the relationship and contained veiled threats as to how compromise on the part of Canberra 'would be conducive to a better atmosphere'.[79] The Australian government rejected the disputes and used them to gain support in the international arena.[80]

CHINA: STRATEGIC COMPETITOR

This was not an isolated event as the Chinese embassy in Canberra was involved in so-called 'Wolf Warrior' diplomacy on numerous occasions, including in relation to countering accusations aired in the Australian Parliament of horrific human rights abuses against the Uighur people in Xinjiang.[81] 'Wolf Warrior' refers to a series of movies that are very popular in China and portray China as confident and assertive on the international stage and include the motto 'whoever offends China shall be punished'.[82] As such, 'Wolf Warrior' diplomacy is viewed as being aggressive and frankly not very diplomatic. China also pursued this strategy against Australia in international fora such as the UN Human Rights Commission where it accused Australia of 'severe human rights violations'.[83] These accusations were connected to war crimes allegations investigated by Australian authorities and represented disingenuously by the Chinese embassy. Another low point in relations occurred in 2020 when the Chinese foreign ministry tweeted a doctored image of an Australian soldier slashing the throat of an Afghan child, which prompted a strong rebuke from Prime Minister Morrison, who described it as 'repugnant' and demanded that it be removed,[84] but it remains online.

Accommodating China in the 'rules-based order'

Much of the diplomatic irritation and tension between Australia and China occurred over issues relating to the 'rules-based order'. The 2017 Foreign Policy White Paper unequivocally supported US global leadership and identified the convergence between the United States', Australia's and the international community's interests in the US continuing to anchor the 'rules-based order'. This included making 'practical and meaningful military commitments' to defending the present order, which linked to Australia's longstanding support for US led-coalition operations. It connected respect for the UN Convention on the Law of the Sea directly to the 'rules-based order', which was a criticism of China's perceived belligerence regarding the findings of the Permanent Court of Arbitration in relation to the South China Sea.[85]

There was acknowledgement in Canberra that some change to the international order was 'inevitable, necessary and appropriate to reflect the greater weight of countries such as China' but in practice declaratory policy repetitively supported the US-led order.[86] In supporting the status quo, AFP aimed to 'encourage China to exercise its power in a way that enhances stability, reinforces international law and respects the interests of smaller countries'.[87] Meanwhile, Australia strongly supported the reinvigoration of the Quadrilateral Dialogue (Quad) with India, Japan and the US to strengthen the free and open Indo-Pacific region, alongside like-minded states. The Quad leaders' 2021 meeting statement noted that: 'We strive for a region that is free, open, inclusive, healthy, anchored by democratic values and unconstrained by coercion,'[88] which was clearly a pointed criticism of Beijing.

Australia's 2017 Foreign Policy White Paper referred to the 'rules-based order' four times, in contrast with the 2016 Defence White Paper, where it was mentioned 52 times, highlighting the securitization of foreign policy.[89] China's first publicly released Defence White Paper did not even mention Australia, highlighting how asymmetric relations were.[90] China argued that it was a defender of international order, which placed Beijing in direct opposition to Canberra and Washington's concerns about China's role as a revisionist power.[91] At the Shangri La Dialogue in 2017, Lieutenant General He Lei, Vice President of the Academy of Military Science of the Chinese People's Liberation Army, noted that:

China has signed onto more than 23,000 bilateral agreements and more than 400 multilateral agreements with related parties in the world, and it is also a member of all specialized agencies in the United Nations, which demonstrates that China is a country that abides by, supports and defends international and regional rules.[92]

Chinese declaratory policy supported world order when it suited, but Australian policy-makers increasingly responded negatively to cases where China was perceived to be challenging the status quo in Asia. There was no better example of this than the South China Sea dispute.

CASE STUDY 6.1: CHINA'S CLAIMS IN THE SOUTH CHINA SEA

Canberra has consistently voiced concerns over China's occupation and militarization of islets in the South China Sea.[93] Australia joined the chorus of support for the findings of the 2016 Permanent Court of Arbitration that contradicted China's sovereignty claims and has highlighted the importance of freedom of navigation to the maintenance of the 'rules-based order'. This reflected support for the maintenance of the sovereignty status quo, but also because free trade required freedom of navigation and two-thirds of Australia's exports travelled through the area, so any potential attempt to limit movement was viewed negatively in Canberra. Australia's response to construction on the islets, their subsequent militarization and the unilateral declaration of an Air Defence Identification Zone around them was consistent with this approach.[94] In 2013, Foreign Minister Julie Bishop opposed the 'coercive or unilateral actions to change the status quo in the East China Sea' and the Chinese government pressured Australia 'to correct its mistake immediately' or risk damaging relations.[95] Australia did not compromise, tensions rose and Prime Minister Turnbull's 'reset' in relations followed, with little impact on rising bilateral tensions.

The Australian Navy has transited through the Chinese claimed area regularly and vessels have been routinely intercepted by the Chinese Navy. This form of sparring was commonplace between Chinese forces and its neighbours and competitors, such as Japan or the US, but Australia did not quite fit this mould. Australia was not a claimant in the South China Sea dispute but has supported its US ally (and Japanese friend in another dispute with China over islands) and was building closer diplomatic relations with Vietnam, which is a claimant.

A 2018 Australian naval visit to Vietnam via an area claimed by China prompted a strong Chinese response that indicated a hardening of relations.[96] While Australia has not conducted 'freedom of navigation operations' (FONOPs) within the 12 nautical mile zones claimed by China around the islets, the Australian Navy has come close enough to be challenged by Chinese Navy vessels.[97] At the time, Prime Minister Turnbull noted: 'We maintain and practise the right of freedom of navigation and overflight throughout the world, and in this context, naval vessels on the world's oceans including the South China Sea, as is our perfect right in accordance with international law.'[98]

Clearly, the Australian government had firmed its position in relation to Beijing reneging on President Xi Jinping's 2015 commitment to not militarize the Spratly Islands. In this context, there was also pressure from the US to conduct FONOPs.[99] Australia has supported US requests to intervene in other conflicts and this fitted the longstanding pattern in Strategic Culture of supporting 'great and powerful friends' and their strategic interests. In this case, as with others, it was framed as also being in Australia's interest. Declaratory policy was also aligned as the Foreign and Defence White Papers echoed a commitment to undertake such activities in the name of upholding the 'rules-based order'. However, while ordering the navy to transit through the area, Canberra has resisted conducting a FONOP. An Australian FONOP is not an unlikely possibility, and in the context of strained relations, it would be likely to provoke a reaction from China in excess of the previous 'tit for tat' exchanges.

Australia's stance on the South China Sea dispute in the face of significant economic and diplomatic risks highlighted the potential for the attitudes of the protagonists in a multi-layered dispute to firm rather than provoke compromise. In the context of a lack of trust and the lack of deep 'people-to-people' links, Canberra's stance highlighted a significant vulnerability in bilateral relations with China. The types of diplomatic confidence-building mechanisms that Liberal Internationalists tout were under-developed in Australia–China relations, while the Realist emphasis on (economic) interests was also not enough of a driver of AFP to promote compromise. Rather, a potent mixture of Strategic Cultural threat perceptions and Liberal Internationalist values was evident in policy-makers taking a position on the South China Sea that seemed highly likely to damage Australia's relationship with China.

The (lack of) institutionalized security relations

A parallel strategic development to China's economic growth was its increased defence spending, modernization of forces and the development of a regional and global strategy. There have been long-held concerns about China's lack of transparency in relation to grand strategy and broader intentions, including specific details of defence spending and the capabilities of weapons systems. China produced its first publicly available Defence White Paper in 2015, but as much interest was shown in what was left out as what was included in this short document.[100] There have always been wide variations in estimates of Chinese defence spending amongst international analysts and the only consensus was that it is rising rapidly and would likely overtake the US by 2050. The 2016 Defence White Paper estimated that this would occur by 2035.[101]

Despite the dramatic growth in the Chinese military, a key characteristic of Australia's foreign relations with China is the low level of institutionalized security cooperation. The web of bilateral security agreements that characterize relations with the US and Japan is absent in relations with China. When viewed through this lens, relations appear narrow and circumscribed by other considerations. Unlike other relationships, military diplomacy is so under-developed that it cannot act as a basis for overcoming concerns about a lack of transparency and building confidence in China's intentions.

For China, military diplomacy with other states is a key plank of foreign policy and one that has increased dramatically over the last few years.[102] President Xi Jinping has noted its central role in protecting China's 'sovereignty, safety and developmental interests'.[103] Commonplace military diplomatic activities utilized by China include joint operations (especially United Nations Peacekeeping Operations (UNPKO) and Humanitarian Assistance and Disaster Relief), specialized training, and port calls by naval vessels.

Defence cooperation

Below the level of institutionalized security relations are a range of defence cooperation activities that can provide an insight into the health of bilateral relations. Considering the longstanding diplomatic relations between China and Australia, a certain level of defence cooperation would be expected. From 2003 to 2016, Australia was China's fifth largest defence cooperation partner with 16 exercises, six naval port calls and 59 senior level visits.[104] These activities increased in frequency from 2012, in step with China's emphasis on military diplomacy. However, cooperation with Australia equated to only 2.9 per cent of China's total programme, highlighting how widespread Chinese activities were with other states and how small Australia's part of the programme was. COVID-19 pandemic restrictions impacted all forms of face-to-face collaboration, but it was telling that recent reporting in Australia on Chinese military visits focused not on collaboration but rather on spy vessels arriving off the coast of Queensland while Australia was exercising with US and other forces.[105]

Dialogues and staff exchanges

Australia and China hold an annual foreign and strategic dialogue, the fifth of which occurred in 2018. There are also regular visits by senior defence personnel and most of these occur in China. While COVID-19 travel restrictions limited the opportunity for face-to-face dialogue, most activities with other states pivoted to online formats. This was not the case with China and several dialogues were publicly suspended by China due to the broader cooling of relations.[106] This limited the capacity of military diplomacy to provide a diplomatic connection with China.

China and Australia's militaries undertook regular educational exchanges at all levels in China's National Defence University and colleges, and Australia's military colleges. However, only small numbers of officers at all levels were involved in these educational activities, which ranged from short courses to degree level offerings. Some involved language immersion as well as specialist training, which was essential if future cooperation was to grow. These attempts to build military diplomatic links addressed the longstanding weakness in 'people-to-people' links. However, despite decades of exchanges, it was difficult to identify an *esprit de corps* between the militaries and unclear whether significant cultural barriers had been overcome. Furthermore, the contrast between relations with China and other militaries, which involved extensive military diplomacy and joint operations, could not be more striking.

Defence procurement

As of 2023, Australia's annual defence budget was A$48.7 billion, involved more than 10 per cent increases over the previous five years and put spending over 2 per cent of GDP. The Department of Defence has been implementing an ambitious upgrade programme to fulfil the 2016 White Paper strategy and 2020 Force Structure Plan, which included the two largest procurement programmes in Australia's history.[107] This equipment was designed to counter equally armed opponents in high-level scenarios, such as war with China in Northeast Asia. Unsurprisingly, despite this large expenditure, not one significant item of defence equipment was sourced from China. Furthermore, the only expenditure on Chinese manufactured goods in the Australian defence organization was on consumables that could be described as dual use (that is, not specifically designed for military use).

The Australian defence establishment has made numerous decisions to *not* purchase equipment from China. In theory, Realist rational actors would preference purchases based on quality, price and availability. The lack of purchases from China may be because Chinese equipment is not 'fit for purpose' or it may be that the lack of expenditure on Chinese military technology is telling insofar as there is a preference for purchasing Western equipment. The longstanding pattern developed during the Cold War was for Australia to acquire key equipment from its ally, former security guarantor, and other European suppliers. Buying US and European equipment also facilitates interoperability, allowing Australia to fight alongside its security guarantor. Defence procurement preferences also feed into the debate over the 'China Choice': Canberra has chosen to strengthen security relations with 'great and powerful' allies and like-minded friends despite its extensive economic interests in China, and China has decided to punish Australia for doing so.

Joint operations and joint exercises

Defence exercises are a key indicator of the strength of institutionalized bilateral defence relations. It is striking that despite 50 years of diplomacy, Australia has only peripherally been involved in joint operations with Chinese forces. Australia no longer has a significant footprint in UNPKO, where China is increasingly active, so this avenue for cooperation does not exist. One opportunity for joint operations occurred in 2009 when Australia pledged a warship and surveillance aircraft to counter-piracy operations off the coast of Somalia. However, Australia participated in a coalition taskforce while China was independently involved and there was little close collaboration between forces.

More recently, Chinese vessels cooperated with Australian authorities during the search for Malaysian Airlines MH370 in 2014 in the Southern Indian Ocean, but even this interaction was marred by mistrust. China's involvement in the search led to speculation about China spying on Australia, highlighting the deep-seated suspicion that exists below the façade of diplomatic relations.[108] As such, the lack of significant joint military operations with China was in contrast to Canberra's long commitment to coalition operations in Iraq and Afghanistan alongside the US or increasing joint activities with Japan.

Aside from joint operations, exercises provide an opportunity for militaries to work alongside each other towards a common goal. As with other areas of collaboration, these activities were curtailed by the COVID-19 pandemic. Prior to this, a much-touted example of growth in this area was Exercise Pandaroo, which alternated between being held in Australia and China. Pandaroo 2018 involved 10 junior soldiers from each military and was described by the Chinese defence attaché as 'promot[ing] the mutual understanding and trust between the two armed forces'.[109] Pandaroo followed the creation of the trilateral Kowari exercise that began in 2014 and also involved US forces. Both involved 10 junior soldiers from each military in survival training, such as mountaineering, kayaking and abseiling. These adventure activities were very narrow in scope. They involved team-building activities rather than approximating the active combat that Australia is routinely involved in training for with the US and other defence partners.

In 2018, China sent a warship to Exercise Kakadu for the first time. Kakadu was Australia's largest maritime military exercise, involving over 3,000 personnel and 21 ships from 28 states. This exercise involved a mixture of humanitarian and warfighting operations, including anti-submarine warfare. China's frigate with 163 personnel on board represented the largest contribution to exercising with Australia to date. China may well have appreciated the invitation given that it was disinvited from the United States' Rim of the Pacific (RIMPAC) exercise in 2018. RIMPAC is the world's largest maritime exercise and China has only participated twice. Kakadu 2020 was cancelled due to COVID-19 and in a sign of diplomatic tension, China was not invited to the 2022 exercise, which was Australia's largest to date.

If military diplomacy was a strong priority for both parties, then the one area that should be highly represented, but was not, was exercising. In the last few years, exercising with China has begun but it has been very limited. The scope was also circumscribed in scope with none of the 16 exercises conducted between 2003 and 2016 involving combat operations. Only one ad hoc naval exercise involved 'live fire activities'. Bilateral and multilateral exercises with Japan and the US, such as Talisman Sabre and RIMPAC, involve tens of thousands of personnel while exercises with China involve only a handful. The reluctance to assist China in building combat capabilities through exercises highlights the underlying suspicion and threat from China that characterizes Strategic Culture and is prudent from a perspective of Realism. It also focuses attention on the lack of confidence-building mechanisms that might be developed if a Liberal Internationalist approach were taken to the rise of China. Revelations in 2022 that ex-Australian and US air force personnel had been training the Chinese highlighted the depth of this suspicion.

The limited scope of defence cooperation, especially when compared to Australia's relations with friends and former foes alike, is telling. The narrowness of relations might seem surprising for a diplomatic relationship of 50 years, but it highlights the role that China has taken as a source of threat in Australian Strategic Culture. Clearly, China was not seen a potential security partner or guarantor, and this has been a constant for many years even if Canberra had not outwardly made a 'China Choice'. Cold War conflict abated after the withdrawal of troops from Vietnam and rapprochement with Beijing in 1972. However, mutually beneficial trade was the focus of engagement rather than security cooperation. By contrast, economic *and* security cooperation with Australia's other Asian former foes has increased dramatically in recent years. Relations with Japan are discussed in Chapter 8, where there was potential for ever closer defence cooperation to shift to a quasi-alliance. Similarly, defence cooperation with Vietnam was steadily increasing and while an alliance was not on the agenda, the two states are drawn together by common threats, with China figuring prominently for both. This highlighted that the cultural similarities with 'great and powerful friends', the US and UK, were only one element needed to build *esprit de corps* between militaries and that the value of shared threat perceptions should not be underestimated.

Despite the lack of operational examples, the declaratory policies of both governments identified closer defence cooperation as a priority. The Chinese government regularly expressed support for strengthening the defence aspects of the 2013 Comprehensive Strategic Partnership and Australian declaratory statements highlighted that this was 'vital'.[110] The 2016 Defence White Paper noted that: 'The Government will seek to deepen and broaden our important defence relationship with China while recognising that our strategic interests might differ in relation to some regional global security issues.'[111]

Analysts noted that the Chinese military's 'role in these military diplomatic trends [cultivation of influence] appears to be a slower-moving manifestation of broader Chinese strategy',[112] and in a case of 'taking two steps forward and one back', these activities are increasingly viewed in Canberra as potentially threatening. Furthermore, the post-2020 diplomatic freeze had a significant impact on any attempt at building closer security cooperation. The reality was that China-Australia defence cooperation is very limited and narrow in scope. Defence relations are best described as cordial and business-like – very different words than would be used to describe relations with security partners such as the US.

Rising perceptions of non-military threats to Australia from China

Beijing and Canberra have long been concerned about the shallowness of 'people-to-people' links and nascent defence diplomacy was part of a mutual attempt to build closer foreign relations. This shallowness is a potential vulnerability when the relationship is under strain, which has been the case since the later 2010s. In this context, Chinese 'influence' activities in Australia have become more contentious than otherwise might have been the case.

Cyberattacks

Over the last decade, cyberattacks against critical infrastructure and government sites have been increasing in frequency. There was no doubt that cybercrime was on the rise, but the government became increasingly concerned with examples that could be viewed as precursors to cyberwarfare by 'state-based actors'. These activities differed from cybercrime insofar as they were perpetrated by state actors rather than transnational criminals and did not use tactics such as denial of service for financial gain, but rather concentrated on probing vulnerabilities in strategic areas and accessing sensitive information. Illegal information gathering has focused on Australia's foreign and defence policies, defence equipment and, most recently, political parties and the Chinese diaspora in Australia.

That these attacks were increasing was of concern, but equally, the fact that the government openly identified the threat from state-based actors highlighted a firming of diplomacy, especially regarding attacks from China. To the backdrop of controversy over statements about Australia defending Taiwan, Defence Minister Peter Dutton identified the 'staggering' level of Chinese espionage in Australia.[113] Despite the general prohibition on discussing intelligence matters in the government, the Australian Signals Directorate revealed that between 2015 and 2018, there were 1,097 cyberattacks on government networks that were serious enough to warrant an operational response.[114] While these activities were far from traditional military threats, the foreign minister noted that they could lead to an escalation that could trigger a war.[115]

The government has also been more regularly publicly identifying attacks and explicitly pointing to them being state sponsored rather than launched by transnational criminals. As alluded to by Dutton's comments, it was likely that the Australian Cyber Security Centre (ACSC), set up in 2014 to meet this challenge, has much more information than was being released and this has fuelled domestic debate about the threat from China. The attacks on the Australian Parliament and major political parties in February 2019, announced in a bipartisan statement by Prime Minister Morrison and Opposition Leader Bill Shorten, highlighted the very real threat to critical information systems. Russia's attempts to influence the 2016 US election have been widely reported and by implication this attack by what the government called a 'sophisticated state actor'[116] could impact Australian elections.

There has been increasing speculation that China was responsible for targeting Australian government and businesses and surveilling ethnic Chinese diaspora in Australia.[117] Most often there was a lack of evidence supporting these claims, as the attacks were designed to be untraceable. Similarly, if they were detected, then the means used by Australian security agencies to do so were also sensitive. What was clear was that the government was signalling the increasing scale of attacks to the perpetrators, the Australian public and allies alike. China was treated as the key suspect, despite publicly denying involvement.[118] This was unsurprising given the rumoured hacking activities of the People Liberation Army's Unit 61398 against the US and UK.[119]

The hacking of the Australian Parliament was viewed as an escalation of an ongoing campaign. Less than three months earlier, Australia joined 12 other states in expressing 'serious concern' over China's 'sustained cyber intrusions'.[120] The foreign minister also reminded China of its 2015 no-hacking pledge at the G20 meeting. Clearly, China's respect of multilateral commitments under the banner of the 'rules-based order' was under question. Similarly, it was noted that the sensitive nuclear submarine technology that would be shared with Australia under the 2020 AUKUS agreement would likely be a target of Chinese cyberattacks requiring greater vigilance by Australian security services.

Chinese influence operations in Australia

> Covert, coercive and corrupting (Prime Minister Malcolm Turnbull describing influence operations in Australia).[121]

In addition to cyber threats, the Australian Security Intelligence Organization (ASIO) reported an increase in influence operations undertaken by foreign powers aimed at furthering their national political and diplomatic agendas. In 2017, ASIO noted 'foreign powers clandestinely seeking to shape the opinions of members of the Australian Public, media organisations, and government officials' and also harassing their diaspora community.[122] By 2019, the ASIO director general, Duncan Lewis, took the unprecedented step of identifying foreign interference as 'an existential threat' to Australia.[123] The Chinese United Work Front Department was associated with much of the activity in Australia and elsewhere.[124]

The threat from influence operations in the 2016 US presidential election brought the issue to prominence, but there has been a long history of concern in Australia. Initially, awareness was raised of Chinese informants applying pressure to pro-Taiwanese, pro-Tibetan and Falun Gong supporters resident in Australia, many of whom were Australian citizens. Claims of a network of over 1,000 agents and informants revealed by a Chinese defector in 2005 raised eyebrows within and outside government.[125] In practice, this influence has played out in numerous ways:

> We might find greater attention than normal directed at One Nation or Fraser Anning – as well as the strategic promotion of Green candidates in certain

places to push political discussion further right and further left at the same time.[126]

Recent overseas events have seen social media accounts, such as Facebook, used to support particular candidates or promote particular issues that can disrupt or influence voting in democratic elections. These tactics could be particularly effective in marginal seats in Australia where the stakes are higher because a few votes could influence the outcome of an electoral contest. In the lead-up to the 2016 US elections, over 5 million paid ads were placed on Facebook within a 10-day period. None of the groups involved reported this activity to the Federal Electoral Commission and one was later found to be a Russian entity.[127]

University collaboration as a battleground in influence operations

Universities have also been a battleground for influence activities and have provided the government an opportunity to criticize Chinese Communist Party operations in Australia. The most significant threat identified has been the collaboration between Chinese military scientists and their Australian counterparts. There were concerns that these collaborations involve deception on the part of the Chinese military and have significant risks and costs in relation to intellectual property and espionage.[128] As tensions rose, it was feared that collaboration may in fact be strengthening Australia's key strategic competitor and for this reason the US government has acted on concerns.[129] In 2019, US universities began limiting collaboration with Huawei, and Australian universities followed suit in curtailing cooperation with Chinese researchers.

There have been claims that Chinese student associations have been used to monitor and control students in Australia.[130] Academic freedom has also been threatened as academics critical of China have reportedly been faced with aggressive social media campaigns.[131] Within Australian universities themselves, Confucius Institutes funded by Beijing have long been the target of criticism in relation to their potential to exercise undue influence over issues critical of China. With the advent of the Foreign Influence Transparency Scheme, the 13 institutes in Australia's universities were contacted by the Attorney General's Department to alert them of their legal obligations to report activities that could be interpreted as attempting to influence the Australian political system.[132]

Conflict over the significance of China also flared amongst China researchers in Australian universities. Notable examples are the heated debate between Hugh White and Clive Hamilton at a La Trobe University seminar and the debate over the 'anonymous Xinjiang paper' in 2021, where academics were caught up in what ostensibly appeared to be propaganda.[133] Australian academics were also central to making the case that China was in fact committing significant human rights abuses against Uighurs in China.[134] In addition, a range of generalist books have been written by White, Hamilton and David Brophy that have popularized debate over Chinese influence operations in Australia.[135]

The foreign minister and the head of DFAT's forthright comments about these issues in 2017 highlighted an escalation in rhetoric by the Australian government and a strategy of openly identifying the perpetrators of influence activities.[136]

These criticisms elicited a strong rebuke from the Chinese ambassador to Australia, who retorted that the 'fabricated' allegations were 'made out of thin air'.[137] Needless to say, these direct accusations were not welcomed in Beijing and the Chinese press has been increasingly critical of the Australian government's actions. A good example of this is the response to the refusal to grant citizenship to Chinese billionaire Huang Xiangmo, which led to the charge that: 'Huang has once again fallen victim to a renewed wave of anti-China hysteria, aimed at increasing fear mongering and hatred toward China and Chinese business throughout the country.'[138] These exchanges heralded a cooling of relations from 2018. Debate continued over the source of tension, with Andrew Robb, a former Coalition cabinet member, blaming the government for 'toxic relations'. However, his credibility was questioned due to his appointment by Chinese firm Landbridge on leaving Parliament, reportedly on a A\$800,000 salary.[139] As time passed and relations soured further, it became less important to discover the origins of the rift and more pertinent to explain its escalation.

The Chinese-language media in Australia has also been identified as playing a role in monitoring the Chinese diaspora in an attempt to limit dissent.[140] The use of Chinese WeChat and Weibo accounts that connect users in China with the Australian diaspora to influence how news (especially about China) is editorialized was viewed as being akin to soft interference.[141] As 600,000 people of Chinese descent in Australia speak Mandarin at home, this platform has the potential to speak directly to a large audience. Influencing these people was important as they could potentially influence electoral outcomes. There was speculation about this in the 2016 federal election and the 2019 New South Wales state election, where the Opposition Leader Michael Daley's comments about Chinese students taking Australian jobs was reportedly treated as being racist and broadcast to WeChat users in several key electorates.[142]

The institutional response to influence (and cyber) activities

The government's response to China's influence activities was to strengthen domestic legislation and policing of both influence and interference operations. This response has been gradual and cumulative and came to a head in 2017. Numerous incidents firmed resolve by Australian policy-makers, the most recent being the cyberattacks on Australia's Parliament and political parties. Prior to this, issues such as human rights, self-determination in Tibet, and the arrest and treatment of prisoners have caused tension and revealed attempts to use influence to leverage outcomes that suit Beijing's interests.

Notable examples of influence operations from 2017 that caused concern include revelations that donors close to the Chinese Communist Party were leveraging influence over the South China Sea. The Chinese government reportedly pressured the opposition with electoral fallout (amongst diaspora communities) for not supporting an extradition treaty.[143] The forced resignation of Labor Senator Sam Dastyari was a low point. Dastyari was accused of supporting China's interests by mouthing packaged talking points on the South China Sea. He was also accused of revealing sensitive information about intelligence-gathering operations against his Chinese contacts to them.[144] Coalition politicians were targeted in equal measure with donations and lucrative consultancies and board positions.[145]

Prime Minister Malcolm Turnbull was galvanized into action by the revelations of 2017. He was a firm advocate of reform, noting that security agencies 'lack the legislative tools they [need and] . . . our system as a whole has not grasped the nature and magnitude of the threat'.[146] While China was the focus of these incidents, the policy to counter them explicitly broadened the focus to all foreign interference activities and ensured that the role of foreign diaspora populations in Australia was not singled out or exaggerated, so as to make them the targets of legislation.

ASIO Director-General Duncan Lewis noted that: 'there's a pressing requirement to deter hostile foreign spies who are conducting espionage and foreign interference against Australian interests'.[147] Andrew Hastie, the chair of the Joint Parliamentary Committee on Intelligence and Security in 2018, was forthright in claiming that 'in Australia it is clear that the Chinese Communist Party is working to covertly interfere with our media and universities and also to influence our political processes and public debates'.[148] The chorus of voices led to action, all of which impacted relations with Beijing.

Initiatives such as the 2018 Foreign Influence Transparency Scheme, which identified influence activities by foreign entities and individuals, have also signalled the government's resolve.[149] The enabling legislation was unprecedented as it criminalized unregistered influence activities.

Russian meddling in US elections brought the issue of foreign interference to the mainstream. Commentators noted that: 'Australia has led the democratic pushback against quiet intrusions from authoritarian states, especially China.'[150] This included coalescing support for action through the Five Eyes intelligence-sharing network that links Australia, Canada, New Zealand, the UK and the US.[151] Five Eyes was a key resource in countering China's hybrid warfare, and network vulnerabilities were likely to be a core target of Chinese cyberwarfare.[152] It also was the target of Chinese ire as a Chinese government spokesmen noted: 'No matter how many "eyes" you have, be careful not to be poked and get blind by harming China's sovereignty, security and development interests.'[153] As this outburst attests, the strengthening of Australia's longstanding security relationships in the face of Chinese pressure, such as the Quad with India, Japan and the US, and the creation of new arrangements such as AUKUS, caused frustration in Beijing.

CASE STUDY 6.2: CHINA'S INFLUENCE ACTIVITIES IN AUSTRALIA

There is no precedent for a mid-sized, open, multicultural nation standing its ground against a rising authoritarian superpower that accounts for a large proportion of its migrants and one in every three of its export dollars.[154]

Countering China has led to a range of institutional responses but also involved public acknowledgement of activities and public statements of attribution for activities. China has been mentioned in numerous government statements, but more often China has been implicated through the media, presumably on the advice of leaked sources in the Australian government.

There has also been direct engagement with the issue from a wide section of the community. For example, when parliamentary committees have deliberated over the issue of influence, some academics have criticized the impact of increasing government regulation on debate.[155] However, the dominant view in public commentary was that China was exercising undue influence. This aligns with the US view, but it is clear that Australian policy-makers were not simply following the US lead, which has been an enduring criticism regarding other strategic issues. Canberra was protecting its own interests against Chinese influence activities.

China's involvement in cyberattacks and influence operations has exposed a very real vulnerability in Australia's democratic systems. The government has been addressing these issues, but well-publicized examples of foreign states taking advantage of these vulnerabilities stoked the heightened threat perceptions inherent in Strategic Culture. These hark back to the Cold War concerns over communist influence in Australia. Furthermore, the public perception that China was a key perpetrator of attacks aligns with the traditional fear of an 'alien' Asian threat from the North. This existed alongside the more orthodox threat perceptions developed from China's conventional military activities in the South China Sea and elsewhere. It also highlighted the vulnerability to hybrid warfare that uses non-military tactics such as influence activities to target societal defences and vulnerabilities which has become another front in the geostrategic and geoeconomics competition.[156]

Conclusion

It was a truism that the geopolitical and geoeconomic challenges posed by China's rise are central to the future of international affairs. However, conjecture over whether Canberra would have to make a choice in the future did not allow for the persistent influence of Strategic Culture on AFP. Australian and Chinese policy-makers have made numerous choices to deepen trade relations and to build 'people-to-people' links. Despite these initiatives, the differences between the two political cultures transcend the complementarity of their economies. National self-interest drives trade relations and this fits neatly with a Realist perspective, but the seemingly intransigent barriers to closer relations point to the enduring influence in AFP of Liberal Internationalist values and the heightened threat perceptions that characterize Australia's Strategic Culture.

The Chinese president was acutely aware of the tension between ideas and cultures. When addressing a joint sitting of the Australian Parliament, he put the challenge succinctly:

Many people applaud China's achievements and have great confidence in China, while some others have concerns about China – and there are also people who find fault with everything China does. I think these diverse views are to be expected. After all, China is a large country of over 1.3 billion people. It is like the big guy in the crowd. Others naturally wonder how the big guy will move and act, and they may be concerned that the big guy may push them around, stand in their way or even take up their place.[157]

President Xi Jinping went on to say that, 'We have every reason to go beyond a commercial partnership to become strategic partners who have a shared vision and pursue common goals.'[158] Despite this declaratory rhetoric, it seems that the reasons to not move beyond a transactional trade-based relationship remain stronger than ever. It may be as much China's choice as Australia's whether to maintain an economic marriage of convenience that has been highly lucrative, strategic and beneficial for both parties, or to shift to outright strategic competition.

7

Background to Japan:
Threat and trading partner

Introduction

Relations with Japan have matured significantly in recent years. The consensus in Canberra and Tokyo is that relations have been mutually beneficial. Early relations were instrumentally focused on trade.[1] Two-way trade has declined in relative terms because other economies have grown to become increasingly important over time, but gross trade is still growing and Japan remains one of Australia's top three trading partners. However, there is a shift underway and the trajectory of relations is now focusing more on security. Bilateral security relations are edging closer to something akin to an alliance and shared threat perceptions of China are driving much of the invigoration of what has been a relatively instrumental bilateral trade relationship. This analysis fits neatly with a Realist conception of maximizing national interests to increase material power.

Japanese officials have described the mutually beneficial security relationship as a 'quasi-alliance', but Canberra has been more circumspect. This may be a hangover from the military threat from Japan during the Second World War being a foundational element of Australian Strategic Culture.[2] The perceived threat from Japan in the first half of the twentieth century shaped the development of Strategic Culture, so this shift towards alliance is significant and under-theorized: it may require a pluralistic explanation combining Realism, Liberal Internationalism and Strategic Culture. Meanwhile, operationally, both states are acting to extend bilateral security activities in new ways that are akin to an alignment, but a formal alliance appears some way off. Japan and Australia's strategic interests are coinciding in relation to managing both the rise of China and the maintenance of US regional engagement. Securitization of the relationship is also evident in minilateralism as Australia now has a clear triangular security relationship with Japan and the US, while a Quad with India is also becoming an institutional reality.

A distinctive element of this chapter and the next are that they reconcile Australia and Japan's realization of shared *strategic* interests with Australia's Strategic Culture. Specifically, debate over institutionalizing the security partnership is connected to Japan's potential repudiation of Article 9 of its constitution[3] (which prohibits the creation of an offensive military force), and the role that the constitution historically played in providing a guarantee that Japan would not re-militarize and threaten Australia. Rather than Japan's return to what is called a 'normal nation' being seen as a challenge to the Strategic Culture, militarization in the face of the rise of China is being welcomed and encouraged in Canberra. It is not viewed as a challenge to Strategic Culture, but rather a restatement of its core principles because Japan is being redefined as a 'like' power; a democracy supportive of the 'rules-based order', allied with the US and increasingly threatened by China.

The relationship with Japan is so central to Australian foreign policy (AFP) that it is split into two chapters. The first (this chapter) focuses on the history of bilateral relations, and can be read as a primer to the following chapter on the challenges and opportunities evident in present relations.

Background/history

Australia's first century of relations with Japan influenced the formation of a unique Strategic Culture. Early contacts with 'Asians' during the Victorian Gold Rush in the 1850s failed to differentiate between Chinese and Japanese immigrants, with both being treated with disdain. Racism towards Asians was the norm and these attitudes were institutionalized by the White Australia Policy that was enacted at the birth of federation in 1901 (see Box 7.1).[4]

The racism reflected the ignorance and fear of a white Settler society in an unfamiliar region. This influenced the attitude that Australia was an Anglo-Saxon (white) outpost in an 'alien' region that needed to protect itself from numerically superior but culturally inferior Asian races. Japan's Second World War threat to Australia quickly removed any sense that Asian militaries were inferior and this stoked Strategic Cultural fear of the North.

In the early decades of the twentieth century, Australian policy-makers were deaf to persistent entreaties by the Japanese to be exempted from the White Australia Policy. These approaches were based on Japan's own feelings of exceptionalism in relation to superiority over the other 'races' in Asia.[5] These

BOX 7.1: THE WHITE AUSTRALIA POLICY

- Inaugurated by Australia's first prime minister, Edmund Barton upon federation in 1901.
- Institutionalized immigration restrictions against Asians and Pacific Islanders.
- Relaxed somewhat after the Second World War to accept southern European immigration.
- A source of tension with Asian states.
- Dismantled in the 1970s after regional decolonization was well underway.

attitudes formed the basis for the extreme nationalism that prompted Japanese imperial expansion in the Second World War. These Japanese attitudes also foreshadowed the close relations that developed after the Second World War based on Japan and Australia being the 'odd men out'[6] who don't quite fit in Asia and are dependent on alliances with the US to guarantee their security.

During this period, Australian policy-makers were blind to the great differences between Asian cultures and the Japanese Empire personified fears of numerically superior, culturally 'alien' others to Australia's north.[7] In 1908, Defence Minister Thomas Ewing asserted that 'between the white and yellow man there is racial hatred . . . They are destined to be enemies for all time.'[8] At this time, referring to 'yellow' skin became racist shorthand for Asians. This sentiment highlights that the rise of modern industrialized Japan strongly influenced the development of the heightened threat perceptions that became a key aspect of Australian Strategic Culture.

Japan's defeat of Russia in 1905 as a wakeup call for Canberra

The Japanese victory in the Russo-Japanese War in 1905, which involved the defeat of the Russian Pacific fleet, shocked Australian policy-makers and prompted early plans to defend Australia.[9] Up to this date, it was assumed that European military technology, strategy and tactics were far superior to any potential challengers. This defeat foreshadowed the stunning victory of Japanese imperial forces as they marched and sailed across Asia in 1941–42. In both cases, analysts did not predict the swift and comprehensive defeat of European imperial forces and profoundly underestimated Japan due to racism.

At the turn of the twentieth century, Japanese vessels that arrived in Australian ports on goodwill visits were met with curiosity and interest by the Australian populace, as was the US 'Great White Fleet' in 1908.[10] By contrast for policy-makers, the latter prompted calls for closer links while the former prompted suspicion and militarization through the creation of an independent naval squadron in 1911. Again, the Japanese influence on the development of Australia's formative Strategic Culture was clear. Russia was a European empire that had been viewed by Canberra as a potential threat and the defeat of the Russian navy in Asia by an Asian power highlighted Australia's vulnerability. It also reinforced feelings of indefensibility due to Australia's geographic distance from Britain, its 'great and powerful friend' and security guarantor. At the time, Britain was more concerned about European geopolitics than the rise of Japan,[11] and another lesson for Canberra of the rise of Japan was the need to closely engage Australia's allies in its interests. The need to keep 'great and powerful' friends focused on Canberra's interests still resonates today. Interestingly, it also provides a point of connection to Japan as Tokyo is also faced with trying to ensure that the US remains engaged in Asia.

The next significant interaction between Japan and Australia occurred during the First World War. Rather than being an enemy Japan joined the Allied Entente in 1914 and provided support to the British war effort, including sending a naval squadron to the Mediterranean.[12] Closer to home, Japanese naval vessels operated with British and Australian vessels to hunt the German raider SMS *Emden*. HMAS *Sydney* eventually sunk SMS *Emden* in the Cocos Islands, thereby removing a significant threat to allied shipping. Japanese naval vessels went on to escort Australian troop transports across the Indian Ocean to fight in Europe. This naval cooperation could have been reasonably predicted to reduce distrust and encourage a positive response to Japanese entreaties, but policy-makers had an entrenched 'mindset' towards Japan that was not easily changed.[13] It was not widely known amongst the general public how closely Australia had collaborated with Japan in the First World War and heightened threat perceptions persisted. This highlights the cognitive dissonance of Strategic Culture – its capacity to replicate itself in the face of unwelcome facts.

Despite Japan's efforts, Australian policy-makers were not willing to treat Japan as an equal in the Versailles Peace Treaty negotiations that concluded the First World War.[14] Australian policy-makers manoeuvred to take trusteeship over Germany's Pacific possessions, such as German New Guinea, and actively worked to limit Japanese ambitions to expand its influence over Pacific islands that were deemed strategically important to Australia. This geographic shield was an example of the policy of strategic denial in its proximate neighbourhood that Australia practises to this day, only at this time Japan was the great power being excluded (and at present Japan is viewed as a security partner against Chinese influence).

Diplomatic distrust grew between Tokyo and Canberra, but at this time the Japanese were responding to Australian exclusionary diplomacy.[15] Distrust and tension were compounded during the inter-war years (1918–39) when Australia supported attempts to economically isolate Japan and Australia's coal embargo of the 1930s became a point of contention between the two states.[16] In the search for resources, Japan invaded Manchuria (1931) and eyed the possessions of European empires in the Asia-Pacific.

1942: Canberra's worst nightmare comes true

The Second World War in Europe began in 1939, but in the Pacific war broke out on 7 December 1941, when Japan attacked the US base at Pearl Harbour in Hawaii. Japan proceeded to attack and occupy British and US outposts across the Asia-Pacific, which led to heightened threat perceptions in Australia. Through a mixture of skill, surprise, guile and the distraction to European powers caused by the Second World War in Europe, the Japanese Empire quickly defeated all European forces in Asia. The empire dramatically expanded in a short period of time to exercise control over most of Asia. As such, the northern geographic shield that Canberra constructed in its strategy since the First World War disappeared almost overnight, stoking the fears of the North that frame Strategic Culture.

The occupation of British colonies in Hong Kong and Malaya in 1941 and the defeat and capture of British and Australian forces in Singapore in April 1942

BACKGROUND TO JAPAN

struck at the heart of the fears inherent in Strategic Culture. An 'alien' Asian power had swept aside all Allied and/or European forces in the region and there were no friendly forces standing between Australia and invasion. Furthermore, most of Australia's seasoned troops were in Europe and the Middle East fighting for the British Empire, and the Japanese assault through Asia was so swift that there was no time to train and arm significant local defence forces. The alliance 'insurance policy' with the UK had failed to deliver in Australia's time of need and Australia was all but defenceless. Even the US Pacific Fleet had been mauled at Pearl Harbour and its land forces had been defeated in the Philippines. The upside to this was that US General Douglas MacArthur had moved his command to Australia, signalling the beginning of the US strategic partnership with Australia.

Australia feared a Japanese invasion and attacks on Darwin and Sydney stoked the fears inherent in Australia's Strategic Culture. Darwin was bombed for the first time in February 1942 and in July reservists were promptly sent to Papua New Guinea (PNG) to repel a Japanese overland invasion on the Kokoda Track. For the first time and possibly the only time in history, threats to Australia that frame Strategic Culture were not exaggerated: they were imminent.

While Australia was holding the tide against Japanese advances on the Kokoda Track, the US quickly regrouped after the Japanese surprise attack against Pearl Harbour and joined Australia to halt the Japanese advance. A series of decisive naval battles in the Coral Sea on the approaches to PNG and at Midway Island, coupled with stalemate on land in PNG and the Solomons at Guadalcanal, halted the Japanese advance. Japanese troops and vessels earmarked for the invasion of Fiji to cut Australia–US supply lines and potentially attack Australia were bogged down and destroyed and the imminent threat eased. Attacks on Darwin and Sydney in 1942 represented the southernmost air and naval attacks undertaken by Japanese imperial forces.

The imminent threat of invasion eased but Australia's resolve did not. As the tide turned in the war, the Australian public recoiled as atrocities committed in the name of the Japanese emperor became common knowledge.[17] There were numerous examples of Japan disregarding international laws and conventions, beginning with the surprise attack on the US base in Pearl Harbour, which led to US participation in the war, to numerous atrocities against civilians in Nanjing, China and prisoners of war (POWs) across Asia. A measure of this belligerence was that more Australian soldiers died while in captivity than in combat.[18] A case that galvanized the nation was the sinking of the Australian Hospital Ship *Centaur*, off Queensland near Stradbroke Island. This attack against a vessel clearly identified as a hospital ship led to the deaths of 268 wounded soldiers and crew, including many nurses. This war crime reinforced the perception of Asian cultures as 'alien' to civilized/Australian values.[19] Another significant event was the discovery of a photo in 1944 of an Australian soldier, identified as Sergeant Leonard Siffleet, being beheaded. Such was the public anger that the racism towards Asians remained ingrained in Australian public opinion and policy. The allied victory in the Second World War did not appease public attitudes towards the Japanese or Asians in general. As Arthur Calwell noted in 1948, 'while I

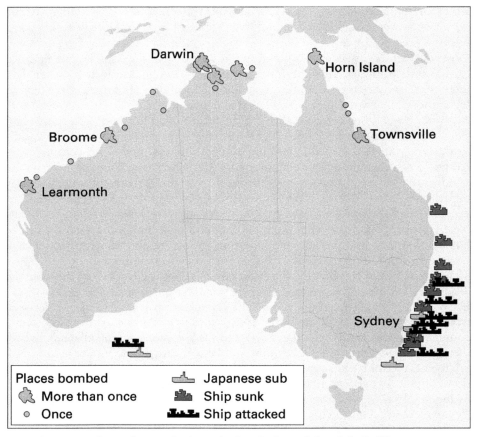

MAP 7.1 *Australia under attack: Australia bombed, strafed and shelled.*[20]

remain Minister for Immigration, no Japanese will be permitted to enter this country'.[21]

With the dropping of atomic bombs in 1945 on Hiroshima and Nagasaki, Japan was eventually defeated by the US and its allies. However, victory did not breed a sense of security in Canberra. As Patience notes: 'the ever-present sense of Asia's threatening proximity had been amplified throughout the long years of the war and continued to aggravate a sense of vulnerability in Australia's foreign and defence planning'.[22] This vulnerability drives Strategic Culture, and therefore it is surprising just how far relations have evolved over the last 80 years from Japan being identified as an existential threat. Japan directly influenced Australia's Strategic Culture by providing a very real existential threat that stoked underlying fears about being indefensible in an 'alien' region. This pattern persists to this day, with various powers such as Indonesia and China becoming the source of this threat from the 'North'.

Conclusion

During the Cold War, bilateral relations slowly thawed as trade relations grew. Economic links drove the relationship, but over time, security grew in importance. This slow shift in relations was driven as much by Canberra as it was Tokyo. Both states had core interests elsewhere and did not necessarily prioritize relations. Furthermore, the instrumentalism of Realism that focused on shared trade interests sat uneasily with influences of Strategic Culture that identified Japan as a threat well into the Cold War era. The evolution in relations from centring on trade to security forms the focus of the next chapter. The open question is whether Australian Strategic Culture can accommodate Japan as a quasi-ally, which highlights the role of shared threat perceptions in driving change in AFP.

8

Japan:
'Special' strategic partner?

Introduction

Generalizations about relations between Australia and Japan focus on their foundation in threats in the Second World War, the dramatic increase in post-war trade and the shared position as US allies in the region. However, the relationship is maturing and there is reason to broaden our understanding of the character of the bilateral relationship. Australia and Japan have declared that they have a 'Special Strategic Partnership'.[1] Australia's 2017 Foreign Policy White Paper clarifies the essence of this partnership:

> A 'Special Strategic Partner' of Australia, Japan is a democratic, trade oriented nation with which we share values and interests, including through our alliances with the United States. Together we are working to achieve a stable region underpinned by open economies and the rule of law. As close partners, each other is invested in the success of the other.[2]

Japan's Ministry of Foreign Affairs (MOFA) echoes these sentiments, focusing on 'fundamental values and strategic interests'.[3] Thus declaratory policy identifies Australia and Japan as defenders of the 'rules-based order' in the Indo-Pacific region.

Closer relations have grown over time and evolved with the strong support of successive prime ministers of both countries, shaped by geopolitical change. The evolution in relations is reflected in declaratory policy that has become increasingly detailed, practical and focused on security. Table 8.1 highlights that in the past 25 years, each respective administration has strengthened declaratory policy agreements.

Prime Ministers Scott Morrison and Shinzō Abe extended already close relations, with Abe describing Australia as an 'indispensable security partner'.[4] The centrepiece of present efforts is an agreement to facilitate increased defence cooperation through exercises, exchanges and training. Prime Minister Morrison was the first foreign leader to meet incoming Japanese Prime Minister Yoshihide Suga in November 2020 and secured the Reciprocal Access Agreement (RAA). The RAA had been negotiated since 2014 and paves the way for much greater

TABLE 8.1 *Australia–Japan policy agreements by administration*

Malcolm Fraser	Takeo Miki	Basic Treaty of Friendship and Cooperation (1976)
Paul Keating	Tomiichi Murayama	Joint Declaration on the Australia–Japan Partnership (1996)
John Howard	Junichiro Koizumi	Australia–Japan Creative Partnership and Australia-Japan Joint Statement on Cooperation to Combat International Terrorism (2003)
John Howard	Shinzō Abe	Japan–Australia Joint Statement on Security Cooperation (2007)
Kevin Rudd	Yasuo Fukuda	Joint Statement on Comprehensive Strategic, Security and Economic Partnership (2008)
Malcolm Turnbull	Shinzō Abe	Joint Statement on Next Steps of the Special Strategic Partnership (2015)
Scott Morrison	Yoshihide Suga	Reciprocal Access Agreement (RAA) (2020)
Anthony Albanese	Fumio Kishida	Joint Declaration on Security Cooperation (2022)

military diplomacy. A measure of its significance is that it is only the second such agreement negotiated by Japan (alongside the one with the US). Furthermore, reportage described it as a 'defence pact' and connected it directly with the joint response to the rise of China.[5]

The delay in signing the agreement was reportedly due to Australia's stance against the death penalty, which Japan still practises.[6] This issue was also identified in relation to Indonesia; in both cases, Australia's Liberal Internationalist values were compromised in the name of the national interest. In the case of Japan, exempting Australian servicemen and women from the death penalty is more of a Realist protection of the national interests than part of a concerted Liberal Internationalist campaign to influence other states to prohibit the death penalty.

By 2022, Tokyo's and Canberra's concerns were overcome by the intensification of geopolitical competition with China, and the Joint Declaration on Security Cooperation signed on Prime Minister Kishida's visit to Perth paved the way for much closer defence cooperation. The declaration updated the 2007 agreement and sent a firm declaratory signal to China about the closeness of the security relationship. Increased exchanges between military forces were proposed, including joint training and exercising in Australia. In addition, the Declaration paved the way for greater trilateral cooperation with the US. The US aspect of this cooperation was foreshadowed in meetings prior to Prime Ministers Kishida's visit. In sum, the 2022 Declaration elevated the security aspects of the relationship to new heights and highlighted that while trade continued to underpin relations, it was no longer the focus of bilateral diplomacy.

The Japanese government's view of Australia

Japanese declaratory policy towards Australia mirrors that of Australia by highlighting the shared interests in trade, security and development cooperation:

> With the region facing a variety of issues, the 'Special Strategic Partnership' between Japan and Australia, which share fundamental values and strategic interests, is more important than ever. The two countries' strategic visions toward maintaining and strengthening a free and open international order based on the rule of law in the Indo-Pacific region are aligned in wide-ranging areas.[7]

Beyond the broader Indo-Pacific, there was growing awareness of the coincidence of security and development assistance interests in the South Pacific, which are identified in Chapter 12 as being central to Australia's national interests. A measure of this potential for increased cooperation was that a draft Pacific strategy was produced in an attempt to coordinate activities more closely.[8]

Japan has become increasingly assertive in expressing its concerns over security issues and is on a path to normalizing its foreign policy. In 2013, Prime Minister Abe noted in a speech that 'Japan bears a sublime responsibility to the world and faces numerous challenges to address.' He went on to say: 'I pray for tranquillity in the seas of Asia. To help ensure this, I dedicate myself body and soul to creating a Japan that is economically strong, unshakeable in its will, and as open as can be to the outside world.'[9] Even a decade earlier this type of statement would have been unusual, but the sentiment has become normalized as part of Japan's approach to foreign policy. Furthermore, a few decades earlier it would have pricked the ears of Australian foreign policy-makers who at that juncture may still have harboured lingering fears of a remilitarized Japan. It seems that this threat scenario from Japan that was so intertwined in Strategic Culture has been so thoroughly replaced by China that the militarization of Japan and its return to the international community as a 'normal nation' is welcomed in Canberra.

Should Canberra support Japan becoming a 'normal nation'?

There has been longstanding debate in international relations over whether Japan should become a 'normal nation'.[10] That is, whether it should remove self-imposed limitations on its foreign policy to exercise all the rights and responsibilities of statehood. To prevent a repeat of Japanese imperial expansion, the post-war constitution prohibited militarization and it could be argued that this constrains Japan's capacity to cooperate internationally, especially with allies.

After the Second World War, Tokyo focused on industrialization and trade facilitation and this export orientation led it to strongly support a Liberal Internationalist free trade regime. On trade, Japan became a 'normal nation' decades ago. However, a single-faceted focus on one element of international affairs does not equate to being a 'normal nation'. Japan already exercises normative influence in the international community through 'soft power' in areas

BOX 8.1: JAPAN'S SLOW RETURN TO 'NORMAL NATIONHOOD'

- Sovereignty defines a state's rights and obligations and it includes the right to shape the international arena.
- States seek to influence international affairs through a range of tools, from ideational aspects of soft power to material power through the application of military force.
- Japan has been constitutionally prohibited from exercising the right of belligerence (to wage wars) other than in the case of self-defence.
- In recent years, this limitation in Article 9 of the Constitution has been stretched by support (short of involvement in active combat) for US operations in the Middle East.
- The question is, should Japan cast off these prohibitions on its behaviour, and should Canberra support this shift?

such as human rights and poverty alleviation in its overseas development assistance (ODA).

The question is whether it should remilitarize to become an actor in international politics commensurate with its longstanding economic power. Japan has now reached the point where in many respects it has passed a threshold to become a 'normal nation', and we may be witness to the beginning of a new era. Furthermore, due to Japan's relative size, being the world's third largest economy, if it exercised military power commensurate with its economy, it could be considered a great power.

There are two aspects of a return to normality that impact on Australian foreign policy (AFP) and Strategic Culture. The first relates to Japan's engagement with international and regional diplomacy promoting Liberal Internationalist norms, and the second to national defence and international security. Furthermore, the present strategic context behind the debate, the rise of China as a threat to the 'rules-based order', is central to how analysts view the question of whether Japan should become a normal nation. By contrast, for Australia's Strategic Culture, the historical strategic context of Japan influencing threat perceptions appears to have faded. This shift relates to both the rise of Japan as a 'normal nation' with many shared values and interests in maintaining the 'rules-based order' in the Indo-Pacific, and also the rising threat from China.

For some time, Japan has been exercising normative influence on international affairs with a focus on non-proliferation of nuclear and other weapons of mass destruction, and human security. Canberra has willingly cooperated with Tokyo on this agenda,[11] which has a firm Liberal Internationalist foundation, but this agenda does not represent a compromise of national interests as it does not undermine Australia's vital interests. Japan's diplomatic approach focuses on 'soft power' such as working through multilateral institutions of international governance. As such, Japan has been a firm supporter of strengthening a 'rules-based order' and has moved well beyond its historical focus on strengthening Liberal Internationalist free trade regimes.

The evolution of shared interests

Australia's longstanding emphasis on the 'rules-based order' and trade liberalization has ensured a coincidence of interests with Japan that has seen close cooperation in the UN and other international fora. The two states have also worked to shape and strengthen regional order through fora such as the Asia Pacific Economic Cooperation (APEC) forum and the Association of Southeast Asian Nations (ASEAN) Regional Forum (ARF). While much of the focus has been on buttressing the regional Liberal Internationalist economic order, there is potential for greater norm-setting cooperation on human security issues, such as managing humanitarian assistance and disaster relief (HADR) in the South Pacific and freedom of navigation in the South China Sea.[12] These are areas where China's influence is viewed as a threat to Australia's interests and the emphasis on these issues has become more pronounced in Australia and Japan's foreign policies.[13]

Ultimately, diplomatic cooperation reflects affinity and/or shared interests. Shared trade and, more recently, security interests have become the diplomatic ties that bind Australia and Japan. By contrast, much has been done to manage cultural relations, but a divide remains. This is similar to the divide that exists with other Asian states, such as China and Indonesia discussed in Chapters 6 and 10, with the clear distinction that Japan is no longer viewed as a potential military threat.

Bridging the cultural divide

Japanese aggression and atrocities during the Second World War (discussed in Chapter 7) have left a bitter legacy that has led policy-makers to be sensitive to any potentially inflammatory cultural activities.[14] Multiple apologies were expressed by political leaders and Tokyo's soft power diplomacy has focused on benign issues such as human security.[15] Australia and Japan signed a Cultural Agreement in 1974 and the Basic Treaty on Friendship and Cooperation in 1976. Both agreements were aimed at multiple audiences, including those in Japan suspicious of the sincerity of Australian diplomacy and those in Australia that remembered the threat posed by Japan and atrocities during the war. Due to the persistent influence of Strategic Culture, some Australians harboured underlying racist attitudes that might be changed through 'people-to-people' links, education and awareness.[16] This is a similar prescription as applied to similar attitudes towards other Asian states detailed in the chapters on China and Indonesia.

Since the 1980s, tourism, immigration and educational exchanges have been developed, sponsored or supported by successive governments to build awareness. Public opinion has shifted somewhat, but relations remain largely driven from the

Tourism and immigration

Before COVID-19 impacted tourism, Japan was the fifth largest tourism market for Australia in number of arrivals and spending. In the year ending January 2020, over 500,000 Japanese tourists, or 0.4 per cent of the population, visited Australia. In percentage terms, this is on par with the US, but below the top four countries in numbers and percentage of the population. In terms of the total spend, Japanese tourists spent over A$2 billion.[17] By contrast, 332,000 Australians travelled to Japan, which was the eighth most popular destination.[18] Numbers have not rebounded since COVID-19 but these figures from immediately prior highlight the potential for growth.

In 2017 there were over 50,000 Japanese-born residents in Australia. This equates to the thirty-eighth largest migrant group in Australia, and this is relatively small compared to other states. In percentage terms, this represents a very small proportion of both Australia and Japan's populations. The small number of migrants likely reflects the preferences of Japanese that is relevant to all destinations and not just Australia.

Tourism and immigration statistics highlight the limits of attempts to build cultural understanding because there is little demand for people to undertake this type of immersion. Government programmes can try to encourage the development of 'people-to-people' links but while incentives might be attractive, this does not mean that there is organic growth in relations. Citizens of states other than Japan are much more interested in travelling and residing in Australia and vice versa. The impact of COVID-19 has been to freeze these trends and there is little likelihood of a dramatic change in the near future. As such, the diplomatic benefits of cultural literacy gained through travel and residence are minor.

Educational exchanges

Student mobility between Australia and Japan has grown to be a major source of cultural exchange that can promote awareness. It is also a significant source of income for Australia. Interestingly, unlike other large education relationships such as with China or India, student exchange is not limited to tertiary students and many more high school and primary school students visit Australia each year than their university counterparts. This interest may be attributable to the fascination with Australia that shapes Japanese public opinion. It also highlights the type of 'people-to-people' programme that can work.

In 2017, prior to the COVID-19 pandemic, Japanese students represented 1 per cent of the Australian student market, down from 3 per cent a decade earlier. The number of Japanese students has been eclipsed by Indian and Chinese students. There has been phenomenal growth in the education market, but the

Japanese share started from a small base and has remained steady in gross numbers rather than keeping pace with growth in this market.[19] This exchange has been thoroughly disrupted by COVID-19 and due to a range of reasons including geopolitics, China's share of the market is not likely to return in the near future. Despite this shift in the complexion of the market, it also does not mean the Japan will be a major market, but rather new players such as India are growing strongly.

The emphasis on student mobility has obvious economic impacts but it is more difficult to measure the impact on cultural diplomacy. It is certainly possible that if positive, student experiences cannot hurt relations, but the impact is very difficult to quantify. Regardless, student mobility has been an enduring theme in bilateral agreements that seek to promote mutual understanding, which highlights the few levers that governments have to build 'people-to-people' links. As such, it fits with Liberal Internationalist values.[20]

Public opinion

Japanese coverage of Australia and vice versa in popular media is generally quite limited and superficial. Disasters, security and quirky cultural qualities dominate the limited coverage. For example, the 2011 Fukushima nuclear disaster was the largest story on Japan reported in Australia in decades. The Japanese press regularly reports on seemingly strange Australian creatures, bush fires and shark/crocodile attacks in Australia. In addition, seemingly quirky habits, trends or inventions regularly pop up in the media and act to reinforce stereotypes on both sides.[21]

Polling in 2020 showed that Japan was the equally most trusted state to act responsibly, along with the UK (87 per cent) and there was very little mistrust towards Japan. Feelings towards Japan are also warm (74 per cent), with only a few states registering more highly, and all of them our old friends and allies. When compared to traditional international allies and friends, Japan does not register highly. Only 1 per cent of respondents see Japan as Australia's best friend internationally. However, in the region Japan is viewed by far as Australia's best friend by 43 per cent of respondents. This is far in excess of the second and third best friendships being Singapore (21 per cent) and Indonesia (15 per cent).[22] Japanese Prime Minister Fumio Kishida was the third most trusted leader after the French and New Zealand leaders.[23] However, 10 per cent of respondents also did not recognize the Japanese prime minister by name.

Polling from 2013 showed that while China's threatening behaviour towards Japan in the East China Sea registered negatively with the Australian public, less than 40 per cent of respondents thought that Australia should join the US in supporting a conflict with China.[24] Polling from 2022 shows that a majority of Australians believe that the Quad (involving Australia, India, Japan and the US) makes Australia and the region safer.[25] This validates the approach taken by successive governments with respect to the institutionalization of security. However, one issue that has proved divisive, but not necessarily decisive, is Japan's whaling.

CASE STUDY 8.1: WHALING – DOMESTIC POLITICS, ENVIRONMENTAL CREDENTIALS AND A CLASH OF CULTURES

Australia has been a vocal opponent of whaling and has often led initiatives in international fora to curb the practice, such as the moratorium on commercial whaling in the International Whaling Commission (IWC).[26] Over time, many whaling nations have responded to international pressure and ended commercial whaling. However, Japan has persisted under the guise of 'scientific whaling', leading to ongoing tension between the governments. In 2010, Australia launched proceedings against Japan in the International Court of Justice (ICJ) for alleged breaches of the International Convention for the Regulation of Whaling in the Southern Ocean Sanctuary. The case hinged on the credibility of Japan's 'scientific' whaling claims and in 2014 the ICJ found that Japan had breached the convention.[27] Japan promptly continued 'scientific' whaling under the guise of a new programme, leading to condemnation by anti-whaling nations, including Australia.

Public condemnation of whaling in Australia blurred the divide between domestic politics and international diplomacy when the Sea Shepherd environmental group funded a fleet of vessels to disrupt the Japanese whaling fleet. These vessels operated out of Australian ports and used vigorous tactics to intercept Japanese whalers. Some of these actions were potentially dangerous to both sides and in 2010 a Sea Shepherd vessel was sunk. This led to claims and counter-claims as the Japanese government applied pressure to the Australian government to curb what it labelled as 'pirate' vessels operating from its ports. The Australian government's response was lukewarm and certainly did not satisfy Japan. Foreign Minister Julie Bishop noted that 'the fact that the Sea Shepherd visits Australian ports or some of the Sea Shepherd fleet might be registered in Australia is not indicative in any way of the Australian government's support for the organisation.'[28]

In December 2018, Japan signalled its intention to pull out of the IWC, announcing that it would no longer conduct 'scientific' whaling in the Southern Ocean, but also announced plans to begin whaling in its exclusive economic zone (EEZ). Japan's chief cabinet secretary Yoshihide Suga (who would go on to be prime minister) cited cultural reasons for resuming whaling. This provides an insight into the types of issues that have historically formed irritants in Australia–Japan relations.[29] The Australian government stated that it was 'extremely disappointed' and this was dispassionately reported in the Japanese press.[30] This public rebuke followed the Australian government's previous response to disquiet in Australia prompted by the 2017 release of footage of Japanese whalers killing a minke whale. At the time, Australia's environment minister was 'deeply disappointed', but that sentiment was diluted by the fact that the government had fought for five years to stop the release of the images, claiming that they would damage relations with Japan.[31]

Whaling is an issue that has elicited strong and emotional condemnation in Australia, highlighting the dramatic cultural differences between Australia and Japan. However, these cultural issues are overshadowed by shared trade and security interests and point to historical perceptions of a threat from 'alien' Asian values that are represented in Australia's Strategic Culture. Whaling is an issue where the government has aligned foreign policy initiatives with domestic public opinion.[32] It has also been a relatively low-cost initiative as it does not appear to have impacted on the broader relationship with Japan, other than mild diplomatic rebukes being met with denial. Unlike either China or Indonesia, Japan has not sought to escalate diplomatic tension over this issue or any other. Furthermore, by stopping whaling in the Southern Ocean, Japan largely removed the objections in Australia, which highlights how proximity counts in foreign policy. If Japan continues to whale in its EEZ, this does not appear to be a major concern to Australians.

It is also worth noting that the focus of the minor diplomatic tension has been on whaling only, and not on other environmental issues such as tuna over-fishing, which would give more credence to Australia's environmental credentials.[33] While Australia has attempted to build its image as an environmentally responsible state by shaming Japan, neither state has benefited in the sense of supporting its normative credentials. Environmental posturing has domestic and international benefits, and as such fits the Liberal Internationalist mould of 'being seen' to be a good international citizen. However, in the face of Australia's weak stance on tuna fishing or climate change, it is hard to argue that Canberra prioritizes environmental issues. This weakens any conclusion that the government's response to whaling was evidence of Liberal Internationalist tendencies.

Diplomatic collaboration in international and regional fora

Australia has worked alongside or closely with Japan in regional and international multilateral fora promoting trade, humanitarianism, climate change and regional architecture. Both states have focused their efforts in the UN system on limiting the proliferation of weapons of mass destruction (WMD). For instance, in 2002, Australia and Japan (alongside the Netherlands) co-sponsored the 'Friends of the CTBT' (Comprehensive Nuclear Test Ban Treaty) Foreign Ministers' Meeting that was organized on the margins of the UN General Assembly and has become a regular forum for supporting non-proliferation.[34] In 2010, Australia and Japan co-sponsored the Non-Proliferation and Disarmament Initiative (NPDI), which brought together 12 states united by their shared interest in strengthening non-proliferation. The primary focus has been on implementing the Non-Proliferation Treaty (NPT) action plan, but a wide range of cooperative activities have been undertaken.[35]

Australia and Japan are also significant ODA donors. This support has been through intergovernmental organizations as well as direct bilateral aid. There is a definite altruistic strain in development assistance that connects to Liberal Internationalist values and Australian and Japanese foreign policy, especially when it is directed towards the South Pacific. However, there is also a firm national interest at stake for both nations that has become more pronounced. For instance, Japan's 2013 National Security Strategy noted: 'As an advanced, liberal and democratic nation, based on the principle of human security, Japan will actively utilize its overseas development assistance (ODA) in supporting democratization.'[36] For Australia's part, the 2013 closure of AusAID, its dedicated development assistance agency, and the rise of the 'aid for trade' approach to ODA, highlighted mixed motives in relation to Liberal Internationalist values and the national interest (which are discussed in Chapter 12 on the South Pacific).

Regional security cooperation

Australia and Japan also shared interests in building a regional security community and have supported various initiatives over the last 30 years to build awareness of shared interests.[37] Both have been external partners/observers in initiatives such as the ARF (1994), the East Asia Summit (2005) and the ASEAN Defence Ministers' Meeting Plus (ADMM-Plus; 2007). Some concrete cooperation on HADR evolved out of the ADMM-Plus, but in practice these initiatives have not been effective confidence-building mechanisms in significant security issues, such as easing concerns over the rise of China, or US regional engagement. As such, bilateral, trilateral and quadrilateral security cooperation has been used to focus on more cohesive groups of like-minded states, such as the Quad.

Multilateral diplomatic collaboration can be contrasted with the bilateral and multilateral trade and security collaboration that has been a major feature of Australia–Japan relations. It also highlights Japan's strategy of harnessing normative power and influence by building a reputation for dealing with humanitarian issues and global challenges such as non-proliferation.[38] The use of ODA also fits this approach to using soft power to further foreign policy goals, which include building credentials as a 'normal nation' while also countering growing Chinese influence.[39]

Overall, Japanese and Australian approaches have been closely aligned and highlight Liberal Internationalist values in the foreign policies of both states, although this approach is much more pronounced for Japan. Cooperation on these issues is fundamentally different to the instrumentalism of trade and security, which fits more neatly within a Realist frame of maximizing narrowly defined national interests. As such, multilateral cooperation on global and regional security issues has deepened the awareness of broader shared interests, which can overcome lingering historical fears of Japanese aggression that influenced the development of Australia's Strategic Culture.

Prime ministerial relations and high-level diplomacy

Public diplomacy between Australia and Japan has been driven from the highest levels.[40] Robert Menzies was the first prime minister to visit Japan in 1957 and this was reciprocated by Prime Minister Nobusuke Kishi visiting Australia. From that time there have been over 25 visits by Australian prime ministers and over 10 by Japanese prime ministers. COVID-19 led to a virtual meeting in July 2020, but Prime Minister Morrison travelled to Japan in December 2020 to be the first foreign leader to meet incoming Prime Minister Yoshihide Suga. This high-level diplomacy mirrors relations with Indonesia and China, but it is different insofar as there is an appreciable slow shift towards more comprehensive relations, as with the US.

A significant symbolic example of close prime ministerial relations occurred with respect to the death and funeral of former prime minister, Shinzō Abe, in September 2022. The tragic assassination of Abe prompted widespread condemnation and messages of sympathy from Australia. Abe was remembered as being responsible for the strengthening of Japan-Australia relations. However, Prime Minister Albanese and three former prime ministers (John Howard, Tony Abbott and Malcolm Turnbull) travelled to Japan for his state funeral. For Albanese this was his second trip to Japan in less than six months. That the former prime ministers also attended was an unprecedented show of support that highlighted just how far diplomatic relations had grown and also how central personal relationships between senior leaders have been to cementing closer ties.

Beyond the increasingly regular prime ministerial visits, the centrepiece of high-level collaboration has been the annual 2+2 ministerial meetings inaugurated in 2010. These meetings have been a catalyst for turning declaratory sentiments about closer relations into concrete initiatives. Their foundation in 2010 coincides with the most recent phase in relations where security institutionalization has been the key priority. There have also been numerous reciprocal visits by a wide cross-section of ministers. Recent visits have covered the portfolios of foreign affairs, defence, trade, tourism, industry, international development and treasury. The focus of these meetings has been firmly on trade and investment, but this is shifting to concentrate more on foreign affairs and defence.

As with the first tentative steps that built trade relations, the current emphasis on security institutionalization has been driven by high-level diplomacy. Prime Ministers John Howard and Ryutaro Hashimoto proposed annual prime ministerial meetings in 1997 to elevate public diplomacy and these have been used to good effect in recent years. Japan's longstanding prime minister, Shinzō Abe, met with successive Australian prime ministers to further the agenda and a series of agreements and arrangements have been negotiated. Prime Minister Malcolm Turnbull visited Japan in January 2018 focusing on regional security issues (such as North Korea) and strengthening bilateral security cooperation. Finalizing ongoing negotiations on a bilateral security agreement was emphasized by the two of them and this goal was achieved in December 2020 at the first prime ministerial meeting after Abe left office due to ill-health.

Trade institutionalization: Normal economic relations as a springboard to normal security ties

For much of the post-Second World War era, Japan was the world's second largest economy after the US, only to be overtaken by China in recent years. Considering the utter destruction of the Japanese economy by the Second World War, this is a major testament to Japanese innovation and industry. Trade was central to the birth of post-war relations and remains a central plank in the relationship. In 1957, Australia and Japan signed the Australia–Japan Agreement on Commerce, which in many ways was a visionary agreement considering the signatories were former enemies whose memories of the war had hardly faded. It was followed by the Basic Treaty of Friendship and Cooperation Between Australia and Japan (NARA, 1976) and both agreements are credited with developing trade opportunities with Japan that provided the foundation for the development of a free trade agreement (in 2015).[41]

Within a decade of the Agreement on Commerce, trade had flourished and Japan had become one of Australia's top three trading partners. This development was aided in a large part by trade with the UK declining as it integrated into the European Union. By the 1990s, Japan became Australia's number one trading partner. 2017 marked the sixtieth anniversary of the Agreement on Commerce and the complementary nature of trade remains central to close relations. Australia and Japan's complementary economies are central to the success of the relationship: Australia has focused on agricultural and natural resource exports, such as iron ore and natural gas, while Japan has focused on manufactured goods, such as passenger vehicles and light trucks and has needed Australian natural resources to do so. This is similar to Australia's relationship to China and in marked contrast to trade with the US, where the focus is on services.

Australia and Japan also share liberal economic outlooks as Japan is an advanced export-oriented industrialized economy organized along capitalist market principles. This is quite unlike China and provides an insight into how the trade relationship provided the bridge to closer diplomatic relations, especially as Japanese militarization and aggression in the 1930s and 1940s was central to the development of Australia's Strategic Cultural fear of an 'alien' Asian state to the north. Trade providing the bridge highlights how Realist national interests, which are free of values and sentimentality, can influence policy.

A measure of the close trade relations was the negotiation of a free trade agreement (FTA), the Japan–Australia Economic Partnership Agreement (JAEPA), which entered into force in January 2015. Free trade agreements are a central part of Australia's comprehensive trade engagement strategy, which has seen the successful negotiation of FTAs with ASEAN and nine individual states. Declaratory policy notes that 'Australia is the only major developed country with [FTAs with] all major North Asian Markets',[42] and modelling has shown that they have and will have a significant positive impact on the Australian economy.[43] Australia's DFAT describes the relationship as 'an extensive and mature partnership in trade and investment, which both countries seek to deepen', and these sentiments are echoed by Japan's MOFA.[44] Significantly, the free trade agreement also fits with Japan's FTA strategy with other developing states.[45]

Trade foreground

In 2017, two-way trade amounted to A\$61 billion. Until recently, Japan ranked as the number one trading partner for Australia and had done so for over 40 years but changing geoeconomic trends have seen China supplant Japan as Australia's number one export destination. A snapshot of the trade relationship can be seen in Figure 8.1.

Australia is Japan's sixth largest two-way trading partner, while Japan ranks third for Australia. Australia is Japan's third largest source of imports and tenth largest export destination (Table 8.2).

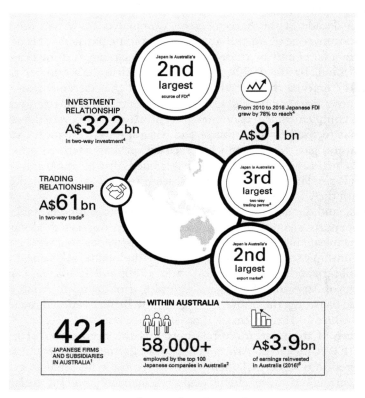

FIGURE 8.1 *Japan and Australia – by numbers.*[46]

TABLE 8.2 *Japan's pre-COVID19 global merchandise trade relationships*[47]

Japan's principal export destinations, 2019		Japan's principal import sources, 2019	
1. United States	19.9%	1. China	23.5%
2. China	19.1%	2. United States	11.3%
3. Republic of Korea	6.6%	3. *Australia*	6.3%
10. *Australia*	2.1%	4. Republic of Korea	4.1%

Australia and Japan have always had highly complementary economies and this has not altered over time. Australia maintains a significant trade surplus with Japan, with Japanese demand for Australian natural resources, such as iron ore, outpacing Australian demand for Japanese manufactured goods, such as cars (see Table 8.3). Australia is the largest energy supplier to Japan, literally fuelling Japan's industrial development.

Foreign direct investment

Australia has been a beneficiary of the growth and globalization of the Japanese economy in a number of ways. In relation to FDI, the gross amount of Japanese FDI has steadily grown over time (see Table 8.4), as has the share of total Japanese foreign investment that this represents.

The total stock of Japanese investment in Australia is over A\$240 billion, which represents a surplus of over A\$100 billion in Australia's favour. On a year-by-year basis, Japan is the second largest investor in Australia, with A\$91 billion in 2017.[48] Significantly, this is second to the US (A\$190 billion) and greater than the UK (A\$83 billion). The latter two states are, or were, longstanding security partners entwined through history and central to assuaging the fears in Strategic Culture. As such, there is a great deal of symmetry with these two 'great and powerful friends'. That Japan is such a significant investor speaks to economic opportunities and the trust that has been built in the 60 years since trade was institutionalized in 1957, and can be contrasted in the low level of investment from China.

This FDI has a significant impact on economic growth in Australia. Japanese firms hold assets worth A\$119 billion and employ nearly 60,000 staff in over

TABLE 8.3 *Major Australian pre-COVID19 exports and imports*[49]

Major Australian exports, 2019–20 (A\$m)		Major Australian imports, 2019–20 (A\$m)	
Natural gas	19,302	Passenger motor vehicles	7,208
Coal	14,431	Refined petroleum	3,106
Iron ores and concentrates	7,038	Goods vehicles	1,549
Beef, f.c.f.	2,422	Rubber tyres, treads and tubes	766

TABLE 8.4 *Australia's pre-COVID19 investment relationship with Japan*[50]

Australia's investment relationship with Japan, 2019 (A\$m)	Total	FDI
Australia's investment in Japan	139,567	1,653
Japan's investment in Australia	241,091	116,102

400 subsidiaries.[51] Japanese firms also reinvest a higher proportion of their profits in Australia than other investors (A$3.9 billion in 2016, equating to 4.3 per cent of the Japanese FDI stock in Australia). This makes the net surplus in investment from Japan a key contributor to Australian economic growth, second only to the US and well ahead of investment from China.

Cooperation in regional trade institutionalization

In the 1990s, Australia and Japan cooperated in the creation of the Asia Pacific Economic Cooperation (APEC) forum. APEC was a significant initiative to grow trade between the 'Asian Tiger' economies and promote a trade liberalization agenda at the regional level. Since 2012, Australia and Japan also worked with other members of ASEAN to negotiate the Regional Comprehensive Economic Partnership (RCEP) grouping covering all significant economies in the Indo-Pacific. The RCEP involves ASEAN, China, Japan, New Zealand and the Republic of Korea. It includes nine of Australia's top 14 trading partners who account for approximately 30 per cent of global gross domestic product (GDP) and population.[52] In 2022, the RCEP came into force for 12 of the 14 original parties and India has the option of negotiating entry in the near future.

To the backdrop of the looming trade war between the US and China, Prime Minister Malcolm Turnbull visited Japan in 2018 and reaffirmed support for the Trans-Pacific Partnership (TPP), which was signed later in 2018. President Trump had pulled the US out of the TPP in 2017. Despite this setback, Japan persisted diplomatically and rallied the remaining 11 members to retain the agreement, which was rebadged as the Comprehensive Progressive Agreement for Trans-Pacific Partnership (CPTPP).

Despite the withdrawal of the US, Canberra has strongly supported the CPTPP. Australia's support of Japan's lead on the CPTPP speaks to Australia's declared interest in encouraging the trade aspects of a Liberal Internationalist 'rules-based order', including open trade through free markets. It also highlights lingering questions about the US support for free trade that arose in the late 2010s, which were causing uncertainty, especially in the face of concern over the place of alliances in Trump's foreign policy.[53] For domestic political reasons, the Biden administration has not joined the CPTPP but did launch the Indo-Pacific Economic Framework (IPEF) in 2022. Like the CPTPP the IPEF encompasses 40 per cent of global trade and includes eight of Australia's top trading partners. Australia and Japan became founding members thus continuing the free trade agenda alongside their US ally.

This level of multilateral economic cooperation between Australia and Japan provides evidence of what Canberra means by the sentiment that 'each country is invested in the success of the other'.[54] However, the level of investment and the coincidence of economic and security interests highlights that the diplomatic relationship is far more significant than the instrumental economic interaction that characterized relations in the first decades after the Second World War.

The 'Special Strategic Partnership' avowed between the two states is becoming a security alignment and has elements of collaboration that are akin to the core relationships with 'great and powerful friends' that have characterized Strategic Culture. Instrumental economic interactions fit neatly with a Realist paradigm on maximizing interests, and the close cooperation fits a Liberal Internationalist and neo-Realist perspective of creating or using institutional architecture to suit the interests of the international community and/or national interests. These interests are increasingly reflected in bilateral security relations.

Bilateral security institutionalization: operationalizing the 'Special strategic partnership'

> In recent years our defence relationship has grown rapidly. Australia will continue to boost defence engagement with Japan, including in maritime security and in research and development.[55]

Given the history of the Japanese Empire's belligerence during the Second World War, security cooperation was much slower to develop than trade. In fact, much of the growth in Australia's close relations with its 'great and powerful friend', the US, was prompted by defeating Imperial Japan and deterring the potential rise of Japan as a threat in the future. However, despite these less than auspicious foundations, security relations have grown exponentially in recent years with institutionalization well underway.

The shift to institutionalized security relations points to the influence of the threat from China in both Japan[56] and in Australia. Shared threats can be the glue that binds states in the international arena but Australia and Japan also share responses to these threats, namely alliances with the US. However, questions have been raised over the credibility of the security guarantee from Australia's 'great and powerful friend'/Japan's, ally prompted by the Trump administration's foreign policy.[57] Both issues are unifying factors in the Australia–Japan relationship (and trilateral alliance relations are discussed later).

Shared threat perceptions and Australia's Strategic Culture

A key distinction between Australia and Japan arises from Japan's geography and history: Japan is geographically proximate to China and North Korea, Japan and China/North Korea have a long history of conflict, and mutual threat perceptions have been identified by Japan, China and North Korea. In contrast to Japan, Australia sits on the edge of Asia, a region that it has never felt a part of. However, despite being thousands of kilometres away from Northeast Asia, heightened threat perceptions drive Australian strategic policy. As noted, these threat perceptions characterize Australia's Strategic Culture and have morphed from a generalized fear of Asia to the Japanese Empire and then Communist China, both during the Cold War and presently.

Significantly, Australia and Japan's shared threat perceptions align Realist shared interests between the two states that might ordinarily have been expected to be negated by Australian Strategic Culture. That is, threat perceptions from

146 AUSTRALIAN FOREIGN POLICY

Asia that are inherent to Strategic Culture are no longer triggered by Japan, and its seems that Strategic Culture is evolving and Japan's position as a democracy, an ally of the US and growing security partner exempts it from being identified as an 'alien' threat. Despite growing shared security interests, security institutionalization between former enemies is still noteworthy, especially where Australia's Strategic Culture was so strongly shaped by the experience of being threatened with invasion by Japan in the Second World War. As such, security relations with Japan test key aspects of Strategic Culture and highlight the influence of Realist emphases on shared interests over the reliance on permanent alliances with 'great and powerful friends' that have shaped AFP. The question is whether these two foci of relations are in tension or reinforce one another.

The process of security normalization has been gradual, mirroring China's rise and increasing assertiveness, and this conforms with a Realist analysis.[58] Just as China has been more assertive in the South China Sea and increased its participation in UN peacekeeping, so has Japan eased the self-imposed limitations first on participation in peacekeeping, and more recently allowing its military forces to defend themselves and others. Beyond self-defence from the perceived threat of China, Japan's security interests are primarily maritime and relate mainly to maintaining freedom of navigation for trade. Protecting maritime trade has relied on a Liberal Internationalist strategy of promoting the 'rules-based order', especially in the Indo-Pacific where trade could be disrupted by China.

Japan's longstanding territorial disputes with China and Russia have ensured that security interests have remained a concern and its Strategic Culture is shifting towards identifying as a maritime power.[59] Maritime disputes have escalated, with increasing incursions by Chinese forces along with tensions over the disputed Senkaku Islands and China's occupation of the Spratly Islands, highlighting the importance of maintaining sovereignty and freedom of navigation. The Realist prescription focuses on strengthening alliances and alignments, and defence self-reliance. This emphasises the coincidence of interests between Canberra and Tokyo and also the similar responses to threats.

Japan's Strategic Culture and closer defence cooperation

Japan's Strategic Culture provides insights into how it faces Australia. The historical legacy of an expansionist militaristic empire and its defeat casts a long shadow over foreign policy, as do the implications of economic growth to great power levels. Japan's constitutional limitation to self-defence has shaped its strategic outlook as it has been dependent on the US for security, leading to fears of abandonment if the US failed to follow through on security guarantees.[60] However, the rise of China, calls by the US for greater burden-sharing in the alliance and questions about US resolve have prompted a gradual change in Japan's posture.[61]

Japan's Strategic Culture is focused on the geographical proximity and historical animosity with China. Like Australia, Japan cannot escape its geography and threat perceptions in relation to China's actions and ambitions have strongly influenced Japanese foreign policy for centuries. However, unlike Australia, Japan's position in Northeast Asia places it adjacent to the source of its threat, which highlights how enlarged or exaggerated Australian threat perceptions are in comparison. As self-imposed limitations on the use of force in international affairs are relaxed, as they were in 2015, Japan approaches international affairs differently and this is reflected in defence cooperation. For example, Prime Minister Shinzō Abe used the 2015 provisions for collective self-defence to extend protection to Australian military forces on joint operations, an arrangement second only to the US. As such, shared threat perceptions and fear of abandonment in their respective Strategic Cultures provides motivation for evolution in Australia–Japan defence relations.

China: shared threat perceptions as a catalyst for closer defence cooperation

Attitudes in Canberra and Tokyo towards the rise of China have evolved and this is evidenced in the shift from being overly sensitive to China's concerns over bilateral cooperation in the 1990s. This sensitivity led to downplaying and rescheduling activities and the abandonment of the Quad in 2008. However, bilateral relations have evolved, leading to cooperation unencumbered by diplomatic sensitivities from the late 2000s. Institutionalization followed this sentiment.

The Japan-Australia Joint Statement on Security Cooperation (2007) began the contemporary process of intensified security cooperation and institutionalization. Annual 2+2 ministerial meetings between foreign and defence ministers were developed as a mechanism to operationalize the high-level political commitment to closer security relations. In 2010, an Acquisition and Cross Servicing Agreement was signed. An Information Security Agreement followed in 2013. This was followed by the Agreement Concerning the Transfer of Defence Equipment and Technology of 2014, which provided a framework for the ultimately unsuccessful submarine contract tender in 2015. There is some debate over whether Japan was given indications that it was the preferred tenderer,[62] but there is no sense that any lingering Strategic Cultural bias shaped the outcome. Canberra's decision did not have a discernible negative impact on the bilateral defence relationship.

Security institutionalization has been designed to broaden and deepen practical defence cooperation. While it has proceeded apace, it has facilitated bilateral activities such as training, exchanges and exercises. For example, Japanese forces have participated in major Australian exercises such as Talisman, Sabre and Kakadu and forces have conducted joint patrols in the South China Sea. In addition, from 1990, Australian and Japanese forces have deployed alongside one another on UN and HADR operations in states such as Iraq, South Sudan, the Philippines as well as the Fukushima earthquake of 2011. Australian diplomatic and military diplomatic responses to Fukushima were acknowledged as an important shift in the tone of bilateral relations.

BOX 8.2: AUSTRALIAN SUBMARINES AND SHARED INTERESTS

- Canberra put out tender for conventional submarines to replace the Collins Class.
- Japanese and Australian officials worked closely together during the tender process.
- Ultimately, a French company won the contract in 2016.
- The French contract was then discontinued and the 2021 AUKUS agreement paved the way for Australia to acquire nuclear-powered submarines from either the UK or US or both.
- Australian submarines to operate in Northeast Asia alongside the US and Japanese forces.
- Japan did not benefit from the submarine contract, but the shift to nuclear vessels aligns with Japanese interests as it will allow closer cooperation.

A poignant example of the dramatic shift in security relations was Prime Minister Abe's visit to Darwin in November 2018. The Japanese prime minister laid a wreath in memory of the 243 people who were killed during the first Japanese attack on Australian soil in February 1942. In his remarks, he noted: 'Thanks to the devoted efforts of many, Japan and Australia have achieved reconciliation and have become special strategic partners driving regional peace and prosperity.'[63] These words would have been unimaginable until very recently and reflect the dramatic change in foreign policy since the Second World War. Even less imaginable would have been the fact that negotiations on a security agreement were underway. The visit to Darwin by Prime Minister Abe was seen as a symbol of the relationship moving on from Japan's failed bid to supply submarines to Australia.

A measure of the closeness of relations was that by 2022, Canberra was pushing for Japan to be treated as the quasi-fourth member of AUKUS. Defence Minister Richard Marles noted: 'now we are poised to build the Japan–Australia relationship as a powerful force in its own right', describing the relationship as 'foundational'.[64]

The debate over amending Article 9 (and AFP)

Canberra acknowledges that the decision about whether to amend Article 9 of the Constitution is a matter for the Japanese government.[65] It is such a momentous decision that there has been considerable domestic debate about whether to go down this path.[66] However, debate over Article 9 also has a significant international dimension as it has ramifications for regional and international security.

BOX 8.3: THE PROHIBITION ON BELLIGERENCY

Article 9 prohibits Japan from developing the type of offensive military forces that would allow it to be a 'belligerent' and wage war like most other 'normal' nations.

'(1) Aspiring sincerely to an international peace based on justice and order, the Japanese people forever renounce war as a sovereign right of the nation and the threat or use of force as means of settling international disputes. (2) In order to accomplish the aim of the preceding paragraph, land, sea, and air forces, as well as other war potential, will never be maintained. The right of belligerency of the state shall not be recognized.'

This prohibition was reinforced by a limitation of spending 1 per cent of its GDP on defence expenditure which was repealed in 2022.

Debate over Article 9 is captured by the question: Should Japan become a 'normal' nation? Normality in a security sense relates to the capacity and sovereign right of Japan to defend itself *and* wage war to achieve its national interests. This would involve a maritime strategy that intersected and coincided with Australia's interests.

Japan currently possesses a Self Defence Force (SDF) focused on national defence. Defence spending, at approximately US$40 billion, remains within the 1 per cent GDP envelope, but still makes it the world's eighth largest defence budget. Furthermore, in 2022, Prime Minister Kishida proposed doubling the defence budget to 2 per cent of GDP by 2027, which would greatly expand the resources available for weapons upgrades. In terms of personnel, the SDF is the eighteenth largest military. The SDF possesses potent capabilities and is ranked as the fifth largest navy on earth. At the height of fears about Japan prior to the First World War, its navy was the third largest on earth but rather than being viewed as a threat, the benefits of interoperability are now highlighted by Canberra.

The SDF has grown from a modest force to a highly capable military that has already blurred distinctions between defence and offence. Much of the SDF's equipment is defensive or dual-use (both defensive and offensive) and there have been some notable shifts in recent years. For instance, the navy's helicopter landing ships have been defined as defensive yet have the capacity to launch fifth-generation F35 fighter jets, which have significant defensive and offensive capabilities. Similarly, submarines are dual-use, but the production of larger vessels with greater range provides Japanese policy-makers offensive options. These options are likely to grow if Australia acquires nuclear submarines that can deploy alongside SDF forces.

The collective self-defence of allies

In September 2015, the Japanese Diet passed legislation formalizing the SDF's participation in UN peacekeeping operations and allied/coalition operations but stopped short of repealing Article 9. However, allowing the SDF to be involved in the collective self-defence of allies (including Australia) was certainly not envisaged by the framers of the article. That is, Japanese forces undertaking coalition operations have been explicitly allowed to fight alongside allies if they are attacked. This change was designed to facilitate swift responses to crises on the Korean Peninsula, but critics point out that it has significant potential implications in relation to deployments with the US in places such as Iraq and Afghanistan. If the institutionalization of the Australia–Japan 'quasi alliance' becomes more concrete, then the same considerations would apply to independent Australian or Japanese operations. However, it must be noted that the ANZUS alliance already commits Australia to defend US forces in the 'Pacific Area' and that would include the more than 50,000 US personnel based in Japan.

Previously, Japanese forces were not able to participate in active combat and had limited self-defence options, let alone offensive options. As such, in deployments to Iraq, Afghanistan and elsewhere, they required other states' militaries to provide force protection. In what could be seen as a pointed irony based on the experience of the Second World War, in 2005 Australian forces deployed a task force of 450 troops to take on this role in Iraq.[67] Roles were reversed from the First World War, where Japanese naval vessels guarded Australian troop transports transiting across the Indian Ocean to fight in Europe.

Officially, 'Australia welcomed and supported Japan's recent passage of 'Legislation for Peace and Security', which enables Japan to contribute even more actively to securing the peace, stability and prosperity of the region and the world in line with its policy of a 'Proactive Contribution to Peace'.[68] The Australian 2017 Foreign Policy White Paper noted:

> We expect Japan ... steadily to pursue reforms to its defence and strategic policies over the decade. Australia supports these reforms and Japan's efforts to improve its security capabilities and to play a more active role in the security of the region.[69]

Australia's 2016 Defence White Paper also contained this positive sentiment on security normalization and foreshadowed that it would 'deepen and broaden our growing security cooperation with Japan'.[70]

The Quadrilateral Security Dialogue

Japan and Australia began trilateral meetings with India in 2015, which also spurred the re-invigoration of an arrangement known as the Quadrilateral Security Dialogue (Quad), which comprised Australia, Japan, India and the US. In the 1990s, Canberra was sensitive to Beijing's perceptions of the Quad as a form of strategic encirclement and discontinued cooperation but by the mid-2010s, these concerns had been overtaken by strategic change. Australia's 2017 Foreign Policy White Paper noted:

We strongly encourage India's strategic engagement with East Asia and the United States. We will work with India in the East Asia Summit (EAS) and build on the growing strategic collaboration between Australia, India and Japan.[71]

Following the explicit identification of China as a threat in the US National Security Strategy, the Trump administration highlighted that a 'free and open Indo-Pacific' (FOIP) was central to its approach to the region.[72] Congress passed the Asia Reassurance Initiative Act of 2018, aiming to support allies in the region in the face of both perceptions of China's increasingly assertive actions in the South China Sea and claims of domestic interference by several countries, including Australia. The Act focuses on maritime security and explicitly supports the Quad by emphasizing that:

> the security dialogue between the United States, Australia, India, and Japan is vital to address pressing security challenges in the Indo-Pacific region in order to promote – (A) a 'rules-based order' (B) respect for international law; and (C) a free and open Indo-Pacific.[73]

This messaging was important for both Japan and Australia, which needed reassurance of US commitment to regional security to assuage fears of alliance abandonment associated with their Strategic Cultures. The support for what has been variously termed a free, inclusive, open, 'stable and prosperous Indo-Pacific' aligned with Australia's 2017 Foreign Policy White Paper[74] and subsequent 2+2 foreign and defence ministerial consultations with Japan.

From trilateral defence cooperation with the US to trilateral security agreements?

Trilateralism has been used to extend relations beyond the 'hub and spokes' model. The 'hub and spokes' refers to the US post-Second World War San Francisco Treaty system that was built on bilateral security guarantees between asymmetric partners, with the US dominant in each. Originally, trilateral cooperation was narrowly focused on dialogue and tentative in scope.[75] The Trilateral Security Dialogue (TSD) and the US–Japan–Australia Security and Defense Cooperation Forum (SDCF) were inaugurated in 2001. As with the Quad, trilateral cooperation was viewed with suspicion by China, which for a time limited its development due to sensitivities in Canberra and Tokyo. This did not mean that it was not significant, but it was constrained due to the geopolitical context. Over time, geopolitical conflict intensified, Canberra's and Tokyo's sensitivities towards China waned, and opportunities for trilateral cooperation expanded.[76]

The 2016 Defence White Paper and 2017 Foreign Policy White Paper emphasized the importance of working with sub-regional groupings and highlighted the value of trilateral cooperation with the US and Japan. Declaratory policy stated that, 'Australia remains strongly committed to our trilateral dialogues with the United States and Japan and, separately, with India and Japan.'[77] The value of Australia's and Japan's respective alliances with the US and the links they bring were routinely noted in statements from prime ministerial meetings and the 2+2 dialogues.[78]

Trilateralism is also evident operationally. Much of Australia and Japan's defence equipment is sourced from the US or derived from US platforms. A prime example is the F-35 Joint Strike Fighter (JSF), a fifth-generation fighter – of the Indo-Pacific states, only Japan, Australia and South Korea have been able to acquire it. Similarly, joint naval patrols and exercises have highlighted the value of integrated defence platforms. As such, defence acquisitions have reinforced the value of interoperability with US forces, and by extension with Australian forces.[79]

An Australia–Japan 'quasi-alliance'?

The pace of change in the relationship is fuelling speculation in both Australia and Japan over whether a 'quasi-alliance' is forming around the 'wheel' of the orthodox US alliance 'hub and spokes'.[80] Some US allies have been content to be spokes in the wheel and rely on the US guarantee of security as the hub. Australia and Japan's bilateral security cooperation demonstrates that the hub and spokes may evolve into a networked alliance.

The development of an alliance between Australia and Japan has great significance for how alliances are conceived as it would institutionalize connections around the alliance wheel. Security institutionalization would effectively create a third side of separate bilateral relations to bolster the triangular relationship. Functionally, it would create new dynamics with the senior alliance partner (the US) and potential competitors (namely China).

A prime example of the significance of evolving trilateralism is obligations between Australia and Japan that are separate but connected to the US alliances. For both states, this would assuage some of the fears of abandonment that characterize their respective Strategic Cultures. However, commentators have questioned whether an alliance could undermine strategic stability in the region.[81] The institutionalization of a 'quasi-alliance' may also influence perceptions of allies and potential competitors alike about the credibility of US extended deterrence. As with trilateral relations with the US and Japan, a 'quasi-alliance' could be viewed by strategic competitors such as China as a form of hedging against US decline, and as such would fit a Realist approach to strategic balancing by both Australia and Japan.[82] That is, up to now Canberra and Tokyo have relied wholeheartedly on US guarantees but a separate bilateral alliance would provide another level of insurance against mutual threats.

It is not simply China's rise shaping security institutionalization, but also the perceptions of the two dependent allies of the US response to China's rise. This was particularly the case during the Obama administration when China moved to militarize the South China Sea. Policy-makers are circumspect and focused on national interests, so this trend may be a rare example of the reliance on 'great and powerful friends' being impacted by strategic change. However, unlike the last liminal moment in allegiances when Australia shifted from the UK to the US from

1942 to 1951 (on security if not cultural or economic issues), in this case the US alliance is being bolstered by greater collaboration between allies.

This approach fits the US declared policy of 'burden-sharing' first enunciated in Nixon's Guam Doctrine in 1969[83] and reiterated by the Trump administration with respect to US allies, in particular NATO, spending more on defence.[84] In the 1960s and 1970s, the US envisaged drawing down from the Vietnam War and was disinclined to commit forces to wars on the Asian landmass. It called on allies (namely Japan, South Korea and Australia) to do more to share the burden of their defence. Nixon's comments were prompted by a conversation with Prime Minister Andrew Gorton of Australia, highlighting that this issue was not new, and that ambiguity in relation to the US commitment to Asia prompted a shift towards greater defence self-reliance in Australia.[85] Trump continued this trend, prompting Prime Minister Abe to emphasise the alliance and this positively influenced relations with Australia, which was similarly fearful of China and US disengagement.[86]

Conclusion

One hundred years after Defence Minister Thomas Ewing predicted that 'white and yellow man ... are destined to be enemies for all time',[87] the identity of threats has shifted from Japan to Indonesia, Asian Communism and mercantilist China. In the Second World War, Australia and Japan were bitter enemies. Australia feared an imminent Japanese invasion and attacks on Darwin and Sydney stoked the fears inherent in Australia's Strategic Culture. During the Cold War, relations thawed and economic and security relations grew. Economic links drove the relationship, but over time security grew in importance. The incremental growth in bilateral cooperation has been accelerating, driven by a shifting focus from trade and international diplomacy to security.

Trade remains an important foundation after the Cold War, but the relationship has strengthened and transformed. Central to this shift is the strategic challenge posed by the rise of China, and in particular, China's rise against questions of US resolve to maintain the alliance relationships that have underpinned strategic stability in the Indo-Pacific. Security institutionalization of the 'Special Strategic Partnership' may point to a response to a liminal moment prompted by geostrategic and geoeconomic change. It also tests several aspects of Strategic Culture, including reliance on immutable alliances with 'great and powerful friends' and treating 'alien' Asia as the source of threat.

The growing closeness of relations with a former enemy seems to challenge the continuity of Strategic Culture, but this challenge may be more apparent than real. It highlights the intersection of Realist and Liberal Internationalist interests with the threat perceptions that drive Strategic Culture. The Japan of today is far from the ultra-nationalistic Japan that sought an empire in the middle of the last century. Australian threat perceptions now focus on China's geopolitical and geoeconomic ambitions; an Asian state remains the target of the threat and Australia's response is more sophisticated insofar as it has found that Japan and many Asian states fit the ancient proverb that 'your enemy's enemy is your friend', which is closely associated with Realist geopolitics.[88]

In this chapter, the capacity of Strategic Culture to adapt to changing threat perceptions has been tested, but there is much more to this shift in relations than simply 'positivist' *Realpolitik*. Strategic Culture is not immutable, but equally, change has been gradual. Japan is not a permanent enemy just as the UK is not a permanent ally. However, the condition for change is that allies, or 'quasi-allies', must share threat perceptions and values. Japan's alignment with Liberal Internationalist values and the 'rules-based order' since the Second World War, and the identification of China as the current existential threat, have allowed Tokyo to be repositioned as a security partner with shared threat perceptions and outlook. This means greater security institutionalization, such as Japan joining the Five Eyes intelligence-sharing network, is likely. Five Eyes is a secretive intelligence-sharing network set up during the Cold War by the US, UK, Canada, Australia and New Zealand to respond to shared threats. Joining Five Eyes would be significant because it has been identified by China as a mechanism used to marshal opposition to Beijing. If not this initiative, then others will signal a warming of relations.

The Australian and Japanese governments have explained the transformation of the relationship in terms that reflect Realism, Liberal Internationalism and Strategic Culture: 'The Prime Ministers reaffirmed the special strategic partnership between Japan and Australia, based on common values and strategic interests including democracy, human rights, the rule of law, open markets and free trade.'[89]

Australia is supporting the rise of Japan as a 'normal' nation and the 'quasi-alliance' is likely to become real in the near future. As such, the historical determinism of Strategic Culture has been qualified by particular geopolitical conditions, specifically threat perceptions and the trust in the credibility of the security guarantee of the 'great and powerful friend' in the face of the rise of a potentially threatening 'alien' state in the region. This evolution in relations is in sharp contrast with the relationship with China and highlights the underlying securitized basis of AFP.

9

Background to Indonesia: The fractured history of diplomacy and the dynamic of diplomatic slight and escalation

Introduction

> There are few neighbouring countries in the world as different as Indonesia and Australia. The gulf between their history, culture, economy and politics almost guarantees that relations between the two countries are likely to be difficult and fraught with the danger of misunderstanding.[1]

This quote from the Joint Standing Committee on Foreign Affairs, Defence and Trade highlights that Australia's relationship with Indonesia is perplexing and paradoxical. Despite the efforts of successive Australian governments, Indonesia remains 'a stranger next door'.[2] Indonesia is Australia's nearest Asian neighbour with many shared economic and security interests that have the theoretical potential to lead to close relations, yet the relationship remains distant. This distance largely defies the emphasis on maximizing national interests in the theories traditionally used to explain international relations.[3]

The enduring distance between neighbours

In contrast to Australia's path to nationhood, Indonesia fought for independence from a colonial power. It is the most populous Muslim nation on earth and as such, the historical and cultural distance between Australia and Indonesia is vast and plays into the definition of Asian 'other' ingrained in Australian society[4] and Strategic Culture. This distance lies in tension with the incremental growth in shared security interests, which may provide the bridge to closer relations as the implications of the rise of China become more apparent. However, despite rising tensions in the South China Sea, Indonesia has resisted identifying China as a threat due to Indonesia's own unique Strategic Culture of independence and non-interference, as well as its growing trade interests with respect to China.[5] As such, there is little indication that the pattern of bilateral military diplomacy developed by Canberra and Jakarta in relation to counter-terrorism could be leveraged in relation to geopolitics. As with other areas of the relationship, there is potential for enhanced cooperation in this regard, but also the question of why the potential has not been realized to date.

Unrealized potential

The bilateral relationship has been characterized as having great potential for trade growth by generations of politicians, commentators and analysts,[6] but in reality, this potential is largely unrealized as the relationship remains pragmatic and transactional. As such, the focus of this chapter and the next is diplomacy and security rather than trade. Despite the Indonesian President Joko Widodo describing Australia as Indonesia's 'closest friend',[7] diplomatic relations regularly fluctuate between benign and diplomatically hostile, with public opinion in both states nearly always lagging well behind government attempts to build closer ties. It could *not* be said that Australians even characterize Indonesia as a neighbour,[8] the notable exception being disaster diplomacy where Australians respond generously.

Relations are regularly tested by events that are best described as diplomatic gaffes in Canberra, but Indonesia's reflexive defensive response escalates them into significant missteps.[9] This dynamic of slight and escalation is unique in Australia's foreign relations, highlighting both a blind spot in Australian foreign policy (AFP) in relation to Indonesia's interests and Jakarta's heightened sensitivity to actions that it interprets as impinging on its sovereignty. A prime example of this occurred in 2004 with Australia's unilateral declaration of a 1,000 nautical mile maritime identification zone that included Indonesian waters. Predictably, Jakarta viewed the declaration as an infringement of sovereignty, which led to diplomatic protests and a souring of relations.[10] Similarly, Canberra's 2009 agreement to allow US troops to rotate through Darwin had the unintended consequence of impacting on Indonesia's strategic interests with fears that the forces could be used to respond to tension in West Papua and to protect the US Freeport mine if it was threatened by a civil disturbance.[11] Finally, Canberra's announcement of the AUKUS nuclear submarine agreement in 2021 shocked Jakarta into action with respect to its longstanding support for nuclear non-proliferation. These sorts of diplomatic blind spots largely defy theorization in relation to Realism or Liberal Internationalism and highlight Canberra's historical and cultural emphasis of the threat perceptions that characterize Strategic Culture.

The relationship is punctuated by regular crises. Indonesia's sensitivity to regular Australian actions that might reflect diplomatic clumsiness rather than challenges to sovereignty impacts what could generally be seen as benign, if not warm, relations. What is more interesting is that these diplomatic spats often occur publicly – a public gaffe by Australia is followed by a public rebuke by Indonesia. This dynamic is worthy of scrutiny, as despite close geographic proximity, the generally benign relationship has not been close or based on mutual affinity. Furthermore, despite recurrent tension, the underlying relationship has proved to be quite resilient.[12] These trends are more significant given largely unrealized potential for mutual benefits to be gained from the close relations that many Indonesianists in Australia regularly proclaim.

The fact that there has been a vocal Indonesia lobby in Australia is an important aspect of relations that also deserves scrutiny due to the persistence of cultural distance; it appears that elite-led advocacy and initiatives have failed to influence widely-held Strategic Cultural beliefs that identify Indonesia as a potentially threatening 'Asian other'. The necessity of shared culture and history to build affinity is absent in relations with Indonesia and human rights concerns reinforce this distance. Declaratory policy seeks to strengthen relations, but simultaneously government documents have identified a threat to Australia coming 'from or through'[13] Indonesia and public opinion has consistently identified Indonesia as a military threat.[14] Despite this persistent cultural barrier, the government's essentially Realist approach to enhancing security and economic cooperation through top-down institutionalization has failed to take root, although it has had the notable side effect of largely drowning out the human rights concerns of Liberal elites and public opinion. While a similar trade-off is evident regarding trade and human rights in relation to China, with China trade is far more significant and the threat perceptions in Canberra and the general population have shifted from nascent to real.

Two-way trade has grown in recent decades but remains moderate considering the proximity and complementarity of economies. This is surprising given the growth in Indonesia's economy and predictions that it will be the fourth largest economy by 2050.[15] Australian businesses have generally missed out on capitalizing on Indonesia's growth, largely of their own accord. Bilateral trade has also not been immune to the fallout of the regular diplomatic fractures between the two neighbours, a prime example being Prime Minister Julia Gillard's 2015 ban on live cattle exports due to questions over animal welfare. There has been a level of economic cooperation and collaboration through regional and international organizations and, in the absence of other bilateral measures, this international collaboration could be seen as a defining characteristic of relations even if it has not delivered the expected bilateral trade volumes.

Bilateral security relations are similarly benign with a declaratory focus on avoiding significant sovereignty gaffes and an operational focus on countering fundamentalist terrorism and transnational crime (especially in relation to human trafficking). Australia and Indonesia have developed shared security interests in both the 'War on Terror' on their doorsteps and managing asylum seekers, leading to unprecedented defence/security cooperation.[16] Border security is a sovereignty issue for Indonesia and as much a cultural and economic issue for Australia, reinforcing the sense of differing interests. Furthermore, when talk of potential turns to security relations, there is a nascent coincidence of interests in relation to managing an increasingly confident rising China that is gaining more emphasis. However, Jakarta's approach and strategy in relation to China's rise has been very different to Australia's insofar as China has not been openly identified as a potential military threat, so a word of caution is required.[17] Jakarta has been concerned with Chinese incursions in the Natuna Sea and the Joint Statement from Widodo's 2020 visit to Australia noted 'serious concerns about developments

158   AUSTRALIAN FOREIGN POLICY

in the South China Sea, including the continued militarisation of disputed features'.[18]

A distinctive aspect of this chapter and the next is that they engage with the persistent advocacy that argues that relations with Indonesia *should* be closer, and that despite it not occurring to date, this potential *will* be realized. This has been a regular refrain for decades. The fact that the potential has not been realized indicates that there is inherent tension in the bilateral relationship and, potentially, in how we analyse and theorize it. In particular, the largely Realist triumph over Liberal Internationalist values in the relationship and focus on trade potential is worthy of emphasis. Therefore, the question of why relations are not closer will be a recurring theme. A pluralistic theoretical approach will be applied critically to reflect on the distance between Australia and Indonesia.[19] However, at the outset it must be noted that unlike other relationships, Strategic Culture does not provide a convincing explanation for relations and it seems that the influence of geographic proximity is a unique variable that has been under-theorized. Beyond 'high' theory, scholars of comparative politics use a 'conditions of cooperation' framework whereby similarities in history, politics and extensive economic collaboration are considered to create an enabling environment for cooperation.[20] This contention is worth examining as it may provide insights into why relations are distant and highlight the value of shared security interests in building closer ties.

At several points in recent memory, relations with Indonesia have been at the forefront of Australian foreign policy, but otherwise attention has been sporadic and fits several identifiable historical patterns. Namely, the exigencies of geographic proximity tempered by political and economic distance, increased securitization of relations, and slight and escalation in public diplomacy leading to highly institutionalized 'top-down' initiatives to repair relations.

Historical background: The institutionalization of sensitivity to Indonesian sovereignty

Before Indonesia's independence, the East Indies was the imperial possession of the Netherlands, a key competitor to the British Empire in the Asia-Pacific region. Before Australia's independence in 1901, the imperial possessions and trading houses of other European empires formed the basis of threat perceptions, and the East Indies straddled strategic sea routes between Australia and other British outposts in the region, in particular the naval base in Singapore. Trade was the key to strategic cooperation and the Dutch East India and British East India companies competed to extract resources from the colonies. This means that in sharp contrast to Australia's diplomatic relationships with China, the South Pacific and the US, Indonesia is unique in that the threat from the Dutch Empire prior to federation in 1901. Furthermore, perceptions of threat from Japanese forces in the Dutch East Indies during the Second World War had a formative influence on threat perceptions from the 'north' that characterize Strategic Culture, and this may at least partially explain the tension that appears inherent in the contemporary diplomatic relationship.

BACKGROUND TO INDONESIA

While the British Empire gradually became more powerful and acquired several Dutch possessions, the East Indies remained a valuable outpost for the Dutch. During the Second World War, the Japanese invaded the East Indies in 1941 and defeated the Allies by early 1942. As with Singapore, Allied forces were overwhelmed, destroyed or captured, with remnants of the Dutch colonial administration operating from Australian territory for the duration of the war. The Japanese occupation prevented Allied forces from occupying staging points to participate in key battles to the north and provided natural resources to support the Japanese war effort. As such, the Japanese invasion and occupation was a key element making 1942 a liminal year for Canberra.[21] The significance of 1942 is discussed in detail in Chapter 3. Suffice to say, battles in and around the Indonesian archipelago and what was then known as Papua and New Guinea symbolized Australia's battle for survival, and bitter fighting in Dutch and Portuguese Timor and Kokoda have a central place in Australian military history and its national image.

Ultimately, the Japanese were defeated, but in the process Dutch control over the East Indies had been terminally weakened. In 1945, Indonesian nationalist forces challenged Dutch sovereignty by fighting for independence while Allied powers attempted to manage a peaceful transition from Japanese rule. Australia diplomatically intervened and strongly supported a negotiated settlement through the UN whereby Indonesia gained independence in 1949. This settlement did not include Netherlands New Guinea or Portuguese East Timor, but these were incorporated by Jakarta into Indonesia, in 1969 and 1975 respectively. However, these annexations did not receive strong support in Canberra and divisions over the balance between supporting either the stability of the Indonesian nation or human rights/self-determination of ethnic groups provided the basis for future tension between Realists and Liberal Internationalists, and between pro- and anti-Indonesia lobbyists within and outside the Australian government and academia.

Canberra's embrace of the US Domino Theory in the Cold War came close to home with the rise of Communism in Indonesia in the 1960s. The Domino Theory posited that Communist insurgencies would cause the downfall of Asian states and lead to them toppling like dominos lined up in a row.[22] An attempted coup in 1965 prompted a violent purge by the Indonesian army of Communists and leftists. Approximately half a million people were killed, President Sukarno was toppled, and General Suharto took control and subsequently led the country for three decades. While Australia did not actively support the killings, Canberra has been accused of being complicit, with Prime Minister Harold Holt reportedly commenting: 'With 500,000 to 1 million Communist sympathisers knocked off, I think it is safe to assume a reorientation has taken place.'[23] Suharto's overthrow of Sukarno and his staunch anti-Communism identified him as someone that Canberra (and Washington) could work with. Sukarno's removal was perceived to be in Australia's interests as he was associated with the Communists and had supported a confrontation in Borneo in 1962 over the formation of Malaysia, which saw Australian and Indonesian military forces engage in active combat, including Australian special forces operating clandestinely within Indonesian territory.[24]

The dynamic of slight and escalation

During Suharto's long 30-year rule, the dynamic of slight and escalation first became a characteristic of the bilateral relationship. Maintaining strong relations was clearly seen as being in Australia's national interests by successive prime ministers, but events such as the West Papua 'referendum' in 1969 and occupation of Portuguese East Timor in 1975 were viewed negatively by Australian public opinion, putting pressure on the bilateral relations.[25] The government's Realist approach to the national interest differed from the public's Liberal Internationalist attitudes on human rights and self-determination, and Australian media reportage of abuses often inflamed the situation. For instance, press allegations of corruption levelled against members of Suharto's family in the mid-1980s caused a significant rift. This pattern of a slight on Australia's part followed by an escalation by Indonesia was repeated regularly, and in particular in relation to human rights abuses such as the 1991 Santa Cruz massacre or 1998 referendum on independence in East Timor.

The 1991 Santa Cruz massacre (also known as the Dili massacre) had a profound impact on public perceptions of Indonesia in Australia, complicating foreign policy. In November 1991, a confrontation between Indonesian military forces and mourners (from a previous extra-judicial killing) quickly escalated when several hundred soldiers opened fire on protestors in the Santa Cruz cemetery in Dili, East Timor. Estimates of deaths vary widely from 50 to 250, with an equal number of people wounded or 'disappeared'.[26] The Australian public was sensitive to human rights abuses in Timor for several reasons, not least of which were the historical connection to the Timorese through resistance to Japanese occupation in the Second World War, the existence of a large and vocal diaspora population in Australia, and lingering mistrust over the contentious deaths of Australian journalists during the Indonesian occupation in 1975. Furthermore, it has been estimated that tens of thousands of Timorese were killed or 'disappeared' during the Indonesian occupation from 1975,[27] which sat uneasily with the Liberal Internationalist values expressed by many Australians.[28]

Public opinion was critical of the Indonesian military's treatment of civilians, but the government's responses were muted. Successive governments were also less vocal in relation to international condemnation from other states. The scale of the Dili massacre, and the fact that it was witnessed and filmed by international press and other observers, made it difficult to ignore, but this was the approach taken by Canberra unless there was no other alternative. It could be argued that this response reflects a Realist preference for non-interference in domestic issues, but equally it was judged not to be in Australia's interests to fracture relations with its nearest Asian neighbour.

The public response to the Santa Cruz massacre was too difficult for the Australian government to ignore, but the response was half-hearted at best. Other than a few condemnatory declaratory statements, the government walked a tightrope designed to not fall foul of Jakarta, which opened itself to charges of appeasement. Stability was valued over human rights,[29] no matter how uncomfortable this made some elements in the Labor Party government. Prime

BACKGROUND TO INDONESIA

Minister Paul Keating noted at the time that it was 'an appalling lapse of control by individual security forces on the ground in Dili rather than deliberate policy instructions from Jakarta'.[30] Foreign Minister Gareth Evans succinctly repeated the position that it was 'an aberration, not an act of state policy'.[31] This approach to downplaying human rights violations followed consistent denials from the Fraser government when East Timor was invaded and only lost currency amongst Australian leaders, albeit briefly, when the militia-backed violence after the independence referendum in 1998 escalated. The approach of successive governments supported longstanding criticisms of appeasement in relation to human rights violations in East Timor and West Papua.[32] Canberra's withering response to human rights violations can be contrasted with Indonesia's reflexive defence of its sovereignty, but both responses highlight the Realism that drove policy in both capitals.

Military diplomacy and security institutionalization to the backdrop of human rights violations

Against the backdrop of human rights violations, successive governments encouraged military diplomacy between the Australian Defence Force (ADF) and Tentara Nasional Indonesia (TNI) – or Indonesian National Military. While defence cooperation had grown throughout the 1980s. it took until 1995 to see security cooperation institutionalized. The Keating government's Agreement on Maintaining Security (AMS) was signed in 1995. The AMS was controversial insofar as it was secretly negotiated, testament to the sensitivities in Australia about defence cooperation.

With the memory of the fallout of the Santa Cruz massacre barely faded, the Mantiri affair erupted in 1994: an Indonesian general who appeared to condone the massacre was proposed as the incoming Indonesian ambassador to Australia. The public furore eventually caused the nomination to be withdrawn, but not before media attention and vocal public protest had soured bilateral relations. The Mantiri affair led to an escalation with regard to Jakarta's 'tit for tat' response in the nomination of Australian ambassadorial candidates, yet also provided the context within which the AMS could be seen as a demonstration of relations being repaired. This event highlights a pattern of negotiating declaratory initiatives to institutionalize initiatives (usually by Australia) that could repair relations. This pattern is repeated often in the turbulent relationship and it will a key point of interest in the coming decades as Indonesia surpasses Australia economically.

Essentially, the AMS provided a framework within which existing defence cooperation could be formalized and extended. It facilitated the parties providing declaratory support in times of threat, but did not compel binding action beyond consultation if 'adverse challenges' were faced by either party. The secrecy of the negotiations and focus on 'adverse challenges' was controversial in Australia because they could be interpreted as being *internal* challenges, such as in East Timor and West Papua, and politicians and commentators alike pointed to the diplomatic problems this might cause in relation to further suppression of human rights. Alternative wording, such as the inclusion of 'external' in the phrase, was proposed as being more appropriate after the text was released and the lack of parliamentary scrutiny in Australia imposed by the secrecy of negotiations might be blamed for this ambiguity,[33] which came into stark relief when violence erupted during the 1998 East Timor crisis.

Despite the controversy and its non-binding nature, the AMS was strategically significant as it was Indonesia's first bilateral security agreement. The AMS signalled a minor redefinition of the post-independence focus on the Non-Aligned Movement (NAM) and ASEAN and a growing awareness of more challenging security issues in the post-Cold War environment, particularly in relation to managing the rise of China.[34] The NAM was created by states that wanted to avoid the divisive and dangerous aspects of the bipolar divide of the Cold War, where warring camps faced off in a geostrategic conflict that bound them to take 'sides'. Indonesia's Strategic Culture elevates diplomatic independence as a key national interest.[35]

Indonesia had undertaken defence cooperation but eschewed any form of alliance entanglements, and while the AMS was not an alliance, it did institutionalize responses to shared threats. Given Indonesia's membership of NAM and sensitivity over sovereignty issues, bilateral security cooperation was destined to develop slowly and spasmodically. By contrast, for Australia it completed a ring of agreements with all its close neighbours and provided some continuity in security relations in the event of President Suharto leaving office. This occurred in 1998, but the AMS did not survive the 'betrayal' felt by Indonesia over Australia's leading role in the Timor independence referendum and subsequent International Force in East Timor (INTERFET) operation in 1999.

Australia's 'betrayal' over East Timor (1998–99)

Australia's role in East Timor's independence is the single most significant event in bilateral relations with Indonesia. Furthermore, the impacts of the 'betrayal' are never far from the surface of relations to this day. There is debate over whether Canberra could have predicted that Prime Minister's John Howard's letter to President B.J. Habibie suggesting that greater autonomy options for East Timor should be canvassed would lead to independence. Even if it was an unintended consequence, the 1998 'Howard letter' provided the spark at a time when Indonesia was vulnerable due to the post-Suharto transition to democracy.

BOX 9.1: THE HOWARD LETTER (1998)

- Sent by Prime Minister John Howard to President B.J. Habibie.
- Ostensible aim to resolve diplomatic tension in Australia–Indonesia relations by resolving status of Timor in Indonesia.
- Context of ongoing political tension in East Timor.
- Delivered at a time of domestic upheaval in Indonesia after the fall of Suharto.
- Rather than securing more autonomy for Timor within Indonesia, a referendum led to independence.
- Significant source of tension in relations with Canberra.

BOX 9.2: INTERNATIONAL FORCE EAST TIMOR (INTERFET), SEPTEMBER 1999

- An ad hoc peacekeeping mission formed in response to violence that occurred during the UN-brokered East Timor Special Autonomy Referendum.
- International condemnation of violence by Indonesian-backed militias prompted intervention.
- A UN-approved but not UN-led peace-making mission.
- John Howard offered to the UN that Australia would lead the operation
- Multinational force overwhelmingly formed by Australians with contingents from 22 states.
- Insecurity about how Indonesian military and militias would react, but order was quickly restored.
- Caused significant breach in relations.
- Often used by critics of the US alliance to claim that the US did not materially support the Australian intervention, but significant naval assets were involved, rather than 'boots on the ground'.

As Indonesia moved towards an independence referendum in East Timor, violence and intimidation occurred but was effectively ignored by Canberra. However, once the overwhelming vote in favour of independence was announced, the violence escalated and this demanded a response. While human rights violations were undoubtably occurring in East Timor, the pressure on the government from the Australian media and public opinion was a decisive factor that forced Canberra's hand. This highlights the recurring theme also evidenced in relation to asylum seekers and climate change, whereby the rights or welfare of non-citizens are not the main factor influencing AFP.

Australia eventually led a peace-making mission which owed much of its initial success to the longstanding military-diplomatic relations that had been built between the ADF and TNI over previous decades. The worst-case scenario of open conflict between Indonesia and Australia was averted, but the diplomatic damage was done. Australia's 'reluctant' involvement and intervention was a direct challenge to Indonesian sovereignty, which is why it impacts relations to this day. The Australian Parliament has described the situation as a 'complex misunderstanding',[36] but this is an extreme understatement that highlights the persistence of the dynamic of slight and escalation in relations. Regardless of whether Australia was a 'reluctant saviour' for the Timorese, as critics claim,[37] it was entirely predictable that any attempt to influence Indonesian domestic affairs would be seen by Jakarta as meddling and would be met with resistance that would likely cause a breach in relations.

The Bali bombings and the identification of shared
threat perceptions (2002)

The terrorist bombings in Bali in October 2002 brought the 'War on Terror' to Australia's neighbourhood. The carnage caused outrage in Australia and prompted the government to increase counter-terrorism cooperation with Indonesia. Cooperation included a dramatic increase in official development assistance (ODA) and collaboration led to easing tensions between Canberra and Jakarta. As such, the Bali bombings are an important watershed in Australia–Indonesia relations and AFP. The bombing of nightclubs frequented by foreigners, especially Australians, was viewed by many as an attack on Australia itself as Bali had long been a playground for tourists looking for a cheap holiday. Of the 202 people killed in the attacks, 88 were Australian and 38 were Indonesian.

For Indonesia, the attacks symbolized the rise of a potent internal threat to sovereignty (stability and territorial integrity), which is a sensitive issue in Indonesian Strategic Culture.[38] For Jakarta, the bombings had a significant economic impact as Bali was a tourist conduit to developed countries and a major source of foreign exchange. For Canberra, they highlighted the threat to citizens in the region. The bombings shocked ordinary Australians as many had holidayed in Bali and the bombings galvanized public opinion in support of the 'War on Terror' internationally. This response to instability in Australia's neighbourhood was reminiscent of the response to the Domino Theory during the Cold War, with Islamic fundamentalist terrorism replacing Communism as the amorphous threat from the 'alien' 'north'. As with the rise of Suharto's anti-Communism during the Cold War, Jakarta's response to the bombings identified Indonesia as an ally in meeting this new threat. As such, military diplomacy was a familiar tool that Canberra used to strengthen the counter-terrorism capacity of the Indonesian military. Again, the maintenance of regional stability was Australia's primary national interest and it overshadowed lingering concerns about the TNI's human rights record, which had the potential to become a diplomatic issue with respect to the independence movement in West Papua.

During the subsequent joint investigation, the Bali bombers were adamant that they were not specifically targeting Australians, but rather Americans, and this was supported by the simultaneous bombing of the US Consulate. Osama Bin Laden's statement that the attacks were retribution for Canberra taking the lead with respect to the INTERFET intervention in East Timor appeared to confirm Australia's fears. However, this threat can be discounted as an opportunist attempt to globalize the terrorist threat by connecting Jemaah Islamiyah in Indonesia with Al-Qaeda's global campaign against the West.

The bombings were primarily a locally led internal threat to Indonesian sovereignty, and while Canberra may have associated the them with the global 'War on Terror' that it had wholeheartedly joined after the 9/11 attacks on the US in 2001, Indonesia viewed them as an internal threat to national cohesion, akin to others in areas such as Aceh and West Papua. As such, they stoked fears in Jakarta with respect to the internal cohesion of Indonesia. Therefore, despite Australia and Indonesia having different motives, protecting sovereignty was elevated in both capitals as they viewed the terrorist threat through a narrow Realist lens of threats to sovereignty.

Counter-terror collaboration between Australia and Indonesia had already been steadily increasing since the 9/11 attacks on the US. The Bali bombings were a catalyst to closer cooperation, further eroding the remaining animosity in Jakarta with respect to Australia leading the INTERFET intervention in East Timor. Australia and Indonesia worked extremely closely together on the investigation and subsequently developed comprehensive counter-terrorism cooperation. The target of the threat may have been viewed differently in Canberra and Jakarta, but the shared nature of the threat was clear. This securitization and militarization of relations allowed shared threat perceptions to grow based on a shared terrorist enemy that replaced the Communist threat from the Cold War era. This highlighted Canberra's enduring national interest in fostering stability in Indonesia that sidelined Liberal Internationalist values in relation to human rights in general, and specifically sovereignty questions such as national self-determination in West Papua. The evolution in diplomatic cooperation also points to the possibility of closer relations developing if another shared threat presented itself, such as from an expansionist China.

The significance of the Bali bombings is different for the two states, but they did provide a catalyst to building closer relations. It may seem that fighting terrorism is the essence of this new bond, but the common denominator for both Canberra and Jakarta is the maintenance of stability in Indonesia. However, this resort to *Realpolitik* is the lowest common denominator in relations because it is narrowly focused on threats. It also highlights the dramatic cultural differences between the two neighbours in relation to Liberal Internationalist values because Indonesia's war on *domestic* terror is the latest example of sovereignty protection that has also allegedly involved questionable human rights practices. The legacy of the Bali bombings is also divisive: Bali continues to be a favoured Australian holiday destination, but the future of the bombing site has not been secured and differences in approaches to publicly memorializing the dead have become apparent.[39]

Howard's doctrine of pre-emption as a threat to Indonesia (2002)

The leadership of INTERFET in East Timor shows that Australia was not always so sensitive to Indonesia's sovereignty reinforcing the dynamic of slight and escalation. Prime Minister Howard's comments on pre-emption show that this lack of sensitivity was not an isolated example. In December 2002, soon after the Bali bombings, Howard stated that Australia could pre-emptively strike terrorist forces in another country if they posed an imminent threat. This was a reflection on the US intervention in Afghanistan as a response to the Taliban's unwillingness to cooperate against the Al-Qaeda forces operating there.

Not surprisingly, Howard's comments were viewed negatively in Indonesia (as well as in other Asian states). Jakarta warned that Australia had no right to pre-emption and should not flout international law by threatening to attack terrorists in neighbouring states. This incident is an example of Indonesia's sensitivity about sovereignty intersecting with Australia's exaggerated threat from the 'north'

BOX 9.3: THE US DOCTRINE OF PRE-EMPTION

- Policy elevated in White House's National Security Statement in 2002.
- A clear response to the Taliban providing safe haven to Al-Qaeda in preparing to attack the US on 11 September 2001.
- Argues that if a state or group within a state is going to attack the US, then the US is justified in pre-emptively attacking and neutralizing the threat.
- Does not have a sound basis in international law but can be justified by self-defence provisions of laws of war.
- The question is how to prove an imminent threat and who gets to decide?

and militarized foreign policy. Furthermore, the predictable offence that the comments would provoke was ignored, as were the implications for Australia's Liberal Internationalist support for a 'rules-based order' which pre-emption challenged.

In discussing pre-emption, Howard was following US President George W. Bush's lead in relation to the 'War on Terror' with respect to Al-Qaeda launching the 9/11 attacks from Afghanistan. Canberra's embrace of pre-emption highlighted differences in threat perceptions between Australia and Indonesia. Indonesia focused on domestic threats while Australia was concentrated on international threats, which could occur within Indonesia and could technically justify pre-emption if Jakarta was unable or unwilling to respond to them. This added a twist to the contentious strategic guidance from the 1960s that identified a threat to Australia coming 'from or through' Indonesia.[40]

The terrorist attacks in Bali continue to cast a shadow over bilateral relations and highlight both shared interests and the differences between Indonesia and Australia. The differences align with Indonesia being seen as an Asian 'other' in Strategic Culture. However, unlike Imperial Japan and Communist/Mercantilist China, Indonesia is on Australia's doorstep and this proximity counts. Proximity interrupts other influences on foreign policy, whether Realist, Liberal Internationalist or Strategic Cultural, and it has been under-theorized in AFP. Canberra and Indonesia cannot escape the fact that they are near neighbours, but that they have not built neighbourly relations.[41]

Australia's response to the Boxing Day tsunami as a bridge to closer relations (2004)

The importance of proximity was also evident in a very different way in the next significant event in bilateral relations. On Boxing Day in 2004, a tsunami struck the Indian Ocean region and Indonesia was the hardest hit, with over 160,000 deaths and countless casualties. Australian support was swift and responsive

BACKGROUND TO INDONESIA

involving the provision of critical resources such as medical supplies, clean water, and water purification and sanitation, but was also mindful of the need to support Jakarta in facing the long-term challenges ahead.[42]

Canberra's response was measured, providing A$68 million in emergency aid to tsunami-affected countries. In contrast, the Australian public donated A$313 million, with A$42 million through CARE Australia alone. The public response was noted in Canberra, providing a clear signal that more needed to be done to assist a proximate neighbour. The government then provided a five-year, A$1 billion reconstruction fund to Jakarta through the Australia–Indonesia Partnership for Reconstruction and Development (AIPRD). Australia was the second largest donor to tsunami-affected states after the US and the majority of government and private donations were earmarked for Indonesia. The swift response by the people and Government of Australia to the tsunami, and the design of relief efforts to be sensitive to Indonesian sovereignty concerns, ensured that relations were back on an even keel.

West Papuan asylum seekers as a wedge in relations (2006)

There were regular irritants in the bilateral relationship that conformed to the dynamic of slight and escalation that framed diplomacy. Another such significant divisive event was the arrival of 43 West Papuan asylum seekers in Queensland in January 2006. The group was quickly found to have valid claims to refugee status and was provided with protection visas and settled in Australia. This response caused a rift in relations because by acknowledging a reasonable fear of persecution (as defined by the UN Refugee Convention), the government appeared to be criticizing Indonesia's treatment of West Papuan independence activists.

Predictably, Jakarta was not pleased with Canberra's actions in granting refugee status. Sensitivities were such that when criticized by Jakarta, the Australian prime minister deflected the decision onto the bureaucrats in the Immigration Department. The prime minster tried to avoid the political storm and in a compromise for Jakarta, quietly agreed to process future arrivals offshore. Given Indonesia's sensitivity over sovereignty, any question of Canberra supporting self-determination in West Papua was destined to disrupt relations. That the asylum seekers were quickly found to have valid grounds for fearing persecution is evidence of Liberal Internationalist ethics in Australia's domestic policy, but the tenuous position of West Papua in AFP has not been tested recently.

In privileging maintaining stability in relations with Jakarta instead of defending human rights, Canberra identified its core national interests while responding to Indonesia's sensitivity to sovereignty challenges. This case study and the others presented here highlight that Australia's support for military intervention to support national self-determination in East Timor could be seen as an aberration rather than a norm characterizing relations. This approach conformed closely with the *Realpolitik* that characterises classical Realism. The stability of Indonesia is Australia's prime interest and as such, assisting Indonesia in protecting its sovereignty is prime. This approach rationalized courting President Suharto despite ongoing human rights concerns and downplaying numerous breaches of human rights conventions in Timor or West Papua.

Realpolitik, sovereignty, liberal rights, human rights and media freedom

Canberra's inconsistent and withering response to human rights abuses in Indonesia is telling. It reveals a tension particularly within the Australian Labor Party over the balance to be struck between Liberal Internationalist values central to party ideology and *Realpolitik* in international affairs, where national interests are privileged over values. The national interest defined in these narrow Realist terms focuses on defending the Australian state and protecting and improving the welfare of Australian citizens. If need be, the welfare of non-Australians can be defined as a secondary priority and this is precisely how Australian governments have viewed the rights to self-determination of numerous groups within Indonesia.

Australia's free and vibrant press and domestic civil society groups have revealed the awkward truth about the priority successive governments have placed on stability in relations with Indonesia. On occasion, Indonesian attempts at maintaining domestic stability have shocked Australian and international public opinion and caused strains in bilateral relations. Unlike similar situations in China or Myanmar, this has led to a withering response from Australian policy-makers. Several diplomatic breaches have been directly attributable to investigative journalism. Examples include the allegations in the 1980s of corruption against President Suharto's family, the reportage of Indonesian-backed militias during East Timor's independence referendum in 1998, and coverage of the treatment of live cattle exports in 2011 that resurfaced in 2021. Other diplomatic gaffes have been exaggerated by press coverage and the ABC has been singled out for criticism by Indonesian politicians.[43]

The post-Suharto democratization of Indonesia from 2008 also led to a relaxation of media controls that has ensured that increasing media freedom is cutting both ways. Jakarta recognized that there might be some 'pent up dissent' towards Australia that is now more freely expressed in Indonesia.[44] This is evident in protests where flag burning occurs, often in front of the Australian embassy in Jakarta. In the past, media would have been more likely to be used as an orchestrated voice of the government in public diplomacy, but the development of press freedom means that criticisms of Australia are more likely aimed at both Australia and the domestic Indonesian audience. Therefore, the long-standing action-reaction dynamic in relation to diplomatic gaffes and escalated responses can be more pronounced when local media inflames the situation.

The consistent response of successive governments in downplaying human rights issues in Indonesia highlights the triumph of *Realpolitik* over Liberal Internationalist values in AFP towards Indonesia. The 1999 INTERFET intervention to support Timorese independence by John Howard, a Liberal prime minister who would not have been predicted to have elevated Liberal Internationalist values in foreign policy, could be seen as a miscalculation with unintended consequences. Subsequent AFP in relation to West Papua and the institutionalization of sovereignty protecting bilateral agreements, such as the 1995 Agreement on Maintaining Security, 2006 Lombok Treaty and 2014 Joint

BACKGROUND TO INDONESIA

Understanding, highlight that Canberra's response to Timorese independence was an aberration rather than the norm. The East Timor intervention highlights that the most likely event that could force Canberra into taking decisive action would be a major human rights violation that is captured by the press and broadcast through Australian TV and social media.

Conclusion

What makes Australia's uneasy relationship with Indonesia more significant is that it is also about to be rebalanced, as Indonesia is predicted to overtake Australia economically and militarily in coming decades. As such, the confident vantage of superiority from which Canberra has viewed the regular rifts in relations will shift to one where Indonesia will dominate and how this shift will play out is unpredictable. From this perspective, analysts have argued that Australia needs to leverage off its strength to incorporate as much multilateral engagement it can in the relationship before the situation reverses.

The theme of the great potential for stronger relations permeates government documents and reviews, persisting despite may years of official efforts to bridge cultural gaps. The shallowness and patchiness of 'people-to-people' links is a reoccurring theme, as the Joint Committee of Foreign Affairs, Defence and Trade noted: 'At the political and people-to-people levels, the relationship needs considerable strengthening.'[45] The next chapter on present relations with Indonesia will explore this unrealized potential to the backdrop of the dynamic of slight and escalation that has loomed large in bilateral relations. The historical record on diplomatic relations highlights Canberra's focus on stability in relations and willingness to compromise on human rights norms; whether this tension can be sustained is also worthy of further scrutiny.

10

Indonesia:
Proximity and the unrealizable
potential of dissimilar neighbours

Introduction

> Of all the important interests that Australia and Indonesia share, none is more significant than their shared interest in security, a reality brought home in one resounding blow by the Bali bombing in October 2002. This shared interest alone is a compelling reason for being good neighbours. Notwithstanding this, it needs to be noted that it is quite clear that there are factors such as events in East Timor which play as heavily on the minds of Indonesia when contemplating the bilateral relationship as Bali does for both of us.[1]

The sober appraisal of the Australian Joint Committee of Foreign Affairs, Defence and Trade is sidestepped by the government's optimistic declaratory policy.

Geographic proximity has always been the founding rationale for diplomacy between Australia and Indonesia. However, geography has no ideology and was not enough to overcome Australia's Strategic Cultural fear of Asia. Cold War security cooperation with President Suharto's Indonesia brought the two neighbours together based on shared anti-Communism which drove the relationship. Of course, these shared interests could not outlast the fall of Communism in 1989 and over time, shared interests morphed into combatting Islamic fundamentalist terrorism. The evolution in relations from anti-Communism to counter-terrorism forms a key backdrop to this chapter, as does the challenges that China poses to the Indo-Pacific and 'rules-based order' more generally.

Key thematic questions addressed in the chapter build on the background provided in Chapter 9. A significant question framing bilateral relations is: as relations mature will Canberra and Jakarta outgrow the historical dynamic of slight and escalation? What does the priority afforded to stable relations with Indonesia say about the place of Liberal Internationalist values in AFP? How can the tensions between public opinion toward human rights and national interests be reconciled? Why is the potential for closer relations never realised? Will the rise of China be the catalyst to realise the potential of closer relations?

The Comprehensive Strategic Partnership (2005–)

Successive governments have identified the potential for closer relations to develop, but do not openly question why this has not come to pass. The centrepiece of bilateral relations is the Joint Declaration on a Comprehensive Strategic Partnership (CSP) between Australia and the Republic of Indonesia. The CSP was signed in 2005 and renewed in 2018. The 2018 preamble notes:

> Our historical ties are deep – from Makassan seafarers trading with the Aboriginal peoples of northern Australia centuries ago, to Australia's support for Indonesia's quest for independence in the 1940s ... We have supported each other in times of adversity: through the bombings in Bali in 2002, the tsunami in Aceh in 2004 and the bushfires in Victoria in 2009 ... Our Comprehensive Strategic Partnership builds on the 2006 Lombok Treaty, a cornerstone of the relationship underscoring our support for the sovereignty, territorial integrity, national unity and political independence of each nation.[2]

The CSP prioritizes trade, 'people-to-people' links, and shared national and regional security interests. The 2005 version asserts that Australia and Indonesia are 'close neighbours and friends', but while the former is irrefutable, the latter is questionable. Despite declaratory statements such as this, the shallowness of 'people-to-people' links and trade can be juxtaposed with security interests to highlight the key weaknesses and strengths in the relationship, and these form the basis of the rest of this chapter.

Bilateral security institutionalization and cooperation as a tool for normalizing fractured relations

> The Bali bombings of 12 October 2002 brought home to both Indonesia and Australia, devastatingly and unmistakably, how closely the interests of both countries lie.[3]

Canberra's response to the Bali bombing in 2002 and Boxing Day tsunami in 2004 cemented the path to normalized relations between Australia and Indonesia after the fracture caused by Australia's support for Timorese independence in 1998. Counter-terrorism is a shared interest, albeit with the two parties having different perspectives about the nature of the threat (whether it be primarily domestic and/or international). In recent years, the implications of the rise of China have also highlighted the existence of shared geostrategic interests akin to those that bound the relationship during the Cold War.

Bilateral defence cooperation has grown as a response to countering Islamic fundamentalist terrorism and transnational crime, especially in relation to human trafficking. Both the 2015 Indonesian and 2016 Australian Defence White Papers identified the importance of strengthening these shared interests.[4] More recently, maritime security aspects of the 'rules-based order' and the development of the Indo-Pacific as a frame to shape strategic outlooks have further solidified links.[5] As such, security, more than economics or cultural links, provides the glue that

172   AUSTRALIAN FOREIGN POLICY

holds the relationship together and the significance of shared security interests is increasing.

The level of bilateral defence cooperation is not widely publicized, but joint maritime and land exercises occur each year, as do small-scale training activities and reciprocal attendance at defence colleges. Of particular note is the training of Indonesian special forces by Australian special forces, which has occurred for over 25 years. Military diplomacy of this sort has been institutionalized through the Indonesian-Australian Defence Alumni Association, which has over 2,000 members. One area of cooperation that was a cause of concern during the Cold War was the training of Indonesian special forces by Australia's Special Air Service (SAS). This is noteworthy as these forces are Indonesia's most highly trained and capable have been accused of alleged human rights abuses in Timor, West Papua and elsewhere. Canberra has been criticized for this aspect of defence diplomacy, but it has not stopped. More recently, post-Bali bombings Australia (and the US) has funded Indonesia's specialist counter-terrorist unit (Detachment 88), which has been extremely effective in neutralizing terrorist threats to Indonesia.

Indonesia's non-alignment and defence cooperation

Defence cooperation has occurred to the backdrop of Indonesia's longstanding membership of the Non-Aligned Movement (NAM) and Association of Southeast Asian Nations (ASEAN). Both of these organizations privilege a Realist version of sovereignty, territorial integrity and the principle of non-interference in domestic affairs. As such, Liberal Internationalist values in relation to human rights are not considered priorities in national or international affairs. Given this context, the increasing level of institutionalized security cooperation with Australia is testament to both the strength of mutual security interests and Canberra's recent success in not impinging upon Indonesian sensitivities surrounding sovereignty and territorial integrity. Canberra would prefer that the dynamic of slight and escalation, whereby Australia's responses to issues such as East Timorese independence fractured relations, was consigned to history.

The Australian government was at pains to highlight the fact that formal defence relations did not collapse in the aftermath of the INTERFET intervention in East Timor from 1999. This was also the case during the Indonesia-Malaysian confrontation in the 1960s, when Australian and Indonesian forces were involved in active combat against one another in Borneo. Military diplomacy did not collapse, but shots were fired. This highlights a level of pragmatism evident in public diplomacy that can be ascribed to the reality of two states coexisting in close proximity. This pragmatism aligns with Australia's emphasis on maintaining stability in relations. However, it can sit uneasily with respect to Indonesia's sensitivity over sovereignty that is regularly exhibited in the diplomatic dynamic of slight and escalation.

A prime example of the potential for tension based on differing strategic outlooks is the AUKUS agreement of 2021. AUKUS was a response to Australia's insecurity over the rise of China, but Indonesia believes that acquiring nuclear submarines will lead to greater regional instability.

Canberra did not consult with Indonesia, and this would not be expected of such a sensitive agreement. However, when Indonesia was notified just prior to the public announcement, it was clear that Jakarta had some concerns. These concerns focused on the potential for a nuclear accident, as submarines often transit unseen through the Indonesian archipelago, and concerns about the impact on the non-proliferation of nuclear technology and weapons.

Mixed diplomatic messages came from Jakarta culminating in representations to the UN Non-Proliferation review conference. Canberra responded to Indonesia's concerns and made a submission to the conference. The outcome was that greater transparency and oversight was needed on the transfer of nuclear submarine technology, but the practical impact of this is unclear. Meanwhile, the AUKUS partners are accelerating cooperation, which will likely see increased US and UK nuclear submarine activity in the region.

The Lombok Treaty and non-interference in sovereign affairs

Bilateral security communiques routinely reference the importance of the 2006 Lombok Treaty. The Agreement Between the Republic of Indonesia and Australia on the Framework for Security Cooperation (known as the 'Lombok Treaty') was Prime Minister Howard's attempt to realign diplomacy after the East Timor fracture in relations by reaffirming Indonesia's sovereignty. The key element of the Lombok Treaty was non-interference in each party's sovereign affairs. As noted, sovereignty issues are a key sensitivity in the relationship and the trigger for many diplomatic slights. Post-Timor, the most notable challenge for Indonesia is pressure for self-determination in West Papua and Canberra's resolve has been regularly tested by press reports on human rights obligations. This has led to extreme sensitivity on Australia's part.

In this context, the Lombok Treaty can be seen as a bilateral version of the non-interference provisions of the ASEAN Treaty of Amity and Cooperation (TAC) that form a centrepiece of Indonesian foreign policy. There is debate over whether the Lombok Treaty prohibits Australian responses to human rights issues in Indonesia as Indonesian policy-makers attest.[6] However, in practice successive Australian governments have navigated a careful path whereby human rights issues are not completely ignored, but are also not publicly mentioned and any reference to sovereignty is sacrosanct.

Spying and sovereignty

The 2014 Joint Understanding on a Code of Conduct[7] prohibiting intelligence gathering against one another was the Australian government's attempt to assuage Indonesia after spying revelations. In 2013, leaked Australian Signals Directorate (ASD) files identified a strategy of tapping the Indonesian President and senior cabinet ministers' phones. This caused publicly vented irritation in Jakarta, especially when it was revealed that President Susilo Yudhoyono's wife was targeted, and this led to another cooling of relations. The Indonesian ambassador to Australia was recalled by Jakarta for seven months, ostensibly because Canberra would not engage with the allegations or openly prohibit further activity, and the

Joint Understanding was another example of an institutionalized response to the dynamic of slight and escalation in relations.

Military ties were suspended again in 2017 after complaints from Indonesian military personnel enrolled in Australian defence training programmes about 'inflammatory' course materials that referenced West Papua. However, the suspension seemed to be limited in nature rather than a full breach of the sort that occurred over the spying scandal of 2013. The statement by Indonesia's defence minister, Ryamizard Ryacudu, cautioning against allowing 'insignificant rats [to] disrupt the relationship between countries'[8] appeared to reveal that domestic politicking in Indonesia may be partially to blame for the diplomatic breach. Meanwhile, political leaders on both sides attempted to ease tension and the Joint Understanding was designed to help normalize relations during times of crisis.

Institutionalized defence cooperation

Institutionalization of defence cooperation has proceeded apace with approximately 15 high-level dialogues and 18 exercises occurring annually. High-level dialogues include the foreign and defence ministers' 2+2 meeting, the sub-regional defence ministers' Meeting on Counter-Terrorism and the ASEAN-Special Summit Counter-Terrorism Conference. The joint Memorandum of Understanding on Countering Terrorism and Violent Extremism was renewed in 2018 for another five years to coordinate activities in this area of central importance to both states. A key initiative in practical cooperation was the joint Jakarta Centre for Law Enforcement Cooperation (JCLEC), opened in 2004 in the wake of the Bali bombings. The JCLEC has trained over 28,000 officials from 80 regional states.

A renewed Australia–Indonesia Defence Cooperation Program (DCP) was signed in February 2018. Australia's new strategic focus on the Indo-Pacific concentrated on shared maritime security interests, challenges to the 'rules-based order' and the peaceful resolution of disputes through international law. The emphasis on norms of international law was a direct reference to agreements such as the 1982 United Nations Convention on the Law of the Sea (UNCLOS), and was aimed at China's actions in militarizing the South China Sea. As such, Australia's defence minister Linda Reynolds, noted that Australia and Indonesia 'both have a stake in managing growing strategic competition between great powers in the Indo-Pacific', and highlighted shared interests in countering 'a resurgence of terrorism and violent extremism',[9] thereby reinforcing the ongoing relevance of the key shared threat.

The renewed DCP came on the back of the Joint Declaration on Maritime Cooperation signed in February 2017, and the subsequent Maritime Cooperation Plan of Action. These agreements focus on maritime trade and developing greater maritime security interoperability. Significantly, the Plan of Action involved 'navy to navy cooperative activities, including assisting mutual efforts to combat transnational organised crimes committed at sea'.[10] This points to the importance of strong bilateral links to counter transnational crime, including the human trafficking of asylum seekers that is such a politically divisive issue

INDONESIA: PROXIMITY AND THE UNREALIZABLE POTENTIAL 175

in Australia (see Chapter 15) and cannot be effectively managed without Indonesian cooperation. It was also mooted that Australia and Indonesia would begin joint maritime patrols of the sort that Indonesia has developed with Malaysia and the Philippines in the Sulu Sea. Australia has also been keen to connect bilateral initiatives with Indonesia, such as the Cyber Policy Dialogue with ASEAN-Regional Forum (ARF) activities in areas such as the Inter-Sessional Meeting on ICT Security, which Indonesia hosted in late 2019.

Military diplomacy underpinning diplomatic tensions

As public diplomacy between Canberra and Jakarta has been regularly disrupted, military diplomacy has often acted to balance domestic pressures.[11] Military diplomacy has long been a key element of the relationship, not least because of the foundation of modern Indonesia as a military dictatorship.[12] From this perspective, close relations between Indonesian and Australian military officers at all levels deepens the development of personal relations at political levels. However, military diplomacy became more complex and fragile in the post-democratization, post-East Timorese independence era, when the influence of the military in government was reduced and when the *esprit de corps* between militaries was tested by Australia's leadership of INTERFET.

At times the defence relationship has been described as 'volatile',[13] which mirrors the longstanding dynamic of diplomatic slight and escalation and provides an insight into the health of foreign relations at any given time. Differences in the culture and role of the military in the two countries create the potential for misunderstanding and tension. While the defence relationship survived the most recent serious downturn in the bilateral relationship over the crisis in East Timor, it was damaged by it. It is an open question whether this damage was permanent. According to the Australian Department of Defence, 'the East Timor crisis reduced the level of mutual confidence in the defence relationship', which could only be slowly rebuilt even with the stimulus of the post-9/11 counter-terror cooperation.[14]

The emphasis on security institutionalization and military diplomacy has largely been driven by Australia and, in many respects, this continues a trend from the era when Indonesia was a military dictatorship. In declaratory statements, the governments often highlight that their extensive cooperation on counter-terrorism has been increasingly close since the Bali bombings in 2002. This cooperation has grown in breadth and complexity as new issues arose, such as the belief that terrorists were posing as asylum seekers (especially from Sri Lanka) and concerns over the impact of returning jihadis from the war in Syria. This security cooperation reflects shared threat perceptions akin to those against Communism in the Cold War. As maritime security cooperation continues to grow, it may be that managing the rise of China becomes another mutual security issue to bind relations. All of these issues align with a Realist conception of national interests, but if shared threat perceptions of China grow, then this issue would also reflect the longstanding threat from the 'north' that characterises in Strategic Culture. When combined with Jakarta's sensitivity to slight and reflexive escalation of diplomatic breaches, this essentially

176 AUSTRALIAN FOREIGN POLICY

Realist focus on stability in Canberra has limited the scope for an evolution in relations.

Joint regional security cooperation and institutionalization with Indonesia

The security emphasis of bilateral relations is reflected in joint regional security cooperation, but this is far less developed than bilateral cooperation. Furthermore, the sensitivity over Indonesia's human rights record and practices has limited the possibility of multilateral diplomatic cooperation on humanitarian issues through organizations such as the UN, which Australia undertakes with numerous states including Japan.

Australia is connected to Indonesia through the ARF, which was founded in 1994. The ARF brought together ASEAN members with dialogue members and observers to discuss regional security issues. The ARF is important for Australia as it allows engagement on security issues that would be considered too divisive for ASEAN itself, due to the respect for the TAC that limits interference in the domestic affairs of its member states. The ARF's focus on creating a regional security community and preventative security reflected Australia's priorities in the 1990s. This push to 'Asianize' Australia and Australian foreign policy was closely connected with the government of Prime Minister Paul Keating and Foreign Minister Gareth Evans, which activated the Labor party tradition of Liberal Internationalism,[15] but lost emphasis during the Howard years and never had any appreciable impact on Strategic Culture.

The ARF involvesd regular meetings of senior officials and a range of subsidiary meetings, which cover counter-terrorism and transnational crime, disaster relief, maritime security, and non-proliferation and disarmament. There is also a biennial exercise testing the capacity to respond to natural disasters. Canberra joined the ASEAN Defence Ministers' Meeting Plus (ADMM-Plus) in 2007. However, developing shared regional security interests with Indonesia and other Indo-Pacific states has proved elusive, as evidenced by inaction in crises such as that of the Rohingya refugees in Myanmar. The ARF has also not evolved to effectively manage recent challenges, such as the rise of China and militarization of the South China Sea.

The limits of institutionalized security cooperation with Indonesia

Australia and Indonesia collaborate instrumentally in regional fora and have acted to extend regionalism and develop regional architecture. In part, activities to extend regionalism are an outcome of Australia not being welcomed into ASEAN, which is Indonesia's (and South-East Asia's) premier forum for economic activity. Australian efforts to develop regional architecture have been sensitive to complement ASEAN or focus on areas that don't fit into its remit (trade institutionalization is covered separately below).

A prime example of a co-sponsored initiative is The Bali Process on People Smuggling, Trafficking in Persons and Related Transnational Crime. The Bali Process was developed in 2002 as a policy forum to raise awareness of human

INDONESIA: PROXIMITY AND THE UNREALIZABLE POTENTIAL

trafficking and develop responses to it. It involves 49 members made up of heavily impacted states, partner states, intergovernmental organizations and civil society groups. It is institutionalized through the Regional Support Office in Bangkok and operationalized through the Consultation Mechanism, Good Offices, Technical Experts Group and the Task Force on Planning and Preparedness. Indonesia hosted the Seventh Bali Process Ministerial Conference in August 2018, which reaffirmed the 2016 Bali Process Declaration on People Smuggling, Trafficking in Persons and Related Transnational Crime (2016 Bali Declaration).

Institutionalized security cooperation has grown significantly since the 'War on Terror' began in 2001, but it has largely been a top-down approach. Furthermore, the strength in relations relates to instrumental bilateral defence cooperation rather than collaborating with Indonesia to develop a regional approach to shared challenges. Despite the failure to convert the potential for closer relations into a reality, efforts have continued to cement closer links. Successive Australian governments and the elite-led Indonesia lobby in Australia regularly lamented the shallowness of cultural links and have attempted to engineer 'people-to-people' links through educational exchanges and official development assistance (ODA). This top-down approach highlighted Canberra's sensitivity to public opinion and the importance of taking a pragmatic approach to downplaying Indonesian human rights violations whilst recognizing Indonesian sensitivity to sovereignty issues.

Attempts to bridge the cultural divide

There are regular reminders of the cultural differences between Australia and Indonesia, such as the imposition of Sharia law in Aceh in 2001, or the new Criminal Code in 2022, but Indonesian human rights abuses have never been far from the surface of Australian public attitudes towards Indonesia. The reporting of the 1965–66 communist purge, where hundreds of thousands were killed, followed by numerous incidents in East Timor and West Papua, has produced a legacy of public ill-will that is difficult for the government to overcome. Canberra's prescription has been that 'people-to-people' links will bridge the cultural divide. A range of initiatives have been put in place to achieve this end, focusing on education, overseas development assistance and tourism; however, the cultural distance between both states is resistant to change.

Public opinion: somewhat less than friends

Public opinion provides an insight into just how fraught and dualistic the relationship is, expressing both a desire for stronger ties, and mistrust and threat.[16] This dualism had been a recurrent theme in public opinion, with Indonesia being seen as a military threat to Australia but at the same time a security partner collaborating to counter shared threats (from terrorism to human trafficking). Multiple polls over the last 30 years have identified Indonesia as a potential military threat to Australia; this only became a minority opinion in the last decade (as China rose in prominence).[17] This polling aligns neatly with concerns about indefensibility against threats from the 'north' that characterize Strategic Culture and highlights the difficulty in the government maintaining a pragmatic Realist approach to promoting stability in relations with Indonesia. These attitudes also stoke the Liberal Internationalist critique that pervades public opinion of downplaying human rights in Indonesia for the sake of maintaining good diplomatic relations.

Regular concern is expressed in government circles over 'the level of misunderstanding and even mistrust ... in the relationship', with the policy prescription being 'much better communication and much deeper understanding ... at both the political and at the people-to-people levels'.[18] At the level of public opinion, commentators have noted the 'mutual popular ignorance and misconception, with many Australians still seeing Indonesia as a potential aggressor, and many Indonesians' perceptions of Australia being limited to media coverage of flag burnings and myths about a continuing White Australia policy'.[19] Clearly, there is a low base from which the government has hoped to make inroads.

Australian public opinion on Indonesia is revealing and mirrors many of the tensions in the diplomatic relationship. Overall, Australians feel moderate 'warmth' towards Indonesia (at 57° on the Lowy Institute feelings thermometer), but until the very recent fallout in relations this is below China. It is well below traditional allies such as the UK (77°) or growing friends such as Japan (74°). This is up from a decade ago when the warmth towards Indonesia was below 50 per cent, but the rise has been slow.[20] Polls show similar but lower results for trust in whether Indonesia will act responsibility on the international stage.[21]

On the issue of friendship, no respondent in the 2022 Lowy Poll believed that Indonesia was Australia's best international friend, and this was behind China (one respondent). When the focus is narrowed to being a best friend in Asia, Indonesia is rated at 15 while Singapore is 21 and both are eclipsed by Japan with 43 respondents.[22] Friendship, warmth and trust are elusive and difficult to measure but these figures stand in sharp contrast to old friends such as the UK, allies such as the US and rising partners such as Japan. Despite the discussion of friendship in declaratory policy, the underlying feelings in Australia are quite different and this gulf has not been breached by decades of well-meaning focus on 'people-to-people' links.

A core reason for the lack of warmth towards Indonesia is reminders of cultural or political differences. This aligns with Strategic Culture, and has not evolved to account for changes in Indonesia over the last 20–30 years. For example, most Australians do not believe that Indonesia is a democracy and this attitude has persisted despite increasing coverage of recent Indonesian elections.[23] At the same time, there is a popular perception that trade with Indonesia is important to Australia, which matches the rhetoric of 'potential' used by the government and Indonesia lobby, but not the reality of day-to-day relations.

A key tension in the relationship is enduring perceptions of threat from Indonesia. This could change from a direct military threat to more specifically, an association with Communism during the Cold War and Islamic fundamentalist terrorism since 2001. For sizeable segments of the Australian population, Indonesia is viewed as an outright military threat, or an ideological/religious threat, while also being seen as a potential saviour in defending against a larger threat further afield.[24] There is hope and advocacy amongst some analysts that the balance can tip towards Indonesia being seen as an ally,[25] especially against China, but as it stands, this hope aligns with other arguments about potential that are yet to be realized.

Indonesia as an ally in the 'War on Terror'

On the significant issue of counter-terrorism, the belief that 'Indonesia is a dangerous source of violent Islamic terrorism' has declined from 54 per cent to 44 per cent over recent years, but 44 per cent of Australians disagree, so the population is neatly divided on this issue.[26] While 41 per cent think that 'the Indonesian government has worked hard to fight terrorism',[27] a sizeable proportion of Australians (32 per cent) disagree. Criticism about Indonesia's ability or willingness to confront Islamic fundamentalist terrorism highlights a significant gap between Australian perceptions and the reality of Indonesia, which is steadfast in its domestic war against terror. This gap is problematic insofar as counter-terrorism cooperation has been central to the growth of stronger bilateral relations over the last 15 years. If the relationship is viewed through a purely instrumental Realist lens, then Canberra's interest in the counter-terrorist credentials of the Indonesian government is important to counter domestic Liberal Internationalist concerns about human rights. However, government-led initiatives to strengthen security relations are not matched by public perceptions of the cost of compromising human rights in the name of *Realpolitik*.

Even with successes in counter-terrorism, the cultural difference with Indonesia has been regularly put on stark display in relation to the 'War on Terror'. A Senate Standing Committee found that: 'In a world where the issue of relationships between Muslim and non-Muslim countries is highly volatile, a solid relationship between Australia and Indonesia is of great value to Australia.'[28] The dynamic of slight and escalation has the potential to become more fraught for Canberra if it took on a religious tone. For Australia, the particular concern would be if there was a misunderstanding of Australia's intentions and a belief that it has 'a hostile view of the Islamic world or Indonesia's part in it'.[29] An example of the type of issue that could inflame Indonesia's Islamic sensitivities was the Morrison government's proposal to move the embassy in Israel to Jerusalem, which had religious undertones and had a significant negative impact on bilateral relations.

Media coverage in Indonesia and Australia

Australian coverage of Indonesia (and vice versa) in popular media is generally quite narrow and superficial. Despite being neighbours, proximity has not led to a high volume of reciprocal news coverage of shared interests in press reportage. In Australia, incidents of human rights violations, terrorist threats, natural disasters, Australian drug traffickers and animal cruelty dominate coverage of Indonesia. A particularly strong example is the 2011 ABC *Four Corners* exposé of the methods by which Australian live cattle exports were killed.[30] The public response caused Prime Minister Julia Gillard's government to ban exports with dramatic impacts throughout the industry in both Australia and Indonesia. This narrow and largely negative coverage of Indonesia is made worse through access to images of protesters being shot at in the Dili massacre, animals being killed with machetes or flag burning outside the Australian embassy. The Gillard government's response is another example of Liberal Internationalist values in Labor foreign policy intersecting with domestic public opinion.

Growing press freedom and the rise of social media in Indonesia is putting pressure on bilateral relations. For example, the Australian ambassador was questioned over Senator Fraser Anning's comments blaming Muslim immigration after the Christchurch Mosque massacre in March 2019.[31] While comments by a right-wing senator should not have been an issue, the depiction in the media of the Australian coat of arms behind the senator was misinterpreted in Indonesian social media as a sign of official Islamophobia and the Indonesian government believed that it needed to be countered.[32]

CASE STUDY 10.1: DRUG TRAFFICKING AND DEATH SENTENCES – PUBLIC OPINION, SOVEREIGNTY AND CULTURAL SENSITIVITY

Australia outlawed the death penalty in 1966 and has taken a stance against it in the international arena, especially in relation to sentences given to Australian drug smugglers. A particularly good example is the Barlow and Chambers executions in Malaysia in 1986. In such cases, senior Australian government ministers made bids for clemency that were unsuccessful and soured already-strained relations. However, the fate of the Bali terrorist bombers (2001) and Bali Nine drug smugglers (2005) put pressure on Canberra's commitment for several reasons, not least of which was the sensitivity to issues that could be perceived as undermining Indonesian sovereignty. President Joko Widodo pre-emptively stated that he would not approve clemencies, which made the situation more complex for Australian policy-makers.

BOX 10.1: THE BALI NINE DRUG SMUGGLERS

- A group of young casual catering employees from Sydney recruited by a drug syndicate to smuggle drugs.

- Australian Federal Police (AFP) became aware of the syndicate and surveilled planners in Sydney and on earlier trips to Bali.
- In April 2005, the AFP provides information to Indonesian authorities on nine alleged smugglers.
- Indonesian police surveil alleged smugglers and arrest them at airport bound for Australia.
- The group in possession of 8.3 kg of heroin – a capital crime in Indonesia.
- There is heightened public scrutiny of trial due to death sentences.
- Indonesian sovereignty of display with regards to death sentences for drug smuggling.
- Despite pleas for clemency, two Australians are executed by firing squad.

Another inconvenient factor in the Bali Nine case was the criticism that the Australian Federal Police (AFP) had shared information with Indonesian authorities that led to the arrests, rather than apprehending them on their return to Australia where they would not have faced the death penalty. This turn of events at least questioned the political judgement of the AFP insofar as Australian citizens were involved. However, public revulsion of the terrorist bombers and condemnation for the drug smugglers made the situation easier for the Australian government. Ultimately, the Bali bombers – Amrozi bin H. Nurhasyim, Ali (Murkhas) Ghufron and Imam Samudra – were executed in 2008 and two of the Bali Nine, Andrew Chan and Myuran Sukumaran, were executed in 2015.

The contrast with the prison sentences given to terrorists or drug smugglers is telling. For every person executed, many more are imprisoned, sometimes for lengthy sentences. As with the death penalty, public opinion has largely supported these sentences. In these cases, the Australian government has been happy to accept that justice has been done. However, the release of several of the Bali bombers early in their sentences had the potential to disrupt relations from the Australian side. For example, Umar Patek, a convicted bombmaker and member of Jemaah Islamiyah, was released very near the twenty-year anniversary of the bombings in December 2022. In these cases, the government publicly made diplomatic representations, but the tone was muted and was sensitive to both Australian public opinion and Indonesia's sovereignty concerns. As such, they did not trigger a slight in relations and stable diplomatic relations were maintained.

In none of these cases, were relations with Indonesia disrupted, therefore achieving the AFP's primary aim of maintaining stability. The executions led to some domestic criticism of the Australian government's commitment to universalist human rights, but as noted, the there was little public sympathy for terrorists or drug smugglers. From a Liberal Internationalist perspective, Australia's credentials in relation to the death penalty were shown to be lacking and *Realpolitik* prevailed so that the sovereignty of Indonesia was upheld.

Despite longstanding attempts by the Australian government to build positive cultural awareness, public opinion brings into relief the significant cultural differences between the two neighbours. There is also an imbalance between the role and function of the media in Australian and Indonesian societies, with media reportage in Australia often acting to undermine government attempts at both building closer relations and appeasing Indonesian sensitivities over sovereignty. There is an underlying desire to build closer relations, with the narrative of 'potential' resonating in public opinion in relation to a Realist conception of national interests. However, it coexists with a high level of mistrust, suspicion and threat, which aligns with Strategic Culture. That said, curiously it is often Liberal Internationalist concerns over issues such as human rights and animal welfare, rather than traditional military threats, that reinforces distrust.

Cultural immersion or transactional education

International education exchange is another area that the Australian government posits can be used to overcome cultural barriers. The question is, does it function this way for Indonesia or is it a more transactional arrangement, as with other aspects of bilateral relations? Successive reports and reviews have identified the need to strengthen 'people-to-people' links with Indonesia, and education is highlighted as a key priority.[33] COVID-19 disrupted international education flows, but in 2017, 8,650 Indonesian students studied in Australia and spent A$833 million doing so. This represents 0.8 per cent of the Australian student market and the seventh largest source of income for Australia. The number of Indonesian students was eclipsed by Indian and Chinese students and while there has been phenomenal growth in the education market, the Indonesian share started from a small base and has not kept pace with this growth.[34] This is despite the growth in the Indonesian middle class, who form the main market for international education.

Notwithstanding the dominance of the Chinese and Indian markets, Indonesia has consistently been in the top 15 sources of foreign students for Australia (by numbers), representing approximately one-third of Indonesian students who travel abroad to study. While some of Australia's traditional markets, such as the US, are in decline, the Indonesian market is predicted to grow and there has been significant growth in student numbers visiting Australia in recent years (8.5 per cent from 2015 to 2018).[35] Austrade views education as a key aspect of Australia's 'brand' in Indonesia: considerable efforts have been taken to grow this market and this will continue in the post-COVID-19 world.

The Australia Awards programme has been the centrepiece of educational exchange between Australia and Indonesia, with 300 scholarships (or approximately 20 per cent of the total) offered to Indonesian students in 2018 with an additional 500 short-term places offered. The Australia Awards built on the history of the original 1950s Colombo Plan, which also used educational exchange to build 'people-to-people' links.[36] Similar projects have been put in place for teachers, such as the Australia–Indonesia Institute's BRIDGE Project.

The Australia–Indonesia Institute was founded by the Australian government in 1989, at the height of the Hawke/Keating Labor government's attempts at increasing Asian integration. Its mission is to build intercultural awareness through 'people-to-people' links. Canberra instituted the New Colombo Plan (NCP) in 2014, which seeks to encourage Australian students to travel to Asia to increase their cultural literacy. This was a response to the decline in cultural immersion by Australian students in Asia (and can be connected to the decline of Asian language studies in Australia since the peak of the 1990s). The NCP has been popular and by 2020, approximately 60,000 students had studied abroad, although COVID-19 interrupted the programme.[37] A key aim was to increase the two-way flow of students to Asia as most exchange traffic was from Asia to Australia, but it is too early to tell whether this will have a measurable impact on perceptions of Indonesia represented in public opinion.

Due to the complexities of measuring intercultural awareness, it is difficult to evaluate the impact of educational exchange. Evidence suggests that Australia is the foreign destination of choice for Indonesian students, as many more travel to Australia than to larger markets such as the US.[38] Surprisingly, some studies of Indonesian students in Australia have found that educational exchange actually led to greater awareness and acceptance of diverse groups within Indonesia rather than building links to Australia or the creation of a cosmopolitan identity.[39] Indonesian students in Australia often connect closely with other Indonesian students (through student societies, etc. and shared accommodation) rather than with the broader Australian community. This could have benefits in relation to stability within Indonesia, but wouldn't fulfil the aim of building 'people-to-people' links between the countries.

The emphasis of successive Australian governments on international education has been an enduring theme in bilateral agreements that seek to promote mutual understanding through enhanced 'people-to-people' links. This aligns the national interest with Liberal International values.[40] Government efforts have been institutionalized through organizations/groups such as the Australia–Indonesia Institute, the Australia–Indonesia Centre and the Australia–Indonesia Youth Association. However, as with tourism, the small numbers of Indonesians studying in Australia and the narrow scope of their experience limits the efficacy of education as a form of cultural diplomacy. There have been notable exceptions, such as Indonesian Foreign Minister Marty Natalegawa, who completed a PhD at the Australian National University, and the Australian Awards aim to emulate this form of support for Indonesia's leaders of tomorrow, but there is not enough evidence yet to evaluate whether the potential of this programme will be realized. What is evident is that the potential of previous programmes has been lauded by successive Australian governments while at the same time Indonesian literacy in Australia has declined.[41]

Official development assistance: 'pursuing national interest and extending Australia's influence'[42]

A key difference between Australia's diplomacy with Indonesia and other key relationships that are dominated by security and trade is that Australia is also a major ODA donor to Indonesia. In the 1990s and 2000s, Australia was Indonesia's fourth largest source of ODA, but this changed with the 25 per cent increase in aid after the Bali bombings.[43] Indonesia is the second largest recipient of Australian ODA behind Papua New Guinea, which highlights that proximity does count. In 2022–23, Australian ODA to Indonesia was A$307 million, or approximately 6.6 per cent of total outlays, and focused on economic partnership, governance and poverty alleviation. The evolution of the relationship to Canberra's support for an 'aid for trade' approach that involved economic partnership was demonstrated by efforts to improve the productivity and sustainability of the Indonesian economy.

Economic projects focus on both national economic institutions and infrastructure, as well as on increasing competitiveness, reducing transaction costs and improving economic participation, right down to the village and individual levels. Development priorities are captured by Figure 10.1. Representative projects include the Australia–Indonesia Partnership for Promoting Rural Incomes through Support for Markets in Agriculture, and the Water and Sanitation for Low Income Communities Project.

Projects also support more orthodox development priorities, epitomized by the UN Sustainable Development Goals (SDGs), such as access to clean water and sanitation. Gender remains prominent in the programme, as do measures designed to strengthen health systems and reduce extreme poverty and inequality. These ODA programmes have highlighted the legacy of focusing on more traditional development challenges that fit squarely in a Liberal Internationalist framework of

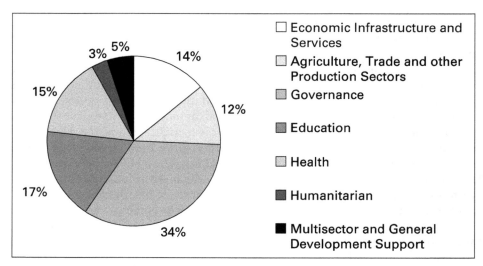

FIGURE 10.1 *Australian ODA to Indonesia.*[44]

universal human rights. The emphasis is on improving the wellbeing of 'ordinary' Indonesians, often amongst the most vulnerable groups and those in rural areas.

In addition, many of these programmes were implemented in partnership with large intergovernmental organizations, such as the UNICEF Rural and Remote Education Initiative for Papuan Province, or the World Bank education programmes, highlighting the willingness to develop multilateral solutions to complex development challenges. This approach dilutes the diplomatic benefit gained from using bilateral programmes that can be credited directly to Canberra, but meets best practice for ODA. Humanitarianism is evident in AFP towards Indonesia, but it sits awkwardly with a Realist focus on stability and maximizing the national interest return on aid 'investments'. There are plentiful examples whereby Australia's national interests trump Liberal Internationalist values, most notably when the Indonesian government is responsible for human rights violations that are unpalatable to Australian public opinion.[45]

Canberra's abiding interest in stability is also evident in ODA to Indonesia: 'A prosperous, stable and growing Indonesia is good for regional stability, security, trade and cooperation.'[46] Therefore, Australia 'support[s] Indonesia's efforts to tackle inequality and maintain social stability, promote tolerance and pluralism, and counter violent extremism'.[47] Stability links ODA's traditional human security focus with the present emphasis on promoting economic growth. A link has been posited between economic growth, poverty alleviation, strengthening institutions of governance and a reduction in Islamic radicalism that could potentially lead to a terrorist threat to Indonesia and Australia. The 'aid for trade' agenda reflects the socialization of the Australian government's domestic neoliberal agenda into ODA (see Chapter 13), but also reflects securitization by elevating the maintenance of stability and counter-terrorism into a development space that was previously dominated by improving human welfare.

Tourism and immigration

Tourism has the potential to build cultural awareness, but it can also reinforce prejudices so analysts must be careful in evaluating claimed benefits. If the interaction is positive, it aligns with the Australian government's approach to building 'people-to-people' links. By contrast, for Indonesia tourism is more instrumental insofar as it is a major source of foreign exchange income, and it is conveniently centred on Bali. Before the COVID-19 pandemic travel restrictions were enacted in Australia and Indonesia, approximately 1.3 million Australians visited Indonesia (mostly Bali) each year, boosting the economy by A$1.8 billion, making Indonesia Australia's second most popular destination.[48] Australians represented roughly 8 per cent of inbound tourists and Indonesia expected this to grow. In contrast, 187,000 Indonesians visited Australia, spending A$756 million, which represented the twelfth largest market for inbound arrivals and the seventeenth largest by spending. This asymmetry in numbers and spending shows that tourism was more economically significant for Indonesia than Australia.

There was strong growth of 42 per cent in tourism from Indonesia over the last five years prior to the pandemic and, as with other areas of the relationship, it was predicted that there is potential for the numbers to continue growing.[49] Predictions were in part due to the growth in the affluent middle class in Indonesia, but despite this potential, in gross and percentage terms, the Indonesian tourist market was underperforming compared with other countries. This highlighted the unrealized potential in the relationship and the Australian government's attempts to develop the relationship. Furthermore, the complete collapse of tourism caused by the COVID-19 epidemic highlighted Indonesia's reliance of Bali on tourism. In 2022, tourist numbers rose dramatically but are nowhere near pre-pandemic levels. The long-term insecurity over tourism in the future means that this aspect of relations is not likely to be repaired in the foreseeable future.

In 2019, there were over 88,000 Indonesian-born residents in Australia,[50] forming the twentieth largest migrant group. In percentage terms, this represents a very small proportion of both Australia's and Indonesia's populations. At roughly 90,000 residents, the small number of Indonesians is striking when compared to a population of approximately 280,000,000. It is noteworthy that despite all the potential associated with proximity and complementary economies, there has been so little permanent or semi-permanent migration.

Tourism and immigration statistics highlight how narrow 'people-to-people' links are with Australia's populous neighbour. There has been a structural barrier limiting links due to poverty in Indonesia, but one key conclusion is that Indonesia's growing middle class is choosing to travel elsewhere. Attempts to build enduring 'people-to-people' links through this avenue have been undermined by the lack of demand for authentic immersion by Australians rather than cheap package holidays in Bali. This form of mass tourism does not necessarily change attitudes in a positive way for either Australian or Indonesians. The citizens of states much further afield are much more interested in travelling and residing in Australia and vice versa. This is in stark contrast with educational choices, where proximity counts more for Indonesia.

Counter-terrorism travel warnings as a source of tension

Due to the transactional economic factors for Indonesia, the impact of terrorism on tourism is intimately connected to efforts to increase cooperation with Australia on counter-terrorism. The Bali bombings in 2002 severely disrupted the tourism trade, and while it quickly returned to its growth trajectory, it is in Indonesia's interests that there are no further disruptions to tourism. For Jakarta, Australia's Department of Foreign Affairs and Trade (DFAT) Smartraveller advice to citizens is problematic, because it varies from exercising 'a high degree of caution . . . because of the high threat of terrorist attack' to 'reconsider your need to travel.'

> We continue to receive information indicating that terrorists may be planning attacks in Indonesia. Attacks could occur at anywhere, anytime. Indonesian authorities continue to arrest terrorists in advanced stages of attack planning.[51]

These warnings have been a longstanding source of irritation in Jakarta[52] and have only recently dropped to 'exercise a high degree of caution . . . due to security risks'. Recent Smartraveller advice from 2022 notes: 'The terrorist threat in

Indonesia is ongoing. Attacks could happen anywhere and anytime. This includes places that Westerners visit...including Bali.'[53] From Canberra's standpoint, the protection of Australians abroad has received greater emphasis since the 'War on Terror' began after the 9/11 attacks on the United States in 2001 and therefore Indonesia's capacity to prevent repeat attacks against citizens and property remains a priority. Due diligence requires warning, but the advice is also an impediment to tourism. This highlights the impact of elevated threat perceptions, which characterize Australia's Strategic Culture, on bilateral relations with Indonesia.

Tourism has been treated as another area where there is great potential, but as with other areas in the relationship, it is highly transactional and focused largely on economic gains for Indonesia. As with counter-terrorism, Australia–Indonesia interests on tourism differ. A focus on tourism growth is shared, but the Australian government's attempts to build 'people-to-people' links is largely unilateral, while Indonesia is interested in foreign exchange. The whole approach has been brought into relief by the collapse of tourism and immigration due to the COVID-19 epidemic and it is unlikely that the potential, if real, will be realized in the near future.

The limits of 'people-to-people' links between culturally dissimilar neighbours

The coverage of human rights abuses in Indonesia in the Australian media highlight an uncomfortable truth for the government, and one which the public has steadfastly refused to forget. The limits of the mantra that 'people-to-people' links will improve awareness has been tested in bilateral relations, and it may be that when combined with the essentially liberal attitudes of ordinary Australians (in relation to self-determination and human rights), the influence of cultural difference and similarity posited by Strategic Culture is more powerful than government/elite-led promotion of national self-interest. Tourism, immigration and educational exchanges have grown slowly from a small base, but public opinion has hardly shifted. This further questions the impact of 'people-to-people' links as relations remain largely driven from the top down, and the exigencies of *Realpolitik* have not shifted public opinion.

The Australian government's prescription has been that 'people-to-people' links will bridge the cultural divide, but the perception of Indonesia as an 'Asian other' identified through Australia's Strategic Culture is much more difficult to alter despite shared security interests in the 'War on Terror'. Nonetheless, high-level diplomacy has remained a core mechanism for maintaining cordial – if not always warm – relations and repairing the fallout from instances where a slight by Australia has caused an escalation in tension in Jakarta.

Prime ministerial relations and high-level diplomacy

A recurrent theme in bilateral relations with Indonesia is that they are driven by a top-down approach and this is clear from an overview of attempts to manufacture 'people-to-people' links. These shallow connections can be contrasted to the more comprehensive links Australia shares with states with which it has historical and cultural affinity (which is dealt with in depth in other chapters). As such, building *authentic* 'people-to-people' links would be ideal, but public diplomacy at the prime ministerial/presidential level is an important element of relations over which leaders have more control. There is a sound historical basis for this pattern of high-level diplomacy insofar as Indonesia was governed by two dictators for the first 53 years after independence, with President Suharto himself being in power for 31 years. Successive Australian governments successfully courted Suharto, knowing that in an authoritarian state influence needed to be created at the top. However, close relations with a dictator led to persistent criticisms from Liberal Internationalists in politics and the media concerned about human rights violations. This pattern of pragmatism in public diplomacy between Canberra and Jakarta continues to shape relations and in evidenced in the almost complete silence over the human rights situation in West Papua.

Prime ministerial/presidential relations provide a litmus test for the health of relations. Much has been made of the Keating-Suharto and Turnbull-Widodo partnerships due to a range of observable outcomes prompted by their close relationships (such as the 1994 Agreement on Maintaining Security). Prime Minister Paul Keating made his first overseas trip to Jakarta and elevated the relationship to the top foreign policy priority.[54] It is true that close partnerships can build 'interpersonal trust', reset damaged relationships and accelerate diplomatic change,[55] but they are also fragile as personal relationships do not necessarily survive changes in government. Close partnerships can also be contrasted with times where there is little apparent affinity between leaders, such as between Abbott and Widodo, and where relations broke down, as with Howard and Habibie.[56] Anthony Albanese was the latest prime minister to make his first overseas trip to Indonesia in 2022, but it remains to be seen whether this form of diplomatic theatre can paste over the regular cleavages in the relationship.

Superficially, the health of public diplomacy can be tested through the frequency and outcomes of state visits. This was certainly the case with China, where high-level visits collapsed after the breakdown in relations in 2018. Recent visits include state visits to Australia by the Indonesian President in 2017 and 2020, and attendance at the G20 in 2014 and ASEAN–Australia Special Summit in 2018. President Widodo used his speech to the Australian Parliament in 2020 to focus on practical means of strengthening the relationship, which may highlight an understanding of the unrealized potential in the relationship from Jakarta.

The Australian prime minister visited Indonesia in 2018, where the leaders announced the finalization of the Indonesia–Australia Comprehensive Economic Partnership Agreement (IA-CEPA). The bilateral relationship was strengthened through the renewal of the CSP in 2018. Prime Minister Albanese followed the recent pattern of visiting Indonesia after his election in 2022. Despite tensions over the AUKUS, the vision from the bilateral meetings was very warm and positive, including a bicycle ride around the Presidential Palace in Jakarta. Annual leaders' meetings do not occur with all diplomatic partners and this signals the centrality of relations to AFP.

Indonesian and Australian ministers and high-level officials also meet regularly during bilateral visits. Recent visits have involved ministers of foreign affairs, trade, tourism and investment/trade; minister of home affairs with coordinating minister for political, legal and security affairs; and ministers of defence. Beyond ad hoc visits, a series of high-level meetings have been developed to maintain the relationship, including the Indonesia–Australia annual leaders' meeting, the foreign and defence ministers' 2+2 meeting (the seventh of which occurred in Jakarta in 2021), and the Ministerial Council on Law and Security (the seventh of which occurred in Jakarta in 2021). These meetings reflect the evolution of relations from initiatives developed by the Keating government in the early 1990s to institutionalized relations such as the Australia–Indonesia Ministerial Forum (AIMF).

In addition to high-level visits, Australian and Indonesian ministers and officials regularly meet on the sidelines of regional fora, such as the East Asia Summit (from 2005), Subregional Meeting on Counter-terrorism Bali Democracy Forum and ASEAN Australia Special Summit. These bilateral side meetings provide important opportunities to engage in private and public diplomacy and are particularly useful when relations are strained, which is a regular occurence due to the dynamic of slight and escalation. Side meetings are also reinforced by the broader cultural and professional collaboration in events such as the Indonesia Australia Dialogue (IAD) between leaders in business, media, academia and the broader community, the fourth of which was held in Sydney in 2018.

High-level meetings diversify interactions and build 'people-to-people' networks that have the potential to offset the transactional nature of other aspects of the relationship. However, top-down approaches have inherent weaknesses, not the least of which is the risk of hinging the health of the bilateral relationship on relations between leaders. As Indonesia becomes more powerful and globalized, its public diplomacy is increasing and becoming more diversified, making it difficult to measure the health of bilateral relations as other states are competing to gain influence. Canberra is increasingly facing a more competitive diplomatic environment and notwithstanding periodic good relations between leaders, the foundations of relations are not necessarily as firm as they could be.

Trade institutionalization: Regional integration over bilateral trade

> Indonesia will move from being the 16th largest economy into the top 10 by 2030, and be the fourth largest by 2050. By 2030, around 70 per cent of Indonesians will be of working age, supporting a consuming class of around 135 million people and business opportunities will be worth approximately $US1.8 trillion.[57]

Numerous Australian government and advocacy reports highlight the abundant opportunities that exist in Indonesia's burgeoning economy, but regardless of this potential trade relations have not flourished. Indonesia is currently the world's sixteenth largest economy and is predicted to become the fourth largest by 2050.[58] Despite having significant government support, complementary economies and the benefits of proximity, Indonesia is Australia's thirteenth largest trading partner while Australia is Indonesia's eleventh largest export market and eighth largest import market.

Trade orientation

Two-way trade between Australia and Indonesia focuses on natural resources, agricultural products and services, and within these areas trade is quite complementary (see Table 10.1). For instance, prior to the disruption caused by COVID-19, education dominated Australian services exports while travel dominated services imports.

At best, the trend in two-way trade could be termed stable. While Australian exports to Indonesia have slightly increased over the last five years, Indonesian exports to Australia have slightly declined since 2014 (see Table 10.1). Considering that Indonesia's economy has been growing at over 5 per cent over the last five years, these figures are telling. In this context, two-way trade could be described as stagnant because Indonesia's export-led growth is occurring primarily with other trading partners. The implications are that Indonesia's economy is growing through trade with other states and that proximity to Australia does not count significantly in trade relations (see Table 10.2). This is also the case for Australia where exports are generally sent elsewhere and imports are generally sourced from elsewhere. The potential convenience of proximity is not being realized and, despite the numerous efforts at trade institutionalization mentioned below, the statistics do not point to market forces bringing the two economies together.

Foreign direct investment (FDI) as a window to the impact of cultural difference on trade

Australia–Indonesia FDI is very modest. About 2,500 Australian businesses export to Indonesia, but only 10 per cent of these have subsidiaries in the country. Market access limitations inhibiting trade could be viewed as largely self-imposed, influenced by differences in business cultures and the complexity of the domestic regulatory environment. Barriers to bilateral trade point to the value of the free trade agreement (FTA) signed with Indonesia in 2019, but the open question is whether changes to the regulatory environment will actually promote bilateral trade.

Australia has the potential to benefit from the sustained growth in the Indonesian economy and if it does not occur through two-way trade, it could occur through investment; foreign direct investment (FDI) could provide additional capital to facilitate growth. That said, the potential to increase two-way investment and foreign direct investment should not be overstated because they are more underdeveloped than other economic activities (see Table 10.3). The small outflows of investment from Indonesia mean that its visibility in Australia as a trade partner is not significant. However, Australian investment in Indonesia has steadily grown over time and FDI to Indonesia has grown significantly since the lows after the global financial crisis (GFC) in 2008.

TABLE 10.1 *Australia's pre-COVID-19 pandemic trade and investment relationship with Indonesia*[59]

Australian merchandise trade with Indonesia, 2018–19 (A$m)			Total share	Rank	Growth (yoy)
Exports to Indonesia	6,609		1.8%	12th	–2.6%
Imports from Indonesia	5,057		1.6%	15th	12.3%
Total merchandise trade (exports + imports)	11,666		1.7%	14th	3.3%
Major Australian exports, 2018–19 (A$m)		**Major Australian imports, 2018–19 (A$m)**			
Coal	835	Crude petroleum			826
Live animals (excl seafood)	691	Refined petroleum			657
Crude petroleum	643	Tobacco, manufactured			361
Wheat	403	Monitors, projectors & TVs			191
Australia's trade in services with Indonesia, 2018–19 (A$m)			Total share	Rank	Growth (yoy)
Exports of services to Indonesia	1,757		1.8%	13th	8.7%
Imports of services from Indonesia	4,413		4.3%	6th	16.8%
Major Australian services exports, 2018–19 (A$m)		**Major Australian services imports, 2018–19 (A$m)**			
Education-related travel	935	Personal travel excluding education			3,730
Personal travel excluding education	458	Transport			297

192 AUSTRALIAN FOREIGN POLICY

TABLE 10.2 *Indonesia's pre-COVID-19 pandemic merchandise trade relationships*[60]

Indonesia's principal export destinations, 2019		Indonesia's principal import sources, 2019	
1. China	15.1%	1. China	24.1%
2. Japan	10.8%	2. Singapore	11.4%
3. United States	10.2%	3. Japan	9.5%
13. Australia	*1.6%*	*8. Australia*	*3.1%*

TABLE 10.3 *Australia's pre-COVID-19 pandemic investment relationship with Indonesia*[61]

Australia's investment relationship with Indonesia, 2018 (A$m)	Total	FDI
Australia's investment in Indonesia	5,632	2,283
Indonesia's investment in Australia	1,076	1

Investment decisions are made for a range of reasons, including projected profitability, risk and trust. The profit motive is assumed to be the prime driver of investment and in the light of advocacy for the potential to develop trade, the light exposure of Australia in Indonesia is significant. Factors such as corruption, a challenging regulatory environment and terrorism have impacted the perceptions of Australian businesses. Clearly, Indonesia is not viewed as a positive destination for investment. These same perceptions that limit investment in Indonesia drive the high level of two-way investment between Australia and the US. This pattern indicates that it is highly unlikely that the potential for greater investment will be realized. Despite the negotiation of a bilateral FTA, business sentiment is not in step with the government's policy prescriptions, highlighting that the top-down approach to closer relations based on pragmatic security considerations and proximity has not positively influenced private sector investment and trade decision-making.

Trade and investment facilitation through a bilateral free trade agreement?

Indonesia's growth trajectory and economic potential has long been attractive to Canberra and with this in mind, the IA-CEPA was negotiated to reduce almost all barriers to free trade. It was signed in March 2019 after 12 rounds of negotiations spanning nine years. It is comprehensive insofar as it includes all aspects of economic activity (goods, services and investment) and it found strong support in the Australian business community. It is so recent that its impact remains to be seen, but generally conforms with a Liberal Internationalist free trade agenda. However, it does not include human rights protections (e.g. workers' rights) commonplace in such agreements. This highlights the sensitivities in the bilateral relationship to any initiative that could be seen as meddling in Indonesian sovereignty and the acknowledgement that attempting to uphold human rights standards may limit the scope of cooperation.

That Canberra was willing to set aside human rights provisions that routinely appeared in other agreements was reminiscent of the Asian Values debates of the 1990s.

BOX 10.2: THE ASIAN VALUES DEBATE

- Came to prominence in the 1990s but has since faded.
- Response by several key leaders in the region to Australian Liberal Internationalism, especially Prime Minister Mahathir Mohamad of Malaysia.
- Rebuttal of the western universality of human rights.
- Focus on 'Asian' values such as discipline, building consensus, communitarianism versus individualism, respect for elders, government paternalism.
- Denial of a state's responsibility to elevate human rights over other interests.
- Attempt to limit imposition of human rights norms in regional organizations and agreements.
- Identifies Australia as an outsider trying to meddle in Asia.

In the 1990s, the influential Indonesia lobby within government and academia, accepted the notion promoted by Malaysia and Indonesia that Liberal Internationalist values, such as human rights, might not be universally applicable. Recent diplomatic initiatives with Indonesia (and China, for that matter) reveal that human rights of key strategic/trading partners will not drive AFP.

Regional trade institutionalization

While bilateral trade has not met expected potential, Australia and Indonesia have a long history of regional trade collaboration, which may have facilitated trade growth with third parties. Australia and Indonesia are both founding members of the Australia-led 1989 Asia–Pacific Economic Cooperation forum (APEC). APEC was born during an intensive period of interest in building regional architecture in the 1980s and 1990s. Prime Minister Bob Hawke and Foreign Minister Gareth Evans were central to the conception and inauguration of APEC. The centrepiece of APEC is the annual leaders' meeting, the first of which involved 12 regional leaders and was held in Canberra in 1989.

Initially, APEC was an initiative to grow trade between the 'Asian Tiger' economies and close partners through a trade liberalization agenda. It has subsequently grown to have 21 members from around the Pacific Rim and several intergovernmental dialogue members, including ASEAN and the Pacific Islands Forum (PIF). Negotiating an APEC Free Trade Area of Asia-Pacific (FTAAP) is regularly discussed, but has not been achieved. Negotiations may have stalled because APEC members are members of many of the other regional trade arrangements, such as ASEAN, the Comprehensive and Progressive Agreement for Trans-Pacific Partnership (CPTPP) and the Regional Comprehensive Economic Partnership (RCEP) grouping.

The diplomatic context within which APEC was born is instructive of the limits of Australian 'middlepowermanship' under the Labor governments of the 1980s and 1990s.[62] APEC is an inclusive intergovernmental organization that connects Australia with Asia as part of the government's strategy of enhanced regional integration. Australia was never offered full membership of ASEAN, so Australian policy-makers proposed APEC as a new regional agreement with broader membership. It was based on the ASEAN Post Ministerial Conference format, which was created to facilitate dialogue with non-members.

While not being a full member, in 1974 Australia became ASEAN's first dialogue partner. If treated as a group, ASEAN is Australia's third-largest trading partner. Relations with ASEAN have grown steadily over time and diversified into political areas such as counter-terrorism. Australia and ASEAN signed a strategic partnership agreement in 2014 and biennial summits have been held since 2016. However, Australia is not a member of ASEAN and this highlights that there are limits to Australia's ability to achieve its interests in the Indo-Pacific. Former prime ministers Keating and Rudd both suggested that Australia should join,[63] but no invitation has been forthcoming. Indonesia is a leading member of ASEAN and it is telling that Canberra has not been able to leverage off the bilateral relationship to gain membership of the pre-eminent regional organization. The clear message is that Australia is not part of Asia and this reinforces the alienation from Asia that characterizes Strategic Culture. Both Realism and Liberal Internationalism would posit closer economic relations as essential to achieving Australian prosperity, while Liberal Internationalists would also suggest that trade liberalization could also lead to other forms of liberalization. However, there are limits to how welcome Australia is in regional fora and no sign that Jakarta has attempted to smooth Canberra's entry.

Australia and Indonesia are also members of the ASEAN-Australia–New Zealand Free Trade Area (AANZFTA) that entered into force in January 2010. The genesis of the idea can be traced back to 1993. This agreement has brought Australia and New Zealand (NZ) together with 11 ASEAN members to reduce tariffs and transaction costs. This was Australia's first multi-country FTA and was negotiated (with NZ) as an agreement with the Australia–New Zealand Closer Economic Relations Agreement (CER) and ASEAN. While all ASEAN members are eligible to join, only nine have signed, which again highlights the limits of Canberra's influence. It may also highlight the crowded regional economic architecture that may have led to member fatigue.

INDONESIA: PROXIMITY AND THE UNREALIZABLE POTENTIAL 195

From 2012, Australia worked with ASEAN to negotiate the pan-Asian RCEP grouping. This is the world's largest free trade area involving ASEAN, China, Japan, New Zealand and the Republic of Korea. Australia worked closely with Indonesia, ASEAN's coordinator of negotiations, to further talks, which led to the agreement being signed in November 2020. The RCEP is the world's largest trade block, which accounts for approximately 30 per cent of global GDP and population and includes nine of Australia's top 14 trading partners.[64] It also excludes the US, and therefore provides a counter to the protectionism exhibited in the trade war between the US and China that developed during the Trump administration in the later 2010s. As such, it reinforces Australia's interests in supporting Liberal Internationalist free trade regimes that provide the economic prop for the 'rules-based order' that Canberra has identified as a key foreign policy interest.

Despite the benefits of proximity and numerous initiatives institutionalizing bilateral and regional cooperation, the level of economic interaction between Australia and Indonesia has not reached a state where trade with each other is more significant than trade with other states. The potential for growth in bilateral trade commensurate with the growth in Indonesia's economy has not been realized. As such, trade can be characterized as involving instrumental economic interactions slowly growing from a low base. Despite regular claims of the great potential for increased trade, this potential is largely unrealized and past experience indicates that the likelihood of Australia benefiting from Indonesia's economic growth trajectory is low.

Conclusion

Australia and Indonesia are close neighbours, strategic partners, and friends, committed to working together to build a prosperous and stable region.[65]

This statement from the Australian Department of Foreign Affairs obscures the complexity in relations. Australia cannot escape its geography as it is a close neighbour, but if measured by relations with other traditional partners, Canberra and Jakarta are far from friends.

In many ways, Australia's relations with Indonesia defy orthodox theorizing through Realist or Liberal Internationalist lenses. The relationship is so unbalanced that it does not fit with theories designed to explain the behaviour of great powers with complementary resources and interests in maximizing their power and influence. The COVID-19 crisis provided opportunities for closer cooperation but this is the latest example of a long history of unrealized potential. There still appears to be more potential for cooperation than actual engagement.[66] Indonesia's security interests are primarily internal and maritime, relating mainly to domestic challenges to sovereignty and internal cohesion. While Australia is geographically proximate to Indonesia to the south and strategically looks north, Indonesia is firmly focused on its north. Indonesia looks north economically and strategically, looks inwardly in relation to challenges to sovereignty, and benefits from a southern neighbour so benign that it does not figure in its foreign policy unless there is a crisis, which occurs regularly through a pattern of slight and escalation.

Generations of Australian policy-makers and Indonesia lobbyists in the foreign affairs and academic establishments have attempted to engineer closer relations based on the exigencies of proximity, the huge economic potential of Indonesia and deeply ingrained fears of Indonesia becoming a threatening neighbour. One reason that this potential has not been realized is that Indonesia neatly fits with the 'Asian other' that characterizes Strategic Culture. Even the cultivation of friendly anti-Communist dictatorship during the Cold War or a post-9/11 moderate counter-terrorist power could not negate the impact of Australia's threat perceptions. This contradiction highlights the bankruptcy of the mantra of Indonesia's potential in AFP. Past experience of persistent top-down attempts at institutionalizing stronger 'people-to-people' links demonstrates the limits of this approach to developing closer bilateral ties. That said, the shared history of anti-Communism and counter-terrorism shows that maintaining and developing a shared security outlook offers the greatest potential for assuaging the fears identified in public opinion and Strategic Culture.

Australia and Indonesia have been enemies before and Canberra has an abiding interest in ensuring that relations do not sour again. Relations are closer than ever but are not by any means warm, and avoiding the longstanding dynamic of slight and escalation will become more significant as Indonesia becomes the dominant partner in the bilateral relationship in the near future. Canberra is aware of Indonesia's strategic potential and Australia has advocated for Indonesia to be given a permanent seat on the Security Council,[67] but is not prepared for the implications of being the lesser partner. The worst-case scenario of an Indonesia with aggressive nationalistic aspirations would be a nightmare for Canberra and despite decades of institutionalization, the foundations for cooperation remain weaker than any other key bilateral relationship.

The 'War on Terror' provided a bridge to overcome the cultural divide and the Bali bombings were used to great diplomatic advantage, but distrust and disengagement remains. Indonesia's proximity does not negate the strong influence of Strategic Culture evident in other relationships because the threat from a proximate neighbour is more existential than the imagined threat from the 'north'. Pragmatic instrumentalism characterizes trade and security interactions, which aligns more neatly within a Realist frame of maximizing narrowly defined national interests. The focus of both Strategic Culture and Realism on defending the national interest demands something as radical as a defence alliance against a common foe as the only prescription to negate the potential of Indonesia to be such a proximate existential threat.

Realpolitik has its limits and for Australia requires continued security guarantees from the US, and some analysts have identified potential to connect increasing security cooperation with the ANZUS alliance.[68] Indonesia's growing concern over China's challenge to the 'rules-based order' in the South China Sea may provide a bridge to building closer relations in an era when Canberra's worst-case scenario is that US decline may lead to its withdrawal from the Indo-Pacific. Adapting the shared threat perceptions that have been built around the Islamic fundamentalist threat that developed during the 'War on Terror' provides a window to how Strategic Culture could position Indonesia similarly to how the relationship with Japan is evolving, but this will involve a significant investment in shaping Australian public opinion. If the government/elite-led efforts to date are anything to go by, there are significant challenges to be overcome. Proximity provides no guarantee of potential being realised.

11

Background to the South Pacific: The diversity of the South Pacific as seen from Canberra

Introduction

Australia's relations with the South Pacific have always been under-theorized[1] and what academic Joanne Wallis describes as the increasingly 'crowded and complex'[2] region makes it even more so. The dominant Realist strains in International Relations theory focus on the behaviour of great powers towards one another, or between them and lesser powers, and previous chapters have reflected on this dynamic from Australia's position as a medium power. Some intellectual effort has been applied to understanding how medium powers deal with great powers and diplomacy, and in this regard Australia's 'middlepowermanship' is intertwined with the Liberal Internationalist values in Australian foreign policy (AFP). In stark contrast is the lack of theorizing about how medium powers, such as Australia respond to lesser powers, such as Pacific Island Countries (PICs).

It is noteworthy that from Canberra's vantage point, the South Pacific is viewed through both the lens of bilateral relationships and as a region that is engaged with as a whole (and this dualistic approach frames the way this chapter is structured). The way AFP frames the South Pacific differs markedly from Australia's other key relationships (which are viewed bilaterally) due to the interplay of proximity, history and the dramatic asymmetry between Australia and PICs. The influence of these three contextual factors is not privileged in International Relations theories such as Realism and Liberal Internationalism, but does figure in Strategic Culture, and as such, together they provide insights into Canberra's approach to the South Pacific.

Beyond this background context, three overarching themes characterize relations with the region. First, the diversity of both the region and of Australia's approach to it. Second, Australia's leadership aspirations and sensitivity to foreign influence in the region and by extension the threat that strategic competitors could pose from the region. And third, Australia's role as the primary regional development and security partner. The emphasis placed on achieving Australia's interests in relation to these three themes has varied over time, but increasingly reflects the geostrategic competition with China that is also shaping other diplomatic relationships. Canberra perceives that this competition is playing out

BACKGROUND TO THE SOUTH PACIFIC

in the South Pacific and its 2018 foreign policy 'Step-up' reveals that tensions exist between the three themes.[3] These tensions can be explained by the dominant Realist approach to AFP, the Liberal Internationalist values that coexist and Australia's underlying Strategic Culture.

To tease out the interplay between these three contextual factors and three themes, several case studies covering key region-wide issues are examined in the following chapter, as are two bilateral relationships that are representative of the diversity in approaches by Australia to the region. Examples of the growing confidence of Pacific Island leaders in interacting with and shaping AFP, and external powers challenging Australian dominance, will also be canvassed to provide a complete picture of the state of play in AFP towards the South Pacific. This chapter will provide the background to relations with the South Pacific that provides the context for current diplomacy.

A diverse region

This chapter mirrors AFP insofar that it encompasses a region rather than one bilateral diplomatic relationship, which is not how the Indo-Pacific, North America, Europe or other regions are treated in AFP. What follows is a brief overview of South Pacific geography, demography, economy and history. The aim is not to provide a comprehensive overview of the region, but rather a snapshot of the diplomatic terrain that Canberra operates within, as the diversity of the region is striking and has shaped AFP approaches.

Geography

The dominant European understanding of geography focuses on landscapes. This bias is understandable given the fact that the sovereignty over geographically bounded territory has so strongly shaped European history and foreign policy outlooks. Furthermore, it is warfare over territory that has spurred the study of International Relations. This mindset must be challenged when looking at the *seascape* in which PICs inhabit, and this is precisely what contemporary conceptions of the Blue Pacific or Pacific continent do.[4] Historically, landscapes involve proximity and a level of connectedness and contest that shaped European history and have framed the study of International Relations and foreign policy. This focus on defending territorially bounded states from contiguous neighbours is not present in most of the South Pacific due to their isolation from one another and other centres of international power for most of their history, and also conversely due to their late history of colonization relative to Africa, Asia or South America.

Land borders have shaped European political development, as have the vast distances between PICs. Globalization is focused on the centres of international exchange and from the perspective of trade flows the South Pacific was and continues to be a backwater. The relatively recent interconnectedness that modern transport and information technology has brought has been uneven and patchy. The recent history of decolonization, mostly in the 1970s and 1980s, meant that most PICs do not have lengthy experience of diplomatic relations and the regional organizations that represent them do not have longevity or the stability of organizations in other regions, such as the EU or ASEAN.

Due to the isolation and diversity of the region, the metropolitan powers – Australia and New Zealand – and outside powers have relied on regional institutions to gain access to PICs as they have grouped Melanesian, Polynesian and Micronesian states for the purposes of diplomatic coordination and the delivery of official development assistance (ODA) to provide essential services and to respond to natural disasters. However, internal instability within the region's first institution, the South Pacific Commission (SPC) and its offshoot, the Pacific Islands Forum (PIF) has impacted on the ability of external states and metropolitan powers such as Australia to engage in region-wide diplomacy.[5]

The South Pacific includes two large states, Papua New Guinea (PNG) and Fiji, with sizeable economies and populations, but most states are smaller island groups. Together Fiji and PNG encompass more than 90 per cent of most regional statistics such as landmass, population and GDP. Despite their small size, the exclusive economic zones (EEZs) of PICs are vast, encompassing roughly 10 per cent of the world's oceans and representing an area three times the size of European EEZs. In this respect, the isolation and separation of islands and atolls represents a potential strength, leading to the conception of the Blue Pacific Continent. Large EEZs also provide PICS a bounty of resources, such as fishing rights, where land-based natural resources are limited for most. However, these resources are also a potential source of weakness with respect to outside powers wanting to take advantage of them. One of the best examples of this double-edged sword is phosphate mining on Nauru, with tuna fishing rights continuing to provide an apt case.

BOX 11.1: COLONIALISM, NEO-COLONIALISM AND PHOSPHATE MINING ON NAURU

- Pre-independence Nauru was a German protectorate.
- Valuable phosphate fertilizer discovered in 1900.
- Phosphate mined by a British company with licensing fees to the German government.
- Germany loses Nauru after the First World War and it becomes a League of Nations mandated territory jointly administered by Australia and New Zealand (1920).
- Nauru becomes independent in 1968, buys the phosphate mining company and invests profits in a trust fund for future generations.
- Phosphate runs out (becomes unviable) and much of Nauru is left a mining wasteland.
- Phosphate trust fund mismanaged and long-term income stream collapses.
- Nauru dependent on aid and vulnerable.
- Nauru accepts Australian offshore detention centres in 2002 as part of a multimillion-dollar deal providing Canberra a palatable alternative to onshore detention.

The South Pacific is dotted with thousands of islands, islets and atolls, the largest of which are home to the culture, government and commerce of PICS. By contrast, most of the thousands of islands, etc. are uninhabited. Several PICs, including the Federated States of Micronesia (FSM), Fiji, Kiribati, Samoa, the Solomon Islands, Tonga, Tuvalu and Vanuatu are archipelagic states. Other than PNG and Fiji, the landmass of most PICs is very small and nowhere near the area of a European city. For example, PNG is 462,840 km^2 and Fiji 18,274 km^2, while Tuvalu has a landmass of 21 km^2. Populations and population densities also vary enormously, with PNG having a population of over 9.4 million (density 20 per km^2), Fiji 903,000 (49 per km^2) and Tuvalu 12,000 (393 per km^2). By contrast, Australia's landmass is 7,692,000 per km^2: all Pacific islands could fit into New South Wales (NSW) with an area larger than Victoria left over. Australia's population is 25.8 million with a density, that of Australia is 3 per km^2, which is dramatically lower than anywhere in the Pacific, but population densities in Australian cities are on par with many PICs.

Most national borders in the Pacific are not based on natural land boundaries formed by geographic features such as mountain ranges and rivers. The Pacific seascape involves small islands dotted over large expanses of ocean with national boundaries determined by a range of factors, including the happenstance of map-making during colonial times. For the most of history, inter-island trade and diplomacy was limited due to the large distances involved and they have therefore focused on inward developments. A focus inward encouraged sub-national differences to take on a level of significance that was never 'homogenized' by a dominant group. This lack of homogenization has led to weak identification with the modern states developed after independence was gained from colonial powers in the late twentieth century.[6]

Where islands are close enough to have facilitated travel by small sailing vessels, there have been conflicts akin to those that punctuate the nation-building episodes in European history, such as between Tonga and Fiji, but diplomacy and conflict between 'nations' did not characterize the history of the South Pacific. Most PICs did not face the arrival of explorers, imperial powers and missionaries as unitary actors. That is, generally they did not have the shared national histories and identities that characterized relations between European powers, and this continues to shape how they face Australia and other powers today. The individual histories of colonization are more significant than a sense of shared response that unified some indigenous peoples in the face of colonial encroachment into their lands.

The implications of this lack of political inter-connectedness, as understood in the development of European statehood, can be seen in the fragility of Pacific regionalism. For example, in 2021, the PIF, the pre-eminent regional organization, faced significant internal tension over the selection of its secretary general.[7] The threatened withdrawal of the Federated States of Micronesia from the PIF threatened to split the organization, and this took several years to be resolved through consensus, which has been the Pacific Way[8] in the past. The limits of regionalism are also clear in the largely bilateral roll out of COVID-19 vaccines, where longstanding relationships with ex-colonial and trustee powers, such as

Australia, France, New Zealand and the US, had the most significant impact on availability to PICs.

Geography, trade and identity

Historically, the challenges posed by geography have meant that economic interdependence between many PICs has also been weak. Most large-scale economic activity, whether imports or exports, occurs between PICs and economies outside the region. As such, colonial patterns of economic interaction persist whereby large-scale extraction of natural resources was exported, such as in the case of Fiji's sugar industry or oil and gas in PNG. However, the overall export-oriented industry or the sort that conforms with a neoliberal economic model is limited, as are import substitution ventures, due largely to the small size of domestic markets.

Geographic necessity means that most Pacific Islanders remain involved in subsistence agriculture and fishing. Furthermore, subsistence means that 'place' is closely associated with identity, and together with religion, locality provides key means of identification. Place has often been very localized and the European processes of national homogenization of populations that occurred through centuries of war have not occurred across the Pacific, meaning that many sub-national forms of identification are as meaningful as 'national' identities. Public displays of nationalism are often limited to international sporting events (in particular, rugby) and patriotism of the sort experienced in Western democracies is hardly evidenced.

Demography[9]

The South Pacific is divided into three seemingly distinct ethnic and linguistic areas, although there is some debate over the ethnic, cultural or geographic boundaries between them. Despite the isolating aspects of geography noted above, common roots can be found due to longstanding maritime pathways to discovery and settlement. The South Pacific is divided between two broad language groups, with approximately 9 million speaking Papuan languages and under 2.5 million speaking Austronesian languages. Thus, language differentiates Melanesia from Polynesia and Micronesia. However, clear distinctions are not as significant as they might seem, as within these two broad language groups there are hundreds of distinct languages, with over 850 languages spoken in PNG alone. Given the history of tribal conflict within, if not as much between, many PICs, these differences in language may be just as divisive as language has been unifying in European history. Melanesia is the most populous ethnic or cultural area as it incorporates Fiji, PNG, the Solomon Islands and Vanuatu. It also involves almost all the landmass of PICs, but not the largest seascape, which is in Polynesia (See Map 11.1).

Education

Educational participation and literacy rates average in the 80-percentile range across the region, but rates vary widely between and within individual states.

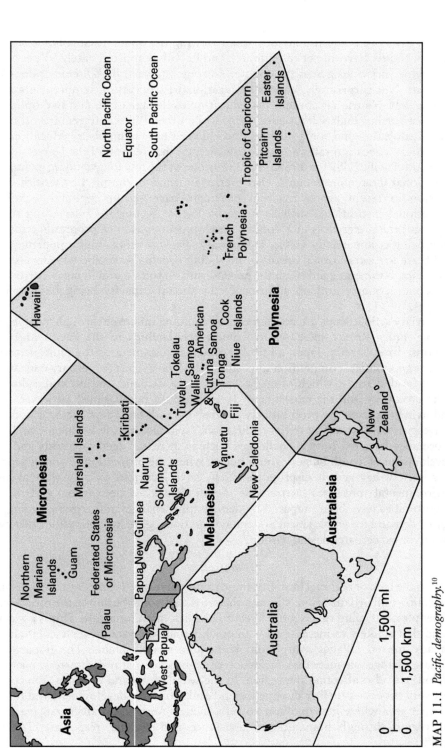

MAP 11.1 *Pacific demography.*[10]

Again, diversity is the watchword when viewing the South Pacific. Some states, such as Nauru, have 96 per cent literacy, and PNG has approximately 65 per cent, with wide variations across the country. In contrast, Australia's literacy rate is 99 per cent. Not surprisingly, national educational participation requirements also vary widely. Nauru has compulsory education to the age of 16 and two optional years of further high school education, while other PICs only require primary school education and some, such as PNG, do not have compulsory education.

Tertiary education rates are quite low, despite the creation of the University of the South Pacific (USP) in 1968. The USP is one of the few longstanding examples of regional interconnectedness. However, even it has been mired by tension and division in recent years. External providers have set up regional technical educational institutions, such as Australia Pacific Technical College, and these represent the preferences in a donor's development assistance programme rather than being commercially viable. Donors also provide scholarship opportunities, and these are a traditional means of providing benefits to Pacific Islanders while also being boomerang aid (with the expenditure on tuition and living occurring in the donor country and no additional educational capacity being built in the Pacific).

Tertiary scholarships are also a means of building influence through 'people-to-people' links. Recent increases in Chinese scholarships to the Pacific and the response by Australia, Japan and other states, is testament to the multiple tools used as geopolitical competition intensifies. The final avenue for tertiary education is self-funded study, which often occurs in New Zealand and Australia due to their proximity and the existence of large diaspora populations. However, fees and living expenses are prohibitively expensive for all but a few Pacific islanders.

Despite slow growth in tertiary education, rapid increases in healthcare and life expectancy have led to new challenges, such as increased aged care costs and the development of 'youth bulges'. Youth bulges, where the proportion of young people in a society has grown disproportionately, have increased existing societal and environmental pressures across the South Pacific. Employment and other opportunities have been outpaced by demographic changes and growth leading to unmet demand for employment and intergenerational gaps in expectations that can lead to or exacerbate societal tension.[11]

Urbanization

Due to the lack of regional mobility, these trends have often contributed to internal migration and urbanization. Climate change is also contributing to the movement of peoples, but again this is more likely to be intra- than interstate. This is a recent trend that is likely to increase pace so quickly that some states, such as Fiji, have already moved villages away from vulnerable coastal plains. The impacts of climate change on increased incidence of significant natural disasters, such as cyclones, is also affecting the region. In the wake of natural disasters, the costly recovery processes further disrupt societal and economic development and this is another area where metropolitan powers, such as Australia, actively engage with the region through humanitarian assistance and disaster response (HADR) activities.

BACKGROUND TO THE SOUTH PACIFIC

As with other trends, urbanization is also occurring unevenly across the Pacific. In smaller states, all population growth is akin to urbanization, because there is not a large amount of arable land available for development. In states with larger landmasses, such as PNG, Fiji and the Solomon Islands, the capitals and centres of economic activity are attracting large numbers of unskilled workers. In Fiji, urbanization has exceeded 50 per cent of the population and is centred around the capital, Suva.

Urbanization is putting pressure on existing fragile infrastructure and challenging laws about property ownership, as large informal settlements spring up around capital cities. The growth in density of informal settlements has also adversely impacted on public health, with the COVID-19 pandemic being the latest significant challenge facing these communities. By contrast, in Australia, urbanization is the norm: over 90 per cent of the population live in a few cities and over 80 per cent of the population live on the coastal strip of land between the dividing range and the Pacific Ocean. Of these, two-thirds live in eight capital cities and 40 per cent live in the two largest cities, Melbourne and Sydney.

Religiosity

Organized religion was brought to the region by European missionaries in the nineteenth century and the region remains predominantly Christian. In all PICs, over 80 per cent of the population is Christian and in many, more than 90 per cent identify as Christian. The most popular faiths are Anglican, Catholic, Jehovah's Witness, Mormon and Wesleyan Methodist. The Wesleyan missionaries were particularly active in the nineteenth century and they have been joined by various denominations in all PICs. In the early days of colonization, there was significant competition for souls and in many places missionaries actually paved the way for the arrival of Western empires and trading companies.

While Christianity remains dominant, growth has been in religions that have arrived more recently, such as Mormonism. Mormonism is the fastest growing faith in the Pacific. Other faiths, such as Islam and Hinduism, exist in small numbers primarily in Fiji. Even there they are only a large minority amongst the Indo-Fijian community. The Jewish faith is the only religion largely unreported in the region.

It is important to note that European religion has also become interwoven with 'place' and traditional indigenous belief systems that were often polytheistic and focused on ancestors, family and sometimes animism. Sorcery was once widespread in many parts of Melanesia and continues to influence behaviour alongside religions brought from elsewhere. Traditional healing is commonplace and occurs alongside Western medical interventions, often interacting in surprising ways,[12] as in the case of COVID-19 vaccine hesitancy in PNG.[13]

In contrast to the lack of demographic diversity of the South Pacific, Australia is a multicultural society where religious belief is declining and a quarter of the population identify as irreligious. Within this multicultural society, Indigenous Australians currently make up approximately 3 per cent of the total and have been largely displaced and marginalized. As a nation predominantly made up of immigrants and the descendants of immigrants, Australian civic identity is not intertwined with place, with the implication that land ownership is a commercial proposition rather than an identity for most.

While local identity remains the mainstay of Pacific societies, Australia has built a form of civic nationalism that focuses on the state and thus coincides with the historical evolution of multicultural democracies elsewhere. This can be strongly contrasted with many PICs, where nationalism and a national identity do not come naturally to most people, and the penetration of the state into traditional ways of life and thinking is far more limited, trailing off the further from the capital that people live. However, unlike most other states, Australia is founded on a white settler society which provides Strategic Culture with many of its most potent characteristics, such as heightened threat perceptions from 'alien' Asia. The Australian state could be viewed as continuing the white settler legacy and Canberra has to be sensitive to not be labelled by Pacific islanders as neo-colonizers.

Economics, trade and official development assistance (ODA)

As noted, PIC economies involve a high level of subsistence activity, whether farming or fishing, with commercial agriculture often focused on meeting local demand. Beyond subsistence economics, export-oriented industries are largely limited to PNG and Fiji, as is large-scale natural resource extraction (such as mining). Logging is prominent in PNG and the Solomon Islands, and export-oriented fishing occurs across the Pacific with a focus on tuna.

The South Pacific's large EEZs provide many states with income from fisheries, and this is a major source of income for those that straddle tuna fishing grounds. These large fisheries have also prompted highly institutionalized multilateral cooperation to ensure that stocks are managed sustainably. For example, the Western and Central Pacific Fisheries Commission was established by a UN convention and has 26 members, including Australia. Australia's support for monitoring illegal and unreported fishing acknowledges the importance of fisheries income for PICS and is designed to address regional concerns about threats to these fisheries. Sustainable management of forestry is under-developed, largely because forest reserves are national rather than regional issues. Furthermore, some South Pacific governments have been implicated in mismanagement and unsustainable forestry practices.

The focus on subsistence economics, domestic demand and export-oriented fisheries is in marked contrast to Australia, which has an export-oriented economy focused on natural resources and agriculture. While the high volume of economic activity in Australia provides significant government revenue through taxes and charges, all PICs have limited sources of government revenue and run current account deficits. These structural issues were revealed in the weak capacity of PICs to rely on reserves to pay for COVID-19 pandemic relief and the need to borrow to unprecedented levels of their gross domestic product (GDP).

Most PICs are ODA dependent, with varying impacts on their long-term sustainability. In per capita terms and in terms of the ratio of ODA to gross national income (GNI), PICs receive more ODA than any other region on earth. On average, each Pacific islander received just under US$1,000 a year and just under 20 per cent of PIC national incomes are derived from ODA.[14] Key donors are Australia, China, Japan, New Zealand, the US and France. In the case of the latter two donors, the majority of ODA is targeted at their dependent or freely associated territories in the region (American Samoa, French Polynesia, Guam, New Caledonia, Northern Mariana Islands, and Wallis and Futuna). This skews the generalizability of ODA statistics from these great powers (which means that their ODA is not shared across the Pacific). Their focus on dependent territories also highlights the importance of ODA from Australia and China that is distributed to PICs based on other interests, with geopolitics being identified as a more significant driver of ODA flows for these states.

In addition, several PICS have experienced debt distress due to concessional loans (which China prefers to use instead of granting ODA). It is difficult to measure China's ODA and concessional loans to the region, but China has become the fourth largest donor (and second largest if the US and France are discounted).[15] Due to the high levels of ODA and the persistence of development challenges, there is some critique in the literature of the failure of PICs to convert ODA dollars into development or economic outcomes. Besides responses to natural disasters, ongoing deprivation is the focus and most ODA was targeted to meeting the Sustainable Development Goals (SDGs). Externally-led agendas are reflected in Canberra's focus on 'aid for trade' with the idea or hope being that PICs will become sustainable export-oriented economies. Therefore, PICs will become less of a burden on Australia or less of a target for external powers seeking to play out geopolitical contests in Australia's backyard. This hope has not been realized and this might be partly due to the high level of ODA dependence.

The following chapter will delve into more detail of the current state of relations and uses this background chapter as a springboard to do so. The South Pacific region is of central interest to AFP, but its diversity poses challenges unlike the other core diplomatic relationships with medium or great powers. This leads a to a combination of regional and bilateral approaches to engaging with PICs, and the efficacy of this approach has been strained by tensions between Australia's concern over rising geopolitical competition and Canberra's failure to respond wholeheartedly to climate change, the region's prime security interest.

Proximity, history and Canberra's diverse approaches to the region

Proximity is the context that Canberra cannot escape, but that does not mean that it is always reflected in the attention placed on relations within the region. As with Indonesia (see Chapters 9 and 10), Australia is bound to the South Pacific through geography, and this has shaped historical relations and present priorities. However, unlike Indonesia, the asymmetries in relations with PICs are dramatic and unlikely to change (a snapshot of present asymmetries will be discussed below). The unevenness in capacity, power and potential has placed Canberra in a unique position in relation to its other major diplomatic relations, one of being the dominant power. In fact, Australia could be considered a *superpower* in the South Pacific.

Acting from a position of dominance is unusual for Australian policy-makers, and they have not necessarily always exercised this role with diplomatic grace. Policy-makers would at most characterize their position relative to others as a middle or medium power. As noted in Chapter 1, Realism focuses on relative power and being a medium power has limits on the diplomatic 'art of the possible'. At, best a Liberal Internationalist middle power can be creative and strategic in shaping multilateral diplomacy to suit its preferences. Australia exhibits both of these tendencies in its foreign policy and Australia's unique response to its power relative to potential threats and allies is captured in its Strategic Culture. For the most part, this Strategic Culture is viewed in relation to the region to the north that Australia feels threatened by, yet grateful for its economic dynamism. Simultaneously, Australia has looked outside the region for a culturally similar great and powerful friend to act as security guarantor.

With the focus of AFP in Europe, Asia and elsewhere, the South Pacific is often almost invisible in Australia's strategic outlook, until a coup or natural disaster demands attention (although this appears to be changing). Australia has claimed a leadership role in relation to defence and security by providing a guarantee of sorts in relation to supporting PICs against 'unwelcome' outside interference. A problem arises, however, if PICs and Australia have different views of what is unwelcome. The scope of action was laid out in policy documents such as the 1989 Australia's Regional Security statement, where armed intervention to maintain order and protect Australian citizens and interests was countenanced.[16] By the 1990s, Canberra's thinking had firmed, with the 1997 Australia's Strategic Policy statement extending a security guarantee to PNG and, by extension, other Pacific Islands.[17]

There are numerous examples of military and diplomatic intervention over the decades, but the most routine examples of Australia's self-appointed role are evidenced in responses to perceived 'meddling' in Australia's 'backyard' by external powers. A prime example of this was Australia's leadership of a global campaign to stop French nuclear testing in the Pacific in the mid-1990s, but the present response to China also fits this longstanding pattern of strategic denial.[18] For example, the 1997 Australia's Strategic Policy noted:

> Australia's basic geo-strategic interests in Papua New Guinea and the smaller island states of the Southwest Pacific are similar to the interests we have in Indonesia – to prevent their territory being used as a base close to Australia for attacks upon us ... Australia's relative safety from armed attack at present owes much to the common interests we share with these countries, and to freedom from external pressures on their sovereignty.[19]

The open question has been to what extent this outside interference piques Australia's interests because of the impact on the welfare of PICs or the potential security threat to Australia. For example, one of the first acts of the First World War was against German signals station in what was then Papua. In the Second

BACKGROUND TO THE SOUTH PACIFIC

World War, Australian forces were actively involved in halting the Japanese advance on land at Kokoda and Milne Bay, while the navy operated alongside the US in the Battle of the Coral Sea off what is now the Solomon Islands. The Kokoda campaign is central to Australia's national imagination of itself, so much so that Prime Minister Paul Keating suggested that it should be elevated in importance alongside the legend of Gallipoli. However, at the time PNG was not an independent state in need of defence: PNG was the battleground where, in 1942, the existential Japanese threat to Australia was repelled, and this binds Australia to the South Pacific as the strategic space where forward defence and strategic denial can occur to keep threats from Australia's shores.[20] It must be noted that these interventions were not about defending Pacific interests, because these areas were territories of European empires a long way from being decolonized. Similarly, Australia acted to counter perceptions of Soviet encroachment during the latter half of the Cold War in the late 1980s, also due to Australian threat perceptions.

From the perspective of internal stability, Australia has also militarily and diplomatically intervened in the South Pacific on numerous occasions. For example, intervention occurred in response to coups in Fiji in 1987, 2000 and 2006 and state fragility in PNG from 1989 and the Solomon Islands from 2003. Post-decolonization Australia's self-appointed role as a regional policeman has been increasingly challenged by Pacific leaders. Canberra's present focus on countering China is testing Australia's leadership credentials because South Pacific leaders do not necessarily see threats from a geopolitical perspective. As such, China may simply be another development partner playing by different rules. The tension between Australia's interest in strategic denial in the region[21] and interests defined by the PICs themselves (such as climate change) provide a backdrop to AFP towards the region.

By contrast to strategic matters, the South Pacific has been the recipient of significant Australian ODA for generations and this underlying historical role as a benefactor provides a firm foundation for Canberra's claim to exercise leadership in the region. This asymmetrical relationship stretches back to colonial times before Australia's independence when several British possessions in the South Pacific were administered from Australia. The links were so close at this time that when Australian federation was being debated in the 1890s, it was proposed that PNG and Fiji could be united with the Australian colonies. ODA and HADR support for PICs has been a constant that has not waxed and waned based on shifting priorities in Canberra. From this perspective, proximity counts, but so do other drivers of engagement in Canberra, such as leadership aspirations and threat perceptions.

Conclusion

Historically, Australia's response to the South Pacific has generally been reactive. There have been regular local political crises, natural disasters and interventions from outside powers where the relative calm in the South Pacific has been shattered, and these events have prompted a more robust response from Canberra.

However, in the past the calm between crises has often seen Canberra treat the region with benign neglect. This pattern may have ended and the next chapter will test Australia's level of commitment to the region.

With the onset of climate change, regional environmental crises have occurred with greater regularity, as has Australia's willingness to intervene to manage them. Canberra's greater attentiveness also coincides with the rise of China in the region from the mid-2000s. Geopolitical competition has ensured that the pattern of benign neglect, punctuated by emergency responses to isolated events, appears to have shifted so that the South Pacific has become a permanent priority in AFP. This shift will be documented in the next chapter through several case studies, namely the Regional Assistance Mission to the Solomon Islands (RAMSI) intervention from 2003 to 2018, the sanctions following the Fiji coup from 2006 to 2014, and Canberra's Pacific 'Step-up' from 2018.

12

South Pacific:
Australia's 'hegemonic' credentials
under challenge

Introduction

A key challenge for Canberra in dealing with the diversity of the South Pacific discussed in the previous chapter is that Australian foreign policy (AFP) is aimed at multiple audiences in Australia, the South Pacific, as well as to allies and potential adversaries beyond, all with different interests and expectations. Diplomatic messaging to different audiences sometimes leads to tensions and apparent contradictions in AFP towards the South Pacific, especially in relation to the influence of China and climate change.[1]

Key thematic questions canvassed in this chapter include: How does AFP towards the South Pacific differ from other relationships? Can Canberra escape its colonial past to develop sound diplomatic partnerships in the South Pacific? How does Australia's 'great power' role in the South Pacific impact on foreign policy? How can Australia compete with China in the battle for influence in the South Pacific?

Leadership *for whom?*

Since federation, Australia has viewed itself as a regional leader and this is symbolized by Prime Minister Scott Morrison echoing John Howard in calling the South Pacific 'our patch'.[2] This self-appointed leadership role involves responsibilities and obligations, but Pacific Island Countries (PICs) have often been disappointed to find that Australia's priorities are not always focused on obligations to the Pacific. Australia is not a PIC, but rather could be seen as a neighbour seeking to be treated as an insider. From this perspective, Australia – and New Zealand (NZ) – are treated as metropolitan powers, as distinct to outside powers. As geopolitical contest intensifies, this is an important distinction in relation to outside powers such as China, Indonesia or Russia. More is expected from Australia than from outside powers in relation to official development assistance (ODA) and preferential trade, while the overarching responsibility for security, including humanitarian assistance and disaster response (HADR), is taken for granted.

If we transpose the observations from Australia's relations with allies and other great powers, it is clear that the US alliance is never far from the minds of Australian policy-makers. In the South Pacific, this plays out in a unique way because Canberra assumed the responsibility of managing the South Pacific (alongside NZ) in the name of Western interests under the Canberra Pact in 1944.[3] New Zealand gave up this responsibility in the 1980s when it challenged the US strategy of nuclear deterrence, leading to their suspension from the ANZUS alliance, and Australia willingly filled the void. An official recognition of this role is evident in the 'secret' Radford-Collins Agreement from the 1950s, which identifies responsibility for the management of sea lanes of communication in the South Pacific to Australia. As such, Australia's leadership can be contextualized in relation to larger geopolitical competition (at first during the Cold War and now with a new Cold War with China underway). It is also apparent that proximity and history are important contextual factors that must be taken into account in analysing AFP in the South Pacific. This means that AFP has an audience in Washington, DC that cannot be discounted and Canberra's leadership credentials do not simply reflect Australian public opinion or attitudes of PICs, but also the perceptions of an alliance partner. In this manner, Australia's ability to speak on behalf of PICs and its responsibility to act on their behalf has strategic significance beyond day-to-day diplomacy.

In South Pacific capitals, Canberra's self-appointed sense of responsibility has been interpreted as paternalism and while this can be welcomed, it can equally become a source of tension. The growing confidence and assertiveness of PIC leaders, and the availability of alternative options for ODA, finance and diplomatic support from states such as China, means that Canberra's capacity to exercise leadership is being challenged. In this context, simply doing more of the same in AFP is likely to be counterproductive due to the possibility of charges of neo-colonialism. This is most evident in Canberra's response to climate change, which angered PICs. Criticism softened with compromises made by the newly elected Albanese government, but PICs are rightly sceptical and it remains to be seen whether Australia follows through on domestic targets. The responses of PICs to Australia's approach to climate change also highlights that Canberra will be held to a higher account than other diplomatic partners because it is viewed as a regional partner and friend. China may be able to do more to substantively combat climate change by cutting its significant level of carbon emissions, but it is not treated as a regional power and not held to account in the way that Australia is.

Australia as a neo-colonial bully or saviour?

Australian diplomacy is regularly criticized from within the region as being insensitive, patronizing and/or heavy handed. Examples abound and this dynamic is by no means new. For example, in the 1990s, Prime Minister John Howard claimed a 'special responsibility' for the Pacific,[4] which justified military intervention and ODA, but also embedded Australia's good governance agenda in the ODA programme. A focus on issues such as good governance and gender may have reflected best practice in international development but did not always align with the priorities identified by PIC leaders. This was followed by a shift in priority to 'aid for trade', which also may have not been the priority in PICs.

Furthermore, Australia's behaviour has often been particularly insulting given the hierarchical nature of South Pacific societies and their reverence for leaders ('big men'). In the mid-1990s, a classified Australian intelligence briefing paper was inadvertently left at a meeting of Pacific leaders and fell into the hands of journalists. The report, meant for Australian political leaders' eyes only, was highly critical of the probity of Pacific leaders, describing them as corrupt drunks who mismanaged Pacific economies to the brink of bankruptcy. The prime minister of Fiji, Sitiveni Rabuka, was particularly vocal in his criticism of Canberra's 'disrespect'.[5] Other PIC leaders were less public in their criticism, due in part to asymmetries in relation to their ODA dependence, but this did not mean that Canberra's attitudes had not undermined relations. This dynamic is similar to the slight and escalation that occurs with Indonesia (discussed in Chapter 10), but in this case the uneven nature of relations and Pacific Way of consensus pushes tensions behind closed doors.

In addition to being insensitive to regional hierarchies, Australian comments are also regularly characterized as patronizing. This has two levels with respect to the natural interests of PICs and their relative weakness in being able to both engineer sustainable development trajectories and respond to natural disasters.[6] For example, in 2015, Australia's immigration minister, Peter Dutton, made a joke to the prime minister about PICs having 'water lapping at their doors' that was overheard by a microphone and led to a chorus of criticism.[7] In 2018, the environment minister insulted the former president of Kiribati, Anote Tong, by suggesting the Pacific leaders were always searching for cash and offered to get her chequebook to pay him.[8] More recently, in response to the deadlock at the 2019 PIF leaders' meeting in Tuvalu, Australia's deputy prime minister, Michael McCormack, dismissively responded to Pacific concerns about climate change by saying that they could 'come here and pick our fruit'.[9] The pent-up frustration amongst PIC leaders was clear from the 2019 PIF meeting, which ended with the host passionately warning: 'don't expect that [Australia] comes and we bow down'.[10]

A key element of the critique of AFP is the use of 'megaphone diplomacy', whereby undiplomatic statements are made to the press from afar, and the Morrison and Albanese governments have been careful to not fall into this trap. Australia's view of itself contrasts with increasingly sensitive regional attitudes to Australia's clumsy diplomacy, especially in relation to climate change, which PICs view as an existential threat, but Australia has only been willing to effectively address very recently.

Canberra consistently proclaims a sense of responsibility for the Pacific, which could be described as a 'Special Relationship' of the sort developed by great powers with each other or lesser powers,[11] but one where proximity and asymmetry coincide to shape a sense of obligation, albeit one that has the potential to be described as paternal and patronizing. Australia has been accused of being the US 'Deputy Sheriff' in the South Pacific but this does not do justice to the hegemonic role Australia plays as the sheriff in relation to natural disasters and political crises.[12]

CASE STUDY 12.1: METROPOLITAN VERSUS GEOGRAPHIC IDENTITY: WEST PAPUA AND SOUTH PACIFIC IDENTITY

An unresolved issue for the South Pacific is the treatment of West Papua, which highlights how fundamentally Australia is not a PIC. Protest in West Papua has occurred since the discredited referendum saw Indonesia take control in 1969 and violence has regularly flared up. Many Pacific Islanders believe that West Papuans should be brought into the regional narrative, rather than treating them as an Indonesian or Southeast Asian problem. South Pacific leaders, especially those from Vanuatu, have been increasingly vocal in criticisms of alleged human rights abuses.[13] There has been division in the region about how to respond, especially between Melanesian states with closer relations to Indonesia, and this has played out in different responses in various fora. There is support for greater autonomy or independence and this has caused tension in key regional organizations, including the PIF, the Melanesian Spearhead Group (MSG) and the Pacific Islands Development Forum (PIDF). In addition, the Pacific Small Island Developing States (PSIDS) grouping in the UN has allowed PIC concerns to be aired on the international stage.

In 2019, PIF leaders called on Indonesia to allow a fact-finding visit by the UN High Commissioner for Human Rights, an issue that has previously been sidelined by Canberra. It may be no coincidence that increasing confidence amongst PIC leaders in relation to regional interests on issues such as climate change is spilling over into other issues that Australia (and other outside powers) have been able to moderate in the past. In this case, Vanuatu has exercised significant leadership in maintaining a strong position that has previously been watered down or completely excluded by Australia. Consensus is becoming harder to engineer when the mood has shifted to frustration with a lack of action by Indonesia, and those such as Australia who are unwilling to support action. This builds the perception that Australia is more an outsider than a neighbour and undermines Australian attempts to connect AFP with Australia's participation in a South Pacific family. As such, the unresolved West Papua issue highlights another weakness in Australia's ability to influence the region; soft power requires the acquiescence of those being influenced and the levers of Australia's 'soft' and 'hard' power in the region are under challenge both from within the region and by outside powers such as China.

China does not claim to support human rights – in fact, it's record on human rights in areas such as Xinjiang is shocking. Regardless, Canberra is held to a higher standard than China by PICs. This is the nightmare scenario for Canberra that feeds the threat perceptions inherent in Strategic Culture, whereby a potentially hostile power gains a tactical foothold that can be leveraged into a strategic challenge. The inability to capitalize on Australia's hard security power and shared history to gain influence in the South Pacific has also been an enduring theme in AFP and one that has perplexed policy-makers and commentators alike.[14] Meanwhile, the geopolitical contest with China intensifies.

The treatment of West Papua also highlights that the patchy application of Liberal Internationalist values in foreign policy can do reputational harm. Canberra is critical of China's record on human rights but has not been willing to address the issue with Indonesia due to the pressing national interest of maintaining stability and good relations (discussed in Chapter 10). In this context, Canberra cannot afford to alienate PICs, but that is exactly what occurred over climate change at the 2019 PIF leaders' meeting. As with climate change, Australia has other international interests that impacted on its approach to West Papua, namely the protection of the relationship with Indonesia that is extremely sensitive to any interference over human rights. The protection of the relationship with Indonesia has been prioritized in AFP and this is evidence of a Realist/Strategic Cultural prioritization of protecting Australia's security from threats 'from or through Indonesia'[15] over domestic human rights concerns. Unfortunately Canberra's approach also impacts relations with the South Pacific.

Australia's membership of the PIF versus the double standard China can leverage off as an outsider

A key difference between Australia and its strategic competitors was that Australia was a full member of the pre-eminent regional organization, the PIF, and to have its credentials challenged at a time when it wanted to leverage off proximity and history was highly problematic. Even more galling was when Anote Tong, former president of Kiribati, called for Australia's suspension from the forum by comparing Australia's behaviour to Fiji's in the 2000s (when it had a military coup).[16] Canberra had achieved regional support through the PIF for its sanctions regime against Fiji for eight years and the suggestion that its behaviour was comparable demonstrated how fragile influence is and how quickly regional dynamics can change.

PIC leaders have foreshadowed that they will not ignore Canberra's uncompromising stance on climate change, so this issue will require concerted effort; the benign neglect that Australia has often shown in the past will not suffice. Similarly, Canberra's criticism of China was turned back on itself when the prime minister of Fiji, Frank Bainimarama, accused Australia of 'chequebook diplomacy'. This is a charge usually levelled at China and Taiwan in relation to their attempts to try to use ODA and other inducements to buy diplomatic recognition for one against the other. To level the charge against Australia is particularly effective, given the good governance agenda whereby China's destabilizing foreign policy initiatives, for instance in relation to 'debt-trap' diplomacy, have been consistently criticized.[17]

China has become increasingly aware of the cleavages in the South Pacific and has leveraged them to gain influence in the region. Part of the fallout from the 2019 PIF was a series of unguarded comments by China's diplomats about Australia's behaviour, which they claimed represented the Pacific view of Australia. The Chinese Foreign Ministry noted that 'it wasn't the first time that leaders of the Pacific Island Countries resented Australia's behaviour'.[18] China has been escalating the war of words and Australia's regional leadership credentials have been a prime target. Furthermore, there is a real vulnerability for Canberra due to the stark domestic decisions relating to climate change that would need to be made to satisfy PIC leaders.

The Albanese government's climate change commitments in 2022 were well received. The government committed to a 43 per cent cut in emissions by 2030 and becoming net zero by 2050. This met international expectations and changed Australia from being a pariah to a partner on climate change. However, these commitments needed to be backed up by action and it remains to be seen whether the government can achieve them without radically transforming the Australian economy away from export-oriented extraction of natural resources. Regardless of the declaratory policy shift on climate change, if Canberra is not willing to compromise on climate change *to the level required by PICs*, then a wholesale shift in approach would be needed to try to work around the blockages in relations.

This episode is telling insofar as it revealed a double standard in relation to China's record on climate change. At over 30 per cent of the global total, China's emissions dwarf Australia's (1 per cent) and cuts to their emissions would significantly impact the trajectory of climate change. However, China was not held to account by PICs on emissions, even when the Chinese Foreign Ministry weighed in to criticize Australia's diplomacy. This led the New Zealand foreign minister to openly defend Australia against this apparent double standard. Regardless, as a metropolitan power claiming leadership credentials, Australia is judged differently to China.

The diplomatic acrimony the 2019 PIF reveals that there is a basis for the sense of a Pacific family that Canberra hopes to connect with, which means PICs are profoundly disappointed with Australia's stance as they want Canberra to be convinced to comprehensively change policy even if this will not materially impact on the threats they face, such as rising sea levels. This belief and hope demonstrates the natural affinity that comes with historical ties and proximity that outside powers cannot hope to build regardless of chequebook diplomacy involving increased ODA. The PIC response to Australia also highlights that there are limits to how much a wayward Pacific family member, so to speak, will be excused for aberrant behaviour. Therefore, Canberra must be aware of how much goodwill and political capital it has expended in the past by not wholeheartedly compromising on climate change, and how much it will lose if it doesn't follow through on recent commitments.

CASE STUDY 12.2: THE ACRIMONIOUS 2019 PIF AS A TURNING POINT IN AUSTRALIA'S RELATIONS WITH PICS

Claims of bullying and neo-colonialism are never far from the surface of diplomacy in the South Pacific, and are often levelled when Canberra attempts to achieve its interests through regional fora such as the PIF. There was acrimony during the fiftieth meeting in Tuvalu in 2019 in relation to the failure to compromise to reach a consensus on climate change. In the face of rising

SOUTH PACIFIC: AUSTRALIA'S 'HEGEMONIC' CREDENTIALS 217

frustration amongst PIC leaders over the lack of a meaningful global response to climate change, Australia was viewed as being intransigent as it brought to the negotiating table several 'red lines' over which it was not willing to compromise.

Australia's 'red lines' included not being willing to phase out coal mining or make binding commitments to limit global warming to under 1.5°C, as suggested by the Intergovernmental Panel on Climate Change (IPCC). The 12-hour marathon negotiations produced a compromise leaders' communique, which was promptly followed by a stronger unofficial statement (the Kainaki II Declaration) that was agreed by PICs but not endorsed by Australia.[19] Ultimately, the outcome highlighted that Australia's national interest was intimately entwined in the continuing export of hydrocarbons and that this would be prioritized over PIC interests.

This statement of Australia's Realist domestic economic interests may have seemed brutal to PIC leaders and climate change activists in Australia, but it reflects a consistent message that is only brutal insofar as it is seldom expressed so clearly. The prime minister was representing the Australian people and domestic political considerations are prime: he pointedly noted that he is 'accountable to the Australian people'.[20] This position was teased out in heated debate between the Australian prime minister, Scott Morrison and his host the prime minister of Tuvalu, Enele Sopaoga, where the latter charged: 'You are concerned about saving your economy in Australia . . . I am concerned about saving my people in Tuvalu.'[21] Morrison's response that a strong Australian economy was necessary to provide continued ODA has neo-colonial tones and did not appease PIC leaders.

Morrison's stance was not simply about electioneering and public opinion, but rather a long-term reflection on the economic growth trajectory needed to maintain the prosperity that supports the Australian way of life. While the opposition in Australia attempted to score political points from the tension at the PIF, they ultimately admitted that they too were wedded to a continued reliance on coal for export income and domestic electricity production.[22] An unequivocal prioritization of economic interests hardly ever occurs in international affairs because it is not diplomatic, but in the case of not phasing out coal, the prime minister was on firm ground.

There has been strong sentiment in Australia for many years to respond to climate change, but not if this undermines prosperity. Furthermore, as with many advanced developed countries, a technological fix is often sought to manage the challenge, rather than a more fundamental shift in economic activity or social expectations. A technological fix is ostensibly what was on offer when Morrison pledged A$500 million to PICs for climate change mitigation and adaptation to the region on the eve of the PIF, but it was viewed as a band aid by PICs.

What's even more illuminating for AFP is that this statement of economic interests is potentially in tension with a Realist/Strategic Cultural focus on military security: in this case, the strategic denial of competitors in the South Pacific. Despite the obvious priority of gaining PIC support for managing geostrategic competition with China, this priority was not enough to force compromise in the overarching focus on the prosperity and welfare brought by

Australia's hydrocarbon-led, export-oriented trade policy. This highlights that in sharp contrast to the South Pacific, Canberra does not perceive an existential threat from climate change and its threat perceptions are focused on orthodox military threats. As such, they are amenable to national military security responses, such as armament and alliance, rather than by reference to a Liberal Internationalist ethic of multilateralism. Despite the obvious contradiction in their stance due to being the largest greenhouse gas emitter, this is yet another point that China is willing to take advantage of, with Beijing highlighting Australia's 'obsolete Cold-War mentality and zero-sum game mindset'.[23]

In the aftermath of the acrimonious 2019 PIF meeting, the prime minister of Fiji, Frank Bainimarama, accused Australia of being 'insulting and condescending' and the prime minister of Tuvalu, Enele Sopoaga, described Australia's approach as 'neo-colonial' and 'very un-Pacific'. He went on to comment regarding the fruit-picking comments: 'I don't think that the Tuvaluan people are paupers to come crawling under that type of very abusive and offensive language.'[24] The most sensitive criticism, related to Australia's leadership credentials, was to question: 'what is the point of these guys [Australia] remaining in the Pacific Island Leaders Forum?'[25] Australia's claims of family bonds with the Pacific, or *vuvale* in Fijian, a central plank in the present 'Step-up' policy, were roundly criticized in an unprecedented show of public division.

More significantly for AFP, China has also used the tension in Australia's relations with the South Pacific as part of their broader diplomatic, economic and geostrategic conflict with Australia. Furthermore, this conflict with Canberra is connected to Australia's support for the 'rules based order' and US alliance (see Chapter 4). This would be a counterproductive tactic if reducing diplomatic tension in bilateral relations between China and Australia is Beijing's aim, as it strikes a diplomatic blow. For instance, at a low point in the present diplomatic 'freeze', a Chinese delegation asserted that 'in Fiji, they think China respects them more than you respect them'.[26] Undiplomatic public statements like this characterize tensions in bilateral relations and highlight that the geostrategic battleground is broader than simply the trade sanctions China has imposed on Australia.

The fallout from the 2019 PIF highlights a number of trends that AFP has to grapple with. First, PIC leaders are increasingly confident in identifying and acting on their interests, and less likely to be influenced by external powers.[27] Second, by extension, Canberra's capacity to sway opinion has waned and attempts at building influence are becoming more complex. Third, the climate change 'elephant in the room' is in the spotlight. Australia's late compromises on climate change question its capacity to 'speak' for the PICs or represent them in international fora. Fourth, Australia's leadership credentials are under threat from powers it defines as inimical to its interests, namely China, but potentially from Russia as well, and AFP's underlying focus on traditional geostrategic threats may be making this situation worse.

In sum, the South Pacific is more 'crowded and complex'[28] and this challenges many of the assumptions underpinning AFP towards the Pacific to date. There are limits to both the influence gained from asymmetry that characterizes the Realist tendencies in relation to the region, and the altruism and paternalism that is reflective of the Liberal Internationalist aspect of AFP that was so important to how the South Pacific is framed domestically. Finally, the threat perceptions that drive Strategic Culture have been triggered due to the proximity of the China 'threat' and this is driving a securitized view of the South Pacific and one whereby military diplomacy will play an increasingly important part.[29]

The South Pacific is strategically significant to Australia insofar as it is treated as Australia's area of primary strategic concern, and this explains the strategic denial of geopolitical competitors practised so consistently. As such, Canberra is sensitive to the geostrategic competition shaping Australia's bilateral relations with China playing out in the South Pacific. This fits a long-established pattern whereby a period of benign neglect of the region is followed by a reset and at present, this is reflected in a concerted effort to develop a cohesive Pacific foreign policy to protect Australia's interests. There could be no effective 'Step-up' without effective action on climate change, and this came with the election of the Albanese government in 2022.

Australia's South Pacific 'Step-up'

Perceptions of increased Chinese influence in the South Pacific grew over the 2000s and Canberra wanted to strengthen ties with the region, but this could not happen in earnest until sanctions against Fiji were lifted in December 2014. Fiji was the most vocal opponent of Australia's claims to leadership within the region and is therefore integral to the success of any new initiatives. The implementation of the Turnbull government's 2016 Pacific 'Step-up' was delayed due to domestic political manoeuvring and did not really gain pace until Prime Minister Scott Morrison put his stamp on it in 2018. Since then, Morrison made the Pacific a priority. When visiting Fiji in January 2019, he said that 'to step up you have to show up',[30] and he and his ministers have followed through on this commitment. However, despite this flowery rhetoric, it was not until the Albanese government was elected that barriers to closer relations could be broken down. Furthermore, Foreign Minister Penny Wong's frenetic pace of visits to South Pacific capitals redefined what it meant to 'show up'.

Notwithstanding the barrier imposed by the inability to compromise on climate change, the Morrison government made significant strides in re-engaging with the South Pacific. A series of annual leaders' meetings were instituted to deliver on the pledge of maintaining regular high-level diplomacy. This was a direct response to criticisms of earlier prime ministers, who generally only ventured into the Pacific for the annual PIF leaders' meetings and whose non-attendance at many PIF meetings was treated as a diplomatic snub.

Scott Morrison made his first overseas trip to the South Pacific, was the first prime minister to visit Fiji for a generation, and the first ever to visit twice in a year, when he used 'rugby diplomacy' to reconnect with Prime Minister Bainimarama after the war of words over climate change at the 2019 PIF meeting in Tuvalu. One clear trend in AFP is that Canberra has generally treated the Pacific with benign neglect until a crisis occurs. It then responds like a fireman arriving to put out a fire that is well and truly alight. As the crisis is resolved, Australia then withdraws to focus on other more pressing foreign policy priorities elsewhere. The Morrison government was well on the way to combatting this perception amongst PIC leaders, especially with respect to Australia's long sanctions against Fiji, and the key diplomatic challenge was the disruption caused by geostrategic competition with China.

The Albanese government was elected at a time of heightened geopolitical competition with China in the South Pacific. In fact, China signed a security agreement with the Solomon Islands in the midst of the election campaign, which appeared to be a tactical decision to take advantage of a government in caretaker mode. This agreement caused alarm in Canberra, and amongst strategic analysts, who dwelled on a worst-case scenario whereby a Chinese base would disrupt sea lanes of communication with the US during a future conflict. China went on to try to negotiate a region-wide security agreement but failed to get traction, in part due to the concerns of PICs about being drawn into a geopolitical contest.

The China threat (to Australia's interests) in the South Pacific

Australia's renewed interest in the South Pacific corresponds with a firming of opinions in the security establishment in Canberra over the potential threat posed by China. Most commentary focused on geostrategic issues and saw the Pacific as a potential battleground.[31] However, Prime Minister Morrison is also credited with providing high-level political will, in a similar way as Foreign Minister Julie Bishop did, in elevating the relative position of the Pacific in AFP to the point where it could be viewed as a top priority. Much has been made of Morrison's missionary experience in Fiji in his youth, and his shared love of rugby, but regardless of whether these connections were central to decision-making, the government has maintained a level of engagement with the South Pacific that showed no sign of waning.

In this case, proximity is clearly a key driver of AFP, as was the personal attitudes of leaders that aligned with Australia's Strategic Culture. Similarly, a strategy that includes developing personal relationships and affinity speaks to South Pacific concerns about Australian neo-colonial bullying and does not fit easily with orthodox International Relations perspectives on how states achieve their interests. After the election of the Albanese government in 2022, this approach was accelerated by Foreign Minister Penny Wong in her frenetic diplomacy to counter Chinese entreaties. The message was that Canberra was listening to Pacific concerns and listening was followed by tangible actions in relation to climate change, security and labour mobility.

Subsequently, Australia signed bilateral security agreements with PNG and Vanuatu focused on dialogue and security issues identified as priorities by PICs such as humanitarian assistance and disaster response. That these agreements were signed so quickly highlights the success of the government's approach, and also the willingness of PICs to partner with Australia. However, in the case of PNG, the agreement simply complements already extensive practical defence cooperation.

A whole-of-government approach

A key characteristic of the 'Step-up' initiative is the focus on a whole-of-government approach from Australia towards the South Pacific. Previously, the development focus of AFP in the region was evident insofar as Australia's dedicated ODA agency, the Australian Agency for International Development (AusAID), had been a central implementer of foreign policy in the region. Other departments and areas were also integral in providing specialist support for Australia's interests, especially from the Department of Foreign Affairs and Trade (DFAT) and the Department of Defence (DOD) during HADR operations.

Following the absorption of AusAID into DFAT in 2013, decision-making became more centralized and, in the light of perceptions of a rising geopolitical challenge from China, more securitized. In 2018, the Office of the Pacific was created to coordinate all government stakeholders in delivering the 'Step-up'. The new approach made the implementation of the regional engagement aspects of the 2016 Defence White Paper and 2017 Foreign Affairs White Paper a priority and signalled a comprehensive and long-term commitment. The open question is whether this attention will challenge previous cases of heightened tension that faded into benign neglect.

The Foreign Policy White Paper views integration within the region and with Australia as being 'vital' to building a sustainable future of PICs.[32] As such, the 'Step-up' gives voice to an underlying integrative impulse in AFP towards the South Pacific that focuses on Australia leading attempts to more closely connect security, economic and developmental activities. This integrative tendency gives voice to Australia's leadership ambitions, and the fact that it is framed on Australia's terms highlights the inbuilt weakness and limitation in the approach, because in the White Paper and 'Step-up' responding effectively to halt climate change was not prioritized, but assisting PICs to adapt to climate change were included through initiatives such as labour mobility programmes.

From this perspective, ongoing initiatives, such as the Pacific Agreement on Closer Economic Relations (PACER and PACER+), were incorporated as planks in a whole-of-government approach to the region with the new Australian Infrastructure Financing Facility for the Pacific (AIFFP), coordinated HADR and multi-agency response to transnational crime. Australia's conceptualization of a South Pacific 'family' would connect PICs to take greater advantage of economies of scale in areas where the sustainability of one bilateral approach, or one economy, aligned with neo-liberalism and was questionable in the South Pacific context.

Importantly for Canberra, it was envisioned that Australia's leadership credentials would be boosted by this comprehensive reset of AFP. While the 'Step-up' represents a concerted effort on the part of the Morrison and Albanese governments, it must be noted that it also represents the latest in a long line of attempts to encourage integration and sustainability, such as the Howard government's 2005 Pacific Plan and the Rudd government's Port Moresby

Declaration in 2008. Therefore, we must be mindful of the fact that Pacific leaders have seen commitments such as these from Canberra only to see them fade away into benign neglect.

The Australian Infrastructure Financing Facility for the Pacific (AIFFP)

One *new* initiative in the 'Step-up' was the creation of the AIFFP. The infrastructure facility is a departure from Australia's practice of gifting ODA because it involves gifts and loans. The focus is also different insofar as the aim is to respond to infrastructure needs identified by the PICs themselves rather than Australia's traditional emphasis on building capacity to tackle particular social and governance challenges, such as gender inequality. As such, it is a clever innovation that aligns the shift to 'aid for trade' within AFP with the demands of PICs that have been increasingly met by China, which, unlike Australia, treats concessional loans for infrastructure as ODA.

The incorporation of infrastructure in ODA also highlights the continuing shift from AusAID's focus on governance and capacity-building, with gender programmes being the clearest point of continuity. AusAID was absorbed into DFAT in 2013 for largely domestic political and bureaucratic reasons, and therefore caution is needed in relation to attributing too much of the 'aid for trade' agenda in the 'Step-up' to external factors, such as countering China's influence in the region. As such, the 'aid for trade' approach can be attributed to a domestic neoliberal economic agenda that can be harnessed to achieve Australia's national interests in countering China. This shifts emphasis from Liberal Internationalist agendas and altruism to a more Realist focus on national interests.

There are questions about the efficacy of providing loans for ODA, and in the lead up to the AIFFP announcement, this had been a key criticism of China's approach to ODA. Development practitioners have been concerned both about whether development outcomes could be delivered through loans and about the long-term sustainability of this approach, as the track record in the South Pacific was not overly positive.[33] The issue became politicized and public debate in Australia concentrated on the allegedly insidious aims of China entrapping PICs. The focus was on unsustainable lending, which could lead to 'debt traps', whereby China could leverage PICs due to unfulfillable repayment obligations.[34] These arguments were exaggerated by rumours in 2018 that China was negotiating setting up a military base in Vanuatu and they highlighted the strategic denial mindset in AFP.[35] China's negotiation of a defence cooperation agreement with the Solomon Islands, announced during the 2022 Australian federal election campaign, brought these fears to a head.

Public opinion towards the South Pacific

The government is on firm ground with public opinion strongly supporting both Australia's long-term approach to the South Pacific and of Canberra's recent

SOUTH PACIFIC: AUSTRALIA'S 'HEGEMONIC' CREDENTIALS

'Step-up' initiative. For example, large majorities of respondents in the 2022 Lowy Poll believed that Australia should pay for COVID-19 vaccines and HADR for Pacific islanders (86 per cent and 93 per cent respectively).[36] According to the 2019 Lowy Poll, a firm majority (75 per cent) continued to support Australia's interventionist stance whereby military forces would be used to restore law and order and respond to humanitarian crises. A large majority (88 per cent) agreed with the strategic appraisal that a Chinese base in the Pacific would pose a 'critical threat' to Australia's interests, demonstrating the strategic denial apparent in Australia's Strategic Culture has been internalized in (or originates in) public opinion.[37] As such, it is not surprising that 73 per cent believed that 'Australia should try to prevent China from increasing its influence in the Pacific' and 82 per cent think that ODA should be used to counter Chinese influence.

Interestingly, while the public firmly believed that meeting the geopolitical challenge posed by China in the Pacific was a priority, the population was divided over whether more ODA should be spent on the South Pacific (48 to 49 per cent).[38] However, this stance should also be treated with caution, as it has been demonstrated that the Australian public consistently overestimates how much is spent on ODA (see Chapter 13). For instance, in 2019, the Australian public thought that 14 per cent of the federal budget was spent on ODA and believed that it should be adjusted down to 12 per cent, but the 2019 ODA budget was in fact less than 1 per cent.[39]

The following sections will develop the present implications of the 'Step-up' in key policy areas of security, ODA and trade.

Security cooperation: Defence and humanitarian assistance and disaster response (HADR)

Defence cooperation has been a mainstay of AFP in the South Pacific for decades. It is noteworthy that defence cooperation is not counted as ODA, so it represents additional resources being targeted to the region through military diplomacy. The Defence Cooperation Programme (DCP) has involved a broad spectrum of activities, from personnel exchanges and exercises to the provision of defence equipment and HADR. Donating defence infrastructure has always been a key element of the engagement, in contrast to ODA where capacity-building has been the focus (until recently at least). The pattern of engagement has involved ongoing military diplomacy, building 'people-to-people' links supported by the strategic provision of equipment, such as patrol boats, and services, such as maritime surveillance.

Recent defence infrastructure projects that are aligned with the 'Step-up' include the joint development of the Lombrum naval base on Manus Island in PNG and the Black Rock HADR facility in Fiji. The A$170 million Lombrum project was mutually beneficial for Australia/US and PNG. For Australia, it was evidence of the geopolitical contest with China and allowed Australia to cooperate with its ally, the US, in doing so. In comments he was forced to retract for

224   AUSTRALIAN FOREIGN POLICY

diplomatic reasons, the chief of the PNG Defence Force confirmed this strategic necessity.[40]

For PNG, the Lombrum base redevelopment provided necessary infrastructure for the patrol boats donated by Australia. It was a also convenient injection of resources into the province since the Manus Island Regional Processing Centre closed (see Chapter 15). Similarly, the development of Fiji's Black Rock base was widely viewed as a response to China (which was reportedly interested in developing the base),[41] while also providing Fiji with essential infrastructure to support its deployments to UN peacekeeping operations.

CASE STUDY 12.3: THE PACIFIC MARITIME SECURITY PROGRAMME AND PACIFIC SUPPORT FORCE

A key defence infrastructure project that cemented Australia's position as a security partner of choice was the provision of 22 patrol boats to 11 PICs through the Pacific Patrol Boat Project in the 1980s. After 30 years' service, these vessels reached the end of their useful life and were replaced by new Guardian Class patrol boats through the 2017 Pacific Maritime Security Programme (PMSP). The PMSP will cost Australian taxpayers over A$2 billion over the next 30 years. The first boat was delivered to PNG in 2018, with subsequent deliveries of 19 vessels to 12 PICs. The new vessels are more capable and tailored to the needs of PICs insofar as they have greater capacity to independently respond to local maritime contingencies, including HADR.

These vessels are one element of the broader PMSP, which includes in-country support, training, exchanges and maritime surveillance by Australian aircraft. Together, the PMSP is aimed at enhancing maritime intelligence and interoperability with Australia and other PICs. These projects also enhance Australia's position as the partner of choice in security affairs, which was a key aim of the 2016 Defence White Paper. As with the earlier programme, these vessels have been being gifted to PICs, which is consistent with Australia's approach to ODA. However, the greatest strategic benefit to Australia is that this second iteration of the programme has cemented Australia's position as a security partner of choice for two generations. Competing powers such as China can offer niche equipment and infrastructure, but this integrated programme is comprehensive and affordable, and epitomizes strategic denial as it crowds out the influence of others.

In mid-2019, the creation of the Pacific Support Force (PSF) was announced to collaborate more closely with PICs. Its focus was on the states with the two largest militaries, PNG and Fiji, but cooperation with Vanuatu, which does not have a military, was also foreshadowed. The PSF is a dedicated unit within the Australian Army's First Division based in Brisbane. Its focus is on training and it is modelled on the army's approach to military diplomacy honed in Afghanistan. As geostrategic competition heated up across the region, Canberra sought to institutionalize security arrangements by updating and developing new defence and security cooperation agreements with PICs such as PNG and Vanuatu (both in 2022). Australia's great and powerful friend, the US, was also firming relations and Canberra welcomed the Biden administration's Declaration on US–Pacific Partnership in September 2022. In the stroke of a pen, the US achieved what the Chinese attempted earlier in the year when China's foreign minister visited the region with a draft agreement in hand, only to be rebuffed by PIC leaders.

Australia as a regional policeman: Regional Assistance Mission to the Solomon Islands (RAMSI) and the Enhanced Cooperation Programme (ECP)

Australia's post-Cold War military interventions in the region include Bougainville from 1989, East Timor from 1998 and the Solomon Islands from 2003. There were also administrative and diplomatic interventions in PNG in 2006 and sanctions against Fiji from 2006 to 2014. The intervention in the Solomons ended in 2017 and had a significant impact on AFP and Pacific security; as such, it will be dealt with in depth.

Prior to the intervention, Canberra denied requests for support from the Solomon Islands government for several years, but quickly reversed its stance by leading the RAMSI from 2003. This shift highlighted the impact of the 9/11 attacks on the US in 2001 on Australia's strategic outlook[42] and Canberra's securitization of domestic instability in the South Pacific. Instability in the proximate region was perceived as a direct threat to Australia's national interests (see the discussion of how this trend played out in Indonesia in Chapter 10).

The RAMSI operation was conceived with little DFAT input and represented the Howard government's search for non-institutionalized options to foreign policy challenges.[43] At the time, the Australian Defence Force (ADF) was engaged

BOX 12.1: RAMSI AT A GLANCE, 2003–17

- Began with an Australia-led military and police intervention in 2003.
- Followed by state-building efforts largely funded by Australian and NZ ODA.
- Lasted 14 years with ongoing security support from Australia.
- One death of an Australian soldier.
- Cost Australia taxpayers approximately A$3 billion.
- Coalition comprising Australia, New Zealand and member states of the Pacific Islands Forum, namely Federated States of Micronesia, Fiji, Kiribati, Marshall Islands, PNG, Tonga, Tuvalu, Vanuatu.
- Involved approximately 2,200 personnel (military and police), the vast majority of whom were Australian.

in active combat operations in Afghanistan and Iraq, and it was argued that it could devote newly honed skills to this relatively straightforward intervention in Australia's 'backyard'. Other than one notable reversal in the security situation in 2006, the ADF and, subsequently, Australian police were able to create a secure enabling environment for development activities to occur. The state-building tasks undertaken by DFAT and other departments were challenging aspects of the operation as administrative and judicial systems were restored and strengthened, and a significant effort was applied to rebuilding faith amongst Solomon Islanders in the rule of law.[44]

The commitment is ongoing, as Canberra negotiated a security treaty with the Solomon Islands guaranteeing continuing support, including the possibility of military intervention at the invitation of the Government of the Solomon Islands, after the final withdrawal of forces in 2017. This arrangement was called into question by Australia's response to rioting in the Solomons in 2019. In 2019, domestic tensions sparked by the shift in diplomatic recognition from Taiwan to China boiled over, leading to riots in Honiara with Chinatown being the target of looting and arson. The reasons for the rioting had as much to do with underlying domestic tensions as they did to diplomatic recognition, but the point was that law and order broke down and Australia intervened alongside other Pacific forces. For the Chinese government, the fact that Chinatown and other Chinese assets were burned called into question the efficacy of Canberra's policing response, especially in a time of heightened geopolitical competition.

What followed was the 2022 security agreement between China and the Solomon Islands. The key aim for the Chinese was to train Solomon Islands security forces to respond to future challenges and to provide an avenue to deploy forces to defend Chinese assets if need be. The ramifications of the agreement were profound. Canberra tried to scupper the agreement, but the Solomons did not bow to external pressure. The US also applied pressure and the Chinese played the sovereignty card to defend the actions of the Solomons. While the issue seemed to be completely in the realm of foreign policy, the agreement was signed to the backdrop of disquiet in the Solomons, so domestic politics was a key driver of the agreement.

The newly elected Albanese government reinvigorated the 'Step-up' and the first priority was stabilizing the situation in the Solomons. Foreign Minister Penny Wong attempted to get the Solomons government to reverse the decision but to no avail. However, she did get a clear statement from the Solomons that the agreement would not lead to the development of a Chinese base there. Honiara may have been surprised at how the worst-case scenario of a Chinese military base quickly came to dominate commentary about the agreement and quickly halted speculation with an unequivocal statement of the parameters of the agreement. The agreement stood but it was no different to the bilateral agreement between Honiara and Canberra with respect to facilitating bilateral policing cooperation.

The 2005 Enhanced Cooperation Programme (ECP) was an Australian governance-strengthening intervention in PNG designed to counter perceptions of state fragility. The ECP occurred in the context of the overarching perception of there being an 'arc of instability' in the Pacific that Australia was responsible for and threatened by and it came on the heels of the 2003 RAMSI intervention.[45]

The billion-dollar operation involved Australian police and civil servants being embedded into the PNG police and judicial system. It was approved by PNG under pressure from Australia but for the personnel involved, the vast differences between fragility in PNG and the hollow state in the Solomon Islands became apparent very quickly.[46]

The operation unravelled in May 2005 almost before it began when the PNG Supreme Court found that the immunity granted to Australian Federal Police officers was unconstitutional. In the wake of the decision, the AFP unceremoniously packed up and left PNG. Concerns in Canberra about the fragility of the PNG state persisted and targeted policy interventions continued, but they were much more measured and focused more on building local capacity than intervening from the outside. The ECP was a clear example of the limits to Australia's influence, regardless of either a claimed regional leadership role, or significant spending on ODA to the region. The implications of Canberra's response to the coup in Fiji in 2006 was similar insofar as the domestic response was not welcoming for Australian intervention leading to an impasse.

Canberra's longstanding willingness to deploy resources and personnel, including by placing them in harm's way, highlights a significant commitment to maintaining stability in the region. However, the focus has firmly been on Canberra's priority in relation to orthodox security threats to Australia posed by instability in PICs, rather than non-traditional human security issues that might more reflect the day-to-day interests of Pacific Islanders. This highlights the essentially Realist lens through which Australian policy-makers view security, in contrast to their Pacific counterparts. Maintaining regional security and stability is an important aim of AFP, but the military security implications for Australia of state fragility and/or collapse are never far from the minds of Australian policy-makers. Furthermore, the strategic denial of competitors such as China remains a priority, despite the apparent Liberal Internationalist intentions in ODA.

Official development assistance (ODA) to PICs

Australia's ODA budget as a percentage of gross national income (GNI) has been declining over the last decade, but the South Pacific has been largely quarantined from the impacts of this trend (ODA is dealt with in detail in Chapter 13). The 2022–23 ODA budget to the Pacific was A$1.38 billion. Until relatively recently, ODA to the region has remained remarkably stable at about 27 per cent of the total budget but rose to 30 per cent under the 'Step-up'.[47] Part of this shift is that the region has been quarantined from cuts to the total budget under the Morrison government (that is, the cuts have impacted elsewhere). Furthermore, the budget to the Pacific grew under the Albanese government. This highlights the policy preferences of the government, whereby ODA is not prioritized but when it is used proximity counts, as does the role ODA can play in maintaining influence to counter China.

ODA is focused on bilateral programmes, but the government acknowledges that there are many issues that are best addressed multilaterally through the Pacific Regional Programme (PRP). Bilateral programmes are implemented through Country Plans and the PRP is guided by an Aid Investment Plan 2015–16 to 2018–19. The Aid Plan focused on partnerships with key regional organizations with a technical focus including the Pacific Islands Forum Secretariat (PIFS), Secretariat of the Pacific Community (SPC), University of the South Pacific (USP), Forum Fisheries Agency (FFA) and the Secretariat of the Pacific Regional Environment Programme (SPREP). These relationships have been institutionalized through formal partnership agreements.

The Aid Plan has four aims to counter the challenges facing PICs, namely 'economic growth', 'effective regional institutions', 'healthy and resilient communities' and 'empowering women and girls'. The Aid Plan's rationale included the bleak assessment:

> Geographic isolation and small and dispersed populations make the delivery of even basic goods and services logistically difficult and expensive. Natural disasters and economic shocks hinder economic development. Little progress has been made toward the Millennium Development Goals, and the private sector is typically small with large informal economies. Violence, a lack of women in leadership roles and constrained financial opportunities limit women's economic participation.[48]

Clearly, the government was pessimistic about progress in the South Pacific, feeding into Australian stereotypes of corruption and incompetence discussed in the previous chapter. Despite criticisms of Australia's national interests driving ODA, its position as the largest donor to the region highlights the importance of Canberra's role as a significant benefactor. Until recently, it was assumed that this largesse built on asymmetry would be translated into influence, but this is being questioned by the rising confidence of PIC leaders in identifying their interests and protecting them, and the role of China and other powers in providing PICs with diplomatic alternatives to Australia.

The description of ODA as an 'investment' and the emphasis on economic growth, private sector activity and mutual obligation is in line with the government's 'aid for trade' approach (detailed in Chapter 13). This tone captures the shift from a more Liberal Internationalist altruistic approach to ODA where ODA is a gift, to a more neoliberal model where encouraging self-reliance and sustainability are the aims. While Canberra's implementation of the AIFFP can be viewed as a geopolitical response to China's perceived 'debt-trap diplomacy', it must also be noted that it aligns with the government's domestic neoliberal economic agenda insofar as loans are provided for economically viable projects rather than ODA gifts to support less immediately realizable capability-building aims.

It is also noteworthy that by 2019 all of the DFAT's aid investment plans had expired, while the ODA aspects of the 'Step-up' continued apace. This points to the shift from a technocratic approach to ODA delivery to the geopolitical emphasis of the programme. That is, regular planning measures were neglected while the government continued to use ODA to attempt to maintain influence in the region.

Trade and economic institutionalization: PACER+ and the limits of integration

Australia's trade with the South Pacific is tiny, representing approximately 1.5 per cent of its total trade. Investment in the region is less than 1 per cent of Australian investment overseas. Therefore, an extremely important contextual point that frames AFP is that trade with the South Pacific is insignificant for Australia compared with other relationships (and this is also the case for its strategic competitors). However, the trade volumes with Australia are not insignificant for PICs.

The asymmetry between Australia and the region is stark. According to the World Bank, in 2018, the GDP of the Pacific was US$33.7 billion (statistics from this date are used to overcome distortions caused by COVID-19). Of this, PNG represented US$23.4 billion and Fiji US$5.5 billion. This means that the rest of the PICs have a combined GDP of US$4.8 billion. Australia's GDP was US$1.432 trillion, meaning that Pacific GDP was equivalent to 0.2 per cent of Australian GDP and the GDP of small PICs is equivalent to 0.003 per cent of Australian GDP. This is certainly insignificant and puts paid to PIC calls for Canberra to limit economic growth to combat climate change. Furthermore, Australian GDP has continued to grow past US$1.5 trillion, but South Pacific GDP has not recovered from the COVID-19 pandemic.

Australia's largest export in 2018 was coal and the GDP of the whole South Pacific was less than Australia's exports of coal every year (US$45.66 billion). This is an important consideration in relation to managing climate change: Canberra's interest in maintaining Australia's export-oriented prosperity would be severely challenged by curtailing climate change-inducing exports and successive governments have decided that it is not in Australia's interests to do so. As noted earlier, these vested interests pose a real challenge in engaging with PICs who see climate change as an existential threat. The Albanese government appears to have shifted policy in relation to setting a credible emissions reduction target of 43 per cent from 2005 levels by 2030 and net zero emissions by 2050, but it remains to be seen whether this involves curtaining exports of climate change-inducing natural resources.

The low trade volumes means that Realist assumptions that trade interests drive Australia's relations with the South Pacific should be discounted from the outset. By contrast, for most PICs, Australia is a significant trading partner and is one of their top five import and export destinations. Australia's key trade competitors in the South Pacific are Singapore and China, with the former exporting processed food and most of the refined energy supplies to the region, and the latter focusing on merchandise trade, both of which are complementary to the Australian economy's focus on natural resources and services. As such, there is little direct trade competition with China and therefore Strategic Cultural historical factors and geopolitics rather than geoeconomics should be viewed as the prime rationale for strategic competition.

PACER+

The centrepiece of trade relations between Australia and the Pacific for nearly 20 years has been the Pacific Agreement on Closer Economic Relations (PACER) and its update aptly named PACER+. PACER came into force in 2001 and promoted trade liberalization above all, leading some PIC leaders to criticize it for promoting the neoliberal interests of the larger metropolitan economies. PACER+ was negotiated between 2009 and 2017 and finally signed without the participation of the region's two largest economies, Fiji and PNG. The absence of the region's two largest economies meant that it only covered 14 per cent of regional trade.

While PACER+ can be connected to the 'Step-up', its lineage can be traced back to the 1981 South Pacific Regional Trade and Economic Cooperation Agreement (SPARTECA), highlighting that regional trade institutionalization has long been on Canberra's agenda. PACER+ is a free trade agreement covering goods, services and investment. The agreement is comprehensive when viewed through the eyes of an export-oriented advanced economy but was not as attractive to many PICs, as it did not handle the key issue of labour mobility, which for many is a significant potential source of foreign earnings. One way of handling limited growth prospects and demographic challenges, such as a youth bulge, is to export labour in return for foreign currency remittances that can be used to develop small business infrastructure.

The neglect of labour mobility in PACER+ and its central importance for PICs meant that the Australian government was forced to deal with the issue through a range of other mechanisms, such as the Pacific Australia Labour Mobility Scheme (PALMS) that brought Pacific Islanders to work in Australia, and the Australia–Pacific Technical Coalition that trained them in the South Pacific. For Canberra, these separate programmes afforded far more flexibility, especially if numbers/quotas need to be reduced due to an economic downturn in the future. The combined impact of the reduction in backpacker labour due to COVID-19 and pressure from PICs led to a range of innovations in the Seasonal Worker Programme (SWP) and other schemes designed to streamline processes and respond to criticisms of the treatment of workers. Most importantly, the numbers of Pacific Islanders given access to these schemes increased.

Labour schemes have long been a source of tension between PICs and Canberra. Historically, these labour schemes were built on mutual short-term economic benefits but did not confer any enduring immigration rights to workers. However, this is mooted to change under the Albanese government. Numbers steadily grew over the last decade from a few hundred to the cap of about 12,000 and they were mainly sourced from Vanuatu, Tonga and Timor Leste.[49] In the same way that Canberra's unwillingness to respond to climate change has impacted relations with PICs, so too have barriers to the flow of people. Canberra has closely regulated Pacific labour through various schemes (e.g. the SWP), slowly increasing numbers in line with New Zealand's approach, but the COVID-19 pandemic and division in the agricultural sector over whether backpackers should be privileged over Pacific Islanders has slowed the process.

That Canberra persisted with PACER+ as a regional free trade agreement that only covered 14 per cent of South Pacific trade when it focused on bilateral agreements with other major trading partners speaks volumes to the way trade relations with the Pacific are viewed. Australia may be a firm supporter of the Liberal Internationalist 'rules-based order' with free trade at its centrepiece, but political will and compromise has not been applied to developing a truly regional free trade agreement, largely because it may not be in Australia's interests to do so. Furthermore, the fact that it took eight years to negotiate speaks to growing confidence of small PICs in standing up for their national interests and the inability of Australia to convince more powerful PICs to sign onto an Australian-sponsored initiative which they did not see as having merit. As such, it also highlights that PIC leaders are increasingly aware of how their interests differ from those of Australia (economic as well as security and environmental) and are willing to act to protect them.[50] There is a history of this attitude in the South Pacific, such as the 2003 Pacific Island Countries Trade Agreement (PICTA), which sat alongside PACER but excluded Australia and New Zealand.

Australia's lack of prioritizing trade with PICs belies a realistic appraisal of the economic potential of the region, which is in tension with the 'aid for trade' agenda that frames development assistance with the region. If the aim was simply to promote regional trade and self-reliance, then the fact that the markets are small would not influence AFP. It also highlights a tension in the geoeconomic analyses of the interests of extra-regional powers in the Pacific that are targets of Australian strategic denial. The very small trade volumes and apparent lack of potential also means that caution should be exercised when viewing the motives of other actors, such as China, in the South Pacific. Trade is often cited as a key driver of foreign interest in the region, but for a state such as China, the lack of significant trade volumes points to other geopolitical motives that align with Strategic Culture and a Realist appraisal of Australia's interests. PIC diplomatic independence is gaining strength, in part due to the alternatives offered by Australia's strategic competitors, namely China, and this is a cause for concern in Canberra.

Bilateral relations overview

Due to the diversity of relations with PICs, two case studies are used to illustrate AFP in the region. By all measures, Australia is a superpower in the South Pacific, but as noted earlier, this Realist power differential has not always played out to suit Canberra's preferences. One reason for this is the diversity between PICs themselves and the following case studies tease out these themes. The first is Fiji, a PIC that often exercises regional leadership and which successfully opposed Australia's diplomatic preferences and sanctions from 2006 to 2014. Fijian resistance also provided the context within which China began to challenge Australian influence in the South Pacific. The second case study of Nauru highlights how structural asymmetries can play out in foreign policy whereby Australia was able to export its asylum seeker problem to a PIC at a relatively small cost. Both

Bilateral relations with Fiji as a representative example of larger PICs

Fiji is an archipelagic state 3,500 km north-east of Canberra, made up of 850 islands and islets, many of which are uninhabited. The land area of Fiji is 18,200 km², making it about a quarter of the size of Tasmania. It has a population of approximately 905,000, of whom 90 per cent live on the two largest islands.

Fiji is a Melanesian state but approximately a third of the population are of Indian background. These Indo-Fijians are the descendants of indentured workers brought by the British colonists in the late nineteenth and early twentieth centuries to work in the sugar cane industry. There are significant differences between the Indo and Fijian populations with respect to measures such as life expectancy and educational participation and attainment. There is also very little inter-marriage, so they remain quite distinct. Despite marked differences in the ethnic groups within Fiji, educational participation for Fijians as a whole is above the regional average, as is life expectancy. By most measures, it is the second largest PIC (after PNG) and by many measures the most 'developed'.

Fiji amicably gained independence from the UK in 1970 and became a republic during its first coup in 1987. Post-colonial relations with the UK were strong, as technical support was provided to strengthen the organs of the state. In the years after independence, many key roles in the government were held by British diaspora or administrators from the UK, New Zealand and Australia. Links with the UK and Commonwealth continue, but in the last decade the Fijian government has distanced itself from ex-colonial powers, due largely to perceptions of interference in the sovereign affairs during the sanctions years of 2006–14 after the coup in 2006. This included changing the currency and an aborted attempt to remove the Union flag from the national flag.

Fiji and Australia have longstanding public diplomacy links through colonial administration, trade, the Commonwealth and sporting competitions, but military diplomacy has also framed the relationship. During the Second World War, New Zealand was focused on defending Fiji while Australia was in PNG, so Australia's links grew in the post-independence era through training and military aid. Significantly, this military diplomacy included supporting Fiji's first peacekeeping operation in 1978, which formed a key part of its post-independence nation-building strategy. Close 'people-to-people' links built through military diplomacy were disrupted by Australian sanctions against Fiji during 2006–14, but have grown since, albeit on a footing more focused on Fiji's interests in the tourism market. The COVID-19 pandemic completely collapsed Pacific tourism but prior to 2020, Australia was Fiji's largest source of tourists and tourist dollars. Over 370,000 Australians visited in 2018–19, representing 42 per cent of the market. Tourism comprised 40 per cent of Fijian GDP, so it was a significant source of income and foreign exchange, the loss of which has had dire economic impacts. Fiji was known as a family holiday destination, in contrast to Bali's reputation as a party destination, and many Australian tourists are return visitors. The positive impact of tourism on

Australian public opinion towards the Pacific should not be underestimated, especially since there is a conspicuous absence of a large Pacific diaspora in Australia to influence how the Pacific is viewed domestically. Despite their geographic proximity, Pacific islanders comprise less than 1 per cent of the Australian population.

CASE STUDY 12.4: AUSTRALIAN SANCTIONS AGAINST FIJI

On several occasions, tension has arisen in bilateral relations corresponding with coups in Fiji in 1987, 2000 and 2006, triggering Australian concerns over maintaining regional stability. On the first two occasions, political sanctions were instituted, and diplomatic pressure was applied publicly and through diplomatic channels; within a few months the situations had largely been resolved and relations normalized. However, in 2006 the breach was not resolved due to both the persistence of significant domestic political challenges in Fiji and an assertion of sovereignty by the Fijian interim government that resented Australian meddling.

In December 2006, Commodore Frank Bainimarama, the chief of the military, dissolved Fiji's democratically elected government and installed himself as the head of an interim government. Australia imposed 'smart sanctions', targeting members of the regime and the military more broadly, but stopped short of economic sanctions, ostensibly to reduce the impact on ordinary Fijians.[52] The interim government was uncompromising and applied a 'Look North' policy to develop new friends and diplomatic partners, including China.[53] The diplomatic impasse was made worse by reversals on the part of Bainimarama in relation to the proposed date for elections. Canberra wanted to punish Fiji but did not want to escalate the situation, and so Fiji was suspended from the PIF and Commonwealth, but no additional sanctions were instituted.

Sanctions are only effective if implemented comprehensively and in this case Canberra focused on withholding the benefits of bilateral cooperation rather than broadening their application. The interim government quickly worked around the 'smart sanctions' and developed partnerships with states as diverse as China, South Korea, Indonesia and the United Arab Emirates, which turned the sanctions into a mere inconvenience. However, the diplomatic war of words continued unabated and megaphone diplomacy inflamed issues. The situation was not resolved until Foreign Minister Julie Bishop unilaterally relaxed sanctions in 2014 immediately prior to elections in Fiji being held.

A key criticism of the sanctions was that they dragged on despite not having the intended impact on Fiji. Australian public opinion did not share the government's zeal in maintaining sanctions and by 2012, a firm majority (79 per cent) of respondents to the Lowy Poll supported re-engaging with Fiji.[54] Lowy polling in Fiji itself in 2012 also revealed that there was firm support for the Fijian interim government, which caused obvious irritation in Canberra.[55] However, sanctions continued, regardless of their ineffectiveness or unpopularity.

The bilateral relationship with Fiji provides an insight into Australia's relations with PICs as Fiji has the political and economic potential to lead and to resist unwelcome external pressure from Canberra. The changing nature of relations with Fiji offers a window into South Pacific attitudes towards Australia because Fiji is strong and confident enough to face Australia without fear of the costs of losing favour. This independence is based on indigenous attitudes to neo-colonialism, a low level of ODA dependence and economic viability. The resistance to Australian sanctions from 2006 to 2014 cemented these attributes and attitudes. This was clearly evidenced in relation to Prime Minister Bainimarama's critical response to Canberra's failure to compromise on climate change at the 2019 Tuvalu PIF.

Fiji's defence of formal sovereignty fits an orthodox Realist model and reflects a heightened sensitivity by recently decolonized states. Fiji's independence came at a time when the wisdom of granting statehood to potentially unsustainable states was being queried in the UN system. As such, Fiji's response to diplomatic slights and coercion captures PIC sensitivities, but only Fiji and PNG are willing and/or able to openly respond to challenges from greater powers. Interestingly, Canberra's megaphone diplomacy and reactive response to diplomatic slights is akin to the dynamic discussed in relation to Indonesia in Chapter 10. In both cases, Canberra has not necessarily fine-tuned its approach or messaging to allow for states that are sensitive about defending their formal sovereignty.

Australia's pressure on Fiji could be painted as a Liberal Internationalist defence of the 'rules-based order' and human rights, but this would not do justice to Canberra's motivation to be seen as the predominant power in the region. This human rights rhetoric is not convincing due to the very 'Pacific' nature of the 2006 coup. That is, unlike violent coups in Africa and elsewhere, nobody lost their lives and the political coercion that followed was relatively low level yet insidious. In addition, the Howard government was not known for defending Liberal perspectives in foreign policy towards other international political crises involving coups, such as in Burma and Thailand.[56] Similarly, Canberra was criticized for military interventions, such as Iraq, where support for the US alliance was a prime Realist and Strategic Cultural motivator.

In the case of the South Pacific, the influence of proximity is central to AFP (as is also apparent in relation to Indonesia) and this disrupts orthodox theorizing. In this case (and unlike Indonesia), the strategic denial of unwelcome competitors is a clear priority. Canberra's strategic motivation highlights the influence of asymmetrical relations on AFP, which has allowed Canberra to routinely diminish the sovereignty of PICs and to view the South Pacific through the lens of threats to Australia. Canberra's motives can be explained by its Realist and Strategic Cultural focus on geopolitical competition and threats are therefore central to understanding Australia's use of sanctions. Fiji's confident defence of sovereignty explains how this approach stalled and failed from 2006 to 2014. The long-term ramifications of the protracted diplomatic conflict can be seen in the nature of the 'Step-up' and Morrison's pronouncement that AFP would be informed by a *vuvale* (family) relationship, which upholds sovereignty by eschewing interference in domestic affairs.[57]

Bilateral relations with Nauru as a representative example of a small PIC

Nauru is a Micronesian coral island located on the equator 4,500 km north-east of Australia. At 21 km^2 in size, Nauru is the smallest PIC and the third smallest state on earth. Due to phosphate mining for most of the twentieth century, the centre of the island is uninhabitable. Only a small coastal strip is arable land and it produces coconuts, fruit and vegetables. The fishing grounds surrounding the island have been damaged by the by-products of mining and overfishing of the remaining fragile stocks.[58]

Nauru was populated approximately 3,000 years ago by Micronesian and Polynesian people and had a population of approximately 800 when colonized by Germany in 1888 under an arrangement with the British Empire. Annexation brought European rule to the island that was experiencing civil unrest in the wake of the introduction of alcohol and firearms by whalers and traders. Colonization also brought epidemic diseases, missionaries and prospectors who discovered phosphate fertilizer, which was mined from 1906, causing widespread environmental degradation. With defeat in the First World War, Germany lost its empire and in 1920, Nauru became a League of Nations mandated Trust Territory administered by Australia, New Zealand and the UK.

Australia had occupied Nauru soon after the First World War broke out in 1914 and Australia led the trustee administration that operated from 1920 to 1947. In the Second World War, Nauru's phosphate was a valuable war material for Australia and so the Germans attacked it in December 1940. Nauru was invaded by Japan in August 1942 and the population was treated with brutality, with many deported to serve as labourers on Japanese bases elsewhere in the Pacific. Nauru was not strategically significant to the war and was isolated and bypassed by the allies as they contained and ultimately defeated Japan. In September 1945, Australian forces arrived to accept the surrender of Japanese forces in Nauru two weeks after Japan's official surrender. Australia's connection with Nauru fits neatly with the strategic denial and support for alliances in Strategic Culture. Nauru was not of interest in and of itself, but rather was a venue for contest between Australia and the German and Japanese empires in the South Pacific.

After the Second World War, Nauru returned to being a jointly managed Trust Territory led by Australia, this time under the auspices of the UN. Phosphate mining continued as the main source of economic activity as Nauru moved towards independence in 1966. Nauru became a republic but did not join the UN until 1999 and continued to use the Australian dollar as its currency. Appeals from its courts were referred to the Australian High Court until as recently as 2018. Nauru has no military and Australia is nominally responsible for its defence.

The Government of Nauru acquired the phosphate mining companies soon after independence and profited greatly, but as these finite resources ran out, mismanagement and corruption were discovered in relation to the Nauru Phosphate Royalties Trust, which was created to provide a sustainable long-term income once the resources ran out (which ultimately occurred in 2006). By the 1990s, Nauru was effectively bankrupt and successful attempts to get legal restitution from Australia, New Zealand and the UK for environmental degradation did not provide enough resources to develop sustainable alternatives.

CASE STUDY 12.5: NAURU'S ROLE IN AUSTRALIA'S 'PACIFIC SOLUTION'

Recent relations with Nauru have focused on the Australian detention centre that Nauru agreed to host as part of Canberra's 'Pacific Solution' (see Chapter 15). The Pacific Solution was the Howard government's attempt to manage the impact in Australia of the international problem of increasing refugee flows. The plan was an ad hoc response to the Tampa crisis where a freighter picked up asylum seekers at sea and sought to bring them to Australia. Canberra hastily negotiated Memoranda of Understanding (MOU) with PNG and Nauru to relocate asylum seekers without them setting foot on Australian territory. The government's argument was that transiting them away from Australia would not activate international obligations to determine the refugee status of asylum seekers and ultimately resettle refugees.

The aim of this offshore processing regime was to stop the flow of refugees by removing the incentives driving people smugglers and asylum seekers alike. It was a dramatic restatement of the sovereign right to control borders with Howard stating that 'We will decide who comes to this country.'[59] This fits the orthodox Realist perspective whereby the territorial integrity and political independence of statehood is elevated over other more Liberal Internationalist values. In a situation reminiscent of the approach to climate change, Canberra received domestic and international criticism and condemnation for this approach,[60] but persisted in elevating the national interest nonetheless.

This position reflected an extremely divided domestic polity on this issue and due to compulsory voting, populism influenced policy. Several Labor governments voiced strong criticisms of the asylum seeker policy while in opposition, but on election, the Rudd Labor government did not immediately repeal the policy and it was only phased out in 2008 when the flow of asylum seekers had become a trickle. However, it was reinstated by the Gillard Labor government in 2010. Being accused of being 'soft' on refugees was akin to being soft on national security issues such as terrorism, and these issues highlight one of the few clear examples of the influence of domestic politics on AFP. In a case of what was politicized as 'illegal' immigration, asylum seekers became potential threats in ways that resonated with the attitudes in Strategic Culture towards an 'alien' other.

Immigration, illegal or otherwise, will be dealt with in detail in Chapter 15, but for the purposes of this chapter, it must be noted that along with PNG, Nauru was integral to managing a potentially significant electoral problem for successive Australian governments.[61] For over a decade, Nauru acted as a solution to a domestic political issue for Australia but this had domestic and regional implications for both states as there was disquiet in the region over offshore processing. For many observers, it became a quintessential example of Canberra throwing its weight around and taking advantage of its asymmetrical relationship with Nauru, and Nauru's vulnerability in the face of economic challenges in which Australia was implicated.[62]

Clouds on the horizon for AFP at the 2018 Nauru PIF

The 2018 PIF held in Nauru was eventful and illuminating in relation to bilateral relations with Australia in a number of ways. Rising geopolitical tensions were on display when a Chinese representative attempted to address the meeting and was rebuffed by the host, President Baron Waqa of Nauru. China reportedly gained an invitation at the behest of diplomatic allies such as Fiji, but overestimated their position and were rebuffed. Beijing's representative was ejected from the meeting under diplomatic protest with Waqa describing China as 'insolent'.[63]

This incident drew attention to the ongoing chequebook diplomacy between China and Taiwan, because Nauru was one of the few states that diplomatically recognized Taiwan. Nauru had also see-sawed between recognizing China and Taiwan between 2012 and 2015, thereby receiving ODA from both parties. Belief that there could be a truce between China and Taiwan in this diplomatic competition was shattered in the most undiplomatic of exchanges. This exchange foreshadowed increased pressure from China, which saw the Solomon Islands and Kiribati shift recognition to China in 2019.

Climate change was also high on the agenda, but as the meeting occurred soon after the Boe Declaration was signed, the focus was on implementation planning. The Leaders' Communique did include the familiar reference to climate change being 'the single greatest threat to the livelihood, security and wellbeing of Pacific people',[64] but no concrete commitments were demanded and open conflict with Australia was avoided. Canberra's success at watering down references to climate change were noted, but frustration was building, especially from the host of the next meeting, Prime Minister Enele Sopoaga of Tuvalu and (as noted earlier) a storm had erupted at the 2019 meeting.

The Nauruan government also continued to put pressure on press freedoms to manage publicity over hosting the Australian 'regional processing centre'. Nauru banned the Australian Broadcasting Corporation (ABC) from attending, due to alleged 'bias and unethical reporting'[65] and otherwise charged journalists exorbitant sums for visas, which also included tight conditions. For instance, journalists were banned from speaking to asylum seekers. In an unfortunate incident, a NZ journalist was arrested for breaching these conditions, bringing unwanted attention to the issue. This prompted a strong response in Australia, but Prime Minister Turnbull took a firm Realist stance by supporting Nauru's right to decide who enters the country. He also stated that he would not participate in megaphone diplomacy, which has long been a criticism of Australia by PIC leaders, but in this case, it was not clear that defending a liberal value such as press freedom in another state was as important as the maintenance of Australia's 'Pacific Solution' in Nauru.

Geopolitical contest and local threat perceptions

The tension at the 2019 PIF highlighted that regional threat perceptions are firmly focused on climate change. Climate is treated as an existential threat to PICs and is enshrined in the PIF's 2018 Boe Declaration, which focuses on the threat to the 'livelihoods, security and wellbeing of Pacific peoples'.[66] Most PICs do not rate orthodox military security threats highly, so much so that only three PICs have militaries. Only two PICs have significant forces (Fiji and PNG), albeit with a focus on peacekeeping and internal security. Other threats, from transnational crime, illegal fishing, human trafficking, money laundering, cybersecurity and terrorism, do rate with PICs, but the level of concern varies widely. Furthermore, the level of response to many of these threats has sometimes been driven by outside expectations (in the case of terrorism) and often with outside support (with resources from development partners being allocated to activities such as combating illegal, unreported and unregulated fishing).

In contrast, AFP towards the South Pacific focuses on strategic denial and development, and presently the two have been combined as a response to China. Military diplomacy, infrastructure loans and traditional gifted ODA are all connected in a whole-of-government response to perceptions that China is increasing its influence. Australia's approach in trying to lock in support is in tension with the traditional 'friends to all, enemies to none' approach adopted by many PICs, whereby all external powers are seen as potential development partners and the national interest in securing development assistance trumps geopolitics. This is one key reason why the South Pacific has been such a battleground in the contest between China and Taiwan over diplomatic recognition. In this case, PIC leaders were reviewing the best outcomes for their states in a manner that could be seen as quite Realist and mercenary. As captured aptly by Lord Palmerston, states should have 'no eternal allies . . . and no perpetual enemies'.[67]

From this perspective, China's competition with the US globally, and with Australia and the US in the South Pacific, can be seen by PIC leaders as an opportunity to attract additional resources. Most commentators view the 'Step-up' as a direct response to perceptions of China's increasing influence, but analysts must also be mindful of longstanding South Pacific diplomatic practices, and local agency in attracting ODA should not be underestimated.[68] The warning signs for Canberra were clear from the 2019 PIF, with pointed comments from regional leaders such as Prime Minister Tuila'epa Malielegoai of Samoa, who noted that: 'Our friends and their friends are our friends. But their enemies are not our enemies.'[69] The narrow lens of strategic competition through which many policy-makers in Canberra view the South Pacific may actually undermine Australia's leadership credentials.

Conclusion

Australian foreign policy towards the South Pacific displays the tension between Canberra's claimed leadership and threat perceptions. Australia primacy is being questioned both from within the South Pacific and from outside powers gaining influence in the region. Sanctions against Fiji from 2006 to 2014 coincided with perceptions that Australian influence was waning with respect to other powers, so the success of the 'Step-up' with Fiji and the South Pacific is essential for the achievement of AFP priorities. Australia's dominance and sometimes domineering approach has led to charges of neo-colonialism, which reveals the intersection of Liberal Internationalism in the form of ODA, and a more Realist definition of the national interest, as evidenced in initiatives such as military diplomacy, infrastructure loans and 'aid for trade'. Climate change is the litmus test for Australian policy-makers and how Canberra maintains its fossil fuel-driven development path while appeasing PICs will shape the geostrategic contest with China in the years to come.

13

The politicization of official development assistance as a foreign policy tool

Introduction

> We cannot continue to live beyond our means and Australia's aid program is no exception. Australians are a generous people but they expect Government to impose the same rigours and tests of value for money on our aid program as we do on areas of domestic spending and they want to see results.[1]

The quote from Foreign Minister Julie Bishop highlights the tension within Australian foreign policy towards the provision of official development assistance (ODA). Official development assistance can be viewed both as an altruistic responsibility of developed states to assist developing states and as an instrument of policy designed to further the national interest. The tension is more apparent than real as in practice ODA is both altruistic and also aligned to the national interest.

Australia has provided international aid since the Second World War when the Liberal Internationalist current of thought in Australian foreign policy (AFP) came to the fore. The post-war environment was associated with the proliferation of multilateral organizations, such as the United Nations (UN), which Australia strongly supported. The archetypal aid project from this time was the Colombo Plan (1950), which brought thousands of young people from Asia to Australia for education and cultural immersion. In the minds of many, aid at this time was viewed as a form of charity within the international community, akin to charity within a national community. For governments, however, the promotion of democracy in the face of international Communism was a priority, as was the development of infrastructure for economic growth. From the very beginning, politics was intertwined with altruism as the purpose of aid in AFP.

Over time, aid grew into a multi-billion-dollar industry and the practice of international development was supported by the growth of an academic discipline. Aid management became increasingly technocratic and evidence-based, with progressive Liberal Internationalist theories of change influencing decision-making. With the professionalization of development assistance, the label 'aid', with its paternalistic connotations, altered to become 'official development assistance'.

BOX 13.1: AID AND OFFICIAL DEVELOPMENT ASSISTANCE

Official development assistance (ODA) is the technical term used in the development sector to describe developed government financial support for development projects in developing countries. In practice, ODA and aid are interchangeable, but in the sector the term 'assistance' is preferred to 'aid'.

In recent years, the way ODA was portrayed by the Australian government has shifted from a largely technocratic form of altruism to a policy tool closely tied to achieving the national interest. As noted, politics and diplomacy were always central to ODA policies, but since the election of Prime Minister Tony Abbott's Coalition government in 2013, the focus on national interests has become more explicit. This trend is clearly captured by the 'aid for trade' agenda and the push for ever greater ODA 'effectiveness' in relation to achieving national interests. The politicization of ODA is another area that sits alongside the treatment of climate change and asylum seekers in allowing analysis of the enduring themes in AFP. The integration of the Australian Agency for International Development (AusAID) into the Department of Foreign Affairs and Trade in 2013; Australia's bid to take up a rotational seat on the United Nations Security Council (UNSC) between 2009 and 2012 (granted in 2012); and the Pacific 'Step-Up' to counter China from 2016, all provide fertile ground for analysis of the place of ODA in AFP.

The government's approach to ODA provides an insight into the tensions that exist between goals that are best described as Realist and Liberal Internationalist in foreign policy. Official development assistance provides insights into the ideology of governments because they have a greater capacity to shape policy and budgeting in this area than in other areas that were more closely aligned with domestic constituencies (such as education, health or defence).[2] As ODA has increasingly been framed as a tool used for competition against the threat posed by China in the South Pacific,[3] it has also highlighted the enduring influence of the threat perceptions that characterize Australian Strategic Culture.

Thematic questions addressed in this chapter include: In what sense could Australia been seen as a Liberal Internationalist in exercising 'middlepower-manship' through ODA? Have national interests trumped international and/or global responsibilities? And, how does public opinion influence foreign policy-making on ODA?

In this chapter, the present Labor government's approach will be compared with that of previous Labor and Coalition governments to identify trends. While comparisons and contrasts between governments of different persuasions are instructive, they are not as clear as may be assumed for two reasons. The first is due to a general trend towards neoliberalism in government which connects ODA to the national interest.[4] The second is a sustained constrained budgetary environment has limited government options. What is becoming increasingly clear is that ODA is being used more openly to achieve foreign policy goals and that attempts to maintain or build a bipartisan consensus between Coalition and Labor governments on elevating altruism has been disrupted by the Coalition's emphasis on ODA as a tool to achieve a narrow Realist perspective of the national interest.

ODA policy also provides the opportunity to reflect on foreign policy as the boundary between the international/global and domestic policy realms. In this regard, the present policy highlights the weakness of international norms in penetrating the Australian polity and influencing AFP. There appears to be little international normative pressure that can alter domestic policy settings. This is similar to climate change, where ever increasing pressure only prompted deflection through Prime Minister Morrison's 'Australian way' deemed wholly unsatisfactory by commentators.[5] Another connection between climate change and ODA is what it tells us about the influence of public opinion on ODA, and there are some surprising trends that highlight ignorance and division in the Australian polity on Liberal Internationalist issues.

A snapshot of Australian ODA in the shadow of COVID-19

Official development assistance has historically been approximately around 1 per cent of the federal budget. In 2020–21, it was below 1 per cent. After a decade of growth from 2004, Australia's ODA programme peaked under the previous Labor government at A\$5 billion in 2013 and has declined every year since, returning to a level not seen for a decade (in real terms adjusted for inflation).

The Albanese government elected in May 2022 promised to increase ODA. This is a common message heard from incoming Labor governments and in 2022–23, A\$4.5 billion was allocated in the federal budget. While the gross figure increased once inflation was accounted for, this did not represent a significant increase.

Canberra's emergency response to COVID-19

Canberra's emergency response to COVID-19 was temporary, so it should be viewed in context of longstanding trends in ODA. That said, it also revealed the priority afforded to the proximate region in AFP. In the context of a budget freeze, the maintenance of ODA levels to the Pacific throughout the pandemic pointed to the importance that Canberra afforded to the 'Step-Up'. ODA to the South Pacific was exempted from cuts elsewhere in the budget and responding to the COVID-19 pandemic in the Pacific became the focus of Australia's 2020 Partnerships for

Recovery strategy. This strategy acknowledged that: 'How our neighbourhood emerges from this crisis will determine Australia's economic and strategic circumstances for decades to come,'[6] and this justified a significant whole-of-government approach to the pandemic. However, this strategy did not signal a new approach as it was also aligned with the 2018 Pacific 'Step-Up' and increasing anxiety about China's influence that coincided with both China's trade sanctions and the open identification of China as a military threat. Caution was warranted in identifying a focus on the human security of Pacific Islanders and Southeast Asians when their welfare was closely connected to Australia's longstanding threat perceptions. This nexus between national security and ODA altruism highlighted the pluralistic approach needed to contextualize AFP, as Realist national interests, Strategic Cultural threats from the 'north', and Liberal Internationalist rights altruism and leadership all coincided in Canberra's COVID19 Partnerships for Recovery.

The geographic focus of ODA

The majority of ODA in 2022–23 was directed to Australia's nearest neighbours in the South Pacific (A$1.38 billion) followed by Asia (A$738 million).[7] Most funds were allocated to bilateral programmes, but regional programmes remained a key delivery mechanism where cross-cutting themes such as gender equality were addressed. Papua New Guinea (PNG) remained the largest bilateral programme with A$479 million, followed by Indonesia with A$266 million. The Solomon Islands rounded off the top three bilateral programmes with A$103 million.[8] These three states have been the major beneficiaries of Australian ODA for some time. In line with the government's Pacific 'Step-Up', the region receives the largest amount of ODA, aligning with the government's argument that it has the capacity to do greater good by concentrating its ODA. This emphasis on concentrating resources is reinforced by the fact that ODA makes up a significant amount of the gross national income (GNI) for several regional states (for example, 11 per cent for Nauru, 10 per cent for Tuvalu and 9.4 per cent for the Solomon Islands). In fact, half of the 15 most aid-dependent states on earth are Pacific Island countries (PICs), and questions about the efficacy of aid to the Pacific[9] are swept aside by geopolitics and the interests expressed by Strategic Culture. In Australian ODA proximity counts, connecting with the emphasis in Strategic Culture on maintaining stability in Australia's area of primary strategic concern and aligning with a Liberal Internationalist sense of responsibility for less well-endowed neighbours.

Australia's three major ODA recipients have also seen ad hoc increases in ODA due to natural disasters, such as the COVID-19 pandemic and the 2004 Indian Ocean tsunami, and through cooperation with Australia's diplomatic priorities, such as Indonesia assisting with interdicting what the government termed 'unauthorized arrivals' since 2001, or PNG hosting the Manus Island Regional [asylum seeker] Processing Centre (2001–8, 2012–17), or the Solomon Islands recovering from political instability with the support of the

Australian-funded Regional Assistance Mission to the Solomon Islands (RAMSI) from 2001 to 2017. It is also noteworthy that the top three beneficiaries form part of the so-called 'arc of instability', a term coined in the 2000s to describe the threat to Australia posed by state fragility in Indonesia to PNG and the Pacific.[10]

From the standpoint of geopolitical competition, the PICs are perceived as being vulnerable to Chinese influence 'bought' through ODA, or, more accurately, 'concessional loans', as these are China's preferred mechanism. In the case of PNG, the loss of Australian funding due to the closure of the Manus Island Regional Processing Centre (caused by the decline in numbers of asylum seekers) was quickly replaced by funding for the redevelopment of the Lombrum Naval Base (also located on Manus Island). The additional support offered by Canberra provides continuity and stability and will assist PNG in responding to humanitarian emergencies. However, maintaining the position of security 'partner of choice' is also Canberra's key foreign policy priority, so this funding highlights the blend of self-interest and altruism in Australia's ODA programme. It is almost impossible to disaggregate altruism from national interests,[11] but it is clear that the successive governments have put greater emphasis on the latter.

The tightening geographic scope of Australia's ODA programme is indicative of strategic priorities. As the overall budget declined over the last decade, the Middle East and South and West Asia shared the brunt of cuts with a more than 50 per cent decline over the last three years.[12] This reflects a government commitment to the proximate region[13] but also appears a response to the critique of spreading the budget too thin by donating small amounts to Africa and Latin America. The Pacific was spared budget cuts, highlighting the importance of the 'Step-Up' to AFP and the Morrison Coalition government's lack of interest in promoting Australia's middle power credentials. From 2008 to 2012, the previous Gillard and Rudd Labor governments had used ODA in a successful campaign to gain a rotational seat on the UNSC, with the aim of furthering national and globalist ideals. While the former Labor governments were aiming to practise creative middle power leadership and advocacy in the UN, the Coalition government was much more tightly focused on promoting national interests. As such, the difference between Labor promoting Australia's middle power credentials and the Coalition's focus on effectively using Australia's status as a *medium* power was on display.[14]

The difference between middle and medium powers reflects an ideational divide over the purpose of foreign policy, which links to discussions of ODA and the national interst (see Chapter 2).

> ## CASE STUDY 13.1: POLITICIZING ODA TO WIN A UNITED NATIONS SECURITY COUNCIL (UNSC) SEAT
>
> The focus on the proximate region was treated as a core national interest. However, it was also an attempt by the Morrison Coalition to criticize the previous Labor government's forays into Africa and Latin America to support their (ultimately successful) bid to win a rotational seat on the UNSC. From 2009 to 2011, Australia's ODA to Africa increased dramatically from A\$102.7 million to A\$393.5 million, an increase of 380 per cent in two years, which placed Australian ODA well above its two UNSC seat competitors, Finland and Luxembourg. Both were longstanding donors to Africa but did not spend as much as Australia during this period. At the same time, Australian ODA to Latin America jumped from A\$5 million to A\$50 million dollars in one year (2009 to 2010).
>
> In an act of expediency, Australia's ODA to Africa and Latin America then promptly declined after the UNSC campaign was completed. The Coalition foreign minister who took over from the Labor incumbent noted that the previous government's ODA policy had 'been spread far too thinly across the globe for reasons often not related to poverty alleviation, thus putting at risk our ability to achieve results in the geographic region where I believe we have a primary responsibility'.[15] The incoming Abbott government took on the semi-permanent UN seat won through Labor's ODA diplomacy, but promptly cut ODA to Africa and was criticized for being seen to be a close US ally on the UNSC rather than a middle power advocate for globalist Liberal Internationalist values.

ODA by sector

In recent years, there have been small increases to strategic areas in the ODA budget, including humanitarian emergencies and refugees. This also reflects the focus on the Pacific, where humanitarian assistance and disaster response (HADR) operations are routine. The precise amounts provided to particular bilateral programmes can vary based on local conditions; for example, the percentage of the bilateral programme to the Solomon Islands spent on governance reflects the transition to independence after the nearly 15-year-long RAMSI that ended in 2017.

The focus on stability is clear as the largest allocation is to effective governance. In announcing the reorientation of ODA in 2020, the minister for international development and the Pacific noted the connection between ODA and the national interest: 'when our partners are more prosperous and strong, and stable and secure, our region is strong, and therefore we are strong'.[16]

Prior to the emergency response to COVID-19, the first three of Australia's development programme investment priorities – infrastructure, agriculture and governance – had an explicit focus on 'aid for trade'. Support for economic activity broadly defined (infrastructure, trade, fisheries and water) was the largest single strategic priority.[17] The Albanese government renamed spending by 'sector' versus 'investment priority' and this reflects a reframing on the purpose of ODA more akin to a Liberal Internationalist development paradigm, where the human security of recipients is elevated in importance.

When drawing conclusions about the shift in substantive ODA priorities from Coalition to Labor governments, caution is warranted for several reasons. First, the declaratory policy framing spending may shift but the underlying spending does not necessarily shift. Second, the Coalition government's ideological preference for neoliberal economics means that economic security is conceived narrowly with a preference for export-oriented industries that can be supported through 'aid for trade' initiatives. Labor may simply shift focus to smaller-scale localized economic activity. Third, the ODA budget stands at less than 1 per cent of the 2022–23 federal budget while defence spending was approximately 6 per cent and growing faster than ODA. Also, historically, the ODA budget did not reflect the international stability operations undertaken by the Department of Defence, Australian Border Force (and its predecessors) and the Australian Federal Police, and considerable sums were spent in areas such as Afghanistan and Iraq supporting traditional military security and sovereignty interests.

CASE STUDY 13.2: HUMANITARIAN ASSISTANCE

In the humanitarian budget, a preference is displayed towards bilateral delivery of emergency assistance versus the use of multilateral agencies, such as the UN and civil society organizations, including the Red Cross. In fact, nearly 80 per cent of the humanitarian budget is allocated bilaterally and 20 per cent is allocated to intergovernmental and civil society groups. The UN is a major recipient of this ODA, but the pooled nature of UN humanitarian appeals means that most of the funds allocated by Australia are likely to go to areas of great need such as Ukraine and the Middle East (Iraq, Lebanon, the Syrian Arab Republic, Jordan and the Palestinian territories) rather than proximate areas that are defined by the government as being more strategic recipients of ODA.

The focus on bilateral delivery in crises acknowledges the capacity of the Australian Defence Force (ADF) to deliver ODA in complex humanitarian emergencies (such as cyclones). Bilateral delivery also ensures that the national interest benefits are maximized insofar as Australia is seen as the source of the ODA rather than simply donating to a pool of funds distributed by an intergovernmental or non-governmental organization. Equally noteworthy is that in emergency situations such as cyclone Winston in Fiji in 2016, much of this ODA is delivered by the ADF, so some of it amounts to re-purposing resources from the defence budget.

Regional and global programmes

In addition to bilateral programmes, the government supports several regional and global programmes and partnerships with intergovernmental organizations, such as the World Bank. The Department of Foreign Affairs and Trade manages Australia's ODA programme, but it is delivered through other federal departments, and numerous partners based in Australia, both internationally and in the recipient states. The largest partners delivering Australian ODA are multilateral organizations, commercial suppliers, Australian government agencies, non-government organizations (NGOs), academic institutions and the recipient governments themselves.

The largest regional budget is in the Pacific (followed by Southeast and East Asia) and these programmes reinforce both the focus on 'aid and trade' and the Pacific 'Step-Up'. In 2020, the new Australian Infrastructure Financing Facility for the Pacific (AIFFP) began operation, with A$1.5 billion available in loans and A$500 million in grants. By 2022–23, this had increased to a total of A$4 billion. While not ODA *per se*, these are not inconsiderable sums and operate in the context of countering Chinese concessional loans that are often treated in geopolitical analyses as being akin to ODA.[19]

The humanitarian assistance budget is also illuminating insofar as it highlights the preference for an area that is closely identified with Liberal Internationalist altruism. That is, an area where the direct, often emergency, need of recipients drives ODA contributions. In 2022–23, Australia allocated A$639 million to humanitarian programmes, making this sector the fourth largest in the ODA budget. However, it still only represented less than 15 per cent of the budget.

How Australian ODA compares

In terms of the gross amount allocated to ODA, Australia rated thirteenth in 2022, down from ninth in 1996. All the countries who spend more than Australia (bar Canada, Japan and the US) are European. Six have higher GNIs than Australia. In gross terms, government claims that Australia is a generous ODA giver is defensible and we will see later that this perception aligns with public opinion.

Measuring ODA as a percentage of GNI is the benchmark in the ODA sector as it allows international comparisons to be drawn using the relative size of the donor's economy. Governments came together at the UN in the 1970s and pledged to aim for ODA budgets of 0.7 per cent of GNI, but this goal has proved illusory. Between 1995 and 2021, Australia's relative international position has declined from 0.34 per cent to 0.22 per cent of GNI, shifting Australia from the ninth to the twenty-first most generous donor. It is noteworthy that in 1995, Australia was above average and now it is below average. From a political standpoint, the Labor government improved the longstanding decline in GNI when it took office in 2006, but this improvement in ODA as a percentage of GNI declined again once the Coalition won office in 2013.[20] The open question is whether this will change under the Albanese government.

Australia's GNI is the ninth largest internationally, which places Australia's generosity behind its wealth,[21] but as noted, most donors are European and many states with higher GNI are not major donors (such as Qatar, which leads the GNI table, and Bermuda). Of the 19 more generous states as a percentage of GNI, 10 have higher GNIs than Australia, which highlights that almost half of states more generous than Australia by this measure are less wealthy. By 2021, most other states spending less than 0.2 percent of GNI on ODA were either facing political crises or relatively new to providing ODA.[22] These trends challenge Australia's middle power credentials because successive governments have failed to prioritize ODA for needy non-citizens over national budgetary priorities.

The per capita figures provide an interesting comparison to GNI. In 1995, Australia was the eighth most generous donor in the Organization for Economic Cooperation and Development (OECD) on a per capita basis, spending US$116 (at 2016 prices). By 2021, Australia was 18th and spending US$114:[23] Both Australia's gross spend per capita and relative spend had declined. As with the GNI figures, the per capita spend peaked under Labor in the mid-2000s and declined after the Coalition took office in 2013, although the correlation is not as stark. Regardless of debate over which measure should be used, Australia's commitment to ODA has been criticized internationally as it has become the second least generous donor in the OECD.[24]

ODA policy and implementation

> The purpose of the aid program is to promote Australia's national interests by contributing to sustainable economic growth and poverty reduction.[25]

In June 2014, the Abbott Coalition government launched the 'New Aid Paradigm' to reorient Australia's ODA strategy on the national interest. The official aims of the ODA programme were consistent with previous aims in relation to prosperity, poverty and stability, but the most noteworthy shift was that the role of national interest considerations was elevated in declaratory policy. In contrast, the international drivers of ODA, such as the Sustainable Development Goals (SDGs), were not emphasized in the government's policy speeches and declaratory policy announcing the 'New Aid Paradigm.'

ODA and the national interest

The strategic framework that guided ODA delivery focuses on 'promoting prosperity, reducing poverty, enhancing stability', but the strategic decisions about the prioritization of ODA were to be based on four tests.[26] The first test developed to guide ODA decisions was:

> Pursuing national interest and extending Australia's influence. Australia's longer-term strategic and economic objectives will guide aid allocation decisions. Considerations will include an assessment of the costs of regional instability and insecurity, including financial, humanitarian, political and

health-related risks, prospects to strengthen trade and investment, and the potential to extend Australia's influence.[27]

Other tests were titled the 'Impact on Promoting Growth and Reducing Poverty', 'Australia's Value-add and Leverage' and 'Making Performance Count'.[28] These tests oriented ODA more closely to the national interest than the previous government and ended the Rudd and Gillard government's declaratory policy focus on middle power leadership promoting globalist Liberal Internationalist goals. The Albanese government may return to more Liberal Internationalist values, but in a constrained budgetary environment this will be challenging.

As noted earlier, the geographic scope of the programme has also tightened to focus on Australia's core interests in the Asia-Pacific (interestingly the term Indo-Pacific is not yet used to define ODA delivery). The shift was justified as being more closely aligned with the national interest because 'stronger growth, prosperity and stability in the region is of direct benefit to Australia, Australians and citizens of our neighbouring countries', and Australia could also have a bigger impact by concentrating ODA on traditional partners.[29]

Neoliberal management and budgeting

The aid program is not charity ... we will not pretend that aid alone is a panacea for poverty.[30]

Neoliberal economics was the ideological preference of Coalition governments in domestic politics, with the emphasis being on market-oriented solutions. It quickly became clear that the ODA sector would be a target for policy reform such as privatizing ODA delivery. Institutionally, the sector was reformed dramatically with Australia's dedicated ODA agency, the Australian Agency for International Development (AusAID), being merged into the Department of Foreign Affairs and Trade in 2013.[31] This reform was not based on one of the numerous government or independent reviews of ODA policy that have occurred regularly but rather reflected the policy preferences of the newly elected Coalition government. It 'aligned aid and trade and diplomacy' in the name of the national interest, but equally allowed new public management (NPM) reforms that had long driven public sector reform in Australia and other developed states to be imposed on the ODA sector.[32]

A version of 'public value' that had evolved in the NPM literature was also applied, with a very strong focus on the national interest. AusAID's mandate had always existed under the umbrella of the national interest, but focused on delivering development outcomes and programmes emphasizing good governance, local capacity-building and gender equality for recipients. Alignment with best practice in the global ODA industry was understandable but AusAID's independence from the Department of Foreign Affairs and Trade had meant that it was perceived as having drifted too far away from the national interest to focus on the recipients of ODA as key stakeholders. The 'new' aspect of the

Coalition's 'New Aid Paradigm' reflected the ideological preferences of the Coalition and the longstanding neoliberal economic management that had become the orthodoxy in government. As such, promoting export-oriented economic growth and self-help amongst ODA recipients aligned closely with Liberal party ideology.

In addition to institutional reform, Coalition governments also imposed neoliberal budget stringency across the foreign affairs portfolio and this impacted on the ODA budget. This form of neoliberalism had been implemented across government portfolios for some time, but ODA was one area where it had not impacted as deeply. On launching the 'New Aid Paradigm', the then foreign minister made arguments that epitomized the ideology of Coalition governments. For example, she noted that 'The previous Labor Government as borrowing money from overseas, to fund an ODA programme to send money back overseas – \$1 billion each and every month is borrowed to pay the interest on Labor's debt.'[33] The policy result was that the ODA budget was to be 'stabilized' at A\$5 billion for two years and then capped to grow with the inflation rate. This ensured that the graduated increases promised by Labor for their next term, but not delivered while in office, would never go ahead. In addition, the budget was in fact cut and dropped below A\$5 billion rather than being 'stabilized'.[34]

The Morrison Coalition government argued that this was a 'generous' allocation that placed Australia in the top ten donors amongst OECD states.[35] Critics focused on the failure to match the promised Labor increases to reach 0.5 per cent of GNI by 2015, which many commentators treated as cuts when they were in fact simply promises of the opposition. Kevin Rudd made this pledge during the 2010 federal election campaign but even though the GNI increased under the Rudd and Gillard governments, it did not come close to 0.5 per cent of GNI. In an attempt to obscure the reality, governments focused on gross ODA spending rather than the accepted measure (GNI), which allowed ODA to be benchmarked against economic activity. The focus on GNI is ODA industry best practice but for Canberra it does not provide a favourable impression of Australian ODA.

The 'New Aid Paradigm' and the national interest

The 'New Aid Paradigm' focused on 'aid for trade' initiatives, enhanced private sector involvement in ODA delivery and enhanced performance measures. The policy aligned with OECD best practice[36] and reflected development literature on changes in the nature of inequity in the region, by focusing on adapting ODA to relieving poverty in states that have grown from least developed to become middle-income. Two-thirds of Australia's ODA recipients had achieved middle-income status and ODA had become less a driver of development than a support for domestic economic activity and international investment. From a geopolitical standpoint, the 'New Aid Paradigm' also recognized that China had gone from a recipient of ODA to an ODA giver on par with Australia,[37] and presumably it would overtake Australia in the near future.

Much of the 'New Aid Paradigm' was not *new* insofar as it reflected continuity, especially in relation to improving ODA effectiveness, which had had bipartisan support. For example, Prime Minister Howard's Coalition government had set up the Office of Aid Effectiveness (OAE) in 2006 to oversee the performance of ODA. As such, the governance of Australia's ODA programme is reviewed closely to allow continuous improvement. The Department of Foreign Affairs and Trade's (DFAT) 2014 performance framework provided clear targets and reflected the neoliberal trends in governance that have influenced all aspects of government service delivery. Of particular note in the DFAT framework is a geographic focus on the Asia/Indo-Pacific and on poverty reduction, gender equality ('empowering women and girls') and reducing corruption. Increasing prosperity is the priority and the private sector is identified as a key partner in delivering the programme.[38]

'Aid for trade'

'Aid for trade' acknowledged the increased flows of investment in the developing world that had eclipsed ODA flows. 'Aid for trade' sought to focus on the alleviation of poverty by encouraging domestic economic growth. The neoliberal assumption underpinning this 'new' approach to ODA was that economic growth would reduce poverty and that ODA investments in economic infrastructure and regulatory reform could support the private sector in creating jobs, which would in turn increase prosperity. The then foreign minister cited OECD and World Trade Organization (WTO) research 'that 1 USD invested in aid for trade is associated with an increase of nearly 8 USD in additional exports from all developing countries'.[39] The 'aid for trade' agenda was reinforced by the 2017 Foreign Policy White Paper's focus on the trade and investment aspects of maintaining a 'rules-based' international order.[40] This export-oriented neoliberal economic strategy mirrored the government's domestic approach to economic management, but its applicability in all settings, particularly the South Pacific, was debatable.

While the focus was clearly on improving the economic sustainability of Indo/Asia-Pacific states, another positive outcome was that A$1 in Australian ODA delivered a A$7.10 increase in Australian exports to recipient states.[41] This meant that 'aid for trade' also improved Australia's longstanding export-oriented growth strategy. Similarly, Australia's use of education as ODA has undoubtably benefited recipients individually and regionally through interventions such as the Australia–Pacific Training Coalition (APTC). New iterations of the Colombo Plan, such as the Australia Awards, have seen thousands of scholarships given to regional applicants to study in Australia (over 3,100 in 2020 alone), benefiting the Australian university sector whilst being counted by the government as ODA. Australia's ODA has been criticized as being 'Boomerang aid'.[42] That is, it is ostensibly spent to support developing countries but comes back to Australia as goods and services produced by Australian companies. While there is grounds for criticism, it is clear that this sort of economic return fits the government's neoliberal focus on ODA.

The international institutional setting

While the national interest is evident across much of the ODA programme, a more Liberal Internationalist focus on altruism in ODA is most apparent in the engagement with international organizations and partners. The Australian ODA programme is guided by national policy priorities, yet also aligned with the UN's 17 Sustainable Development Goals (SDGs).[43]

BOX 13.2: THE SDGS AND ODA

In 2015, UN members agreed that the 17 SDGs should guide best practice in ODA delivery. Most states including Australia agreed to the framework as there is little debate that 'ending poverty and other deprivations must go hand-in-hand with strategies that improve health and education, reduce inequality, and spur economic growth'. The open question is to what extent Canberra has incorporated the SDGs in ODA. This is more significant given Canberra's use of ODA as part of the geostrategic competition with China in the South Pacific.

ODA policy makes multiple references to SDGs as aspirational goals which Australia is working towards. However, the OECD has noted that the alignment with the SDGs in Australian ODA is incomplete.[44] This gap highlights that this international framework may relate to a theory of developmental change that is not the prime driver of Australia's ODA strategy. The 2022 ODA budget mentions various forms of sustainability, but there is a strong focus on promoting sustainable economic growth that aligns with the 'aid for trade' agenda rather than the SDGs. For instance, the Department of Foreign Affairs and Trade notes that the programme in the Pacific 'will focus on promoting sustainable, inclusive and private-sector led economic development, enhancing security cooperation and deepening people-to-people links'.[45] The provision of alternative finance through the AIFFP also points to the claim that Chinese aid is leading to 'unsustainable debt', which will lead to 'Debt Trap' diplomacy in the Pacific.[46]

In practice, Australia's multilateral cooperation is focused through a number of UN programmes and issue-based partnerships with NGOs. For example, Australia has long supported both the Global Fund to fight AIDS, Tuberculosis and Malaria, and GAVI, the Vaccine Alliance. Its level of support for multilateral ODA delivery has broadly tracked its commitment to ODA more generally, but the figures are tiny compared to the overall programme. For example, in 2022–23, less than A$70 million was provided to UN agencies out of a budget of A$4.4 billion (see Table 13.1). The fact that most of Australia's COVID-19 diplomacy in the Indo-Pacific was delivered bilaterally highlights the emphasis on national interests because it can be identified as coming from a particular donor rather than a large organization. Australia also supports intergovernmental organizations focused on development, such as the World Bank and Asian Development Bank, which provide development finance. With the election of the Albanese government, these commitments have continued but remain small.

THE POLITICIZATION OF OFFICIAL DEVELOPMENT ASSISTANCE

Australia's politicized approach to ODA

The use of ODA as a tool in a broader foreign policy strategy can be identified through a case study that connects ODA aims and geostrategic goals. In the case of China in the South Pacific, orthodox Realist geopolitics are on display, as are underlying threat perceptions that characterize Australia's unique Strategic Culture. Added to these themes is a history of support for PICs that comes from a mix of considerations, including long relationships, many originating before federation, and a sense of responsibility (bordering on paternalism) that is founded in the connection between the Liberal Internationalist values in AFP and proximity to 'near neighbours'.

TABLE 13.1 *ODA delivered through UN agencies, 2022–23*[47]

Agency	A$m
UN Women	7.8
United Nations Children's Fund (UNICEF)	19.0
United Nations Development Programme (UNDP)	13.0
United Nations Population Fund (UNFPA)	9.2
United Nations Programme on HIV and AIDS ((UNAIDS)	4.5
World Health Organization (WHO)	15.0

CASE STUDY 13.3: COUNTERING CHINESE INFLUENCE IN THE PACIFIC

Canberra's fears of rising Chinese influence are more complex due to China and Taiwan's cheque book diplomacy where ODA has been used to gain or prevent political recognition of Taiwan by PICs. This longstanding competition flared in 2019, with the Solomon Islands and Kiribati agreeing to switch allegiances from Taiwan to China. Australia has a one-China policy, but China's threats to forcibly reunite with Taiwan are a key part of the larger geopolitical competition between the US and China. The perception that China is increasing influence over those islands caused concern in Canberra. In addition, the most recent round of competition comes with the added inducement of an invitation to join China's 'Belt and Road Initiative'. President Xi's original 2013 concept of a modern silk road to form a belt and road linking China with Central Asia included several maritime pivot points in the Indian Ocean. The inclusion of the South Pacific in the maritime belt and road is a relatively new development that coincides with increased competition with Taiwan and Australia in the South Pacific.

There are numerous tangible examples of Canberra using the ODA programme to achieve political interests. The overall amount of ODA donated to the Pacific has grown from A$1.1 billion in 2017–18 to A$1.4 billion in 2022–23. Australian ODA to PNG and the Solomon Islands increased in traditional areas. In addition, funding was boosted through the funding of the Coral Sea Cable system, a submarine internet link that was negotiated to stall an agreement to accept a Chinese-funded cable that was perceived to be a threat to Australia's interests. In addition, ODA to the Pacific was quarantined from cuts elsewhere in the budget and from 2020, responding to the COVID-19 pandemic in the Pacific became the focus of Australia through the Partnerships for Recovery strategy.[48]

Another good example of Canberra's politicized use of ODA is the shift in the complexion of ODA to include infrastructure. Historically, Australia's ODA programme had moved away from infrastructure projects, such as roads, dams and wharves, to focus on capacity-building efforts. This approach aligned with good practice in the development arena, such as the SDGs, whereby improving the capacity of locals in the governance, education and health arenas was deemed an effective method of achieving positive developmental change. In contrast, China has had an advantage in the South Pacific insofar as it provided ODA, or more accurately, long-term loans at concessional rates managed through its Export Import (EXIM) bank. These were attractive to local elites for a number of reasons, including the fact that they met local political infrastructure demands without the stringent governance provisions that Australian ODA projects entailed.

In 2018, the Australian government announced a new A$2 billion infrastructure facility to meet the needs of the Pacific. Widely viewed as a direct response to China's use of ODA to grow influence in the region, it initially involved A$1.5 billion in loans and A$500 million in grants but quickly grew to A$4 billion. This was a significant shift from Australia's traditional focus on ODA as a gift to ODA as a loan, which also matches China's approach. Other recent infrastructure projects include: the submarine internet cable linking PNG and the Solomon Islands to the world through the Australian network, airports, ports, highways, and the long-term electrification of PNG that aims to provide electricity to 70 per cent of the population by 2030.

There is a strong focus on HADR in the Pacific, including A$500 million for renewable energy and climate resilience announced before the 2019 Pacific Islands Forum (PIF) Leaders' Summit in Tuvalu. However, Canberra's highly politicized diplomacy was undermined by its stance on coal and attempts to water down international efforts to counter climate change, including in the PIF itself.[49]

The question of just how much strategic competition with China is influencing ODA has been the focus of recent research and it is clear that 'China is changing the way Australia's political elites think about aid.'[50] This focus on national interest calculations is also clear in emergency responses such as COVID-19 diplomacy.

CASE STUDY 13.4: COVID-19 DIPLOMACY AND CHINA

While it is difficult to disaggregate altruistic and national interest motives since they often overlap, a clear implication of Australia's COVID-19 diplomacy was that it was to counter perceptions that China was gaining influence through COVID-19 elsewhere in Asia and Africa.[51] COVID-19 brought into relief the importance of bilateral relations; the multilateral COVAX facility only provided 20 per cent of a state's needs at most, so most PICs relied on longstanding diplomatic relations to gain access to supplies for the majority of their populations. While there was pressure from the development sector to focus Australia's ODA on global vaccine equity,[52] the government focused on its proximate neighbours. Canberra allocated about of a third of the US per capita to COVAX and concentrated resources on the South Pacific.[53] Canberra justified its regional approach by the need to focus efforts, but this approach also aligned with the broader Pacific 'Step-Up' policy, with PNG, Timor Leste and Fiji given priority for distribution of Australian-produced vaccines. The pandemic was framed as a threat to Australia[54] and therefore prioritizing an emergency response domestically and internationally was firmly within Australia's interests, which fits with the high-level threat perceptions that characterize Strategic Culture.

Australia was willing and able to deliver, not least due to domestic resistance to using locally-produced vaccines. That is, a potentially difficult public policy decision (whether to supply Australian citizens or donate doses to neighbours) was avoided by the fact that there was excess supply in Australia. Despite mixed awareness and support for ODA as discussed below, the government was on firm ground with clear public support for assisting Pacific islanders despite the domestic challenges posed by the pandemic. Pandemic diplomacy reaped rewards for PICs because they had low capacity to respond to the COVID-19 pandemic and their situation was made worse by the disruption to trade and tourism, on which many PICs relied heavily. At the same time, China was practising its own COVID-19 diplomacy in Africa and Asia and there were rumours of China offering vaccines to PICs. Canberra's prompt action effectively blocked Chinese vaccine diplomacy, a point that Beijing openly confirmed.[55]

Public opinion and political incentives

The influence of public opinion on policy is less clear than national interest considerations in relation to issues such as geopolitical competition. The majority of Australians support the idea of ODA but are largely ignorant of the details. Therefore, they do not form a significant domestic constituency supporting ODA with respect to other public policy priorities such as education or healthcare. Furthermore, since the COVID-19 pandemic, many politicians harbour concerns that increasing ODA will have negative electoral consequences.[56] Therefore, the influence of public opinion from 'below' on the ODA programme can be questioned. In contrast, anecdotal support for altruistic gift-giving is evidenced in public donations to domestic NGOs, such as Amnesty International and World Vision.[57]

Historically, a large minority of Australians have felt that Australia has provided too much ODA; less than 20 per cent think that Australia should provide more. However, in 2022, in the shadow of the COVID-19 pandemic, a slight shift was detected, with those thinking that Australia provides too much declining to about 26 per cent and those thinking that Australia gives too little rising to over 24 per cent.[58] The public has also consistently displayed a lack of awareness by wildly overestimating the size of the ODA budget, often by a magnitude of up to ten, which if accurate would make it on par with the defence budget. When informed about the exact amount of ODA that Australia provides, respondents think that the level is about right, changing their opinion from thinking that Australia was being too generous. However, in contrast, this has not led to the view that Australia should be more generous.

Interestingly, a recent study that connected spending to China's influence in the Pacific also revealed that people don't think that more aid should be given to counter China.[59] It is clear that people are concerned about the potential threat from China and the threat in Australia's 'back yard', the South Pacific. However, these concerns are not strong enough to motivate greater generosity, even when people are informed about how much they had exaggerated the true level of ODA in their estimations. A key response to China's ODA in the Pacific was to think that a greater proportion of the present ODA budget should be directed towards the Pacific, and this mirrors the government's post-2013 policy.[60] A fascinating twist to this research is that despite the concerns about China, this did not mean that the majority believed that ODA should be focused on achieving Australia's national interests, but rather maintained a traditional focus on humanitarian concerns.

In the case of ODA, there is no democratic deficit as there exists with climate change. That is, government policy is largely aligned with public opinion. There is a moderate constituency amongst the public and development practitioners supporting ODA for altruistic purposes, and these supporters are more likely to vote for the Labor Party or Greens. These attitudes align closely with Liberal Internationalist values and were more apparent under Labor governments because they were more closely aligned with the party ideology. It also must be noted that the differences between Coalition and Labor policies on ODA may be more apparent in the declaratory rhetoric than the substantive approach to achieving the national interest – that is, Labor policy statements appear more supportive of the Liberal Internationalist aims of ODA, but this does not necessarily alter national interest priorities.[61] However, in the absence of a broad-based ODA constituency, there is little ground for creating an ODA platform as part of an electoral contest. The incoming Albanese government has suggested that ODA will be stabilized, but in real terms this does not mean that ODA will increase greatly.

Differences in policy preferences between Labor and Coalition governments are more akin to the response to climate change, where parties can safely 'preach to the converted' but are unlikely to gain large numbers of votes from elevating party preferences on ODA. There have been criticisms of ODA's declining transparency,[62] especially in relation to ODA being so closely or openly tied to the national interest, but it is not surprising that these have not gained traction even amongst the Labor government.

Conclusion

Official development assistance provides an insight into the complexity of foreign policy-making as Liberal Internationalism would seem to be the driving altruistic force but Realism and Strategic Culture are clearly evident in elevating national interest considerations. From a theoretical standpoint, ODA highlights the pluralism needed to try to adequately explain foreign policy strategies and outcomes. This pluralistic approach shows that differences in declaratory policy between the Coalition and Labor parties should not be over-emphasized.

Analysing the role of ODA in AFP also highlights the difficulty of using conclusions about a single issue to generalize about AFP more generally. From a practical standpoint, ODA fits into a larger foreign policy strategy that changes over time and is strongly influenced by factors such as the state of the economy, the ideology of political parties and academic/industry best practice.

Australia's response to the COVID-19 pandemic had a significant impact on ODA insofar as resources were redirected within the budget to tackle the issue. However, unlike most OECD donors, it did not lead to an increase in ODA. The government's pandemic response highlighted existing trends, including the increased focus on the South Pacific from the 'Step-Up' and heightened concern over China's influence in the Pacific, which led to a level of competitive COVID-19 diplomacy, which benefited PICs. As such, the national interest has become more intwined with ODA priorities including responding to humanitarian emergencies.

ODA has been closely aligned with the Coalition government's neoliberal ideology and the threat perceptions that drive Realism and Strategic Culture. Claims that Australia should exercise creative 'middlepowermanship'[63] or good international citizenship are associated with Labor governments and may be elevated in the Albanese government's ODA policy; this mirrors the treatment of climate change and asylum seekers. However, a note of caution is needed. While there are clear differences in the approach to ODA (theory of change) between the Labor and Coalition governments, the focus on the national interest remains. This is highly Realist while also aligning with Strategic Culture insofar as strategic denial of China in the South Pacific is a key aim. ODA was not viewed by the government as charity and it is seldom claimed that it is provided for altruistic aims, even though the majority of programmes are designed with developmental best practice in mind.

An interconnected range of factors explain the evolution of a pluralistic foreign policy stance on ODA. Official development assistance has never been a high priority for government or voters, and as such, has been open to foreign policy politicization. While there is significant domestic support for ODA, it is based on a high level of ignorance about the size and nature of the programme and an underlying focus on ODA as charity rather than ODA as a tool for achieving the national interest. This means that ODA has not been a key issue at elections. ODA policy reinforces existing preferences and increases or cuts to the ODA programme closely align with the preferences of the voting bases of the two key parties, meaning that little electoral gain can be developed in this area. In the absence of a strong domestic constituency, ODA can be used by governments to achieve foreign policy goals, such as winning a rotational seat on the UNSC or countering Chinese influence in the South Pacific. As such, ODA provides a very useful insight into the diplomatic priorities of the day which are supporting the neoliberal 'aid for trade' agenda and strategic stability in Australia's proximate region.

14

Realism and the limits of climate securitization in Australian foreign policy

Introduction

Australia on its own won't cool the climate. (Prime Minister Morrison, 2019)[1]

Debate over to what extent Australia should respond to climate change has led to division and inaction in Canberra. Until very recently, the national interest has been cited for not responding in a manner that undermined prosperity, but with the election of the Anthony Albanese government this appears to have changed. However, appearances can be deceptive.

In 2020, Australian greenhouse gas emissions dipped to levels not seen since 1995, but this was due largely to the impact of lockdowns owing to the COVID-19 pandemic. The year before, 2019 was the fourth hottest year on record[2] and was dominated by the disastrous 'Black Summer' bushfire season. These facts were used by the government and opponents alike for political point scoring, but didn't impact Australian foreign policy (AFP) towards climate change.

The politicization of climate change provides a case study for how the key themes intersect in AFP. The central place of climate change in the 2007 federal election, the subsequent failure of Prime Minister Kevin Rudd's 2009 Conference of the Parties (COP) campaign in Copenhagen, and the reversals under the Gillard, Turnbull and Morrison administrations, highlight the role of foreign policy as the boundary between domestic politics and international relations. Climate change policies and politics provide salient examples of the limits of Liberal Internationalist 'middlepowermanship and 'good international citizenship' when partisan politics is at play and Australia's core national interests are threatened. AFP on climate change also highlights the democratic deficit that can occur when public opinion and enduring Realist foreign policy goals clash. In this case, maintaining economic prosperity through a neoliberal export-oriented trade policy has been elevated over other interests.

The responses of successive governments to climate change have caused much debate and division domestically, but from a foreign policy standpoint most of the tension over climate change has occurred in international fora, such as the UN. Australia's uncompromising stance was shared by many like-minded states until the late 2010s, but as opinion strengthened in the 2020s against those holding out against taking significant action, Australia's response was singled out for criticism, especially in its proximate region (South Pacific) (see Chapter 12). By the time of the election of the Albanese government, Australia could no longer hold out against rising international pressure, but the question is whether the commitment to cut emissions is more apparent than real. Canberra has now committed to reducing emissions by shifting to renewables, but not to limiting the exports of climate change-inducing commodities that fuel Australia's prosperity.

Thematic questions addressed in this chapter include: Has Australia's stance on climate change undermined its interests, especially in the South Pacific? In what sense could Australia be seen to be exercising 'middlepowermanship' on climate change? Have national interests trumped international/global responsibilities? How does public opinion influence foreign policy-making in Canberra? Does the Albanese government climate compromise also compromise economic prosperity?

A snapshot of Australian emissions: The basis for debate

Almost every aspect of climate change policy in Australia is divisive, beginning with the fundamental question of what is being measured. Much debate occurs between those who would prefer to refer to gross emissions, per-capita figures or figures that include both domestic *and* exported emissions.

Gross emissions

In gross terms, Australia in 2022 is the world's thirteenth largest economy yet eleventh largest emitter of CO_2 (487 million tonnes).[3] This equated to an increase on the year before based on increased post COVID-19 economic activity. However, it was 21 per cent below 2005 levels (the baseline for the Paris Agreement).[4] Therefore, Australia's emissions have reduced since the Paris Agreement and are quite closely aligned with national economic activity. From this perspective, Australian emissions appear commensurate with its economic activity and earlier commitments. However, these commitments have been overtaken by events, in particular the aim of constraining global temperature increases to 1.5°C by 2030. As it stands, if every state aligned with Australia's climate commitments, then temperatures would likely rise to 3°C with catastrophic impacts on the environment.[5]

Comparative gross emissions

Comparatively, Australia emits 1.4 per cent of total global emissions. Therefore, it could be argued that Australia can do little to effect change in global climate change. Even a 50 per cent cut in emissions (beyond what any government has promised) would not have a significant practical impact. This is one rationale behind the inaction by successive governments. However, this ignores the impact that support for norms can buttress for the 'rules-based order' and encourage others to comply. These other states, such as China and the US, can have a material outcome on global emissions if they compromise. Failure to compromise on a technical issue of practicality also ignores the ideational leadership of 'middlepowermanship', which aligns with Liberal Internationalist values in AFP. Therefore, a compromise on climate change was simply the right thing to do, but it took until the election of the Albanese government in 2022 for this to occur.

Per-capita emissions

From one standpoint, Australia's 16 tonnes of CO_2 per person makes it the highest emitter per capita. Australia has the world's fifty-fifth largest population, so by this measure, Australia's emissions are much higher than would be expected from a country with a similar population. Australia's per capita emissions are greater than all other developed economies, including the US, which has the world's second largest economy. However, Australia's economy is unlike most developed states insofar as it heavily concentrated on the export of agricultural and natural resources (versus manufactured goods or services). As such, Australia's emissions include those expended to produce and export these commodities and the export of these commodities is essential to Australia's continuing prosperity.

Given the very different bases for measuring Australia's impact on climate change, critics of Canberra's climate policy therefore prefer to focus on emissions in per capita terms. The significant mismatch in gross terms is used to highlight what they perceive to be an increased responsibility to meaningfully act to counter climate change, while others would prefer to downplay the issue by focusing on gross emissions. From the standpoint of gross emissions, Australia is a minor player and does not stand out from other polluters.

The missing emissions – exports of climate change-inducing commodities and Australian prosperity

Measures of national emissions do not include the export of the fossil fuels responsible for climate change. Some critics of Canberra's stance highlight that continuing to export (and profit from) climate change-producing fuels implicates Australia in worsening the problem versus working to solve it. If exported commodities are included, Australia's carbon footprint increases from 1.4 per cent of global emissions to over 5 per cent, putting it on par with the fifth largest gross polluter, Russia. On a per capita basis, this would place Australia even higher at more than four times its nearest rival, the US.[6] If exported fossil fuels are accounted for, Australia would be amongst the nine states responsible for emitting 66 per cent of global emissions.[7] The imbalance between imports and exports is shown in Figure 14.1.

The role of exports is significant from the standpoint of emissions and public policy as Australia is the sixth largest fossil fuel producer. Australia is the largest exporter of coal (29 per cent of total international exports) and in 2019, Australia became the largest exporter of liquified natural gas (LNG), valued at A\$49 billion. In 2022, this was valued at A\$93 billion. This is unlikely to change without government regulation as already-buoyant exploration and investment in both coal and gas is predicted to increase over the next ten years but may decline

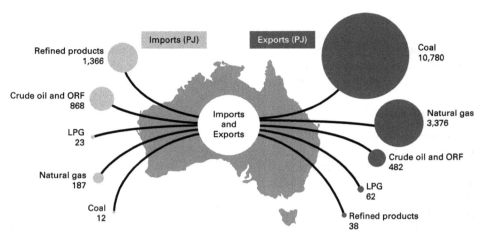

FIGURE 14.1 *Australian pre-COVID19 energy imports and exports, 2019.*[8]

sharply thereafter due to global efforts to reduce emissions. If emissions from projected developments are included with current domestic emissions and exports, then Australia would be responsible for 13 per cent of the allowable emissions of all states under the Paris Agreement.[9] For those seeking to tackle climate change, Australia's emissions and export-oriented, fossil fuel-dependent trade trajectory comes under scrutiny, and the failure to comprehensively act or lead highlights tensions between a narrow Realist focus on the national interest and Liberal Internationalist values.

In a similar vein to the focus on gross emissions, Australian governments have argued that a moratorium on Australian coal exports would not have any impact because importers would simply buy coal from elsewhere.[10] Emissions are measured when the commodities are burnt and are therefore included in the figures for Australia's key export markets, such as China and Japan. The point is that Australia could impact global emissions if the government regulated the export of these commodities. However, that would involve a dramatic change in Australia's commitment to free trade and market mechanisms. Canberra wanted to protect Australia's prosperity for as long as possible and therefore relied on market demand. That is, when importers curbed the use of fossil fuels, then demand would drop as would prices, which would render exports uneconomic.

The key public policy challenge for Canberra is that curbing emissions would have to occur without curbing exports of fossil fuels. To do otherwise would have a significant impact on Australian gross domestic product (GDP) and prosperity, and would require a significant restructure of the economy in order to maintain current Australian standards of living. Australia's cost-benefit analysis is unlike most other states, especially developed states, as their economies are not so dependent on exporting fossil fuels. As such, the incentives to compromise are not great. This was exemplified by statements in 2020 by the new Resources Minister Keith Pitt on the need to export more coal and gas to maintain living standards: 'We should use every opportunity to utilise the common wealth for the common good.'[11] Similarly, one of the government's responses to the war in the Ukraine was to donate 70,000 tonnes of coal, highlighting its ongoing necessity.

The present international institutional framework

The 1997 Kyoto Protocol to the 1992 United Nations Framework Convention on Climate Change (UNFCCC) was to expire in 2020, so in 2015 a total of 196 states, including Australia, negotiated and signed onto its successor, the Paris Agreement. As with all previous international agreements on this divisive issue, the Paris Agreement was reached after significant, sometimes acrimonious, debate. In negotiations, Australia was part of a group of fossil fuel producers and consumers that worked to limit measures that would adversely impact their development paths. In a clear display of Realism, national economic interests were protected over globalist interests; Australian interests over those most impacted by the effects of climate change. Of particular note for AFP was the ongoing rise of South Pacific activism and advocacy for cuts to emissions that would meaningfully address climate change due to the present and predicted impacts on Pacific Island Countries (PICs). Until 2022, Australia was not prepared to compromise, and this perceived intransigence contributed to tensions between Australia and PICs (discussed in detail in Chapter 12).

The Paris Agreement called on states to act to limit global temperature rises by at least 2°C by 2030, with the aspiration being reaching a 1.5°C threshold. The reasoning behind these targets was based on scientific predictions that were no longer debatable, and commitments were based on predicting the overall level of global emissions that could be produced between 2015 and 2030 and still constrain temperature rises. Most states, including Australia, made pledges to cut emissions, but these were not large enough to even reach the 2°C target, let alone 1.5°C. This led to domestic and international criticism of Canberra's stance, but prosperity was put before Liberal Internationalist values of the common good.

In Paris, the longstanding principle of 'common but differentiated responsibility' for previous emissions and present actions to combat climate change was upheld. As such, it was acknowledged that historical emissions provided benefits for developed states that meant they had greater responsibility for making cuts at present, even though late-industrializing developing states may actually be producing a greater share of present emissions. However, in the absence of offering differentiated targets, the Paris Agreement continued to provide only moral force for developed countries such as Australia to take action. It is this principle that opens the door for debate over the position of exported fossil fuels in the national targets of exporters. A position that Canberra has steadfastly rejected in all negotiations.

The overarching aim of reaching zero emissions by 2050 was enshrined in the Paris Agreement, but the focus has been on the 2030 timeframe and meeting commitments to 2030 became increasingly politicized as the deadline neared. While the international community had moved to acknowledge the need for greater cuts in emissions by 2030, Australia was still debating 2030 targets and whether to commit to net zero emissions by 2050. At this stage, the UN 'Emission

Gap Report 2020' noted that a three-fold increase in commitments would be needed to constrain temperature rises to 2°C and a five-fold increase would be needed to achieve 1.5°C.[12]

The difference between the upper and lower temperature commitments of 2°C and 1.5°C is significant, as it will have a major impact on practical efforts to combat climate change. It also highlights the limits of political will amongst many states, including Australia, to commit to any action that would likely impede economic prosperity. This brings into stark relief that lack of aspiration to progressive leadership on climate change that would mark Australia as a 'good international citizen' actively practising 'middlepowermanship' to deliver a global 'good'. This sort of aspiration has not been expressed since the Rudd government of 2009. Rather, Canberra has joined the majority of conservative states seeking to limit any negative impacts on national interests. Furthermore, the definition of national interests was narrowly focused on material resources and fitted a Realist frame of thinking about maximizing relative national wealth to protect security rather than a Liberal Internationalist focus on broader human security perspectives.

Australia's response to international pressure

Australia's lack of engagement with the multilateral process was aptly captured by Prime Minister Morrison's non-attendance at the 2019 UN Climate Summit in New York, even though he was in the US visiting President Donald Trump at the time. Similarly, in a speech to the UN General Assembly earlier in 2019, the prime minister announced that Australia would be pulling out of the Green Climate Fund (which provides finance to mitigate the impacts of climate change on vulnerable states). This followed the government fighting off a divisive and politically damaging challenge by PICs at the annual Pacific Islands Forum (PIF) Leaders' Summit in Tuvalu in August 2019, where PICs tried to raise expectations beyond the Paris Agreement commitments by specifically targeting the closure of coal mines and limiting coal energy production.[13] The government preferred to provide bilateral climate adaptation aid directly to PICs, to the tune of A$500 million, than to join multilateral actions, such as the Green Climate Fund. Presumably this strategy was connected to the geopolitical tension with China whereby Canberra wanted to try to build influence in the South Pacific. However, it did not achieve the aim of placating PICS (see Chapter 12).

Recent government policy

Climate change received passing mention in the 2017 Foreign Policy White Paper, which acknowledged the risk that climate change poses to Australia and the region, in particular PICs. The 2016 Defence White Paper echoed this position and noted the potential challenges Australia might face as its neighbours were impacted by climate change.[14] However, no connection was made between Australia's approach to emissions and these potential threats, and the Foreign Policy White Paper contended that 'Australia has comprehensive policies to reduce domestic emissions while maintaining our economic competitiveness'.[15] Furthermore, the Foreign Policy White Paper proposed allocating official development assistance (ODA) to mitigation and adaptation efforts of vulnerable states but did not provide details.

In 2018, the Senate Committee on Foreign Affairs, Defence and Trade held an inquiry that reported the significant risk posed by climate change to Australian national and human security.[16] There was also a chorus of civil society reports highlighting these issues. However, these reports had no appreciable impact on policy and were largely ignored by the government. This led a former Chief of the Defence Force to note that the Coalition has been 'breathtakingly complacent' in their response to the inquiry, and this was echoed by retired senior officials.[17] The 2019 bushfires in Eastern Australia also brough the risks to public prominence and evidence mounted. For example, the CSIRO's 2022 'State of the Climate' report found that climate change was causing 'an increase in the risk of natural disasters from extreme weather, including "compound extremes", where multiple extreme events occur together or in sequence, thus compounding their impacts'.[18] The CSIRO also found that Australian average temperatures had already risen by 1.5°C since 1910. Regardless, Canberra's stance did not change.

In declaratory policy, the Morrison government maintained the aspiration of cutting emissions to 26–28 per cent below 2005 levels by 2030. This would track to meet the goals of the 2015 Paris Agreement. In order to achieve these targets, a range of initiatives were put in place. In 2019, the government replaced the Emissions Reduction Fund (ERF) with the A$3.5 billion Climate Solutions Package that it asserted would meet Australia's international commitments, but this initiative was criticized as being a rebranding of existing initiatives that actually starved them of funding.[19] In addition, the emphasis was placed on abatement programmes such as carbon capture and greater use of hydrogen rather than legislating to reduce emissions. Recent predictions highlighted that Australia would in fact exceed these commitments (by reaching about 30–38 per cent cuts), but in order to achieve 1.5°C, it was predicted that Australia would have to make much more significant cuts, to the order of 75 per cent.[20] Furthermore, exceeding targets was not attributable to federal government policy, but rather that this is the result of state government programmes, such as domestic solar and wind power, rather than federal government action.[21]

Regardless of the government's repeated assurances, analysts such as the Climate Transparency Group noted that despite continual reference to meeting its Paris commitments, the government was not likely to come close to meeting those targets.[22] In fact, it was predicted that emissions would actually be 8 per cent higher than 2005 and there was little sign of this changing as:

the Australian government dismissed the findings of the IPCC Special Report on Global Warming of 1.5°C, discontinued its funding to the Green Climate Fund (GCF), ignored the call by the UN Secretary General and its Pacific Island neighbours to increase its climate action, let alone the expressed desire of Australians for more action – and its emissions continue to increase, despite Government protestations to the contrary.[23]

There was a significant tension between declaratory and operational policy (what Canberra says and what it does) on climate change that remains unresolved. To claim that it was achieving its targets, the government relied on the contentious practice of carrying over credits from the levels that Australia was meant to achieve by 2020 from the Kyoto Agreement into present planning. That is, 'surplus' emissions that were not emitted in the earlier period were treated as 'carry over credits', meaning that over 50 per cent of the emissions reductions Australia needed to achieve by 2030 would come from a technical surplus from an earlier accounting period. Furthermore, Australia had negotiated very generous targets under the earlier Kyoto Protocol, meaning that the surplus came at little cost to the Australian economy. In practice, the use of 'carry over credits' meant that Australia would not undertake the cuts needed to global emissions to reach either the 1.5°C or 2°C temperature targets. As such, the national interest was firmly on display and critics noted that 'if all other countries were to follow Australia's "Highly Insufficient" current policy trajectory, warming could reach over 3°C and up to 4°C', rather than the 1.5–2°C sought by the Paris Agreement.[24]

By taking this uncompromising stance, Australia was singled out for its intransigence at the 2019 COP meeting in Madrid and was characterized by climate scientists and activists as a state that was not actively supporting measures to manage climate change. These charges continued to be laid against Canberra at the Glasgow COP in 2021.[25] In contrast, other developed states had made significant commitments to cut emissions and many had adjusted them in line with the expectations of the Paris Agreement. For example, the UK's target was 68 per cent and the US target was 50–52 per cent. After the election of Joe Biden in 2020, there was commentary about the pressure that the US was putting on Australia to act and this connected Canberra's response to climate change with the maintenance of security through the US alliance that is so valued by Realism and Strategic Culture. While these cuts and new international commitments were still not enough to ensure temperature rises of 2°C were reached, Australia still lagged. Australia did not adjust its 2030 targets and was late in agreeing to net zero. This meant that on the eve of the Glasgow COP in 2021, Australia was ranked last (thirty-first) amongst developed states for its response to climate change.[26]

The Morrison government was under pressure to commit to net zero before the Glasgow COP in November 2021 and the sources of pressure were telling. The key pressure on government to not compromise came from members of the Coalition government, particularly the National Party part of the Coalition. As the Glasgow COP neared, it became increasingly clear that Australia's position was diplomatically and domestically unsustainable and the Nationals ensured that the interests of their regional/agricultural constituency was protected. This pitted them against several actors with which they would usually be aligned, including the prime minister and the large mining companies that were calling for compromise. The Nationals provided the prime minister with an ultimatum of sorts, which involved a range of protections for rural communities and no shift in 2030 commitments. From an international standpoint, pledging net zero by 2050 was not revolutionary, and from the standpoint of climate science, this pledge was insufficient to limit climate change to 2°C, let alone the 1.5°C target. However, making this pledge involved significant domestic compromises and was clearly not an example of 'middlepowermanship'.

Canberra's intransigence was already firmly in the sights of domestic and international civil society critics, but pressure from the private sector and other states also increased substantially. While there had been murmurs from business,[27] it was not until 2021 that key Australian businesses openly entered the political debate. The about-turn by NewsCorp in October 2021 was incredibly influential, as it had hitherto been highly critical of first, the concept of climate change and second, doing anything substantive to respond if it would undermine Australian prosperity. This removed an influential mouthpiece for critics of compromise. This shift coincided with concerted campaigns by key mining companies to reposition and 'green' themselves. The BHP board consulted shareholders and was seemingly surprised by the level of support for initiatives such as significant cuts to production emissions. Fortescue CEO Twiggy Forrest embarked on a campaign focusing on repositioning operations to hydrogen production and attempted to shame Chinese President Xi Jinping into attending the Glasgow COP.

On the international front, there were suggestions that Europe might impose climate tariffs on Australian imports. Public statements from the US and the COP host, the UK, indicated significant commitments were expected from all, but this was interpreted as singling out Australia.[28] Given the recent announcement of the AUKUS security treaty of such importance to Australia, the pressure from these allies had greater importance than pressure from numerous intergovernmental organizations, such as the UN, which had failed to shift Australian policy. This should not be a surprise, given the government's unwillingness to heed often damning criticisms of human rights bodies in relation to Australia's asylum seeker policies, such as mandatory detention. This highlights that on a key public policy issue that crosses the domestic/international divide, the pressure-points for government were both domestic and international, but both focused on more Realist concerns in relation to Australia's economic prosperity and military security than any Liberal Internationalist conception of normative good.

The election of the Albanese government in 2022 and compromise on climate change

The election of the Albanese government in May 2022 heralded a major shift in policy, but it remains to be seen whether it is more apparent than real. There is no doubt there was a shift in declaratory policy and this was well received internationally, and particularly in the South Pacific. The government committed to a 43 per cent cut in emissions by 2030 and reaffirmed the previous government's commitment to becoming net zero by 2050. The 43 per cent cut was much larger than the Morrison government's pledge of 26–28 per cent below 2005 levels. Furthermore, the government enshrined these targets in legislation through the Climate Change Bill in August 2022.

The Albanese government's climate change commitments met international expectations and changed Australia overnight from being a pariah to a participant in efforts to mitigate climate change. Canberra has now committed to reducing emissions by shifting to renewables, but not to limiting the exports of the climate change-causing commodities that fuel Australia's prosperity. As such, the government is relying on an ambitious shift to renewable energy within Australia to meet targets and expects global market mechanisms to slowly shift demand away from these commodities as other states bring more renewables online.

The reason to be cautious is twofold. First, declaratory statements need to be backed up by action and the government's plan needs to be implemented quickly. Second, these commitments meet expectations but do not exceed them and if other states only did what Canberra has pledged, then temperatures will still rise by 3°C. As such, this shift is not dramatic and certainly doesn't provide an example of creative 'middlepowermanship'.

Regardless of the detail, the declaratory policy shift on climate change did have a positive impact on the perceptions of PICs, which was one of the concerns of the incoming government with respect to geopolitical competition with China. It was also noteworthy that Prime Minister Albanese did not attend the COP in Egypt but rather prepared for an intensive series of meetings in Asia the next week, which also focused on security and relations with China.

Australia's minimalist response to climate change

Over the last 20 years, there has been political debate over whether climate change was real or manmade, but this has long passed from the mainstream. That said, climate denial still exists in the fringes of Australian polity. The focus shifted to what can and/or should be done about climate change and at what cost to Australia's prosperity. Division centred on what can be characterized as minimalist and maximalist perspectives of how to respond. The minimalist response focuses on the minimum that can be done to meet the letter, if not spirit, of international agreements whilst protecting Australian prosperity. The maximalist approach refers to efforts to meaningfully address climate change in ways that would actually halt or reverse the process. The former approach has dominated government policy other than for a brief period in the late 2000s, when Prime Minister Rudd capitalized on a spike in public opinion to attempt to innovate domestically and in foreign policy.

Proponents of responding to climate change in a meaningful maximalist way view it as a global issue that has local impacts. These impacts include the increased incidence of adverse climactic disasters such as cyclones, droughts and bushfires, and these outcomes have been securitized as threats to states. Predictions are that current emissions cuts are more likely to see the earth warming by 3°C and the Australian Academy of Science has found that impacts for Australia could be profound.[29]

Climate securitization

The expectation amongst climate maximalists is that the nature of the threat will be accepted and this will prompt a proportionate response, but in practice, the response has been inhibited by national interests and climate change has not been effectively securitized in the Australian mindset.[30] This means that it has not been elevated to the level of a national security threat that would trigger a significant government response, explained elsewhere in AFP as a Realist or Strategic Cultural militarization of threats, such as that posed by China.

The 2019 bushfires in Australia highlighted the limits of how much the government was willing to accept a connection between climate change and natural disasters. In this severe natural disaster, key government figures challenged both the climate science that pointed to increased incidence and intensity of bushfires[31] and also popular commentary linking the fires to the government's climate change policy.[32] Prime Minister Morrison repeated the argument drawn from gross rather than per capita measures of emissions: 'I am sure you would also agree that no response by any one government anywhere in the world can be linked to one fire event.'[33]

With the exception of a short period in Kevin Rudd's prime ministership in 2009, successive Australian governments have chosen to not take a lead internationally on climate change.[34] This does not mean that Australian governments have not engaged with the issue of climate change in international fora, but rather that they have done so in a manner that has allowed them to protect national interests, narrowly defined in economic terms.[35]

Australian governments have ensured that Australia's development path was not encumbered by restrictions to economic growth and have done so by negotiating targets that have not imposed a significant cost on the Australian economy. As such, Canberra has complied with the letter of international agreements in a minimalist manner. The attempt to use 'carry-over credits' is a case in point. This lack of leadership brings into relief claims that Australia's 'middlepowermanship' leads to intellectual effort and coalition-building being applied to international challenges to achieve creative outcomes. In this case, policy creativity was used to ensure that Australia's climate change obligations did not undermine its economic growth. It may be that the Liberal Internationalist values in foreign policy are more likely to be represented by Labor governments, such as Rudd's 2009 COP campaign and the election of the Albanese government in 2022.

The limits of Labor leadership on climate change

As noted earlier, the exception to Canberra's intransigence on climate policy was the Rudd Labor government, as the then prime minister identified climate change as 'the great moral challenge of our generation'[36] and followed declaratory statements with concrete action. For example, in 2009, Rudd ratified the Kyoto Protocol (which his conservative predecessor John Howard refused to do) and brought in a number of schemes to reduce Australia's carbon footprint and to encourage the development of renewable energy. An ambitious national renewable energy target was also set for 2020.

Rudd attempted to influence global negotiations, taking an unprecedentedly large delegation to the Copenhagen Climate Summit in 2009, but was thwarted by geoeconomics and national interests, which showed the limits of creative 'middlepowermanship' when framed as a choice between international 'goods' and national interests. The international outcome was a very public defeat that was punctuated by claim and counterclaim by the parties involved, concluding in a memorable undiplomatic critique of China by Rudd.[37] Domestically, the deadlock sounded the death knell for the then government's Carbon Pollution Reduction Scheme (CPRS). This failure was the only time that an Australian government aspired to transformational/progressive leadership in the climate arena.

In 2014, the Tony Abbott Coalition government repealed the previous Labor government's 'carbon tax' and in 2015 reduced the 2020 renewable energy target, but despite the half-hearted approach to climate change, the original target was met regardless of political posturing. According to the International Renewable Energy Agency, Australia led the world in the percentages of renewable electricity production that was brought online in 2019, with more than double its nearest competitor.[38]

State leadership on climate change

The above achievements were based on wind power and a ten-fold increase in solar energy production, including record-breaking levels of rooftop solar. Due to the perceived lack of federal leadership, state governments have driven much of the innovation in responding to climate change while federal governments have watered down international negotiations. All state and territory governments have made their own emissions reductions targets, such as Victoria legislating to meet the Paris Agreement's target of zero emissions by 2050. A positive side effect of this state government-sponsored path to renewables was that by 2020, the cost of producing renewable energy was declining, therefore removing one of the key barriers to the greater uptake of renewables, paving the way for future increases if government programmes were maintained.

While state governments led, there were some grounds for the scepticism of the commitment of successive federal governments to climate change programmes. Some of these schemes were politicized and problematic in various ways. For example, in 2009, the Rudd government's 'pink batts' scheme, so named after the colour of the subsidized ceiling insulation, was introduced, along with initiatives focused on encouraging more efficient energy use such as installing energy-efficient light bulbs. There was debate over the efficacy of these schemes and controversy over the industry that sprung up to implement them. Efforts to generalize solar energy production through rooftop solar subsidies also faced similar debate and were often led through state government intervention. Despite its obvious limitations, this decentralized approach has delivered surprising results, with rooftop solar uptake reaching 20 per cent of households and increasing by 30 per cent in 2020. However, it did mean that there was no overarching federal legislative framework guiding efforts to reduce emissions.

These initiatives led the world and as such, Australia was on a path to exceed its 2030 international commitments, but the opportunity to scale up existing projects has not been embraced in Canberra. The Labor government also implemented a Carbon Pricing Scheme in 2012, but it was incredibly divisive:

dubbed by critics as a 'carbon tax', it was repealed in 2014 after a Coalition government won office, leaving no demand-led carbon abatement programmes in Australia. As such, on the eve of the Glasgow COP in 2021, Australia was the only developed country in the G20 without some sort of carbon pricing scheme.

In practice, this meant that while Australia was involved in the negotiations of international climate agreements such as the Kyoto Protocol, the motivation was to ensure that Australia did not face targets that suffocated growth. Even so, Canberra then did not ratify the Protocol and the government took the implausible stance that it was still meeting the targets even though it did not sign the international agreement. However, the reason it could meet the targets without taking substantive action was that Canberra had negotiated such good terms in the first place. On election, Kevin Rudd quickly signed the Protocol, but at this stage this was more an act of political symbolism achieving an election promise rather than an initiative that would lead to deeper cuts to Australian emissions. This pattern of under-promising and then delivering underwhelming results continues to this day, so that the government can declare that it is meeting its international climate change commitments without constraining the economy. The fact that these commitments reflect the nature of compromise in multilateral negotiations and are not significant enough to halt climate change to 1.5°C highlights how far from a maximalist approach the government has positioned itself. Climate maximalists, such as the head of the International Energy Agency, roundly criticized Australia's position.[39] More importantly for Canberra, the outcome did not significantly impact on Australia's national interests, which are equated with the ongoing economic growth trajectory,[40] largely because the climate change-inducing fossil fuels are exported to other states and form part of their carbon footprint. However, this calculus is changing.

The continuing reliance on fossil fuels for exports and domestic energy

Australia's role in exporting fossil fuels is seen by many maximalists as a disingenuous response to climate change; this argument has had an impact on foreign policy as it has been strongly expressed by PICs. The natural resources such as coal, natural gas and petroleum reflect 8 per cent of Australia's GDP and 70 per cent of exports, but the greenhouse gasses produced by them are accounted for in the recipient state. As such, Australia evades responsibility for the impact on climate change, but there is growing pressure to limit the impact through the closure of mines and through decommissioning coal-fired power plants and halting the creation of new ones. The Australian government has been unwilling to take any of these actions. Despite the impressive uptake of renewable energy in the last five years, coal alone was still responsible for producing 78 per cent of Australia's electricity generation in 2018 but by 2021, 28 per cent of power was produced by renewables.[41]

Table 14.1 highlights the dominance of fossil fuels, especially coal, in Australia's energy production, and the localization of renewables through state-based wind and solar schemes.[42]

TABLE 14.1 *Australian pre-COVID 19 electricity generation, 2018*[43]

Fuel type	GWh	Share (%)
Fossil fuels	**212,066**	**81.1**
Black coal	120,601	46.1
Brown coal	35,962	13.8
Gas	50,245	19.2
Oil	5,259	2.0
Renewables	**49,339**	**18.9**
Hydro	17,452	6.7
Wind	16,266	6.2
Bioenergy	3,539	1.4
Solar PV, small-scale	9,942	3.8
Solar PV, large-scale	2,139	0.8
Total	**261,405**	**100**

While the use of renewables increased, new fossil fuel projects were also approved and the support for the Adani Carmichael coal mine in Queensland in 2019 was a symbolic focus for the frustration in sections of the community. The approval of what was planned to be the largest mine on earth incensed many climate change campaigners in Australia and overseas, but these attitudes did not negatively impact the Coalition government. In fact, support for the mine was credited with influencing the Coalition re-election in the 2019 election. Government support for fossil fuel exploration and production accounted for over A\$29 billion a year in subsidies and tax offsets, representing 2.3 per cent of GDP.[44] This trend showed no sign of changing with projects such as Adani receiving preferential treatment in relation to speedy approvals and development of supporting infrastructure.

The 2019 'Production Gap Report' found that large producers such as Australia will extract 50 per cent more fossil fuels than needed to maintain warming at the Paris Agreement's threshold of 2°C and 120 per cent more than needed to stabilize temperatures at the more ambitious 1.5°C target. Coal is the largest contributor to the gap and Australia is the largest exporter of coal (29 per cent of total exports). Australia is the largest exporter of liquified natural gas and the sixth largest fossil fuel producer. If exported fossil fuels are accounted for, then Australia is amongst the nine states responsible for emitting 66 per cent of emissions.[45] This highlights why Australia's small level of emissions is not as significant as the impact of the use of exported fossil fuels in production elsewhere.

Motivations for change: Elections, public opinion and environmental costs

There has been significant criticism from domestic analysts, activists and media of the government's stance on climate change. It has been a commonly held belief that public opinion influences policy, so it is worth reviewing to what extent public opinion has shaped climate policy. There has been broad awareness amongst the general public and the business community that Australia's efforts to counter climate change were inadequate.[46] These opinions related to both the general approach and very specific reference to international commitments, such as the Kyoto Protocol or Paris Agreement. Notably, youth more strongly supported effective climate change action and their participation in climate strikes from 2019 received strong rebukes from the government.

Numerous polls have been conducted on the issue and the results were remarkably consistent. According to the Australia Institute's 2019 'Climate of the Nation' poll:

- 81 per cent of respondents were concerned that climate change will lead to more droughts and flooding (up from 78 per cent in 2018);
- 78 per cent of respondents thought that climate change would lead to water shortages in cities, up 11 percentage points in two years (67 per cent in 2017);
- 64 per cent of respondents thought Australia should have a net zero emissions target by 2050;
- 62 per cent of respondents supported levying fossil fuel exports to fund local climate change adaptation; and
- 54 per cent of respondents thought that Australia should not wait until other major emitters like the US and China act on climate change.[47]

According to Australia Institute polling in 2021, support for action on climate change has not wavered despite the impact of the COVID-19 pandemic.[48] The ABC's Vote Compass highlights the increasing support for governmental action on climate change over time.[49] However, at the same time there is hesitance over the costs of responding to climate change, and despite the divisive debate around Australia's response to 2030 and 2050 cuts announced at the 2021 COP, most Australians feel that the government is doing enough to counter climate change.[50]

Public opinion was highly educated about climate change and supported action, but the strength of support for taking action without major emitters was weaker, indicating that the government narrative about Australia's small amount of gross emissions and inability to materially impact on the issue may have struck a chord with a large portion of the public.

Despite the pronounced increase in interest in government action on climate change over time, action only eventuated very recently. Segments of the Coalition (especially the National Party) were opposed to taking a maximalist approach to climate change, and at several junctures internal politicking impacted on leadership, including in the case of Prime Minister Turnbull's political demise in 2018. On both sides of politics, climate change policy was implicated in the removal of prime ministers and electoral defeats/victories of the last seven prime ministers from 2010 to 2019.[51] As noted earlier, only in one case, Kevin Rudd in 2009, was the correlation between victory and climate policy a positive one, even though this did not translate into effective federal legislative action or international law.

From the perspective of electoral contest, in 2021 the Labor Opposition Leader Anthony Albanese produced a clear alternative to the government by committing to a 43 per cent cut in emissions by 2030.[52] This would represent a meaningful response to meeting the more ambitious 1.5°C target that was watered down in negotiations. The opposition also explicitly disagreed with the use of contentious 'carry over credits' and has stated that it would not bring back a divisive 'carbon tax'. The opposition painted the government as being influenced by 'climate sceptics' and has taken the moral high ground, but the limits of this position were highlighted in the fallout over criticism of PICs following the 2019 Pacific Islands Forum. When pressed, Penny Wong, the former minister for climate change in the Rudd and Gillard governments, could not deny that Labor would continue Australia's development path based on coal; there would be no federally mandated closure of plants and mines, or limitations on exports. Similarly, Labor's Bob Hawke and Paul Keating did not match their rhetoric with legislative action.[53] The opposition's position shows how divisive climate change policy is in Australia and international observers have lamented the impact of domestic politics in shaping a minimalist approach to climate change in the country.[54]

Polling highlights a key reason why the Morrison government did not compromise and also why the opposition has not been able to gain traction on this issue.[55] Countering climate change is an incredibly divisive issue in Australia, but it is also one that aligns very closely with traditional political allegiances. A very high majority of both Labor and Greens voters support greater action on climate change (96 and 99 per cent respectively) but only a small majority of Coalition voters (59 per cent) share their beliefs. Other issues were likely to be greater priorities for Coalition voters (that is, they did not vote primarily based on climate change policies), so the policies of the major parties were low risk in that they were 'preaching to the converted' in their political bases. This means that governments since at least John Howard's in the 1990s have been able to deflect the need for maximalist action by acknowledging the issue, yet equivocating due to the cost to Australia's national (economic) interests, which strikes a chord across political boundaries.[56]

The politicized nature of climate policy and the lack of meaningful response to it highlights a truism of politics in relation to the limits of Liberal Internationalism and domestic voting patterns: votes are cast primarily on local issues. From the perceptive of foreign policy issues shaping voting patterns, the agenda was crowded and contested, and it is debatable how much foreign policy issues influence voting patterns in the first place.[57] Furthermore, within the domestic policy-making arena, large, well-funded lobby groups and some mainstream media outlets worked together to limit effective climate action.[58] This has occurred in various ways, such as through political donations to both major political parties and the editorial position taken by influential media. The vested interests of fossil fuel industry groups and the unions representing workers in these areas also overlap and they have applied pressure equally to the Coalition and the Labor Party.[59]

Voters were not ignorant of the threat of climate change and aspired to respond in a Liberal Internationalist manner, but often focused on the economic costs of taking a maximalist position, particularly when these costs were personalized at an individual level.[60] They may also focus on more immediate impacts and/or those that fit more localized interests and/or a more traditional military threat spectrum, which aligns with Realism and Strategic Culture.

The failed securitization of climate change in AFP

From the 2000s, there was an attempt to securitize climate change to influence international and national efforts towards a maximalist approach to the issue. Securitization relates to a process whereby efforts were made to bring an issue that has hitherto been treated as peripheral to security concerns of states to become a central priority. Securitization requires advocates to champion the elevation of a particular issue to become a mainstream concern and requires policy-makers (and public opinion) to be convinced of the gravity of the threat. For climate change, advocates were invariably outside of orthodox decision-making channels and were attempting to influence those on the inside (such as politicians) who could affect change. These advocates could be from civil society, intergovernmental organizations or specialist epistemic communities of scientists, and they often worked in coalitions.[61] Most recently, the issue was championed by former senior defence officials, but these voices also failed to appreciably shift government policy.[62]

As part of a process of securitization, any debate over the nature and significance of the threat was treated as part of the problem itself. That is, divisive debates were intimately connected to the scientific realities of climate change. In Australia, this occurred in relation to climate sceptics and advocates alike. Debate often occurred nonetheless because policy-makers and security practitioners were not convinced of the validity of elevating a non-traditional, non-military security challenge, such as climate change, in national security agendas.[63] The defence establishment was focused on orthodox military threats and conceptual confusion occurred when the orthodox (Realist) focus on military security was diluted by climate issues. From the perspective of orthodox threats, climate change had the potential to redirect limited resources to areas defined as peripheral to their narrow military security concerns.[64] Securitization has been attempted and failed to get traction in the climate area in Australia, but had a long history in relation to other global human security concerns such as HIV and AIDS.

Securitization in practice: contrasting the AIDS epidemic of the 1990s, climate change from the 2000s and the COVID-19 pandemic

There are a number of reasons why it was not surprising that the securitization of climate change did not gain traction in Australia. A case study of the way issues have been securitized in the past is instructive for how climate change was treated in Australia. In the early 1990s, academics and development practitioners became increasingly concerned about the spread of the AIDS epidemic and its potential to have strategic impacts. It was argued that the epidemic would have a profound impact on fragile or failed states, especially in Africa, and that this would have global impacts.[65] In a short space of time, the organs of global governance and new purpose-built intergovernmental organizations were predicting a catastrophic future if the epidemic spread unchecked. Preliminary studies based on partial data appeared to back up this catastrophic picture, with the result being that the international community was mobilized, and over the next 30 years billions of dollars in ODA was despatched to counter the HIV and AIDS epidemic. As such, a public health issue was elevated to become a national security issue, not simply where the threat appeared to physically present itself (primarily in Africa), but globally.

Securitization of HIV and AIDS occurred in two parts. The first related to the impact on degrading the efficacy of militaries and the likelihood of increased conflict and war in fragile states. The second part occurred when a local threat was then connected to the national security of great powers due to the increased role of peacekeeping and peace-making operations in Africa.[66] There was also a temporal aspect to this issue: it coincided with the end of the Cold War, where the possibility of reduced international tension was countenanced, as was the likelihood of greater threats from failed and failing states. Thus, a space was created to include non-traditional threats in security planning.

At this time, Australia was involved in peacekeeping operations, but the global impacts of the HIV and AIDS epidemic did not resonate in the Australian security or policy-making communities. The government did provide significant financial support for the global fight against HIV and AIDS through its ODA budget, but the issue had the greatest impact when proximity was connected to threats in relation to impacts in the South Pacific, such as in Papua New Guinea (PNG). Despite some commentary catastrophizing the issue, it was not successfully securitized in Australia and the national interest remained a key driver of health ODA.[67] A major effort was applied to countering the epidemic in PNG, but it was treated as a public health issue and the policy approach taken in Canberra was to increase targeted ODA. As such, HIV and AIDS did not transition to become a national security threat in Australia.

Part of the reason for this was that the impacts of HIV and AIDS were being felt elsewhere, and Australia had great capacity to respond locally to protect Australian citizens. Both of these conditions apply to climate change: the greatest impacts are seen to be occurring elsewhere and Australia's adaptive capacity is viewed as a cost-effective solution. This capacity and reserves of resources was on display in the response to the COVID-19 pandemic, where Australian citizens were prioritized through a radical budgetary support package and a closure of borders that firmly reinforced sovereign rights. This again highlights the dominance of a Realist approach over the broader globalist tendencies in Liberal Internationalism: the human security of Africans or even Papua New Guineans was treated as fundamentally different to threats to Australian citizens.

The limits of Liberal Internationalism with respect to the welfare of others

As the threats posed by climate change were largely perceived in Australia at a global level until the 2020s. This highlights a key attribute of securitization as it argues from the general (global level) to the particular (local impacts). As with HIV and AIDS, the globalization of climate change is a key aspect of the messaging associated with the threat, but it has also prompted quite different responses depending on how global issues are perceived in a particular polity. This conforms with the examples of HIV and AIDS and COVID-19, where a perceived global threat was not effectively localized in Australia and achieved far more attention (and resources) elsewhere. One attempt to localize responses to climate change was the principle of differentiated historical responsibility for causing climate change, leading to diminished responsibility for the need to act now. It was argued that developing states such as China or Brazil, which could be viewed as late industrializers, were not as implicated in the historical production of climate change-inducing gases and therefore had a diminished responsibility for responding to the problem.

This was an important perspective for Australia because it effectively meant that those countries would continue industrializing to 'catch up', while developed states that were early industrializers, such as Australia, would have to curtail their present development path. As noted earlier, this principle was rejected by Canberra on the grounds of its low gross emissions and the inability of Australia to materially impact on climate change when compared to other, larger emitters. Canberra's response to attempts to limit its export-oriented, fossil fuel-driven development path was to negotiate generous targets and then apply 'carry over credits' to institutionalize a minimalist approach that would not meaningfully impact on reducing climate change.

As with HIV and AIDS and COVID-19, Australia's advanced economy and wealth was seen as offering technological fixes to reduce emissions (for example, through 'clean' coal, carbon sequestration in forests or hydrogen). Technological innovation was also viewed as providing the capacity to both mitigate and adapt to climate change. Furthermore, the narrow politicized debate within the Australian policy-making community also limited technological options, such as nuclear power, which is an option to facilitate a shift to a maximalist response, but it requires a major shift in political will. In the meantime, other innovative approaches to reducing emissions have not been taken.[68] As such, climate change continues to be primarily viewed as an environmental issue and has not made the jump to be viewed as a national security issue demanding an emergency response.

This can be contrasted with perceptions of rising Chinese influence in the South Pacific, which has shaped foreign policy responses (see Chapter 6 and 12).

Another similarity between climate change and HIV and AIDS is that the impact in the South Pacific brought Australia's policy into clear relief. Even if national impacts in Australia were downplayed due to technological fixes, the threats to near neighbours had the potential to make the global threat real. This is how the 2016 Defence White Paper and 2017 Foreign Policy White Paper connected climate change to AFP.[69] However, it was done in a cursory manner and the focus was firmly on using non-military instruments, such as ODA, to promote resilience, mitigation and adaptation in the South Pacific. As such, the threat to PICs remained a threat at a distance.

Conclusion

Australia is the world's largest exporter of coal and liquified natural gas, and the sixth largest fossil fuel producer. If exported fossil fuels are accounted for, then Australia is amongst the nine states responsible for emitting 66 per cent of emissions.[70] Despite being implicated in the problem of climate change, successive governments have shown little interest in leading international efforts to create regimes that can meaningfully curb emissions. As such, any claim of exercising creative 'middlepowermanship' or good international citizenship does not have credibility in AFP towards climate change. Even the Albanese government's compromise on climate change can be seen as a minimalist response where Canberra was playing catch up for years of inaction rather than taking the lead. A Liberal Internationalist emphasis on global issues and human security is absent.

A range of factors contribute to the maintenance of a largely Realist foreign policy stance on climate change. International pressure grew over time and had some influence on Albanese's compromise, but ultimately appeals to Liberal Internationalist values were not strong enough to overcome the overwhelming focus on protecting Australian prosperity, and that has not changed. While there is significant domestic awareness and advocacy, this does not necessarily reach into the ballot box, where more parochial economic interests prevail. Furthermore, traction has not been gained in AFP due to the failure to effectively securitize climate change in Australian security and policy-making communities, which would activate the threat-driven emphasis inherent in Australia's Strategic Culture. The missing link in climate policy in Australia is effective leadership and public advocacy that prompts change. Ultimately, a stubborn refusal by voters and politicians alike to compromise national prosperity is a barrier that has not been overcome to date. The emphasis on Realist national interests may be damaging relations with PICs, but Albanese's declaratory shift, ODA and technological fixes remain the prescription despite the negative impact that AFP could have on limiting Chinese influence, further highlighting how entrenched narrow economic national interests are in AFP.

15

Asylum seekers as a threat to Australian sovereignty: Buttressing realism and the intergenerational appeal of strategic culture

Introduction

In the early 2000s, an influx of asylum seekers to Australia became a divisive 'wedge' issue that highlighted the boundary between domestic and foreign policy that characterizes International Relations. The politicization of asylum seekers in elections became a key legacy of John Howard's Coalition government (1996 to 2007) and its ongoing divisiveness also reveals the impact of the ideology of successive Labor and Coalition governments on Australian foreign policy (AFP). As with official development assistance (ODA) and climate change, the public policy towards asylum seekers provides a litmus test of the theoretical perspectives used to explain AFP.

As numbers of arrivals declined in the late 2010s, the policy 'problem' appeared to have been resolved for Australia, in sharp contrast to many other states nearer the sources of upheaval and political oppression, but just how this came about, and whether it is really resolved, is open to debate. With the wind down of 'offshore processing' in 2019, there is the opportunity to reappraise the refugee debate through the lens of the themes that explain AFP. However, any appraisal has to occur against the backdrop of the fact that the underlying policy is being maintained even in the absence of significant numbers of arrivals. The maintenance of offshore processing was costing the equivalent of A\$3.4 million per asylum seeker per annum in 2021, which was deemed politically expedient by Scott Morrison's Coalition government because it allowed the system to be quickly reactivated. Furthermore, the election of Anthony Albanese's Labor government did not lead to a change in policy.

Thematic questions addressed in this chapter include: What does AFP towards asylum seekers tell us about whether Realist national interests and Strategic Culture have trumped Liberal internationalist responsibilities? In the context of intense politicization, how does domestic electoral politics, civil society and public opinion influence foreign policy-making? If Australia cannot be said to be a 'good international citizen', then what is the resulting imact on the achievement of national interests?

Background to Australia's hard-line policy on asylum seekers

In parallel to ODA (discussed in Chapter 13), Australia has supported refugee resettlement since the Second World War when the Liberal Internationalist values in AFP became prominent. This approach aligns with the concept of 'good international citizenship' identified with Labor party ideology.[1] Good international citizenship relates to acting in, and being seen to act in, a manner that meets the expectations of progressive international norms, with respect to issues such as human rights.

The institutional basis for support for refugees was becoming a signatory to various post-war international agreements, the most important of which was the International Refugee Convention (1954). Since then, over 800,000 refugees have been resettled in Australia. The refugee crisis as a result of the Second World War saw millions of people move throughout Europe and Asia and this intersected with Australia's feeling of isolation and vulnerability, which was piqued by the vivid experience of the threat from Japan. For strategic and economic reasons, Canberra wanted to quickly increase Australia's population, but it also maintained a strong sense of cultural superiority and a racist immigration policy, which epitomised the focus on culturally similar 'great and powerful friends' inherent in Strategic Culture.

Strong domestic support for the restrictive 'White Australia Policy' intersected with the need for population growth leading to Labor Immigration Minister Arthur Calwell's call to 'populate or perish'. This policy shift led to the immigration policy being tweaked to encourage more British people to emigrate and also to allow for increased numbers of southern Europeans, from Greece and Italy. It is clear that accepting these immigrants and refugees could be treated as an altruistic Liberal Internationalist act by Canberra while also resolving a significant public policy issue. However, 'populate or perish' was also a direct Realist defence of the national interest, which also coincided with the threat focus from the 'north' that characterizes Australian Strategic Culture. As such, the pluralistic initial response to refugee immigration (reflecting both Liberal Internationalist and Realist/ Strategic Cultural perspectives) aligns with the treatment of ODA detailed in Chapter 13 and climate change in Chapter 14, as does the subsequent toughening of government policy in both areas.

Post-Second World War immigration involved an influx of 'ten pound' poms, so-called because they were given subsidized transport to Australia at a cost of £10 as part of the Assisted Passage Migration Scheme. Versions of this programme, such as 'Bring out a Briton', existed until 1982, highlighting the very strong cultural and racial connection to Britain and the British Empire/Commonwealth.

This connection to the 'mother' country stands in contrast to the alienation from the Indo-Pacific region within which Australia is located.

Versions of the British assisted passage programme were also developed for Greece, Italy and Turkey to meet the demand for labour during the immediate post-war boom and a range of language and other tests were used to shape the complexion of immigrants so that they were as culturally similar as possible, an approach whose lineage remains evident in present immigration and citizenship tests. The perception of strategic need, driven by the vulnerability inherent in Strategic Culture, saw 'whiteness' redefined and eventually led to the dismantling of the White Australia Policy in the 1970s. The White Australia Policy was increasingly seen as conflicting with Liberal Internationalist foreign policy values, but restrictions remained nonetheless.[2] As such, immigration policy highlights the apparent tension in AFP where Liberal Internationalism operated alongside narrower conceptions of the national interest in Realist thought and Strategic Culture.

The first major test of the resolve of the government to control who attempted to immigrate to Australia without applying beforehand was the Vietnamese 'boat people' in the 1970s. The end of the Vietnam War saw thousands of anti-Communist South Vietnamese flee the victorious Communist regime and small numbers of them reached Australia. This posed a problem for Malcolm Fraser's Coalition government as the Vietnamese did not meet Australia's stringent immigration requirements, such as English language proficiency. The issue was complicated by the fact that Australia was implicated in this conflict insofar as successive governments had strongly encouraged US engagement to combat the creeping threat of Communism as part of the 'Domino Theory'. Australian support for the war included 'boots on the ground', with over 50,000 Australian troops serving, of whom 500 were killed. Australian troops were withdrawn in 1972, the war ended in 1975, and its end was the first covered on television, so the Australian public were aware of the nature of the conflict. The first boatload of refugees arrived in Darwin soon after the fall of Saigon in 1976. Over 2,000 South Vietnamese arrived over the next five years.

With the defeat of the South to Communist northern forces, there was little debate over whether these 'boat people' were refugees and in contrast to the 2000s, while they were sometimes termed 'irregular arrivals', they were not effectively securitized as a threat. That said, the attitudes that became policy in the 2000s were nascent in some policy statements from this earlier era, but they did not drive policy. For example, in 1977, Ted Robertson, the Labor senator for the Northern Territory, warned that the government needed to unambiguously 'make it clear . . . that Australia is not going to open the floodgates . . . we will have to find a way of showing our sympathy while stopping the flood of what basically are illegal immigrants'. Federal opposition leader Gough Whitlam followed by describing the Vietnamese as 'queue jumpers' in the 1977 election,[3] which was the first in Australia where refugee policy displayed the potential to become a politically divisive 'wedge' issue.[4] Ultimately, the Vietnamese were not welcomed with open arms, but they were welcomed nonetheless. However, as with earlier immigrants or refugees, the expectation was that they would assimilate to the Australian way of life, which reflected the legacy of the White Australia Policy.

Mandatory detention of asylum seekers was introduced by Prime Minister Paul Keating's Labor government in 1992 in response to an influx of asylum seekers from Southeast Asia, but it was not overly utilized and numbers of asylum seekers remained small. Significantly, it was not politicized, which may be due to the small numbers involved.

The next policy challenge was a spike in arrivals from 1999 to 2001, which prompted the Pacific Solution whereby 'offshore processing' of asylum seekers was introduced. There was a further spike in numbers arriving in Australia in 2011, which led to the reintroduction of mandatory 'offshore processing'. The foreign policy responses to these two more recent spikes in numbers forms the focus of this chapter.

The international context: Refugee flows and Australian foreign policy

Figure 15.1 clearly identifies the present scale of the international public policy challenge, which is a far cry from the 1.5 million refugees that existed in 1951 when the United Nations High Commission for Refugees (UNHCR) was created. Refugee numbers have grown steadily since the Second World War, with an estimated 8.2 million in 1980 versus 89 million forcibly displaced people in 2021.[5] Over a quarter of displaced people, or about 27 million, were refugees, a number which approximates the population of Australia. International flows influence attempts to claim asylum in Australia and present numbers have returned to well below the peak of 60 million in 2014. Figure 15.1 also highlights the relatively small commitment Australia has to refugee resettlement at present. For example, Australia participates in the UN's refugee resettlement programme, but only comparatively small numbers are accepted (approximately 13,500 a year, most of which are offshore applicants). Even at the height of the 2011 peak in attempts to reach Australia that prompted the reintroduction of 'offshore processing' and the tightening of the policy to make it mandatory, Australia only received a very small percentage of applicants to developed states. However, in gross number, Australia remains in the top five recipients of refugees amongst developed countries.

According to the UNHCR, in 2021 most asylum seekers originated from Syria, Venezuela, Afghanistan and South Sudan, and most were resident in neighbouring states such as Turkey, Colombia and Pakistan. Most seek to be resettled in the US, Germany and France. These trends highlight the fact that most vulnerable people live far from Australia and most apply to neighbours, states that are welcoming and where opportunities are perceived to exist. From these perspectives, Australia does not figure in the top 10 potential hosts and none of the top 10 areas that people flee are in the Indo-Pacific region. For example, nearly 90 per cent of Afghan refugees are resettled in neighbouring states, including almost a million

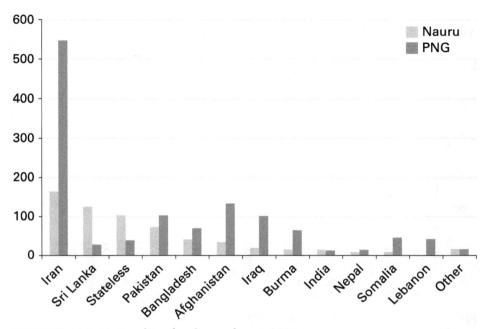

FIGURE 15.1 *Nationality of asylum seekers in 2015.*

in Iran, while Australia hosts 11,900. Australia continues to receive large numbers of asylum claims (39,400 in 2021) but most of these originate from air arrivals not by the more contentious sea route and only 23 per cent of these claims are found to be valid, in contrast to the approximately 80 per cent of applicants whose claims were processed while offshore because they arrived by boat.[6] Australia also has a relatively slow process and a large number of outstanding claims.[7]

The nationality of asylum seekers in Australia is quite different to global trends with a strong focus on Middle Eastern states with large diaspora populations already present in Australia. Figure 15.1 shows their nationality at the height of 'offshore processing' in 2014–15.[8] The large number of stateless people highlights Canberra's concerns about verifying the identity of asylum seekers.

The number of asylum seekers reaching Australia

Since August 2013, when the mandatory 'offshore processing' policy was introduced, over 4,100 people were sent to PNG and Nauru. Most of these, over 3,100, were sent after the policy was tightened so that arrivals by boat would not be resettled in Australia even if they were subsequently determined to be refugees. Offshore processing was wound down in the late 2010s when approximately 500 asylum seekers were housed in 'offshore processing' centres. These numbers are a far cry from the peak number of 2,450 (1,273 in PNG and 1,177 in Nauru) in

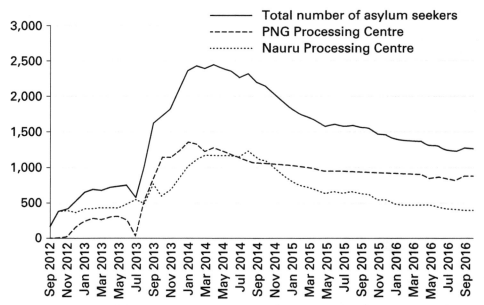

FIGURE 15.2 *'Offshore processing' in PNG and Nauru.* Source: https://www.aph.gov.au/About_Parliament/Parliamentary_Departments/Parliamentary_Library/pubs/rp/rp1617/Quick_Guides/Offshore

2014. Figure 15.2 highlights trends in 'offshore processing', including the notable peak in 2014 that followed the decision by Kevin Rudd's Labor government to transfer all asylum seekers to offshore centres. By 2020, over 200 people remained in the programme, the majority of whom had been determined to be refugees,[9] but did not have the right to resettlement due to prohibitions written into Australian legislation.

More than 4,000 people had been processed by PNG and Nauru and relocated. The majority were moved to Australia for medical treatment, but nearly 1,000 were transferred to the US under the agreement made with Barak Obama's administration (see below), several hundred were deported, whether forcibly or voluntarily with financial support from the Australian government, and 17 died offshore. Of those deported, 33 have been reported to have died.[10] The inhumanity of these statistics were highlighted by critics of the hard-line policy, but the core tenets of the policy were not relaxed.

The international institutional setting

Australia is party to the 1951 Geneva Convention Relating to the Status of Refugees and 1967 Protocol Relating to the Status of Refugees. These agreements define refugee status and protect refugees against refoulement (return to the place they are fleeing). They also prohibit arbitrary detention and punishment for the act of seeking asylum and critics of government policy, such as Amnesty International, have repeatedly focused on these aspects of the Convention and Protocol (e.g. Article 31), and other international agreements such as the International Covenant on Civil and Political Rights.[11] The UNHCR oversees the placement of refugees in 'receiving' states such as Australia, but it is entirely Australia's choice who and how many are offered resettlement in Australia. The UNHCR does not grant refugees the right to resettlement, but rather simply determines refugee status and conditions impacting the status of refugees.

Successive governments have agreed that Australia would fulfil its UNHCR obligations to accept refugees as a 'receiving' state, but would not accept those who arrived on Australian shores without being processed in a second country adjacent to their home country. The term 'queue jumpers' became a derogatory term for those who did not apply to the first state they arrived in after escaping persecution. It was popularized by the Howard Coalition government, but actually coined by the former Labor prime minister Gough Whitlam in the 1970s, highlighting the long history of politicization of the issue in Australia.

The Howard government claimed that asylum seekers were required to have their cases adjudicated in the first state they arrived at having left their home, but this is not a condition within international agreements. The government repeatedly used this claim to counter the moral criticisms of Australian policy, and this became a key aspect of the politicized debate. Other international and domestic criticisms of the Pacific Solution and 'offshore processing' focused on the physical treatment of refugees,[12] such as whether the conditions under which they were transported for processing and boat turnbacks were counter to Australia's obligations under the 1914 International Convention for the Safety of Life at Sea (SOLAS).[13] None of these criticisms influenced successive governments to overturn the policy, which highlights the elevation of sovereignty in the national interest and the domestic drivers of foreign policy.

The practice of offshore processing

The following section looks at the key elements within the approach of successive governments to asylum seekers. Debate over immigration, whether illegal or otherwise, in Australia has become highly politicized and this is reflected in the language used by protagonists, so from the outset it is worth noting where the battle lines were drawn.

The language of division used to frame AFP: 'unauthorized arrivals', asylum seekers, refugees and illegal immigrants

The public policy context was that in the early 2000s, increasing numbers of people were attempting to get to Australia to claim asylum within Australia's legal jurisdiction (rather than in a state adjacent to where they were allegedly persecuted). The fact that many had travelled great distances at such cost led

Prime Minister John Howard's government to query their motives and claim that they were illegal *economic* migrants attempting to subvert Australian immigration processes. The government framed these people as illegal immigrants and 'unauthorized arrivals', and argued that they should have sought a determination on their refugee status in whatever state they fled to first.

The term 'unauthorized arrival' was used by the Howard government to denote those who arrived in Australia without following official immigration processes. In practice, this term sought to dehumanize these people as they were not referred to as *people*. Technically, they could be arrivals by boat or plane, but in practice the focus was always on boat arrivals because their identity could not necessarily be positively identified (in contrast to plane arrivals who had to apply for a visa before arriving and then attempt to change it once on Australian soil). It was reasonable to expect that the act of fleeing a war zone might limit the capacity to provide identity documents, but this was not the primary consideration of the government. As such, the public policy debate over the technicalities of the Liberal Internationalist right to asylum was less a debate than the statement of two diametrically opposed perspectives of the function of foreign policy in achieving Australia's national interests. The positions involved a plaintive appeal by critics of the policy to humanize it by respecting international norms with respect to asylum, especially when women and children were involved. By contrast, support for the hard-line policy by successive governments of both political persuasions involved an archetypal Realist restatement of sovereignty. Support also connected to Australia's Strategic Culture with respect to the threat perceptions generated by culturally dissimilar 'alien' outsiders (whether from Asia or elsewhere).

BOX 15.1: THE POLITICIZATION OF TERMS TO DESCRIBE ASYLUM SEEKERS

- **Unauthorized arrival:** a term coined by the Howard government to distinguish between those who do *not* follow orderly rules for seeking asylum from those who do. A key rule was that an asylum seeker should claim asylum in the first country they transit to rather than transiting to third countries such as Australia. These people were also labelled 'queue jumpers'.
- **Asylum seeker:** a person who wants to have their case for political asylum determined by a responsible body.
- **Refugee:** a person whose case for asylum has been determined by a responsible body to be valid.
- **Illegal immigrant:** a person who does not follow orderly immigration rules and is not determined to have a claim to asylum. These people were often claimed to be economic migrants.

Outside of government statements, the terms 'unauthorized maritime arrival', 'irregular maritime arrival', 'irregular entrant' and 'asylum seeker' were used by opponents of the government's policy to humanize and de-politicize these people. These terms focus on the fact that may have legitimately needed to escape persecution and were attempting to have their refugee status determined so they could gain access to resettlement opportunities. Once a determination was made by relevant authorities (whether the UN or other intergovernmental agencies or domestic authorities), then a person was either classified as a refugee or had their application denied.

According to the Convention and Protocol Relating to the Status of Refugees (Refugee Convention), a refugee is a person who has 'a well-founded fear of being persecuted for reasons of race, religion, nationality, membership of a particular social group or political opinion, is out-side the country of his nationality and is unable or, owing to such fear, is unwilling to avail himself of the protection of that country'.[14] Refugees have the right to claim asylum and to be resettled by agreeable states, but states are not obliged to accept refugees.

Notably for Australia's case, refugees are also protected against refoulement (forcible removal to wherever they were fleeing from). The implication of government policy and much of the divisive commentary in Australia was that many 'unauthorized arrivals' had no basis for claiming refugee status in Australia and as such were not asylum seekers *per se*, but rather immigrants driven by economic means to illegally bypass national immigration processes. Therefore, the government would detain them offshore (outside of Australia's legal jurisdiction) and avoid responsibilities under the Refugee Convention to process and accept those found to have legitimate claims to refugee status. However, this interpretation was criticized in international fora, such as the UN Human Rights Committee, for being very selective and disingenuous in its application.[15] The counter-argument was that their refugee status was unknown until their applications were processed by appropriate authorities and therefore their status as asylum seekers needed to be respected when they arrived on Australian shores.

Key aspects of Canberra's approach to asylum seekers

Australia's approach to asylum seekers was directly connected to the numbers of arrivals as the four major shifts in policy coincided with peaks and troughs in these numbers. The first peak occurred in 2001 and it led to the Pacific Solution. The following trough led to the repeal of the Pacific Solution in 2009, but it was quickly followed by its reintroduction and strengthening through mandatory offshore processing. The subsequent trough saw a decline in the numbers of asylum seekers and refugees housed in the Pacific through medical and other arrangements culminating in the Medivac Bill of 2019, which saw most remaining asylum seekers transferred to Australia for medical treatment or approved for future transfer (see below).

Before detailing the history of Australia's asylum seeker policy, another note on nomenclature is required in relation to the terms used to explain the implementation of government asylum seeker policy.

This chapter focuses on the policy developed by the Howard government and successive governments whereby asylum seekers attempting to transit *by boat* to Australia were transferred to a third country, and the language used to describe this policy is as contested as the policy itself. The Coalition government invented the term 'offshore processing' to describe the mechanism developed to avoid obligations to review applications in Australia, which could entail obligations to accept refugees until they were accepted elsewhere. The places asylum seekers were housed were described as 'regional processing centres' or identified by their location, as in the 'Nauru Regional Processing Centre'. In contrast, domestic critics, including on occasion the Labor Party while in opposition, have described these places as 'detention centres'. Despite criticism whilst in opposition, it was the Rudd Labor government that implemented the policy of 'mandatory detention'.

In practice, *detention* quickly became mandatory offshore *processing* (even though this term was not used) because in 2015 and 2016, the detention centres in PNG and Nauru became 'open' insofar as asylum seekers were not forcibly detained within them and could move around and live in local communities. This was in part due to the fact that they were so geographically isolated that escape was improbable, but also because there was little incentive to escape because asylum seekers needed to wait for their refugee applications to be processed and failed applicants were able to access resources to be voluntarily deported. Despite these differences, the popular description of the process used the stronger term

BOX 15.2: THE LANGUAGE OF DETENTION

- **Offshore processing:** the procedure for determining asylum claims that did not involve claimants having their cases adjudicated in Australia, but rather transited them to third countries. This approach also did not grant successful refugees the right to resettlement in Australia.
- **Mandatory detention:** the firm approach whereby all asylum seekers (termed 'unauthorized arrivals' by the Howard government) were mandatorily detained while their status was determined. For many this became indefinite detention because even if they were found to be refugees, they were not granted the right to be resettled in Australia.
- **Regional proceeding centres and detention centres:** the terms used respectively by successive governments and critics to describe the places where asylum seekers were detained offshore.
- **The Pacific Solution:** the umbrella term used to describe the policy whereby asylum seekers intercepted outside of Australia's migration zone were transited and housed in processing centres in the Pacific. These were located on PNG's Manus Island and on Nauru. As such, these Pacific islands provided Canberra the foreign policy solution to their deeply politicized asylum seeker public policy problem.

'detention centres'. The difference in language highlights both the politicization of asylum seekers in Australia and also the impact of domestic politics on foreign policy. Australia's Strategic Cultural fear of 'alien' outsiders can be seen insofar as the Howard government elevated the national interest in choosing who came to Australia and alluded to the threat of opening the 'flood gates', which could lead to potential terrorist threats from 'unauthorized arrivals'.

The Pacific Solution: the temporary emergency response that securitized asylum seekers

The so-called Pacific Solution was a response to an increase in asylum seekers attempting to land on Australian territory to have their refugee status applications assessed. The Howard government negotiated two offshore arrangements with neighbouring states as part of the Pacific Solution in 2001. One involved developing a centre on Manus Island in PNG and the other a centre in Nauru. Both were negotiated quickly to provide the government with a powerful credible deterrent to people smugglers in order to 'stop the boats'. However, both involved significant negotiation, legislation and regulation (in both Australia and the host nations) and significant long-term budgetary support from Australia. For example, Nauru received tens of millions of dollars of additional ODA. Both centres were initially very basic, involving military-style tents and cots, but conditions improved gradually as infrastructure was built.

The government sought to reduce the incentives to both those attempting to arrive in Australia and the people smugglers who transited them. This was achieved by stopping them from being eligible to make a claim for resettlement in Australia even if they were determined to be legitimate refugees. This involved changes to the Migration Act in 2001 that excised territory (Christmas Island, Ashmore Reef and Cocus [Keeling] Islands) from Australia's migration zone for the purposes of denying asylum seekers access to the courts. In practical terms, this meant that if an asylum seeker arrived in one of these places, they would not be treated as arriving in Australia and therefore would not trigger a process whereby they could be resettled in Australia if found to have a case for refugee status. This approach to modifying the migration zone was deemed a success and was expanded when a suspected illegal entry vehicle (SIEV) arrived on Melville Island off Darwin in 2014. The SIEV was towed away under the turnback policy (whereby boats were physically turned back from entering Australian waters or landing on Australian territory), and Melville Island was quickly excised from the Australian migration zone.

The Pacific Solution was a challenging public policy response for a number of reasons, not least due to the diplomacy needed to negotiate with two regional states. However, the operational requirement for the Australian Defence Force (ADF) to intercept small boats along Australia's long northern coastline (especially facing Indonesia and Sri Lanka) and transfer them to the Pacific was also a significant undertaking. The Pacific Solution was also costly in human and budgetary terms as well as reputationally. The human cost of offshore processing is inestimable but domestic critics pointed out that the loss of liberty, insecurity, delays, despair, dislocation and forced relocation led to increased self-harm, suicide, family breakdown and other humanitarian impacts that questioned Australia's respect for international norms.[16] Canberra's approach was routinely criticized in international fora and its reputation for supporting Liberal Internationalist foreign policy values was challenged by the treatment of asylum seekers and the states that hosted the Pacific Solution.[17]

Boat turnbacks, temporary protection visas, deportations and third-country resettlement

Successive governments employed other deterrent measures in addition to offshore processing that further highlight the priority afforded to 'stopping the boats' that is best explained through the lenses of Realism and Strategic Culture.

Boat turnbacks

In October 2001, in the face of increasing numbers of SIEVs, the government announced that vessels that arrived in Australian waters would be turned back to wherever they came from. This was a message to people smugglers and to Indonesia, which was generally either the last port of call for these boats or where they originated. In practice, the new policy meant that SIEVs would be towed back towards Indonesian territorial waters (12 nautical miles from shore) and set adrift. Turnbacks were often greeted with violence by asylum seekers, many of whom may already have been transferred to Australian naval vessels. While desperation was understandable, this violence did nothing to support the asylum seekers' case in the eyes of Australian public opinion and further politicized the already charged issue.

The first turnback was SIEV 5 on 19 October 2001, the same day that SIEV X sank with the loss of 353 lives (more of this later). Several other vessels were turned back in 2001 and 2003 and then the policy was used sporadically from 2013 to 2018. In total, six SIEVs were turned back in 2001–3 and 33 in 2013–18, with a total of 1,420 people on board. Interestingly, the average size of the numbers smuggled dropped considerably over this period from 123 to 25, which reflected some success. The turnback policy was unpopular domestically, led to murmurs of dissent from within the Royal Australian Navy (RAN), which was responsible for actually turning back the boats, and attracted international criticism.[18] However, despite these Liberal Internationalist criticisms, the policy was steadfastly maintained. In fact, one of the first foreign policy acts of the incoming Albanese government in May 2022 was to authorize the turnback of a boat from Sri Lanka.

Temporary protection visas

For those asylum seekers who arrived by boat and were then found to be refugees, the government brought in a category of 'bridging' visa that was also designed to act as a disincentive. The Howard government inaugurated temporary protection visas (TPVs) in 1999, which were revoked by the Rudd government in 2008 and reinstituted by the Abbott government in 2013. Temporary protection visas allowed 'unauthorized arrivals' who were found to be refugees to be settled in Australia but only afforded them limited rights. These visas were reviewed every three years so that refugees could be returned home if conditions in their state of origin improved for them.

TPV holders could access limited government benefits and had the right to work, but did not have the right to family reunion or travel outside of Australia, the first of which was a key aim for many asylum seekers. As such, TPVs were a disincentive to many asylum seekers who were processed offshore. They were also implicated in risky journeys by unaccompanied women and children who did not have the capacity to reunite with their family members in Australia through family reunion visas because their husbands were in offshore detention or did not have the right to reunion.[19] During the first stage of their operation, over 11,000 refugees were placed on TPVs, 95 per cent of whom eventually received permanent protection. However, two decades after the influx of asylum seekers that prompted these changes, over 30,000 people were still living in the community on TPVs or are otherwise awaiting determination of asylum claims. In November 2022, the right of people on TPVs to travel outside Australia was granted, which provided the opportunity for those isolated from their families to reunite, but otherwise the conditions did not change.

Deportations

Forcibly returning asylum seekers who had been sent for offshore processing was another element of Canberra's approach designed to create a credible disincentive to people smugglers and asylum seekers. Some asylum seekers that the government deemed did not meet their protection requirements were forcibly returned to their countries of origin, such as the case of Tamils and Sinhalese who arrived by boat after the Easter 2019 terrorist attacks in Sri Lanka. Others were deported to a third state.

The government argued that these people did not meet Australia's non-refoulement obligations under the Refugee Convention, presumably because they were determined to be economically motivated or had arrived in territory excised from Australia's migration zone. However, their deportation was shrouded in secrecy and, as they were routinely arrested on their return, UN and human rights NGOs expressed concern for their welfare.[20] Despite these concerns, the numbers of forcibly deported failed asylum seekers more than doubled from 2010 to over 1,700 in 2016 while their percentage of total applications also increased from 30 to 35 per cent.[21] Some asylum seekers chose to return to their states of origin, highlighting their frustration and acceptance of the challenges of ever being resettled in Australia or elsewhere. For example, 303 returned in 2014 and 63 in 2015, the majority of whom were from Iran and Iraq.[22] The government provided inducements to encourage this 'choice'.

Third-country resettlement

One problematic aspect of offshore processing and the prohibition on entry to Australia was that this removed options for resettlement for those subsequently found to be refugees. Most asylum seekers granted refugee status in PNG or

Nauru had no option for resettlement, which critics argued exacerbated into medical problems (especially mental health issues) which led to the Medivac Bill against the wishes of the government in 2019 (see below).

Successive governments used diplomacy to search for resettlement options. Several Pacific islands were already housing asylum seekers during processing but these were developing states, so they were not good options for resettlement. Attempts to broker arrangements to resettle refugees with Asian states failed. In 2011, an attempt was made to negotiate an arrangement with Malaysia to take 800 'irregular boat arrivals' in return for taking 4,000 refugees from Malaysia, but this was stymied by the Australian High Court. A 2014 agreement with Cambodia was short-lived. This highlighted the government's lack of leverage with Asian states, many of whom had their own refugee or internally displaced persons challenges and also were not inclined to provide Canberra with a face-saving option due to criticism of Australia's hard-line approach to asylum seekers.

In 2013, New Zealand offered to take some refugees from offshore detention, but this was not accepted until 2022. Presumably, Canberra was concerned that refugees would be able to gain access to Australia in the future through the visa free travel arrangements that exist between Australia and New Zealand. A few refugees were privately sponsored by Canadians, and the government was inclined to support this avenue, but the numbers involved were small.

Interestingly, the only palatable offer that Canberra took up was from Australia's 'great and powerful friend'. In 2016, Prime Minister Malcolm Turnbull found US President Barack Obama receptive to Australia's foreign policy predicament and willing to provide support. The arrangement was for a certain number of 'unauthorized arrivals' who were subsequently found to be refugees and housed in offshore processing centres on Manus Island in PNG and Nauru to be resettled in the US. By 2021, a total of 980 refugees had been resettled in the US and 21 approved for resettlement had been transferred to Australia under the Medivac Bill. This willingness to cooperate on security issues of concern to each party highlights the closeness of the relationship with the US and provides a clear example of leveraging good relations with Washington to achieve Australia's national interests.

Three reasons for the politicization of asylum seekers

Many areas within AFP have bipartisan support, but the situation with asylum seekers is problematic. While the policy remained remarkably constant despite changes in government, there was the potential for division. More Labor voters were likely to support Liberal Internationalist foreign policy values such as human rights in foreign policy (and ODA) and to advocated for a relaxation of the hard-line policy. However, the policy had broad general support across the electorate. This created electoral 'wedging' opportunities for the Coalition. As such, unlike other areas of the foreign policy portfolio, AFP towards asylum seekers became highly politicized.

The politicization of offshore processing was threefold.

Offshore processing as an effective foreign policy response to increasing numbers of asylum seekers?

First, successive governments wanted to provide a credible disincentive to people smugglers who were active in profiting from the wish of asylum seekers to settle in Australia. The distances involved in reaching transit points to Australia in Indonesia and the complexity of transiting across open ocean to Australia necessitated organization, infrastructure and knowledge that individual asylum seekers could not hope to possess, so a veritable industry grew up around transiting them from political hotspots far afield to Australia. The government's language focused on breaking the people smugglers' 'business model', which made it seem like transnational criminals were profiting from Australia's generosity, but this language like much in this area obscured the complexity.[23] Offshore processing was the initial disincentive, but from July 2013 the government strengthened the policy through TPVs, etc. so that no one arriving by boat would be resettled in Australia even if their application for refugee status processed offshore was successful. This approach targeted both supply and demand factors in the 'business model' and was accompanied by a strident advertising.

The policy had some impact because the numbers of asylum seekers quickly declined dramatically. However, some caution is warranted in this conclusion as the policy shift also coincided with changes in the conditions that provoked displacement. That is, the intensity of conflict in Iraq and Afghanistan declined and the civil war in Sri Lanka ended. So, it may have been that the 'push' factors felt by potential asylum seekers reduced their inclination to travel to attempt to gain asylum in Australia.

Border protection and sovereignty

The second reason for instituting offshore processing was that border protection issues had risen in prominence among the electorate due to the perception that Australia was being 'flooded' by asylum seekers. The clear implication from government policy initiatives was that Australia's sovereignty was being undermined. Probably the clearest statement of this position occurred in the election campaign of 2001 when Prime Minister Howard's speeches focused on the defence of Australian sovereignty and were clear statements of Realism that also reflected Australia's unique Strategic Culture in relation to 'alien' threats and indefensibility. Howard noted that national security 'is also about having an uncompromising view about the fundamental right of this country to protect its borders ... we will decide who comes to this country and the circumstances in which they come'.[24]

Successive governments securitized asylum seekers as a threat to Australia and this was reinforced by the militarized response to *MV Tampa* in 2001, where the elite Special Air Service (SAS) were used to divert the ship away from Australian ports. The asylum seekers aboard the *Tampa* were moved to an Australian navy vessel and this incident prompted the government to announce that a refugee processing centre would be built on Christmas Island foreshadowing the Pacific

Solution. In public opinion, this strong restatement of the primacy of Australian sovereignty and an enhanced emphasis on border protection was reinforced by the 9/11 terrorist attacks on the US. Howard's narrative of choosing who could come to Australia included explicit and implicit references to the threat of terrorists and criminals using people smuggling networks to arrive in Australia. Due to their participation in the civil war in Sri Lanka, Tamil asylum seekers could be defined in this way, which reinforced the government's claims, even if these asylum seekers had only used these tactics against their government in the context of an asymmetrical civil war.

Public opinion and foreign policy

The third reason for supporting offshore processing was electoral insofar as it aligned with the attitudes of a large segment of the general public. Attitudes did soften over time as the volume of asylum seekers declined, and there was always greater division over the treatment of children, especially their detention. However, the Howard government was on firm ground electorally when it stopped the *MV Tampa* from delivering 440 asylum seekers that it had picked up in international waters when their boat sank between Indonesia and Australia in August 2001 and attempted to divert them away from Australian territory. Known as the Tampa Affair, this incident provoked strong condemnation amongst sections of the population and internationally, but is also credited with swinging and firming some voters to the incumbent government because beforehand Labor had a commanding lead in the polls. Government approval peaked with 77 per cent of Australians supporting the handling of the Tampa Affair and 71 per cent supporting mandatory detention.[25]

It is difficult to precisely disaggregate the influence of the Tampa Affair on the 2001 election because it occurred the month before the 9/11 terrorist attacks on the US, and therefore the impact of the two events is intertwined. However, it is clear that it had an independent impact and when intertwined with the rise of international Islamic fundamentalist terrorism,[26] both issues reinforced the government's strong stance. The 'War on Terror' led to a significant restatement of sovereignty and like many states, Canberra connected the control of who could reside in the state with these broader international trends. The fact that asylum seekers were effectively dehumanized explains how successive tragedies such as SIEV X or SIEV 223 in 2010, which involved the deaths of hundreds of 'non-Australians', did not lead to a dramatic shift in foreign policy.

CASE STUDY 15.1: AUSTRALIA'S SEE-SAWING FOREIGN POLICY ON ASYLUM

The use of AFP to manage Canberra's asylum problem, such as the Pacific Solution and TPVs, was connected not only to the numbers of asylum seekers arriving in Australia, but also to wedge politics and electioneering.

Rudd's repeal and Gillard's reinstatement and escalation of the Pacific Solution

By the time the Howard government lost the election in 2006, the 'flood' of asylum seekers had turned to a trickle, with only 25 arrivals in 2007–8. The offshore processing centres were closed by Prime Minister Kevin Rudd's government in 2008 as part of an election commitment which could be said to reflect Liberal Internationalist foreign policy values in domestic politics and AFP. This decision had great symbolism and was met with strong approval by the segment in the population who had been strongly against the Pacific Solution, which they viewed as an abrogation of Australia's responsibilities under the Refugee Convention. However, coincidentally by 2008 the numbers of asylum seekers had also declined and the Pacific Solution was seen to have achieved its aims, so there was little policy cost to closing the processing centres unless this prompted another surge in asylum seekers.

By the mid-2000s, all of the initial asylum seekers from the *MV Tampa* had been relocated from Nauru (to Australia and elsewhere) and the centre was only used to house a few Rohingya and approximately 80 Tamils from the Christmas Island Regional Processing Centre. Therefore, when the arrangement with Nauru was ended by Rudd, this was seen as much as an ideological decision by the incoming Labor government to end the Pacific Solution as a prudent response to changed conditions. Therefore, this shift was pragmatic but nonetheless is an example of the Liberal Internationalist foreign policy values that are more likely to be expressed in a Labor government's foreign policy.

A few years later in 2011, the Labor leadership and prime ministership had transferred to Julia Gillard and the numbers of 'irregular entrants' had increased dramatically from 25 in 2008–9 to in excess of 5,000 in 2009–10. The Coalition opposition blamed this rapid increase on Labor's softening of border protection arrangements, but it also coincided with international conditions that led to an increase in numbers to the highest levels for a decade.[27] As shadow minister for population and immigration when in opposition, Gillard had opposed the Pacific Solution, but once in government she quickly moved to limit the impact of 'wedge' politics by taking a hard-line approach that mirrored the Coalition opposition.

The Gillard government then sought to renew the Pacific Solution by another name and 'regional processing' resumed in Nauru in September 2012 and in PNG in November 2012. Rudd resumed the Labor leadership and prime ministership in 2013 and quickly negotiated a Regional Resettlement Arrangement with PNG and Nauru involving mandatory detention as a further disincentive. Again Australia's Pacific friends came to the rescue by providing a solution for the Rudd government's domestic political problem.

The politicized nature of foreign policy towards asylum seekers was on display as this decision occurred two months before an Australian federal election and was seen as a direct response to the Coalition opposition's announcement of a stronger approach. However, it was significant that the Gillard government's declaratory policy introduced a humanitarian rationale in relation to drownings during the dangerous journey and the safety of children and downplayed the Coalition government's focus on sovereignty. This highlighted the Labor government's sensitivity to Liberal Internationalist values, at least in public diplomacy.

Accurate figures are hard to verify, but it may be that over 1,500 asylum seekers drowned on route to Australia[28] and the SIEV X drowning of hundreds of children and women struck a chord with the Australian population, sufficient to allow a softening in rhetoric, but not enough to prompt the government to end the tough policy. There were some concessions though, for example, initially female asylum seekers were housed in both centres, but after July 2013 females and children were all processed and housed on Nauru.

The Abbott government's re-introduction of TPVs

The election victory by Tony Abbott's Coalition in September 2013 signalled a return to an uncompromising approach to border protection to involve a refusal to consider resettlement. In practice, this meant that asylum seekers attempting to reach Australia by boat would be processed offshore and if their claims to refugee status were approved, they would be eligible to resettlement through the UNHCR, but not to Australia. Border protection involving mandatory detention and a 'zero tolerance' approach was exemplified by Operation Sovereign Borders (2013), which advised that it 'is a military-led border security operation ... committed to protecting Australia's borders, combating people smuggling in our region, and preventing people from risking their lives at sea'.[29] The militarization of the policy continues and this highlights the connection to the threat perceptions that characterize Strategic Culture.

Business as usual under the Albanese government

The election of the Albanese government in May 2022 had the potential to see a wholesale shift in Canberra's approach to asylum seekers, but history was working against any great shift. Like the Rudd government in the 2010s, the Albanese government did make some key changes that signalled a more humane approach. However, like the Rudd government these changes were made in the context of very few new arrivals and a shift in public policy focus to issues such as the potential for conflict with China, the war in the Ukraine and climate change.

Soon after the election, the policy on refugees travelling overseas was relaxed, which provided hope to many refugees who had been trapped on TPVs in Australia. However, the architecture of offshore processing remained. For example, one of the first foreign policy acts of the incoming government was to turn back a SIEV and the navy issued a strong warning to potential asylum seekers and people smugglers:

> My message to people smugglers attempting illegal maritime ventures to Australia is clear, don't risk your life on a dangerous journey, Australia's policies have not changed, a legal and safe pathway is the only way to a life in Australia (Rear Admiral Justin Jones, Commander of Operation Sovereign Borders).[30]

CASE STUDY 15.2: CHILDREN AS PAWNS IN POLICY

The safety of children was a persistent theme in the narrative of asylum since 2001. Both supporters of the hard-line response and their critics highlighted the plight of children. Two key events firmed attitudes and highlighted division over the value placed on sovereignty and protecting borders (connected more closely with Realism and Strategic Culture) and human rights (linked more to Liberal Internationalist foreign policy values).

'Children Overboard'

The first event was the so-called 'Children Overboard' affair of 7 October 2001. At the height of the influx of SIEVs, the minister for defence, Peter Reith, released photos that purportedly showed asylum seekers on SIEV 4 throwing their children overboard when confronted by the Royal Australian Navy. The alleged actions of the people on SIEV 4 shocked the public and were used by the government to firm support for the tough stance on 'unauthorized arrivals' in the lead up to the 2001 election. Public opinion was shocked by the imagery, which supported the Howard government's hard line. The Australian public was left to wonder what sort of person would throw their children overboard on the high seas?

Investigative journalism and a subsequent Senate Select Committee report revealed that the event had not taken place as asserted by the government. In fact, the photographs were of a different incident (where the vessel was in fact sinking). The government discovered the error, largely due to internal reporting

---

BOX 15.3: KEY EVENTS IN THE 'CHILDREN OVERBOARD' AFFAIR

- SIEV 4 entered Australian waters from Indonesia.
- Australian Navy attempted (but failed) to persuade SIEV 4 to leave.
- Australian Navy boarded and turned back the vessel.
- Fourteen asylum seekers jumped into the water to attempt to force rescue and detention in Australia.
- Order was restored and SIEV 4 sent on its way.
- In deteriorating weather, and after being sabotaged, SIEV 4 could not be repaired by the Australian Navy and sank.
- All 253 asylum seekers were rescued from the water by the Australian Navy and transited to Christmas Island.
- Photos purportedly showing asylum seekers throwing children overboard were released, influencing public opinion.

by the navy,[31] but Canberra did not correct the record. The Senate Committee review of events was 'struck by the minister's keenness to persist with the original story in the face of repeated advice that there was no evidence available to corroborate it'.[32] The politicization of asylum seekers in the context of an election campaign saw the government perpetuate falsehoods that depersonalized them for electoral gain.

SIEV X

The second event that framed attitudes towards children asylum seekers was the sinking of SIEV X. This tragic and contentious event was known as 'A certain maritime incident' from the title of the Senate Committee's report. The committee examined the sinking in the context of very close cooperation between the ADF and Australian intelligence agencies and Indonesian authorities to mount disruption activities within Indonesia itself and to run extensive aerial patrol missions in Indonesia's exclusive economic zone (EEZ), but not its territorial waters. At the time, several vessels, including SIEV 6 and 7, were interdicted by the navy, but not SIEV X despite credible intelligence that a vessel had set sail and foundered.[33]

Since the introduction of the hard-line policy in 2001, the place of children in detention – whether offshore or in Australia – was always contested and less defensible than the treatment of adults. The high proportion of children and women who died was a consequence of the government policy limiting the family reunion of asylum seekers living in Australia on TPVs.[34] Those asylum seekers and refugees already in Australia were separated from their families, who often remained in refugee camps overseas and made the perilous journey to reunite with them.

BOX 15.4: KEY EVENTS IN THE SIEV X TRAGEDY

- People smugglers used an unseaworthy and overloaded vessel to transport asylum seekers from Indonesia to Christmas Island (Australia).
- On 2 October 2001, SIEV X foundered in a storm and 46 survivors were rescued but 353 people died, including 146 children and 142 women.
- Led to questions about Australian collaboration with Indonesian authorities in deterring people smugglers.
- Highlighted the perilous journeys that asylum seekers were willing to take despite Canberra's tough approach to border protection.
- Reinforced politicization of asylum seeker policy during an election campaign.

The SIEV X tragedy eventually led the government to compromise its hard-line mandatory approach, but only in relation to children. Nonetheless, small numbers of children were detained and processed in the centres under the post-2012 mandatory detention regime. The numbers of children in the detention system fluctuated significantly with 100–200 detained at any given time between October 2012 and March 2015. At other times, smaller numbers of children were kept in detention. A similar trend is evident in relation to female detention with between 200 and 300 detained during this period, reflecting family units with multiple male and female children.[35] A concerted campaign by the Refugee Council of Australia amongst others was launched in 2018 and the government relented with the last child leaving Nauru in February 2019. The compromises in managing the children of asylum seekers represented an isolated example of Liberal Internationalist foreign policy values in relation to children's rights directly shaping policy, albeit at a time when the refugee crisis had diminished and the policy was seen to have succeeded in 'stopping the boats'.

CASE STUDY 15.3: SOVEREIGNTY, THREAT PERCEPTIONS AND UNAUTHORIZED AIR ARRIVALS IN A 'WAR ON TERROR'

While the focus of debate on 'unauthorized arrivals' was on arrivals by sea, there has been a parallel trend in air arrivals that provides a useful test of several aspects of government policy. In 2020, it was revealed that over 50,000 asylum seekers who had arrived by plane had failed to receive temporary protection visas and were awaiting deportation. Most of those deported were voluntary deportations reflecting an acceptance of the outcome of failed asylum claims. These asylum seeker arrivals can be distinguished from the boat arrivals as they had valid identification and most had valid visas (unless they were from countries with a visa waiver) when they arrived. These visa overstayers arrived ostensibly to holiday, study or visit relatives, but once onshore they then claimed asylum. In January 2020 alone, over 1,900 air arrivals claimed asylum. Most (546) were from Malaysia, followed by China (309) and India (255).

Onshore applicants have their applications processed differently to boat arrivals to excised territories and have access to an appeals process, which can extend the time that they are in Australia before being deported. In contrast to arrivals by boat, more than 90 per cent of these claims are found to have no basis. There are major criticisms of the process because applicants can work in Australia until their claims and appeals are heard, in contrast to those who attempt to arrive by sea. The government has been criticized for the apparent double standard in relation to the treatment of air and boat arrivals, and has defended the integrity of the visa system as less than one per cent of travellers to Australia each year claim asylum.[36] Furthermore, air arrivals didn't form part of the government's aim of breaking the people smugglers' 'business model'.[37]

Plane arrivals have always been an issue, but they have been more consistent over time and this lack of fluctuation and the fact that they arrive with valid identification papers has not triggered the same threat response as boat arrivals. The 'War on Terror' involved a strong practical restatement of sovereignty, including much stronger vetting of plane passengers. In practical terms, this meant that not only did they have valid identification documents but also a convincing rationale for travel. According to the logic of border protection, this dramatically reduced the risk of a threat developing to Australia and also reduced the percentage of asylum seeker applicants to less than 1 per cent.

Air arrivals were treated as a different class by the government, and it appears that this aligned with public opinion because the conditions of air arrivals never became a significant public policy issue. Here was no double standard as such in relation to the treatment of air versus boat arrivals, but rather the tough treatment of boat arrivals highlights the centrality of sovereignty and security in government thinking, which aligns with both Realism and Strategic Culture.

Public/international opinion and a lack of political incentives to compromise

The offshore processing/detention policy met with domestic and international criticism from UN agencies and human rights organizations. For example, an Amnesty International report 'found a toxic mix of uncertainty, unlawful detention and inhumane conditions creating an increasingly volatile situation on Nauru, with the Australian Government spectacularly failing in its duty of care to asylum seekers'.[38] The riot at the Manus Island Regional Processing Centre in 2014 which led to the death of one detainee, injuries to 60 others and millions of dollars in damage, highlights the frustration experienced by asylum seekers and the punitive response to it by the government reinforced the unwillingness to compromise border protection as a key plank of sovereignty. Criticism was especially vocal when the Labor government reinstated the policy in 2013, which seemed more at odds with the party's Liberal Internationalist foreign policy values than the hard-line approach taken by Coalition governments. This highlights the brutal realities of foreign policy-making on divisive issues that have electoral implications. The narrative of being tough on unauthorized arrivals (and terrorism) became part of electoral contests,[39] and the high cost of doing so, at roughly A\$1.1. billion in 2016–17 for example, was not electorally divisive. Similarly, revelations in 2021 that the maintenance of offshore processing was costing the equivalent of A\$3.4 million per asylum seeker did not cause political problems for the government.

Domestic sensitivities also provoked changes to the policy itself in relation to the detention of children, and whether asylum seekers were actually physically detained, with Nauru becoming an open centre in October 2015 and Manus

Island following suit in May 2016. This meant that asylum seekers could move freely around the area where the processing centre was established but were not free to leave the state. In practice, this meant that there was a rapid decline in numbers living within the centres with only a handful present in Manus from 2017 and Nauru from 2018. In addition, for various reasons, approximately 50 asylum seekers who had not been awarded refugee status were moved by PNG authorities from Manus to a separate detention centre in Port Moresby. However, as they were taken into PNG custody, their welfare was no longer treated as an issue by Australian government officials.

As with ODA, immigration has never been a top priority for voters, but this does not mean that it has not been open to foreign policy politicization. Other than the Tampa Affair/2001 election, immigration has not appeared in the top 10 priorities for voters with core domestic issues such as education and taxes dominating. There is general support for humanitarian resettlement, but this occurs within the context of stronger support for border protection and control over how many, who and when refugees arrive in Australia. While the general public does not focus on sovereignty as a prime national interest, and is not aware of particular International Relations theories, it is abundantly clear that the response to the public policy challenge is more akin to the government's focus on treating boat arrivals as a form of illegal immigration. It is acknowledged that these people may be asylum seekers, but while many acknowledge that they should be treated more generously, there is no evidence that a government would be electorally punished for not doing so. A proportion of the population believe that they should be treated more humanely and most of these would be Labor or Greens voters, which partially explains the softer rhetoric and humane themes introduced by Labor politicians, even when the substance of their policy stances differed little from the Coalition.

CASE STUDY 15.4: HUMANIZING ASYLUM SEEKERS THROUGH THE RISE AND FALL OF THE MEDIVAC BILL 2019?

The Medivac Bill was passed in February 2019 amidst acrimonious parliamentary and public debate. The Bill operated for nine months of 2019 while the Morrison government did not have a majority in Parliament. Medivac sought to depoliticize medical transfers of asylum seekers from offshore detention to Australia by placing the emphasis for initial review and appeals on medical practitioners. The minister for home affairs still had the right to refuse the transfer on security grounds, but this had to be established in the face of a compelling medical case supported by two doctors and reviewed by a medical board.

The Morrison government strongly argued that the Bill undermined Australia's border security. This was because it removed the minister of home affairs' discretion in approving medical transfers and did not have clear provisions for returning transferees who recovered in Australia. The opposition noted that since 2015 to 2018, the pace of medical transfers had slowed while medical need had increased (Figure 15.3). As such, they were criticizing the slowness of determinations of refugee status by the PNG and Nauruan governments.

Before the Medivac Bill was passed, 12 people had died while awaiting approval to travel to Australia for medical care. During the short life of the Medivac provisions, 418 applications were approved and 192 asylum seekers were actually transferred to Australia for treatment. The approved applications represented two-thirds of the asylum seekers being held offshore. By the end of 2019, none of those relocated to Australia remained in hospital, but rather than being returned to offshore processing centres, most were living in community detention in Australia. A small number were being detained in local facilities for security reasons. As noted earlier, 21 of the refugees approved for transfer to the US under the Obama deal actually transferred to Australia under Medivac. Notably, 57 asylum seekers who were not approved for transfer to the US were also transferred to Australia under Medivac.[41]

Medivac was a clear reflection on human rights that reflects Liberal Internationalist foreign policy values. In the seven years prior to the Medivac Bill, over 1,300 asylum seekers and their families had been transferred to Australia under the previous system involving ministerial approval. No evidence of them having a negative impact on Australia's community was provided by the government during debate over the Bill. Furthermore, only a few were returned offshore once their treatment was completed and there were no returns after April 2018. In addition, in contrast to the previous Labor government's relaxation of offshore processing, which appears to have emboldened human traffickers leading to an increase in arrivals, the Medivac Bill was not followed by an increase in new arrivals. Rather, it appears that sovereignty concerns were the main reason for resistance, which continues the Howard government's refrain that 'we shall decide who comes'.

Critics note that Medivac was a response to conditions created by Canberra's tough stance on asylum seekers. It would not be needed if not for the inability to find resettlement options for asylum seekers detained offshore and then granted refugee status, but who were denied access to Australia under the 2012

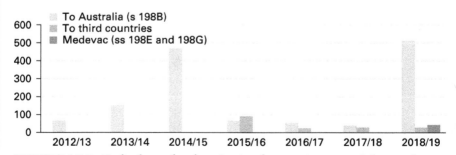

FIGURE 15.3 *Medical transfers from 'regional processing centres'. Source: Senate, Migration Amendment (Repairing Medical Transfers) Bill 2019 [Provisions]*[40]

policy. Clearly, refugee resettlement or the welfare of asylum seekers were not key considerations driving AFP. The humanitarian question posed by the ill-health of refugees in mandatory detention did not sway successive governments in their steadfast support for defending its vision in the national interest, in this case protecting the welfare of Australian citizens.

In December 2019, the Morrison government reached a deal with cross-bench senators to repeal the Medivac Bill and also to allow asylum seekers to be relocated to New Zealand. The government gained Senator Lambie's crucial support in repealing the Medivac Bill. Lambie was clear that her constituents 'don't want deals done over humanity'.[42] However, there was speculation that the secret deal that gained her support was framed in the terms of national security. At that time, there were still 464 asylum seekers in Nauru and PNG, 418 of whom had outstanding applications for transfer under the Medivac legislation.[43] In a similar arrangement to that negotiated with President Obama, and begrudgingly followed through by the Trump administration, New Zealand had offered to take up to 150 refugees a year from Manus Island and PNG. However, as the arrangement only covered those who had been granted refugee status that left some failed asylum seekers in PNG with little option for resettlement.

From the government's perspective, the repeal of Medivac restored Australia's border security regime. This meant that the minister for home affairs regained the discretionary power to decide whether an asylum seeker was repatriated to Australia for medical treatment, thus reducing the influence of the medical profession. If past practice was repeated, this meant that fewer asylum seekers would be transferred to Australia as the medical grounds used to bring those deemed unwell were no longer valid.

Critics such as GetUp noted that Medivac had saved lives, the implication being that lives would be lost needlessly.[44] The Senate report on the repeal of the Bill was split down political lines, highlighting the continuing domestic division over the treatment of asylum seekers.[45] The government was focused on border protection, which fits an orthodox Realist approach on sovereignty and a narrow definition of national interests and the securitization of 'unauthorized arrivals' as a threat aligns with Strategic Culture. In contrast, dissenting reports by Labor and the Greens evoke more Liberal Internationalist foreign policy values in relation to human rights obligations.[46] For example, Labor argued that the repeal represented a 'flouting of Australia's international obligations' and the Greens concluded that:

> The Medevac repeal Bill shows that the government puts political imperatives ahead of people's medical needs. They have made the crass calculation that some lives are worth sacrificing for broader political outcomes, despite their legal and moral obligations.[47]

The Medevac Bill case study has highlighted that caution is needed when connecting Labor's softer, more Liberal Internationalist rhetoric to foreign policy outcomes. The rhetoric has not translated into policy in the past, and in fact Labor governments have tightened the policy for electoral reasons. Therefore, Liberal Internationalist foreign policy values in foreign policy are apparent, but were trumped by a Realist definition of the national interest combined with a Strategic Cultural fear of 'alien' outsiders who could potentially pose a threat to Australia.

Conclusion

The policy approaches of Australian governments towards asylum seekers have responded relative to the volume of people attempting to arrive by sea with several clear peaks in the mid-1970s, early 2000s and early 2010s. During the peaks, both Coalition and Labor governments responded with strident legislative and diplomatic initiatives that reveal the character of Australian public policy on the boundary between domestic politics and international relations. A firm foreign policy response to asylum seekers fits very neatly with Australian Strategic Culture where culturally dissimilar peoples or states are viewed as direct threats to Australia. Furthermore, border protection in the context of a 'War on Terror' brought alive Realism's focus on formal sovereignty, and the Howard government's Pacific Solution set in train an approach whose legacy is felt to this day.

The Labor Party appears inclined at least in their declaratory rhetoric to refer more to Liberal Internationalist foreign policy values, especially while in opposition. However, in practice, polling demonstrated that a firm approach to asylum seekers was needed to secure electoral victory. Furthermore, as the minority of voters inclined to support a more humanist approach to asylum seekers were more likely to be Labor voters, then Labor was at a disadvantage because Coalition polices reflected broad public opinion in favour of strong border protection. As such, border protection became a classic domestic 'wedge' issue where the parties moved to the right with ever more strident responses to asylum seekers to gain electoral advantage.

Policy initiatives such as the Pacific Solution, TPVs, mandatory detention, third-party refugee swaps, etc. were innovative solutions to the policy problem and all of them were effective to a degree in limiting the flow of asylum seekers. At the same time, all did not reflect a focus on Liberal Internationalist foreign policy values, but rather a narrow Realist focus on sovereignty and threats that is aligned with Strategic Culture. In addition, other domestic factors, such as the state of the economy (i.e. unemployment), had less impact on policies aimed at asylum seekers than the exaggerated threat perceptions captured by Strategic Culture, which allowed asylum seekers to be securitized and the response to them militarized. This response is quite unlike the approach to climate change in Chapter 14, where the long timeframe, etc. allowed a focus on economic growth to dominate considerations.

While there were critics in Australia and internationally, there was little sustained pressure to change the hard-line approach to asylum seekers. There was less Liberal Internationalist reference to Australia's responsibility to exercise a form of creative 'middlepowermanship' or good international citizenship to resolve the public policy issue than other matters, such as ODA or climate change. Instead of reversing Coalition policies, Labor governments were responsible for a range of initiatives that made the plight of asylum seekers more tenuous and while their declaratory policy was softer, it did not translate into concrete policy reforms. Clearly, the interests of Australian citizens, especially those who were voters (in marginal electorates) were put above any sense of Liberal Internationalism towards vulnerable asylum seekers. In addition, normative pressure from international agreements, such as the Refugee Convention and the UNHCR, did not influence policy and successive governments elevated sovereignty concerns over respect for the letter and spirit of international agreements.

The policy towards asylum seekers allows reflection on foreign policy as the boundary between global/international and domestic policy realms. In this regard, the elevation of sovereign interests highlights the weakness of international norms in penetrating the Australian polity and influencing Australian foreign policy, which was also the conclusion in relation to ODA and climate change. It seems there is little that international normative pressure can do to shift a policy stance that is largely viewed as being in Australia's national interests, and the defence of national interests has become enshrined in AFP. This position is Realist in nature, but given credibility by the unique attributes of Strategic Culture encouraging the elevation of Australia's national interests over other perspectives.

Overview and conclusion: Australia's foreign policy DNA

This survey of Australian foreign policy (AFP) has revealed the diversity of the challenges and opportunities posed by maintaining key bilateral and regional relations and responding to key international public policy issues. A high level of continuity was revealed, which may seem surprising, but highlights both the enduring influence of core national interests and the inertia in foreign policy-making; the greatest predictor of what Australia will do tomorrow is what policy-makers did in the past. Another enduring theme is the way that Realist and Liberal Internationalist perspectives can be seen operating simultaneously in AFP. Realism is arguably the default explanation for state behaviour in the discipline of International Relations, but values count. Liberal Internationalism and maintaining the 'rules-based order' imbue the outlooks of policy-makers, as does the influence of Australia's unique Strategic Culture. Only a pluralistic account can truly make sense of AFP and bringing history, geography and culture into considerations is essential.

The 'unbreakable alliance' with the US

Australia's relations with the US are pivotal for understanding AFP. Since the Second World War when the mantle of being Australia's 'great and powerful friend' shifted from London to Washington, the relationship with the US has shaped AFP. The institutionalization of security ties through the ANZUS alliance provides the foundation stone for relations but it is a potent mixture of security, trade, values and culture that binds Australia to the US. Furthermore, while the US is the dominant partner, it is a partnership based on consent. Successive generations of Australian policy-makers and analysts have queried the centrality of the alliance to AFP and it has stood the test of time. This continuity itself queries the idea that there are no permanent alliances in international relations, only permanent interests. Australia and the US appear to have an 'unbreakable alliance' that adapted to dramatic strategic change at the end of the Second World War, the Cold War and its end, the post-Cold War disorder and rising geopolitical tension with China, which may in fact become a fully-fledged new Cold War. Australian and US interests have largely coincided and when there have been differences, they have not caused a fracture in relations.

For over 75 years, the US response to liminal moments in international affairs, such as the end of the Second World War, the US withdrawal from the Vietnam War in 1973, the end of the Cold War in 1989 and the post-2001 'War on Terror', has been central to how Canberra reviews its security. The latest event is the integration of rising China into the international system, and similarly Australia has clearly defined its interests and looks to the US to support it in the face of a rising regional hegemon. From the US perspective, Australian support has confirmed its strategic preferences and provided legitimacy to actions taken to support the 'rules-based order'. This coincidence of interests is a longstanding pattern that shows no sign of changing. However, if any event was likely to do so, it would be the wedging that China has undertaken to weaken US alliances. Significantly, the close relationship also endured the unpredictability of Trump's foreign policy. Alliance credibility requires trust and stability and allies from Europe to Asia felt pressure on the credibility of their alliance guarantees.

A key glue that binds the relationship is a coincidence of interests focused on a Liberal 'rules-based order', even though both states are willing to compromise Liberal values in the national interest. However, it is the security realm that has cemented close relations. The US provides the antidote for the deep-seated insecurity that Australia feels in relation to the 'alien' Asian other to the 'north'. This relationship provides a militarizing influence on AFP, but one that has been embraced by Canberra even before the US became Australia's 'great and powerful friend'. Australia has been willing to contribute forces to US operations overseas and provide access to joint facilities in Australia, and these contributions have been strengthened in recent years. With the rise of China and perceived decline of the US, Realists might suggest downgrading the alliance, but Canberra has taken the opposite tack, and this highlights the centrality of Strategic Cultural values to Australia's foreign policy DNA. The implications of Canberra standing up to China's increasingly coercive trade measures are likely to frame AFP for the near future and US support has been and will be essential to weathering the storm.

China – trading partner and strategic competitor

The rise of China has posed great opportunities and challenges for Australian policy-makers. Popular debate has long raised the prospect of Canberra having to make a 'China Choice' – a choice between the economic prosperity gained from trade with China and the security provided by the US alliance. However, if there was a 'China Choice' for Canberra, it was made some time ago and the ramifications were seen in the breakdown in relations in the early 2020s. For Canberra, the 'China Choice' was not so much a choice as an inevitable rupture due to the Strategic Cultural characteristics that interact with Realist focus on interests and a Liberal Internationalist deference to the 'rules-based order'. The debate actually needs to be inverted as it has been China's choice to rupture relations. Beijing's actions have prompted numerous incremental decisions in Canberra designed to protect Australia's sovereignty from unwelcome pressure.

China's foreign policy towards the South China Sea, Japan, Taiwan and the South Pacific have played into concerns about authoritarian states threatening the Liberal Internationalist 'rules-based order' that Australia has comfortably operated within since the Second World War. This does not mean that China is a revisionist power seeking to undermine the system, but rather a rising hegemon seeking to reorder relations to suit its preferences. That China is acting in a manner commensurate with its rapidly growing power is not surprising, but neither is it surprising that this behaviour would trigger threat perceptions from Canberra in relation to the 'alien' Asian other that has characterized Strategic Culture since before federation in 1901. Furthermore, in the Indo-Pacific, China sits alongside Japan as a major diplomatic partner with which Australia had been at war (during the Korean War of the 1950s), but while relations with Japan have been completely recalibrated, attempts to build closer links with China have been constrained by the dramatic differences in political systems and outlooks. Despite significant efforts by governments in the 1980s and 1990s, 'people-to-people' links with China are stunted and show no sign of warming.

China's military modernization and increasing confidence in using military force as a tool of foreign policy in the South China Sea and elsewhere did not go unnoticed in Canberra. Furthermore, actions by Canberra to support the 'rules-based order' or like-minded Indo-Pacific states further complicated relations, as China demanded subservience as part of its hegemonic aspirations in the region. Beijing's moves to influence domestic politics and control the diaspora in Australia were met with concern by Canberra which responded to by tightening foreign ownership rules and introducing foreign interference legislation that was interpreted by Beijing negatively. Canberra also supported the maintenance of the 'rules-based order' in the South China Sea, sponsored the WHO investigation into the origins of the COVID-19 pandemic, highlighted human rights violations of the Uighur people in Xinjiang, and diplomatically rebuked Beijing over its national security laws and the crackdown against protest in Hong Kong. China responded by punishing Australia with discriminatory tariffs, which led Canberra to take a case against China to the World Trade Organization.

Despite increasing coercive trade measures in the earlier 2020s, China remained Australia's largest trading partner, largely because there were some commodities that Beijing could not source elsewhere. As such, China's economic coercion highlighted differences in the way authoritarian states can use trade as a diplomatic lever. This is in contrast with Liberal-minded states that cannot direct economic activity in relation to import or export preferences unless a legitimate sanctions regime is in place. Given the dependence on trade with China, it may have been surprising that Canberra resisted Chinese pressure, but this highlights the limits of the Realist explanation for foreign policy behaviour that focuses too closely on material interests. In many ways, it would have been in Australia's interests to compromise, and much of the 'China Choice' debate was focused on the seeming inevitability of Australia acquiescing to Chinese coercion. However, Canberra had long made its 'China Choice' and was more than willing to trade with China, but continued to rely on the security insurance policy with its 'great and powerful friend', the US.

OVERVIEW AND CONCLUSION: AUSTRALIA'S FOREIGN POLICY DNA   309

Despite perceptions of US decline and concerns about the credibility of the US alliance that peaked during the Trump administration, Canberra chose to stand against domestic and international actions by Beijing that it defined as being inimical to its interests and may even foreshadow future aggression. This was not surprising because China remained the embodiment of the 'alien' Asian threat from the 'north' that is a central characteristic of Strategic Culture. Whether China chooses to further punish Australia remains to be seen but the die has been cast in Canberra: values do count in AFP, but they are not necessarily Liberal Internationalist values. In no uncertain terms, Canberra has restated the value placed on sovereignty and the maintenance of the Australian way of life, and allies such as the US and quasi allies such as Japan have become more central to Australia's security.

The 'Quasi-Alliance' with Japan

Australia's relationship with Japan highlights the need for a hybrid or pluralistic understanding of the usefulness of theory in explaining foreign policy. Only a combination of Realism, Liberal Internationalism and Strategic Culture can explain the trajectory of bilateral relations. Trade is the foundation stone, but security is becoming more significant to the point where we are witnessing the formation of a 'quasi-alliance'. Trade fits neatly with a Realist perspective of maximizing national interests in relation to economic power and also to the need for alliances, as long as they don't undermine Australia's trade interests. However, in this case a 'quasi-alliance' with Japan is actually one of the factors that is shaping the decline in good relations with China. That is, China sees initiatives such as the Quad or the institutionalization of bilateral security relations between Australia and Japan as inimical to its interests.

Canberra's attempts at encouraging closer relations are founded on a long history of trade, but have only been able to progress because Japan is being perceived more as a 'like' nation to Australia. Japan is an established democracy that promotes Liberal Internationalist values and respects the 'rules-based order' in the Indo-Pacific, while also being allied to the US and possessing high-level threat perceptions in relation to China. Australia supports Japan becoming a 'normal nation' and joining the international community in ways that are commensurate with its economic power, with the key being increased defence spending and defence cooperation. For example, Japan's focus on official development assistance (ODA) in the South Pacific has been welcomed by Australia, and this is in stark contrast to concerns about increasing Chinese influence.

Canberra's shift in sentiment outwardly appears to contradict a number of longstanding Strategic Cultural traits, but it in fact highlights the cognitive dissonance inherent in Australia's unique formulation of Strategic Culture. That is, the capacity of Strategic Culture to capture evolving sentiment and adapt to changing circumstances, such as aligning with a state that has been the embodiment of the 'alien' Asian threat from the 'north'. In fact, Japan was integral to the formation of Australian Strategic Culture. The threat posed by Japan in the Second World War quickly removed any perception of Asian inferiority in Australia and this stoked Strategic Cultural fear of the 'north'. Additionally, the swift defeat of British forces in the region highlighted Australia's vulnerability and prompted greater fear of abandonment. Furthermore, in 1942, the threat from Japan was existential and not exaggerated. So the rise of industrialized Imperial Japan strongly influenced the development of the heightened threat perceptions that became a key element of Australian Strategic Culture, yet by 2022 relations with Japan were closer than ever.

Imperial Japan personified the 'alien' other from the 'north' on Australia's doorstep, but modern Japan highlights the fact that Japan and Australia are the 'odd men out'[1] in Asia – democratic, Liberal Internationalist, but dependent on alliances with the US, an external 'great and powerful friend', to guarantee their security from a threatening region. Both states are concerned about abandonment by the US and seek to enmesh the US in the region. Security institutionalization of relations through the 'Special Strategic Partnership' point to a unique response in both Canberra and Tokyo to a liminal moment prompted by geostrategic and geoeconomic change. As such, changes in Japan's political culture exempt it from being identified as an 'alien' threat.

Realism and Liberal Internationalism partially explain why Australia would find Japan an attractive partner due to trade and respect for the 'rules-based order', but the adaptation of Strategic Culture provides the missing element in explaining moves towards developing a 'quasi-alliance'. Japan is no longer a military threat because it is a 'like' democratic state allied to Australia's ally and similarly threatened by China. In the face of this threat, Japan's strategic culture is changing and aligning with Australia's outlook. As such, support for Japan becoming a 'normal nation' directly suits Australia's interests, and not simply from the point of instrumentalism. It is not just because 'your enemy's enemy is your friend' but rather because economic and security interests and Liberal values connect the two states, and shared threat perceptions and fears of abandonment are a potent glue binding Canberra and Tokyo closer together.

Australia is supporting the rise of Japan as a 'normal nation' and the 'quasi-alliance' is likely to become a full alliance in the near future. As such, the historical determinism of Strategic Culture has been qualified by particular geopolitical conditions, specifically threat perceptions and the trust in the credibility of the security guarantee of the 'great and powerful friend' in the face of the rise of a potentially threatening 'alien' state in the region. This evolution in relations is in sharp contrast with the relationship with China and highlights the underlying securitized basis of AFP.

Proximity, with and distance, from Indonesia

Australia's uneasy relationship with Indonesia highlights a tension between geographic proximity and cultural difference. In international affairs, it is unusual to have two neighbours that are so close yet so distant in many ways. Despite not identifying with the Asian region, Australia cannot escape its geography and Indonesia is pivotal as the bridge between Australia and Southeast Asia. In contrast to relations with Japan, cultural barriers have not broken down and until quite recently, it was commonplace to view Indonesia as a military threat. As such, Indonesia fits the 'alien' other to the 'north' that has so strongly influenced AFP since federation and before. Interestingly, Indonesia and its predecessor, the Dutch East Indies, has a unique place in AFP because of its identification as a colony of a competing European empire, the staging point for the Japanese Empire to pose an existential threat to Australia during the Second World War and, post-independence, a potential threat itself.

Proximity is a double-edged sword and has been viewed as a positive attribute of relations by many policy-makers and analysts. However, while these Indonesianists have been vocal advocates of the great potential for closer relations to develop, they have been disappointed by the reality of the incremental growth in links and their pragmatic and transactional nature. Relations remain narrow and instrumental and it is noteworthy that trade has not been the catalyst for the development of closer relations, as with Japan. However, despite the top-down approach of successive Australian governments aimed at building relations, the great potential seems unrealizable for a range of reasons.

The focus of this book is bringing Australian Strategic Culture into the analysis of AFP, but it must be noted that it may be elements of Indonesia's Strategic Culture that interact to limit the realization of the potential for closer relations. Indonesia has elevated sovereignty issues in its foreign policy and has been sensitive about Australia's Liberal Internationalism in relation to human rights. Indonesia has many internal security concerns, and Jakarta prioritizes maintaining the integrity of the nation, and therefore Australia's support for independence in Timor Leste has cast an enduring shadow over relations. The outcome is that there is a dynamic of slight and escalation in diplomatic relations that occurs regularly and has not been overcome by traditional diplomatic means, such as trade, high-level meetings, military diplomacy, tourism, immigration, education and other 'people-to-people' links.

This failure to build closer relations is problematic for Canberra, especially as Indonesia begins to outpace Australia economically and builds stronger international ties. This failure can be explained by the unease with which Canberra's Liberal tendencies views Indonesia and through the historical and cultural emphasis of Strategic Culture, which focuses on threat, alienation and indefensibility. Realism explains just how cordial relations have been maintained despite regular diplomatic breaches.

Over time, Australian governments have shied away from promoting Liberal Internationalist human rights in diplomatic relations with Indonesia, including in relation to national self-determination in West Papua. This may have placated Jakarta to a degree but the wounds from Australia's support for Timorese independence run deep. Otherwise, Canberra has employed an essentially Realist approach to enhancing security and economic cooperation through top-down institutionalization, which has simply failed to take root. This approach is similar to that taken with China, but China is both Australia's number one trading partner and source of threat.

Security cooperation with Indonesia has grown, especially in relation to shared threats and interests focused on countering fundamentalist Islamic terrorism and human trafficking, but the level of institutionalization remains shallow due largely to differing threat perceptions and outlooks, namely Indonesia's focus on internal security and membership of the non-aligned movement. This may change if Indonesia identifies China as a threat, but Jakarta's approach to date has been muted despite tensions in the South China Sea. There remains hope in Canberra that the relationship may reach its potential but as Indonesia grows to surpass Australia economically, turbulence is likely to remain a central aspect of diplomacy.

Climate change and China as challenges to Australian hegemony in the South Pacific

The key themes that guide AFP towards the South Pacific, proximity, history and asymmetry, are enduring. In contrast to relations with other states where bilateral relations dominate diplomacy, Australia has a truly regional approach to the South Pacific that is complementary to its established bilateral relationships. This regional approach relates to the asymmetry of being the largest donor as well as the fact that PICs actively collaborate through regional institutions such as the Pacific Islands Forum (PIF).

Australia's proximity to the South Pacific means that historical ties connect with its colonial history and the legacy of British colonialism in states such as PNG and Fiji. This legacy of colonialism has led to a sense of responsibility, which can sometimes be applied clumsily. The asymmetry with the region has led to a level of paternalism that has prompted criticisms of neo-colonialism, but despite this Australia is viewed as a valued development partner. Australia is also the first responder in times of natural disaster, such as cyclones, and political crises, such as the riots in the Solomon Islands in November 2021. Canberra highly values being the 'security partner of choice' and maintaining this position against rising Chinese influence has been a key driver of AFP towards the South Pacific. Proximity and the historical sense of responsibility makes Canberra's relations with the South Pacific unique when compared to other states as Australia is not an equal or smaller power and finds itself in the position of a hegemonic power. Australia is the preponderant power in the South Pacific as it is vastly more powerful than all South Pacific states combined, and has consistently acted to maintain this position when it feels threatened by strategic competitors.

Historically, AFP towards the South Pacific has wavered between benign neglect and emergency responses to disasters and political instability. Humanitarian assistance and disaster response (HADR) operations cement Australia's role as the partner of choice for most PICs and this aligns well with AFP's stated priorities. However, Canberra has increasingly felt challenged by China's activity in the region and perceived rising Chinese influence as a challenge to its regional leadership role. This has led to a Pacific 'Step-up', which equates to a whole-of-government approach that is a thinly veiled response to China. This policy became entrenched by 2018 and may consign to history the seesawing days of benign neglect and emergency response.

Canberra is responding to the geopolitical challenge posed by China. Although this could be connected to Canberra being the United Sates' 'Deputy Sheriff' in the region, this characterization does not do justice to Australia's enduring interests in the strategic denial of unwelcome competitors in the region. In this respect, Australia's interests may coincide with US interests, but are formed independently of them. Australia's position fits neatly with a Realist attempt to maximize power, but the impact of proximity on Australia's leadership aspirations and sense of responsibility is best explained with reference to historical patterns that characterize Strategic Culture. The role of ODA as a key mechanism for maintaining influence complicates matters as it has historically reflected Liberal Internationalist values.

ODA for the national interest

Due to its association with altruism, a state's approach to ODA is thought to provide an insight into the level of influence that Liberal Internationalist values play in foreign policy. However, in recent years, the narrative in Australian ODA policy has shifted to focus on achieving Australia's national interests. This subverts assumptions about the purpose of ODA to be altruistic when it suits Canberra's interests. This shift corresponds with Australia's dedicated aid agency, AusAID, being incorporated into Department of Foreign Affairs and Trade from 2013. After this date, the effectiveness of ODA was measured more closely and government statements began to focus more on connecting effectiveness to achieving the national interest. This did not mean that the long history of focusing on Liberal Internationalist values such as good governance and gender equality ended, but rather that national interest measures became more prominent and neo-liberal approaches to self-help, such as 'aid for trade', were emphasized.

ODA was also focused more closely on Australia's proximate region with cuts to the programme being felt disproportionately outside of the South Pacific. As concerns regarding China's increasing influence in the South Pacific increased, the government announced the Pacific 'Step-up' and from 2018 the purpose of this policy became clearer. The 'Step-up' saw priority spending on projects that aligned with maintaining Australian influence in the South Pacific. This included the introduction of an infrastructure investment fund, which reversed the longstanding focus of ODA on capacity-building to concentrate on infrastructure – this was a direct counter to China's preference for infrastructure projects in the South Pacific that aligned with its own Belt and Road Strategy.

Aligning ODA more closely with the national interest highlights the tensions that always existed in these projects. They may have been designed with development best practice in mind, but ultimately ODA projects were managed by the funder and results counted. Value for money was equated to effectiveness and it was not a major shift to connect value for money to achieving the national interest. This means that ODA became more closely aligned with core priorities in AFP as it was seen as a tool for achieving the national interest. As such, the Liberal Internationalist values that influence development practice remain but have been tempered by national interest considerations that are more akin to a Realist approach to ODA. However, due to the threat perceptions from China and the aim of maintaining strategic denial of unwelcome powers in the South Pacific, Strategic Culture is also a partial explanation for ODA priorities.

Climate change and the national interest

Australian foreign policy towards climate change provides a useful test of the interplay between various elements of the national interest. Climate change is a non-traditional global security issue and as such, is not amenable to traditional national approaches to military threats. International cooperation is required to respond to climate change and, while imperfect, has been gathering momentum since the 1990s. Australia is in an unusual position internationally due to the overwhelming focus of its economy on exporting commodities that are implicated in the production of climate change-inducing emissions. This could be in relation to coal or liquified natural gas, or iron ore, which requires energy-intensive industry to be turned into steel. This means that any attempt at limiting these commodities would have a negative impact on Australia's export-oriented strategy and general economic welfare. Furthermore, with a large landmass and highly developed scientific capabilities, Australia has often responded to challenges through technological innovation. In the case of climate change, this has involved focusing on adaptation and technological solutions to reduce emissions, rather than wholesale alterations to economic activity. This means that the choices faced by Australia were different to most states that had different economic outlooks and Australia was more similar to other fossil fuel-exporting states (such as oil exporters in the Middle East) and more aligned with high emitters who required fossil fuels to power their industry (such as China). As such, it appears that a narrow Realist analysis of national interests has driven Australia's response to climate change.

The upshot of Australia's unusual outlook on climate change was that successive governments have concluded that it was not in Australia's interests to make major concessions on climate change. Furthermore, all debate was muddied by the fact that Australia itself was a very small net emitter, even though on a per-capita basis its emissions were very high and it exported a large volume of commodities that contributed to climate change in other jurisdictions (where they were exported to). Successive governments acted to weaken the international climate change regime to suit Australia's interests, but Australia still met its targets due to a range of factors such as negotiating low targets during the Kyoto process and the impact of the uptake of renewable energy at the state level.

Other than for a brief period during Kevin Rudd's prime ministership in 2009, Canberra has not led on climate change and it certainly wouldn't be seen as an example of a Liberal Internationalist state exercising creative 'middle powermanship'. In fact, Australia's stance has been criticized by the international community, but until very recently this has not influenced policy-making. For example, at the

OVERVIEW AND CONCLUSION: AUSTRALIA'S FOREIGN POLICY DNA 315

2021 Conference of the Parties in Glasgow, Australia agreed to net zero emissions by 2050 but failed to adjust its 2030 commitments or to produce a credible plan for how to achieve net zero. Until recently, the government's stance has also been out of alignment with public opinion, although public opinion has wavered on the issue when it comes to accepting the costs. This highlights both the lack of impact of public opinion on AFP and the fact that the government had little to lose electorally because opposition parties did not provide an alternative.

The election of the Albanese Labor government in 2022 changed everything and nothing at the same time. The incoming government immediately shifted tack and softened declaratory policy, which is important symbolically and characteristic of Labor governments. The government followed this up with a commitment to an emissions reduction target of 43 per cent by 2030 and net zero emissions by 2050. Furthermore, it was legislated in the Climate Change Bill 2022. This was a significant shift from the Morrison government and was received well domestically, internationally, and particularly in the South Pacific. The commitment was far from middle power leadership, but did align Australia with the developed world. Canberra finally signalled that Australia was willing to bear its share of the cost of reducing global temperatures and slowing climate change, which was an international public good. It had all the hallmarks of Liberal Internationalism, since despite bushfires and floods, Australia did not characterize itself as being vulnerable to climate change. That is, climate change had not been securitized, but the government had finally conceded that Australia must take action. This led to a very Pacific PIF meeting, unlike Morrison's last trip to the South Pacific. However, many questions remained in relation to the implementation of the policy in Australia, and the legislation did not limit the export of climate change-inducing commodities, which left the hard decisions to the market.

If climate change had been securitized, it may have triggered a response in relation to the role of threat perceptions in driving policy so clearly evidenced in Australia's Strategic Culture. However, the multiple threats from climate change are not military in nature and have never gained currency in the Australian polity. In Australia's neighbourhood, Pacific Island Countries (PICs) do identify climate change as an existential threat and Canberra has been facing increasing pressure from PICs to respond effectively, but this has also failed to shift policy. There is a security dimension to pressure from PICs as Canberra is concerned about rising Chinese influence in the region, but this also has not tipped the balance in Canberra in favour of taking action that would damage Australia's growth trajectory. As such, Strategic Cultural fears of threats from the 'north' have not been activated by attempts to securitize climate change and Australia's response is best explained by Realism.

Asylum seekers and Australian national interests

An influx in asylum seekers in the late 1990s led to one of the most divisive political episodes in Australian domestic and foreign affairs. The increase in arrivals of asylum seekers by boat was driven by increased global conflict in the early 2000s. Sources of asylum seekers included the Middle East associated with the 'War on Terror' and operations in Iraq and Afghanistan, and also the renewal of civil war in Sri Lanka from 2005 to 2009. The peak in these arrivals also coincided with a low point in relations with Indonesia following the Australian-led INTERFET intervention in Timor Leste between 1999 and 2000. At this time, Jakarta may not have been as diligent in managing asylum seekers transiting Indonesia en route to Australia. While the numbers were low compared to states neighbouring the key conflict zones, they had a significant political impact in Australia nonetheless.

John Howard was prime minister when the issue of asylum seekers came to a head. The 2001 deployment of the Australian Navy and SAS to prevent asylum seekers who had been rescued by the *MV Tampa* from landing in Australia symbolized the beginning of the politicization of the issue. The subsequent policy of mandatory detention and the Pacific Solution whereby all asylum seekers were denied due process in Australia and were processed offshore in Nauru and PNG, capture the essence of the public policy challenge and the fact that it straddled the domestic/foreign policy divide.

Australia's stance on asylum seekers was extremely divisive domestically and brought international condemnation, but despite a few alterations by Labor governments, the hard-line approach to asylum seekers prevailed. As such, it is clear that Liberal Internationalist values or public opinion did not lead the policy to be more humanitarian due to the fact that the electorate was divided on party lines. In general, Coalition voters were more supportive of a hard-line approach while Labor voters were more interested in a more humanitarian stance, but many Labor voters also believed in strong border protection, so Labor was not in a position to implement a policy that compromised the hard-line approach. On occasion compromises were made, but subsequently reversed when the numbers of asylum seekers increased, as with Prime Minister Julia Gillard's re-implementation of the Pacific Solution.

Over time, the numbers of asylum seekers attempting to arrive in Australia dwindled and this could be attributed to both the hard-line policy and the easing of tensions in conflict zones. However, Coalition governments claim that they 'stopped the boats' and this resonated with a majority of the electorate. Neither international condemnation nor vocal public opinion impacted on the policy and this did not change despite some major stains on Australia's international reputation, such as the 'Children Overboard' affair and the loss of the lives of numerous asylum seekers trying to circumvent Australia's border protection forces. This highlights that the Liberal Internationalism in AFP has limits, and this is similar to how climate change was viewed.

The politicization of asylum seekers used the language of sovereignty in relation to Prime Minister Howard's key claim that 'we shall decide who comes' to Australia. The tough stance was also connected to the 'War on Terror' insofar as it was argued that the inability to verify the identity of some asylum seekers opened up Australia to the threat of terrorists infiltrating their ranks. However, little evidence was provided for this claim other than the fact that many asylum seekers came from states embroiled in civil wars and insurgencies (such as

Afghanistan, Iraq and Sri Lanka). Underlying the harsh declaratory policy rhetoric was the fact that for many Australians, asylum seekers were connected to the 'alien' other that influenced threat perceptions and as such were connected to the threat perceptions that characterize Strategic Culture.

Australia's foreign policy DNA

Australia's bilateral and regional relationships, as well as case studies of foreign policy behaviour, reveal that no single theoretical perspective provides a convincing explanation of AFP. In most relationships and issues, a pluralistic approach is needed to make sense of AFP. Analysts and students of AFP alike can enrich their understanding of AFP if the systemic patterns revealed by Realism and Liberal Internationalism are combined in a hybrid approach. Only then can the peculiarities of AFP be understood and connections to Australia's geography, history and culture that form Australia's unique Strategic Culture be examined. AFP is constrained by the 'art of the possible' in the international system in relation to relative power and persuasion, but we cannot make sense of AFP without understanding the Strategic Culture within which policy-makers in Canberra operate.

The Labor tradition in AFP aspires to Liberal Internationalist values and the 'middlepowemanship' needed to lead progressive change in international affairs. However, middlepowermanship has been largely absent in Australia's approach to asylum seekers, climate change and ODA. Rather Realism is evident in the restatement of sovereignty in Operation Sovereign Borders, the support for the US led 'rules-based order' and 'coalitions of the willing,' and the persistence of an export-oriented strategy reliant on the profits from climate change inducing commodities. Realist strategies to maximise medium power are part of Australia's foreign policy DNA.

The fears inherent to Strategic Culture are not easily altered, despite the realities of Australia's geography and connections to Asia. The threat perceptions developed by settler-colonialists provide an inheritance that shapes and narrows the policy landscape to this day. Attempts to Asianize AFP have singularly failed and Australia remains an Anglo-Saxon outpost on the edge of Asia. These underlying attitudes prevail despite globalisation and the success of Australian multiculturalism. The ever-present fears generated by proximity to threats from 'alien' cultures to the 'north' have not been relieved by the benefits of geography. Australia is an island continent far from threatening powers, and has not faced an existential threat since the Japanese Empire in 1942. However, rather than celebrating the benefits of Australia's geography, the isolation from 'great and powerful friends' continues to drive alliances, alignments and defence spending. Threat perceptions, that are often exaggerated by fears of abandonment and indefensibility are part of Australia's foreign policy DNA.

The latest in a long line of threats is China and Canberra's positioning in advance of a looming conflict is driving much of AFP, especially in the South Pacific. Conflict is by no means inevitable, and will likely be driven more by

Beijing and Washington than Canberra, but the pattern of aligning with the 'great and powerful friend' to counter threats to the 'rules-based order' is clear. Encouraging and reinforcing the leadership of its 'great and powerful friend' is part of Australia's foreign policy DNA.

Generations of Australian foreign policy makers have elevated the national interest to be the moral value of the state. The national interest can change, especially at liminal strategic moments in history, but if past practice is the best predictor of the future, then a revolution in AFP is unlikely. Policy inertia with respect to the national interest is part of Australia's foreign policy DNA, but provides the best opportunity to shape foreign policy for the challenges of the future.

NOTES

1 The Australian foreign policy context

1   Hans Morgenthau, *Politics Among Nations: The Struggle for Power and Peace* (New York: Knopf, 1948).
2   Barry Buzan, Charles Jones and Richard Little, *The Logic of Anarchy: Neorealism to Structural Realism* (New York: Columbia University Press, 1993).
3   Hedley Bull, *The Anarchical Society* (London: Macmillan, 1977).
4   John Mearsheimer, 'Reckless States and Realism,' *International Relations* 23, no. 2 (2009): 241–256.
5   Graham Allison, 'Conceptual Models and the Cuban Missile Crisis,' *American Political Science Review* 63, no. 3 (September 1969): 689–718.
6   Brian Rathbun, *Reasoning of State: Realists, Romantics and Rationality in International Relations* (Cambridge: Cambridge University Press, 2019).
7   Nicolo Machiavelli, *The Prince* (London: Penguin, 2011); Thomas Hobbes, *Leviathan* (London: Penguin, 2017); Henry Kissinger, *Diplomacy* (New York: Simon & Schuster, 1997).
8   Morgenthau, *Politics Among Nations* (1948), 166.
9   Herbert Simon, *Models of Bounded Rationality* (Cambridge, MA: MIT Press, 1982).
10 Roland Paris, 'The Right to Dominate: How Old Ideas About Sovereignty Pose New Challenges for World Order,' *International Organization* 74, no. 3 (2020): 453–489.
11 Stephen Krasner, *Power, the State and Sovereignty Essays on International Relations* (New York: Routledge, 2009), 89–110.
12 Derek Croxton, 'The Peace of Westphalia of 1648 and the Origins of Sovereignty,' *International History Review* 21, no. 3 (September 1999): 569–591.
13 Diana Panke, *Unequal Actors in Equalising Institutions: Negotiations in the United Nations General Assembly* (London: Palgrave Macmillan, 2013).
14 Jess Gifkins, 'R2p in the UN Security Council: Darfur, Libya and Beyond,' *Cooperation and Conflict* 51, no. 2 (2016): 148–165.
15 Catherine Jones, *China's Challenge to Liberal Norms: The Durability of International Order* (London: Palgrave Macmillan, 2018), 139–175.
16 Brian Rathbun, 'The Rarity of Realpolitik: What Bismarck's Rationality Reveals about International Politics,' *International Security* 43, no. 1 (2018): 7–55.
17 John Bew, *Realpolitik: A History* (Oxford: Oxford University Press, 2016).
18 John Mearsheimer, *The Great Delusion: Liberal Dreams and International Realities* (New Haven, CT: Yale University Press, 2018).
19 Rebecca Strating, 'Enabling Authoritarianism in the Indo-Pacific: Australian Exemptionalism,' *Australian Journal of International Affairs* 74, no. 3 (2020): 301–321; Megan Price, 'Norm Erosion and Australia's Challenge to the Rules-based Order,' *Australian Journal of International Affairs* 75, no. 2 (2021): 161–177.
20 Barry Buzan, 'From International System to International Society: Structural Realism and Regime Theory Meet the English School,' *International Organization* 47, no. 3 (1993): 327–352.
21 Nicholas Michelsen, 'What is a Minor International Theory? On the Limits of "Critical International Relations".' *Journal of International Political Theory* 17, no. 3 (2021): 488–511.
22 Shannon Brincat, 'On the Methods of Critical Theory: Advancing the Project of Emancipation Beyond the Early Frankfurt School,' *International Relations* 26, no. 2 (2012): 218-245.
23 Valerie Hudson and Benjamin Day, *Foreign Policy Analysis: Classic and Contemporary Theory*, (Lanham: Rowman and Littlefield, 2020).

NOTES

24 Henry Palmerston, 'Speech' (Speech to the London House of Commons, 1 March 1848).
25 Scott Burchill, *The National Interest in International Relations Theory* (New York: Palgrave Macmillan, 2005).
26 Robert Jervis, *Perception and Misperception in International Politics* (Princeton, NJ: Princeton University Press, 2017), 13–57.
27 See, for instance, Jack Snyder, *The Soviet Strategic Culture: Implications for Nuclear Options* (Santa Monica, CA: Rand Corporation, 1977).
28 Edward Kaplan, *To Kill Nations: American Strategy in the Air-Atomic Age and the Rise of Mutually Assured Destruction* (Ithaca, NY: Cornell University Press, 2015).
29 Junko Kato, 'Institutions and Rationality in Politics – Three Varieties of New-Institutionalists', *British Journal of Political Science* 26, no. 4 (October 1996): 553–582.
30 See, for instance, Snyder, *The Soviet Strategic Culture* (1977); Ken Booth, *Strategy and Ethnocentrism* (Florence: Taylor & Francis, 2014).
31 Graham Allison, 'Conceptual Models and the Cuban Missile Crisis', *American Political Science Review* 63, no. 3 (September 1969): 689–718.
32 Kerry Longhurst, *Germany and the Use of Force* (Manchester: Manchester University Press, 2004), 17.
33 Jeffrey Lantis, 'Strategic Culture: From Clauzewitz to Constructivism', in *Strategic Culture and Weapons of Mass Destruction*, eds. Jeannie Johnson, Kerry Kartchner and Jeffrey Larsen (New York: Palgrave, 2009), 32–52.
34 Colin Gray, 'Strategic Culture as Context: The First Generation of Theory Strikes Back,' *Review of International Studies* 25, no. 1 (1999): 49–69.
35 Ibid.
36 Alastair Johnston, 'Thinking About Strategic Culture', *International Security* 19, no. 4, (Spring 1995): 32–45.
37 Ibid., 32–64.

2 Australia's strategic culture

1 T.B. Millar, *Australia in Peace and War: 1788–1977* (Canberra: Australian National University Press, 1978).
2 Adam Lockyer and Michael D. Cohen, 'Denial strategy in Australian strategic thought,' *Australian Journal of International Affairs*, 71, no. 4, (2017): 423–439.
3 Alan Bloomfield, 'Time to Move On: Reconceptualizing the Strategic Culture Debate,' *Contemporary Security Policy* 33, no. 3 (2012): 437–461; J. Lantis and A. Charlton, 'Continuity or Change? The Strategic Culture of Australia,' *Comparative Strategy* 30, no. 4 (2011): 291–315; Stuart Poore, 'Australia,' in *Neorealism Versus Strategic Culture*, eds. John Glenn, Darryl Howlett and Stuart Poore (New York: Routledge, 2018); Alan Bloomfield and Kim Nossal, 'Towards an *Explicative Understanding* of Strategic Culture: The Cases of Australia and Canada,' *Contemporary Security Policy* 28, no. 2 (2007): 286–307; Michael Wesley and Tony Warren, 'Wild Colonial Ploys? Currents of Thought in Australian Foreign Policy,' *Australian Journal of Political Science* 35, no. 1 (2000): 9–26.
4 Graeme Cheeseman, 'Australia: The White Experience of Fear and Dependence,' in *Strategic Cultures in the Asia-Pacific Region*, eds. Ken Booth and Russell Trood (Basingstoke, Macmillan, 1999), 273–298.
5 Gareth Evans and Bruce Grant, *Australia's Foreign Relations in the World of the 1990s* (Melbourne: Melbourne University Publishing, 1991), 326.
6 Geoffrey Blainey, *The Tyranny of Distance: How Distance Shaped Australian History* (Sydney: Macmillan, 1967).
7 Michael O'Keefe, 'Australia and Indonesia: The Persistence of Distance Between Proximate Neighbours,' in *Australia on the World Stage: History, Politics, and International Relations*, eds. Bridget Brooklyn, Benjamin Jones and Rebecca Strating (London: Routledge, 2022): 157–170.
8 Gwenda Tavan, *The Long, Slow Death of the White Australia Policy* (Melbourne: Scribe, 2005).
9 Gwenda Tavan, 'Testing Times: The Problem of History in the Howard Government's Australian Citizenship Test,' in *Does History Matter? Making and Debating Citizenship, Immigration and*

NOTES

Refugee Policy in Australia and New Zealand, eds. Klaus Neumann and Gwenda Tavan (Canberra: Australian National University Press, 2009), 125–143.

10 Brian Farrell, *The Defence and Fall of Singapore 1940–1942* (Stroud: Tempus, 2006).

11 Noordin Sopiee, 'The Development of an East Asian Consciousness,' in *Living with Dragons,* ed. Greg Sheridan (St Leonards: Allen & Unwin, 1995), 180–193.

12 Richard Higgott and Kim Nossal, 'Odd Man In, Odd Man Out: Australia's Liminal Position in Asia Revisited – a Reply to Ann Capling,' *The Pacific Review* 21, no. 5 (2008): 623–634.

13 Damian Kingsbury and Leena Avonius, *Human Rights in Asia: A Reassessment of the Asian Values Debate* (New York: Palgrave Macmillan, 2008).

14 Stephen Fitzgerald, *Is Australia an Asian Country?* (St Leonards: Allen & Unwin, 1997).

15 David Walker and Agnieszka Sobocinska, *Australia's Asia: From Yellow Peril to Asian Century* (Crawley, WA: University of Western Australia Publishing, 2012).

16 James Jupp, 'From "White Australia" to "Part of Asia": Recent Shifts in Australian Immigration Policy towards the Region,' *International Migration Review* 29, no. 1 (1995): 207–228.

17 Craig Wilcox, *Australia's Boer War: The War in South Africa, 1899–1902* (Melbourne: Oxford University Press, 2002).

18 Charles A. Willoughby, *Reports of General Macarthur: The Campaigns of Macarthur in the Pacific,* Vol. 1 (Washington, DC: US Government Print Office, 1994 (1966)), 23, https://history. army.mil/html/books/013/13-3/index.html.

19 Ibid., 23.

20 J.L.S Girling, 'Vietnam and the Domino Theory,' *Australian Outlook* 21, no. 1 (1967): 61–70.

21 Michael O'Keefe, 'Teaching Australian Foreign Policy through the Lens of Strategic Culture,' *Australian Journal of International Affairs* 73, no. 6 (2019): 532–538.

22 Michael O'Keefe, 'Enduring Tensions in the 2000 Defence White Paper,' *Australian Journal of Politics and History* 49, no. 4 (2003): 532–534.

23 Australian Capital Territory, *Parliamentary Debates,* House of Representatives United States of America Terrorist Attacks Speech, 17 September 2001, 30739-30742 (John Howard, Prime Minister).

24 'Security Treaty between Australia, New Zealand and the United States of America (ANZUS),' in *Australia Treaty Series 1952, no. 2,* signed 1 September 1, 1951, entered into force 29 April 1952 (Canberra: Department of External Affairs, 1952).

25 John Birmingham, 'A Time for War: Australia as a Military Power,' *Quarterly Essay* QE20 (December 2005); Graeme Cheeseman and St John Kettle, eds., *The New Australian Militarism: Undermining our Future Security* (Leichhardt: Pluto Press, 1990).

26 'China Fires Back at Julie Bishop Over "Irresponsible" Remarks,' *The Australian,* November 27, 2013.

27 Australian Department of Foreign Affairs and Trade, *2017 Foreign Policy White Paper* (Canberra: Commonwealth of Australia, 2017), 7, 58, 63, 105.

28 Christine De Matos and Robin Gerster, *Occupying the 'Other': Australia and Military Occupations from Japan to Iraq* (Newcastle Upon Tyne: Cambridge Scholars Publishing, 2009).

29 Gary Smith and St John Kettle, eds., *Threats Without Enemies: Rethinking Australia's Security* (Leichardt: Pluto Press, 1992).

30 Paul Dibb, *Review of Australia's Defence Capabilities: Report for the Minister of Defence* (Canberra: Australian Government Publishing Service, 1986); Australian Department of Defence, *The Strategic Basis of Australian Defence Policy* (Canberra: Australian Department of Defence, March 1971), para 160.

31 Paul Dibb and Richard Brabin-Smith, 'Indonesia in Australian Defence Planning,' *Security Challenges* 3, no. 4 (2007): 67–93.

32 Department of Defence, *The Defence of Australia, 1987* (Canberra: Australian Government Publishing Service, 1987).

33 Gary Smith and St John Kettle, eds., *Threats Without Enemies: Rethinking Australia's Security* (Leichardt: Pluto Press, 1992).

34 Dibb, *Review of Australia's Defence Capabilities* (1986).

35 Michael Evans, *The Tyranny of Dissonance: Australia's Strategic Culture and Way of War 1901-2004,* Study Paper no. 306 (Canberra: Land Warfare Studies Centre, February 2005).

36 Dibb, *Review of Australia's Defence Capabilities* (1986); Department of Defence, *The Defence of Australia, 1987* (Canberra: Australian Government Publishing Service, 1987).

NOTES

37 Gary Smith and St John Kettle, eds., *Threats Without Enemies: Rethinking Australia's Security* (Leichhardt: Pluto Press, 1992).

38 Australian Department of Defence, *2020 Defence Strategic Update* (Canberra: Australian Government Publishing Service, 2020): 14–15.

39 J.L.S Girling, 'Vietnam and the Domino Theory,' *Australian Outlook* 21, no. 1 (1967): 61–70.

40 Malcolm Booker, *The Last Domino: Aspects of Australia's Foreign Relations* (Melbourne: Collins, 1976).

41 Merze Tate, 'The Australian Monroe Doctrine,' *Political Science Quarterly* 76, no. 2 (June 1961): 264–284.

42 Robert Jervis, *Perception and Misperception in International Politics* (Princeton, NJ: Princeton University Press, 2017), 13–57.

43 Allan Gyngell, *Fear of Abandonment: Australia in the World Since 1942*, (Melbourne: Black Inc, 2017).

44 John Curtin, 'The Task Ahead,' *Herald*, 27 December 1941, 10.

45 Danielle Chubb and Ian McAllister, *Australian Public Opinion, Defence and Foreign Policy: Attitudes and Trends since 1945* (Singapore: Palgrave Macmillan, 2021).

46 Michael O'Keefe, 'The Militarisation of China in the Pacific: Stepping up to a New Cold War?,' *Security Challenges* 16, no. 1 (2020): 94–112.

47 See, for example, Duncan MacCullum, 'The Alleged Russian Plans for the Invasion of Australia, 1864,' *Journal of the Royal Australian Historical Society* 44, no. 5 (1959): 301–322.

48 Alex Davis, 'Making a settler colonial IR: Imagining the "international" in early Australian International Relations,' *Review of International Studies* 47, no. 5 (December 2021): 637–655.

49 Stuart Ward, *Australia and the British Embrace: The Demise of the Imperial Ideal* (Melbourne: Melbourne University Publishing 2001), 13–40.

50 David Lee and Christopher Waters, eds., *Evatt to Evans: The Labor Tradition in Australian Foreign Policy*, (St Leonards: Allen & Unwin, 1997).

51 John Holmes, 'Is there a Future for "Middlepowermanship"?,' in J.K. Gordon, ed., *Canada's Role as a Middlepower* (Toronto: Canadian Institute of International Affairs, 1966).

52 'Fraser, Malcolm, Statement on the World Situation,' Transcript 4135, PM Transcripts: Transcripts from the Prime Ministers of Australia, updated 1 June 1976.

53 Henry Albinski, *Australian External Policy Under Labor: Content, Process and the National Debate* (St Lucia: University of Queensland Press, 1977); Michael Wesley, *The Howard Paradox: Australian Diplomacy in Asia 1996–2006* (Sydney: ABC Books, 2007).

54 Andrew Carr, 'Is Australia a Middle Power? A Systemic Impact Approach,' *Australian Journal of International Affairs* 68, no. 1 (2014): 70–84.

55 Carl Underer, 'The "middle Power" Concept in Austrlaian Foreign Policy,' *Australian Journal of Politics adn History* 53, no. 4 (2007): 538–551.

56 Allan Patience, *Australian Foreign Policy in Asia: Middle Power or Awkward Partner?* (London: Palgrave Macmillan, 2018), 1–16.

57 Jeffrey Robertson, 'Middle-Power Definitions: Confusion Reigns Supreme,' *Australian Journal of International Affairs* 71, no. 4 (2017): 355–370; Mark Beeson, Alan Bloomfield and Wahyu Wicaksana, 'Unlikely Allies? Australia, Indonesia and the Strategic Cultures of Middle Powers,' *Asian Security* 17, no. 2 (2021): 178–194.

58 Andrew Cooper, Richard Higgott and Kim Nossal, *Relocating Middle Powers: Australia and Canada in a Changing World Order* (Vancouver: University of British Columbia Press, 1993).

59 James Cotton and John Ravenhill, eds., *Middle Power Dreaming: Australia in World Affairs 2006–2010* (Melbourne: Oxford University Press, 2011).

60 Patience, *Australian Foreign Policy in Asia* (2018), 233–255.

61 Gabriele Abbondanza, 'Australia the "Good International Citizen"? The Limits of a Traditional Middle Power,' *Australian Journal of International Affairs* 75, no. 2 (2021): 178–196.

62 Australian Department of Foreign Affairs and Trade, *Australia's Regional Security* (Canberra: Commonwealth of Australia, 1989).

63 Derek MacDougall, 'Australia and Asia Pacific Security Regionalism: From Hawke to Keating to Howard,' *Contemporary Southeast Asia* 23, no. 1 (April 2001): 81–100.

64 Evans and Grant, *Australia's Foreign Relations in the World of the 1990s* (1991).

NOTES

65 Gary Smith and 'Liberal's Realist Tradition,' *Austrlian Journal of Politcs and History*, 51, 3, 2005, 459–72.
66 Benjamin Reilly, 'The Return of Values in Australian Foreign Policy,' *Australian Journal of International Affairs* 74, no. 2 (2020): 116–123.
67 Hans Morgenthau, *Politics Among Nations: The Struggle for Power and Peace* (New York: Knopf, 1948).
68 John Howard, 'Australia's International Relations – Ready for the Future' (Speech, National Convention Centre, Canberra, 22 August 2001).
69 David McCraw, 'The Howard Government's Foreign Policy: Really Realist?,' *Australian Journal of Political Science* 43, no. 3 (September 2008): 465–480.

3 Background to the United States

1 Maria Malksoo, 'The Challenge of Liminality for International Relations Theory,' *Review of International Studies* 38, no. 2 (2012): 481–494.
2 Rebecca Strating, 'Enabling Authoritarianism in the Indo-Pacific: Australian Exemptionalism,' *Australian Journal of International Affairs* 74, no. 3 (2020): 301–321.
3 Stockholm International Peace Research Institute, 'Military Expenditure Database,' February 2020–2021, accessed December 2022.
4 Stuart Ward, ed., *British Culture and the End of Empire* (Manchester: Manchester University Press, 2001).
5 John Curtin, 'The Task Ahead,' *Herald*, Melbourne, 27 December 1941, 10.
6 Charles A. Willoughby, *Reports of General Macarthur: The Campaigns of Macarthur in the Pacific* (Washington, DC: US Government Print Office, 1994 (1966)), 23–24.
7 Ibid., 24.
8 Christine De Matos and Robin Gerster, *Occupying the 'Other': Australia and Military Occupations from Japan to Iraq* (Newcastle upon Tyne: Cambridge Scholars Publishing, 2009).
9 J. Girling, 'Vietnam and the Domino Theory,' *Australian Outlook* 21, no. 1 (1967): 61–70.
10 Peter Edwards, *Australia and the Vietnam War* (Sydney: New South Publishing in association with the Australian War Memorial, 2014).
11 'Disintegration of the Malay Barrier and the Threat to Australia,' Plate 08, Charles A. Willoughby, *Reports of General Macarthur: The Campaigns of Macarthur in the Pacific* (Washington, DC: US Government Print Office, 1994 (1966)), 24.
12 Australian Department of Defence, *Australian Defence* (Canberra: Australian Department of Defence, 1976), 11.
13 Christine De Matos and Robin Gerster, *Occupying the 'Other'* (2009).
14 White House, 'U.S. Strategic Framework for the Indo-Pacific,' 5, accessed 2 March 2021.
15 White House, *National Security Strategy of the United States of America, December 2017* (2017), 3, 46.
16 Peter Hartcher, '"Just Not Going to Happen": US Warns China over Australian Trade Stoush,' *The Age*, 16 March 2021.
17 Stephen Dziedzic, 'US to Partner with Australia, Papua New Guinea on Manus Island Naval Base,' *ABC News*, 17 November 2018.
18 US Department of State. 'U.S. Relations with Australia, Bilateral Relations Fact Sheet Bureau of East Asian and Pacific Affairs,' 2021, accessed 2 March 2021.
19 White House, 'Readout of President Joseph R. Biden, Jr. Call with Prime Minister Scott Morrison of Australia,' News Release, 3 February 2021.
20 Australian Department of Foreign Affairs and Trade, *2017 Foreign Policy White Paper* (Canberra: Commonwealth of Australia, 2017), 38–39.
21 Stephen Walt, *The Origins of Alliances* (Ithaca, NY: Cornell University Press, 1987).
22 Office of the Prime Minister of Australia, '70 Years of ANZUS and Our Alliance with the United States,' News Release, 1 September 2021.
23 Brendan Taylor, 'Unbreakable Alliance? ANZUS in the Asian Century,' *Asian Politics & Policy* 8, no. 1 (2016): 75–85.
24 Bill Clinton, 'Speech to the Australian Parliament' (Speech, House of Representatives, Parliament House, Canberra, 20 November 1996).

324 NOTES

25 Embassy of Australia. 'Australian and the United States Relations,' 2021.
26 Embassy of Australia. 'History of Mateship,' 2021.
27 White House, *National Security Strategy* (2017), 46.
28 Special Service Division, Services of Supply, United States Army, *Instructions for American Servicemen in Australia 1942* (Washington, DC: War and Navy Department, 1942), 4.
29 Ibid., 15–17 (emphasis added).
30 Ned Price, 'Secretary Blinken's Call with Australian Foreign Minister Payne,' News Release, 27 January 2021.
31 Robert Menzies, 'Visit to the US Senate by Hon. Robert Gordon Menzies,' *Congressional Record* 84th Cong., 1st sess., Vol. 101, Pt 3 (16 March 1955), 3020–3021.
32 Price, 'Secretary Blinken's Call with Australian Foreign Minister Payne,' 2021.
33 Australian Department of Foreign Affairs and Trade, *2017 Foreign Policy White Paper*, chapter one (2017); Scott Morrison, 'Remarks, Ceremonial Welcome, White House – Washington D.C.: Transcript' (Speech, Washington DC, 29 September 2019); Scott Morrison, 'Address, Aspen Security Forum – 'Tomorrow in the Indo-Pacific': Transcript' (Speech, 5 August 2020).
34 Anthony Galloway, 'We Won't Trade Away Values: Payne,' *The Age*, 20 March 2021, 10.
35 White House, *National Security Strategy* (2017), 17.
36 Simon Jackman, Zoe Meers, Shaun Ratcliff, and Jared Mondschein, *Public Opinion in the Age of Trump,* The United States Studies Centre (18 December 2019), https://www.ussc.edu.au/analysis/public-opinion-in-the-united-states-and-australia-compared.
37 Ibid., 11–13.
38 Strating, 'Enabling Authoritarianism in the Indo-Pacific,' (2020): 301–321; Stewart Firth, 'Australia's Policy Towards Coup-Prone and Military Regimes in the Asia-Pacific: Thailand, Fiji and Burma,' *Australian Journal of International Affairs* 67, no. 3 (2013): 357–372.
39 Kori Schake, *America vs the West: Can the Liberal World Order be Preserved?* (Melbourne: Penguin Press, 2018).
40 Joe Biden, 'Remarks by President Biden on America's Place in the World' (Speech, US Department of State Headquarters, Harry S. Truman Building, Washington, DC, 4 February 2021).
41 Brendan O'Connor, *Anti-Americanism: History, Causes, Themes* (Westport, CT: Praeger, 2007).
42 William Tow, 'Deputy Sheriff or Independent Ally? Evolving Australian-American Ties in an Ambiguous World Order,' *Pacific Review* 17, no. 2 (2004): 272.

4 United States

1 Neville Meaney, 'Look Back in Fear: Percy Spender, the Japanese Peace Treaty and the ANZUS Pact,' *Japan Forum* 15, no. 3 (June 2003): 399–410.
2 Australian Department of External Affairs. 'Security Treaty Between Australia, New Zealand and the United States of America (ANZUS),' in *Australia Treaty Series 1952, no. 2*, signed 1 September 1951, entered into force 29 April 1952 (Canberra: Department of External Affairs).
3 Ibid.
4 Ibid.
5 Peter Layton, 'America's New Alliance Management,' *Australian Outlook*, 8 March 2017.
6 US Congress, House, *John S. McCain National Defense Authorization Act for Fiscal Year 2019*, HR 5515, 115 Cong., 2nd sess., *Congressional Record* 208 (3 January 2018), 421.
7 Paul D. Wolfowitz, 'ANZUS Alliance,' *Department of State Bulletin* 85 (1985): 65–66.
8 Hugh White, *The China Choice: Why America Should Share Power* (Collingwood, VIC: Black Inc., 2012).
9 Stephan Frühling, 'Is ANZUS Really an Alliance? Aligning the US and Australia,' *Survival* 60, no. 5 (2018): 199–218.
10 Dougal Robinson, 'A Sustained Tantrum: How the Joint Chiefs of Staff Shaped the ANZUS Treaty,' *Australian Journal of International Affairs*, 74, no. 5 (2020): 495–510.
11 Peter Hartcher, 'There's Good News, Bad News and Worse News about Donald Trump', *The Age*, 2 April 2019.
12 Reuben Steff and Alan Tidwell, 'Understanding and Evaluating Trump's Foreign Policy: A Three Frame Analysis,' *Australian Journal of International Affairs*, 74, no. 4 (2020): 394–419.

NOTES

13 Peter Hartcher, 'I Asked Would the US Defend Australia If We Were Attacked? The Answer is Sobering', *The Age*, 26 January 2021.

14 Brice Harris, 'United States Strategic Culture and Asia-Pacific Security,' *Contemporary Security Policy 35*, no. 2 (2014): 290–309.

15 Eric Heginbotham, *The US China Military Scorecard* (Washington, DC: Rand, 2017).

16 Fredrik Doeser and Joakim Eidenfalk, 'Using Strategic Culture to Understand Participation in Expeditionary Operations: Australia, Poland, and the Coalition against the Islamic State,' *Contemporary Security Policy 40*, no. 1 (2019): 4–29.

17 Stockholm International Peace Research Institute, 'Arms Industry Database,' December 2018, 2021.

18 Derek Woolner, *Lessons of the Collins Class Submarine Program for Improved Oversight of Defence Procurement*, Research Paper 3, 2001-02 (Canberra: Parliamentary Library, 18 September 2001).

19 Australian National Audit Office, 'Air Warfare Destroyer Program', Audit Report No. 22, 2013–14 (Canberra: Australian National Audit Office, 2014).

20 Nick McKenzie, Angus Grigg and Chris Uhlmann, 'China Uses the Cloud to Step Up Spying on Australian Business,' *The Age*, 20 November 2018.

21 *Global Times*. 'Five Eyes Alliance Plotting Against China Will Backfire on Themselves,' *Global Times*, 14 December 2020.

22 Des Ball, *A Base for Debate: The US Satellite Ground Station at Nurrungar* (Sydney: Allen & Unwin, 1987).

23 Brendan O'Connor, *Anti-Americanism: History, Causes, Themes* (Westport, CT: Praeger, 2007); Michael Denborough, ed., *Australia and Nuclear War* (Canberra: Croom Helm, 1983).

24 Australian Capital Territory, *Parliamentary Debates*, House of Representatives Ministerial Statements, 20 February 2019, 1087–1091 (Christopher Pyne, MP).

25 Commonwealth of Australia, *Howard Ministries, Cabinet Submissions*. Cabinet Submission JH97/0423 - Establishment of a Joint Australia - United States Relay Ground Station at Pine Gap - Decision JH97/0423/NS (Canberra: National Archives of Australia, 1996–1997).

26 Australian Capital Territory, *Parliamentary Debates*, House of Representatives Ministerial Statements, 20 February 2019, 1087–1091 (Christopher Pyne, MP).

27 Bert Chapman, 'US Marine Corps Battalion Deployment to Australia: Potential Strategic Implications,' *Security Challenges 13*, no. 1 (2017): 1–18.

28 White House, Office of the Press Secretary, 'Remarks by President Obama to the Australian Parliament, Parliament House, Canberra, Australia,' News Release, 17 November 2011.

29 Aiden Warren and Adam Bartley, *U.S. Foreign Policy and China* (Edinburgh: Edinburgh University Press, 2021): 97–99.

30 Angus Martyn, 'The Right of Self-Defence under International Law – the Response to the Terrorist Attacks of 11 September,' *Current Issues Brief 8*, 2001–02, 12 February 2002.

31 Australian Capital Territory, *Parliamentary Debates*, House of Representatives United States of America Terrorist Attacks Speech, 17 September 2001, 30739-30742 (John Howard, Prime Minister).

32 Ibid.

33 Michael Brissenden, 'Tony Abbott Makes First Visit to Afghanistan as PM, Says Australia's Longest War is Ending,' *ABC News*, 29 October 2013.

34 Martyn, 'The Right of Self-Defence under International Law,' 2002.

35 Fergus Hanson, *The 2008 Lowy Institute Poll: Australia and the World*. The Lowy Institute (23 September 2008), 11–12.

36 Nicole Brangwin, Marty Harris, and David Watt, *Australia at War in Afghanistan: Revised Facts and Figures*, Parliamentary Library (Canberra: Department of Parliamentary Services, 12 September 2012).

37 Fiona Hilferty, Ilan Katz, Fredrik Zmudzki, Miranda van Hooff, Ellie Lawrence-Wood, Amelia Searle, Geoff Evans, Ben Challinor, and Adrian Talbot, *Homelessness Amongst Australian Veterans: Summary of Project Findings*, Australian Housing and Urban Research Institute (May 2019).

38 Watson Institute for International and Public Affairs, Brown University, 'Costs of War: Afghan Civilians,' Brown University, 2021.

NOTES

39 Anthony Galloway, 'Australia to Withdraw All Troops from Afghanistan after Biden's Vow to End War,' *Sydney Morning Herald*, 15 April 2021.
40 Karen Middleton, *An Unwinnable War: Australia in Afghanistan* (Melbourne: Melbourne University Publishing, 2011).
41 Michael Ong, 'Iraq: Issues on the Eve of War,' *Current Issues Brief* 19, 2002–03, 18 March 2003.
42 Tony Kevin, 'Australia Started the War Before it Started', *Sydney Morning Herald*, 22 April 2004.
43 Bob Woodward, *Plan of Attack* (New York: Simon & Schuster, 2004).
44 Watson Institute for International and Public Affairs, Brown University, 'Costs of War: Iraqi Civilians,' 2021.
45 Alan Beaumont, 'Our Military and Diplomatic Elders on Truth in Democracies and the Downside of Invading Iraq,' *Sydney Morning Herald*, 10 August 2004.
46 Henry Albinski, *Politics and Foreign Policy in Australia: The Impact of Vietnam and Conscription* (Durham, NC: Duke University Press, 1970).
47 *SBS News*. 'Australia is US Deputy-Sheriff: Mahathir,' *SBS News*, 23 August 2013.
48 Peter Hartcher, '"Just Not Going to Happen": US Warns China over Australian Trade Stoush,' *The Age*, 16 March 2021.
49 Alan Ryan, *'Primary Responsibilities and Primary Risks:' Australian Defence Force Participation in the International Force East Timor*, Study Paper No. 304 (Land Warfare Studies Centre, November 2000), 76.
50 Australian Civil-Military Centre, *Afghanistan: Lessons from Australia's Whole-of-Government Mission* (Canberra: Commonwealth of Australia, November 2016), 30.
51 Henry Palmerston, 'Speech' (Speech to the London House of Commons, 1 March 1848).
52 Charles Miller, 'Public Support for ANZUS: Evidence of a Generational Shift?,' *Australian Journal of Political Science* 50, no. 3 (June 2015): 442–461.
53 Danielle Chubb and Ian McAllister, *Australian Public Opinion, Defence and Foreign Policy: Attitudes and Trends since 1945* (Singapore: Palgrave Macmillan, 2021).
54 Simon Jackman, Zoe Meers, Shaun Ratcliff, and Jared Mondschein, *Public Opinion in the Age of Trump*, The United States Studies Centre (18 December 2019).
55 Ibid.
56 Natasha Kassam. *Lowy Institute Poll 2022*. The Lowy Institute (29 June 2022), 6.
57 Natasha Kassam. *Lowy Institute Poll 2020*. The Lowy Institute (24 June 2020); Alex Oliver, *Lowy Institute Poll 2018*. The Lowy Institute (20 June 2018); Alex Oliver, '*Lowy Institute Poll 2016*. The Lowy Institute (21 June 2016).
58 Kassam. *Lowy Institute Poll 2020* (2020), 8.
59 Ibid., 8.
60 Natasha Kassam. *Lowy Institute Poll 2022* (2022), 6.
61 Ibid., 6–7.
62 Alex Oliver, *Lowy Institute Poll 2013*. The Lowy Institute (24 June 2013).
63 Bates Gill and Tom Switzer, 'The New Special Relationship: The U.S.-Australia Alliance Deepens,' *Foreign Affairs*, 19 February 2015.
64 Jackman, et al., *Public Opinion in the Age of Trump* (2019).
65 Richard Gowan, *Australia in the UN Security Council*, The Lowy Institute (12 June 2014.
66 United Nations Security Council, 'Security Council Resolution 2139,' 22 February. New York: United Nations Security Council, 2014.
67 US Department of State, *Voting Practices in the United Nations 2017: Report to Congress Submitted Pursuant to Public Laws 101-246 and 108-447* (Washington, DC: March 2018).
68 Scott Morrison and Donald Trump, 'Remarks by President Trump and Prime Minister Morrison of Australia at Arrival Ceremony' (Speech, South Lawn, White House, Washington, DC, 20 September 2019).
69 Michael Green, Peter Dean, Brendan Taylor, and Zack Cooper, *The ANZUS Alliance in an Ascending Asia*. Centre of Gravity Series No. 23 (Canberra: The Australian National University, July 2015).
70 Mark Latham, 'Labor and the World' (Speech, The Lowy Institute, Sydney, 7 April 2004).

NOTES

71 National Archives of Australia. *Cabinet Submission 170 – Review of ANZUS –Decisions/Der and 634* (Canberra: Commonwealth of Australia, 24–30 1983).
72 Kevin Rudd, 'ANZUS and the 21st Century,' *Australian Journal of International Affairs 55*, no. 2 (June 2001): 301–315.
73 Commonwealth of Australia, *Defence Strategic Review*, Canberra, 2022.
74 Jackman, et al., *Public Opinion in the Age of Trump* (2019).
75 John Kehoe and Laura Tingle, 'US "Stunned" by Port of Darwin Sale to Chinese,' *Australian Financial Review*, 17 November 2015.
76 Greg Miller 'This Was the Worst Call by Far: Trump Badgered, Bragged and Abruptly Ended Phone Call with Australian Leader,' *Washington Post*, 2 February 2017.
77 US Bureau of Economic Analysis. 'U.S. International Trade in Goods and Services: Australia,' updated 1 January 2023.
78 Australian Department of Foreign Affairs and Trade, 'United States Fact Sheet,' updated August 2021.
79 Australian Department of Foreign Affairs and Trade, *Australia's Trade Since Federation* (Canberra: Australian Department of Foreign Affairs and Trade, 2016).
80 US Bureau of Economic Analysis. 'U.S. International Trade in Goods and Services: Australia,' updated 1 January 2023.
81 Ibid.
82 Ibid.
83 Ibid.
84 Australian Bureau of Statistics, *340120DO005 Migration, Australia 2016–2017*, Canberra, October 2018.
85 Austrade, Australian Government, *International Visitors in Australia* (Canberra, Commonwealth of Australia, 2018); Australian Bureau of Statistics, *3401.0 Overseas Arrivals and Departures, Australia*, Canberra, May 2018.
86 Australian Bureau of Statistics, *5368.0.55.004 International Trade: Supplementary Information, Calendar Year, 2017*, Canberra, updated 25 May 2018

5 Background to China

1 John Fitzgerald, *Big White Lie: Chinese Australians in White Australia* (Sydney: University of New South Wales Press, 2007).
2 Graeme Davison, *The Use and Abuse of Australian History* (St Leonards, NSW: Allen & Unwin, 2000).
3 Robert O'Neill, 'Setting a New Paradigm in World Order: The United Nations Action in Korea,' in *In from the Cold: Reflections on Australia's Korean War*, eds. John Blaxland, Michael Kelly and Liam Brewin Higgins (Canberra: Australian National University Press, 2020), 29–48.
4 Ibid.
5 National Museum Australia, Defining Moments Korean War, accessed 20 February 2023. https://www.nma.gov.au/defining-moments/resources/korean-war.
6 Ministry of Patriots and Veterans Affairs Korea, Casualties, accessed 20 February 2023. https://www.mpva.go.kr/english/contents.do?key=987.
7 Robert Manne, *The Petrov Affair* (Melbourne: Text Publishing, 2004); Nick McKenzie, Paul Sakkal and Grace Tobin, 'Defecting Chinese Spy Offers Information Trove to Australian Government,' *The Age*, 25 November 2019.
8 Commonwealth of Australia and People's Republic of China, 'Joint Communique of the Australian Government and the Government of the People's Republic of China Concerning the Establishment of Diplomatic Relations between Australian and China,' News Release, 1 December 1972.
9 Paul Dalgleish, 'Bob Hawke: Guide to Archives of Australia's Prime Ministers' (Canberra: National Archives of Australia, 2021), 21.
10 Xi Jingpin, 'Address by the President of the People's Republic of China' (Speech, Parliament House, Canberra, 17 November 2014).

6 China

1   'China' and 'Beijing' are used throughout as shorthand for the Government of the PRC and they do not refer to the Chinese people.

2   Hugh White, *The China Choice: Why America Should Share Power* (Melbourne: Black Inc., 2012).

3   Allan Gyngell, 'History Hasn't Ended: How to Handle China,' *Australian Foreign Affairs* no. 7 (2019): 5–27; Richard McGregor 'Trade Deficits: How China Could Punish Australia,' *Australian Foreign Affairs* no. 7 (2019): 54–74.

4   White, *The China Choice* (2012); David Brophy, *China Panic: Australia's Alternative to Paranoia and Pandering* (Melbourne: Black Inc., 2021); Clive Hamilton, *Silent Invasion: China's Influence in Australia* (Melbourne: Hardie Grant, 2018).

5   Linda Jakobson and Bates Gill, *China Matters: Getting it Right for Australia* (Melbourne: Black Inc., 2017).

6   Hamilton, *Silent Invasion* (2018); Peter Hartcher, 'Red Flag: Waking Up to China's Challenge,' *Quarterly Essay* 76, (2019).

7   Tourism Research Australia, 'Latest International Visitor Survey (IVS) Results,' 2018.

8   Australian Bureau of Statistics, *Census 2021* (Canberra 2022).

9   Nick Baker, 'Australia "Missing Out" as Students Continue to Shun Learning Chinese,' *SBS News*, 12 March 2019.

10   Consulate General of the PRC in Perth. 'Australia Targets Chinese Journalists, Scholars, Pushes Anti-China Witch-Hunt,' News Release, 10 September 2020; Natasha Kassam and Jennifer Hsu, *Being Chinese in Australia: Public Opinion in Chinese Communities* (Sydney: The Lowy Institute, 2021).

11   Australian Bureau of Statistics. 'International Trade: Supplementary Information, Calendar Year, 2017: Table 7.4 International Trade in Services, Credits, Calendar Year by Country and Travel Service, $M – Education,' updated 25 May 2018.

12   Australian Department of Education and Training, 'Where Do International Students Come From and What Do They Study,' 2019.

13   Australian Department of Education and Training, 'Research Snapshot: China – Outbound and Inbound International Students,' updated August 2016 .

14   Junfang Xi, Weihuan Zhou, and Heng Wang, 'The Impact of the China–Australia Free Trade Agreement on Australia's Education Exports to China: A Legal and Economic Assessment,' *World Economy* 41, no. 12 (2018): 3503–3523.

15   Xi Jingpin, 'Address by the President of the People's Republic of China' (Speech, Parliament House, Canberra, 17 November 2014).

16   Min Hong, 'A Comparative Study of the Internationalization of Higher Education Policy in Australia and China (2008–2015)', *Studies in Higher Education* 45, no. 4 (2020): 768–779.

17   Bradley McConachie, 'Australia's Use of International Education as Public Diplomacy in China: Foreign Policy or Domestic Agenda?', *Australian Journal of International Affairs* 73, no. 2 (2019): 198–211.

18   Christopher Pokarier, 'Cross-Border Higher Education in the Australia–Japan Relationship,' *Australian Journal of International Affairs* 6, no. 4 (December 2006): 552–573.

19   Marina Yue Zhang, 'Students in China Heed Their Government's Warnings Against Studying in Australia,' *The Conversation*, 8 July 2020.

20   Martin Choi and Catherine Wong, 'China-Australia Relations "Will Not Be Helped" by Foreign Influence Register,' *South China Morning Post*, 21 February 2019.

21   Alex Oliver, *Lowy Institute Poll 2018*. The Lowy Institute (20 June 2018), 6–8, 10, 12; Natasha Kassam, *Lowy Institute Poll 2022*. The Lowy Institute (29 June 2022), 6–8, 12–15, 18.

22   Natasha Kassam, *Lowy Institute Poll 2022* (2022), 13.

23   Natasha Kassam, *Lowy Institute Poll 2021*. The Lowy Institute (23 June 2021), 17.

24   Fergus Hanson, *Lowy Institute Poll 2009*. The Lowy Institute (12 October 2009), 8.

25   Natasha Kassam, *Lowy Institute Poll 2021* (2021), 13.

26   Alex Oliver, *Lowy Institute Poll 2018* (2018), 12; Natasha Kassam, *Lowy Institute Poll 2021* (2021), 15.

NOTES

27 Ibid., 12.

28 Fergus Hanson, *Lowy Institute Poll 2009*. The Lowy Institute (12 October 2009), 8.

29 Alex Oliver, *Lowy Institute Poll 2018* (2018), 10, 12.

30 Alex Oliver, *Lowy Institute Poll 2018* (2018), 10, 12; Natasha Kassam, *Lowy Institute Poll 2021* (2021), 15.

31 Natasha Kassam, *Lowy Institute Poll 2021* (2021), 13.

32 Xi Jingpin, 'Full Text of Xi Jinping's Report at 19th CPC National Congress' (Speech, 19th National Congress of the Communist Party of China, 18 October 2017), emphasis added.

33 Shen Yujia, 'Australia Tearing Up Formal Belt and Road Deal has Little Exemplary Effect,' *Global Times*, 22 April 2021.

34 Xi, 'Address by the President of the People's Republic of China' (2014).

35 Michael O'Keefe, 'The Militarisation of China in the Pacific: Stepping Up to a New Cold War?,' *Security Challenges* 16, no. 1 (2020): 94–112.

36 For example, see Australian Department of Foreign Affairs and Trade. 'News, Speeches and Media: Correcting the Record,' 2021.

37 Xi, 'Address by the President of the People's Republic of China' (2014).

38 Malcolm Turnbull, 'Speech at the University of New South Wales, Sydney – 7 August 2018' (Speech, University of New South Wales, Sydney, 7 August 2018).

39 Australian Department of Foreign Affairs and Trade, *Trade and Investment at a Glance 2020* (Canberra: Commonwealth of Australia, 2020), 11.

40 Ibid., 17.

41 Australian Department of Foreign Affairs and Trade, 'China Fact Sheet,' updated August 2021.

42 Department of Foreign Affairs and Trade, *2017 Foreign Policy White Paper* (Canberra: Commonwealth of Australia, 2017), 26.

43 Tommy Chai, 'How China Attempts to Drive a Wedge in the U.S.-Australia Alliance,' *Australian Journal of International Affairs* 74, no. 5 (2020): 511–531.

44 Martin Choi and Catherine Wong, 'China-Australia Relations "Will Not Be Helped" by Foreign Influence Register,' *South China Morning Post*, 21 February 2019.

45 Kirsty Needham, 'Australian Coal in the Firing Line of Chinese 'Environmental' Crackdown,' *The Age*, 20 March 2019.

46 Turnbull, 'Speech at the University of New South Wales, Sydney (2018).

47 Darren Gray, 'Wine, Lobster, Copper . . . What's at Stake in Our Trade Tensions with China,' *The Age*, 6 November 2020.

48 Peter Hartcher, ' "Just Not Going to Happen": US Warns China Over Australian Trade Stoush,' *Sydney Morning Herald*, 16 March 2021.

49 Scott Morrison, 'Press Conference – Newquay Airport, United Kingdom' (Speech, Newquay Airport, United Kingdom, 13 June 2019).

50 Shuji Nakayama, Setsuo Otsuka, and Issaku Harada, 'US–China Tariff Showdown Uproots Global Supply Chains,' *Nikkei Asia*, 24 August 2018.

51 Kirsty Needham, 'Fears the United States Could Displace Australian Coal in China,' *The Age*, 21 March 2019.

52 Australian Department of Foreign Affairs and Trade, *International Investment Australia 2021* (Commonwealth of Australia: Canberra, 2022), 10.

53 *ABC News*. 'National Security Cited as Chinese Oz Minerals Deal Blocked,' *ABC News*, 27 March 2009.

54 Foreign Investment Review Board, *Protecting the National Interest, Guidance 11* (Canberra: Commonwealth of Australia, 2020).

55 Tim Biggs and Jennifer Duke, 'China's Huawei, ZTE Banned From 5G Network,' *Sydney Morning Herald*, 23 August 2018.

56 Angus Grigg, 'Australia's Defence Department Bans Chinese App WeChat,' *Australian Financial Review*, 11 March 2018.

57 Adam Ni, 'Australia a Potential Target in US–China Fight Over Huawei,' *ABC News*, 30 January 2019.

58 Jane Golley and Guo Chunmei, 'Australia–China Bilateral Relations: Mixed Messages,' *Contemporary International Relations* 25 no. 5 (2015): 4.
59 Ibid., 1–27.
60 Natasha Kassam, *Lowy Institute Poll 2021* (2021), 12.
61 Jeffrey D. Wilson, 'Resource Nationalism or Resource Liberalism? Explaining Australia's Approach to Chinese Investment in Its Minerals Sector,' *Australian Journal of International Affairs* 65, no. 3 (2011): 283–304.
62 Foreign Investment Review Board, *Foreign Investment Review Board Annual Report 2017–18* (Canberra: Commonwealth of Australia, 2017), 40.
63 Foreign Investment Review Board, *Foreign Investment Review Board Annual Report 2019–20* (Canberra: Commonwealth of Australia, 2021), 38.
64 Dallas Rogers, Chyi Lin Lee, and Ding Yan, 'The Politics of Foreign Investment in Australian Housing: Chinese Investors, Translocal Sales Agents and Local Resistance,' *Housing Studies* 30, no. 5 (2015): 730–748.
65 Dallas Rogers, *The Geopolitics of Real Estate: Reconfiguring Property, Capital and Rights* (London: Rowman & Littlefield, 2016).
66 Australian Department of Foreign Affairs and Trade, *International Investment Australia 2021* (2022), 10.
67 Dallas Rogers, Alexandra Wong, and Jacqueline Nelson, 'Public Perceptions of Foreign and Chinese Real Estate Investment: Intercultural Relations in Global Sydney,' *Australian Geographer* 48, no. 4 (2017): 437–455.
68 Foreign Investment Review Board, *Foreign Investment Review Board Annual Report 2009–10* (Canberra: Commonwealth of Australia, 2011), 16.
69 Foreign Investment Review Board, *Foreign Investment Review Board Annual Report 2019–20* (2021), 38.
70 Foreign Investment Review Board, *Foreign Investment Review Board Annual Report 2017–18* (2017), 11, 27; Foreign Investment Review Board, *Foreign Investment Review Board Annual Report 2019–20* (2021), 39.
71 Turnbull, 'Speech at the University of New South Wales, Sydney (2018).
72 'PM Meets Dalai Lama in Sydney,' *SBS News*, 24 February 2015.
73 *SBS News*. 'Kadeer Hopes for Democracy and Freedom,' *SBS News*, 24 February 2015.
74 *SBS News*. 'China Arrest Aussie Mining Boss for Spying,' *SBS News*, 24 February 2015.
75 *SBS News*. 'US to Boost Military Activities in Australia,' *SBS News*, 26 February 2015.
76 *The Australian*. 'China Fires Back at Julie Bishop Over "Irresponsible" Remarks,' *The Australian*, 27 November 2013.
77 Tim Biggs and Jennifer Duke, 'China's Huawei, ZTE Banned From 5G Network,' *Sydney Morning Herald*, 23 August 2018.
78 Michael O'Keefe, 'The Militarisation of China in the Pacific (2020): 99.
79 Jonathan Kearsley, Eryk Bagshaw, and Anthony Galloway, '"If You Make China the Enemy China Will Be the Enemy": Beijing's Fresh Threat to Australia,' *Sydney Morning Herald*, 18 November 2020.
80 Jonathan Kearsley and Eryk Bagshaw, "Not Here to Be Bullied': UK Weighs in on China Hitlist,' *The Age*, 26 November 2020.
81 Eryk Bagshaw and Anthony Galloway, '"Horrific Abuses": Uighur Report Reveals First-hand Accounts of Torture,' *The Age*, 3 February 2021.
82 Peter Connelly, 'Chinese Evacuations and Power Projection (Part 2): A Movie Genre Is Born,' *The Strategist*, 14 December 2018.
83 Xiu Lin, 'China Urges Australia to Face up to Severe Human Rights Violations at UN Body,' *Global Times*, 8 July 2020.
84 Eryk Bagshaw, 'China Should be "Totally Ashamed": Scott Morrison Demands China Take Down Post,' *The Age*, 30 November 2020.
85 Australian Department of Foreign Affairs and Trade, *2017 Foreign Policy White Paper* (Canberra, Commonwealth of Australia, 2017), 7, 58, 63, 105.
86 Ibid., 7.

NOTES

331

87 Ibid., 39.

88 Office of the Prime Minister of Australia. 'Quad Leaders' Joint Statement: The Spirit of the Quad,' News Release, 12 March 2021.

89 Australian Department of Defence, *2016 Defence White Paper* (Canberra: Commonwealth of Australia, 2016).

90 State Council of the People's Republic of China, *China's Military Strategy* (Xinghua: State Council of the People's Republic of China, 2015).

91 White House, *National Security Strategy of the United States of America, December 2017* (2017), 25.

92 *China Daily*. 'China Defender of International, Regional Rules: Senior Chinese Military Official,' *China Daily*, 6 June 2017.

93 'China Fires Back at Julie Bishop Over "Irresponsible" Remarks,' *The Australian*, 27 November 2013.

94 Australian Department of Foreign Affairs and Trade, *2017 Foreign Policy White Paper* (2017), 61.

95 'China Fires Back at Julie Bishop Over "Irresponsible" Remarks,' 2013.

96 Andrew Greene, 'Australian Warships Challenged by Chinese Military in South China Sea,' *ABC News*, 20 April 2018.

97 Ibid.

98 Ibid.

99 *The Australian*. 'US Tells Australia to Take on China Over Disputed Islands,' *The Australian*, 24 July 2018.

100 State Council of the People's Republic of China, *China's Military Strategy* (2015).

101 Australian Department of Defence, *2016 Defence White Paper*, 49.

102 Kenneth Allen, Phillip C. Saunders, and John Chen, *Chinese Military Diplomacy 2006–2016: Trends and Implications*, China Strategic Perspectives 11. Center for the Study of Chinese Military Affairs, Institute for National Strategic Studies, National Defense University (Washington DC: National Defense University Press, 2017).

103 Xi Jinping, 'Speech at the All Military Diplomatic Work Conference' (Speech, 29 January 2015).

104 Kenneth Allen, Phillip C. Saunders, and John Chen, *Chinese Military Diplomacy 2006–2016: Trends and Implications*, China Strategic Perspectives 11. Center for the Study of Chinese Military Affairs, Institute for National Strategic Studies, National Defense University (Washington DC: National Defense University Press, 2017), 3.

105 Andrew Greene, 'Second Chinese Spy Ship Approaches Australia to Monitor Military Exercises after Being on Our Radar "for Some Time",' *ABC News*, 18 July 2021.

106 Michael Smith and Andrew Tillett, 'China Payback Kills Dialogue,' *Australian Financial Review*, 6 May 2021.

107 Australian Department of Defence, *2016 Integrated Investment Program* (Canberra: Commonwealth of Australia, 2016).

108 Gavin Fernando, 'Security Experts Claim a Chinese Vessel Tasked with Finding MH370 is Likely Spying On Us,' *News.com.au*, 24 September 2016.

109 *Xinhua*. 'Australia–China Joint Military Exercise Kicks Off in Canberra,' *Xinhua*, 17 September 2019.

110 Australian Department of Foreign Affairs and Trade, *2017 Foreign Policy White Paper* (2017), 37.

111 Australian Department of Defence, *2016 Defence White Paper* (2016), 44.

112 Kenneth Allen, Phillip C. Saunders, and John Chen, *Chinese Military Diplomacy 2006–2016: Trends and Implications*, China Strategic Perspectives 11. Center for the Study of Chinese Military Affairs, Institute for National Strategic Studies, National Defense University (Washington DC: National Defense University Press, 2017), 60.

113 Ben Packham, 'China Meddling "Staggering," Makes Case for Interference Laws,' *The Australian*, 17 November 2021, 6.

114 Senate Standing Committee on Finance and Public Administration, *Parliamentary Inquiry – Inquiry into the Digital Delivery of Government Services – 14 March 2018, Answer Question on Notice, Department of Defence* (Canberra: Commonwealth of Australia, 14 March 2018).

NOTES

115 David Wroe, 'Cyber Attacks Could Help Trigger a War, Says Marise Payne,' *Sydney Morning Herald*, 11 March 2019.

116 Australian Signals Directorate. 'ACSC Detects Malicious Activity Targeting Political Party Networks,' updated 19 February 2019.

117 Clive Hamilton, *Silent Invasion* (2018).

118 David Wroe, 'Cyber Attacks Could Help Trigger a War, Says Marise Payne,' 2019.

119 Tom Phillips, 'Unit 61398 – The Featureless 12-storey Building Which Houses One of the World's Most Dangerous and Secretive Cyber-hacking Operations,' *Sydney Morning Herald*, 20 February 2013.

120 Tara Cosoleto, 'Australia Joins Global Condemnation of "Serious" China Cyber Hacking,' *SBS News*, 21 December 2018.

121 Australian Capital Territory, *Parliamentary Debates, House of Representatives Official Hansard, No. 17, 2017, Thursday, 7 December 2017, Forty-fifth Parliament First Session – Period* (Canberra: Commonwealth of Australia, 2017), 13146.

122 Andrew Greene, 'ASIO Overwhelmed by Foreign Spying Threats Against Australia in Past Year,' *ABC News*, 18 October 2017 (quote); Australian Security Intelligence Organisation, *ASIO Submission to the Parliamentary Joint Committee on Intelligence and Security, Review of Administration and Expenditure No. 16, 2016–2017*, Submission 5 (Canberra: Commonwealth of Australia, 2017), 4.

123 Jade Macmillan, 'Foreign Interference More of an "Existential Threat" to Australia than Terrorism: ASIO Chief,' *ABC News*, 4 September 2019.

124 Lisa Murray, 'United Front Work Department: China's "Magic Weapon" for Winning Friends,' *Australian Financial Review*, 23 May 2019.

125 US Congress, Joint Hearing Before the Subcommittee on Africa, Human Rights and International Operations and the Subcommittee on Oversight and Investigations of the Committee on International Relations, *Congressional Record*, 109th Cong. 62, 1st sess., Serial No. 109-62 (2005) (Testimony of Yonglin Chen, First Secretary and Consul for Political Affairs, Former Chinese Consulate, Sydney, Australia), 3.

126 Michael Jensen, 'We've Been Hacked – So Will the Data be Weaponised to Influence Election 2019? Here's What to Look For,' *The Conversation*, 21 February 2019.

127 Young Mie Kim, Jordan Hsu, David Neiman, Colin Kou, Levi Bankston, Soo Yun Kim, Richard Heinrich, Robyn Baragwanath, and Garvesh Raskutti, 'The Stealth Media? Groups and Targets Behind Divisive Issue Campaigns on Facebook,' *Political Communication* 35, no. 4 (2018): 515–541.

128 Alex Joske, *Picking Flowers, Making Honey: The Chinese Military's Collaboration with Foreign Universities*, Policy Brief Report No. 10/2018, 30 October (Canberra: Australian Strategic Policy Institute and International Cyber Policy Centre, 2018).

129 White House, *National Security Strategy of the United States of America, December 2017* (2017), 25.

130 Stephen Dziedzic and Andrew Greene, 'China's Soft Power: Julie Bishop Steps Up Warning to University Students on Communist Party Rhetoric,' *ABC News*, 16 October 2017; Nick McKenzie, Richard Baker, Sashka Koloff, and Chris Uhlmann, 'The Chinese Communist Party's Power and Influence in Australia,' *ABC News*, 4 June 2017.

131 Emma Reynolds, 'Tensions Rise as Chinese Government's Influence Infiltrates Aussie Universities,' *News.com.au*, 1 September 2017.

132 Fergus Hunter, 'China Funded Confucius Institutes Targeted Under New Foreign Influence Scheme,' *The Age*, 12 March 2019.

133 Latika Bourke, 'ANU Academic Slammed Over Citation of "Sub-Par" Chinese Genocide Research,' *The Age*, 27 April 2021.

134 James Leibold, 'Surveillance in China's Xinjiang Region: Ethnic Sorting Coercion and Inducement,' *Journal of Contemporary China* 29, no. 1 (2020): 46–60.

135 White, *The China Choice: Why America Should Share Power* (2012); David Brophy, *China Panic: Australia's Alternative to Paranoia and Pandering* (Melbourne: Black Inc., 2021); Clive Hamilton, *Silent Invasion* (2018).

136 Stephen Dziedzic and Andrew Greene, 'China's Soft Power,' 2017.

NOTES

137 Claire Bickers, 'Chinese Ambassador to Australia Cheng Jingye Slams 'Groundless' Foreign Influence Allegations,' *News.com.au*, 15 June 2017.

138 Chen Hong, 'Australia Smearing China with Spying Brush,' *Global Times*, 2 November 2019.

139 Eliza Borello, 'Andrew Robb Blames Former Coalition Leaders for 'Toxic' Relationship with China,' *ABC News*, 12 March 2019.

140 Linda Jakobson and Bates Gill, *China Matters: Getting it Right for Australia* (Melbourne: Black Inc., 2017).

141 Tom Sear, Michael Jensen, and Titus C. Chen, 'How Digital Media Blur the Border Between Australia and China,' *The Conversation*, 16 November 2018.

142 Wanning Sun, 'Chinese Social Media Platform WeChat Could be a Key Battleground in the Federal Election,' *The Conversation*, 28 March 2019.

143 Primrose Riordan, 'China's Veiled Threat to Bill Shorten on Extradition Treaty,' *The Australian*, 4 December 2017, 4.

144 Louise Yaxley, 'Malcolm Turnbull Questions Sam Dastyari's Loyalty Amid Claims He Passed Security Information to Chinese Donor,' *ABC News*, 29 November 2017.

145 Chris Uhlmann and Andrew Greene, 'Chinese Donors to Australian Political Parties: Who Gave How Much?,' *ABC News*, 8 June 2017.

146 Australian Capital Territory, *Parliamentary Debates, House of Representatives Official Hansard, No. 17, 2017, Thursday, 7 December 2017, Forty-fifth Parliament First Session – Period* (Canberra: Commonwealth of Australia, 2017), 13147.

147 *Committee Hansard* (Melbourne, 16 March 2018), 34.

148 Commonwealth of Australia, *Parliamentary Debates, House of Representatives Federation Chamber Bills, Appropriation (Parliamentary Departments) Bill (No. 1) 2018–2019*, Second Reading, Speech, Tuesday 22 May 2018, 4259 (Andrew Hastie, MP).

149 Australian Attorney General's Department, 'Foreign Influence Transparency Scheme,' 2021.

150 Kelsey Munro, 'Australia's New Foreign-Influence Laws – Who Is Targeted?,' *The Interpreter*, 5 December 2018.

151 Andrew Greene, 'Chinese Government Intrusion into Western Universities Sparks Push for Collective Action,' *ABC News*, 15 October 2017.

152 Mikael Wigell, 'Hybrid Interference as a Wedge Strategy: A Theory of External Interference in Liberal Democracy,' *International Affairs 95*, no. 2 (2019): 255–275.

153 Cau Fandi, '"Five Eyes" Could be Poked Blind if China's Security and Sovereignty Harmed, Warns Chinese FM Spokesperson,' *Global Times*, 19 November 2020.

154 Larry Diamond and Orville Schell, *China's Influence & American Interests: Promoting Constructive Vigilance* (Stanford, CA: Hoover Institution, 2018), 149.

155 Concerned Scholars of China. *An Open Letter from Concerned Scholars of China and the Chinese Diaspora: Australia's Debate on 'Chinese Influence'* Canberra, Asia and the Pacific Policy Society, 26 March 2018.

156 Mikael Wigell, 'Hybrid Interference as a Wedge Strategy: A Theory of External Interference in Liberal Democracy,' *International Affairs 95*, no. 2 (2019): 255–275.

157 Xi Jingpin, 'Address by the President of the People's Republic of China' (2014).

158 Ibid.

7 Background to Japan

1 See, for instance, Allan Patience, *Australian Foreign Policy in Asia: Middle Power or Awkward Partner?* (London: Palgrave Macmillan, 2018), 137–181.

2 Yusuke Ishihara, 'Australia: The Challenges of the Japan-Australia Quasi-Alliance,' *East Asian Strategic Review 2016*, National Institute of Defense Studies.

3 Government of Japan. 'The Constitution of Japan,' signed on 3 November 1946, entered into force 3 May 1947. Tokyo, 1947.

4 Gwenda Tavan, *The Long, Slow Death of the White Australia Policy* (Melbourne: Scribe, 2005).

334 NOTES

5   Patience, *Australian Foreign Policy in Asia: Middle Power or Awkward Partner?* (2018), 137–181.
6   Mark Beeson and Hidetaka Yoshimatsu, 'Asia's Odd Men Out: Australia, Japan, and the Politics of Regionalism,' *International Relations of the Asia-Pacific* 7, no. 2 (May 2007): 227–250.
7   Henry Frei, *Japan's Southward Advance and Australia: From the Sixteenth Century to World War Two* (Melbourne: Melbourne University Publishing, 1991).
8   Thomas Ewing (1908), 'Speech by the Honorable TT Ewing, MP Minister of State for Defence' (Speech to the Parliament of the Commonwealth of Australia, Parliament House, Canberra, 29 September 1908).
9   T.B. Millar, *Australia in Peace and War: External Relations 1788–1977* (Canberra: Australian National University Press 1978).
10 David Stevens, 'The Great White Fleet's Visit to Australia,' Sea Power Centre, Royal Australian Navy.
11 Neville Meaney, 'Australia and Japan: The Historical Perspective,' in *The Japanese Connection: A Survey of Australian Leaders' Towards Japan and the Australia–Japan Relationship*, eds. Neville Meaney, Trevor Matthews and Sol Encel (Melbourne: Longman, 1988).
12 Alessio Patalano, ed., *Maritime Strategy and National Security in Japan and Britain: From the First Alliance to Post-9/11* (Leiden: Brill 2012).
13 Patience, *Australian Foreign Policy in Asia: Middle Power or Awkward Partner?* (2018), 147.
14 Naoko Shimazu, *Japan, Race and Equality: The Racial Equality Proposal of 1919* (London: Routledge, 1998), 125.
15 Pam Oliver, 'Allies, Enemies and Trading Partners: Records on Australia and the Japanese, Research Guide' (Canberra: National Archives of Australia, 2004).
16 Kosmas Tsokhas, '"Trouble Must Follow": Australia's Ban on Iron Ore Exports to Japan in 1938,' *Modern Asian Studies* 29, no. 4 (1995): 871–892.
17 Lionel Wigmore, *Australia in the War of 1939–45, Vol. IV: The Japanese Thrust* (Canberra: Australian War Memorial, 1957), 674.
18 Lionel Wigmore, *Australia in the War of 1939–45, Vol. IV:* (1957).
19 Patience, *Australian Foreign Policy in Asia: Middle Power or Awkward Partner?* (2018), 157–159.
20 Australian War Memorial. 'Australia Under Attack: Australia Bombed, Strafed and Shelled,' updated 27 November 2019.
21 Alan Rix, *Coming to Terms: The Politics of Trade with Japan 1945–57* (Sydney: Allen & Unwin, 1986), 180.
22 Patience, *Australian Foreign Policy in Asia: Middle Power or Awkward Partner?* (2018), 161.

8 Japan

1   Australian Department of Foreign Affairs and Trade, *Australia–Japan Strategy for Cooperation in the Pacific* (Canberra: Australian Department of Foreign Affairs and Trade, 2016).
2   Australian Department of Foreign Affairs and Trade, *2017 Foreign Policy White Paper* (Canberra: Commonwealth of Australia, 2017), 40–41.
3   Japanese Ministry of Foreign Affairs, *Diplomatic Bluebook 2020* (Tokyo: Japanese Ministry of Foreign Affairs, 2019), Chapter 2, 6 (1).
4   *Japan Times*. 'Japan, Australia Vow to Step Up Security Times Under Abe's Successor,' *Japan Times*, 8 September 2020.
5   Stephen Dziedzic, 'Australia and Japan Agree "in Principle" to Historic Defence Pact,' *ABC News*, 18 November 2020.
6   Mai Sato and Simone Abel, 'Japan-Australia Pact Highlights Need to Move Away Creatively from Death Penalty,' *The Conversation*, 20 November 2020.
7   Japanese Ministry of Foreign Affairs, *Diplomatic Bluebook 2020* (2019), Chapter 2, 6 (1).
8   Australian Department of Foreign Affairs and Trade, *Australia–Japan Strategy for Cooperation in the Pacific* (2016).
9   Shinzō Abe, 'The Bounty of the Open Seas: Five New Principles for Japanese Diplomacy' (Speech, 18 January 2013).

NOTES

10 William C. Middlebrooks, Jr., *Beyond Pacifism: Why Japan Must Become a 'Normal' Nation* (Westport, CT: Praeger, 2013).

11 Daisuke Akimoto, 'An Analysis of the ICNND: The Japan-Australia Collaboration for Nuclear Abolition,' *Asian Journal of Peacebuilding* 2, no. 1 (May 2014): 97–110.

12 Tomohiko Satake, 'The Japan-Australia Contribution to a Liberal and Inclusive Regional Order: Beyond the "China Gap",' *Australian Journal of International Affairs* 70, no. 1 (2015): 24–36.

13 Australian Department of Defence, *2016 Defence White Paper* (Canberra: Commonwealth of Australia, 2016); Japanese Ministry of Foreign Affairs, *Diplomatic Bluebook 2020* (2019), Chapter 2, 6 (1).

14 Nissim Otmazgin, 'Geopolitics and Soft Power: Japan's Cultural Policy and Cultural Diplomacy in Asia,' *Asia-Pacific Review* 19, no. 1 (2012): 37–61.

15 Kaoru Kurusu and Rikki Kersten, 'Japan as an Active Agent for Global Norms: The Political Dynamism Behind the Acceptance and Promotion of "Human Security",' *Asia-Pacific Review* 18, no. 2 (December 2011): 115–137.

16 Gary Woodard, Moreen Dee, and Max Suich, *Negotiating the Australia–Japan Basic Treaty of Friendship and Cooperation: Reflections and Afterthoughts*, Asia Pacific Economic Papers, no. 362 (Canberra: Crawford School of Public Policy, Australian National University, 2007).

17 Tourism Australia, 'International Market Performance Statistics.'

18 Tourism Research Australia, 'Latest International Visitor Survey (IVS) Results,' 2018.

19 Australian Bureau of Statistics, 'International Trade: Supplementary Information, Calendar Year, 2018: Table 7.4 International Trade in Services, Credits, Calendar Year by Country and Travel Service, $M – Education,' released 24 May 2019.

20 Christopher Pokarier, 'Cross-Border Higher Education in the Australia–Japan Relationship,' *Australian Journal of International Affairs* 6, no. 4 (December 2006): 552–573.

21 Ian McArthur, 'Media Portrayal of the Cultural Relationship between Australia and Japan,' *Australian Journal of International Affairs* 60, no. 4 (2006): 574–589.

22 Natasha Kassam, *Lowy Institute Poll 2022*. The Lowy Institute (29 June 2022), 8.

23 Ibid., 7.

24 Alex Oliver, *Lowy Institute Poll 2013*. The Lowy Institute (24 June 2013).

25 Natasha Kassam, *Lowy Institute Poll 2022* (2022), 4.

26 Marguerite Tarzia and Bill McCormick, 'International Whaling,' Parliament of Australia, 2010.

27 'Australian Attorney General's Department, 'Whaling in the Antarctic Litigation,' 31 March 2014.

28 Katharine Murphy, 'Greg Hunt and Julie Bishop at Odds over Whaling Monitoring,' *The Guardian*, 18 October 2013.

29 Simon Denyer and Akiki Kashiwagi, 'Japan to Leave International Whaling Commission, Resume Commercial Hunting,' *The Washington Post*, 26 December 2018.

30 'Australia "Extremely Disappointed" by Japan's Withdrawal from International Whaling Commission,' *Japan Times*, 26 December 2018.

31 Nicole Hasham, 'The Shocking Japanese Whaling Footage the Australian Government Wanted to Hide,' *Sydney Morning Herald*, 28 November 2017.

32 Michael Heazle, '"See You in Court!": Whaling as a Two Level Game in Australian Politics and Foreign Policy,' *Marine Policy* 38 (March 2013): 330–336.

33 Charlotte Epstein and Kate Barclay, 'Shaming to "Green": Australia–Japan Relations and Whales and Tuna Compared,' *International Relations of the Asia-Pacific* 13, no. 1 (January 2013): 95–123.

34 'CTBT Ministerial Meetings,' Comprehensive Nuclear-Test-Ban Treaty Organization, 2014.

35 Australian Department of Foreign Affairs and Trade, 'Nuclear Issues: Towards a Nuclear Weapons Free World.'

36 Prime Minister of Japan and His Cabinet, *National Security Strategy, December 17, 2013* (Tokyo, 2013).

37 Donna Weeks, 'An East Asian Security Community: Japan, Australia and Resources as "Security",' *Australian Journal of International Affairs* 65, no. 1 (January 2011): 61–80.

38 Y.-K. Heng, 'Beyond "Kawaii" Pop Culture: Japan's Normative Soft Power as Global Trouble-Shooter,' *The Pacific Review* 27, no. 2 (2014): 169–192.

NOTES

39 Andre Asplund, 'Normative Power Japan: Settling for "Chinese Democracy",' *Contemporary Japan* 30, no. 1 (2018): 117–134.

40 David Walton, 'The Role of Prime Ministers in Australia–Japan Relations: Howard and Rudd', *The Round Table* 99, no. 409 (August 2010): 429–437.

41 Peter Drysdale, 'Did the NARA Treaty Make a Difference?,' *Australian Journal of International Affairs* 60, no. 4 (December 2006): 490–505.

42 Australian Department of Foreign Affairs and Trade, *2017 Foreign Policy White Paper* (2017), 59.

43 Centre for International Economics, *Economic Benefits of Australia's North Asian FTAs* (Canberra: Centre for International Economics, 2015), 27.

44 Australian Department of Defence, *2016 Defence White Paper* (2016); Japanese Ministry of Foreign Affairs, *Diplomatic Bluebook 2020* (2019), Chapter 2, 6 (1).

45 Hidetaka Yoshimatsu and Patrick Ziltener, 'Japan's FTA Strategy Toward Highly Developed Countries: Comparing Australia's and Switzerland's Experiences, 2000–09,' *Asian Survey* 50, no. 6 (2010): 1058–1081.

46 Australian Trade and Investment Commission, *Japanese Investment in Australia: A Trusted Partnership* (Canberra: Australian Trade and Investment Commission, 2017.

47 'Japan Fact Sheet,' Australian Department of Foreign Affairs and Trade, February 2021, https://www.dfat.gov.au/sites/default/files/japn-cef.pdf.

48 Australian Trade and Investment Commission, *Japanese Investment in Australia: A Trusted Partnership* (2017).

49 Australian Department of Foreign Affairs and Trade, 'Japan Fact Sheet,' February 2021.

50 Ibid.

51 Ibid.

52 Scott Morrison, 'Regional Trade Deal to Boost Export Opportunities for Aussie Farmers and Businesses,' Press Release, 15 November 2020.

53 Michael Green, *Line of Advantage: Japan's Grand Strategy in the Era of Shinzo Abe* (New York: Columbia University Press, 2022).

54 Australian Department of Foreign Affairs and Trade, *2017 Foreign Policy White Paper* (2017), 41, https://www.dfat.gov.au/sites/default/files/minisite/static/4ca0813c-585e-4fe1-86eb-de665e65001a/fpwhitepaper/pdf/2017-foreign-policy-white-paper.pdf.

55 Ibid., 41.

56 Rikki Kersten, 'Australia and Japan: Mobilising the Bilateral Relationship,' in *Middle Power Dreaming: Australia in World Affairs 2006–2010*, eds. James Cotton and John Ravenhill (Melbourne: Oxford University Press, 2012), 94–110.

57 Michael Green, *Line of Advantage* (2022).

58 Tomohiko Satake and John Hemmings, 'Japan–Australia Security Cooperation in the Bilateral and Multilateral Contexts,' *International Affairs* 94, no. 4 (2018): 816.

59 Alexis Dudden, 'Two Strategic Cultures, Two Japans,' in *Strategic Asia 2016–17: Understanding Strategic Cultures in the Asia Pacific*, eds. Ashley J. Tellis, Alison Szalwinski, and Michael Wills (Washington, DC: National Bureau of Asian Research, 2016), 91–112; Takuya Matsuda, 'Explaining Japan's Post-Cold War Security Policy Trajectory: Maritime Realism,' *Australian Journal of International Affairs* 74, no. 6 (2020): 687–703.

60 Tomohiko Satake and John Hemmings, 'Japan–Australia Security Cooperation in the Bilateral and Multilateral Contexts,' (2018): 821–822.

61 Alexis Dudden, 'Two Strategic Cultures, Two Japans,' in *Strategic Asia 2016–17* (2016), 91–112.

62 *Japan Times*. 'Abe's Failed Submarine Bid,' *Japan Times*, 23 June 2016.

63 Emily Smith, 'Shinzō Abe Arrives in Darwin for First Visit By Japanese Leader,' *ABC News*, 16 November 2018.

64 Matthew Knott, 'Australia in Push to Boost Ties with Japan', *The Age*, 10 December 2022, 9.

65 Government of Japan, 'The Constitution of Japan,' Signed on 3 November 1946, entered into force 3 May 1947. Tokyo, 1947.

66 Alexis Dudden, 'Two Strategic Cultures, Two Japans,' in *Strategic Asia 2016–17* (2016), 91–112.

67 *Sydney Morning Herald*, 'Labor Tested by Japan's Iraq Resolve,' *Sydney Morning Herald*, 1 March 2005.

NOTES

68 Malcolm Turnbull and Shinzo Abe. 'Joint Statement – Next Steps of the Special Strategic Partnership: Asia, Pacific and Beyond,' News Release, 18 December 2015.

69 Australian Department of Foreign Affairs and Trade, *2017 Foreign Policy White Paper* (2017), 41.

70 Australian Department of Defence, *2016 Defence White Paper* (2016), 61.

71 Australian Department of Foreign Affairs and Trade, *2017 Foreign Policy White Paper* (2017), 42.

72 US Department of Defense, 'Transcript: Remarks by Secretary Mattis at Plenary Session of the 2018 Shangri-La Dialogue,' updated 2 June 2018.

73 US Congress, 'Asia Reassurance Initiative Act of 2018.' Public Law No. 115–409, 31 December 2018.

74 Australian Department of Foreign Affairs and Trade, *2017 Foreign Policy White Paper* (2017), 37–48.

75 Tomohiko Satake and John Hemmings, 'Japan–Australia Security Cooperation in the Bilateral and Multilateral Contexts,' (2018): 823.

76 Trent Scott and Andrew Shearer, *Building Allied Interoperability in the Indo-Pacific Region: Discussion Paper 1, Command and Control* (Washington, DC: Center for Strategic and International Studies, 2017).

77 Australian Department of Foreign Affairs and Trade, *2017 Foreign Policy White Paper* (2017), 40; Australian Department of Defence, *2016 Defence White Paper* (2016), 63.

78 Turnbull and Abe. 'Joint Statement,' 2015.

79 Scott and Shearer, *Building Allied Interoperability in the Indo-Pacific Region* (2017).

80 Thomas Wilkins, 'From Strategic Partnership to Strategic Alliance? Australia–Japan Security Ties and the Asia Pacific,' *Asia Policy* no. 20 (July 2015): 81–112.

81 Robert Ayson, 'Australia–Japan: Abbott Uses the "A" Word,' *The Interpreter*, 3 December 2018.

82 Michael Green, *Japan's Reluctant Realism: Foreign Policy Challenges in an Era of Uncertain Power* (London: Macmillan, 2003).

83 Richard Nixon, 'Informal Remarks in Guam with Newsmen, July 25, 1969,' in *Richard Nixon 1969: Containing the Public Messages, Speeches, and Statements of the President,* The Public Papers of the Presidents of the United States. Washington, DC: US Government Printing Office, 1971, 544–549.

84 Peter Layton, 'America's New Alliance Management,' *Australian Outlook*, 8 March 2017.

85 Australian Department of Defence, *Australian Defence* (Canberra: Commonwealth of Australia, 1976).

86 Michael Green, *Line of Advantage* (2022).

87 Thomas Ewing, 'Speech by the Honorable T.T. Ewing, MP Minister of State for Defence (Speech, House of Representatives, Parliament of the Commonwealth of Australia, Canberra, 29 September 1908).

88 Kautilya, *The Arthashastra* (Delhi: Penguin Classics, 2000).

89 Malcolm Turnbull and Shinzo Abe. 'Joint Statement,' 2015.

9 Background to Indonesia

1 Gary Brown, Frank Frost and Steven Sherlock, 'The Australian-Indonesian Security Agreement – Issues and Implications,' Research Paper No. 25, 1995–96 (18 December 1995).

2 Joint Standing Committee on Foreign Affairs, Defence and Trade, Foreign Affairs Sub-Committee, *Near Neighbours – Good Neighbours: An Inquiry into Australia's Relationship with Indonesia* (Canberra: Commonwealth of Australia, 31 May 2004), 1; Tim Lindsey and Dave McRae, eds., *Strangers Next Door? Indonesia and Australia in the Asian Century* (Sydney: Bloomsbury, 2018).

3 Michael O'Keefe, 'Australia and Indonesia: The Persistence of Distance Between Proximate Neighbours,' in *Australia on the World Stage: History, Politics, and International Relations*, eds. Bridget Brooklyn, Benjamin Jones and Rebecca Strating (London: Routledge, 2022), 157–170.

4 Alison Broinowski, *The Yellow Lady: Australian Impressions of Asia* (Melbourne: Oxford University Press, 1992).

5 Yohanes Sulaiman, 'What Threat? Leadership, Strategic Culture, and Indonesian Foreign Policy in the South China Sea,' *Asian Politics and Policy* 11, no. 4 (October 2019): 606–622; Emirza

Adi Syailendra, 'A *Nonbalancing* Act: Explaining Indonesia's Failure to Balance Against the Chinese Threat,' *Asian Security* 13, no. 3 (September 2017): 237–255.

6 H. Soesastro and T. McDonald, eds., *Indonesia-Australia Relations: Diverse Cultures, Converging Interests* (Jakarta: Centre for Strategic and International Studies, 1995); Joint Standing Committee on Foreign Affairs, Defence and Trade, Foreign Affairs Sub-Committee, *Near Neighbours – Good Neighbours* (2004), 1; Kyle Springer, 'Australia Tries to Unlock the Benefits of Proximity with Indonesia,' *The Conversation*, 3 October 2017.

7 Joko Widodo, *Address by the President of the Republic of Indonesia* (Speech, Parliament House, Canberra, Australian Capital Territory, 10 February 2020).

8 Michael O'Keefe, 'Australia and Indonesia: The Persistence of Distance between Proximate Neighbours,' in *Australia on the World Stage: History, Politics, and International Relations*, eds. Bridget Brooklyn, Benjamin Jones, and Rebecca Strating (London: Routledge, 2022), 157–170.

9 Evi Fitriani, 'President Joko Widodo's Foreign Policy: Implications for Indonesia-Australia Relations,' in *Strangers Next Door? Indonesia and Australia in the Asian Century*, eds. Tim Lindsey and Dave McRae (Sydney: Bloomsbury, 2018), 31–54.

10 S. Wiryono, 'An Indonesian View: Indonesia, Australia and the Region,' in *Different Societies, Shared Futures: Australia, Indonesia and the Region*, ed. John Monfries (Singapore: Institute of Southeast Asian Studies, 2006), 16.

11 *Antara News*. 'US Mily [*sic*] Presence in Darwin Arouses Suspicion in Many Quarters,' *Antara News*, 23 November 2011.

12 Greta Nabbs-Keller, 'Understanding Australia–Indonesia Relations in the Post-authoritarian Era: Resilience and Respect,' *Australian Journal of International Affairs* 74, no. 5 (2020): 532–556.

13 Australian Department of Defence, *The Strategic Basis of Australian Defence Policy* (Canberra: Department of Defence, 1971), para 160.

14 Simon Philpott, 'Fear of the Dark: Indonesia and the Australian National Imagination,' *Australian Journal of International Affairs* 55, no. 3 (2001): 371–388.

15 Price Waterhouse Coopers, *The Long View: How Will the Global Economic Order Change by by 2050?* (February 2017).

16 Michael McKenzie, *Common Enemies: Crime, Policy and Politics in Australian-Indonesia Relations* (Oxford: Oxford University Press, 2018), 24–53.

17 Andrew Phillips and Eric Hiariej, 'Beyond the "Bandung Divide"? Assessing the Scope and Limits of Australia–Indonesia Security Cooperation,' *Australian Journal of International Affairs* 70, no. 4 (2016): 422–440.

18 Prime Minister's Office, 'Media Statement: Joint Statement between the Government of the Republic of Indonesia and the Government of Australia,' News Release, 10 February 2020.

19 Michael O'Keefe, 'Australia and Indonesia: The Persistence of Distance between Proximate Neighbours', in *Australia on the World Stage : History, Politics, and International Relations*. Routledge, eds. Bridget Brooklyn, Benjamin Jones, and Rebecca Strating (London: Routledge, 2022), 156–70.

20 Maryanne Kelton and David Willis, 'US–Australia–Indonesia Trilateral Security? Conditions for Cooperation,' *Australian Journal of International Affairs* 73, no. 3 (2019): 289–311; J.D.B. Millar, 'The Conditions for Cooperation,' in *India, Japan, Australia: Partners in Asia*, ed. J.D.B. Millar (Canberra: Australian National University Press, 1968), 195–209.

21 Peter Grose, *1942: The Year the War Came to Australia*, (St Leonards: Allen & Unwin, 2021).

22 J. Girling, 'Vietnam and the Domino Theory,' *Australian Outlook* 21, no. 1 (1967): 61–70.

23 Richard Tanter, 'Witness Denied: Australian Media Responses to the Indonesian Killings of 1965–66,' *Inside Indonesia* 71 (July–September 2002).

24 Peter Dennis and Jeffrey Grey, *Emergency & Confrontation: Australian Military Operations in Malaya and Borneo 1950–1966* (Sydney: Allen & Unwin in association with the Australian War Memorial, 1996).

25 Richard Woolcott, 'Australia–Indonesia Bilateral Relations,' in *Indonesia-Australia Relations: Diverse Cultures, Converging Interests*, eds. H. Soesastro and T. McDonald (Jakarta: Centre for Strategic and International Studies, 1995), 27–34.

26 Human Rights Watch, 'East Timor: The November 12 Massacre and Its Aftermath,' *Asia Watch* 3, no. 26 (12 December 1991).

NOTES

27 Ibid.
28 Des Ball, 'Indonesia and Australia: Strange Neighbours or Partners in Regional Resilience?,' in *Indonesia-Australia Relations: Diverse Cultures, Converging Interests*, eds. H. Soesastro and T. McDonald (Jakarta: Centre for Strategic and International Studies, 1995), 95–131.
29 Ken Setiawan, 'On the Periphery: Human Rights, Australia and Indonesia,' in *Strangers Next Door? Indonesia and Australia in the Asian Century*, eds. Tim Lindsey and Dave McRae (Sydney: Bloomsbury, 2018), 193–210.
30 Paul Keating, *Engagement: Australia Faces the Asia-Pacific* (Sydney: Macmillan, 2000), 129.
31 Australian Capital Territory, *Parliamentary Debates*, House of Representatives Ministerial Statements: East Timor, 23 June 2008, 5583–5584 (Gareth Evans, MP, 1991, quoted by Robert Charles, MP).
32 John Birmingham, 'Appeasing Jakarta: Australia's Complicity in the East Timor Tragedy,' *Quarterly Essay* QE2 (June 2001).
33 Dewi Fortuna Anwar, 'Indonesia's Foreign Policy after the Cold War,' *Southeast Asian Affairs* 1994 (1994): 146–163.
34 Alan Dupont, 'The Australia–Indonesia Security Agreement,' *Australian Quarterly* 68, no. 2 (1996): 49–62.
35 Yohanes Sulaiman, 'Indonesia's Strategic Culture: The Legacy of Independence,' in *Strategic Asia 2016–17: Understanding Strategic Cultures in the Asia-Pacific*, eds. Ashley J. Tellis, Alison Szalwinski and Michael Wills (Washington, DC: National Bureau of Asian Research, 2016), 169–193.
36 Joint Standing Committee on Foreign Affairs, Defence and Trade, Foreign Affairs Sub-Committee, *Near Neighbours – Good Neighbours* (2004), 13–14.
37 Clinton Fernandes, *Reluctant Savior: Australia, Indonesia and the Independence of Timor* (Melbourne: Scribe, 2004).
38 Yohanes Sulaiman, 'Indonesia's Strategic Culture (2016), 169–193.
39 Elisabeth Taylor, Peter Charles Taylor, Saul Karnovsky, Anne Aly and Nell Taylor '"Beyond Bali": A Transformative Education Approach for Developing Community Resilience to Violent Extremism,' *Asia Pacific Journal of Education* 37, no. 2 (2017): 193–204.
40 Australian Department of Defence, *The Strategic Basis of Australian Defence Policy* (1971), para 160.
41 Michael O'Keefe, 'Australia and Indonesia,' (2022).
42 Joint Standing Committee on Foreign Affairs, Defence and Trade, Human Rights Sub-Committee, *Australia's Response to the Indian Ocean Tsunami* (Canberra: Commonwealth of Australia, 2006).
43 Joint Standing Committee on Foreign Affairs, Defence and Trade, Foreign Affairs Sub-Committee, *Near Neighbours – Good Neighbours* (2004), 13–14, https://www.aph.gov.au/Parliamentary_Business/Committees/House_of_representatives_Committees?url=jfadt/indonesia/report.htm#fullreport.
44 Joint Standing Committee on Foreign Affairs, Defence and Trade, Foreign Affairs Sub-Committee, *Near Neighbours – Good Neighbours* (2004), 3.
45 Ibid., viii.

10 Indonesia

1 Joint Standing Committee on Foreign Affairs, Defence and Trade, Foreign Affairs Sub-Committee, *Near Neighbours – Good Neighbours: An Inquiry into Australia's Relationship with Indonesia* (Canberra: Commonwealth of Australia, 31 May 2004), 35.
2 Australian Department of Foreign Affairs and Trade. 'Joint Declaration on a Comprehensive Strategic Partnership between Australia and the Republic of Indonesia,' updated 31 August 2016.
3 Joint Standing Committee on Foreign Affairs, Defence and Trade, Foreign Affairs Sub-Committee, *Near Neighbours – Good Neighbours* (2004), 1.
4 Australian Department of Defence, *2016 Defence White Paper* (Canberra: Commonwealth of Australia, 2016); Evan Laksmana, 'Indonesia in Australia's 2016 Defence White Paper,' *Security Challenges* 12, no. 1 (2016): 165–170.
5 Evan Laksmana, *Reinforcing Indonesia-Australia Defence Relations: The Case for Maritime Recalibration*. The Lowy Institute (2 October 2018).

6 Hugh White, 'The Lombok Treaty: Devil in the Detail,' *The Interpreter*, 7 March 2008.

7 Australian Department of Foreign Affairs and Trade, 'Agreement between Australia and the Republic of Indonesia on the Framework for Security Cooperation,' in *Australia Treaty Series 2008, ATS 3*, signed 13 November 2006, entered into force 7 February 2008 (Canberra: Department of Foreign Affairs and Trade, 2014).

8 Prashanth Parmeswaran, 'Old Shadows in New Australia–Indonesia Military Spat,' *The Diplomat*, 6 January 2017.

9 Linda Reynolds, 'ASPI-FPCI 1.5 Track Dialogue 2019' (Speech, Canberra, 23 July 2019.

10 Australian Department of Foreign Affairs and Trade, *Plan of Action for the Implementation of the Joint Declaration on Maritime Cooperation between the Government of Australia and the Government of the Republic of Indonesia* (Canberra: Commonwealth of Australia, 2017), 4.

11 Guy Wilson, *Defence Diplomacy: The Right Ballast for Australia's Troubled Relations with Indonesia*, Indo-Pacific Strategic Papers (Canberra: Centre for Defence and Strategic Studies, Australian Defence College, 2017), 9–38.

12 Harold Crouch, *The Army and Politics in Indonesia* (Ithaca, NY: Cornell University Press, 1988).

13 Evan Laksmana, *Reinforcing Indonesia-Australia Defence Relations* (2018), 2.

14 Joint Standing Committee on Foreign Affairs, Defence and Trade, Foreign Affairs Sub-Committee, *Near Neighbours – Good Neighbours* (2004), 38.

15 Gareth Evans and Bruce Grant, *Australia's Foreign Relations in the World of the 1990s* (Melbourne: Melbourne University Publishing, 1991).

16 Agnieszka Sobocinska, 'Measuring or Creating Attitudes? Seventy Years of Australian Public Opinion Polling about Indonesia,' *Asian Studies Review* 41, no. 3 (2017): 371–388.

17 Newspoll, *Australian Attitudes Towards Indonesia: Report* (Canberra: Newspoll, 2013); Australian Gallup Polls in Agnieszka Sobocinska, 'Measuring or Creating Attitudes? (2017): 371–388.

18 Joint Standing Committee on Foreign Affairs, Defence and Trade, Foreign Affairs Sub-Committee, *Near Neighbours – Good Neighbours* (2004), 7.

19 Rob Goodfellow, 'Ignorant and Hostile: Australian Perceptions of Indonesia,' *Inside Indonesia* (September 1993): 4–6.

20 Alex Oliver, *Lowy Institute Poll 2018*. The Lowy Institute (20 June 2018); Fergus Hanson, *Lowy Institute Poll 2009*. The Lowy Institute (12 October 2009); Natasha Kassam, *Lowy Institute Poll 2022*. The Lowy Institute (29 June 2022).

21 Fergus Hanson, *Lowy Institute Poll 2009*. The Lowy Institute (12 October 2009); Natasha Kassam, *Lowy Institute Poll 2022* (2022).

22 Ibid.

23 Newspoll, *Australian Attitudes Towards Indonesia: Report* (Canberra: Newspoll, 2013); Natasha Kassam, *Lowy Institute Poll 2022* (2022).

24 Greg Fealy, 'Islam in Australia–Indonesia Relations: Fear, Stereotypes and Opportunity,' in *Strangers Next Door? Indonesia and Australia in the Asian Century*, eds. Tim Lindsey and Dave McRae (Sydney: Bloomsbury, 2018), 149–168.

25 Hugh White, 'The Jakarta Switch: Why Australia Needs to Pin its Hopes (Not Fears) on a Great and Powerful Indonesia,' *Australian Foreign Affairs*, July 2018, 15–46.

26 Alex Oliver, *Lowy Institute Poll 2018* (2018).

27 Ibid.

28 Joint Standing Committee on Foreign Affairs, Defence and Trade, Foreign Affairs Sub-Committee, *Near Neighbours – Good Neighbours* (2004), 3.

29 Joint Standing Committee on Foreign Affairs, Defence and Trade, Foreign Affairs Sub-Committee, *Near Neighbours – Good Neighbours* (2004).

30 *ABC News*, 'A Bloody Business,' *ABC Four Corners*, 8 August 2011.

31 Maani Truu, 'Indonesia Condemns Anning Comments on Christchurch Terror Attack,' *SBS News*, 18 March 2019.

32 Ben Bland, 'Why Jakarta Called in Australia's Ambassador after Christchurch,' *The Interpreter*, 19 March 2019.

33 Joint Standing Committee on Foreign Affairs, Defence and Trade, Foreign Affairs Sub-Committee, *Near Neighbours – Good Neighbours* (2004).

NOTES

34 Australian Bureau of Statistics, 'International Trade: Supplementary Information, Calendar Year, 2018: Table 7.4 International Trade in Services, Credits, Calendar Year by Country & Travel Service, $m – Education,' released 24 May 2019.

35 Ibid.

36 Daniel Oakman, '"Young Asians in Our Homes": Colombo Plan Students and White Australia,' *Journal of Australian Studies* 26, no. 72 (2002): 89–98.

37 Australian Department of Foreign Affairs and Trade, *New Colombo Plan 2020 Scholarships* (Canberra: Department of Foreign Affairs and Trade, 2019), 3.

38 Simon Marginson, 'Global Position and Position-taking in Higher Education: The Case of Australia,' in *Higher Education in the Asia-Pacific: Strategic Responses to Globalization*, eds. Simon Marginson, Sarjit Kaur, and Erlenawati Sawir (Dordrecht, Springer, 2011), 384.

39 Meredith L. Weiss and Michele Ford, 'Temporary Transnationals: Southeast Asian Students in Australia,' *Journal of Contemporary Asia* 41, no. 2 (2011): 243.

40 Christopher Pokarier, 'Cross-Border Higher Education in the Australia–Japan Relationship,' *Australian Journal of International Affairs* 60, no. 4 (2006): 552–573.

41 Paul Thomas, ed., *Talking North: The Journey of Australia's First Asian Language* (Melbourne: Monash University Press, 2018).

42 Australian Department of Foreign Affairs and Trade, *Australian Aid: Promoting Prosperity, Reducing Poverty, Enhancing Stability* (Canberra: Department of Foreign Affairs and Trade, June 2014), 27.

43 Robin Davies, 'The Unexamined Gift: Australia's Aid Relationship with Indonesia,' in *Strangers Next Door? Indonesia and Australia in the Asian Century*, eds. Tim Lindsey and Dave McRae (Sydney: Bloomsbury, 2018), 443–470.

44 Australian Department of Foreign Affairs and Trade, *Indonesia: Development Cooperation Fact Sheet, October 2022* (Canberra: Department of Foreign Affairs and Trade).

45 Michael O'Keefe, 'Australian Intervention in Its Neighbourhood: Sheriff and Humanitarian?,' in *Righteous Violence: The Ethics and Politics of Military Intervention*, eds. Tony Coady and Michael O'Keefe (Melbourne: Melbourne University Publishing, 2005), 75–98.

46 Australian Department of Foreign Affairs and Trade, *Indonesia: Development Cooperation Fact Sheet, October 2022.*

47 Australian Department of Foreign Affairs and Trade, 'Australia's Development Partnership in Indonesia.'

48 Tourism Research Australia, 'Latest International Visitor Survey (IVS) Results,' 2018.

49 Australian Government Austrade, *Market Action Plan – Indonesia* (Canberra: Commonwealth of Australia, 2019), 14.

50 Australian Department of Home Affairs, 'Country Profile – Indonesia,' updated 12 July 2021.

51 Australian Department of Foreign Affairs and Trade, 'Smartraveller: Indonesia,' updated 12 July 2021.

52 Joint Standing Committee on Foreign Affairs, Defence and Trade, Foreign Affairs Sub-Committee, *Near Neighbours – Good Neighbours* (2004).

53 Australian Department of Foreign Affairs and Trade, 'Smartraveller: Indonesia,' updated 12 July 2021

54 Paul Keating, 'Speech by the Prime Minister, the Hon. PJ Keating MP, Jakarta, Wednesday 22 April, 1992' (Speech, Jakarta, Indonesia, 22 April 1992). Canberra: Department for Prime Minister and Cabinet, 1992.

55 Nicholas Wheeler, *Trusting Enemies: Interpersonal Relationships in International Conflict* (Oxford: Oxford University Press, 2018).

56 Sian Troath, 'Bonded but Not Embedded: Trust in Australia–Indonesia Relations, Keating & Suharto to Turnbull and Jokowi,' *Australian Journal of International Affairs* 73, no. 2 (2019): 126–142.

57 Joint Standing Committee on Trade and Investment Growth, *Leveraging on Our Advantages: The Trade Relationship between Australia and Indonesia* (Canberra: Commonwealth of Australia, 2017), 4.

58 Economist Intelligence Unit, *Long Term Macroeconomic Forecasts: Key Trends to 2050* (London: Economist Intelligence Unit, 2015), 3.

NOTES

59 Australian Department of Foreign Affairs and Trade, 'Indonesia Fact Sheet,' updated August 2021.
60 Ibid.
61 Ibid.
62 Hangga Fathana 'Cabinet Papers 1994–95: How a Security Agreement Allayed Australian Anxiety over Indonesia,' *The Conversation*, 1 January 2018.
63 Graeme Dobell, *Special Report: Australia as an ASEAN Community Partner* (Canberra: Australian Strategic Policy Institute, February 2018).
64 Scott Morrison, 'Regional Trade Deal to Boost Export Opportunities for Aussie Farmers and Businesses', Press Release, 15 November 2020.
65 Australian Department of Foreign Affairs and Trade, *Indonesia: Development Cooperation Fact Sheet, October 2022* (Canberra: Department of Foreign Affairs and Trade).
66 Mark Beeson, Alan Bloomfield and Wahyu Wicaksana, 'Unlikely Allies? Australia, Indonesia and the Strategic Cultures of Middle Powers,' *Asian Security* 17, no. 2 (2021): 178–194.
67 Joint Standing Committee on Foreign Affairs, Defence and Trade, Foreign Affairs Sub-Committee, *Near Neighbours – Good Neighbours* (2004), 7.
68 Maryanne Kelton and David Willis, 'US–Australia–Indonesia Trilateral Security? Conditions for Cooperation,' *Australian Journal of International Affairs* 73, no. 3 (2019): 289–311.

11 Background to the South Pacific

1 Jonathan Schultz, 'Theorising Australia–Pacific island relations', *Australian Journal of International Affairs* 68, no. 5 (2014): 548–568.
2 Joanne Wallis, *Crowded and Complex: The Changing Geopolitics of the South Pacific* (Canberra: Australian Strategic Policy Institute, 2017); Jonathan Schultz, 'Theorising Australia–Pacific Island Relations,' *Australian Journal of International Affairs* 68, no. 5 (2014): 548–568.
3 Australian Department of Foreign Affairs and Trade, 'Stepping up Australia's Engagement with Our Pacific Family' (Canberra: Department of Foreign Affairs and Trade, September 2019).
4 Pacific Island Forum Secretariat, *The 2050 Strategy for the Blue Pacific Continent* (Suva, 2022).
5 Stephen Dziedzic, 'What Does the Splitting of the Pacific Islands Forum Mean for Australia?,' *ABC News*, 11 February 2021.
6 Tonga is the notable exception here, where a monarchy faced explorers and remained the key formal institution.
7 Stephen Dziedzic, 'What Does the Splitting of the Pacific Islands Forum Mean for Australia?,' 2021.
8 Ratu Sir Kamisese Mara, *The Pacific Way* (Honolulu, HI: University of Hawai'i Press, 1997).
9 Tintazul. 'Map of Oceania.' Wikimedia Commons, 30 January 2014.
10 Helen Ware, 'Demography, Migration and Conflict in the Pacific,' *Journal of Peace Research* 42, no. 4 (2005): 435–454.
11 For more detail, see Ron Crocombe, *The South Pacific* (Fiji: University of the South Pacific Press, 2001); Donald Denoon, Malama Meleisea, Stewart Firth, Jocelyn Linnekin, and Karen Nero, *The Cambridge History of the Pacific Islanders* (Melbourne: Cambridge University Press, 1997/2008).
12 Tarryn Phillips, Celia McMichael and Michael O'Keefe, '"We Invited the Disease to Come to Us": Neoliberal Public Health Discourse and Local Understanding of Non-communicable Disease Causation in Fiji,' *Critical Public Health* 28, no. 5 (2018): 560–572.
13 Indo-Pacific Centre for Health Security, 'Australian and PNG Community Leaders Tackle Vaccine Hesitancy,' Department of Foreign Affairs and Trade, 2 June 2021.
14 Matthew Dornan and Jonathan Pryke, 'Foreign Aid to the Pacific: Trends and Developments in the Twenty-First Century,' *Asia and Pacific Studies* 4, no 3 (2017): 386–404.
15 Lowy Institute, 'Lowy Institute Pacific Aid Map' (Sydney: The Lowy Institute, 2020).
16 Australian Department of Foreign Affairs and Trade, *Australia's Regional Security* (Canberra: Commonwealth of Australia, 1989).
17 Australian Department of Defence, *Australia's Strategic Policy* (Canberra: Commonwealth of Australia, 1997), 21.

NOTES

343

18 Charles Hawksley, 'Australia's Aid Diplomacy and the Pacific Islands: Change and Continuity in Middle Power Foreign Policy,' *Global Change, Peace & Security* 21, no. 1 (2009): 115–130; Michael O'Keefe, 'The Militarisation of China in the Pacific: Stepping Up to a New Cold War?,' *Security Challenges* 20, no. 1 (2020): 94–112.

19 Australian Department of Defence, *Australia's Strategic Policy* (1997), 10, 13.

20 Australian Department of Defence, *Defending Australia: 1976 Defence White Paper* (Canberra: Commonwealth of Australia, 1976).

21 Adam Lockyer and Michael D. Cohen, 'Denial strategy in Australian strategic thought,' *Australian Journal of International Affairs* 71, no. 4 (2017): 423–439.

12 South Pacific

1 Jenny Hayward-Jones, 'Cross Purposes: Why is Australia's Pacific Influence Waning?,' *Australian Foreign Affairs* 6 (2019): 29–50.

2 Scott Morrison, 'Address – "Australia and the Pacific: A New Chapter"' (Speech, Lavarack Barracks, Townsville, Queensland, 8 November 2018); John Howard, 'Doorstop Interview Samoa,' Transcript 21448, PM Transcripts: Transcripts from the Prime Ministers of Australia, updated 8 August 2004.

3 Commonwealth of Australia and Commonwealth of New Zealand, *Australia–New Zealand Agreement* (Canberra, 21 June 1944).

4 John Howard, 'Doorstop Interview Samoa,' 2004.

5 Quoted in Clyde Farnsworth, 'Australians Make a Candid Error Angering Their Neighbors,' *The New York Times*, 7 August 1997.

6 Matthew Bishop, Rachid Bouhia, George Carter, Jack Corbett, Courtney Lindsay, Michelle Scobie and Emily Wilkinson, *Towards Sustainable Development in Small Island Developing States: Why We Need to Reshape Global Governance*, ODI Working Paper (London: ODI, 2021).

7 Francis Keany, 'Peter Dutton Overheard Joking About Rising Sea levels in Pacific Island Nations,' *ABC News*, 11 September 2015.

8 Dan Conifer, 'Environment Minister Melissa Price Accused of Dinner-time Slur Against Pacific Island Nations,' *ABC News*, 17 October 2018.

9 Paul Karp, 'Australia's Deputy PM Apologises to Pacific for Fruit-picking Comments "If Any Insult Was Taken",' *The Guardian*, 22 August 2020.

10 Kate Lyons, 'Revealed: "Fierce" Pacific Forum Meeting Almost Collapsed Over Climate Crisis,' *The Guardian*, 16 August 2019.

11 Kristin Haugevik, *Special Relationships in World Politics. Inter-state Friendship and Diplomacy after the Second World War* (Abingdon: Routledge, 2018).

12 Michael O'Keefe, 'Australia and the Fragile States on the Pacific,' in *Trading on Alliance Security: Australia in World Affairs 2001–2005*, eds. James Cotton and John Ravenhill (Melbourne: Oxford University Press, 2007), 147–148.

13 Jordan Fennell, 'Vanuatu MP Calls for Pressure on Indonesia to Allow UN Visit to West Papua,' *ABC News*, 12 May 2021.

14 See Joanne Wallis, *Pacific Power? Australia's Strategy in the Pacific Islands* (Melbourne: Melbourne University Publishing, 2017).

15 Australian Department of Defence, *The Strategic Basis of Australian Defence Policy* (Canberra: Department of Defence, March 1971), para 160.

16 Peter Hannam, 'Call for Australia's Pacific Membership to be Suspended over Coal,' *Sydney Morning Herald*, 17 August 2019.

17 US Department of Defense, *Indo-Pacific Strategy Report: Preparedness, Partnerships and Promoting a Networked Region* (Washington, DC: Department of Defense, 2019).

18 Christina Zhou, 'Beijing Suggests Australia Reflect on How It Treats Pacific Neighbours After Climate Change Fallout,' 2019.

19 Pacific Island Forum Secretariat, *Fiftieth Pacific Islands Forum, Funafuti, Tuvalu, 13–16 August 2019* (Funafuti, Tuvalu, 13–16 August 2019), 9.

NOTES

20 Melissa Clark, 'Pacific Leaders, Australia Agree to Disagree About Action on Climate Change,' *ABC News*, 15 August 2019.

21 Ibid.

22 Tom McIlroy, 'Labor Would Have Rejected Pacific Coal Calls: Wong,' *Australian Financial Review*, 19 August 2019.

23 Christina Zhou, 'Beijing Suggests Australia Reflect on How It Treats Pacific Neighbours After Climate Change Fallout,' *ABC News*, 21 August 2019.

24 *Melanesia News*, 'Tuvalu's Prime Minister on Australia's Statements at PIF Retreat,' *Melanesia News*, 19 August 2019.

25 *Straits Times*, '"They Can Pick Fruit": Australia–Pacific Islands Row Deepens Over "Neo-Colonial" Attitude,' *Straits Times*, 19 August 2019.

26 Eryk Bagshaw, 'China Claims Australia the "Pioneer" of a Global Anti-China Campaign,' *The Age*, 24 September 2019.

27 Greg Fry and Sandra Tarte, eds., *The New Pacific Diplomacy* (Canberra: Australian National University Press, 2015).

28 Joanne Wallis, *Crowded and Complex: The Changing Geopolitics of the South Pacific* (2017).

29 Michael O'Keefe, 'The Militarisation of China in the Pacific Stepping Up to a New Cold War?,' *Security Challenges* 16, no. 1 (2020): 94–112.

30 Scott Morrison, 'Remarks, Pacific Skills Portal Launch: Transcript' (Speech, Funafuti, Tuvalu, 14 August 2019).

31 Michael O'Keefe, 'The Militarisation of China in the Pacific Stepping Up to a New Cold War?,' (2020): 94–112.

32 Australian Department of Foreign Affairs and Trade, *2017 Foreign Policy White Paper* (Canberra: Commonwealth of Australia, 2017), 99.

33 Terence Wood and Sabit Otor, 'A Risky Proposition? Australian Aid Loans and the Pacific,' *DevPolicy*, 22 August 2019.

34 Roland Rajah, Jonathan Pryke and Alexander Dayant, 'China, the Pacific, and the "Debt Trap" Question,' *The Interpreter*, 23 October 2019.

35 David Wroe, 'China Eyes Vanuatu Military Base in Plan with Global Ramifications,' *Sydney Morning Herald*, 9 April 2018.

36 Natasha Kassam, *Lowy Institute Poll 2022*. The Lowy Institute (29 June 2022), 5.

37 Natasha Kassam, *Lowy Institute Poll 2019*. The Lowy Institute (26 June 2019); Natasha Kassam, *Lowy Institute Poll 2022* (2022), 5.

38 Natasha Kassam, *Lowy Institute Poll 2019*. The Lowy Institute (26 June 2019).

39 World Vision, 'DFAT Works,' last modified 2021 Australian Government, Department of the Treasury, *Budget 2019–20: Portfolio Budget Statements 2019–20, Budget Related Paper No. 116, Treasury Portfolio* (Canberra: Commonwealth of Australia, 2019); Terence Wood, 'Aid and Australian Public Opinion,' *Asia and the Pacific Policy Studies* 5, no. 2, (2018): 235–248.

40 Marian Faa, 'Australian Defence Force to Fund $175 Million Major Upgrade for Papua New Guinea's Naval Base on Manus Island,' *ABC News*, 15 June 2021.

41 Primrose Jordan, 'Australia Beats China to Fiji Base,' *The Australian*, 7 September 2018.

42 Tarcisius Kabutaulaka, 'Australian Foreign Policy and the RAMSI Intervention in Solomon Islands,' *The Contemporary Pacific* 17, no. 2 (2005): 283–308.

43 Rory McKibbin, 'Australian Security and Development in Solomon Islands,' *Australian Journal of. Political Science* 44, no. 3 (2009): 439–456.

44 Charles Hawksley and Nichole Georgeou, 'Transitional Justice as Police-Building in Solomon Islands: Tensions of State-Building and Implications for Gender,' in *Current Issues in Transitional Justice: Towards a More Holistic Approach*, eds. Natalia Szablewska and Sascha-Domonik Bachmann (Cham Springer, 2015): 133–160.

45 Robert Ayson, 'The "Arc of Instability" and Australia's Strategic Policy', *Australian Journal of International Affairs* 61, no. 2 (2007): 215–231.

46 Sinclair Dinnen and Abby McLeod, 'The Quest for Integration: Australian Approaches to Security and Development in the Pacific Islands,' *Security Challenges* 4, no. 2 (2008): 23–43.

47 Australian Department of Foreign Affairs and Trade, *Australian Official Development Assistance Budget Summary 2022–23* (Canberra: Commonwealth of Australia, 2023).

NOTES

48 Australian Department of Foreign Affairs and Trade, *Aid Investment Plan: Pacific Regional 2015–16 to 2018–19* (Canberra: Commonwealth of Australia, 2014).

49 Richard Curtain and Stephen Howes, *Governance of the Seasonal Worker Programme in Australia and Sending Countries*, Development Policy Centre, Crawford School of Public Policy, ANU College of Asia and the Pacific, The Australian National University (Canberra: Development Policy Centre, 8 December 2020).

50 Greg Fry and Sandra Tarte, eds., *The New Pacific Diplomacy* (2015).

51 Michael O'Keefe, 'Countering Unwelcome Strategic Competitors in the South Pacific: Canberra's Perspective on the Role of Island States in the Indian and Pacific Islands in Realizing Australia's Indo-Pacific Interests,' *Journal of Indo-Pacific Affairs* 5, no. 7 (November/December 2022): 15–31.

52 Michael O'Keefe, 'The Implications of Australia's "Smart Sanctions" Against Fiji 2006 to 2014 for Geopolitical Contest in the South Pacific,' *East Asia* 6 (2021): 63–80.

53 Michael O'Keefe, 'The Strategic Context of the New Pacific Diplomacy,' in *The New Pacific Diplomacy*, eds. Greg Fry and Sandra Tarte (Canberra: The Australian National University Press, 2015): 130.

54 Fergus Hanson, *Lowy Institute Poll 2012: Public Opinion and Foreign Policy*. The Lowy Institute (5 June 2012).

55 Jenny Hayward-Jones, *Fiji at Home and in the World*. The Lowy Institute (6 September 2011).

56 Stewart Firth, 'Australia's Policy Towards Coup-prone and Military Regimes in the Asia-Pacific: Thailand, Fiji and Burma,' *Australian Journal of International Affairs* 67, no. 3 (2013): 357–372.

57 Republic of Fiji and Commonwealth of Australia, *Fiji-Australia Vuvale Partnership* (Canberra: Australian Department of Foreign Affairs and Trade, 2019).

58 Nauru Department of Commerce, Industries and Environment. *Convention on Biological Diversity Sixth National Report of Nauru* (Yaren, Nauru, October 2019).

59 John Howard, 'Address at the Federal Liberal Party Campaign Launch, Sydney' (Speech, Sydney, 28 October 2001).

60 Rebecca Strating, 'Enabling Authoritarianism in the Indo-Pacific: Australian Exemptionalism,' *Australian Journal of International Affairs* 74, no. 3 (2020): 301–321.

61 Michael O'Keefe, 'Countering Unwelcome Strategic Competitors in the South Pacific: Canberra's Perspective on the Role of Island States in the Indian and Pacific Islands in Realizing Australia's Indo-Pacific Interests,' (2022): 15–31.

62 Amnesty International, *Island of Despair: Australia's Processing of Refugees on Nauru* (London: Amnesty International, 2016).

63 Kelvin Anthony and Evan Wasuka, 'Fiji Government Says China and Taiwan Resolve Incident,' *ABC Radio Australia* (Pacific Beat), 21 October 2020.

64 Pacific Island Forum Secretariat, *Forty-Ninth Pacific Islands Forum, Yaren, Nauru, 3–6 September 2018: Forum Communiqué* (Yaren, Nauru, 3–6 September 2018); Pacific Island Forum Secretariat, *Boe Declaration on Regional Security* (Yaren, Nauru, 2018).

65 Government of Nauru, 'Nauru Govt Says Q&A Is a Wakeup Call for ABC Bias and Unethical Reporting,' News Release, July 2018

66 Pacific Island Forum Secretariat, *Forty-Ninth Pacific Islands Forum, Yaren, Nauru, 3–6 September 2018: Forum Communiqué* (Yaren, Nauru, 3–6 September 2018).

67 Henry Palmerston, 'Speech' (Speech to the London House of Commons, 1 March 1848).

68 Chengxin Pan, Matthew Clarke and Sophie Loy-Wilson, 'Local Agency and Complex Power Shifts in the Era of Belt and Road: Perceptions of Chinese Aid in the South Pacific,' *Journal of Contemporary China* 28, no. 117 (2019): 385–399.

69 *The Australian*, 'Their Enemies Are Not Our Enemies: Pacific Nations Won't Join Stand Against China,' *The Australian*, 19 August 2019.

13 The politicization of official development assistance as a foreign policy tool

1 Julie Bishop, 'The New Aid Paradigm' (Speech, Canberra, Australian Capital Territory, 15 October 2019).

NOTES

2 Jack Corbett, *Australia's Foreign Aid Dilemma: Humanitarian Aspirations Confront Democratic Legitimacy* (New York: Routledge, 2017).

3 Michael O'Keefe, 'The Militarisation of China in the Pacific: Stepping Up to a New Cold War?' *Security Challenges* 16, no. 1 (2020): 94–112.

4 Shahar Hameiri, 'Risk Management, Neo-liberalism and the Securitisation of the Australian Aid Program,' *Australian Journal of International Affairs* 62, no. 3 (2008): 357–371.

5 Annabel Crabb, 'Morrison's Climate "Plan" Reveals a Spectacular New Model of Political Leadership in Australia,' *ABC News*, 31 October 31 2021.

6 Australian Department of Foreign Affairs and Trade, *Partnerships for Recovery: Australia's Covid-19 Development Response* (Canberra: Australian Department of Foreign Affairs and Trade, 2020), 1.

7 Australian Department of Foreign Affairs and Trade, *Australian Development Budget Summary 2022–23* (Canberra: Department of Foreign Affairs and Trade, 2022), 7.

8 Ibid.

9 Matthew Dornan and Jonathan Pryke, 'Foreign Aid to the Pacific: Trends and Developments in the Twenty-First Century,' *Asia and the Pacific Policy Studies* 4, no. 3 (July 2017): 386–404.

10 Dennis Rumley, Vivian Louis Forbes and Christopher Griffin, eds., *Australia's Arc of Instability: The Political and Cultural Dynamics of Regional Security* (Dordrecht: Springer, 2006).

11 Michael O'Keefe, 'Australian Intervention in Its Neighbourhood: Sheriff and Humanitarian?,' in *Righteous Violence: The Ethics and Politics of Military Intervention*, eds. Tony Coady and Michael O'Keefe (Melbourne: Melbourne University Publishing, 2005), 75–98.

12 Angela Clare, 'Australia's Foreign Aid Budget 2020–21,' in *Budget Review 2020–21*, Research Paper Series, 2020–21(Canberra: Parliamentary Library, 2021), 70–74.

13 Alex Hawke, 'Address to the Australasian Aid Conference, Canberra' (Speech, Canberra, Australian Capital Territory, 19 February 2020).

14 Dane Moores, 'Australia's Aid Ambition Should Rise with Its Geopolitical Status,' *The Interpreter*, 12 November 2021.

15 Bishop, 'The New Aid Paradigm' (2019).

16 Alex Hawke, 'Address to the Australasian Aid Conference, Canberra' (2020).

17 Australian Department of Foreign Affairs and Trade, *Australian Aid Budget Summary 2019–20* (Canberra: Department of Foreign Affairs and Trade, 2019), 6.

18 Ibid.

19 Denhua Zhang, *Chinese Concessional Loans: Part 1: Perceptions and Misconceptions*, in Brief 2018/23 (Canberra: Australian National University Department of Pacific Affairs, 2018).

20 Development Policy Centre. 'Australia Aid Tracker Comparisons.'

21 Ibid.

22 Stephen Howes, 'Australia Hits (Almost) Rock Bottom in New Global Aid Rankings,' *Devpolicy*, 10 May 2021.

23 Development Policy Centre. 'Australia Aid Tracker Comparisons.'

24 Stephen Howes, 'Australian Aid Ranked Second Last and New Zealand Last Among Traditional Aid Donors,' *Devpolicy*, 21 September 2021.

25 Australian Department of Foreign Affairs and Trade, *Australian Aid: Promoting Prosperity, Reducing Poverty, Enhancing Stability* (Canberra: Department of Foreign Affairs and Trade, June 2014), 1.

26 Australian Department of Foreign Affairs and Trade, *Australian Aid* (2014).

27 Ibid., 27.

28 Ibid., 4.

29 Ibid., 7.

30 Minister for Foreign Affairs, The Hon Julie Bishop MP, 'Re-Shaping Australia's Aid Program,' updated 18 June 2014.

31 Bishop, 'The New Aid Paradigm' (2019).

32 John Alford, 'The Limits to Traditional Public Administration, or Rescuing Public Value from Misrepresentation,' *Australian Journal of Public Administration* 67, no. 3 (2008): 357–366.

NOTES

33 Bishop, 'The New Aid Paradigm' (2019).
34 Ibid.
35 Ibid.
36 Organization for Economic Cooperation and Development and World Trade Organization, *Aid for Trade at a Glance 2019: Economic Diversification and Empowerment* (Paris: OECD Publishing, 2019).
37 Bishop, 'The New Aid Paradigm' (2019).
38 Australian Department of Foreign Affairs and Trade, 'Australia's Development Program' (Canberra: Australian Department of Foreign Affairs and Trade, 2022).
39 Organization for Economic Cooperation and Development and World Trade Organization, *Aid for Trade at a Glance 2013* (Paris and Geneva: WTO and OECD Publishing, 2013), 26.
40 Australian Department of Foreign Affairs and Trade, *2017 Foreign Policy White Paper* (Canberra: Commonwealth of Australia, 2017), 46–97.
41 Sabit Amun Otor and Matthew Dornan, *How Does Foreign Aid Impact Exports in the Long Run?* Discussion Paper No. 62, Development Policy Centre, Crawford School of Public Policy, ANU College of Asia and the Pacific, The Australian National University (Canberra: Development Policy Centre, 17 September 2017).
42 Nicole Georgeou and Charles Hawksley, 'Australian Aid in the Pacific,' *Australian Outlook*, 26 July 2016.
43 United Nations Department of Economic and Social Affairs. *Sustainable Development Goals*. New York: United Nations.
44 Organization for Economic Cooperation and Development, *OECD Development Co-operation Peer Reviews: Australia 2018* (Paris: OECD Publishing, 2018).
45 Australian Department of Foreign Affairs and Trade, *Australian Aid Budget Summary 2019–20* (Canberra: Department of Foreign Affairs and Trade, 2019), 11.
46 Michael O'Keefe, 'Why China's "Debt-book Diplomacy" in the Pacific Shouldn't Ring Alarm Bells Just Yet,' *The Conversation*, 17 May 2018.
47 Australian Department of Foreign Affairs and Trade, *Australian Development Budget Summary 2022–23* (Canberra: Department of Foreign Affairs and Trade, 2022), 7.
48 Australian Department of Foreign Affairs and Trade, *Partnerships for Recovery: Australia's Covid-19 Development Response* (Canberra: Australian Department of Foreign Affairs and Trade, 2020).
49 Michael O'Keefe, 'Pacific Island Nations Will No Longer Stand for Australia's Inaction on Climate Change,' *The Conversation*, 16 August 2019.
50 Terence Wood, Christopher Hoy and Jonathan Pryke, 'Does Chinese Aid Make Australians More Generous?,' *The Interpreter*, 13 August 2019.
51 Denhua Zhang, *China's Coronavirus 'Covid-19 Diplomacy' in the Pacific*, in Brief 2020/10 (Canberra: Australian National University Department of Pacific Affairs, 2020).
52 #End Covid for All, 'Shot of Hope: Australia's Role in Vaccinating the World Against COVID-19'.
53 Dane Moores, 'COVAX Summit: Time for Australia to Recommit to Global, Not Regional, Vaccine Equity,' *Devpolicy*, 31 May2021.
54 Anthony Galloway, Rachel Clun and Lydia Lynch, '"Real Risk to Australia": Vaccines to be Rolled Out to PNG within Days,' *The Age*, 17 March 2021.
55 Natalie Whiting, Marian Faa and Annika Burgess, 'China Accuses Australia of COVID-19 Vaccine Sabotage in the Pacific,' *ABC News*, 6 July 2021.
56 Benjamin Day and Tamas Wells, 'What Parliamentarians Think About Australia's Post-CoVID-19 Aid Program: The Emerging Cautious Consensus in Australian Aid,' *Asia and the Pacific Policy Studies* 8, no. 3 (September 2021): 384–400.
57 Terence Wood, 'NGO Donations: Are Australians Turing Inwards?,' *DevPolicy*, 26 March 2020.
58 Terence Wood, 'Australian Public Opinion About Aid: Is it Changing and Does it Matter?,' *DevPolicy*, 22 December 2022..
59 Terence Wood, Christopher Hoy and Jonatan Pryke, 'Does Chinese Aid Make Australians More Generous?,' *The Interpreter*, 13 August 2019.
60 Ibid.

NOTES

61 Charles Hawksley, 'Australia's Aid Diplomacy and the Pacific Islands: Change and Continuity in Middle Power Foreign Policy,' *Global Change, Peace & Security*, 21, no. 1 (2009): 115–130.

62 Organization for Economic Cooperation and Development, *OECD Development Co-operation Peer Reviews: Australia 2018* (Paris: OECD Publishing, 2018).

63 Sarah Teo, 'Middle Power Identities of Australia and South Korea: Comparing the Kevin Rudd/Julia Gillard and Lee Myungbak Administrations,' *The Pacific Review* 3, no. 2 (2017): 223–224.

14 Realism and the limits of climate securitization in Australian foreign policy

1 Ben Doherty, 'China Accuses Australia of Being a "Condescending Master" in the Pacific,' *The Guardian*, 21 August 2019.

2 Bureau of Meteorology (BOM), *Annual Climate Statement 2020: Fourth Hottest Year on Record* (Canberra: BOM, 8 January 2021).

3 Australian Department of Climate Change, Energy, the Environment and Water, *Australia's Emissions Projections 2022* (Canberra, December 2022).

4 Australian Department of Climate Change, Energy, the Environment and Water, *Australia's Greenhouse Emissions: March 2022 Quarterly Update* (Canberra, March 2022).

5 Climate Action Tracker, 'Australia,' 2019.

6 Paola Yanguas Parra, Bill Hare, Ursula Fuentes Hutfilter and Niklas Roming, *Evaluating the Significance of Australia's Global Fossil Fuel Carbon Footprint* (Melbourne: Climate Analytics: 2019).

7 SEI, IISD, ODI, Climate Analytics, CICERO, and UNEP, *The Production Gap: The Discrepancy Between Countries' Planned Fossil Fuel Production and Global Production Levels Consistent with Limiting Warming to 1.5°C or 2°C* (2019).

8 Australian Department of the Environment and Energy, *Australian Energy Update 2019* (Canberra: Australian Energy Statistics, 2019).

9 Paola Yanguas Parra, Bill Hare, Ursula Fuentes Hutfilter and Niklas Roming, *Evaluating the Significance of Australia's Global Fossil Fuel Carbon Footprint* (Melbourne: Climate Analytics: 2019).

10 Daniel Hurst, 'Malcolm Turnbull: Coal Export Ban "Would Make No Difference to Emissions",' *The Guardian*, 27 October 2015..

11 David Crowe, 'New Resources Minister Calls for More Coal, Gas and Uranium Exports,' *The Age*, 11 February 2020.

12 United Nations Environment Programme, *Emissions Gap Report 2020* (Nairobi: United Nations Environment Programme and UNEP DTU Partnership, 2020).

13 Melissa Clarke, 'Pacific Islands Forum: How Enele Sopoaga and Scott Morrison Lost when Australia Scuttled Tuvalu's Hopes,' *ABC News*, 18 August 2019. https://www.abc.net.au/news/2019-08-18/pacific-islands-forum-2019-climate-change-focus/11417422; Pacific Islands Development Forum, 'Nadi Bay Declaration on Climate Change Crisis in the Pacific,' News Release, 31 July 2019.

14 Australian Department of Defence, *2016 Defence White Paper* (Canberra: Commonwealth of Australia 2016), 41, 48, 55–56; Australian Department of Foreign Affairs and Trade, *2017 Foreign Policy White Paper* (Canberra: Commonwealth of Australia 2017), 33–34, 84.

15 Australian Department of Foreign Affairs and Trade, *2017 Foreign Policy White Paper* (Canberra: Commonwealth of Australia 2017), 84.

16 Senate, Foreign Affairs, Defence and Trade References Committee, *Implications of Climate Change for Australia's National Security* (Canberra: Parliament House Senate Printing Unit, 2018).

17 Chris Barrie, 'Climate Change Poses a "Direct Threat" to Australia's National Security. It Must be a Political Priority,' *The Conversation*, 8 October 2019; see also Australia Security Leaders Climate Group, *Whole-of-Nation Climate-Security Risk Assessment, Missing in Action: Responding to Australia's Climate & Security Failure* (Canberra: Australian Security Leaders Climate Group, 2021).

NOTES

18 Commonwealth Scientific and Industrial Research Organization (CSIRO) and Bureau of Meteorology (BOM), *State of the Climate 2022* (Canberra: CSIRO/BOM, 23 November 2022), 25.

19 Katharine Murphy, 'Scott Morrison to Reboot Tony Abbott's Emissions Reduction Fund with $2bn,' *The Guardian*, 25 February 2019.

20 Climate Council, *From Paris to Glasgow: A World on the Move* (Sydney: Climate Council of Australia Ltd, 2021).

21 Bill Hare, Anna Chapman, Victor Maxwell, Cindy Baxter and Nandini Das, *Australia's 2030 Emissions: States Lead the Way* (Melbourne: Climate Analytics, 2021).

22 Climate Transparency, *Brown to Green Report: the G20 Transition Towards a Net-Zero Emissions Economy 2019* (Berlin: Climate Transparency, 2019).

23 Climate Action Tracker, 'Australia,' 2019.

24 Ibid.

25 Nick O'Malley, 'Australia Awarded "Colossal Fossil" Award as Climate Talks Drag On,' *Sydney Morning Herald*, 13 November 2021.

26 Climate Council, *From Paris to Glasgow: A World on the Move* (Sydney: Climate Council of Australia Ltd, 2021).

27 John A. Mathews, 'Trade Policy, Climate Change and the Greening of Business,' *Australian Journal of International Affairs 69*, no. 5 (2015): 610–624.

28 Nick O'Malley, 'Australia Awarded "Colossal Fossil" Award as Climate Talks Drag On,' 2021.

29 Australian Academy of Science, *The Risks to Australia of a 3°C World* (Canberra: Australian Academy of Science, 2021).

30 Matt McDonald, 'The Failed Securitization of Climate Change in Australia,' *Australian Journal of Political Science 47*, no. 4 (2012), 579–592.

31 K. Hennessy, B. Fitzharris, B.C. Bates, N. Harvey, S.M. Howden, L. Hughes, J. Salinger and R. Warrick, 'Australia and New Zealand,' in *Climate Change 2007: Impacts, Adaptation and Vulnerability. Contribution of Working Group II to the Fourth Assessment Report of the Intergovernmental Panel on Climate Change*, eds. Martin Parry, Osvaldo Canziani, Jean Palutikof, Paul van der Linden and Clair Hanson (Cambridge: Cambridge University Press, 2007), 507–540.

32 Andrew J. Dowdy, Hua Ye, Acacia Pepler, Marcus Thatcher, Stacey L. Osbrough, Jason P. Evans, Giovanni Di Virgilio and Nicholas McCarthy, 'Future Changes in Extreme Weather and Pyroconvection Risk Factors for Australian Wildfires,' *Scientific Reports 9*, no. 1 (2019).

33 Jacqueline Maley, 'Australia's Climate Policies Will Protect Environment and "Seek to Reduce" Hazard of Fires, says Prime Minister,' *The Age*, 2 January 2020.

34 Robyn Eckersley and Matt McDonald, 'Australia and Climate Change,' in *Australian Foreign Policy: Controversies and Debates*, eds. Daniel Baldino, Andrew Carr and Anthony J. Langlois (Oxford: Oxford University Press, 2014), 230–251.

35 Peter Christoff, 'Climate Discourse Complexes, National Climate Regimes and Australian Climate Policy,' *Australian Journal of Politics and History 59*, no. 3 (2013): 349–367.

36 Kevin Rudd, 'Climate Change: Forging a New Consensus,' Transcript of Remarks to the National Climate Change Summit, Parliament House, Canberra (Canberra, 31 March 2007).

37 Rudd at Copenhagen COP: 'Those Chinese fuckers are trying to ratfuck us,' in Marieke Hardy, 'Column on Kevin: May Contain Course Language,' *ABC News*, 15 June 2010.

38 International Renewable Energy Agency (IRENA), *Renewable Capacity Statistics 2021* (New York: IRENA, 2021), 4.

39 Bevan Shields, 'Global Energy Chief Slams Climate Debate in Australia,' *The Age*, 21 December 2019, 1, 10.

40 Matt McDonald, 'The Future of Climate Politics in Australia,' *Australian Journal of Politics and History 59*, no. 3 (2013): 449–456.

41 Bevan Shields, 'Just 2 Per Cent of Britain's Power Now Comes from Coal. In Australia, It's More Like Three Quarters,' *The Age*, 2 January 2020..

NOTES

42 Australian Department of the Environment and Energy, *Australian Energy Update 2019* (Canberra: Australian Energy Statistics, 2019).

43 Australian Department of the Environment and Energy, *Australian Energy Update 2019* (Canberra: Australian Energy Statistics, 2019), 29.

44 David Coady, Ian Parry, Nghia-Piotr Le and Baoping Shang, *Global Fossil Fuel Subsidies Remain Large: An Update Based on Country Level Estimates*. IMF Working Paper No. 2019/089 (Washington, DC: International Monetary Fund, 2 May 2019).

45 SEI, IISD, ODI, Climate Analytics, CICERO, and UNEP, *The Production Gap: The Discrepancy Between Countries' Planned Fossil Fuel Production and Global Production Levels Consistent with Limiting Warming to 1.5°C or 2°C* (2019).

46 Catherine Hanrahan, 'Federal Election 2019: Vote Compass Finds Broad Desire for More Action on Climate Change,' *ABC News*, 15 May 2019.

47 Richie Merzian, Audrey Quicke, Ebony Bennett, Rod Campbell and Tom Swann, *Climate of the Nation 2019: Tracking Australia's Attitudes Towards Climate Change and Energy* (Manuka, ACT: The Australia Institute, 2019), 1.

48 Audrey Quicke, *Climate of the Nation: Tracking Australia's Attitudes Towards Climate Change and Energy* ((Manuka, ACT: The Australia Institute, 2021).

49 https://votecompass.abc.net.au (accessed 13 December 2019).

50 David Crowe, 'Voter Support for More Ambitious 2030 Cuts Eases,' *The Age*, 26 November 2021.

51 Marc Hudson, '"A Form of Madness": Australian Climate and Energy Policies 2009–2018,' *Environmental Politics* 28, no. 3 (2019): 583–589.

52 Australian Labor Party (ALP), *Powering Australia* (Canberra: ALP, 2021), 4.

53 Clive Hamilton, *Running from the Storm: The Development of Climate Change Policy in Australia* (Sydney: University of New South Wales Press, 2001).

54 Bevan Shields, 'Global Energy Chief Slams Climate Debate in Australia,' 2019, 1, 10.

55 https://votecompass.abc.net.au (accessed 13 December 2019).

56 Nathan Young and Aline Coutinho, 'Government, Anti-reflexivity, and the Construction of Public Ignorance about Climate Change: Australia and Canada Compared,' *Global Environmental Politics* 13, no. 2 (2013): 89–108.

57 Matt McDonald, 'Foreign Policy Should Play a Bigger Role in Australian Elections. This is Why it Probably Won't,' *The Conversation*, 24 April 2019.

58 David Holmes and Cassandra Star, 'Climate Change Communication in Australia: The Politics, Mainstream Media and Fossil Fuel Industry Nexus,' in *Handbook of Climate Change Communication: Vol. 1, Theory of Climate Change Communication*, eds. Walter Leal Filho, Evangelos Manolas, Anabela Marisa Azul, Ulisses M. Azeiteiro, and Henry McGhie (Cham: Springer, 2018), 151–170.

59 Marc Hudson, '"A Form of Madness": Australian Climate and Energy Policies 2009–2018,' (2019).

60 Juliet Pietsch and Ian McAllister, '"A Diabolical Challenge": Public Opinion and Climate Change Policy in Australia,' *Environmental Politics* 19, no. 2 (2010): 217–236.

61 See, for example, Climate Council, *Rising to the Challenge: Addressing Climate and Security in the Region* (Sydney: Climate Council of Australia Ltd, 2021).

62 Australia Security Leaders Climate Group, *Whole-of-Nation Climate-Security Risk Assessment, Missing in Action: Responding to Australia's Climate & Security Failure* (Canberra: Australian Security Leaders Climate Group, 2021).

63 Lorraine Elliott, 'Plus ça Change? The Coalition, Labor and the Challenges of Environmental Foreign Policy,' in *Middle Power Dreaming: Australia in World Affairs 2006–2010*, eds. James Cotton and John Ravenhill (Melbourne: Oxford University Press, 2011), 208–223.

64 Michael Thomas, 'Climate Securitization in the Australian Political–Military Establishment,' *Global Change, Peace & Security* 27, no. 1 (2015): 97–118.

65 Michael O'Keefe, 'Lessons from the Rise and Fall of the Military AIDS Hypothesis: Politics, Evidence and Persuasion,' *Contemporary Politics* 18, no. 2 (2012): 239–253.

66 Roxanne Bazergan and Philippa Easterbrook, 'HIV and UN Peacekeeping Operations,' *AIDS* 17, no. 2 (2003): 278–279.

NOTES

67 Adam Kamradt-Scott, 'Securing Indo-Pacific Health Security: Australia's Approach to Regional Health Security,' *Australian Journal of International Affairs* 72, no. 6 (2018): 500–519.

68 Bevan Shields, 'Global Energy Chief Slams Climate Debate in Australia,' 2019, 1, 10.

69 Australian Department of Defence, *2016 Defence White Paper* (Canberra: Commonwealth of Australia, 2016), 41, 48, 55–56; Australian Department of Foreign Affairs and Trade, *2017 Foreign Policy White Paper* (Canberra: Commonwealth of Australia 2017), 33–34, 84.

70 SEI, IISD, ODI, Climate Analytics, CICERO, and UNEP, *The Production Gap: The Discrepancy Between Countries' Planned Fossil Fuel Production and Global Production Levels Consistent with Limiting Warming to 1.5°C or 2°C* (2019).

15 Asylum seekers as a threat to Australian sovereignty

1 Gabriele Abbondanza, 'Australia the "Good International Citizen"? The Limits of a Traditional Middle Power', *Australian Journal of International Affairs* 75, no. 2 (2021): 178–196.

2 Gwenda Tavan, *The Long, Slow Death of the White Australia Policy* (Melbourne: Scribe, 2005).

3 Cited in Klaus Newman, *Across the Seas: Australia's Response to Refugees: A History* (Melbourne: Black Inc., 2015).

4 Katherine Betts, 'Boat People and Public Opinion in Australia', *People and Place* 9, no. 4 (2001): 34.

5 United Nations High Commissioner for Refugees, *Global Trends: Forced Displacement in 2021* (Geneva: Office of the United Nations High Commissioner for Refugees, 2022).

6 Elibritt Karlsen, *Australia's Offshore Processing of Asylum Seekers in Nauru and PNG: A Quick Guide to Statistics and Resources.* Research Paper Series, 2016–17 (Canberra: Commonwealth of Australia, 2016).

7 United Nations High Commissioner for Refugees, *Global Trends: Forced Displacement in 2018* (Geneva: Office of the United Nations High Commissioner for Refugees, 2019).

8 Elibritt Karlsen, *Australia's Offshore Processing of Asylum Seekers in Nauru and PNG: A Quick Guide to Statistics and Resources.* Research Paper Series, 2016–17 (Canberra: Commonwealth of Australia, 2016).

9 Australian Department of Home Affairs, *Statistics of Transitory Persons in Nauru and PNG* (Canberra: Commonwealth of Australia, 31 October 2021).

10 Alex Reilly, 'Explainer: The Medevac Repeal and What It Means for Asylum Seekers on Manus Island and Nauru,' *The Conversation*, 4 December 2019.

11 Amnesty International, 'Nauru Camp A Human Rights Catastrophe With No End In Sight', 'Nauru Camp a Human Rights Catastrophe with No End in Sight.' Amnesty International Australia Nauru Offshore Processing Facility Review 2012. News Release, 23 November 2012.

12 United Nations Human Rights Committee, *International Covenant on Civil and Political Rights, Human Rights Committee: Concluding Observations on the Sixth Periodic Report of Australia* (Geneva: United Nations, 1 December 2017).

13 International Maritime Organization (IMO), *International Convention for the Safety of Life at Sea (SOLAS), 1974* (London: IMO, 1974).

14 United Nations High Commissioner for Refugees. *Convention and Protocol Relating to the Status of Refugees: Text of the 1951 Convention* (Geneva: Office of the United Nations High Commissioner for Refugees, 2010).

15 United Nations Human Rights Committee, *International Covenant on Civil and Political Rights, Human Rights Committee: Concluding Observations on the Sixth Periodic Report of Australia* (Geneva: United Nations, 1 December 2017).

16 David Neil and Michelle Peterie, 'Asylum Seekers, Healthcare and the Right to have Rights: The Political Struggle over Australia,' in *Regulating Refugee Protection through Social Welfare Provision*, ed. Peter Billings, 181–199 (London: Routledge, 2021).

17 Rebecca Strating, 'Enabling Authoritarianism in the Indo-Pacific: Australian Exemptionalism', *Australian Journal of International Affairs* 74, no. 3 (2020): 311–315.

18 Harriet Spinks, *Boat 'Turnbacks' in Australia: A Quick Guide to the Statistics since 2001.* Research Paper Series, 2018–19 (Canberra: Commonwealth of Australia, 2018); Refugee

352 NOTES

Council of Australia. 'Statistics on Boat Arrivals and Boat Turnbacks,' updated 20 November 2021; Royal Australian Navy, *The Royal Australian Navy Leadership Ethic* (Canberra: Commonwealth of Australia, 2010), 36.

19 Sue Hoffman, 'The Myth of Temporary Protection Visas.' *ABC News*, 14 June 2011.

20 United Nations High Commissioner for Refugees, 'UNHCR Legal Position: Despite Court Ruling on Sri Lankans Detained at Sea, Australia Bound by International Obligations,' News Release, 4 February 2015.

21 Jay Song and Neil Cuthbert, *Removal of Failed Asylum Seekers in Australia: A Comparative Perspective*. The Lowy Institute (27 March 2017).

22 Elibritt Karlsen, *Australia's Offshore Processing of Asylum Seekers in Nauru and PNG: A Quick Guide to Statistics and Resources*. Research Paper Series, 2016–17 (Canberra: Commonwealth of Australia, 2016).

23 Cat Baker, *The People Smugglers' Business Model*, Research Paper No. 2, 2012–13 (Canberra: Commonwealth of Australia, 28 February 2013).

24 John Howard, 'Address at the Federal Liberal Party Campaign Launch, Sydney' (Speech, Sydney, 28 October 2001).

25 Katherine Betts, 'Boat People and Public Opinion in Australia', *People and Place 9*, no. 4 (2001): 40–43.

26 Gwenda Tavan, 'Issues that Swung Elections: Tampa and the National Security Election of 2001,' *The Conversation*, 3 May 2019.

27 United Nations High Commissioner for Refugees. *Asylum Levels and Trends in Industrialized Countries: Statistical Overview of Asylum Applications Lodged in Europe and Selected Non-European Countries* (Geneva: Office of the United Nations High Commissioner for Refugees, 2021), 2.

28 Marg Hutton, *Drownings on the Public Record of People Attempting to Enter Australia Irregularly by Boat Since 1998*, updated 2 February 2014.

29 Australian Department of Home Affairs, *Operation Sovereign Borders: Australia's Borders are Closed to Illegal Migration* (Canberra: Commonwealth of Australia, 2020). https://osb.homeaffairs.gov.au/home.

30 Anthony Galloway, 'Albanese Government Turns Round its First Asylum Seeker Boat', *Sydney Morning Herald*, 24 May 2022.

31 The Titheridge Minute, reproduced in Senate Select Committee, *A Certain Maritime Incident* (Canberra: Commonwealth of Australia, 2002), Chapter 6: The failure to correct the record.

32 Senate Select Committee, *A Certain Maritime Incident* (Canberra: Commonwealth of Australia, 2002), Chapter 6: The failure to correct the record.

33 Ibid.

34 Sue Hoffman, 'The Myth of Temporary Protection Visas.' *ABC News*, 14 June 2011.

35 Elibritt Karlsen, *Australia's Offshore Processing of Asylum Seekers in Nauru and PNG: A Quick Guide to Statistics and Resources*. Research Paper Series, 2016–17 (Canberra: Commonwealth of Australia, 2016).

36 David Crowe, 'Plane Asylum Seekers Hit New Peak – 50,000 Waiting to Be Deported.' *The Age*, 16 February 2020.

37 Cat Baker, *The People Smugglers' Business Model*, Research Paper No. 2, 2012–13 (Canberra: Commonwealth of Australia, 28 February 2013).

38 Amnesty International, 'Nauru Camp A Human Rights Catastrophe With No End In Sight', 2012.

39 Janet Phillips, *A Comparison of Coalition and Labor Government Asylum Seeker Policies since 2001* (Canberra: Commonwealth of Australia, 2017).

40 Senate Legal and Constitutional Affairs Legislation Committee, *Migration Amendment (Repairing Medical Transfers) Bill 2019 [Provisions]* (Canberra: Parliament House Senate Printing Unit, 2019).

41 David Crowe and Rob Harris, 'Medevac Deal with Lambie Clears Ground for New Zealand Solution.' *Sydney Morning Herald*, 5 December 2019.

NOTES

42 Jacquie Lambie, '"Tasmanians Don't Want Deals Done over Humanity," Senator Lambie on Medevac Vote.' By Fran Kelly. *ABC Radio National.* Australian Broadcasting Corporation, 15 October 2019.

43 Alex Reilly, 'Explainer: The Medevac Repeal and What It Means for Asylum Seekers on Manus Island and Nauru,' *The Conversation*, 4 December 2019.

44 Asylum Seeker Resource Centre (ASRC), *At What Cost? The Human and Economic Cost of Australia's Offshore Detention Policies* (Melbourne: ASRC, 2019).

45 Senate, Legal and Constitutional Affairs Legislation Committee, *Migration Amendment (Repairing Medical Transfers) Bill 2019 [Provisions]*, Canberra 2019 (https://parlinfo.aph.gov. au/parlInfo/download/committees/reportsen/024304/toc_pdf/MigrationAmendment(Repairing MedicalTransfers)Bill2019[Provisions].pdf;fileType=application%2Fpdf) <Accessed February 12, 2020>

46 Ibid.

47 Ibid.

Overview and conclusion: Australia's foreign policy DNA

1 Mark Beeson and Hidetaka Yoshimatsu, 'Asia's Odd Men Out: Australia, Japan, and the Politics of Regionalism,' *International Relations of the Asia-Pacific* 7, no. 2 (May 2007): 227–250.

BIBLIOGRAPHY

Books

Albinski, Henry. *Politics and Foreign Policy in Australia: The Impact of Vietnam and Conscription.* Durham, NC: Duke University Press, 1970.

Albinski, Henry. *Australian External Policy Under Labor: Content, Process and the National Debate.* St Lucia: University of Queensland Press, 1977.

Ball, Des. *A Base for Debate: The US Satellite Ground Station at Nurrungar.* Sydney: Allen & Unwin, 1987.

Bew, John. *Realpolitik: A History.* Oxford: Oxford University Press, 2016.

Blainey, Geoffrey. *The Tyranny of Distance: How Distance Shaped Australian History.* Sydney: Macmillan, 1967.

Booker, Malcolm. *The Last Domino: Aspects of Australia's Foreign Relations.* Melbourne: Collins, 1976.

Booth, Ken. *Strategy and Ethnocentrism.* Florence: Taylor & Francis, 2014.

Broinowski, Alison. *The Yellow Lady: Australian Impressions of Asia.* Melbourne: Oxford University Press, 1992.

Brophy, David. *China Panic: Australia's Alternative to Paranoia and Pandering.* Melbourne: Black Inc., 2021.

Bull, Hedley. *The Anarchical Society.* London: Macmillan, 1977.

Burchill, Scott. *The National Interest in International Relations Theory.* New York: Palgrave Macmillan, 2005.

Buzan, Barry, Charles Jones, and Richard Little. *The Logic of Anarchy: Neorealism to Structural Realism.* New York: Columbia University Press, 1993.

Cheeseman, Graeme, and St John Kettle, eds. *The New Australian Militarism: Undermining Our Future Security.* Leichardt: Pluto Press, 1990.

Chubb, Danielle, and Ian McAllister. *Australian Public Opinion, Defence and Foreign Policy: Attitudes and Trends since 1945.* Singapore: Palgrave Macmillan, 2021.

Cooper, Andrew, Richard Higgott, and Kim Nossal. *Relocating Middle Powers: Australia and Canada in a Changing World Order.* Vancouver: University of British Columbia Press, 1993.

Corbett, Jack. *Australia's Foreign Aid Dilemma: Humanitarian Aspirations Confront Democratic Legitimacy.* New York: Routledge, 2017.

Cotton, James, and John Ravenhill, eds., *Middle Power Dreaming: Australia in World Affairs 2006–2010.* Melbourne: Oxford University Press, 2011.

Crocombe, Ron. *The South Pacific.* Fiji: University of the South Pacific Press, 2001.

Crouch, Harold. *The Army and Politics in Indonesia.* Ithaca, NY: Cornell University Press, 1988.

Davison, Graeme. *The Use and Abuse of Australian History.* St Leonards, NSW: Allen & Unwin, 2000.

De Matos, Christine, and Robin Gerster. *Occupying the 'Other': Australia and Military Occupations from Japan to Iraq.* Newcastle Upon Tyne: Cambridge Scholars Publishing, 2009.

Denborough, Michael, ed. *Australia and Nuclear War.* Canberra: Croom Helm, 1983.

Dennis, Peter, and Jeffrey Grey. *Emergency & Confrontation: Australian Military Operations in Malaya and Borneo 1950–1966.* Sydney: Allen & Unwin in association with the Australian War Memorial, 1996.

Denoon, Donald, Malama Meleisea, Stewart Firth, Jocelyn Linnekin, and Karen Nero. *The Cambridge History of the Pacific Islanders.* Cambridge: Cambridge University Press, 1997/2008.

BIBLIOGRAPHY

Edwards, Peter. *Australia and the Vietnam War.* Sydney: New South Publishing in association with the Australian War Memorial, 2014.

Evans, Gareth, and Bruce Grant. *Australia's Foreign Relations in the World of the 1990s.* Melbourne: Melbourne University Publishing, 1991.

Farrell, Brian. *The Defence and Fall of Singapore 1940–1942.* Stroud: Tempus, 2006.

Fernandes, Clinton. *Reluctant Savior: Australia, Indonesia and the Independence of Timor.* Melbourne: Scribe, 2004.

Fitzgerald, John. *Big White Lie: Chinese Australians in White Australia.* Sydney: University of New South Wales Press, 2007.

Fitzgerald, Stephen. *Is Australia an Asian Country?* St Leonards: Allen & Unwin, 1997.

Frei, Henry. *Japan's Southward Advance and Australia: From the Sixteenth Century to World War Two.* Melbourne: Melbourne University Publishing, 1991.

Fry, Greg, and Sandra Tarte, eds. *The New Pacific Diplomacy.* Canberra: Australian National University Press, 2015.

Green, Michael. *Japan's Reluctant Realism: Foreign Policy Challenges in an Era of Uncertain Power.* London: Macmillan, 2003.

Green, Michael. *Line of Advantage: Japan's Grand Strategy in the Era of Shinzo Abe* (New York: Columbia University Press, 2022).

Hamilton, Clive. *Running from the Storm: The Development of Climate Change Policy in Australia.* Sydney: University of New South Wales Press, 2001.

Hamilton, Clive. *Silent Invasion: China's Influence in Australia.* Melbourne: Hardie Grant, 2018.

Haugevik, Kristin. *Special Relationships in World Politics. Inter-State Friendship and Diplomacy after the Second World War.* Abingdon: Routledge, 2018.

Heginbotham, Eric. *The US China Military Scorecard.* Washington, DC: Rand, 2017.

Hobbes, Thomas. *Leviathan.* London: Penguin, 2017.

Jakobson, Linda, and Bates Gill. *China Matters: Getting It Right for Australia.* Melbourne: Black Inc., 2017.

Jervis, Robert. *Perception and Misperception in International Politics.* Princeton, NJ: Princeton University Press, 2017.

Jones, Catherine. *China's Challenge to Liberal Norms: The Durability of International Order.* London: Palgrave Macmillan, 2018.

Kaplan, Edward. *To Kill Nations: American Strategy in the Air-Atomic Age and the Rise of Mutually Assured Destruction.* Ithaca, NY: Cornell University Press, 2015.

Kautilya. *The Arthashastra.* Delhi: Penguin Classics, 2000.

Keating, Paul. *Engagement: Australia Faces the Asia-Pacific.* Sydney: Macmillan, 2000.

Kingsbury, Damian, and Leena Avonius. *Human Rights in Asia: A Reassessment of the Asian Values Debate.* New York: Palgrave Macmillan, 2008.

Kissinger, Henry. *Diplomacy.* New York: Simon & Schuster, 1997.

Krasner, Stephen. *Power, the State and Sovereignty Essays on International Relations.* New York: Routledge, 2009.

Lindsey, Tim, and Dave McRae, eds. *Strangers Next Door? Indonesia and Australia in the Asian Century.* Sydney: Bloomsbury, 2018.

Longhurst, Kerry. *Germany and the Use of Force.* Manchester: Manchester University Press, 2004.

Machiavelli, Nicolo. *The Prince.* London: Penguin, 2011.

Manne, Robert. *The Petrov Affair.* Melbourne: Text Publishing, 2004.

McKenzie, Michael. *Common Enemies: Crime, Policy and Politics in Australian-Indonesia Relations.* Oxford: Oxford University Press, 2018.

Mearsheimer, John. *The Great Delusion: Liberal Dreams and International Realities.* New Haven, CT: Yale University Press 2018.

Middlebrooks, William C., Jr. *Beyond Pacifism: Why Japan Must Become a 'Normal' Nation.* Westport, CT: Praeger, 2013.

Middleton, Karen. *An Unwinnable War: Australia in Afghanistan.* Melbourne: Melbourne University Publishing, 2011.

Millar, T.B. *Australia in Peace and War: 1788–1977.* Canberra: Australian National University Press, 1978.

BIBLIOGRAPHY

Morgenthau, Hans. *Politics Among Nations: The Struggle for Power and Peace.* New York: Knopf, 1948.

Newman, Klaus. *Across the Seas: Australia's Response to Refugees: A History.* Melbourne: Black Inc., 2015.

O'Connor, Brendan. *Anti-Americanism: History, Causes, Themes.* Westport, CT: Praeger, 2007.

O'Neill, Robert. *Australia in the Korean War 1950–53: Vol. 2, Combat Operations.* Canberra: Australian War Memorial and Australian Government Publishing Service, 1985.

Panke, Diana. *Unequal Actors in Equalising Institutions: Negotiations in the United Nations General Assembly.* London: Palgrave Macmillan, 2013.

Patalano, Alessio, ed. *Maritime Strategy and National Security in Japan and Britain: From the First Alliance to Post-9/11.* Leiden: Brill, 2012.

Patience, Allan. *Australian Foreign Policy in Asia: Middle Power or Awkward Partner?* London: Palgrave Macmillan, 2018.

Rathbun, Brian. *Reasoning of State: Realists, Romantics and Rationality in International Relations.* Cambridge: Cambridge University Press, 2019.

Ratu Sir Kamisese Mara. *The Pacific Way.* Honolulu, HI: University of Hawai'i Press, 1997.

Rix, Alan. *Coming to Terms: The Politics of Trade with Japan 1945–57.* Sydney: Allen & Unwin, 1986.

Rogers, Dallas. *The Geopolitics of Real Estate: Reconfiguring Property, Capital and Rights.* London: Rowman & Littlefield, 2016.

Rumley, Dennis, Vivian Louis Forbes, and Christopher Griffin, eds. *Australia's Arc of Instability: The Political and Cultural Dynamics of Regional Security.* Dordrecht: Springer, 2006.

Schake, Kori. *America vs the West: Can the Liberal World Order Be Preserved?* Melbourne: Penguin Press, 2018.

Shimazu, Naoko. *Japan, Race and Equality: The Racial Equality Proposal of 1919* London: Routledge, 1998.

Simon, Herbert. *Models of Bounded Rationality.* Cambridge, MA: MIT Press, 1982.

Smith, Gary, and St John Kettle, eds. *Threats Without Enemies: Rethinking Australia's Security.* Leichhardt: Pluto Press, 1992.

Snyder, Jack. *The Soviet Strategic Culture: Implications for Nuclear Options.* Santa Monica, CA: Rand Corporation, 1977.

Soesastro, H. and T. McDonald, eds. *Indonesia-Australia Relations: Diverse Cultures, Converging Interests.* Jakarta: Centre for Strategic and International Studies, 1995.

Tavan, Gwenda. *The Long, Slow Death of the White Australia.* Melbourne: Scribe, 2005.

Thomas, Paul, ed. *Talking North: The Journey of Australia's First Asian Language.* Melbourne: Monash University Press, 2018.

Walker, David, and Agnieszka Sobocinska. *Australia's Asia: From Yellow Peril to Asian Century.* Crawley, WA: University of Western Australia Publishing, 2012.

Wallis, Joanne. *Pacific Power? Australia's Strategy in the Pacific Islands.* Melbourne: Melbourne University Publishing, 2017.

Walt, Stephen. *The Origins of Alliances.* Ithaca, NY: Cornell University Press, 1987.

Ward, Stuart. *Australia and the British Embrace: The Demise of the Imperial Ideal.* Melbourne: Melbourne University Publishing, 2001.

Ward, Stuart, ed. *British Culture and the End of Empire.* Manchester: Manchester University Press, 2001.

Warren, Aiden, and Adam Bartley. *U.S. Foreign Policy and China.* Edinburgh: Edinburgh University Press, 2021.

Wesley, Michael. *The Howard Paradox: Australian Diplomacy in Asia 1996–2006.* Sydney: ABC Books 2007.

Wheeler, Nicholas. *Trusting Enemies: Interpersonal Relationships in International Conflict.* Oxford: Oxford University Press, 2018.

White, Hugh. *The China Choice: Why America Should Share Power.* Melbourne: Black Inc., 2012.

Wigmore, Lionel. *Australia in the War of 1939–45, Vol. IV: The Japanese Thrust.* Canberra: Australian War Memorial, 1957.

358 BIBLIOGRAPHY

Wilcox, Craig. *Australia's Boer War: The War in South Africa, 1899–1902*. Melbourne: Oxford University Press, 2002.

Willoughby, Charles A. *Reports of General Macarthur: The Campaigns of Macarthur in the Pacific*, Vol. 1. Washington, DC: US Government Print Office, 1994 (1966). https://history.army.mil/html/books/013/13-3/index.html.

Woodward, Bob. *Plan of Attack*. New York: Simon & Schuster, 2004.

Book chapters

Ball, Desmond. 'Indonesia and Australia: Strange Neighbours or Partners in Regional Resilience?' In *Indonesia-Australia Relations: Diverse Cultures, Converging Interests*, edited by H. Soesastro and T. McDonald, 95–131. Jakarta: Centre for Strategic and International Studies, 1995.

Cheeseman, Graeme. 'Australia: The White Experience of Fear and Dependence.' In *Strategic Cultures in the Asia-Pacific Region*, edited by Ken Booth and Russell Trood, 273–298. Basingstoke: Macmillan, 1999.

Davies, Robin. 'The Unexamined Gift: Australia's Aid Relationship with Indonesia.' In *Strangers Next Door? Indonesia and Australia in the Asian Century*, edited by Tim Lindsey and Dave McRae, 443–470. Sydney: Bloomsbury, 2018.

Dudden, Alexis. 'Two Strategic Cultures, Two Japans.' In *Strategic Asia 2016–17: Understanding Strategic Cultures in the Asia Pacific*, edited by Ashley J. Tellis, Alison Szalwinski, and Michael Wills, 91–112. Washington, DC: National Bureau of Asian Research, 2016.

Eckersley, Robyn, and Matt McDonald. 'Australia and Climate Change.' In *Australian Foreign Policy: Controversies and Debates*, edited by Daniel Baldino, Andrew Carr, and Anthony J. Langlois, 230–251. Oxford: Oxford University Press, 2014.

Elliott, Lorraine. 'Plus ça Change? The Coalition, Labor and the Challenges of Environmental Foreign Policy.' In *Middle Power Dreaming: Australia in World Affairs 2006–2010*, edited by James Cotton and John Ravenhill, 208–223. Melbourne: Oxford University Press, 2011.

Fealy, Greg. 'Islam in Australia–Indonesia Relations: Fear, Stereotypes and Opportunity.' In *Strangers Next Door? Indonesia and Australia in the Asian Century*, edited by Tim Lindsey and Dave McRae, 149–168. Sydney: Bloomsbury, 2018.

Fitriani, Evi. 'President Joko Widodo's Foreign Policy: Implications for Indonesia-Australia Relations.' In *Strangers Next Door? Indonesia and Australia in the Asian Century*, edited by Tim Lindsey and Dave McRae, 31–54. Sydney: Bloomsbury, 2018.

Hawksley, Charles, and Nichole Georgeou. 'Transitional Justice as Police-Building in Solomon Islands: Tensions of State-Building and Implications for Gender.' In *Current Issues in Transitional Justice: Towards a More Holistic Approach*, edited by Natalia Szablewska and Sascha-Domonik Bachmann, 133–160. Cham: Springer, 2015.

Hennessy, K., B. Fitzharris, B.C. Bates, N. Harvey, S.M. Howden, L. Hughes, J. Salinger, and R. Warrick. 'Australia and New Zealand.' In *Climate Change 2007:Impacts, Adaptation and Vulnerability. Contribution of Working Group II to the Fourth Assessment Report of the Intergovernmental Panel on Climate Change*, edited by Martin Parry, Osvaldo Canziani, Jean Palutikof, Paul van der Linden, and Clair Hanson, 507–540. Cambridge: Cambridge University Press, 2007.

Holmes, David, and Cassandra Star. 'Climate Change Communication in Australia: The Politics, Mainstream Media and Fossil Fuel Industry Nexus.' In *Handbook of Climate Change Communication: Vol. 1, Theory of Climate Change Communication*, edited by Walter Leal Filho, Evangelos Manolas, Anabela Marisa Azul, Ulisses M. Azeiteiro, and Henry McGhie, 151–170. Cham: Springer, 2018.

Holmes, John. 'Is there a Future for "Middlepowermanship"?' In *Canada's Role as a Middlepower*, edited by J.K. Gordon. Toronto: Canadian Institute of International Affairs, 1966.

Kersten, Rikki. 'Australia and Japan: Mobilising the Bilateral Relationship.' In *Middle Power Dreaming: Australia in World Affairs 2006–2010*, edited by James Cotton and John Ravenhill, 94–110. Melbourne: Oxford University Press, 2012.

BIBLIOGRAPHY

Lantis, Jeffrey. 'Strategic Culture: From Clauzewitz to Constructivism.' In *Strategic Culture and Weapons of Mass Destruction*, edited by Jeannie L. Johnson, Kerry M. Kartchner, and Jeffrey A. Larsen, 32–52. New York: Palgrave, 2009.

Marginson, Simon. 'Global Position and Position-Taking in Higher Education: The Case of Australia.' In *Higher Education in the Asia-Pacific: Strategic Responses to Globalization*, edited by Simon Marginson, Sarjit Kaur, and Erlenawati Sawir, 375–392. Dordrecht: Springer, 2011.

Meaney, Neville. 'Australia and Japan: The Historical Perspective.' In *The Japanese Connection: A Survey of Australian Leaders' Towards Japan and the Australia–Japan Relationship*, edited by Neville Meaney, Trevor Matthews, and Sol Encel. Melbourne: Longman, 1988.

Millar, J.D.B. 'The Conditions for Cooperation.' In *India, Japan, Australia: Partners in Asia*, edited by J.D.B. Millar, 195–209. Canberra: Australian National University Press, 1968.

Neil, David, and Michelle Peterie. 'Asylum Seekers, Healthcare and the Right to Have Rights: The Political Struggle over Australia.' In *Regulating Refugee Protection through Social Welfare Provision*, edited by Peter Billings, 181–199. London: Routledge, 2021.

Nixon, Richard. 'Informal Remarks in Guam with Newsmen, July 25, 1969.' In *Richard Nixon 1969: Containing the Public Messages, Speeches, and Statements of the President*, 544–549. The Public Papers of the Presidents of the United States. Washington, DC: US Government Printing Office, 1971.

O'Keefe, Michael. 'Australian Intervention in Its Neighbourhood: Sheriff and Humanitarian?' In *Righteous Violence: The Ethics and Politics of Military Intervention*, edited by Tony Coady and Michael O'Keefe, 75–98. Melbourne: Melbourne University Publishing, 2005.

O'Keefe, Michael. 'Australia and the Fragile States on the Pacific.' In *Trading on Alliance Security: Australia in World Affairs 2001–2005*, edited by James Cotton and John Ravenhill, 131–149. Melbourne: Oxford University Press, 2007.

O'Keefe, Michael. 'The Strategic Context of the New Pacific Diplomacy.' In *The New Pacific Diplomacy*, edited by Greg Fry and Sandra Tarte, 125–136. Canberra: The Australian National University Press, 2015.

O'Keefe, Michael. 'Australia and Indonesia: The Persistence of Distance Between Proximate Neighbours'. In *Australia on the World Stage: History, Politics, and International Relations*, edited by Bridget Brooklyn, Benjamin Jones, and Rebecca Strating, 157–170. London: Routledge, 2022.

O'Neill, Robert. 'Setting a New Paradigm in World Order: The United Nations Action in Korea.' In *In from the Cold: Reflections on Australia's Korean War* edited by John Blaxland, Michael Kelly, and Liam Brewin Higgins, 29–48. Canberra: Australian National University Press, 2020.

Poore, Stuart. 'Australia.' In *Neorealism Versus Strategic Culture*, edited by John Glenn, Darryl Howlett, and Stuart Poore. New York: Routledge, 2018.

Setiawan, Ken. 'On the Periphery: Human Rights, Australia and Indonesia.' In *Strangers Next Door? Indonesia and Australia in the Asian Century*, edited by Tim Lindsey and Dave McRae, 193–210. Sydney: Bloomsbury, 2018.

Sopiee, Noordin. 'The Development of an East Asian Consciousness.' In *Living with Dragons*, edited by Greg Sheridan, 180–193. St Leonards: Allen & Unwin, 1995.

Sulaiman, Yohanes. 'Indonesia's Strategic Culture: The Legacy of Independence.' In *Strategic Asia 2016–17: Understanding Strategic Cultures in the Asia-Pacific*, edited by Ashley J. Tellis, Alison Szalwinski, and Michael Wills, 163–193. Washington, DC: National Bureau of Asian Research, 2016.

Tavan, Gwenda. 'Testing Times: The Problem of History in the Howard Government's Australian Citizenship Test.' In *Does History Matter? Making and Debating Citizenship, Immigration and Refugee Policy in Australia and New Zealand*, edited by Klaus Neumann and Gwenda Tavan, 125–143. Canberra: Australian National University Press, 2009.

Wiryono, S. 'An Indonesian View: Indonesia, Australia and the Region.' In *Different Societies, Shared Futures: Australia, Indonesia and the Region*, edited by John Monfries, 11–19. Singapore: Institute of Southeast Asian Studies, 2006.

Woolcot, Richard. 'Australia–Indonesia Bilateral Relations.' In *Indonesia-Australia Relations: Diverse Cultures, Converging Interests*, edited by H. Soesastro and T. McDonald, 27–34. Jakarta: Centre for Strategic and International Studies, 1995.

360 BIBLIOGRAPHY

Government proceedings and legislation

Australian Capital Territory. *Parliamentary Debates.* House of Representatives United States of America Terrorist Attacks Speech (17 September 2001).

Australian Capital Territory. *Parliamentary Debates.* House of Representatives Ministerial Statements: East Timor (23 June 2008).

Australian Capital Territory. *Parliamentary Debates, House of Representatives Official Hansard, No. 17, 2017, Thursday, 7 December 2017, Forty-fifth Parliament First Session – Period* (Canberra: Commonwealth of Australia, 2017), 13146. https://parlinfo.aph.gov.au/parlInfo/download/chamber/hansardr/716f5e71-dee3-40a3-9385-653e048de81b/toc_pdf/House%20of%20Representatives_2017_12_07_5783_Official.pdf;fileType=application%2Fpdf.

Australian Capital Territory. *Parliamentary Debates.* House of Representatives Ministerial Statements (20 February 2019), 1087–1091.

Australian Department of External Affairs. 'Security Treaty between Australia, New Zealand and the United States of America (ANZUS).' In *Australia Treaty Series 1952, no. 2,* signed 1 September 1951, entered into force 29 April 1952. Canberra: Department of External Affairs, 1952. http://www.austlii.edu.au/au/other/dfat/treaties/1952/2.html.

Australian Department of Foreign Affairs and Trade. 'Agreement between Australia and the Republic of Indonesia on the Framework for Security Cooperation.' In *Australia Treaty Series 2008, ATS 3,* signed 13 November 2006, entered into force 7 February 2008. Canberra: Australian Department of Foreign Affairs and Trade, 2014. http://www.austlii.edu.au/au/other/dfat/treaties/2008/3.html.

Committee Hansard (Melbourne, 16 March 2018). https://www.aph.gov.au/Parliamentary_Business/Committees/Joint/Treaties/OECDTaxMeasuresBEPS/Report_175/Section?id=committees%2Freportjnt%2F024152%2F25708.

Commonwealth of Australia and Commonwealth of New Zealand. 'Australia–New Zealand Agreement,' Canberra, 21 June 1944. https://www.dfat.gov.au/about-us/publications/historical-documents/Pages/volume-07/26-australian-new-zealand-agreement-1944.

Commonwealth of Australia. *Parliamentary Debates, House of Representatives Federation Chamber Bills, Appropriation (Parliamentary Departments) Bill (No. 1) 2018–2019,* Second Reading, Speech, Tuesday 22 May 2018, 4259 (Andrew Hastie, MP). https://parlinfo.aph.gov.au/parlInfo/search/display/display.w3p;db=CHAMBER;id=chamber/hansardr/e7437ebc-d7b3-4d81-a720-4f0c42fff8a9/0173;query=Id:%22chamber/hansardr/e7437ebc-d7b3-4d81-a720-4f0c42fff8a9/0175%22.

Government of Japan. 'The Constitution of Japan.' Signed on 3 November 1946, entered into force 3 May 1947. Tokyo, 1947. https://japan.kantei.go.jp/constitution_and_government_of_japan/constitution_e.html.

International Maritime Organization. 'The International Conference on Safety of Life at Sea, Text of the Convention for the Safety of Life at Sea.' London: International Maritime Organization, 20 January 1914. http://archive.org/details/textofconvention00inte/page/n5/mode/2up?view=theater.

International Maritime Organization (IMO). *International Convention for the Safety of Life at Sea (SOLAS), 1974.* London: IMO, 1974. https://www.imo.org/en/About/Conventions/Pages/International-Convention-for-the-Safety-of-Life-at-Sea-(SOLAS),-1974.aspx.

Parliament of Australia. 'National Security Legislation Amendment (Espionage and Foreign Interference) Bill 2017' (7 December 2017). https://www.aph.gov.au/Parliamentary_Business/Bills_LEGislation/Bills_Search_Results/Result?bId=r6022.

Parliament of Australia. *Parliamentary Debates.* House of Representatives Ministerial Statements (20 February 2019).

Parliament of Australia. *Parliamentary Debates.* House of Representatives Federation Chamber Bills, Appropriation (Parliamentary Departments) Bill (No. 1) 2018–2019, Second Reading, Tuesday 22 May 2018. https://www.aph.gov.au/Parliamentary_Business/Bills_Legislation/Bills_Search_Results/Result?bId=r6104.

United Nations Security Council. 'Security Council Resolution 2139,' 22 February. New York: United Nations Security Council, 2014. https://www.securitycouncilreport.org/atf/cf/%7B65BFCF9B-6D27-4E9C-8CD3-CF6E4FF96FF9%7D/s_res_2139.pdf.

BIBLIOGRAPHY 361

US Congress. *Congressional Record*. 84th Cong, 1st sess., Vol. 101, Pt. 3, 1955.
US Congress. Joint Hearing Before the Subcommittee on Africa, Human Rights and International Operations and the Subcommittee on Oversight and Investigations of the Committee on International Relations. *Congressional Record*, 109th Cong. 62, 1st sess., Serial No. 109–62 (2005) (Testimony of Yonglin Chen, First Secretary and Consul for Political Affairs, Former Chinese Consulate, Sydney, Australia). https://www.govinfo.gov/content/pkg/CHRG-109hhrg22579/pdf/CHRG-109hhrg22579.pdf.
US Congress. 'Asia Reassurance Initiative Act of 2018.' Public Law No. 115–409, 31 December 2018. https://www.congress.gov/bill/115th-congress/senate-bill/2736/text.66_labels.svg#/media/File:Oceania_UN_Geoscheme_Regions.svg.
US Congress, House. *John S. McCain National Defense Authorization Act for Fiscal Year 2019*. HR 5515. 115 Cong, 2nd sess. *Congressional Record* 208, 2018.

Journal articles

Abbondanza, Gabriele. 'Australia the "Good International Citizen"? The Limits of a Traditional Middle Power.' *Australian Journal of International Affairs* 75, no. 2 (2021): 178–196. https://doi.org/10.1080/10357718.2020.1831436.
Akimoto, Daisuke. 'An Analysis of the ICNND: The Japan-Australia Collaboration for Nuclear Abolition.' *Asian Journal of Peacebuilding* 2, no. 1 (2014): 97–110. https://doi.org/10.18588/201405.000021.
Alford, John. 'The Limits to Traditional Public Administration, or Rescuing Public Value from Misrepresentation.' *Australian Journal of Public Administration* 67, no. 3 (2008): 357–366. https://doi.org/10.1111/j.1467-8500.2008.00593.x.
Allison, Graham T. 'Conceptual Models and the Cuban Missile Crisis.' *American Political Science Review* 63, no. 3 (September 1969): 689–718. https://doi.org/10.2307/1954423.
Anwar, Dewi Fortuna. 'Indonesia's Foreign Policy after the Cold War.' *Southeast Asian Affairs* 1994 (1994): 146–163. http://www.jstor.org/stable/27912099.
Asplund, Andre. 'Normative Power Japan: Settling for "Chinese Democracy".' *Contemporary Japan* 30, no. 1 (2018): 117–134. https://doi.org/10.1080/18692729.2018.1422913.
Ayson, Robert. 'The "Arc of Instability" and Australia's Strategic Policy.' *Australian Journal of International Affairs* 61, no. 2 (2007): 215–231. https://doi.org/10.1080/10357710701358360.
Bates, Gill, and Tom Switzer. 'The New Special Relationship: The U.S.-Australia Alliance Deepens.' *Foreign Affairs* (19 February 2015). https://www.foreignaffairs.com/articles/australia/2015-02-19/new-special-relationship.
Bazergan, Roxanne, and Philippa Easterbrook. 'HIV and UN Peacekeeping Operations.' *AIDS* 17, no. 2 (2003): 278–279. https://journals.lww.com/aidsonline/Fulltext/2003/01240/HIV_and_UN_peacekeeping_operations.27.aspx.
Beeson, Mark, and Hidetaka Yoshimatsu. 'Asia's Odd Men Out: Australia, Japan, and the Politics of Regionalism.' *International Relations of the Asia-Pacific* 7, no. 2 (May 2007): 227–250. https://doi.org/10.1093/irap/lcl008.
Beeson, Mark, Alan Bloomfield, and Wahyu Wicaksana. 'Unlikely Allies? Australia, Indonesia and the Strategic Cultures of Middle Powers.' *Asian Security* 17, no. 2 (2021): 178–194. https://doi.org/10.1080/14799855.2020.1846525.
Betts, Katharine. 'Boat People and Public Opinion in Australia.' *People and Place* 9, no. 4 (2001): 34–48.
Bloomfield, Alan. 'Time to Move On: Reconceptualizing the Strategic Culture Debate.' *Contemporary Security Policy* 33, no. 3 (2012): 437–461. https://doi.org/10.1080/13523260.2012.727679.
Bloomfield, Alan, and Kim Nossal. 'Towards an Explicative Understanding of Strategic Culture: The Cases of Australia and Canada.' *Contemporary Security Policy* 28, no. 2 (2007): 286–307. https://doi.org/10.1080/13523260701489859.
Brincat, Shannon. 'On the Methods of Critical Theory: Advancing the Project of Emancipation Beyond the Early Frankfurt School.' *International Relations* 26, no. 2 (2012): 218–245. https://doi.org/10.1177/0047117811423648. https://doi.org/10.1177/0047117811423648.

BIBLIOGRAPHY

Buzan, Barry. 'From International System to International Society: Structural Realism and Regime Theory Meet the English School.' *International Organization* 47, no. 3 (1993): 327–352. https://doi.org/10.1017/S0020818300027983.

Carr, Andrew. 'Is Australia a Middle Power? A Systemic Impact Approach.' *Australian Journal of International Affairs* 68, no. 1 (2014): 70–84. https://doi.org/10.1080/10357718.2013.840264.

Chai, Tommy. 'How China Attempts to Drive a Wedge in the U.S.-Australia Alliance.' *Australian Journal of International Affairs* 74, no. 5 (2020): 511–531. https://doi.org/10.1080/10357718.2020.1721432.

Chapman, Bert. 'US Marine Corps Battalion Deployment to Australia: Potential Strategic Implications.' *Security Challenges* 13, no. 1 (2017): 1–18. http://www.jstor.org/stable/26465613.

Cho, Young Nam, and Jong Ho Jeong. 'China's Soft Power: Discussions, Resources, and Prospects.' *Asian Survey* 48, no. 3 (2008): 453–472. https://doi.org/10.1525/as.2008.48.3.453.

Chou, Mark. 'Projections of China's Normative Soft Power.' *Australian Journal of International Affairs* 69, no. 1 (2015): 104–114. https://doi.org/10.1080/10357718.2014.952706.

Christoff, Peter. 'Climate Discourse Complexes, National Climate Regimes and Australian Climate Policy.' *Australian Journal of Politics and History* 59, no. 3 (2013): 349–367.

Croxton, Derek. 'The Peace of Westphalia of 1648 and the Origins of Sovereignty.' *International History Review* 21, no. 3 (September 1999): 569–591. https://doi.org/10.1080/07075332.1999.9640869.

Day, Benjamin, and Tamas Wells. 'What Parliamentarians Think About Australia's Post-CoVID-19 Aid Program: The Emerging Cautious Consensus in Australian Aid.' *Asia and the Pacific Policy Studies* 8, no. 3 (September 2021): 384–400. https://doi.org/10.1002/app5.338.

Dibb, Paul, and Richard Brabin-Smith. 'Indonesia in Australian Defence Planning.' *Security Challenges* 3, no. 4 (2007): 67–93.

Dinnen, Sinclair, and Abby McLeod. 'The Quest for Integration: Australian Approaches to Security and Development in the Pacific Islands.' *Security Challenges* 4, no. 2 (2008): 23–43. http://www.jstor.org/stable/26459140.

Doeser, Fredrik and Joakim Eidenfalk. 'Using Strategic Culture to Understand Participation in Expeditionary Operations: Australia, Poland, and the Coalition against the Islamic State.' *Contemporary Security Policy* 40, no. 1 (2019): 4–29. https://doi.org/10.1080/13523260.2018.1469709.

Dornan, Matthew, and Jonathan Pryke. 'Foreign Aid to the Pacific: Trends and Developments in the Twenty-First Century.' *Asia and the Pacific Policy Studies* 4, no. 3 (2017): 386–404. https://doi.org/doi.org/10.1002/app5.185.

Dowdy, Andrew J., Hua Ye, Acacia Pepler, Marcus Thatcher, Stacey L. Osbrough, Jason P. Evans, Giovanni Di Virgilio, and Nicholas McCarthy. 'Future Changes in Extreme Weather and Pyroconvection Risk Factors for Australian Wildfires.' *Scientific Reports* 9, no. 1 (2019): 10073. https://doi.org/10.1038/s41598-019-46362-x.

Drysdale, Peter. 'Did the NARA Treaty Make a Difference?' *Australian Journal of International Affairs* 60, no. 4 (2006): 490–505. https://doi.org/10.1080/10357710601006994.

DuPont, Alan. 'The Australia–Indonesia Security Agreement.' *Australian Quarterly* 68, no. 2 (1996): 49–62. https://doi.org/10.2307/20634725.

Epstein, Charlotte, and Kate Barclay. 'Shaming to "Green": Australia–Japan Relations and Whales and Tuna Compared.' *International Relations of the Asia-Pacific* 13, no. 1 (2013): 95–123. https://doi.org/10.1093/irap/lcs019.

Firth, Stewart. 'Australia's Policy Towards Coup-Prone and Military Regimes in the Asia-Pacific: Thailand, Fiji and Burma.' *Australian Journal of International Affairs* 67, no. 3 (2013): 357–372. https://doi.org/10.1080/10357718.2013.788124.

Frühling, Stephan. 'Is ANZUS Really an Alliance? Aligning the US and Australia.' *Survival* 60, no. 5 (2018): 199–218. https://doi.org/10.1080/00396338.2018.1518384.

Georgeou, Nicole, and Charles Hawksley. 'Australian Aid in the Pacific.' *Australian Outlook*, 26 July 2016, accessed 28 November 2022. https://www.internationalaffairs.org.au/australianoutlook/australian-aid-in-the-pacific-islands/.

Gifkins, Jess. 'R2p in the UN Security Council: Darfur, Libya and Beyond.' *Cooperation and Conflict* 51, no. 2 (2016): 148–165. https://doi.org/10.1177/0010836715613365.

BIBLIOGRAPHY

Girling, J.L.S. 'Vietnam and the Domino Theory.' *Australian Outlook* 21, no. 1 (1967): 61–70. https://doi.org/10.1080/10357716708444262.

Golley, Jane, and Guo Chunmei. 'Australia–China Bilateral Relations: Mixed Messages.' *Contemporary International Relations* 25, no. 5 (2015): 1–27. https://aus.thechinastory.org/australia-and-chinaa-joint-report-on-the-bilateral-relationship-with-cicir/australia-china-bilateral-relations-mixed-messages-2015/.

Gray, Colin S. 'Strategic Culture as Context: The First Generation of Theory Strikes Back.' *Review of International Studies* 25, no. 1 (1999): 49–69. https://doi.org/10.1017/S0260210599000492.

Gyngell, Allan. 'History Hasn't Ended: How to Handle China.' *Australian Foreign Affairs* no. 7 (2019): 5–27. https://www.australianforeignaffairs.com/articles/extract/2019/10/history-hasnt-ended.

Hameiri, Shahar. 'Risk Management, Neo-liberalism and the Securitisation of the Australian Aid Program,' *Australian Journal of International Affairs* 62, no. 3 (2008): 357–371. https://doi.org/10.1080/10357710802286817.

Harris, Brice F. 'United States Strategic Culture and Asia-Pacific Security.' *Contemporary Security Policy* 35, no. 2 (2014): 290–309. https://doi.org/10.1080/13523260.2014.928084.

Hawksley, Charles. 'Australia's Aid Diplomacy and the Pacific Islands: Change and Continuity in Middle Power Foreign Policy.' *Global Change, Peace & Security* 21, no. 1 (2009): 115–130. https://doi.org/10.1080/14781150802659473.

Hayward-Jones, Jenny. 'Cross Purposes: Why is Australia's Pacific Influence Waning?' *Australian Foreign Affairs* 6 (2019): 29–50.

Heazle, Michael. '"See You in Court!": Whaling as a Two Level Game in Australian Politics and Foreign Policy.' *Marine Policy* 38 (2013): 330–336. https://EconPapers.repec.org/RePEc:eee:marpol:v:38:y:2013:i:c:p:330-336.

Heng, Yee-Kuang. 'Beyond "Kawaii" Pop Culture: Japan's Normative Soft Power as Global Trouble-Shooter.' *The Pacific Review* 27, no. 2 (2014): 169–192. https://doi.org/10.1080/09512748.2014.882391.

Higgott, Richard A., and Kim R. Nossal. 'Odd Man in, Odd Man Out: Australia's Liminal Position in Asia Revisited – a Reply to Ann Capling.' *The Pacific Review* 21, no. 5 (2008): 623–634. https://doi.org/10.1080/09512740802457351.

Hong, Min. 'A Comparative Study of the Internationalization of Higher Education Policy in Australia and China (2008–2015).' *Studies in Higher Education* 45, no. 4 (2020): 768–779. https://doi.org/10.1080/03075079.2018.1553154.

Hudson, Marc. '"A Form of Madness": Australian Climate and Energy Policies 2009–2018.' *Environmental Politics* 28, no. 3 (2019): 583–589. https://doi.org/10.1080/09644016.2019.1573522.

Ishihara, Yusuke. 'Australia: The Challenges of the Japan-Australia Quasi-Alliance.' *East Asian Strategic Review 2016*, National Institute of Defense Studies (2016), accessed 24 February 2019. http://www.nids.mod.go.jp/english/publication/east-asian/pdf/2016/east-asian_e2016_06.pdf.

Johnston, Alastair I. 'Thinking About Strategic Culture.' *International Security* 19, no. 4 (Spring 1995): 32–64. https://doi.org/10.2307/2539119.

Jupp, James. 'From "White Australia" to "Part of Asia": Recent Shifts in Australian Immigration Policy Towards the Region.' *International Migration Review* 29, no. 1 (1995): 207–228. https://doi.org/10.2307/2547002.

Kabutaulaka, Tarcisius Tara. 'Australian Foreign Policy and the Ramsi Intervention in Solomon Islands.' *The Contemporary Pacific* 17, no. 2 (2005): 283–308. http://www.jstor.org/stable/23722056.

Kamradt-Scott, Adam. 'Securing Indo-Pacific Health Security: Australia's Approach to Regional Health Security.' *Australian Journal of International Affairs* 72, no. 6 (2018): 500–519. https://doi.org/10.1080/10357718.2018.1534942.

Kato, Junko. 'Institutions and Rationality in Politics – Three Varieties of Neo-Institutionalists.' *British Journal of Political Science* 26, no. 4 (October 1996): 553–582. https://doi.org/10.1017/S0007123400007602.

Kelton, Maryanne, and David Willis. 'US–Australia–Indonesia Trilateral Security? Conditions for Cooperation.' *Australian Journal of International Affairs* 73, no. 3 (2019): 289–311. https://doi.org/10.1080/10357718.2019.1570485.

Kim, Young Mie, Jordan Hsu, David Neiman, Colin Kou, Levi Bankston, Soo Yun Kim, Richard Heinrich, Robyn Baragwanath, and Garvesh Raskutti. 'The Stealth Media? Groups and Targets Behind Divisive Issue Campaigns on Facebook.' *Political Communication* 35, no. 4 (2018): 515–541. https://doi.org/10.1080/10584609.2018.1476425.

Kurusu, Kaoru, and Rikki Kersten. 'Japan as an Active Agent for Global Norms: The Political Dynamism Behind the Acceptance and Promotion of "Human Security".' *Asia-Pacific Review* 18, no. 2 (December 2011): 115–137. https://doi.org/10.1080/13439006.2011.630854.

Laksmana, Evan A. 'Indonesia in Australia's 2016 Defence White Paper.' *Security Challenges* 12, no. 1 (2016): 165–170. http://www.jstor.org/stable/26465725.

Lantis, J., and A. Charlton. 'Continuity or Change? The Strategic Culture of Australia.' *Comparative Strategy* 30, no. 4 (2011): 291–315. https://doi.org/10.1080/01495933.2011.605019.

Layton, Peter. 'America's New Alliance Management.' *Australian Outlook* (8 March 2017). https://www.internationalaffairs.org.au/australianoutlook/americas-new-alliance-management-approach/.

Leibold, James. 'Surveillance in China's Xinjiang Region: Ethnic Sorting Coercion and Inducement.' *Journal of Contemporary China* 29, no. 1 (2020): 46–60. https://doi.org/10.1080/10670564.2019.1621529.

MacCullum, Duncan. 'The Alleged Russian Plans for the Invasion of Australia, 1864.' *Journal of the Royal Australian Historical Society* 44, no. 5 (1959): 301–322.

MacDougall, Derek. 'Australia and Asia Pacific Security Regionalism: From Hawke to Keating to Howard.' *Contemporary Southeast Asia* 23, no. 1 (April 2001): 81–100. https://www.jstor.org/stable/25798529.

Malksoo, Maria. 'The Challenge of Liminality for International Relations Theory.' *Review of International Studies* 38, no. 2 (2012): 481–494. https://doi.org/10.1017/S0260210511000829.

Manicom, James, and Andrew O'Neil. 'Accommodation, Realignment, or Business as Usual? Australia's Response to a Rising China.' *The Pacific Review* 23, no. 1 (2010): 23–44. https://doi.org/10.1080/09512740903398322.

Marginson, Simon. 'Global Position and Position Taking: The Case of Australia.' *Journal of Studies in International Education* 11, no. 1 (2016): 5–32. https://doi.org/10.1177/1028315306287530.

Mathews, John A. 'Trade Policy, Climate Change and the Greening of Business.' *Australian Journal of International Affairs* 69, no. 5 (2015): 610–624. https://doi.org/10.1080/10357718.2015.1048782.

Matsuda, Takuya. 'Explaining Japan's Post-Cold War Security Policy Trajectory: Maritime Realism.' *Australian Journal of International Affairs* 74, no. 6 (2020): 687–703. https://doi.org/10.1080/10357718.2020.1782346.

McArthur, Ian. 'Media Portrayal of the Cultural Relationship between Australia and Japan.' *Australian Journal of International Affairs* 60, no. 4 (2006): 574–589. https://doi.org/10.1080/10357710601007042.

McConachie, Bradley. 'Australia's Use of International Education as Public Diplomacy in China: Foreign Policy or Domestic Agenda?'. *Australian Journal of International Affairs* 73, no. 2 (2019): 198–211. https://doi.org/10.1080/10357718.2019.1568388.

McCraw, David. 'The Howard Government's Foreign Policy: Really Realist?'. *Australian Journal of Political Science* 43, no. 3 (September 2008): 465–480. https://doi.org/10.1080/10361140802267258

McDonald, Matt. 'Constructing Insecurity: Australian Security Discourse and Policy Post-2001.' *International Relations* 19, no. 3 (2005): 297–320. https://doi.org/10.1177/0047117805055408.

McDonald, Matt. 'The Failed Securitization of Climate Change in Australia.' *Australian Journal of Political Science* 47, no. 4 (2012): 579–592. https://doi.org/10.1080/10361146.2012.731487.

McDonald, Matt. 'The Future of Climate Politics in Australia.' *Australian Journal of Politics and History* 59, no. 3 (2013): 449–456. https://doi.org/https://doi.org/10.1111/ajph.12026.

McGregor, Richard. 'Trade Deficits: How China Could Punish Australia.' *Australian Foreign Affairs* no. 7 (2019): 54–74. https://www.australianforeignaffairs.com/articles/extract/2019/10/trade-deficits.

McKibbin, Rory. 'Australian Security and Development in Solomon Islands.' *Australian Journal of Political Science* 44, no. 3 (2009): 439–456. https://doi.org/10.1080/10361140903066997.

BIBLIOGRAPHY

Meaney, Neville. 'Look Back in Fear: Percy Spender, the Japanese Peace Treaty and the ANZUS Pact.' *Japan Forum* 15, no. 3 (2003): 399–410. https://doi.org/10.1080/0955580032000124790.

Mearsheimer, John J. 'Reckless States and Realism.' *International Relations* 23, no. 2 (2009): 241–256. https://doi.org/10.1177/0047117809104637.

Michelsen, Nicholas. 'What Is a Minor International Theory? On the Limits of "Critical International Relations".' *Journal of International Political Theory* 17, no. 3 (2021): 488–511. https://doi.org/10.1177/1755088220956680.

Miller, Charles. 'Public Support for ANZUS: Evidence of a Generational Shift?'. *Australian Journal of Political Science* 50, no. 3 (2015): 442–461. https://doi.org/10.1080/10361146.2015.1 052370.

Nabbs-Keller, Greta. 'Understanding Australia–Indonesia Relations in the Post-Authoritarian Era: Resilience and Respect.' *Australian Journal of International Affairs* 74, no. 5 (2020): 532–556. https://doi.org/10.1080/10357718.2020.1725423.

Oakman, Daniel. '"Young Asians in Our Homes": Colombo Plan Students and White Australia.' *Journal of Australian Studies* 26, no. 72 (2002): 89–98. https://doi.org/10.1080/14443050209387741.

O'Keefe, Michael. 'Enduring Tensions in the 2000 Defence White Paper.' *Australian Journal of Politics and History* 49, no. 4 (2003): 532–534. https://doi.org/10.1111/j.1467-8497.2003.00312.x.

O'Keefe, Michael. 'Lessons from the Rise and Fall of the Military Aids Hypothesis: Politics, Evidence and Persuasion.' *Contemporary Politics* 18, no. 2 (2012): 239–253. https://doi.org/10.1080/1356 9775.2012.674340.

O'Keefe, Michael. 'Teaching Australian Foreign Policy through the Lens of Strategic Culture.' *Australian Journal of International Affairs* 73, no. 6 (2019): 532–538. https://doi.org/10.1080/10 357718.2019.1683515.

O'Keefe, Michael. 'The Militarisation of China in the Pacific: Stepping up to a New Cold War?' *Security Challenges* 16, no. 1 (2020): 94–112. https://www.jstor.org/stable/26908770.

O'Keefe, Michael. 'The Implications of Australia's "Smart Sanctions" Against Fiji 2006 to 2014 for Geopolitical Contest in the South Pacific.' *East Asia* 39 (2021): 63–80. https://doi.org/10.1007/s12140-021-09368-9.

O'Keefe, Michael. 'Countering Unwelcome Strategic Competitors in the South Pacific: Canberra's Perspective on the Role of Island States in the Indian and Pacific Islands in Realizing Australia's Indo-Pacific Interests.' *Journal of Indo-Pacific Affairs* 5, no. 7 (November/December 2022): 15–31. https://media.defense.gov/2022/Dec/06/2003126854/-1/-1/1/JIPA%20-%20O'KEEFE. PDF.

Otmazgin, Nissim Kadosh. 'Geopolitics and Soft Power: Japan's Cultural Policy and Cultural Diplomacy in Asia.' *Asia-Pacific Review* 19, no. 1 (2012): 37–61. https://doi.org/10.1080/134390 06.2012.678629.

Pan, Chengxin, Matthew Clarke, and Sophie Loy-Wilson. 'Local Agency and Complex Power Shifts in the Era of Belt and Road: Perceptions of Chinese Aid in the South Pacific.' *Journal of Contemporary China* 28, no. 117 (2019): 385–399. https://doi.org/10.1080/10670564.2018.154 2220.

Paris, Roland. 'The Right to Dominate: How Old Ideas About Sovereignty Pose New Challenges for World Order.' *International Organization* 74, no. 3 (2020): 453–489. https://doi.org/10.1017/S0020818320000077.

Phillips, Andrew, and Eric Hiariej. 'Beyond the "Bandung Divide"? Assessing the Scope and Limits of Australia–Indonesia Security Cooperation.' *Australian Journal of International Affairs* 70, no. 4 (2016): 422–440. https://doi.org/10.1080/10357718.2016.1153601.

Phillips, Tarryn, Celia McMichael, and Michael O'Keefe. '"We Invited the Disease to Come to Us": Neoliberal Public Health Discourse and Local Understanding of Non-Communicable Disease Causation in Fiji.' *Critical Public Health* 28, no. 5 (2018): 560–572. https://doi.org/10.1080/095 81596.2017.1329521.

Philpott, Simon. 'Fear of the Dark: Indonesia and the Australian National Imagination.' *Australian Journal of International Affairs* 55, no. 3 (2001): 371–388. https://doi.org/10.1080/10357710120095225.

Pietsch, Juliet, and Ian McAllister. '"A Diabolical Challenge": Public Opinion and Climate Change Policy in Australia.' *Environmental Politics* 19, no. 2 (2010): 217–236. https://doi. org/10.1080/09644010903574509.

Pokarier, Christopher. 'Cross-Border Higher Education in the Australia–Japan Relationship.' *Australian Journal of International Affairs* 60, no. 4 (2006): 552–573. https://doi. org/10.1080/10357710601007034.

Price, Megan. 'Norm Erosion and Australia's Challenge to the Rules-based Order.' *Australian Journal of International Affairs* 75, no. 2 (2021): 161–177. https://doi.org/10.1080/10357718.2021.1875 983.

Rathbun, Brian. 'The Rarity of Realpolitik: What Bismarck's Rationality Reveals About International Politics.' *International Security* 43, no. 1 (2018): 7–55. https://doi.org/10.1162/isec_a_00323.

Reilly, Benjamin. 'The Return of Values in Australian Foreign Policy.' *Australian Journal of International Affairs* 74, no. 2 (2020): 116–123. https://doi.org/10.1080/10357718.2019.169350 3.

Robertson, Jeffrey. 'Middle-Power Definitions: Confusion Reigns Supreme.' *Australian Journal of International Affairs* 71, no. 4 (2017): 355–370. https://doi.org/10.1080/10357718.2017.129360 8.

Robinson, Dougal. 'A Sustained Tantrum: How the Joint Chiefs of Staff Shaped the ANZUS Treaty.' *Australian Journal of International Affairs* 74, no. 5 (2020): 495–510. https://doi.org/10.1080/10 357718.2020.1721430.

Rogers, Dallas, Chyi Lin Lee, and Ding Yan. 'The Politics of Foreign Investment in Australian Housing: Chinese Investors, Translocal Sales Agents and Local Resistance.' *Housing Studies* 30, no. 5 (2015): 730–748. https://doi.org/10.1080/02673037.2015.1006185.

Rogers, Dallas, Alexandra Wong, and Jacqueline Nelson. 'Public Perceptions of Foreign and Chinese Real Estate Investment: Intercultural Relations in Global Sydney.' *Australian Geographer* 48, no. 4 (2017): 437–455. https://doi.org/10.1080/00049182.2017.1317050.

Rudd, Kevin. 'ANZUS and the 21st Century.' *Australian Journal of International Affairs* 55, no. 2 (2001): 301–315. https://doi.org/10.1080/10357710120066975.

Satake, Tomohiko. 'The Japan-Australia Contribution to a Liberal and Inclusive Regional Order: Beyond the "China Gap".' *Australian Journal of International Affairs* 70, no. 1 (2016): 24–36. https://doi.org/ 10.1080/10357718.2015.1077501.

Satake, Tomohiko, and John Hemmings. 'Japan–Australia Security Cooperation in the Bilateral and Multilateral Contexts.' *International Affairs* 94, no. 4 (2018): 815–834. https://doi.org/10.1093/ ia/iiy028.

Schultz, Jonathan. 'Theorising Australia–Pacific Island Relations.' *Australian Journal of International Affairs* 68, no. 5 (2014): 548–568. https://doi.org/10.1080/10357718.2014.917271.

Sobocinska, Agnieszka. 'Measuring or Creating Attitudes? Seventy Years of Australian Public Opinion Polling About Indonesia.' *Asian Studies Review* 41, no. 3 (2017): 371–388. https://doi. org/10.1080/10357823.2017.1334041.

Steff, Reuben, and Alan Tidwell. 'Understanding and Evaluating Trump's Foreign Policy: A Three Frame Analysis.' *Australian Journal of International Affairs* 74, no. 4 (2020): 394–419. https:// doi.org/10.1080/10357718.2020.1721431.

Strating, Rebecca. 'Enabling Authoritarianism in the Indo-Pacific: Australian Exemptionalism.' *Australian Journal of International Affairs* 74, no. 3 (2020): 301–321. https://doi.org/10.1080/10 357718.2020.1744516.

Sulaiman, Yohanes. 'What Threat? Leadership, Strategic Culture, and Indonesian Foreign Policy in the South China Sea.' *Asian Politics and Policy* 11, no. 4 (October 2019): 606–622. https://doi. org/https://doi.org/10.1111/aspp.12496.

Syailendra, Emirza Adi. 'A *Nonbalancing* Act: Explaining Indonesia's Failure to Balance against the Chinese Threat.' *Asian Security* 13, no. 3 (2017): 237–255. https://doi.org/10.1080/14799855.20 17.1365489.

Tate, Merze. 'The Australian Monroe Doctrine.' *Political Science Quarterly* 76, no. 2 (June 1961): 264–284.

Taylor, Brendan. 'Unbreakable Alliance? ANZUS in the Asian Century.' *Asian Politics & Policy* 8, no. 1 (2016): 75–85. https://doi.org/10.1111/aspp.12232.

BIBLIOGRAPHY

Taylor, Elisabeth, Peter Charles Taylor, Saul Karnovsky, Anne Aly, and Nell Taylor. '"Beyond Bali": A Transformative Education Approach for Developing Community Resilience to Violent Extremism.' *Asia Pacific Journal of Education* 37, no. 2 (2017): 193–204. https://doi.org/10.1080/02188791.2016.1240661.

Teo, Sarah. 'Middle Power Identities of Australia and South Korea: Comparing the Kevin Rudd/Julia Gillard and Lee Myungbak Administrations.' *The Pacific Review* 3, no. 2 (2017): 223–224. https://doi.org/10.1080/09512748.2017.1371210.

Thomas, Michael Durant. 'Climate Securitization in the Australian Political–Military Establishment.' *Global Change, Peace & Security* 27, no. 1 (2015): 97–118. https://doi.org/10.1080/14781158.2015.990879.

Tow, William. 'Deputy Sheriff or Independent Ally? Evolving Australian-American Ties in an Ambiguous World Order.' *Pacific Review* 17, no. 2 (2004): 271–290. https://doi.org/10.1080/0951274042000219851.

Troath, Sian. 'Bonded but Not Embedded: Trust in Australia–Indonesia Relations, Keating & Suharto to Turnbull & Jokowi.' *Australian Journal of International Affairs* 73, no. 2 (2019): 126–142. https://doi.org/10.1080/10357718.2019.1583168.

Tsokhas, Kosmas. '"Trouble Must Follow": Australia's Ban on Iron Ore Exports to Japan in 1938.' *Modern Asian Studies* 29, no. 4 (1995): 871–892. https://doi.org/10.1017/S0026749X00016218.

Walton, David. 'The Role of Prime Ministers in Australia–Japan Relations: Howard and Rudd.' *The Round Table* 99, no. 409 (2010): 429–437. https://doi.org/10.1080/00358533.2010.498979.

Ware, Helen. 'Demography, Migration and Conflict in the Pacific.' *Journal of Peace Research* 42, no. 4 (2005): 435–454. https://www.jstor.org/stable/30042335.

Weeks, Donna. 'An East Asian Security Community: Japan, Australia and Resources as "Security".' *Australian Journal of International Affairs* 65, no. 1 (2011): 61–80. https://doi.org/10.1080/10357718.2011.535602.

Weiss, Meredith L., and Michele Ford. 'Temporary Transnationals: Southeast Asian Students in Australia.' *Journal of Contemporary Asia* 41, no. 2 (2011): 229–248. https://doi.org/10.1080/00472336.2011.553042.

Wesley, Michael, and Tony Warren. 'Wild Colonial Ploys? Currents of Thought in Australian Foreign Policy.' *Australian Journal of Political Science* 35, no. 1 (2000): 9–26. https://doi.org/10.1080/10361140050002809.

Wigell, Mikael. 'Hybrid Interference as a Wedge Strategy: A Theory of External Interference in Liberal Democracy.' *International Affairs* 95, no. 2 (2019): 255–275. https://doi.org/10.1093/ia/iiz018.

Wilkins, Thomas S. 'From Strategic Partnership to Strategic Alliance? Australia–Japan Security Ties and the Asia-Pacific.' *Asia Policy*, no. 20 (2015): 81–112. http://www.jstor.org/stable/24905071.

Wilson, Jeffrey D. 'Resource Nationalism or Resource Liberalism? Explaining Australia's Approach to Chinese Investment in Its Minerals Sector.' *Australian Journal of International Affairs* 65, no. 3 (2011): 283–304. https://doi.org/10.1080/10357718.2011.563779.

Wolfowitz, Paul D. 'ANZUS Alliance.' *Department of State Bulletin* 85 (1985): 65–66.

Wood, Terence. 'Aid and Australian Public Opinion.' *Asia and the Pacific Policy Studies* 5, no. 2 (2018): 235–248. https://doi.org/doi.org/10.1002/app5.230.

Xi, Junfang, Weihuan Zhou, and Heng Wang. 'The Impact of the China–Australia Free Trade Agreement on Australia's Education Exports to China: A Legal and Economic Assessment.' *World Economy* 41, no. 12 (2018): 3503–3523. https://doi.org/doi.org/10.1111/twec.12736.

Yoshimatsu, Hidetaka, and Patrick Ziltener. 'Japan's FTA Strategy Toward Highly Developed Countries: Comparing Australia's and Switzerland's Experiences, 2000–09.' *Asian Survey* 50, no. 6 (2010): 1058–1081. https://doi.org/10.1525/as.2010.50.6.1058.

Young, Nathan, and Aline Coutinho. 'Government, Anti-Reflexivity, and the Construction of Public Ignorance About Climate Change: Australia and Canada Compared.' *Global Environmental Politics* 13, no. 2 (2013): 89–108. https://doi.org/10.1162/GLEP_a_00168.

Newspaper articles and magazines

ABC News. 'National Security Cited as Chinese Oz Minerals Deal Blocked.' *ABC News*, 27 March 2009. https://www.abc.net.au/news/2009-03-27/national-security-cited-as-chinese-oz-minerals/1633314.

BIBLIOGRAPHY

ABC News, 'A Bloody Business', *ABC Four Corners*, 8 August 2011. https://www.abc.net.au/news/2011-08-08/a-bloody-business---2011/2841918.

ABC News. 'Promise Check: We Will Stop the Boats.' *ABC News*, 8 May 2016, RMIT ABC Fact Check. https://www.abc.net.au/news/2014-07-27/we-will-stop-the-boats-promise-check/5474206?nw=0&r=HtmlFragment.

Antara News. 'US Mily [*sic*] Presence in Darwin Arouses Suspicion in Many Quarters.' *Antara News*, 3 November 2011. https://en.antaranews.com/news/77866/us-mily-presence-in-darwin-arouses-suspicion-in-many-quarters.

Anthony, Kelvin, and Evan Wasuka. 'Fiji Government Says China and Taiwan Resolve Incident.' *ABC Radio Australia* (Pacific Beat), 21 October 2020. https://www.abc.net.au/radio-australia/programs/pacificbeat/fiji-china-taiwan-matter-resolved/12797364.

Ayson, Robert. 'Australia–Japan: Abbott Uses the "A" Word.' *The Interpreter*, 3 December 2018.

Bagshaw, Eryk. 'China Claims Australia the "Pioneer" of a Global Anti-China Campaign.' *The Age*, 24 September 2019. https://www.theage.com.au/politics/federal/china-claims-australia-the-pioneer-of-a-global-anti-china-campaign-20190924-p52ufk.html.

Bagshaw, Eryk. 'China Should Be "Totally Ashamed": Scott Morrison Demands China Take Down Post.' *The Age*, 30 November 2020.

Bagshaw, Eryk, and Anthony Galloway. '"Horrific Abuses": Uighur Report Reveals First-Hand Accounts of Torture.' *The Age*, 3 February 2021.

Baker, Nick. 'Australia "Missing Out" as Students Continue to Shun Learning Chinese.' *SBS News*, 12 March 2019. https://www.sbs.com.au/news/australia-missing-out-as-students-continue-to-shun-learning-chinese.

Barrie, Chris. 'Climate Change Poses a "Direct Threat" to Australia's National Security. It Must Be a Political Priority.' *The Conversation*, 8 October 2019. https://theconversation.com/climate-change-poses-a-direct-threat-to-australias-national-security-it-must-be-a-political-priority-123264.

Beaumont, Alan. 'Our Military and Diplomatic Elders on Truth in Democracies and the Downside of Invading Iraq.' *Sydney Morning Herald*, 10 August 2004. https://www.smh.com.au/opinion/our-military-and-diplomatic-elders-on-truth-in-democracies-and-the-downside-of-invading-iraq-20040810-gdjimv.html.

Bickers, Claire. 'Chinese Ambassador to Australia Cheng Jingye Slams "Groundless" Foreign Influence Allegations.' *News.com.au*, 15 June 2017. https://www.news.com.au/national/politics/chinese-ambassador-to-australia-cheng-jingye-slams-groundless-foreign-influence-allegations/news-story/1d14ad59abac3ffe447040aa1b42bf70.

Biggs, Tim, and Jennifer Duke. 'China's Huawei, ZTE Banned from 5g Network.' *Sydney Morning Herald*, 23 August 2018. https://www.smh.com.au/technology/government-implies-5g-china-ban-in-new-security-advice-20180823-p4zz77.html.

Birmingham, John. 'Appeasing Jakarta: Australia's Complicity in the East Timor Tragedy.' *Quarterly Essay*, QE2, June 2001. https://www.quarterlyessay.com.au/essay/2001/06/appeasing-jakarta.

Birmingham, John. 'A Time for War: Australia as a Military Power.' *Quarterly Essay*, QE20, December 2005. https://www.quarterlyessay.com.au/essay/2005/12/a-time-for-war.

Bland, Ben. 'Why Jakarta Called in Australia's Ambassador after Christchurch.' *The Interpreter*, 19 March 2019. https://www.lowyinstitute.org/the-interpreter/why-jakarta-called-australia-ambassador-after-christchurch.

Borello, Eliza. 'Andrew Robb Blames Former Coalition Leaders for "Toxic" Relationship with China.' *ABC News*, 12 March 2019. https://www.abc.net.au/news/2019-03-12/andrew-robb-blames-coalition-leaders-for-toxic-china-relations/10891384.

Bourke, Latika. 'ANU Academic Slammed over Citation of "Sub-Par" Chinese Genocide Research.' *The Age*, 27 April 2021.

Brissenden, Michael. 'Tony Abbott Makes First Visit to Afghanistan as PM, Says Australia's Longest War Is Ending.' *ABC News*, 29 October 2013. https://www.abc.net.au/news/2013-10-29/tony-abbott-makes-first-visit-to-afghanistan-as-prime-minister/5051242?nw=0.

China Daily. 'China Defender of International, Regional Rules: Senior Chinese Military Official.' *China Daily*, 6 June 2017. http://www.chinadaily.com.cn/china/2017-06/03/content_29605400.htm.

BIBLIOGRAPHY

Choi, Martin, and Catherine Wong. 'China-Australia Relations "Will Not Be Helped" by Foreign Influence Register.' *South China Morning Post*, 21 February 2019. https://www.scmp.com/news/china/diplomacy/article/2187165/china-australia-relations-will-not-be-helped-foreign-influence.

Clark, Melissa. 'Pacific Leaders, Australia Agree to Disagree About Action on Climate Change.' *ABC News*, 15 August 2019. https://www.abc.net.au/news/2019-08-15/no-endorsements-come-out-of-tuvalu-declaration/11419342.

Clark, Melissa. 'Pacific Islands Forum: How Enele Sopoaga and Scott Morrison Lost when Australia Scuttled Tuvalu's Hopes,' *ABC News*, 18 August 2019. https://www.abc.net.au/news/2019-08-18/pacific-islands-forum-2019-climate-change-focus/11417422.

Conifer, Dan. 'Environment Minister Melissa Price Accused of Dinner-Time Slur against Pacific Island Nations.' *ABC News*, 17 October 2018. https://www.abc.net.au/news/2018-10-17/melissa-price-denies-insulting-former-kiribati-president/10387494.

Connelly, Peter. 'Chinese Evacuations and Power Projection (Part 2): A Movie Genre Is Born.' *The Strategist*, 14 December 2018. https://www.aspistrategist.org.au/chinese-evacuations-and-power-projection-part-2-a-movie-genre-is-born/.

Cosoleto, Tara. 'Australia Joins Global Condemnation of "Serious" China Cyber Hacking.' *SBS News*, 21 December 2018. https://www.sbs.com.au/news/australia-joins-global-condemnation-of-serious-china-cyber-hacking.

Crabb, Annabel. 'Morrison's Climate "Plan" Reveals a Spectacular New Model of Political Leadership in Australia.' *ABC News*, 31 October 2021. https://www.abc.net.au/news/2021-10-31/morrison-climate-plan-net-zero-new-model-political-leadership/100576698.

Crowe, David. 'New Resources Minister Calls for More Coal, Gas and Uranium Exports.' *The Age*, 11 February 2020.

Crowe, David. 'Plane Asylum Seekers Hit New Peak – 50,000 Waiting to Be Deported.' *The Age*, 16 February 2020. https://www.theage.com.au/politics/federal/airplane-asylum-seekers-hit-new-peak-50-000-waiting-to-be-deported-20200216-p541b1.html.

Crowe, David. 'Voter Support for More Ambitious 2030 Cuts Eases.' *The Age*, 26 November 2021.

Crowe, David, and Rob Harris. 'Medevac Deal with Lambie Clears Ground for New Zealand Solution.' *Sydney Morning Herald*, 5 December 2019. https://www.smh.com.au/politics/federal/medevac-deal-with-lambie-clears-ground-for-new-zealand-solution-20191204-p53gx8.html.

Curtin, John. 'The Task Ahead.' *Herald*, Melbourne, 27 December 1941.

Denyer, Simon, and Akiki Kashiwagi. 'Japan to Leave International Whaling Commission, Resume Commercial Hunting.' *The Washington Post*, 26 December 2018. https://www.washingtonpost.com/world/japan-to-leave-international-whaling-commission-resume-commercial-hunt/2018/12/26/2c32fb20-08c9-11e9-892d-3373d7422f60_story.html?noredirect=on&utm_term=.b9f10e7d09d9.

Doherty, Ben. 'China Accuses Australia of Being a "Condescending Master" in the Pacific.' *The Guardian*, 21 August 2019. https://www.theguardian.com/australia-news/2019/aug/21/china-accuses-australia-of-being-a-condescending-master-in-the-pacific.

Dziedzic, Stephen. 'US to Partner with Australia, Papua New Guinea on Manus Island Naval Base.' *ABC News*, 17 November 2018. https://www.abc.net.au/news/2018-11-17/us-to-partner-with-australia-and-png-on-manus-island-naval-base/10507658.

Dziedzic, Stephen. 'Australia and Japan Agree "in Principle" to Historic Defence Pact.' *ABC News*, 18 November 2020. https://www.abc.net.au/news/2020-11-17/australia-japan-agree-in-principle-to-defence-pact/12891322.

Dziedzic, Stephen. 'What Does the Splitting of the Pacific Islands Forum Mean for Australia?' *ABC News*, 11 February 2021. https://www.abc.net.au/news/2021-02-10/what-does-the-pacific-islands-forum-split-mean-for-australia/13137346.

Dziedzic, Stephen, and Andrew Greene. 'China's Soft Power: Julie Bishop Steps up Warning to University Students on Communist Party Rhetoric.' *ABC News*, 16 October 2017. https://www.abc.net.au/news/2017-10-16/bishop-steps-up-warning-to-chinese-university-students/9053512.

Faa, Marian. 'Australian Defence Force to Fund $175 Million Major Upgrade for Papua New Guinea's Naval Base on Manus Island.' *ABC News*, 15 June 2021. https://www.abc.net.au/news/2021-06-15/major-naval-base-on-png-manus-island-lombrum-adf/100216040.

Fandi, Cau. '"Five Eyes' Could Be Poked Blind If China's Security and Sovereignty Harmed, Warns Chinese Fm Spokesperson.' *Global Times*, 19 November 2020. https://www.globaltimes.cn/content/1207378.shtml.

Farnsworth, Clyde. 'Australians Make a Candid Error Angering Their Neighbors.' *The New York Times*, 7 August 1997. https://www.nytimes.com/1997/08/07/world/australians-make-a-candid-error-angering-their-neighbors.html.

Fathana, Hangga. 'Cabinet Papers 1994–95: How a Security Agreement Allayed Australian Anxiety over Indonesia.' *The Conversation*, 1 January 2018. https://theconversation.com/cabinet-papers-1994-95-how-a-security-agreement-allayed-australian-anxiety-over-indonesia-89143.

Fennell, Jordan. 'Vanuatu MP Calls for Pressure on Indonesia to Allow UN Visit to West Papua.' *ABC News*, 12 May 2021. https://www.abc.net.au/radio-australia/programs/pacificbeat/vanuatu-mp-calls-for-international-pressure-over-west-papua/13340672.

Fernando, Gavin. 'Security Experts Claim a Chinese Vessel Tasked with Finding Mh370 Is Likely Spying on Us.' *News.com.au*, 24 September 2016. https://www.news.com.au/finance/economy/world-economy/security-experts-claim-a-chinese-vessel-tasked-with-finding-mh370-is-likely-spying-on-us/news-story/93b0ee754fbf98b1ce9dada6aadabea6.

Galloway, Anthony. 'We Won't Trade Away Values: Payne.' *The Age*, 20 March 2021.

Galloway, Anthony. 'Australia to Withdraw All Troops from Afghanistan after Biden's Vow to End War.' *Sydney Morning Herald*, 15 April 2021. https://www.smh.com.au/politics/federal/australia-to-withdraw-all-troops-from-afghanistan-after-biden-vows-to-end-war-20210415-p57jeb.html.

Galloway, Anthony. 'Albanese Government Turns Round its First Asylum Seeker Boat', *Sydney Morning Herald*, 24 May 2022. https://www.smh.com.au/politics/federal/albanese-government-turns-around-its-first-asylum-seeker-boat-20220524-p5ao2y.html.

Galloway, Anthony, Rachel Clun, and Lydia Lynch. '"Real Risk to Australia": Vaccines to Be Rolled out to PNG within Days.' *The Age*, 17 March 2021.

Global Times. 'Five Eyes Alliance Plotting against China Will Backfire on Themselves.' *Global Times*, 14 October 2020. https://www.globaltimes.cn/content/1209938.

Goodfellow, Rob. 'Ignorant and Hostile: Australian Perceptions of Indonesia.' *Inside Indonesia*, September 1993, 4–6.

Gray, Darren. 'Wine, Lobster, Copper . . . What's at Stake in Our Trade Tensions with China.' *The Age*, 6 November 2020.

Greene, Andrew. 'ASIO Overwhelmed by Foreign Spying Threats against Australia in Past Year.' *ABC News*, 18 October 2017. https://www.abc.net.au/news/2017-10-18/asio-overwhelmed-by-foreign-spying-threats-against-australia/.

Greene, Andrew. 'Chinese Government Intrusion into Western Universities Sparks Push for Collective Action.' *ABC News*, 15 October 2017. https://www.abc.net.au/news/2017-10-15/chinese-intrusion-on-western-universities-sparks-action/9048456.

Greene, Andrew. 'Australian Warships Challenged by Chinese Military in South China Sea.' *ABC News*, 20 April 2018. https://www.abc.net.au/news/2018-04-20/south-china-sea-australian-warships-challenged-by-chinese/9677908?nw=0&r=HtmlFragment.

Greene, Andrew. 'Second Chinese Spy Ship Approaches Australia to Monitor Military Exercises after Being on Our Radar "for Some Time".' *ABC News*, 18 July 2021. https://www.abc.net.au/news/2021-07-18/second-chinese-spy-ship-australia-monitor-military-exercises/100302198.

Grigg, Angus. 'Australia's Defence Department Bans Chinese App WeChat.' *Australian Financial Review*, 11 March 2018. https://www.afr.com/technology/australias-defence-department-bans-chinese-app-wechat-20180310-h0xay8.

Hannam, Peter. 'Call for Australia's Pacific Membership to Be Suspended over Coal.' *Sydney Morning Herald:*, 17 August 2019. https://www.straitstimes.com/asia/australianz/they-can-pick-fruit-australia-pacific-islands-row-deepens-over-neo-colonial.

Hanrahan, Catherine. 'Federal Election 2019: Vote Compass Finds Broad Desire for More Action on Climate Change.' *ABC News*, 15 May 2019. https://www.abc.net.au/news/2019-05-15/federal-election-vote-compass-climate-change/11110912.

Hardy, Marieke. 'Column on Kevin: May Contain Course Language.' *ABC News*, 15 June 2010.

BIBLIOGRAPHY

Hartcher, Peter. 'There's Good News, Bad News and Worse News About Donald Trump.' *The Age*, 2 April 2019.

Hartcher, Peter. '"Just Not Going to Happen": US Warns China over Australian Trade Stoush.' *The Age*, 16 March 2021.

Hartcher, Peter. 'Red Flag: Waking up to China's Challenge.' *Quarterly Essay*, 76 (2019). https://www.quarterlyessay.com.au/essay/2019/11/red-flag/extract.

Hartcher, Peter. 'I Asked Would the US Defend Australia If We Were Attacked? The Answer Is Sobering.' *The Age*, 26 January 2021.

Hasham, Nicole. 'The Shocking Japanese Whaling Footage the Australian Government Wanted to Hide.' *Sydney Morning Herald*, 28 November 2017. https://www.smh.com.au/politics/federal/the-shocking-japanese-whaling-footage-the-australian-government-wanted-to-hide-20171127-gztg06.html.

Hoffman, Sue. 'The Myth of Temporary Protection Visas.' *ABC News*, 14 June 2011. https://www.abc.net.au/news/2011-06-14/hoffman---the-myth-of-temporary-protection-visas/2757748.

Hong, Chen. 'Australia Smearing China with Spying Brush.' *Global Times*, 2 November 2019. https://www.globaltimes.cn/content/1138476.shtml.

Howes, Stephen. 'Australia Hits (Almost) Rock Bottom in New Global Aid Rankings.' *DevPolicy*, 10 May 2021. https://devpolicy.org/australia-hits-almost-rock-bottom-in-new-global-aid-rankings-20210510-2/.

Howes, Stephen. 'Australian Aid Ranked Second Last and New Zealand Last among Traditional Aid Donors.' *DevPolicy*, 21 September 2021. https://devpolicy.org/australian-and-new-zealand-aid-ranked-last-among-traditional-aid-donors-20210921/.

Hunter, Fergus. 'China Funded Confucius Institutes Targeted under New Foreign Influence Scheme.' *The Age*, 12 March 2019.

Hurst, Daniel. 'Malcolm Turnbull: Coal Export Ban "Would Make No Difference to Emissions".' *The Guardian*, 27 October 2015. https://www.theguardian.com/australia-news/2015/oct/27/malcolm-turnbull-coal-export-ban-would-make-no-difference-to-emissions.

Japan Times. 'Abe's Failed Submarine Bid.' *Japan Times*, 23 June 2016. https://www.japantimes.co.jp/opinion/2016/06/23/commentary/japan-commentary/abes-failed-submarine-bid/#.XHUWFugzY2w.

Japan Times. 'Australia "Extremely Disappointed" by Japan's Withdrawal from International Whaling Commission.' *Japan Times*, 26 December 2018. https://www.japantimes.co.jp/news/2018/12/26/national/australia-extremely-disappointed-japans-withdrawal-international-whaling-commission/#.XG8oXZMzZns.

Japan Times. 'Japan, Australia Vow to Step up Security Times under Abe's Successor.' *Japan Times*, 8 September 2020. https://www.japantimes.co.jp/news/2020/09/08/national/japan-australia-vow-security-ties/.

Jensen, Michael. 'We've Been Hacked – So Will the Data Be Weaponised to Influence Election 2019? Here's What to Look For.' *The Conversation*, 21 February 2019. https://theconversation.com/weve-been-hacked-so-will-the-data-be-weaponised-to-influence-election-2019-heres-what-to-look-for-112130.

Jordan, Primrose. 'Australia Beats China to Fiji Base.' *The Australian*, 7 September 2018.

Karp, Paul. 'Australia's Deputy PM Apologises to Pacific for Fruit-Picking Comments "If Any Insult Was Taken".' *The Guardian*, 22 August 2020. https://www.theguardian.com/australia-news/2019/aug/22/australias-deputy-pm-apologises-to-pacific-for-fruit-picking-comments-if-any-insult-was-taken.

Keany, Frances. 'Peter Dutton Overheard Joking About Rising Sea Levels in Pacific Island Nations.' *ABC News*, 11 September 2015. https://www.abc.net.au/news/2015-09-11/dutton-overheard-joking-about-sea-levels-in-pacific-islands/6768324.

Kearsley, Jonathan, and Eryk Bagshaw. 'Not Here to Be Bullied': UK Weighs in on China Hitlist.' *The Age*, 26 November 2020.

Kearsley, Jonathan, Eryk Bagshaw, and Anthony Galloway. '"If You Make China the Enemy China Will Be the Enemy": Beijing's Fresh Threat to Australia.' *Sydney Morning Herald*, 18 November 2020.

Kehoe, John, and Laura Tingle. 'US "Stunned" by Port of Darwin Sale to Chinese.' *Australian Financial Review*, 17 November 2015.

Kevin, Tony. 'Australia Started the War before It Started.' *Sydney Morning Herald*, 22 April 2004. https://www.smh.com.au/opinion/australia-started-the-war-before-it-started-20040422-gdisim.html.

Knott, Matthew. 'Australia in Push to Boost Ties with Japan', *The Age*, 10 December 2022, 9.

Lin, Xiu. 'China Urges Australia to Face up to Severe Human Rights Violations at UN Body.' *Global Times*, 8 July 2020. https://www.globaltimes.cn/page/202107/1228217.shtml.

Lyons, Kate. 'Revealed: "Fierce" Pacific Forum Meeting Almost Collapsed over Climate Crisis.' *The Guardian*, 16 August 2019. https://www.theguardian.com/environment/2019/aug/16/revealed-fierce-pacific-forum-meeting-almost-collapsed-over-climate-crisis.

Macmillan, Jade. 'Foreign Interference More of an "Existential Threat" to Australia than Terrorism: ASIO Chief.' *ABC News*, 4 September 2019. https://www.abc.net.au/news/2019-09-04/asio-chief-foreign-interference-more-of-a-threat-than-terrorism/11479796.

Maley, Jacqueline. 'Australia's Climate Policies Will Protect Environment and "Seek to Reduce" Hazard of Fires, Says Prime Minister.' *The Age*, 2 January 2020.

McDonald, Matt. 'Foreign Policy Should Play a Bigger Role in Australian Elections. This Is Why It Probably Won't.' *The Conversation*, 24 April 2019. https://theconversation.com/foreign-policy-should-play-a-bigger-role-in-australian-elections-this-is-why-it-probably-wont-115298.

McIlroy, Tom. 'Labor Would Have Rejected Pacific Coal Calls: Wong.' *Australian Financial Review*, 19 August 2019. https://www.afr.com/politics/federal/labor-would-have-rejected-pacific-coal-calls-wong-20190818-p52i9g.

McKenzie, Nick, Richard Baker, Sashka Koloff, and Chris Uhlmann. 'The Chinese Communist Party's Power and Influence in Australia.' *ABC News*, 4 June 2017. https://www.abc.net.au/news/2017-06-04/the-chinese-communist-partys-power-and-influence-in-australia/8584270.

McKenzie, Nick, Angus Grigg, and Chris Uhlmann. 'China Uses the Cloud to Step up Spying on Australian Business.' *The Age*, 20 November 2018.

McKenzie, Nick, Paul Sakkal, and Grace Tobin. 'Defecting Chinese Spy Offers Information Trove to Australian Government.' *The Age*, 25 November 2019. https://www.theage.com.au/national/defecting-chinese-spy-offers-information-trove-to-australian-government-20191122-p53d1l.html.

Melanesia News. 'Tuvalu's Prime Minister on Australia's Statements at PIF Retreat.' *Melanesia News*, 19 August 2019. https://www.melanesia.news/blog/2019/08/19/tuvalus-prime-minister-on-australias-statements-at-pif-retreat/.

Miller, Greg. 'This Was the Worst Call by Far: Trump Badgered, Bragged and Abruptly Ended Phone Call with Australian Leader.' *Washington Post*, 2 February 2017.

Moores, Dane. 'Australia's Aid Ambition Should Rise with Its Geopolitical Status.' *The Interpreter*, 12 November 2021. https://www.lowyinstitute.org/the-interpreter/australia-s-aid-ambition-should-rise-its-geo-political-status.

Moores, Dane. 'Covax Summit: Time for Australia to Recommit to Global, Not Regional, Vaccine Equity.' *DevPolicy*, 31 May 2021. https://devpolicy.org/covax-summit-time-for-australia-to-recommit-to-global-not-just-regional-vaccine-equity-20210531.

Munro, Kelsey. 'Australia's New Foreign-Influence Laws – Who Is Targeted?.' *The Interpreter*, 5 December 2018. https://www.lowyinstitute.org/the-interpreter/australia-new-foreign-influence-laws-who-targeted.

Murphy, Katharine. 'Greg Hunt and Julie Bishop at Odds over Whaling Monitoring.' *The Guardian*, 18 October 2013. https://www.theguardian.com/environment/2013/oct/18/greg-hunt-and-julie-bishop-at-odds-over-whaling-monitoring.

Murphy, Katharine. 'Scott Morrison to Reboot Tony Abbott's Emissions Reduction Fund with $2bn.' *The Guardian*, 25 February 2019. https://www.theguardian.com/australia-news/2019/feb/25/scott-morrison-to-reboot-tony-abbotts-emissions-reduction-fund-with-2bn.

Murray, Lisa. 'United Front Work Department: China's "Magic Weapon" for Winning Friends.' *Australian Financial Review*, 23 May 2019. https://www.afr.com/policy/foreign-affairs/united-front-work-department-chinas-magic-weapon-for-winning-friends-20180523-h10gcp.

Nakayama, Shuji, Setsuo Otsuka, and Issaku Harada. 'US–China Tariff Showdown Uproots Global Supply Chains.' *Nikkei Asia*, 24 August 2018. https://asia.nikkei.com/Economy/Trade-war/US–China-tariff-showdown-uproots-global-supply-chains.

Needham, Kirsty. 'Australian Coal in the Firing Line of Chinese 'Environmental' Crackdown.' *The Age*, 20 March 2019.

BIBLIOGRAPHY

Needham, Kirsty. 'Fears the United States Could Displace Australian Coal in China.' *The Age*, 21 March 2019.

Ni, Adam. 'Australia a Potential Target in US–China Fight over Huawei.' *ABC News*, 30 January 2019. https://www.abc.net.au/news/2019-01-30/huawei-china-us-fight-technology-dominance-australia/10762746.

O'Keefe, Michael. 'Why China's "Debt-Book Diplomacy" in the Pacific Shouldn't Ring Alarm Bells Just Yet.' *The Conversation*, 17 May 2018. https://theconversation.com/why-chinas-debt-book-diplomacy-in-the-pacific-shouldnt-ring-alarm-bells-just-yet-96709.

O'Keefe, Michael. 'Pacific Island Nations Will No Longer Stand for Australia's Inaction on Climate Change.' *The Conversation*, 16 August 2019. https://theconversation.com/pacific-island-nations-will-no-longer-stand-for-australias-inaction-on-climate-change-121976.

O'Malley, Nick. 'Australia Awarded "Colossal Fossil" Award as Climate Talks Drag On,' *Sydney Morning Herald*, 13 November 2021.

Packham, Ben. 'China Meddling 'Staggering,' Makes Case for Interference Laws.' *The Australian*, 17 November 2021, 6.

Parmeswaran, Prashanth. 'Old Shadows in New Australia–Indonesia Military Spat.' *The Diplomat*, 6 January 2017. https://thediplomat.com/2017/01/old-shadows-in-new-australia-indonesia-military-spat.

Phillips, Tom. 'Unit 61398 – the Featureless 12-Storey Building Which Houses One of the World's Most Dangerous and Secretive Cyber-Hacking Operations.' *Sydney Morning Herald*, 20 February 2013. https://www.smh.com.au/technology/unit-61398--the-featureless-12storey-building-which-houses-one-of-the-worlds-most-dangerous-and-secretive-cyberhacking-operations-20130220-2eqj4.html.

Rajah, Roland, Jonathan Pryke, and Alexander Dayant. 'China, the Pacific, and the "Debt Trap" Question.' *The Interpreter*, 23 October 2019. https://www.lowyinstitute.org/the-interpreter/china-pacific-and-debt-trap-question.

Reilly, Alex. 'Explainer: The Medevac Repeal and What It Means for Asylum Seekers on Manus Island and Nauru.' *The Conversation*, 4 December 2019. https://theconversation.com/explainer-the-medevac-repeal-and-what-it-means-for-asylum-seekers-on-manus-island-and-nauru-128118.

Reynolds, Emma. 'Tensions Rise as Chinese Government's Influence Infiltrates Aussie Universities.' *News.com.au*, 1 September 2017. https://www.news.com.au/finance/economy/australian-economy/tensions-rise-as-chinese-governments-influence-infiltrates-aussie-universities/news-story/e7768b0bb1f5953a7608884527387372.

Riordan, Primrose. 'China's Veiled Threat to Bill Shorten on Extradition Treaty.' *The Australian*, 4 December 2017, 4.

Sato, Mai, and Simone Abel. 'Japan-Australia Pact Highlights Need to Move Away Creatively from Death Penalty.' *The Conversation*, 20 November 2020. https://theconversation.com/japan-australia-pact-highlights-need-to-move-away-creatively-from-death-penalty-148436.

SBS News. 'Australia is US Deputy-Sheriff: Mahathir.' *SBS News*, 23 August 2013. https://www.sbs.com.au/news/australia-is-us-deputy-sheriff-mahathir.

SBS News. 'China Arrest Aussie Mining Boss for Spying.' *SBS News*, 24 February 2015. https://www.sbs.com.au/news/kadeer-hopes-for-democracy-and-freedom.

SBS News. 'Kadeer Hopes for Democracy and Freedom.' *SBS News*, 24 February 2015. https://www.sbs.com.au/news/kadeer-hopes-for-democracy-and-freedom.

SBS News. 'PM Meets Dalai Lama in Sydney.' *SBS News*, 24 February 2015. https://www.sbs.com.au/news/pm-meets-dalai-lama-in-sydney.

SBS News. 'US to Boost Military Activities in Australia.' *SBS News*, 26 February 2015. https://www.sbs.com.au/news/kadeer-hopes-for-democracy-and-freedom.

Sear, Tom, Michael Jensen, and Titus C. Chen. 'How Digital Media Blur the Border between Australia and China.' *The Conversation*, 16 November 2018. https://theconversation.com/how-digital-media-blur-the-border-between-australia-and-china-101735.

Shields, Bevan. 'Global Energy Chief Slams Climate Debate in Australia.' *The Age*, 21 December 2019, 1, 10.

Shields, Bevan. 'Just 2 Per Cent of Britain's Power Now Comes from Coal. In Australia, It's More Like Three Quarters.' *The Age*, 2 January 2020. https://www.theage.com.au/world/europe/

just-2-per-cent-of-britain-s-power-now-comes-from-coal-in-australia-it-s-more-like-three-quarters-20200101-p53o71.html.

Smith, Emily. 'Shinzō Abe Arrives in Darwin for First Visit by Japanese Leader.' *ABC News*, 16 November 2018. https://www.abc.net.au/news/2018-11-16/japan-shinzo-abe-darwin-bombing-scott-morrison-prime-minister/10506538.

Smith, Michael, and Andrew Tillett. 'China Payback Kills Dialogue.' *Australian Financial Review*, 6 May 2021. https://www.afr.com/world/asia/china-suspends-a-key-agreement-with-australia-20210506-p57phq.

Springer, Kyle. 'Australia Tries to Unlock the Benefits of Proximity with Indonesia.' *The Conversation*, 3 October 2017. https://theconversation.com/australia-tries-to-unlock-the-benefits-of-proximity-with-indonesia-84284.

Straits Times. '"They Can Pick Fruit": Australia-Pacific Islands Row Deepens over "Neo-Colonial" Attitude.' *Straits Times*, 19 August 2019. https://www.straitstimes.com/asia/australianz/they-can-pick-fruit-australia-pacific-islands-row-deepens-over-neo-colonial.

Sun, Wanning. 'Chinese Social Media Platform WeChat Could Be a Key Battleground in the Federal Election.' *The Conversation*, 28 March 2019. https://theconversation.com/chinese-social-media-platform-wechat-could-be-a-key-battleground-in-the-federal-election-113925.

Sydney Morning Herald. 'Labor Tested by Japan's Iraq Resolve.' *Sydney Morning Herald*, 1 March 2005. https://www.smh.com.au/opinion/labor-tested-by-japans-iraq-resolve-20050301-gdktwk.html.

Tanter, Richard. 'Witness Denied: Australian Media Responses to the Indonesian Killings of 1965–66.' *Inside Indonesia* 71, July–September 2002. https://www.insideindonesia.org/witness-denied.

Tavan, Gwenda. 'Issues That Swung Elections: Tampa and the National Security Election of 2001.' *The Conversation*, 3 May 2019. https://theconversation.com/issues-that-swung-elections-tampa-and-the-national-security-election-of-2001-115143.

The Australian. 'China Fires Back at Julie Bishop Over "Irresponsible" Remarks.' *The Australian*, 27 November 2013.

The Australian. 'US Tells Australia to Take on China over Disputed Islands.' *The Australian*, 24 July 2018.

The Australian. 'Their Enemies Are Not Our Enemies: Pacific Nations Won't Join Stand against China.' *The Australian*, 19 August 2019.

Truu, Maani. 'Indonesia Condemns Anning Comments on Christchurch Terror Attack.' *SBS News*, 18 March 2019. https://www.sbs.com.au/news/indonesia-condemns-anning-comments-on-christchurch-terror-attack/8a0872a1-eef6-405b-a27c-c17a5cb05ab2.

Uhlmann, Chris, and Andrew Greene. 'Chinese Donors to Australian Political Parties: Who Gave How Much?' *ABC News*, 8 June 2017. https://www.abc.net.au/news/2016-08-21/china-australia-political-donations/7766654?nw=0&r=HtmlFragment.

Wade, Matt, and Tony Stephens. 'PM Stung by Roaring Band of Top Brass and Diplomats.' *Sydney Morning Herald*, 9 August 2004, 1.

White, Hugh. 'The Lombok Treaty: Devil in the Detail.' *The Interpreter*, 7 March 2008. http://www.lowyinterpreter.org/the-interpreter/australia-japan-abbott-uses-word.

White, Hugh. 'The Jakarta Switch: Why Australia Needs to Pin Its Hopes (Not Fears) on a Great and Powerful Indonesia.' *Australian Foreign Affairs*, July 2018, 15–46. https://www.australianforeignaffairs.com/articles/extract/2018/07/the-jakarta-switch.

Whiting, Natalie, Marian Faa, and Annika Burgess. 'China Accuses Australia of Covid-19 Vaccine Sabotage in the Pacific.' *ABC News*, 6 July 2021. https://www.abc.net.au/news/2021-07-06/china-accuses-australia-papua-new-guinea-covid-vaccinations/100269320.

Wood, Terence. 'Ngo Donations: Are Australians Turing Inwards?' *DevPolicy*, 26 March 2020. https://devpolicy.org/ngo-donations-are-australians-turning-inwards-20200326.

Wood, Terence. 'Australian Public Opinion About Aid: Is it Changing and Does it Matter?' *DevPolicy*, 22 December 2022. https://devpolicy.org/australian-public-opinion-about-aid-20221202/?utm_source=rss&utm_medium=rss&utm_campaign=australian-public-opinion-about-aid-20221202.

Wood, Terence, and Ryan Edwards. 'Australian Aid Cuts at Odds with Public Opinion.' *DevPolicy*, 18 May 2020. https://devpolicy.org/aid-public-opinion-20210518/.

BIBLIOGRAPHY

Wood, Terence, and Sabit Otor. 'A Risky Proposition? Australian Aid Loans and the Pacific.' *DevPolicy*, 22 August 2019. https://devpolicy. org/a-risky-proposition-australian-aid-loans-and-the-pacific-20190822/.

Wood, Terence, Christopher Hoy, and Jonathan Pryke. 'Does Chinese Aid Make Australians More Generous?' *The Interpreter*, 13 August 2019. https://www.lowyinstitute.org/the-interpreter/ does-chinese-aid-make-australians-more-generous.

Wroe, David. 'China Eyes Vanuatu Military Base in Plan with Global Ramifications.' *Sydney Morning Herald*, 9 April 2018. https://www.smh.com.au/politics/federal/china-eyes-vanuatu-military-base-in-plan-with-global-ramifications-20180409-p4z8j9.html.

Wroe, David. 'Cyber Attacks Could Help Trigger a War, Says Marise Payne.' *Sydney Morning Herald*, 11 March 2019. https://www.smh.com.au/politics/federal/cyber-attacks-could-help-trigger-a-war-says-marise-payne-20190311-p513b3.html.

Xinhua. 'Australia–China Joint Military Exercise Kicks Off in Canberra.' *Xinhua*, 17 September 2019. http://www.xinhuanet.com/english/2018-09/17/c_137474062.htm.

Yaxley, Louise. 'Malcolm Turnbull Questions Sam Dastyari's Loyalty Amid Claims He Passed Security Information to Chinese Donor.' *ABC News*, 29 November 2017. https://www.abc.net. au/news/2017-11-29/sam-dastyari-denies-warning-chinese-donor-of-phone-tap/9205012.

Yujia, Shen. 'Australia Tearing up Formal Belt and Road Deal Has Little Exemplary Effect.' *Global Times*, 22 April 2021. https://www.globaltimes.cn/page/202104/1221826.shtml.

Zhang, Marina Yue. 'Students in China Heed Their Government's Warnings against Studying in Australia.' *The Conversation*, 8 July 2020. https://theconversation.com/students-in-china-heed-their-governments-warnings-against-studying-in-australia-141871.

Zhou, Christina. 'Beijing Suggests Australia Reflect on How It Treats Pacific Neighbours after Climate Change Fallout.' *ABC News*, 21 August 2019. https://www.abc.net.au/news/2019-08-21/beijing-suggests-canberra-self-reflects-after-climate-talks-pif/11434080.

Press releases

Amnesty International. 'Nauru Camp a Human Rights Catastrophe with No End in Sight.' Amnesty International Australia Nauru Offshore Processing Facility Review 2012. News Release, 23 November 2012. https://www.amnesty.org/en/documents/asa42/002/2012/en/.

Amnesty International. 'Shooting Incident at Manus Island Centre Exemplifies the Failure of Offshore Processing.' News Release, 15 April 2017. https://www.amnesty.org.au/australiapng-shooting-incident-manus-island-centre-exemplifies-failure-offshore-processing/.

Commonwealth of Australia and People's Republic of China. 'Joint Communique of the Australian Government and the Government of the People's Republic of China Concerning the Establishment of Diplomatic Relations between Australian and China.' News Release, 1 December 1972. https://pmtranscripts.pmc.gov.au/sites/default/files/original/00003119.pdf.

Consulate General of the PRC in Perth. 'Australia Targets Chinese Journalists, Scholars, Pushes Anti-China Witch-Hunt.' News Release, 10 September 2020. http://perth.chineseconsulate.org/ eng/notc/202009/t20200910_165899.htm.

Government of Nauru. 'Nauru Govt Says Q&A Is a Wakeup Call for ABC Bias and Unethical Reporting.' News Release, July 2018. http://naurugov.nr/government-information-office/ media-release/nauru-govt-says-qa-is-a-wakeup-call-for-abc-bias-and-unethical-reporting.aspx.

Morrison, Scott. 'Regional Trade Deal to Boost Export Opportunities for Aussie Farmers and Businesses.' Press Release, 15 November 2020.

Office of the Prime Minister of Australia. 'Quad Leaders' Joint Statement: The Spirit of the Quad.' News Release, 12 March 2021. https://www.whitehouse.gov/briefing-room/statements-releases/2021/03/12/quad-leaders-joint-statement-the-spirit-of-the-quad/.

Office of the Prime Minister of Australia. '70 Years of ANZUS and Our Alliance with the United States.' News Release, 1 September 2021. https://www.pm.gov.au/media/70-years-anzus-and-our-alliance-united-states.

Pacific Islands Development Forum. 'Nadi Bay Declaration on Climate Change Crisis in the Pacific.' News Release, 31 July 2019. https://cop23.com.fj/nadi-bay-declaration-on-the-climate-change-crisis-in-the-pacific/.

BIBLIOGRAPHY

Price, Ned. 'Secretary Blinken's Call with Australian Foreign Minister Payne.' News Release, 27 January 2021. https://www.state.gov/secretary-blinkens-call-with-australian-foreign-minister-payne/.

Prime Minister's Office. 'Media Statement: Joint Statement between the Government of the Republic of Indonesia and the Government of Australia.' News Release, 10 February 2020.

Turnbull, Malcolm, and Shinzo Abe. 'Joint Statement – Next Steps of the Special Strategic Partnership: Asia, Pacific and Beyond.' News Release, 18 December 2015. https://www.malcolmturnbull.com.au/media/joint-statement-next-steps-of-the-special-strategic-partnership-asia-pacifi.

United Nations High Commissioner for Refugees. 'UNHCR Legal Position: Despite Court Ruling on Sri Lankans Detained at Sea, Australia Bound by International Obligations.' News Release, 4 February 2015. https://www.unhcr.org/en-au/news/press/2015/2/54d1e4ac9/unhcr-legal-position-despite-court-ruling-sri-lankans-detained-sea-australia.html.

White House. 'Readout of President Joseph R. Biden, Jr. Call with Prime Minister Scott Morrison of Australia.' News Release, 3 February 2021. https://www.whitehouse.gov/briefing-room/statements-releases/2021/02/03/readout-of-president-joseph-r-biden-jr-call-with-prime-minister-scott-morrison-of-australia/.

White House, Office of the Press Secretary. 'Remarks by President Obama to the Australian Parliament, Parliament House, Canberra, Australia.' News Release, November 17, 2011. https://obamawhitehouse.archives.gov/the-press-office/2011/11/17/remarks-president-obama-australian-parliament.

Reports

Allen, Kenneth, Phillip C. Saunders, and John Chen. *Chinese Military Diplomacy 2006–2016: Trends and Implications.* China Strategic Perspectives 11, Center for the Study of Chinese Military Affairs, Institute for National Strategic Studies, National Defense University (Washington, DC: National Defense University Press, 2017). https://ndupress.ndu.edu/Portals/68/Documents/stratperspective/china/ChinaPerspectives-11.pdf?ver=2017-07-17-153301-093.

Amnesty International. *Island of Despair: Australia's Processing of Refugees on Nauru* (London: Amnesty International, 2016). https://www.amnesty.org/en/wp-content/uploads/2021/05/ASA1249342016ENGLISH.pdf.

Asylum Seeker Resource Centre (ASRC). *At What Cost? The Human and Economic Cost of Australia's Offshore Detention Policies* (Melbourne: ASRC, 2019). https://asrc.org.au/wp-content/uploads/2013/04/1912-At-What-Cost-report.pdf.

Austrade, Australian Government. *International Visitors in Australia* (Canberra: Commonwealth of Australia, 2018).

Austrade, Australian Government. *Market Action Plan – Indonesia* (Canberra: Commonwealth of Australia, 2019).

Australia Security Leaders Climate Group. *Whole-of-Nation Climate-Security Risk Assessment, Missing in Action: Responding to Australia's Climate & Security Failure* (Canberra: Australia Security Leaders Climate Group, 2021). https://www.aslcg.org/wp-content/uploads/2021/09/ASLCG_MIA_Report.pdf.

Australian Academy of Science. *The Risks to Australia of a 3°C World* (Canberra: Australian Academy of Science, 2021). https://www.science.org.au/files/userfiles/support/reports-and-plans/2021/risks-australia-three-deg-warmer-world-report.pdf.

Australian Bureau of Statistics. *3401.0 Overseas Arrivals and Departures, Australia.* Canberra, May 2018.

Australian Bureau of Statistics. *5368.0.55.004 International Trade: Supplementary Information, Calendar Year, 2017.* Updated 25 May 2018. https://www.abs.gov.au/AUSSTATS/abs@.nsf/DetailsPage/5368.0.55.0042017?OpenDocument.

Australian Bureau of Statistics. *340120DO005 Migration, Australia 2016–2017.* Canberra, October 2018.

Australian Bureau of Statistics. *Census 2021.* Canberra, 2022. https://www.abs.gov.au/census.

Australian Civil-Military Centre. *Afghanistan: Lessons from Australia's Whole-of-Government Mission* (Canberra: Commonwealth of Australia, November 2016). https://www.acmc.gov.au/sites/default/files/2018-07/apo-nid71004-15836_0.pdf.

BIBLIOGRAPHY

Australian Department of Climate Change, Energy, the Environment and Water. *Australia's Greenhouse Emissions: March 2022 Quarterly Update* (Canberra, March 2022).

Australian Department of Climate Change, Energy, the Environment and Water. *Australia's Emissions Projections 2022* (Canberra, December 2022).

Australian Department of Defence. *The Strategic Basis of Australian Defence Policy* (Canberra: Department of Defence, March 1971). https://www.dfat.gov.au/about-us/publications/historical-documents/volume-27/Pages/107-report-by-defence-committee.

Australian Department of Defence. *Australian Defence* (Canberra: Department of Defence, 1976). https://defence.gov.au/publications/wpaper1976.pdf.

Australian Department of Defence. *Defending Australia: 1976 Defence White Paper* (Canberra: Commonwealth of Australia, 1976). https://defence.gov.au/publications/wpaper1976.pdf.

Australian Department of Defence. *The Defence of Australia, 1987* (Canberra: Government Publishing Service, 1987). https://defence.gov.au/publications/wpaper1987.pdf.

Australian Department of Defence. *Australia's Strategic Policy* (Canberra: Commonwealth of Australia, 1997).

Australian Department of Defence. *2016 Defence White Paper* (Canberra: Commonwealth of Australia, 2016). https://www1.defence.gov.au/sites/default/files/2021-08/2016-Defence-White-Paper.pdf.

Australian Department of Defence. *2016 Integrated Investment Program* (Canberra: Commonwealth of Australia, 2016). https://apo.org.au/sites/default/files/resource-files/2016-02/apo-nid65619.

Australian Department of Defence. *2020 Defence Strategic Update* (Canberra: Government Publishing Service, 2020).

Australian Department of the Environment and Energy. *Australian Energy Update 2019*. (Canberra: Australian Energy Statistics, 2019). https://www.energy.gov.au/sites/default/files/australian_energy_statistics_2019_energy_update_report_september.pdf.

Australian Department of Foreign Affairs and Trade. *Australia's Regional Security* (Canberra: Commonwealth of Australia, 1989).

Australian Department of Foreign Affairs and Trade. *Australian Aid: Promoting Prosperity, Reducing Poverty, Enhancing Stability* (Canberra: Department of Foreign Affairs and Trade, June 2014). https://www.dfat.gov.au/sites/default/files/australian-aid-development-policy.pdf.

Australian Department of Foreign Affairs and Trade. *Aid Investment Plan: Pacific Regional 2015–16 to 2018–19* (Canberra: Commonwealth of Australia, 2014). https://www.dfat.gov.au/sites/default/files/pacific-regional-aid-investment-plan-2015-19.pdf.

Australian Department of Foreign Affairs and Trade. *Australia's Trade since Federation* (Canberra: Department of Foreign Affairs and Trade, 2016). https://www.dfat.gov.au/sites/default/files/australias-trade-since-federation.pdf.

Australian Department of Foreign Affairs and Trade. *Australia–Japan Strategy for Cooperation in the Pacific* (Canberra: Department of Foreign Affairs and Trade, 2016).

Australian Department of Foreign Affairs and Trade. *2017 Foreign Policy White Paper* (Canberra: Commonwealth of Australia, 2017). https://www.dfat.gov.au/sites/default/files/minisite/static/4ca0813c-585e-4fe1-86eb-de665e65001a/fpwhitepaper/pdf/2017-foreign-policy-white-paper.pdf.

Australian Department of Foreign Affairs and Trade. *Plan of Action for the Implementation of the Joint Declaration on Maritime Cooperation between the Government of Australia and the Government of the Republic of Indonesia* (Canberra: Commonwealth of Australia, 2017). https://www.dfat.gov.au/sites/default/files/indonesia-australia-maritime-cooperation-action-plan.pdf.

Australian Department of Foreign Affairs and Trade. *New Colombo Plan 2020 Scholarships* (Canberra: Department of Foreign Affairs and Trade, 25 November 2019). https://www.dfat.gov.au/people-to-people/new-colombo-plan/scholarship-program/previous-rounds.

Australian Department of Foreign Affairs and Trade. *Australian Aid Budget Summary 2019–20* (Canberra: Department of Foreign Affairs and Trade, 2019). https://www.dfat.gov.au/sites/default/files/2019-20-australian-aid-budget-summary.pdf.

Australian Department of Foreign Affairs and Trade. *Partnerships for Recovery: Australia's Covid-19 Development Response* (Canberra: Department of Foreign Affairs and Trade, 2020). https://

www.dfat.gov.au/sites/default/files/partnerships-for-recovery-australias-covid-19-development-response.pdf.

Australian Department of Foreign Affairs and Trade. *Australian Aid Budget at a Glance 2019–20* (Canberra: Department of Foreign Affairs and Trade, 2020). https://www.dfat.gov.au/sites/default/files/2019-20-aus-aid-budget-at-a-glance.pdf.

Australian Department of Foreign Affairs and Trade. *Australian Official Development Assistance to the Pacific* (Canberra: Commonwealth of Australia, 2020).

Australian Department of Foreign Affairs and Trade. *Trade and Investment at a Glance 2020* (Canberra: Commonwealth of Australia, 2020). https://www.dfat.gov.au/sites/default/files/trade-investment-glance-2020.pdf.

Australian Department of Foreign Affairs and Trade. *Australian Development Budget Summary 2020–21* (Canberra: Department of Foreign Affairs and Trade, 2021). https://www.dfat.gov.au/sites/default/files/2020-21-aid-budget-summary.pdf.

Australian Department of Foreign Affairs and Trade. *Pacific Step-Up: Stepping up Australia's Engagement with Our Pacific Family* (Canberra: Department of Foreign Affairs and Trade, 2021). https://www.dfat.gov.au/geo/pacific.

Australian Department of Foreign Affairs and Trade. *International Investment Australia 2021* (Canberra: Commonwealth of Australia, 2022).

Australian Department of Foreign Affairs and Trade. *Foreign Affairs and Trade Budget Highlights* (Canberra: Department of Foreign Affairs and Trade, 2022).

Australian Department of Foreign Affairs and Trade. *Australian Development Budget Summary 2022–23* (Canberra: Department of Foreign Affairs and Trade, 2022).

Australian Department of Foreign Affairs and Trade. *Indonesia: Development Cooperation Fact Sheet, October 2022* (Canberra: Department of Foreign Affairs and Trade), accessed 9 December 2022. https://www.dfat.gov.au/sites/default/files/development-cooperation-fact-sheet-indonesia.pdf.

Australian Department of Foreign Affairs and Trade, *Australian Official Development Assistance Budget Summary 2022–23* (Canberra: Commonwealth of Australia, 2023). https://www.dfat.gov.au/about-us/corporate/portfolio-budget-statements/oda-budget-summary-2022-23.

Australian Department of Home Affairs. *Operation Sovereign Borders: Australia's Borders are Closed to Illegal Migration* (Canberra: Commonwealth of Australia, 2020). https://osb.homeaffairs.gov.au/home.

Australian Department of Home Affairs. *Statistics of Transitory Persons in Nauru and PNG* (Canberra: Commonwealth of Australia, 31 October 2021). https://www.homeaffairs.gov.au/about-us-subsite/files/population-and-number-of-people-resettled.pdf.

Australian Government, Department of the Treasury. *Budget 2019–20: Portfolio Budget Statements 2019–20, Budget Related Paper No. 116, Treasury Portfolio* (Canberra: Commonwealth of Australia, 2019). https://treasury.gov.au/sites/default/files/2019-04/pbs_2019-20_combined.pdf.

Australian National Audit Office. *Air Warfare Destroyer Program.* Audit Report No. 22, 2013–14 (Canberra: National Audit Office, 2014). https://www.anao.gov.au/sites/default/files/AuditReport_2013-2014_22.pdf.

Australian Security Intelligence Organization. *ASIO Submission to the Parliamentary Joint Committee on Intelligence and Security, Review of Administration and Expenditure No. 16, 2016–2017.* Submission 5 (Canberra: Commonwealth of Australia, 2017). https://www.aph.gov.au/Parliamentary_Business/Committees/Joint/Intelligence_and_Security/AandENo16/Submissions.

Australian Trade and Investment Commission. *Japanese Investment in Australia: A Trusted Partnership* (Canberra: Trade and Investment Commission, 2017). https://www.austrade.gov.au/International/Invest/Importance-of-Foreign-Direct-Investment/Japanese-investment-in-Australia/report.

Baker, Cat. *The People Smugglers' Business Model.* Research Paper No. 2, 2012–13 (Canberra: Commonwealth of Australia, 28 February 2013). https://parlinfo.aph.gov.au/parlInfo/download/library/prspub/2262537/upload_binary/2262537.pdf;fileType=application/pdf.

Bishop, Matthew, Rachid Bouhia, George Carter, Jack Corbett, Courtney Lindsay, Michelle Scobie, and Emily Wilkinson. *Towards Sustainable Development in Small Island Developing States: Why*

BIBLIOGRAPHY

We Need to Reshape Global Governance. ODI Working Paper (London: ODI, July 2021). https://cdn.odi.org/media/documents/SIDS_sustained_development_WP_jr.pdf.

Brangwin, Nicole, Marty Harris, and David Watt. *Australia at War in Afghanistan: Revised Facts and Figures.* Parliamentary Library (Canberra: Department of Parliamentary Services, 12 September 2012).

Brown, Gary, Frank Frost, and Steven Sherlock. *The Australian-Indonesian Security Agreement – Issues and Implications.* Research Paper No. 25, 1995–96 (18 December 1995). https://www.aph.gov.au/About_Parliament/Parliamentary_Departments/Parliamentary_Library/pubs/rp/RP9596/96rp25#APPENDIX.

Bureau of Meteorology (BOM). *Annual Climate Statement 2020: Fourth Hottest Year on Record* (Canberra: BOM, 8 January 2021).

Centre for International Economics. *Economic Benefits of Australia's North Asian FTAs* (Canberra: Centre for International Economics, 2015). https://www.dfat.gov.au/sites/default/files/economic-modelling-of-australias-north-asia-ftas.pdf.

Clare, Angela. *Budget Review 2020–21.* Research Paper Series, 2020–21 (Canberra: Parliamentary Library, 2021). https://www.aph.gov.au/About_Parliament/Parliamentary_Departments/Parliamentary_Library/pubs/rp/BudgetReview202021/AustraliasForeignAidBudget.

Climate Council. *From Paris to Glasgow: A World on the Move* (Sydney: Climate Council of Australia Ltd, 2021). https://www.climatecouncil.org.au/wp-content/uploads/2021/10/CC_MVSA0279-CC-Report-From-Paris-to-Glasgow_V6-FA_Low_Res_Single_Pages-3.pdf.

Climate Council. *Rising to the Challenge: Addressing Climate and Security in the Region* (Sydney: Climate Council of Australia Ltd, 2021). https://www.climatecouncil.org.au/wp-content/uploads/2021/09/CC_MVSA0274_Climate-Security_V8-FA_Low_Res_Single_Pages.pdf.

Climate Transparency. *Brown to Green Report: The G20 Transition Towards a Net-Zero Emissions Economy 2019* (Berlin: Climate Transparency, 2019). https://www.climate-transparency.org/wp-content/uploads/2019/11/Brown-to-Green-Report-2019.pdf.

Coady, David, Ian Parry, Nghia-Piotr Le, and Baoping Shang. *Global Fossil Fuel Subsidies Remain Large: An Update Based on Country Level Estimates.* IMF Working Paper No. 2019/089 (Washington, DC: International Monetary Fund, 2 May 2019). https://www.imf.org/en/Publications/WP/Issues/2019/05/02/Global-Fossil-Fuel-Subsidies-Remain-Large-An-Update-Based-on-Country-Level-Estimates-46509.

Commonwealth of Australia. *Howard Ministries, Cabinet Submissions.* Cabinet Submission JH97/0423 - Establishment of a Joint Australia - United States Relay Ground Station at Pine Gap - Decision JH97/0423/NS (Canberra: National Archives of Australia, 1996–1997). https://recordsearch.naa.gov.au/SearchNRetrieve/NAAMedia/ShowImage.aspx?B=32383316&T=PDF.

Commonwealth Scientific and Industrial Research Organization (CSIRO) and Bureau of Meteorology (BOM). *State of the Climate 2022* (Canberra: CSIRO/BOM, 23 November 2022). http://www.bom.gov.au/state-of-the-climate/.

Curtain, Richard, and Stephen Howes. *Governance of the Seasonal Worker Programme in Australia and Sending Countries.* Development Policy Centre, Crawford School of Public Policy, ANU College of Asia and the Pacific, The Australian National University (Canberra: Development Policy Centre, 8 December 2020). https://devpolicy.org/publications/reports/Governance_SWP_2020_WEB.pdf.

Diamond, Larry, and Orville Schell. *China's Influence & American Interests: Promoting Constructive Vigilance* (Stanford, CA: Hoover Institution, 2018). https://www.hoover.org/research/chinas-influence-american-interests-promoting-constructive-vigilance.

Dibb, Paul. *Review of Australia's Defence Capabilities: Report for the Minister of Defence* (Canberra: Australian Government Publishing Service, 1986).

Dobell, Graeme. *Special Report: Australia as an ASEAN Community Partner* (Canberra: Australian Strategic Policy Institute, February 2018). https://www.aspi.org.au/report/australia-asean-community-partner.

Economist Intelligence Unit. *Long Term Macroeconomic Forecasts: Key Trends to 2050* (London: Economist Intelligence Unit, 2015).

Evans, Michael. *The Tyranny of Dissonance: Australia's Strategic Culture and Way of War 1901–2004.* Study Paper no. 306 (Canberra: Land Warfare Studies Centre, February 2005).

BIBLIOGRAPHY

Foreign Investment Review Board. *Foreign Investment Review Board Annual Report 2009–10.* (Canberra: Commonwealth of Australia, 2011). https://firb.gov.au/sites/firb.gov.au/files/2015/11/2009-10_FIRB_AR.pdf.

Foreign Investment Review Board. *Foreign Investment Review Board Annual Report 2017–18.* (Canberra: Commonwealth of Australia, 2017). https://firb.gov.au/sites/firb.gov.au/files/2019/02/FIRB-2017-18-Annual-Report-final.

Foreign Investment Review Board. *Protecting the National Interest, Guidance 11* (Canberra: Commonwealth of Australia, 2020).

Foreign Investment Review Board. *Foreign Investment Review Board Annual Report 2019–20.* (Canberra: Commonwealth of Australia, 2021). https://firb.gov.au/sites/firb.gov.au/files/2021-06/FIRB2019-20AnnualReport.

Gowan, Richard. *Australia in the UN Security Council.* The Lowy Institute (12 June 2014). https://www.lowyinstitute.org/publications/australia-un-security-council.

Green, Michael J., Peter J. Dean, Brendan Taylor, and Zack Cooper. *The ANZUS Alliance in an Ascending Asia.* (Canberra: The Australian National University, July 2015). http://sdsc.bellschool.anu.edu.au/sites/default/files/publications/attachments/2015-12/COG_%2323_Web_4.pdf.

Hanson, Fergus. *Lowy Institute Poll 2008: Australia and the World.* The Lowy Institute (23 September 2008). https://www.lowyinstitute.org/publications/2008-lowy-institute-poll-australia-and-world.

Hanson, Fergus. *2009 Lowy Institute Poll 2009.* The Lowy Institute (12 October 2009). https://www.lowyinstitute.org/publications/2009-lowy-institute-poll.

Hanson, Fergus. *Lowy Institute Poll 2012: Public Opinion and Foreign Policy.* The Lowy Institute (5 June 2012). https://www.lowyinstitute.org/publications/lowy-institute-poll-2012-public-opinion-and-foreign-policy.

Hare, Bill, Anna Chapman, Victor Maxwell, Cindy Baxter, and Nandini Das. *Australia's 2030 Emissions: States Lead the Way* (Melbourne: Climate Analytics, 2021). https://climateanalytics.org/media/australia_s_2030_emissions.pdf.

Hayward-Jones, Jenny. *Fiji at Home and in the World.* The Lowy Institute (6 September 2011). https://www.lowyinstitute.org/publications/fiji-home-world-public-opinion-foreign-policy.

Hilferty, Fiona, Ilan Katz, Fredrick Zmudzki, Miranda van Hooff, Ellie Lawrence-Wood, Amelia Searle, Geoff Evans, Ben Challinor, and Adrian Talbot. *Homelessness Amongst Australian Veterans: Summary of Project Findings.* Australian Housing and Urban Research Institute (May 2019). https://www.ahuri.edu.au/sites/default/files/migration/documents/AHURI-Report_Homelessness-Amongst-Australian-contemporary-veterans_Final-Report.pdf.

Human Rights Watch. 'East Timor: The November 12 Massacre and Its Aftermath.' *Asia Watch* 3, no. 26 (12 December 1991). https://www.hrw.org/report/1991/12/12/east-timor-november-12-massacre-and-its-aftermath.

International Renewable Energy Agency (IRENA), *Renewable Capacity Statistics 2021.* New York: IRENA, 2021. https://www.irena.org/publications/2021/March/Renewable-Capacity-Statistics-2021.

Jackman, Simon, Zoe Meers, Shaun Ratcliff, and Jared Mondschein. *Public Opinion in the Age of Trump.* The United States Studies Centre (18 December 2019). https://www.ussc.edu.au/analysis/public-opinion-in-the-united-states-and-australia-compared.

Japanese Ministry of Foreign Affairs. *Diplomatic Bluebook 2020.* (Tokyo: Japanese Ministry of Foreign Affairs, 2019). https://www.mofa.go.jp/policy/other/bluebook/2020/html/chapter2/c020106.html.

Joint Standing Committee on Foreign Affairs, Defence and Trade, Foreign Affairs Sub-Committee. *Near Neighbours – Good Neighbours: An Inquiry into Australia's Relationship with Indonesia* (Canberra: Commonwealth of Australia, 31 May 2004). https://www.aph.gov.au/Parliamentary_Business/Committees/House_of_representatives_Committees?url=jfadt/indonesia/report.htm#fullreport.

Joint Standing Committee on Foreign Affairs, Defence and Trade, Human Rights Sub-Committee. *Australia's Response to the Indian Ocean Tsunami* (Canberra: Commonwealth of Australia, 2006). https://www.aph.gov.au/Parliamentary_Business/%20Committees%20/%20House_of_Representatives_Committees?url=jfadt/tsunamiresponse/prelims.htm.

BIBLIOGRAPHY   381

Joint Standing Committee on Trade and Investment Growth. *Leveraging on Our Advantages: The Trade Relationship between Australia and Indonesia* (Canberra: Commonwealth of Australia, 2017). https://parlinfo.aph.gov.au/parlInfo/download/committees/reportjnt/024065/toc_pdf/Leveragingouradvantages.pdf;fileType=application%2Fpdf.

Joint Standing Committee on Treaties. *Report 186: IA-CEPA and A-HKFTA* (Canberra: Commonwealth of Australia, 2019). https://parlinfo.aph.gov.au/parlInfo/download/committees/reportjnt/024355/toc_pdf/Report186.pdf;fileType=application%2Fpdf.

Joske, Alex. *Picking Flowers, Making Honey: The Chinese Military's Collaboration with Foreign Universities.* Policy Brief Report No. 10/2018, 30 October (Canberra: Australian Strategic Policy Institute and International Cyber Policy Centre, 2018). https://www.aspi.org.au/report/picking-flowers-making-honey.

Karlsen, Elibritt. *Australia's Offshore Processing of Asylum Seekers in Nauru and PNG: A Quick Guide to Statistics and Resources.* Research Paper Series, 2016–17 (Canberra: Commonwealth of Australia, 2016). https://parlinfo.aph.gov.au/parlInfo/download/library/prspub/4129606/upload_binary/4129606.pdf;fileType=application/pdf.

Kassam, Natasha. *Lowy Institute Poll 2019.* The Lowy Institute (26 June 2019). https://www.lowyinstitute.org/publications/lowy-institute-poll-2019.

Kassam, Natasha. *Lowy Institute Poll 2020.* The Lowy Institute (24 June 2020). https://poll.lowyinstitute.org/report/2020/.

Kassam, Natasha. *Lowy Institute Poll 2021.* The Lowy Institute (23 June 2021). https://poll.lowyinstitute.org/report/2021.

Kassam, Natasha. *Lowy Institute Poll 2022.* The Lowy Institute (29 June 2022). https://poll.lowyinstitute.org/report/2022.

Kassam, Natasha, and Jennifer Hsu. *Being Chinese in Australia: Public Opinion in Chinese Communities* (Sydney: The Lowy Institute, 2021). https://charts.lowyinstitute.org/features/chinese-communities/.

Laksmana, Evan. *Reinforcing Indonesia-Australia Defence Relations: The Case for Maritime Recalibration.* The Lowy Institute (2 October 2018). https://www.lowyinstitute.org/publications/reinforcing-indonesia-australia-defence-relations-case-maritime-recalibration-1.

Martyn, Angus. 'The Right of Self-Defence under International Law – the Response to the Terrorist Attacks of 11 September.' *Current Issues Brief* 8, 2001–02 (Canberra: 12 February 2002). https://www.aph.gov.au/About_Parliament/Parliamentary_Departments/Parliamentary_Library/Publications_Archive/CIB/cib0102/02CIB08.

Menzies, Robert. 'Visit to the US Senate by Hon. Robert Gordon Menzies.' *Congressional Record*, 84th Cong., 1st sess., Vol. 101, Pt 3 (16 March 1955), 3020–3021.

Merzian, Richie, Audrey Quicke, Ebony Bennett, Rod Campbell, and Tom Swann. *Climate of the Nation 2019: Tracking Australia's Attitudes Towards Climate Change and Energy* (Manuka, ACT: The Australia Institute, 2019). https://australiainstitute.org.au/report/climate-of-the-nation-2019/.

Millar, T.B. *Australia in Peace and War: External Relations 1788–1977* (Canberra: Australian National University Press, 1978). https://openresearch-repository.anu.edu.au/handle/1885/114800.

National Archives of Australia. *Cabinet Submission 170 – Review of ANZUS –Decisions/Der and 634.* (Canberra: Commonwealth of Australia, 24–30 May 1983).

Nauru Department of Commerce, Industries and Environment. *Convention on Biological Diversity Sixth National Report of Nauru* (Yaren, Nauru, October 2019). https://www.cbd.int/doc/nr/nr-06/nr-nr-06-en.pdf.

Newspoll. *Australian Attitudes Towards Indonesia: Report* (Canberra: Newspoll, May 2013). https://apo.org.au/sites/default/files/resource-files/2013-08/apo-nid35502.pdf.

Oliver, Alex. *Lowy Institute Poll 2013.* The Lowy Institute (24 June 2013). https://www.lowyinstitute.org/publications/lowy-institute-poll-2013.

Oliver, Alex. *Lowy Institute Poll 2016.* The Lowy Institute (21 June 2016). https://www.lowyinstitute.org/publications/lowy-institute-poll-2016.

Oliver, Alex. *Lowy Institute Poll 2018.* The Lowy Institute (20 June 2018). https://www.lowyinstitute.org/publications/2018-lowy-institute-poll.

Ong, Michael. 'Iraq: Issues on the Eve of War. '*Current Issues Brief* 19, 2002–03 (18 March 2003). https://www.aph.gov.au/binaries/library/pubs/cib/2002-03/03cib19.pdf.

Organization for Economic Cooperation and Development. *OECD Development Co-Operation Peer Reviews: Australia 2018* (Paris: OECD Publishing, 2018). https://www.oecd-ilibrary.org/development/oecd-development-co-operation-peer-reviews-australia-2018_9789264293366-en.

Organization for Economic Cooperation and Development and World Trade Organization. *Aid for Trade at a Glance 2013* (Paris: OECD Publishing, 2013). https://www.oecd-ilibrary.org/development/aid-for-trade-at-a-glance-2013_aid_glance-2013-en.

Organization for Economic Cooperation and Development, and World Trade Organization. *Aid for Trade at a Glance 2019: Economic Diversification and Empowerment.* (Paris: OECD Publishing, 2019). https://www.oecd-ilibrary.org/development/aid-for-trade-at-a-glance-2019_18ea27d8-en.

Otor, Sabit Amun, and Matthew Dornan. *How Does Foreign Aid Impact Exports in the Long Run?* Discussion Paper No. 62. Development Policy Centre, Crawford School of Public Policy, ANU College of Asia and the Pacific, The Australian National University (Canberra: Development Policy Centre, 17 September 2017). http://devpolicy.org/publications/discussion_papers/DP62_How-does-foreign-aid-impact-Australian-exports.pdf.

Pacific Island Forum Secretariat. *Forty-Ninth Pacific Islands Forum, Yaren, Nauru, 3–6 September 2018: Forum Communiqué* (Yaren, Nauru, 3–6 September 2018). https://www.un.org/humansecurity/wp-content/uploads/2018/09/49th-Pacific-Islands-Forum-Communiqué.pdf.

Pacific Island Forum Secretariat. *Boe Declaration on Regional Security* (Yaren, Nauru, 2018). https://pacificsecurity.net/wp-content/uploads/2021/02/Boe-Declaration-on-Regional-Security.pdf.

Pacific Island Forum Secretariat. *Fiftieth Pacific Islands Forum, Funafuti, Tuvalu, 13–16 August 2019* (Funafuti, Tuvalu, 13–16 August 2019). https://www.forumsec.org/wp-content/uploads/2019/08/50th-Pacific-Islands-Forum-Communique.pdf.

Pacific Island Forum Secretariat. *The 2050 Strategy for the Blue Pacific Continent* (Suva, 2022). https://www.forumsec.org/2050strategy/.

Parra, Paola Yanguas, Bill Hare, Ursula Fuentes Hutfilter, and Noklas Roming. *Evaluating the Significance of Australia's Global Fossil Fuel Carbon Footprint* (Melbourne: Climate Analytics, 2019). https://climateanalytics.org/media/australia_carbon_footprint_report_july2019.pdf.

Phillips, Janet. *A Comparison of Coalition and Labor Government Asylum Seeker Policies since 2001* (Canberra: Commonwealth of Australia, 2017). https://parlinfo.aph.gov.au/parlInfo/download/library/prspub/3024333/upload_binary/3024333.pdf.

Price Waterhouse Coopers. *The Long View: How Will the Global Economic Order Change by by 2050?* (February 2017). https://www.pwc.com/world2050.

Prime Minister of Japan and His Cabinet. *National Security Strategy, December 17, 2013* (Tokyo: 2013). https://www.cas.go.jp/jp/siryou/131217anzenhoshou/nss-e.pdf.

Quicke, Audrey. *Climate of the Nation: Tracking Australia's Attitudes Towards Climate Change and Energy* (Manuka, ACT: The Australia Institute, 2021). https://australiainstitute.org.au/wp-content/uploads/2021/10/211013-Climate-of-the-Nation-2021-WEB.pdf.

Republic of Fiji and Commonwealth of Australia. *Fiji-Australia Vuvale Partnership* (Canberra: Australian Department of Foreign Affairs and Trade, 2019). https://www.dfat.gov.au/sites/default/files/fiji-australia-vuvale-partnership.pdf.

Royal Australian Navy. *The Royal Australian Navy Leadership Ethic* (Canberra: Commonwealth of Australia, 2010). https://www.navy.gov.au/sites/default/files/documents/Navy_Leadership_Ethic.pdf.

Ryan, Alan. '*Primary Responsibilities and Primary Risks': Australian Defence Force Participation in the International Force East Timor.* Study Paper No. 304 (Land Warfare Studies Centre, November 2000). https://researchcentre.army.gov.au/sites/default/files/sp304_primary_responsibilities_and_primary_risks-alan_ryan.pdf.

Scott, Trent, and Andrew Shearer. *Building Allied Interoperability in the Indo-Pacific Region: Discussion Paper 1, Command and Control* (Washington, DC: Center for Strategic and International Studies, 2017). https://www.csis.org/analysis/building-allied-interoperability-indo-pacific-region-discussion-paper-1.

SEI, IISD, ODI, Climate Change Analytics, CICERO, and UNEP. *The Production Gap: The Discrepancy between Countries' Planned Fossil Fuel Production and Global Production Levels*

BIBLIOGRAPHY

Consistent with Limiting Warming to 1.5°C or 2°C (2019). https://productiongap.org/wp-content/uploads/2019/11/Production-Gap-Report-2019.pdf.

Senate, Foreign Affairs, Defence and Trade References Committee. *Implications of Climate Change for Australia's National Security* (Canberra: Parliament House Senate Printing Unit, 2018). https://www.aph.gov.au/Parliamentary_Business/Committees/Senate/Foreign_Affairs_Defence_and_Trade/Nationalsecurity/Final_Report.

Senate Legal and Constitutional Affairs Legislation Committee. *Migration Amendment (Repairing Medical Transfers) Bill 2019 [Provisions]* (Canberra: Parliament House Senate Printing Unit, 2019). https://parlinfo.aph.gov.au/parlInfo/download/committees/reportsen/024304/toc_pdf/MigrationAmendment(RepairingMedicalTransfers)Bill2019[Provisions].pdf;fileType=application%2Fpdf.

Senate Select Committee. *A Certain Maritime Incident* (Canberra: Commonwealth of Australia, 2002). https://www.aph.gov.au/Parliamentary_Business/Committees/Senate/Former_Committees/maritimeincident/report/index.

Senate Standing Committee on Finance and Public Administration. *Parliamentary Inquiry – Inquiry into the Digital Delivery of Government Services – 14 March 2018, Answer Question on Notice, Department of Defence* (Canberra: Commonwealth of Australia, 14 March 2018). https://www.aph.gov.au/DocumentStore.ashx?id=d191ed6d-ac23-480d-90f9-9bed6d0eedec.

Song, Jay, and Neil Cuthbert. *Removal of Failed Asylum Seekers in Australia: A Comparative Perspective.* The Lowy Institute (27 March 2017). https://www.lowyinstitute.org/publications/removal-failed-asylum-seekers-australia-comparative-perspective#_edn3.

Special Service Division, Services of Supply, United States Army. *Instructions for American Servicemen in Australia 1942.* (Washington, DC: War and Navy Department, 1942).

Spinks, Harriet. *Boat 'Turnbacks' in Australia: A Quick Guide to the Statistics since 2001.* Research Paper Series, 2018–19 (Canberra: Commonwealth of Australia, 2018). https://parlinfo.aph.gov.au/parlInfo/download/library/prspub/5351070/upload_binary/5351070.pdf.

State Council of the People's Republic of China. *China's Military Strategy* (Xinghua: State Council of the People's Republic of China, 2015). http://english.gov.cn/archive/white_paper/2015/05/27/content_281475115610833.htm.

United Nations Department of Economic and Social Affairs. *Sustainable Development Goals.* New York: United Nations https://sdgs.un.org/goals.

United Nations Environment Programme. *Emissions Gap Report 2020* (Nairobi: United Nations Environment Programme and UNEP DTU Partnership, 2020). https://www.unep.org/emissions-gap-report-2020.

United Nations High Commissioner for Refugees. *Convention and Protocol Relating to the Status of Refugees: Text of the 1951 Convention* (Geneva: Office of the United Nations High Commissioner for Refugees, 2010). https://www.unhcr.org/3b66c2aa10.

United Nations High Commissioner for Refugees. *Global Trends: Forced Displacement in 2018* (Geneva: Office of the United Nations High Commissioner for Refugees, 2019). https://www.unhcr.org/globaltrends2018/.

United Nations High Commissioner for Refugees. *Global Trends: Forced Displacement in 2021* (Geneva: Office of the United Nations High Commissioner for Refugees, 2022). https://www.unhcr.org/flagship-reports/globaltrends/.

United Nations High Commissioner for Refugees. *Asylum Levels and Trends in Industrialized Countries: Statistical Overview of Asylum Applications Lodged in Europe and Selected Non-European Countries* (Geneva: Office of the United Nations High Commissioner for Refugees, 2021). http://www.unhcr.org/4e9beaa19.htm.

United Nations Human Rights Committee. *International Covenant on Civil and Political Rights, Human Rights Committee: Concluding Observations on the Sixth Periodic Report of Australia* (Geneva: United Nations, 1 December 2017). http://docstore.ohchr.org/SelfServices/FilesHandler.ashx?enc=6QkG1d%2FPPRiCAqhKb7yhsoAl3%2FFsniSQx2VAmWrPA0uA3KW0KkpmSGOue15UG42EodNm2j%2FnCTyghc1kM8Y%2FLQ4n6KZBdggHt5qPmUYCI8eCslXZmnVlMq%2FoYCNPyKpq.

US Department of Defense. *Indo-Pacific Strategy Report: Preparedness, Partnerships and Promoting a Networked Region* (Washington, DC: US Department of Defense, 2019). https://media.defense.

gov/2019/Jul/01/2002152311/-1/-1/1/DEPARTMENT-OF-DEFENSE-INDO-PACIFIC-STRATEGY-REPORT-2019.PDF.

US Department of State. *Voting Practices in the United Nations 2017: Report to Congress Submitted Pursuant to Public Laws 101-246 and 108-447*. (Washington, DC: US Department of State, March 2018). https://www.state.gov/wp-content/uploads/2019/05/Voting-Practices-in-the-United-Nations-2017.pdf.

Wallis, Joanne. *Crowded and Complex: The Changing Geopolitics of the South Pacific* (Canberra: Australian Strategic Policy Institute, 2017).

White House. *National Security Strategy of the United States of America, December 2017* (2017). https://trumpwhitehouse.archives.gov/wp-content/uploads/2017/12/NSS-Final-12-18-2017-0905.pdf.

Wilson, Guy. *Defence Diplomacy: The Right Ballast for Australia's Troubled Relations with Indonesia*. Indo-Pacific Strategic Papers (Canberra: Centre for Defence and Strategic Studies, Australian Defence College, 2017). https://defence.gov.au/ADC/Publications/documents/digest/Spring_2017/IPSD_Wilson_spring2017.pdf.

Woodard, Gary, Moreen Dee, and Max Suich. *Negotiating the Australia–Japan Basic Treaty of Friendship and Cooperation: Reflections and Afterthoughts*. Asia Pacific Economic Papers, no. 36 (Canberra: Crawford School of Public Policy, Australian National University, 2007).

Woolner, Derek. *Lessons of the Collins Class Submarine Program for Improved Oversight of Defence Procurement*. Research Paper 3, 2001-02 (Canberra: Parliamentary Library, 2001).

Zhang, Denhua. *Chinese Concessional Loans: Part 1: Perceptions and Misconceptions*. In Brief 2018/23 (Canberra: Australian National University Department of Pacific Affairs, 2018). http://dpa.bellschool.anu.edu.au/sites/default/files/publications/attachments/2018-11/ib_2018_23_zhang.

Zhang, Denhua. *China's Coronavirus 'Covid-19 Diplomacy' in the Pacific*. In Brief 2020/10 (Canberra: Australian National University Department of Pacific Affairs, 2020). http://dpa.bellschool.anu.edu.au/sites/default/files/publications/attachments/2020-04/ib_2020_10_zhang_final_0.pdf.

Speeches

Abe, Shinzō. 'The Bounty of the Open Seas: Five New Principles for Japanese Diplomacy.' Speech, 18 January 2013. http://japan.kantei.go.jp/96_abe/statement/201301/18speech_e.html.

Biden, Joe. 'Remarks by President Biden on America's Place in the World.' Speech, US Department of State Headquarters, Harry S. Truman Building, Washington, DC, 4 February 2021. https://www.whitehouse.gov/briefing-room/speeches-remarks/2021/02/04/remarks-by-president-biden-on-americas-place-in-the-world/.

Bishop, Julie. 'The New Aid Paradigm.' Speech, Canberra, Australian Capital Territory, 15 October 2019. https://www.foreignminister.gov.au/minister/julie-bishop/speech/new-aid-paradigm.

Caldwell, Arthur. 'Speech to the Australian Parliament.' Speech, House of Representatives, Parliament House, Canberra, 2 August 1945.

Clinton, Bill. 'Speech to the Australian Parliament.' Speech, House of Representatives, Parliament House, Canberra, 20 November 1996.

Ewing, Thomas. 'Speech by the Honorable T.T. Ewing, MP Minister of State for Defence.' Speech to the Parliament of the Commonwealth of Australia, Parliament House, Canberra, 29 September 1908.

Hawke, Alex. 'Address to the Australasian Aid Conference, Canberra.' Speech, Canberra, Australian Capital Territory, 19 February 2020. https://ministers.dfat.gov.au/minister/alex-hawke-mp/speech/address-australasian-aid-conference-canberra.

Howard, John. 'Australia's International Relations – Ready for the Future.' Speech, National Convention Centre, Canberra, 22 August 2001.

Howard, John. 'Address at the Federal Liberal Party Campaign Launch, Sydney.' Speech, Sydney, 28 October 2001.

Jingpin, Xi. 'Address by the President of the People's Republic of China.' Speech, Parliament House, Canberra, 17 November 2014. https://parlinfo.aph.gov.au/parlInfo/search/display/display.w3p;query=Id:%22chamber/hansardr/35c9c2cf-9347-4a82-be89-20df5f76529b/0005%22.

BIBLIOGRAPHY

Jingpin, Xi. 'Speech at the All Military Diplomatic Work Conference.' Speech, 29 January 2015. http://cpc.people.com.cn/n/2015/0129/c64094-26474947.html.

Jingpin, Xi. 'Full Text of Xi Jinping's Report at 19th CPC National Congress.' Speech, 19th National Congress of the Communist Party of China, 18 October 2017. http://www.chinadaily.com.cn/china/19thcpcnationalcongress/2017-11/04/content_34115212.htm.

Keating, Paul. 'Speech by the Prime Minister, the Hon. PJ Keating MP, Jakarta, Wednesday 22 April, 1992.' Speech, Jakarta, Indonesia, 22 April 1992. Canberra: Department for Prime Minister and Cabinet, 1992.

Latham, Mark. 'Labor and the World.' Speech, The Lowy Institute, Sydney, 7 April 2004.

Morrison, Scott. 'Address – "Australia and the Pacific: A New Chapter".' Speech, Lavarack Barracks, Townsville, Queensland, 8 November 2018. https://www.pm.gov.au/media/remarks-pacific-skills-portal-launch.

Morrison, Scott. 'Remarks, Ceremonial Welcome, White House – Washington D.C.: Transcript.' Speech, Washington DC, 29 September 2019. https://www.pm.gov.au/media/remarks-ceremonial-welcome-white-house-washington-dc.

Morrison, Scott. 'Remarks, Pacific Skills Portal Launch: Transcript.' Speech, Funafuti, Tuvalu, 14 August 2019. https://www.pm.gov.au/media/remarks-pacific-skills-portal-launch.

Morrison, Scott. 'Press Conference – Newquay Airport, United Kingdom.' Speech, Newquay Airport, United Kingdom, 13 June 2019. https://www.pm.gov.au/media/press-conference-newquay-airport-united-kingdom.

Morrison, Scott. 'Address, Aspen Security Forum – "Tomorrow in the Indo-Pacific": Transcript.' Speech, 5 August 2020.

Morrison, Scott, and Donald Trump. 'Remarks by President Trump and Prime Minister Morrison of Australia at Arrival Ceremony.' Speech, South Lawn, White House, Washington, DC, 20 September 2019.

Palmerston, Henry. 'Speech.' Speech to the London House of Commons, 1 March 1848.

Reynolds, Linda. 'ASPI-FPCI 1.5 Track Dialogue 2019.' Speech, Canberra, Australian Capital Territory, 23 July 2019. https://www.minister.defence.gov.au/minister/lreynolds/speeches/aspi-fpci-15-track-dialogue-2019.

Turnbull, Malcolm. 'Speech at the University of New South Wales, Sydney – 7 August 2018.' Speech, University of New South Wales, Sydney, 7 August 2018. https://www.malcolmturnbull.com.au/media/speech-at-the-university-of-new-south-wales-sydney-7-august-2018.

Widodo, Joko. 'Address by the President of the Republic of Indonesia.' Speech, Parliament House, Canberra, Australian Capital Territory, 10 February 2020. https://www.aph.gov.au/Parliamentary_Business/Hansard/Hansard_Display?bid=chamber/hansardr/be8a2537-4a84-4dc2-b27b-28f392b06329/&sid=0001.

Webpages

Australian Attorney General's Department. 'Whaling in the Antarctic Litigation,' 31 March 2014, accessed 29 October 2021. https://www.ag.gov.au/international-relations/international-law/whaling-antarctic-litigation.

Australian Attorney General's Department. 'Foreign Influence Transparency Scheme,' 2021, accessed 17 November 2021. https://www.ag.gov.au/integrity/foreign-influence-transparency-scheme.

Australian Bureau of Statistics. 'International Trade: Supplementary Information, Calendar Year, 2017: Table 7.4 International Trade in Services, Credits, Calendar Year by Country and Travel Service, #dlM – Education,' updated 25 May 2018. https://www.abs.gov.au/AUSSTATS/abs@.nsf/DetailsPage/5368.0.55.0042017?OpenDocument.

Australian Bureau of Statistics. 'Migration, Australia: Estimated Resident Population, Country of Birth – as at 30 June, 1996 to 2018,' updated 3 April 2019. https://www.abs.gov.au/statistics/people/population/migration-australia/2017-18.

Australian Bureau of Statistics. 'International Trade: Supplementary Information, Calendar Year, 2018: Table 7.4 International Trade in Services, Credits, Calendar Year by Country and Travel Service, $M – Education,' released 24 May 2019. https://www.abs.gov.au/statistics/economy/international-trade/international-trade-supplementary-information-calendar-year/2018.

BIBLIOGRAPHY

Australian Customs and Border Protection Service. 'No Way: You Will Not Make Australia Home,' updated 13 September 2013, accessed 18 February 2020. www.customs.com.au.

Australian Department of Education and Training. 'Research Snapshot: China – Outbound and Inbound International Students,' updated August 2016, accessed 3 April 2019. https://internationaleducation.gov.au/research/Research-Snapshots/Documents/China_outbound%20and%20inbound%20tertiary%20students.pdf.

Australian Department of Education and Training. 'Where Do International Students Come From and What Do They Study,' 2019, accessed 19 March 2019. https://internationaleducation.gov.au/research/DataVisualisations/Pages/nationalitySummary.aspx.

Australian Department of Foreign Affairs and Trade. 'Joint Declaration on a Comprehensive Strategic Partnership between Australia and the Republic of Indonesia,' updated 31 August 2016. https://www.dfat.gov.au/geo/indonesia/joint-declaration-comprehensive-strategic-partnership-between-the-commonwealth-of-australia-and-republic-of-indonesia.

Australian Department of Foreign Affairs and Trade. 'Nuclear Issues: Towards a Nuclear Weapons Free World,' accessed 21 February 2019. https://dfat.gov.au/international-relations/security/non-proliferation-disarmament-arms-control/nuclear-issues/.

Australian Department of Foreign Affairs and Trade. 'Australia's Development Partnership in Indonesia,' accessed 10 May 2019. https://dfat.gov.au/geo/indonesia/development-assistance/Pages/development-assistance-in-indonesia.aspx.

Australian Department of Foreign Affairs and Trade. 'Stepping up Australia's Engagement with Our Pacific Family' (Canberra: Department of Foreign Affairs and Trade, September 2019), accessed 12 December 2021. https://www.dfat.gov.au/sites/default/files/stepping-up-australias-engagement-with-our-pacific-family.pdf.

Australian Department of Foreign Affairs and Trade. 'Indonesia Fact Sheet,' updated August 2021. https://www.dfat.gov.au/sites/default/files/indo-cef.pdf.

Australian Department of Foreign Affairs and Trade. 'Smartraveller: Indonesia,' updated 12 July 2021. https://www.smartraveller.gov.au/destinations/asia/indonesia.

Australian Department of Foreign Affairs and Trade. 'China Fact Sheet,' updated August 2021, accessed 9 December 2021. https://www.dfat.gov.au/sites/default/files/chin-cef.pdf.

Australian Department of Foreign Affairs and Trade. 'Japan Fact Sheet,' February 2021. https://www.dfat.gov.au/sites/default/files/japn-cef.pdf.

Australian Department of Foreign Affairs and Trade. 'United States Fact Sheet,' updated August 2021. https://www.dfat.gov.au/sites/default/files/usa-cef.pdf.

Australian Department of Foreign Affairs and Trade. 'News, Speeches and Media: Correcting the Record,' 2021, accessed 2 November 2021. https://dfat.gov.au/news/correcting-the-record/Pages/default.aspx.

Australian Department of Foreign Affairs and Trade. 'Australia's Development Program' (Canberra: Australian Department of Foreign Affairs and Trade, 2022), accessed 5 December 2021. https://www.dfat.gov.au/development/australias-development-program.

Australian Department of Home Affairs. 'Country Profile – Indonesia,' updated 12 July 2021, accessed 5 November 2021. https://www.homeaffairs.gov.au/research-and-statistics/statistics/country-profiles/profiles/indonesia.

Australian Labor Party (ALP), *Powering Australia* (Canberra: ALP, 2021). https://www.alp.org.au/policies/powering-australia.

Australian Signals Directorate. 'ACSC Detects Malicious Activity Targeting Political Party Networks,' updated 19 February 2019, accessed 11 March 2019. https://cyber.gov.au/government/news/parliament-house-network-compromise/.

Australian War Memorial. 'Australia Under Attack: Australia Bombed, Strafed and Shelled,' updated 27 November 2019, accessed 22 February 2021. https://www.awm.gov.au/visit/exhibitions/underattack/bombed.

Australian War Memorial. Aitape, New Guinea. 24 October 1943. A Photograph Found on the Body of a Dead Japanese Soldier Showing NX143314 Sergeant (Sgt) Leonard G. Siffleet of 'M' Special Unit, Wearing a Blindfold and with His Arms Tied, About to Be Beheaded with a Sword by Yasuno Chikao. Canberra: Australian War Memorial, 1943. https://www.awm.gov.au/collection/C21918 [photograph].

BIBLIOGRAPHY

Climate Action Tracker. 'Australia,' 2019, accessed 12 December 2019. https://climateactiontracker. org/countries/australia/2019-12-02/.

Comprehensive Nuclear-Test-Ban Treaty Organization. 'CTBT Ministerial Meetings,' 2014, accessed 28 February 2019. https://www.ctbto.org/the-treaty/ctbt-ministerial-meetings/.

Development Policy Centre. 'Australia Aid Tracker Comparisons 2019,' accessed 22 January 2019. http://devpolicy.org/aidtracker/comparisons/.

Development Policy Centre. 'Australia Aid Tracker Comparisons 2020,' accessed 1 September 2021. http://devpolicy.org/aidtracker/comparisons/.

Development Policy Centre. 'Australia Aid Tracker Comparisons,' accessed 28 November 2022. http://devpolicy.org/aidtracker/comparisons/.

Embassy of Australia. 'History of Mateship,' 2021, accessed 2 March 2021. https://usa.embassy.gov. au/timelines-alliance.

Embassy of Australia. 'Australian and the United States Relations,' 2021, accessed 2 March 2021. https://usa.embassy.gov.au/australia-and-us-relations.

#End Covid for All. 'Shot of Hope: Australia's Role in Vaccinating the World against Covid-19,' accessed 8 November 2021. https://endcovidforall.com.

Fraser, Malcolm. 'Statement on the World Situation.' Transcript 4135, PM Transcripts: Transcripts from the Prime Ministers of Australia, updated 1 June 1976. https://pmtranscripts.pmc.gov.au/ release/transcript-4135.

Howard, John. 'Doorstop Interview Samoa.' Transcript 21448, PM Transcripts: Transcripts from the Prime Ministers of Australia, updated 8 August 2004. https://pmtranscripts.pmc.gov.au/release/ transcript-21448.

Hutton, Marg. 'Drownings on the Public Record of People Attempting to Enter Australia Irregularly by Boat Since 1998,' updated 2 February 2014, accessed 9 November 2021. http://sievx.com/ articles/background/DrowningsTable.pdf.

Indo-Pacific Centre for Health Security. 'Australian and PNG Community Leaders Tackle Vaccine Hesitancy.' Department of Foreign Affairs and Trade, 2 June 2021, accessed 19 November 2021. https://indopacifichealthsecurity.dfat.gov.au/australian-and-png-community-leaders-tackle-vaccine-hesitancy.

Minister for Foreign Affairs, The Hon Julie Bishop MP. 'Re-Shaping Australia's Aid Program,' updated 18 June 2014, accessed 8 November 2021. https://www.foreignminister.gov.au/minister/ julie-bishop/news/re-shaping-australias-aid-program.

Refugee Council of Australia. 'Statistics on Boat Arrivals and Boat Turnbacks,' updated 20 November 2021, accessed 9 December 2021. https://www.refugeecouncil.org.au/asylum-boats-statistics/2/.

Rudd, Kevin. 'Climate Change: Forging a New Consensus.' Transcript of Remarks to the National Climate Change Summit, Parliament House, Canberra (Canberra, 31 March 2007).

Stevens, David, 'The Great White Fleet's Visit to Australia,' Sea Power Centre, Royal Australian Navy. accessed 12 February 2019. http://www.navy.gov.au/history/feature-histories/great-white-fleet%E2%80%99s-1908-visit-australia.

Tarzia, Marguerite, and Bill McCormick. 'International Whaling,' Parliament of Australia, 2010, accessed 21 February 2019. https://www.aph.gov.au/About_Parliament/Parliamentary_ Departments/Parliamentary_Library/pubs/BriefingBook43p/internationalwhaling.

Tourism Australia. 'International Market Performance Statistics,' accessed 22 February 2021. https:// www.tourism.australia.com/en/markets-and-stats/tourism-statistics/international-market-performance.html.

Tourism Research Australia. 'Latest International Visitor Survey (IVS) Results,' 2018, accessed 21 November 2018. https://www.tra.gov.au/International/International-tourism-results/overview.

US Bureau of Economic Analysis. 'U.S. International Trade in Goods and Services: Australia,' updated 2 November 2018. https://www.bea.gov/news/2018/us-international-trade-goods-and-services-september-2018.

US Bureau of Economic Analysis. 'U.S. International Trade in Goods and Services: Australia,' updated 1 January 2023. https://apps.bea.gov/international/factsheet/factsheet.html#601.

US Department of State. 'U.S. Relations with Australia, Bilateral Relations Fact Sheet Bureau of East Asian and Pacific Affairs,' 2021, accessed 2 March 2021. https://www.state. gov/u-s-relations-with-australia/.

388 BIBLIOGRAPHY

Watson Institute for International and Public Affairs, Brown University. 'Costs of War: Afghan Civilians,' 2021, accessed 25 May 2021. https://watson.brown.edu/costsofwar/costs/human/civilians/afghan.

Watson Institute for International and Public Affairs, Brown University. 'Costs of War: Iraqi Civilians,' 2021, accessed 25 May 2021. https://watson.brown.edu/costsofwar/costs/human/civilians/iraqi.

US Department of Defense. 'Transcript: Remarks by Secretary Mattis at Plenary Session of the 2018 Shangri-La Dialogue,' updated 2 June 2018, accessed 9 December 2021. https://www.defense.gov/News/Transcripts/Transcript/Article/1538599/remarks-by-secretary-mattis-at-plenary-session-of-the-2018-shangri-la-dialogue/.

White House. 'U.S. Strategic Framework for the Indo-Pacific,' accessed 2 March 2021. https://trumpwhitehouse.archives.gov/wp-content/uploads/2021/01/IPS-Final-Declass.pdf.

World Vision. 'DFAT Works,' last modified 2021. https://www.worldvision.com.au/get-involved/advocacy/australian-aid.

Miscellaneous

Concerned Scholars of China. *An Open Letter from Concerned Scholars of China and the Chinese Diaspora: Australia's Debate on 'Chinese Influence'*, Canberra, Asia and the Pacific Policy Society, 26 March 2018, accessed November 17, 2021. https://www.policyforum.net/an-open-letter-from-concerned-scholars-of-china-and-the-chinese-diaspora/ [pamphlet].

Dalgleish, Paul. 'Bob Hawke: Guide to Archives of Australia's Prime Ministers.' Canberra: National Archives of Australia, 2021 [research guide].

Lambie, Jackie. '"Tasmanians Don't Want Deals Done over Humanity," Senator Lambie on Medevac Vote.' By Fran Kelly. *ABC Radio National*. Australian Broadcasting Corporation, 15 October 2019. https://www.abc.net.au/radionational/programs/breakfast/tasmanians-don't-want-deals-done-over-humanity-lambie/11602828 [interview].

Lowy Institute. 'Lowy Institute Pacific Aid Map.' Sydney: The Lowy Institute, 2020. https://pacificaidmap.lowyinstitute.org/dashboard [map].

OECD iLibrary. 'OECD International Development Statistics.' OECD, 22 November 2021. https://www.oecd-ilibrary.org/development/data/oecd-international-development-statistics/oda-commitments_data-00068-en [database].

Oliver, Pam. 'Allies, Enemies and Trading Partners: Records on Australia and the Japanese, Research Guide.' Canberra: National Archives of Australia, 2004. https://www.naa.gov.au/sites/default/files/2020-02/research-guide-allies-enemies-trading-partners.pdf [research guide].

'Plaintiff M70/2011 v. Minister for Immigration and Citizenship & Anor, Plaintiff M106 of 2011 by His Litigation Guardian, Plaintiff M70/2011 v. Minister for Immigration and Citizenship and Anor.' Case No. M70/2011, M106/2011, 2011. https://www.hcourt.gov.au/cases/case-m70/2011 [court case].

Stockholm International Peace Research Institute. 'Military Expenditure Database.' February 2020, 2021. https://www.sipri.org/databases/milex [database].

Stockholm International Peace Research Institute. 'Arms Industry Database.' December 2018, 2021. https://www.sipri.org/databases/armsindustry [database].

Tintazul. 'Map of Oceania.' Wikimedia Commons, 30 January 2014. https://commons.wikimedia.org/wiki/File:Oceania_UN_Geoscheme_Regions_with_Zones_and_ISO3166_labels.svg#/media/File:Oceania_UN_Geoscheme_Regions.svg [map].

World Bank. 'World Development Indicators Database.' World Bank, 23 January 2020. https://data.worldbank.org/indicator/NY.GNP.PCAP.PP.CD?most_recent_value_desc=true [database].

Zhao, Lijian. 'Shocked by Murder of Afghan Civilians & Prisoners by Australian Soldiers. We Strongly Condemn Such Acts, & Call for Holding Them Accountable.' Twitter, 30 November 2020. https://twitter.com/zlj517/status/1333214766806888448?lang=en [social media].

INDEX

9/11 terrorist attacks (2001) 23, 55–6, 64

14 disputes, dossier of 108

abandonment, fear of 31

Abbott coalition administration 248, 270, 296

Abbott, Tony 66, 96, 99

Abe, Shinzō 130, 132, 140, 147, 148, 153

academic collaborations 118

Afghanistan 64–7

Agreement on Maintaining Security (AMS) (1995) 161–2

agricultural investment 106

aid *see* official development assistance (ODA)

'aid for trade' 228, 241, 245, 251–2

Aid Investment Plan 228

air arrivals 299–300

Albanese administration
asylum seekers and 290, 296
climate change and 217, 229, 267–8, 316
official development assistance (ODA) and 242, 245
policy positions 27
South Pacific and China 220, 226

Albanese, Anthony 77, 97, 140, 188, 274

alliance premiums/dues 42, 43, 46, 56, 59, 63, 64, 67, 70, 71

anti-Americanism 51–2, 61

'arc of instability' 244

'art of the possible' 6, 9, 10, 11, 13, 34

Asia-Pacific Economic Cooperation (APEC) 144, 193–4

Asia Reassurance Initiative Act (US, 2018) 151

Asian values 19–20, 193

Assisted Passage Migration Scheme 281

Association of Southeast Asian States (ASEAN) 144, 172, 194, 195
Australia–New Zealand Free Trade Area 194–5
Defence Ministers' Meeting Plus (ADMM-Plus) 139, 176
Regional Forum (ARF) 176

asylum seekers 279–306, 316–18
background to hard-line policy 280–2
boat turnbacks 290
deportations 291
international agreements 284–5
international context 282–4
Nauru detention centre 236, 237
offshore processing 279, 283–4, 288–90, 293, 295
politicization of asylum seekers 292–304
air arrivals 299–300
children 297–9
criticism and voter opinions 300–1
Medivac Bill 301–4
see-sawing policies 294–6
temporary protection visas (TPVs) 290–1
terminology used 285–7, 288
third-country resettlement 291–2
West Papuan asylum seekers 167

Australia, characteristics of 29, 41, 50, 247

Australia–China Strategic Economic Dialogue 96

Australia–Indonesia Defence Cooperation Program (DCP) 174–5

INDEX

Australia–Indonesia Partnership for Reconstruction and Development (AIPRD) 167
Australia–Japan Agreement on Commerce (1957) 141
Australia, New Zealand, United States (ANZUS) Treaty 54–74
  activation of 24, 55–6
  benefits of
    coalition operations 64–70
    defence equipment, access to 58–9
    intelligence-sharing 60–1
    joint facilities 61–2
    training and exchanges 62–4
  continuity of 72
  debates on
    bases in Australia 61–2
    military cooperation 70–2
    security guarantee 56–7
    US equipment, suitability of 59–60
  declaratory policy on 47
  public opinion on 72–4
  US personnel in Japan 150
Australia, United Kingdom, United States (AUKUS) agreement 31, 58, 148, 172–3
Australia–United States Defence Trade Cooperation Treaty 58
Australia–United States Free Trade Agreement (AUSFTA) 79–81
Australia–US Force Posture Agreement (2014) 62
Australian Broadcasting Corporation (ABC) 168, 180, 237
Australian Cyber Security Centre (ACSC) 116
Australian Defence Force (ADF) 41, 65, 67, 71, 246
Australian Infrastructure Financing Facility for the Pacific (AIFFP) 222, 246–7, 253
Australian Security Intelligence Organization (ASIO) 117, 120

Bainimarama, Frank 216, 233
Bali Nine case 180–1
Bali Process on People Smuggling . . . 177
Bali terrorist bombings 164–5, 181

Basic Treaty of Friendship and Cooperation Between Australia and Japan (NARA, 1976) 141
Belt and Road Initiative (BRI) 95, 254
Biden administration
  Declaration on US–Pacific Partnership (2022) 225
  Indo–Pacific Economic Framework (IPEF) 144
  leadership of 51
  Manus Island and 46
  relationship with Australia 45, 57, 70, 73, 74, 78, 103
Biden, Joe 47, 51, 77, 94
Bishop, Julie 110, 137, 233, 240
Black Rock base 46, 224
Blainey, Geoffrey 18
'boat people' 281–2
boat turnbacks 290
border controls 236
border protection 293–4, 296
bounded rationality 6–7
Bowen, Chris 92
Boxing Day tsunami (2004) 166–7
'burden-sharing' 31, 45, 46, 153
Bush administration 67–8, 69, 74
Bush, George W. 77, 79, 166
bushfires 269

Calwell, Arthur 19, 127–8, 280
Carbon Pollution Reduction Scheme (CPRS) 270
carbon pricing 270–1
cattle export ban 157, 180
'Centenary of Mateship' (2018) 48
'chequebook diplomacy' 217, 237
child asylum seekers 297–9
China 84–122, 308–10
  Australia–US relationship and 40, 45, 46, 49
  background to relationship with Australia 84–8
  'chequebook diplomacy' 217, 237
  'China Choice' between trade and security 90, 93, 94, 103, 113
  climate change 218
  competition with 254–6
  countering the influence of 254–5

COVID-19 255–6
cultural links 91–7
development loans 244, 247
Five Eyes Agreement and 61, 120
non-military threats, perceptions of
 116–21
 cyberattacks 116–17
 government responses 119–21
 influence operations 117–19
Pacific Islands Forum (PIF) 217–19,
 237
policy activities against 63
recognition of China by Australia
 86–7
security relations, lack of 111–15
Solomon Islands, security agreement
 with 226
South Pacific relationship 207, 214,
 217, 218, 222, 238
threat in the South Pacific 220–1
threat of 24–5, 27–8, 89, 94, 151
'tit for tat' diplomacy,
 characteristics of 107–11
trade links 89, 98–107
 background 98–101
 foreign investment 104–7
 weaponizing of trade 101–4
trade with 81
China–Australia free trade agreement
 (CFTA) 93, 99
Chinese diaspora 92, 119
Christianity in the South Pacific 205
climate change 259–78, 315–16
 Australia's response to 268–72
 elections and 273–5
 emissions, Australian 260–3
 failed securitization of 275–8
 Paris Agreement 263–4
 and population movements 204
 public opinion 273
 recent policy 264–8
 and the South Pacific 215–18, 229,
 237–8, 264
Clinton, Bill 48
coal exports
 emissions and climate change 261,
 262, 271, 272, 278
 slowdown in Chinese customs
 clearance 102, 104
 value of 229

Coalition governments
 and asylum seekers 285, 296
 and climate change 265, 266, 270,
 271, 272, 273–4
 and overseas development
 assistance (ODA) 244, 245,
 247, 248, 249, 250, 251
 and the UN Security Council 75
coastline 29
Cold War
 Communism in Asia 21, 23, 43, 45,
 159
 Communism in China 85–6
 Domino Theory 29–30, 43, 45,
 85–6, 159
 influence of in C21 33
 Japan, relations with 129
 mutually assured destruction
 (MAD) 13–14
 strategic change after 26, 35–6, 37
colonization of Australia 18–19, 20,
 28, 84–5
Communism 19, 21, 23, 30, 43, 45,
 85–6, 159
Comprehensive and Progressive
 Agreement for Trans-Pacific
 Partnership (CPTPP) 144
Comprehensive Strategic Partnerships
 96, 171
Confucius Institutes 118
Constructivism 15
COP (Conference of the Parties)
 meetings 266, 267
counter-terrorism 165, 172, 179, 186–7
counterinsurgency (COIN) operations 65
coups 234
COVID-19 242–3, 255–6
cruise missiles 58
Cuban Missile Crisis (1962) 15
cultural links 82–3, 91–7, 134–40,
 182–3
cultural power 41
Curtin, John 42
cyberattacks 61, 116–17, 119

Darwin
 attacks on 127, 148
 Port 80, 105
 US forces in 45, 63
 visit by Prime Minister Abe 148

INDEX

Dastyari, Sam 119–20
death penalty 131, 180–1
debates method 2–3
declaratory policy 3
decolonization 19, 199–200
defence cooperation
  China 112, 113–14, 115
  Indonesia 172–3, 174–5
  Japan 146–8
  South Pacific 223–7
  US see Australia, New Zealand,
    United States (ANZUS)
    Treaty
defence equipment 58–9, 113
defence exercises 63, 113–15, 147, 172
defence, militarization of 32–3
defence purchases 59–60, 113
  see also submarines
defence spending 41, 111–12, 113, 149
Defence Strategic Review (2023) 29
Defence White Paper (1987) 27
Defence White Paper (2016) 109, 115,
  150, 151
deportations 291
detention centres 236, 237, 288–9
  see also asylum seekers, offshore
    processing
determinism 37
Dibb Review (1986) 26–7
Dili (Santa Cruz) massacre(1991)
  160–1
diplomatic support 74–6, 95, 138–9
diplomatic visits 76–7
Domino Theory 23, 29–30, 43, 45,
  85–6, 159
dossier of 14 disputes 108
drug trafficking 180–1
Dutton, Peter 116, 213

East Indies 158–9
East Timor 70–1, 162–3, 168–9
economy 41
  see also trade links
education market 82–3, 92–3, 135–6,
  182–3, 252
education in the South Pacific 203–4
educational exchanges 113, 135
elections 117–18, 119
emergency assistance 246, 247
emigration 82

emissions 260–3
emissions reductions targets 270
  see also Kyoto Protocol; Paris
    Agreement
epidemics 276–8
equality of states 7, 8
Evans, Gareth 34, 35, 36, 161, 193–4
Evatt, H.V. 48
Ewing, Thomas 125, 153
exchange agreements 62–4
exchanges, educational 113, 135
exclusive economic zones (EEZs) 29,
  200, 206
'exemptionalism,' Australian 9
Exercise Kakadu 114
Exercise Pandaroo 114

'facts' 3
fear of abandonment 31
Fiji 46, 200, 201, 205, 219, 224, 231,
  232–4
First World War 20–1, 48, 51, 125–6
fisheries 206
Five Eyes Agreement 60–1, 120, 154
Forde, Francis 48
Foreign Influence Transparency Scheme
  118, 120
foreign investment 81–2, 104–7,
  143–4, 190, 192
Foreign Investment Review Board
  (FIRB) 80, 104–5
foreign ownership rules 105
foreign policy
  'art of the possible' and 9–11
  building blocks of 6–9
  independence from Britain 33
  national interests and 11–13
  purpose and aim of 11
  see also Strategic Culture of
    Australia
Foreign Policy White Paper (2017)
  109, 130, 151, 221
formal equality 7, 8, 10
formal inequality 8–9
forward defence 32
fossil fuels 261, 262, 271–2, 278
14 disputes, dossier of 108
Fraser administration 161, 281
Fraser, Malcolm 34
'free and open Indo-Pacific' (FOIP) 151

INDEX

free trade 104, 107
free trade agreements (FTAs)
    ASEAN–Australia–New Zealand
        194–5
    Australia–United States 79–81
    China 93, 99
    Indonesia 192–3
    Japan 141
    PACER+ 230–1
    US 49, 79–81
freedom of navigation operations
    (FONOPs) 111

geography of the South Pacific
    199–203
Gillard administration 157, 180, 236,
    244, 295
Gillard, Julia 75, 77
Gold Rushes 84–5
'good international citizenship' 34,
    264, 280
Gorton, Andrew 153
Great War *see* First World War
gross domestic product (GDP) 41, 101,
    229
Guam Doctrine (1968) 45

Hamilton, Clive 90, 118
Hastie, Andrew 120
Hawke administration 87, 183
Hawke, Bob 78, 87, 193–4
He, Lei 110
HIV/AIDS epidemic 276
Holmes, John 34
Holt, Harold 43, 159
Howard administration 225, 251, 279,
    285–6, 289, 290, 294
Howard, John
    asylum seekers 236, 293, 317
    doctrine of pre-emption 165–6
    East Timor and 162–3, 168–9, 173
    Iraq wars 68
    Japanese prime ministers and 140
    Realism of 37
    special responsibility for the Pacific
        212
    support for US 52
    US free trade agreement (AUSTFA)
        79
    'War on Terror' 24, 55–6, 64–5

Huang, Xiangmo 119
Huawei 105
Hull, Cordell 48
human rights abuses 160–1, 168,
    173–4, 177, 214
humanitarian assistance and disaster
    response (HADR) 223, 246,
    247, 255, 313

idealism in domestic politics 34, 37–8
ideational power 34–5, 36, 41
identity 205–6
immigration 82, 84–5, 87–8, 92, 135,
    186
immigration policy 280–1
    see also asylum seekers
indefensibility, sense of 28–31, 56–7
independence 7–8
Indo–Pacific Economic Framework
    (IPEF) 144
Indonesia 155–97, 311–13
    background to relationship with
        Australia 158–67
        Bali terrorist bombings 164–5
        Boxing Day tsunami (2004)
            166–7
        East Timor 162–3, 168–9
        pre-emption doctrine 165–6
        security cooperation 161–2
        slight and escalation 156–7,
            160–1, 168, 174
        West Papuan asylum seekers
            (2006) 167
    cultural links 177–89
        immigration 186
        overseas development assistance
            (ODA) 184–5
        'people-to-people' links 182–3,
            187
        prime ministerial/presidential
            relations 187–9
        public opinion 177–82
        tourism 184–5, 186–7
    distance between Australia and
        Indonesia 155–6
    official development assistance
        (ODA) 243
    Realpolitik in relationship 168–9
    security relations 157–8, 161,
        170–7

Comprehensive Strategic
Partnership (2005–) 171
defence cooperation 172–3,
174–5
joint regional cooperation 176–7
military diplomacy 175–6
non-interference treaty 173–4
spying and sovereignty 174
threat of 26, 157
trade growth unrealized 156, 157
trade links 189–95
balance of trade 190
foreign investment 190–2
free trade agreement 192–3
institutionalization of 193–5
Indonesia–Australia Comprehensive
Economic Partnership
(IA-CEPA) 188, 192–3
Indonesian–Australian Defence Alumni
Association 172
influence operations 117–19, 120–1
infrastructure programmes 254–5
intelligence 60–1, 174
international aid *see* official
development assistance
(ODA)
International Force East Timor
(INTERFET) *see* East Timor
International Relations theory 1–2, 6
international system 6–7
Iraq 67–9

Jakarta Centre for Law Enforcement
Cooperation (JCLEC) 174
Japan 123–54, 310–11
Australia, view of 132
background to relationship with
Australia 123–9
cultural links 134–40
defence spending 149
Five Eyes Agreement, inclusion in
61
'normal nationhood,' return to
132–4, 149
Second World War
defeat of 43, 128
defeat of European forces 126–7
occupation of Nauru 235
occupation of the East Indies 159
threat of 19, 21–2, 30, 42, 127

security relations 145–53
alliance with Australia 152–3
Article 9 of the Japanese
Constitution 148–9
collective self-defence of allies
149–50
defence cooperation 146–8
Quadrilateral Security Dialogue
(Quad) 150–1
threat perceptions 145–6, 147–8
trilateralism 151–2
Self Defence Force 149
'Special Strategic Partnership'
130–1, 144–5
threat of 19, 21, 30, 42
trade links 140–5
whaling 137–8
Japan–Australia Economic Partnership
Agreement (JAEPA) 141
Japan–Australia Joint Declaration on
Security Cooperation (2022)
131
Japan–Australia Joint Statement on
Security Cooperation (2007)
147
Joko Widodo 156, 188
journalism *see* media coverage

Keating administration 161, 183, 282
Keating, Paul 161, 188
Korean War 85
Kyoto Protocol 263, 266, 269, 271

labour schemes 230
languages 92, 203
Latham, Mark 78
Lewis, Duncan 117, 120
Liberal Internationalism, definition of
9–10
Liberal/Labor ideologies 34–8
liminal moments in history
AFP and 12
fear of abandonment and 31
indefensibility and 29, 30
Japan, defeat of 43
Pearl Harbour as 21
Soviet Bloc collapse and 23, 26, 35–6
threat perceptions and 33
'threats without enemies' and 27
US and 39–41

INDEX

literacy rates 203–4
Lombok Treaty (2006) 173
Longhurst, Kerry 15

MacArthur, Gen. Douglas 21, 127
Mahathir Mohamad 70, 193
Malaysian Airlines MH370 114
Manus Island
  asylum processing centre 289,
    300–1
  naval base 46, 223–4
Mares, Richard 148
Marines, deployment of 63–4
maritime cooperation with Indonesia
  175
maritime forces 29
media coverage 93–4, 179–82
media freedom 168, 237
medium powers 34–5, 36, 198, 244–5
Medivac Bill 301–4
Menzies, Robert 48, 86, 139
middle powers 34–5, 244–5
'middlepowermanship' 34, 35–6, 75,
  194, 245, 269–70
migration zone 289
militarization 24, 32–3
military bases 61–2
military cooperation
  Afghanistan 64–7
  debate on 70–2
  First World War 48
  Indonesia 172
  Iraq 67–9
  Second World War 31, 41–2, 43, 48
  Vietnam 45
military diplomacy 175–6
military exercises 63, 113–15, 147, 172
military forces 29
military relations see security relations
military spending 41
military technology 58–9, 71
military training 62–4
miners 84–5
missile launches 61
morality 7
Morgenthau, Hans 7
Morrison administration
  China and 97
  climate change 265, 266
  Indonesia and 179

Medivac Bill 301, 303
official development assistance
  (ODA) 227, 244, 249, 250
Morrison, Scott
  Afghanistan, withdrawal from 67
  China and 103, 109
  climate change and 264, 269
  Japan and 130, 139–40
  South Pacific and 211, 215–16, 219,
    220
  Trump and 77
  US relationship 48–9
mutually assured destruction (MAD)
  13–14, 61

national interest tests 104–5, 248–9
national interests 11–13
National Security Statement (US, 2002)
  166
National Security Strategy (US, 2017)
  45, 48
natural disasters 204, 210, 269
Nauru 200, 231, 235–7, 289, 295
navy 63, 110–11
  see also submarines
neoliberal economics 249–52
'New Aid Paradigm' 251
New Colombo Plan (NCP) 93, 183
New Zealand 56
newspapers see media coverage
9/11 terrorist attacks (2001) 23, 55–6,
  64
Nixon, Richard 45, 153
Non-Aligned Movement (NAM) 162,
  172
nuclear weapons 13–14, 55, 56, 61–2,
  138, 173

Obama, Barack 63, 77, 292
official development assistance (ODA)
  240–59, 314–15
  Bali terrorist bombings and 164
  Indonesia and 184–5
  Japan and 138–9
  policy and implementation 248–53
    international institutional setting
      252–3
    national interest 248–9
    neoliberal economics of 249–52
    politicized approach to 253–6

public opinion 256–7
recent period (2020–) 242–8
  comparison with other countries 247–8
  emergency response to COVID-19 242–3
  geographic focus 243–4
  regional and global programmes 246–7
  by sector 245–6
  South Pacific and 206–7, 209, 222, 227–8
offshore processing *see* asylum seekers, offshore processing
'One China Policy' 87
Operation Enduring Freedom 65
operational policy 3
opinion polls 72–4, 94–5, 105–6, 136, 178, 223, 273
overseas development assistance (ODA) *see* official development assistance (ODA)
overseas residents 82
overseas students *see* education market

Pacific Agreement on Closer Economic Relations (PACER, PACER+) 230–1
Pacific Islands Forum (PIF) 200, 201, 217–19, 237
  2018 meeting 237–8
  2019 meeting 213, 215–16
  Australian membership of 217, 219
  fragility of 201
  and West Papua 214
Pacific Maritime Security Programme (PMSP) 224
Pacific Regional Programme (PRP) 227–8
Pacific Solution 289–90
Pacific Support Force (PSF) 224
Palmerston, Henry 12
pandemics 276–8
  see also COVID-19
Papua New Guinea (PNG) 200, 201, 206, 209, 226–7, 243, 244
  see also Manus Island
Paris Agreement 263–4
Patience, Allan 34, 128

patrol boats 224
Payne, Marise 49
Peace of Westphalia 7
Pearl Harbour 21, 42, 126, 127
people smugglers 293
'people-to-people' links 82, 92, 93, 96, 97, 113, 135, 182, 186, 187
People's Republic of China *see* China
perception of threat 30
  see also threat perceptions
perspectives, of authors 5–6
phosphate mining 200, 235
Pitt, Keith 262–3
Pivot to Asia 63
political ideologies 34–8
political independence 7–8
'populate or perish' 19, 280
population 29, 41, 92, 201, 280
pre-emption doctrine 165–6
prime ministerial/presidential relations
  China 96–7
  Indonesia 187–9
  Japan 130, 139–40
  US 77–8, 79
Progressive Agreement for Trans-Pacific Partnership (CPTPP) 144
public opinion
  on asylum seekers 294, 300
  on China 93–5, 105–7
  on climate change 273
  on Fiji 233
  on Indonesia 160, 177–82
  on Japan 136–8
  on overseas development assistance (ODA) 256–7
  on the South Pacific 222–3
  on US 72–4
  on war in Afghanistan 66–7
  see also anti-Americanism
purchasing power parity (PPP) 41
Pyne, Christopher 62

Quadrilateral Security Dialogue (Quad) 37, 109, 150–1

Rabuka, Sitiveni 213
racism 84, 124, 125, 127
rationality 6
Realism, theory of 9–10, 37, 38
realism in domestic politics 34, 37

INDEX

Realpolitik 9, 51, 165, 168–9
Reciprocal Access Agreement (RAA)
130–1
refugees 167, 236, 280, 281–2, 287
see also asylum seekers
Regional Assistance Mission to the
Solomon Islands (RAMSI)
225–6
Regional Comprehensive Economic
Partnership (RCEP) 144, 195
regional security cooperation 139
regional trade institutions 144, 193–5
Reith, Peter 297
relations between leaders 43, 45
see also prime ministerial/
presidential relations
religiosity of the South Pacific 205–6
renewable energy 270, 272
residential investment 106
Responsibility to Protect (R2P) 8–9
Reynolds, Linda 174–5
Rim of the Pacific (RIMPAC) exercises
63, 114
Robb, Andrew 119
Robertson, Ted 281–2
Rudd administration 236, 288, 295
Rudd, Kevin 75, 77, 78, 250, 269–70,
271
'rules-based order' 49, 51, 83, 102–3,
109–10, 117, 130, 133–4
Russo–Japanese War 125
Ryacudu, Ryamizard 174

sanctions
Australian, against Fiji 233–4
Chinese, against Australia 97,
102–3
Santa Cruz (Dili) massacre (1991)
160–1
scholarships 204, 252
Second World War
Japan
defeat of 43, 128
defeat of European forces 126–7
occupation of Nauru 235
occupation of the East Indies 159
threat of 19, 21–2, 30, 42, 127
military cooperation 31, 41–2, 43,
48
South Pacific 208–9

security relations
China 111–15
Indonesia 157–8, 161, 170, 171–2,
175–6
Japan 139, 145–53
US *see* Australia, New Zealand,
United States (ANZUS)
Treaty
sentences 180–1
settlement, process of *see* colonization
of Australia
slight and escalation dynamic 156–7,
160–1, 168, 174
social media 118, 119, 180
soft power 34–5, 41, 132–3, 133–4
solar energy 270, 272
Solomon Islands 225–6, 243–4
Sopaoga, Enele 215–16
South China Sea dispute 110–11
South Pacific 198–239, 313–14
background to relationship with
Australia 198–210
demography 203–6
diplomatic relations 207–9
economics, trade and ODA
206–7, 209
geography 199–203
bilateral relations 231–7
Fiji 231, 232–4
Nauru 231, 235–7
climate change 215–18, 229, 237–8,
264
criticism of Australian diplomacy
212–13
defence cooperation 223–7
bases 223–4
Enhanced Cooperation
Programme (ECP) in PNG
226–7
Pacific Maritime Security
Programme (PMSP) 224
Regional Assistance Mission to
the Solomon Islands (RAMSI)
225–6
United States and 225
increase in diplomatic effort
Australian Infrastructure
Financing Facility for the
Pacific (AIFFP) 222
step-up 219–22, 223, 226

threat of China 220–1
whole-of-government approach
221–2
official development assistance
(ODA) 227–8, 243
Pacific Islands Forum (PIF) 200,
201, 215–16
and China 217–19, 237
public opinion 222–3
regional leader, Australia as 211–12
threat perceptions 237–8
tourism 232–3
trade links 203, 229–31
West Papua 214–15
sovereign inequality 8–9
sovereignty
Australian border controls 236
Australian, challenges to 61, 62, 93
death sentences and 180–2
Fijian, defence of 234
Indonesian, challenges to 156, 157,
158–9, 162–3, 164–5, 173–4
principle of 7–8, 10, 133
spying *see* intelligence
state-owned enterprises (SOEs) 105
states, definition of 7
Strategic Culture 2, 3, 11, 15–16
Strategic Culture of Australia 17–38
abandonment, fear of 31
alienation from Asia 18–20
core beliefs and practices 17
geographic isolation 18
immigration policy 19
indefensibility, sense of 28–31, 56–7
institutionalizing of 31–2
Liberal/Labor ideologies 34–6
militarization of security and
foreign policy 32–3
permanent threats 25
theory, limits of 36–8
threat of China 24–5, 27–8
threat perceptions, exaggerated
26–8
threat perceptions from Asia 20–3
'War on Terror' 23–4
strategic strike options 58
Strategic Update (2020) 27–8
students *see* education market
submarines 58, 147, 148, 173
Suharto, General 159, 160, 188

Sustainable Development Goals
(SDGs) 252
systemic perspectives 10

Taiwan 87, 217, 237
Tampa Affair 294
temporary protection visas (TPVs)
290–1
'ten pound' poms 281
territorial integrity 7, 8
terrorism 24
see also Bali terrorist bombings;
counter-terrorism; 9/11
terrorist attacks (2001)
third-country resettlement 291–2
threat perceptions 18–19
from Asia 20–3, 25, 145–6
of China 24–5, 27–8, 94, 147–8
of Communism 21, 23, 30
exaggerated 20, 21, 24, 25, 26–8, 60
in Japan 145, 146–7
of Japan 19, 21, 30, 42
permanent threats 25
South Pacific 237–8
'threats without enemies' 27
Tiananmen Square massacre (1989)
87–8
'tit for tat' diplomacy 107–11
tourism 82, 91–2, 135, 185–6, 186–7,
232–3
trade institutions 144, 193–5
see also Australia–United States Free
Trade Agreement (AUSFTA)
trade links
China 98–107
Indonesia 189–95
Japan 140–5
South Pacific 203, 229–31
US 79–82
trade restrictions 102
Trans-Pacific Partnership (TPP) 144
travel warnings 186–7
trilateralism 151–2
troops, deployment of 63–4
Trump administration
alliances 55, 57, 153
Japan and 151
trade agreements 80–1
trade war with China 46, 49, 103,
104

INDEX

Trump, Donald 45, 73, 77, 81, 94, 144, 153
tsunami (2004) 166–7
Tuila'epa Malielegoai 238
Turnbull, Malcolm 77, 107, 111, 120, 140, 144, 237, 292

undue influence 8
United Nations (UN) 8–9
  General Assembly 75
  humanitarian assistance 247
  interventions by 23
  overseas development assistance (ODA) 253
  Security Council 8, 75–6, 95, 249
  Sustainable Development Goals (SDGs) 252
United Nations High Commissioner for Refugees (UNHCR) 285
United Nations Peacekeeping Operations (UNPKO) 113–14
United States of America 39–52, 53–83, 307–8
  alignment with 39–40
  anti-Americanism 51–2, 61
  asymmetry of relationship 50–1
  background to relationship with Australia 41–6
  bases in Australia 61–2
  comparison with Australia 40–1, 50
  cultural links 82–3
  Declaration on US–Pacific Partnership (2022) 225
  diplomatic support 74–6
  diplomatic visits 76–7
  prime ministerial/presidential relations 77–8, 79
  resettlement of refugees 292
  security relationship see Australia, New Zealand, United States (ANZUS) Treaty
  trade links 79–82
  trade war with China 103–4

'unbreakable democratic alliance,' characteristics of 47–52
value of access in Washington 78–9
university collaborations 118
urbanization 204–5

values
  Asian values 19–20
  Liberal Internationalist 34, 35, 36, 40
  shared with the US 48–9
variations in national foreign policy 10–11
Vietnam 110–11, 115
Vietnam War 86, 281
Vietnamese 'boat people' 281–2

war crimes 127
'War on Terror' 23–4, 166, 179, 300
  see also Bali terrorist bombings; Operation Enduring Freedom
weapons of mass destruction 138
  see also nuclear weapons
West Papua 214–15
West Papuan asylum seekers (2006) 167
Westphalian sovereignty 7
whaling 137–8
White Australia Policy 19, 124, 280, 281
White, Hugh 90, 118
Whitlam administration 86–7
Whitlam, Gough 34, 281–2
Widodo, Joko see Joko Widodo
wine exports 102
'Wolf Warrior' diplomacy 109
Wong, Penny 219, 220, 226, 274
workers 230
World Trade Organization (WTO) 102–3

Xi, Jinping 88, 94, 95, 96, 112, 122
Xu, Liping 101

Printed in the USA
CPSIA information can be obtained
at www.ICGtesting.com
LVHW021055241123
764752LV00003B/69